COLLECTING • Figurines from Royal Doulton

Compiled by Stephen Johnson and Wendy Perrott

Editor George Perrott

A Perrot's Price Guide

GEMINI PUBLICATIONS

Published by Gemini Publications Ltd
30a Monmouth Street, Bath, BA1 2AN, England, UK.

Designed by Richard Gale and Stephen Johnson
Cover by Richard Gale
Photography by Photoreel

ISBN 0-9530637-5-5

Printed and Bound in the EU.

TABLE OF Contents

Copyright and Trademarks

ꙮ Acknowledgements ꙮ & Credits

Acknowledgements and Credits

Susie Ryan for researching history and general information on Royal Doulton and assisting the Editor during the three months she worked at Gemini.

Auction Houses that supplied the major information:

PSA. **Potteries Specialist Auctions** 271 Waterloo Road, Cobridge, Stoke on Trent. (See advert)

ASH. **A.S.H. Auctions,** 226 Cobridge Road, Cobridge, Stoke-on-Trent, ST6 3HR.

W&H. **Walton & Hipkiss Auction Dept.** 111 Worcester Road, Hagley, Nr. Stourbridge, West Midlands, DY9 0NG.

Websites that assisted with information:

Liz and Jim at Unforgetables.com Alberta, Canada.

Maureen and Joe at Olde Maine Antiques, NY, USA. (See advert)

Martin Stanton at www.doult.com/Royal_Doulton_figurines.htm Birmingham, England. (see advert)

www.gvcollectiques.co.uk G & V Collectiques Birmingham UK.

www.royal-doulton.co.uk (see advert back cover)

www.ebay.co.uk

And numerous individuals who supplied photographs and useful information.

❧ Foreword ❧

A new era for the Royal Doulton Factory

For nearly 200 years Royal Doulton has represented the epitome of English china, but sadly will be closing the doors at its Nile Street factory in Burslem for the last time by mid 2005. The factory and visitor centre which, in 1998, was named Visitor Attraction of the Year by the Heart of England Tourist Board, will be moving the majority of its production to Indonesia but will keep the high value items, such as the figurines, in its new factory which will be built – together with a new visitor centre – in Festival Park adjacent to Sir Henry Doulton House at Eturia. The current visitor centre enables visitors to walk through and witness the skill of the Doulton workers first hand. It is housed in the original factory buildings dating back to the mid 19th Century and contains the worlds largest display of Royal Doulton figurines from both past and present. This will close by May 2004 and is expected to re-open in 2006 above the new factory.

The untimely closing of the Nile Street factory will result in the loss of approximately 525 jobs, which accounts for nearly 17% of the Group's workforce. About 50 of those staff will transfer to the new site but the remaining workers will inevitably face redundancy. The cost of these redundancies, closure of the old site and subsequent opening of the new site is to be reflected in the charge of £8.5 million, which was identified in the group's 2004 accounts. Partnered with this, Royal Doulton made a £5 million pre-tax loss last year.

If you study the Royal Doulton PLC Annual Report 2003 it is obvious that the company needed to change its strategy to come into line with modern methods of manufacturing or go under, which in realistic terms means to find the most economic method of producing their products by whatever means are necessary. This usually follows the accountant's recommendations. As onlookers, we may not approve of these accounting rules, but today it seems a necessary evil that businesses and indeed countries have to follow to survive.

The restructuring of the company has been going on since Feb 2002. It started with the Royal Albert brand being moved to Jakarta followed by the Baddeley Green site being closed. Eight months later Beswick and Regent unexpectedly followed suit.

Whatever the outcome of these changes we are sure that collectors and dealers alike will join with us and wish Royal Doulton success in the future and that they will go on producing many more attractive and charming ceramics as they have always done.

Gemini Publications

ʒ⁊ Introduction ꙮꙮ

Welcome to 'Collecting Figurines from Royal Doulton'. It is not the first book on this popular subject, and it probably will not be the last, but it is new in the fact that the majority of the pictures are in colour and each figure carries a realistic price guide which represents its current value today.

Royal Doulton have produced more than 4000 of these figures since they first produced 'HN1 Darling'. They are made in a variety of Series and the collector can choose from many subjects. Throughout many years of producing these figures, Royal Doulton designers, painters and staff have shown the experience and skills of a traditional era where quality was supreme. It is almost 100 years since the first figure was produced and during that time collectors throughout the world have avidly collected them. Charles Noke, an experienced modeller from the Worcester factory, was recruited in 1889 but it wasn't until some way into the 20th century that he organised the production of the first 'HN' figures. The 'HN' refers to Harry Nixon who was in charge of the new figure painting department at that time.

We have endeavoured to present this book from the point of view of those who collect Royal Doulton Figurines, leaving out the earlier Doulton Lambeth figures which were mainly produced in the late 19th century and we have concentrated on the collectable figures of the 'HN' series plus the smaller series of 'AIL' (Art is Life) and the 'CL' (Classique Series) and finally the 'M' series (Miniatures).

The majority of collectors buy these figures either directly from the Royal Doulton factory shop or from the many specialist retailers you will find in most major towns and cities. However, there are many collectors who acquire their figures on the secondary market. The secondary market outlets consists of many areas including Auction Houses, Antiques and Collectors fairs, antique shops, flea markets and even boot-fairs, and of course nowadays we have a new source of dealing which takes place on a daily basis on the internet. All these areas of buying and selling makes collecting Royal Doulton figurines much more exciting and nothing is more satisfying to the collector than to find a figure at a bargain price. The fact is that prices of figurines have stabilised over the past few years and a re-adjustment of their valuations needed to be looked at. This book has attempted to do this, with a price band showing the lowest price usually achieved at auction and the higher price expected to be paid at retail level, either in a shop or antique fair. I think this is a fair spread and covers all levels which the buyer or seller can use their own discretion.

The Royal Doulton company has gone through a bad patch over the last few years which has shown in their profits; whether that is because of a general lack of enthusiasm within the collecting fraternity or is it because some people prefer modern collectables like 'Beanie' toys. I for my part think that trade in all types of antiques and collectables have fallen generally. I have seen within the last 4 or 5 years many shops closing down through lack of trade, and Antique and Collectable Fairs losing both customers and stall holders.

There are many different reasons for this lack of interest, I've heard dealers blaming the Swedish furnishing company, Ikea, who they believe have attracted customers away from traditional furnishings. Others blame the internet, which I personally think has done the trade a bit of good. but whatever the reason the fact is that business in the UK antique and collectors trade is suffering, however, this trade has always had its ups-and-downs and eventually the 'ups' will come round again. As a dealer, I have been buying Royal Doulton figurines for the last couple of years, most of them at auction and usually at reasonable prices. Prices are at the lower end at present but I think they will slowly creep back up and feel that now is the time to buy, especially the more desirable ones.

George Perrott
Editor

ℰℱℰ A Short History of ℰℱℰ
Royal Doulton

1815   After completing his apprenticeship at the Fulham Pottery, John Doulton found work at the Vauxhall Walk Pottery in Lambeth. Three years later, he became part-proprietor when in June 1815, Martha Jones (Widow proprietor) took John Doulton and John Watts into partnership.

1820   The pottery became Doulton & Watts when Mrs Jones withdrew from the business.

1826   The business moved to larger premises in Lambeth High Street.

1832   First Reform Act came into being, and the factory made thousands of stoneware 'Reform' bottles and flasks depicting King WIlliam IV, Lord Grey, Lord Brougham and Lord Russell who were closely associated with the Bill.

1835   Henry Doulton, John's second son, aged 15, joins his father in the expanding Doulton company. A highly gifted young man, he eventually became the driving force and was the first potter to appreciate the likely impact of the 'sanitary revolution' and in 1846 Lambeth was the first factory in the world to produce stoneware drainpipes and related wares. Henry's dedication, enthusiasm and far-sightedness were largely responsible for Doulton's rise to world acclaim.

1853   John Watts retired.

1857   The factory was named Doulton & Co., Lambeth.

1867   Paris Exhibition. Some well-shaped vases and jugs were shown, designed by George Tinworth and other students of the Lambeth School of Art, which attracted a great deal of favourable attention.

1871   Four years later the company's wonderfully creative exhibits take the First International Exhibition in London by storm and bring Doulton's artists to the attention of Queen Victoria, beginning the Royal patronage which still continues today.

1871   George Tinworth was employed by Doulton's.

1877   Doulton acquired a major new holding in Pinder, Bourne & Co. Burslem in the heart of the English Potteries, where their new artistic endeavours were to prove even more fruitful.

1878   Paris Exhibition. Doulton awarded Grand Prix. Henry Doulton made Chevalier of the Legion of Honour.

1882   Doulton & Company, Burslem. New company name after Mr Pinder accepts settlement and retires.

1884   Fine bone china becomes Doulton's principal medium. Pieces produced around this date now command fantastic sums at auction.

1885	Henry Doulton receives the Albert Medal of the Society of Arts, personally conferred by the Prince of Wales, later King Edward VII.
1887	Henry Doulton receives a knighthood from Queen Victoria for his services to ceramic art and science – the first potter ever to be accorded such an honour.
1889	Charles Noke (designer) recruited.
1893	Doulton astonishes the world by taking no fewer than 1,500 items to the Chicago Exhibition.
1897	Sir Henry Doulton dies. Henry Lewis Doulton (son) forms a Limited Company.
1901	King Edward VII presents the company with the Royal Warrant and authorises the use of the word 'Royal' to describe all Doulton products - a rarely granted honour.
1902	Leslie Harradine joins Doulton as an apprentice modeller.
1904	After many years of development work the first showing of Flambé takes place at the St. Louis exhibition.
1913	The famous 'HN' figures were launched. Early pieces from the Figures Collection were shown to King George V and Queen Mary during their visit to Burslem. Queen Mary, exclaiming "Isn't he a darling", unwittingly gives the figure 'HN1, Darling', its name.
1934	Having re-established the tradition of Staffordshire figure making, Charles Noke successfully revives another old tradition, that of Toby and Character Jugs.
1939	Mary May (Peggy) Davies joins Doulton as an assistant to Cecil Jack Noke.
1955	Jo Ledger became new art director for Doulton.
1956	Lambeth works and studios close down. Burslem becomes the principle centre of Royal Doulton production
1966	Royal Doulton given the Queen's Award for Technological Achievement.
1968	Minton's of Stoke acquired.
1970	Royal Doulton given the Queen's Award for Export.
1972	Eric Griffiths joins Doulton as the new Director of Sculpture.
1975	British Airways selects Royal Doulton fine bone china for use on its Concorde services.
1978	Royal Doulton given a second Queen's Award for Export.
1980	Royal Doulton International Collectors Club formed to assist and encourage collectors.
1985	Royal Doulton becomes the first bone china in space, as a number of specially commissioned items are launched aboard the Space Shuttle Discovery.
1990	Royal Doulton announce that for every nature sculpture sold, a donation will be made to World Wide Fund for Nature to support their invaluable conservation work.
1993	Royal Doulton became a public limited company and is listed on the London Stock Exchange.
2004	Announcement of the closure of Nile Street Factory in 2005 and the proposal of a new Factory and Visitor centre to be built in 2006 adjacent to its Etruria Headquarters on Festival Park.

Modellers & Designers at Royal Doulton

Modellers and Designers at Royal Doulton.

Without exception, all of the Royal Doulton designers and painters were good at their jobs, but a number were exceptional and I would just like to mention some of these. The first to spring to mind is George Tinworth (1843-1913). After a hard childhood, George at 19 was lucky enough to be offered a place at The Lambeth School of Art. He did very well there under the headmaster, Mr Sparkes, who recognised George's talents and after winning several prizes and medals he exhibited at the Royal Academy, and on a recommendation from Mr Sparkes, George was employed in 1871 by Henry Doulton at the Lambeth Pottery. In 1874 he exhibited 3 large terracotta panels at the Royal Academy and showed 8 smaller panels in the following year.

Tinworth modelled special pieces for important people such as The Archbishop of Canterbury and other such celebrities. These were one-offs and were never copied but he was also known for his famous brown salt-glazed 'Merry Musician' series, which were produced between 1889 and 1912. Charles Noke, who became Doulton's Chief Modeller, was fond of these figures and apparently had a private collection. He was hoping that George Tinworth would have created some models for the 'HN' series but unfortunately Tinworth died in 1913 just at the time that they were being produced for the market. Can you imagine what these figures would have been worth today if he had designed some of them.

Charles J Noke was born in 1858. His father was an antique dealer and specialised in English and Continental porcelain and was a friend of R W Binns who was the head of The Royal Worcester Porcelain Company. He obviously had an influence in Charles joining their company as a apprentice modeller in 1875 under Binns and Hadley. He was hugely influenced by James Hadley, as can be seen in his early Doulton work.

Charles stayed with Worcester for 16 years until 1889 when John Slater asked him to join Doulton at Burslem. He produced a collection of free-standing figures during his first few years at Doulton, a few of which were shown at The Chicago exhibition of 1893. They ranged from 8 to 20 inches high and were made of a variety of Parian porcelain containing Felspar. Unfortunately, they were not very popular with the general public, but today those figures bring top prices at auctions.

As Doulton's chief modeller, Noke was very keen to revive the Staffordshire figure tradition of the 18th century and in 1909 he offered the opportunity to well known sculptors to design small ceramic figures. By 1912 he had collected enough to launch the 'HN' series of models. Harry Nixon was in charge of the figure-painting department and his initials were taken for the series.

Noke decided to launch this series in 1913 to coincide with the visit to the factory of King George and Queen Mary. They were both very impressed and a particular figure by Charles Vyse of a small child was named 'Darling HN1' after Queen Mary picked the figure up and said "Isn't he a darling". This was the beginnings of the 'HN' series of ceramic models which have been produced and sold by Royal Doulton throughout the world ever since. After 52 years of loyal service Charles Noke finally retired in 1941.

Arthur Leslie Harradine was one of the most important sculptors of Royal Doulton. He joined the Lambeth Studios as an apprentice modeller in 1902 and worked under the famous sculptor Albert Toft. In the same year he entered the Camberwell School of Art as a part time student. Charles Noke was impressed by Harradine's Dickens' characters including Pickwick, Micawber, Sam Weller and Uriah Heep and he was fast becoming a respected member of the Royal Doulton Lambeth Studio, which is why it was a big surprise when he suddenly resigned in 1912 after being with Royal Doulton for 10 years. With his brother Percy they moved to Canada to farm 4000 acres of land. Life was hard but they apparently enjoyed it.

The Great War came in 1914 and Harradine found himself in action in France where he was wounded. After the war he decided to establish his own studio so he returned to England with his young family and set up home in Bedfordshire. Charles Noke was keen for Harradine to return to Royal Doulton, but the only way Harradine would work was on a freelance basis from his own studio. It was agreed and continued for 40 years creating many figures that are very collectable today.

Born in Burslem, Mary May (Peggy) Davies grew up in the potteries. She joined Royal Doulton in 1939 as an assistant to Cecil J. Noke. Unfortunately, there were many restrictions on production at Doulton's during the war. Luxury goods were only to be made for export and many of the early figures were discontinued between 1941-1949. Early on in her career, Peggy set herself up as an independent artist with her own studio and produced figures on a contract basis for Doulton. She had a fascination for fashion and history and many of her figures reflect this.

In 1955 Jo Ledger became the new art director for Royal Doulton and he worked directly with Peggy Davies. She produced her much prized Fair Ladies and several outstanding limited editions masterpieces for the collections Les Femmes Fatales, Lady Musicians and Dancers of the World. She was also responsible for themes such as Ballet, Figures of Williamsburg and Kate Greenaway figures.

Doulton continued to grow through the 1950s and a new talent joined by the name of Mary Nichol. She worked from her studio in Devon and supplied a range of historical and nautical characters and street entertainers, which she sent to Doulton's on a regular basis. Mary Nichol and Peggy Davies made between them most of the figures introduced during the 50s and 60s.

Eric Griffiths, the new Director of Sculpture joined Doulton in 1972. He originally trained as a portrait painter, so he preferred to work on a larger scale and he introduced a larger figure, 12 inches high entitled 'Haute Ensemble'.

In 1973 Doulton employed another freelance modeller, Bill Harper, who had many years of experience and he continued Mary Nicoll's range after she sadly died at the age of 52 in 1974. Other sculptors who joined Doulton through the 1970s were Robert Jefferson, Peter Gee, Douglas Tootle, Alan Maslankowski and Robert Tabbenor.

Royal Doulton Figurine Designers

Showing the dates of the first figurine they each produced in the 'HN' series.

HN1	C. Vyse	1913	HN2146	M. Nicoll	1962	HN3272	G. Tongue	1989
HN3	P. Stabler	1913	HN2287	D.B. Lovegrove	1961	HN3358	V. Annand	1991
HN6	C.J. Noke	1913	HN2368	J. Bromley	1968	HN3368	N. Pedley	1991
HN8	G. Lambert	1913	HN2542	E.J. Griffiths	1974	HN3378	T. Potts	1991
HN15	W. White	1913	HN2547	D.V. Tootle	1973	HN3428	A. Munslow	1992
HN18	F.C. Stone	1913	HN2722	W.K. Harper	1974	HN3750	D. Biggs	1995
HN35	A. Toft	1913	HN2824	R. Jefferson	1978	HN3752	A. Dobson	1995
HN39	E.W. Light	1914	HN2861	L. Ispanky	1977	HN3780	J. Jones	1996
HN46	H. Tittensor	1915	HN2877	A. Maslankowski	1979	HN3993	M. Halson	1997
HN59	L. Perugini	1916	HN2906	P. Parsons	1980	HN3996	M. Evans	1998
HN325	F.C. Stone	1918	HN2907	M. Abberley	1980	HN4000	S. Curzon	1998
HN385	S. Thorogood	1920	HN2908	S. Keenan	1980	HN4201A	J. Bromley	2000
HN391	L. Harradine	1920	HN2911	D. Lyttleton	1980	HN4270	M. King	2000
HN1264	J.G. Hughes	1927	HN2919	P. Gee	1981	HN4380	N. Lee	2000
HN1307	H. Fenton	1928	HN2940	R. Tabbenor	1982	HN4430	C. Froud	2002
HN1747	P. Railston	1935	HN2946	B. Franks	1982	HN4511	M. Alcock	2003
HN1774	R. Garbe	1933	HN2970	A. Hughes	1982	HN4540	S. Ridge	2003
HN1890	W.M. Chance	1938	HN3040	D. Brindley	1988	HN4610	N. Welch	2004
HN1992	M. Davies	1947	HN3061	S. Mitchell	1984			
HN1997	R. Asplin	1947	HN3210	P.A. Northcroft	1988			

The reader will notice that the 'HN' numbers do not always follow in sequence as sometimes gaps occur between the numbers. This is because some of the 'HN' series was used on other subjects such as, animals figures, wall-masks and lamp bases and consequently are not shown in this guide.

The Royal Doulton HN Series ran more or less in chronological order for the first 27 years, from 1913 to 1940 covering HN1 to HN1958. After1940 batches of numbers were allocated to individual modellers who sometimes took several years to use up their allotment, therefore it cannot be assumed that one number will automatically follow the other in date order.

Some models were produced in large numbers for many years and consequently are less valuable than those where only a few were made. 'Top of the Hill' HN1833 with four other colourways, designed by Leslie Harradine, was the most popular model that Royal Doulton produced and still very popular today but there are thousands out there. Others were only produced for a year or two and are consequently more elusive and valuation will rise because of their rarity. Many Limited Editions have been produced in the later years and will obviously become more valuable with time. Generally Royal Doulton figurines are still very popular and whatever might happen to the Company, they will always be collected.

❧ Colourways ❧

Since the beginning of Royal Doulton Figurines there has always been the option to collect certain figures in a different variation of colours or glazes. Each figure with a different colour or glaze has a unique HN number, an example being Charles Noke's 'The Moor', which was originally called 'An Arab'. The Moor is available in 7 different colourways and 'An Arab' in 3 different colourways. Noke also tried out various glaze effects on his figures including a glossy red flambé of which 'The Moor' HN3642 is a good example. During the 1920's more master painters joined the figure painting department, the colours changed slightly and the patterns became more impressive. Leslie Harradine's figures of scantily clad ladies were very popular during the Art Deco period and continue to be so. 'The Bather' HN597 was produced in 6 different colourways. 'Negligée' HN1219 was produced in 5 colourways and many more by Harradine were popular including, 'Swimmer' HN1270, 'Lido Lady', 'Susanna', 'Angela' and 'Siesta'.

In the years following the Second World War, whether due to economics or lack of materials at that time, the Royal Doulton collection was streamlined and the alternative colours and glazes became less common. However they were brought back in the 1980s, but mainly for special occasions. These various colourways now appear regularly in the general range, sometimes with a different name.
There are various approaches collectors can apply when collecting Royal Doulton figures; one would be to collect figures from a Series, like Nursery Rhymes which consists of 10 figures, reminding us of our early school days with figures representing Jack and Jill, Little Boy Blue etc. Or one could start with a single figure like 'The Jester' and collect all the various colourways that have been produced from that figure. There is a big range of Series (see index at rear of book) and many interesting figures with a range of colourways to chose from.

Doulton Figurines come in all shapes and sizes and cover many different subjects and eras. Most of them have a brilliant glossy glaze but a matt finish was used for some of the limited edition pieces as it apparently gave them a finer and more detailed definition. A black basalt body in a matt glaze has been used more recently in the modern style 'Images' range but generally the character figures are made from English porcelain, a whiter coloured body which used to be known as English translucent china and was pioneered by the Royal Doulton chemists in 1959. Before English porcelain came along many of the Doulton figures were produced in earthenware, which is more porous and fired at a lower temperature than china.

Marks & Monograms
On Royal Doulton

There is an amazing amount of information on the backstamp marks on each Royal Doulton figure, some of which are self explainatary, but to make it easier we will go through the various marks used since 1913 when these figures were first produced.

Identifying marks

The 'HN' number was first used when Harry Nixon, in charge of the paint shop, used it on the first model 'HN1 Darling'.
The 'HN' reference has been used ever since.

Name of the figure.

Signature of the modeller.

1902-32 Printed on Burslem and Lambeth products (Late 1920s 'Made in England' added)
This mark was first used after King Edward V11 presented a Royal Warrant on the company in 1901.

This year denotes when the figure was first introduced.

From 1999 a new introduction was adopted with the 'First Year of Issue' When a figure is retired a 'Final year of Issue' will appear.

Some standard backstamps used by Royal Doulton.
From 1902 to present.

(1) 1902 to date.
Royal Doulton
Standard printed
mark.

(2) 1930 to date.
Made in England
added.

(3) 1922-1927.
Printed. Mark
without crown.

(4) 1928 Printed mark
for all Fine Bone
china products.

Some early backstamps used by Royal Doulton. From 1913 to c1930

HN1 'Darling'.
Royal Doulton printed mark (1) with hand written model title, designer name and factory. This backstamp lay-out was in use during 1913-20

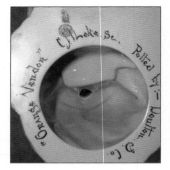

HN72 An Orange Vendor.
Royal Doulton printed mark (1)

HN1325 The Orange Seller.
Royal Doulton printed mark (1)

Some backstamps used by Royal Doulton. From c1930 to date

HN1843 Biddy Penny
Farthing Royal Doulton printed mark (2)

M3 The Paisley Shawl
Royal Doulton printed mark (1) The number '5' shown here is a year number started in 1927 with '1' and ending 1954 making '5' 1931

HN1503 Gwendolen
Royal Doulton printed mark (2)

HN2334 Fragrance
Doulton mark with Registration numbers added. Royal Doulton printed mark (4)

HN2753 Serenade
Royal Doulton printed mark (4)

HN2891 The Newsvendor 1986.
Limited Edition. Royal Doulton printed mark (2)

HN4041 Rebecca
Royal Doulton printed mark (4)

Modern year marks

From 1998 a year logo was introduced dated as follows:-

1998	1999	2000	2001	2002	2003	2004
Umbrella	Top Hat	Fob Watch	Waistcoat	Boot	Gloves	Bottle Oven

Collectors should be aware of a scored line through the backstamp or a small drilled hole through the centre of the lion and crown mark. These defacing marks represent a rejected 'second' piece. These 'seconds' were never sold to the public but they sometimes come onto the market through the employees who were allowed to buy them.

Pictures and Images

Whilst every effort was made by our researcher to provide the whole book with coloured pictures, we became aware that it wasn't entirely possible from the limited sources available to us. However, we have managed to picture more than 70 per cent of the figures in colour and where it was not possible to show the colours, the rest are shown in black and white. Just a few have no pictures at all to match the figure and we apologise for this omission.

However, we are asking our readers to aid us in the next edition by sending in any photographs available for any of the HN figures that are missing in this book. A prize draw will be organised at the end of the year where those people who send in pictures will be put into the draw and the first one out of the hat will receive £100 and the next 20 will receive a free copy of the next edition.

Errors and Omissions.
It would be appreciated if any of the readers of this guide would notify us if they know of any errors and omissions printed in this publication or if any of the information is misleading.

ℰℭ Our Valuation Policy ℰℭ

This is a new publication and we have endeavoured to price the individual pieces from recent sales at either English auction houses or from the internet. This information is shown on many individual figures within the book, which enables us to to give authenticity to our valuation estimates.

All of us know that one swallow does not make a summer, and on that premise, you cannot take an individual sale at auction or on the internet and expect that price to be the general valuation of that particular piece; prices can be high or low, it's all according to whoever is at the auction and how many bidders want the particular item, so taking that into consideration, we have made our valuations within this book on many sales, not just one or two, and from our findings we have decided to show an estimated spread valuation. i.e. £100-150. The first figure being an average of what you might buy at auction, and the second figure what it might be sold at an antiques centre or fair. Obviously, these are average prices and individual buyers and sellers will use their own discretions. The term 'plus comm' is the buyers commission paid at auctions which is added to the sale price; it can differ from 10 to 19.5 per cent plus VAT at any particular auction. In consideration of this, we have averaged a 20 per cent increase on all auction prices in our estimated valuations.

Royal Doulton are constantly selling their recently produced or prestige figures through retail outlets or on their website. Where this occurs in this book, we will show it as 'Royal Doulton web price' and show a retail price for that particular figure. If however, any of these figures have been sold on the secondary market such as at auction we will add that information also.

Foreign currency rates

Currency rates alter from day to day. On 8th October 2004 the rates were as follows against the GB Pound:

US Dollar	1.79	**Euro**	1.45
Canadian Dollar	2.25	**Australian Dollar**	2.46

A simple calculation to find the difference on a daily rate is as follows:

£100 x 1.79 = $179 US Dollars
£100 x 1.45 = €145 Euros
£100 x 2.25 = $225 Canadian Dollar
£100 x 2.46 = $246 Australian Dollar

Example: a Figurine estimated cost £120 would be calculated as follows:

£120 x 1.79 (US current rate) = $214.80 would be the cost in US dollars

To find the rate in reverse, divide the rate,

$100 ÷ 1.79 = £55.87
€100 ÷ 1.45 = £68.97
$100 Canadian ÷ 2.25 = £44.44
$100 Australian ÷ 2.46 = £40.65

❧ How This Book Works ❧

After the reference number 'HN2054' comes the name of the figure, 'Falstaff'. The Version reference applies to the model design, i.e.Second Version was a different model to Falstaff First Version, but each of these versions have different colours (colourways) and each colourway will have a new HN number. The two illustrations below shows that HN2054 Falstaff was Model 353 and had an extra colourway HN618, whereas HN571 Falstaff, First Version, Model 401 has 7 extra colourways which are all the same model 401. In other words 8 versions of the same model each with different colours.

It wasn't possible for our researcher to find all the Model numbers that Royal Doulton prescribed for each model but where we did find them we have shown them against their HN number.

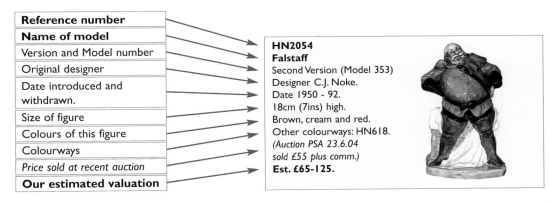

| Reference number |
| Name of model |
| Version and Model number |
| Original designer |
| Date introduced and withdrawn. |
| Size of figure |
| Colours of this figure |
| Colourways |
| *Price sold at recent auction* |
| **Our estimated valuation** |

HN2054
Falstaff
Second Version (Model 353)
Designer C.J. Noke.
Date 1950 - 92.
18cm (7ins) high.
Brown, cream and red.
Other colourways: HN618.
(Auction PSA 23.6.04 sold £55 plus comm.)
Est. £65-125.

HN3710
Primrose
Designer V. Annand.
Date 1996 - 98.
23cm (9ins) high.
Yellow and cream.
Series: Flowers of Love.
(Ebay 28.5.04 sold £86)
Est. £100-150.

HN571
Falstaff
First Version (Model 401)
Designer C.J. Noke.
Date 1923 - 38.
18cm (7ins) high.
Brown and pale green.
Other colourways:
HN575, 608, 609, 619, 638, 1216, 1606.
Est. £1100-1400.

Many Royal Doulton figurines come within a 'Series' There are many of them and they give an extra incentive to collect them. You will find the full range at the back of this book with the index. Above left, there is an illustration of HN3710 Primrose who is part of Series, 'Flowers of Love', which consists of four models, Camellias, Forget-Me-Nots, Primrose and Rose. Some Series have many more figurines within their group. 'Images' for instance have more than 80 models.

HN
SERIES

HN1
Darling
First Version (Model 89)
Designer C. Vyse.
Date 1913 - 28.
19cm (7.5ins) high.
Pale grey.
Other colourways: HN1319,
1371, 1372, 4140.
(Ebay 05/06/04 sold £946)
Est. £1000-1500.

HN5
Picardy Peasant (woman)
Designer P. Stabler.
Date 1913 - 38.
24cm (9.5ins) high.
Grey.
Other colourways: HN4,
17A, 351, 513.
Very rare.

HN2
Elizabeth Fry
Designer C. Vyse.
Date 1913 - 36.
43cm (17ins) high.
Pale blue with green base.
Other colourways: HN2A.
Est. £3000-4000.

HN6
Dunce
Designer C.J. Noke.
Date 1913 - 36.
26.5cm (10.5ins) high.
Pale blue.
Other colourways:
HN310, 357.
Extremely rare.

HN2A
Elizabeth Fry
Designer C. Vyse.
Date 1913 - 36.
43cm (17ins) high.
Pale blue with blue base.
Other colourways: HN2.
Est. £3000-4000.

HN7
Pedlar Wolf
Designer C.J. Noke.
Date 1913 - 38.
19cm (7.5ins) high.
Pale blue and black.
Other colourways: Also
recorded in flambé glaze.
Extremely rare.

HN3
Milking Time
Designer P. Stabler.
Date 1913 - 38.
16.5cm (6.5ins) high.
Pale blue dress, white apron and
pale brown goat.
Other colourways: HN306.
Extremely rare.

HN8
The Crinoline
Designer G. Lambert.
Date 1913 - 38.
16cm (6.25ins) high.
Lilac, yellow and white.
Other colourways: HN9, 9A,
21, 21A, 413, 566, 628.
Est. £1250-1700.

HN4
Picardy Peasant (woman)
Designer P. Stabler.
Date 1913 - 38.
24cm (9.5ins) high.
Blue, white and black.
(Made as a pair with HN13)
Other colourways: HN5, 17A,
351, 513.
Est. £2000-2500.

HN9
The Crinoline
Designer G. Lambert.
Date 1913 - 38.
16cm (6.25ins) high.
Pale green with floral sprays
on skirt.
Other colourways: HN8,
9A, 21, 21A, 413,
566, 628.
Est. £1250-1700.

HN9A
The Crinoline
Designer G. Lambert.
Date 1913 - 38.
16cm (6.25ins) high.
Pale green, no floral
sprays on skirt.
Other colourways: HN8,
9, 21, 21A, 413, 566, 628.
Very rare.

HN13
Picardy Peasant (man)
Designer P. Stabler.
Date 1913 - 38.
24cm (9.5 ins) high.
Blue clothes with white hat.
Other colourways: HN17,19.
(Made as a pair with HN4)
Extremely rare.

HN10
Madonna of the Square
Designer P. Stabler.
Date 1913 - 36.
18cm (7ins) high.
Lilac and brown.
Other colourways: HN10A, 11,
14, 27, 326, 573, 576, 594,
613, 764, 1968, 1969, 2034.
Est. £850-1200.

HN14
Madonna of the Square
Designer P. Stabler.
Date 1913 - 36.
18cm (7ins) high.
Blue and green.
Other colourways: HN10, 10A,
11, 27, 326, 573, 576, 594,
613, 764, 1968, 1969, 2034.
(This figure is a
renumbering of HN10A)
Est. £850-1200.

HN10A
Madonna of the Square
Designer P. Stabler.
Date 1913 - 36.
18cm (7ins) high.
Blue and green.
Other colourways: HN10, 11,
14, 27, 326, 573, 576, 594,
613, 764, 1968, 1969, 2034.
Very rare.

HN15
The Sleepy Scholar
(Also known as The 'Idle Scholar')
Designer W. White.
Date 1913 - 38.
17cm (6.75ins) high.
Cream.
Other colourways: HN16, 29.
(Designed to pair with HN26
'The Diligent Scholar')
Est. £3000-4000.

HN11
Madonna of the Square
Designer P. Stabler.
Date 1913 - 36.
18cm (7ins) high.
Grey.
Other colourways: HN10,
10A,14, 27, 326, 573, 576,
594, 613, 764, 1968,
1969, 2034.
Very rare.

HN16
The Sleepy Scholar
(Also known as The 'Idle Scholar')
Designer W. White.
Date 1913 - 38.
17cm (6.75ins) high.
Pale green and black.
Other colourways: HN15, 29.
Est. £3000-4000.

HN12
Baby
Designer C.J. Noke.
Date 1913 - 38.
12cm (4.75ins) high.
Pale pink.
Extremely rare.

HN17
Picardy Peasant (man)
Designer P. Stabler.
Date 1913 - 38.
24cm (9.5ins) high.
Green hat and trousers.
Other colourways: HN13,19.
Very rare.

HN17A
Picardy Peasant (woman)
Designer P. Stabler.
Date 1913 - 38.
24cm (9.5ins) high.
Green hat and clothes.
Other colourways: HN4,
5, 351, 513.
Very rare.

HN18
Pussy
(Also known as 'The Black Cat')
Designer F. C. Stone.
Date 1913 - 38.
19cm (7.5ins) high.
Pale blue and black.
Other colourways: HN325, 507.
Extremely rare.

HN19
Picardy Peasant (man)
Designer P. Stabler.
Date 1913 - 38.
24cm (9.5ins) high.
Green clothes with white hat.
Other colourways: HN13, 17.
Very rare.

HN20
The Coquette
Designer W. White.
Date 1913 - 38.
23.5cm (9.25ins) high.
Blue/green.
Other colourways: HN20A, 37.
Est. £3000-4000.

HN20A
The Coquette
Designer W. White.
Date 1913 - 38.
23.5cm (9.25ins) high.
Light green.
Other colourways: HN20, 37.
Est. £2300-3000.

HN21
The Crinoline
Designer G. Lambert.
Date 1913 - 38.
16cm (6.25ins) high.
Lemon and green, with
rosebuds on skirt.
Other colourways: HN8, 9,
9A, 21A, 413, 566, 628.
Est. £1250-1750.

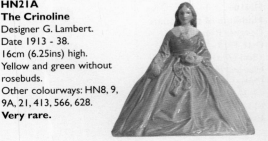

HN21A
The Crinoline
Designer G. Lambert.
Date 1913 - 38.
16cm (6.25ins) high.
Yellow and green without
rosebuds.
Other colourways: HN8, 9,
9A, 21, 413, 566, 628.
Very rare.

HN22
The Lavender Woman
(Also known as 'The Lavender Girl'
and 'Any Old Lavender')
Designer P. Stabler.
Date 1913 - 36.
21.5cm (8.5ins) high.
Pale blue.
Other colourways: HN23, 23A,
342, 569, 744.
Est. £2000-2700.

HN23
The Lavender Woman
(Also known as 'The Lavender Girl'
and 'Any Old Lavender')
Designer P. Stabler.
Date 1913 - 36.
21.5cm (8.5ins) high.
Pale green.
Other colourways: HN22, 23A,
342, 569, 744.
Very rare.

HN23A
The Lavender Woman
(Also known as 'The Lavender Girl'
and 'Any Old Lavender')
Designer P. Stabler.
Date 1913 - 36.
21.5cm (8.5ins) high.
Blue and green.
Other colourways: HN22, 23, 342,
569, 744.
Very rare.

HN24
Sleep
First Version (Model 95)
Designer P. Stabler.
Date 1913 - 36.
20.5cm (8ins) high.
Pale green.
Other colourways: HN24A,
25, 25A.
Est. £1200-1600.

HN27
Madonna of the Square
Designer P. Stabler.
Date 1913 - 36.
18cm (7ins) high.
Mottled blue and green.
Other colourways: HN10,10A,
11, 14, 326, 573, 576, 594, 613,
764, 1968, 1969, 2034.
Very rare.

HN24A
Sleep
First Version (Model 95)
Designer P. Stabler.
Date 1913 - 36.
20.5cm (8ins) high.
Dark blue.
Other colourways: HN24,
25, 25A.
Est. £1200-1600.

HN28
Motherhood
First Version (Model 93)
Designer P. Stabler.
Date 1913 - 36.
20.5cm (8ins) high.
Pale blue.
Other colourways: HN30, 303.
Est. £3000-4000.

HN25
Sleep
First Version (Model 95)
Designer P. Stabler.
Date 1913 - 36.
20.5cm (8ins) high.
Bronze.
Other colourways: HN24,
24A, 25A.
Est. £1200-1600.

HN29
The Sleepy Scholar
(Also known as 'The Idle Scholar')
Designer W. White.
Date 1913 - 38.
17cm (6.75ins) high.
Brown.
Other colourways: HN15, 16.
Est. £3000-4000.

HN25A
Sleep
First Version (Model 95)
Designer P. Stabler.
Date 1913 - 36.
20.5cm (8ins) high.
Bronze. (Fewer firings)
Other colourways: HN24,
24A, 25.
Extremely rare.

HN30
Motherhood
First Version (Model 93)
Designer P. Stabler.
Date 1913 - 36.
20.5cm (8ins) high.
White dress with blue and
yellow pattern.
Other colourways: HN28, 303.
Extremely rare.

HN26
The Diligent Scholar
(Also called the 'Attentive Scholar')
Designer W. White.
Date 1913 - 36.
18cm (7ins) high.
Brown and green.
(Designed to pair with HN15
'The Sleepy Scholar')
Est. £3000-4000.

HN31
**The Return of
Persephone**
Designer C. Vyse.
Date 1913 - 38.
40.5cm (16ins) high.
Grey, brown and blue.
Extremely rare.

HN32
Child on Crab
Designer C.J. Noke.
Date 1913 - 38.
13cm (5.25ins) high.
Pale blue, green and light brown.
Other colourways: Also known in
flambé glaze.
Est. £3000-4000.

HN37
The Coquette
Designer W. White.
Date 1914 - 38.
23.5cm (9.25ins) high.
Pale green floral dress.
Other colourways: HN20, 20A.
Est. £3000-4000.

HN33
An Arab
Designer C.J. Noke.
Date 1913 - 38.
42cm (16.5ins) high.
Dark green, brown and blue.
Other colourways: HN343, 378;
also called 'The Moor', HN1308,
1366, 1425, 1657, 2082,
3642, 3926.
Est. £1700-2300.

HN38
The Carpet Vendor
First Version (Model 163)
Designer C.J. Noke.
Date 1914 - 36.
16cm (6.25ins) high.
Yellow, green and blue.
Other colourways: HN76, 350;
also recorded in a flambé glaze.
Very rare.

HN34
Moorish Minstrel
Designer C.J. Noke.
Date 1913 - 38.
34.5cm (13.5ins) high.
Purple and brown.
(Made as a pair with HN301
'Moorish Piper Minstrel')
Other colourways: HN364,
415, 797.
Est. £1600-2200.

HN38A
The Carpet Vendor
Second Version
Designer C.J. Noke.
Date 1914 - 36.
16cm (6.25ins) high.
Blue, green and yellow
longer patterned carpet.
Other colourways: HN348.
Very rare.

*Picture
not available
at present*

HN35
Charley's Aunt
First Version (Model 161)
Designer A. Toft.
Date 1913 - 36.
18cm (7ins) high.
Black and white.
Other colourways: HN640.
*(Auction PSA 23.6.04 sold
£300 plus comm.)*
Est. £400-550.

HN39
The Welsh Girl
(Also known as 'Myfanwy Jones')
Designer E.W. Light.
Date 1914 - 36.
30.5cm (12ins) high.
Purple, red, black and white.
Other colourways: HN92, 456,
514, 516, 519, 520, 660, 668,
669, 701, 792.
Est. £3000-4000.

HN36
The Sentimental Pierrot
Designer C.J. Noke.
Date 1914 - 36.
14cm (5.5ins) high.
Grey.
Other colourways: HN307.
Est. £3000-4000.

HN40
A Lady of the Elizabethan Period
First Version (Model 165)
(Also known as 'Elizabethan Lady')
Designer E.W. Light.
Date 1914 - 38.
24cm (9.5ins) high.
Orange and brown with pattern.
Other colourways: HN40A,
73, 411.
Very rare.

HN40A
A Lady of the
Elizabethan Period
First Version (Model 165)
(Also known as 'Elizabethan Lady')
Designer E.W. Light.
Date 1914 - 38.
24cm (9.5ins) high.
Brown and orange
without pattern on dress.
Other colourways: HN40, 73, 411.
Very rare.

HN41
A Lady of the Georgian Period
Designer E.W. Light.
Date 1914 - 36.
26cm (10.25ins) high.
Light blue and orange.
Other colourways: HN331, 444,
690, 702.
Est. £1700-2300.

HN42
Robert Burns
First Version
Designer E.W. Light.
Date 1914 - 38.
35.5cm (14ins) high.
Brown, orange, green and yellow.
Extremely rare.

HN43
A Woman of the Time of
Henry VI
Designer E.W. Light.
Date 1914 - 38.
23.5cm (9.25ins) high.
Pale green, yellow and white.
Extremely rare.

HN44
A Lilac Shawl
Designer C.J. Noke.
Date 1915 - 38.
22.5cm (8.75ins) high.
Cream and lilac.
Other colourways: HN44A; 'In
Grandma's Days' HN339, 340, 388,
442; 'The Poke Bonnet' HN362,
612, 765.
Est. £1200-1500.

HN44A
A Lilac Shawl
Designer C.J. Noke.
Date 1915 - 38.
22.5cm (8.75ins) high.
Cream, yellow and lilac.
Other colourways: HN44; also
called 'In Grandma's Days'
HN339, 340, 388, 442; 'The Poke
Bonnet' HN362, 612, 765.
Est. £1200-1500.

HN45
A Jester
First Version (Model 170)
Designer C.J. Noke.
Date 1915 - 38.
25.5cm (10ins) high.
Black, white and yellow.
Other colourways: HN71, 71A, 320, 367, 412,
426, 446, 552, 616, 627, 1295, 1702, 2016, 3922.
(Auction PSA 10.3.04 sold £970 plus comm.
Restoration to hand)
Est. £2500-3500.

HN45A
A Jester
Second Version (Model 171)
Designer C.J. Noke.
Date 1915 - 38.
26cm (10.25ins) high.
Green, white and brown.
Other colourways: HN45B, 55,
308, 630, 1333.
Est. £2500-3500.

HN45B
A Jester
Second Version (Model 171)
Designer C.J. Noke.
Date 1915 - 38.
26cm (10.25ins) high.
Dark red, white and yellow.
Other colourways: HN45A, 55,
308, 630, 1333, also recorded in
black and white.
Est. £2500-3500.

HN46
The Gainsborough Hat
Designer H. Tittensor.
Date 1915 - 36.
22cm (8.75ins) high.
Lilac and purple.
Other colourways: HN46A, 47, 329,
352, 383, 453, 675, 705.
Est. £1700-2300.

HN46A
The Gainsborough Hat
Designer H. Tittensor.
Date 1915- 36.
22cm (8.75ins) high.
Lilac with black patterned collar.
Other colourways: HN46, 47, 329,
352, 383, 453, 675, 705.
Extremely rare.

HN50
A Spook
Designer H. Tittensor.
Date 1916 - 36.
18cm (7ins) high.
Blue/green robe with
black cap.
Other colourways: HN51,
51A, 51B, 58, 512, 625, 1218;
also recorded in flambé
glaze and in miniature.
Est. £1700-2300.

HN47
The Gainsborough Hat
Designer H. Tittensor.
Date 1915 - 36.
22cm (8.75ins) high.
Pale green and cream.
Other colourways: HN46, 46A,
329, 352, 383, 453, 675, 705.
Est. £1700-2300.

HN51
A Spook
Designer H. Tittensor.
Date 1916 - 36.
18cm (7ins) high.
Green robe with red cap.
Other colourways: HN50,
51A, 51B, 58, 512, 625,
1218: also known in flambé
glaze and in miniature.
Est. £1700-2300.

HN48
Lady of the Fan
Designer E.W. Light.
Date 1916 - 36.
24cm (9.5ins) high.
Lilac.
(Designed to pair with HN48A.
Many pairs were issued with
complimentary colour schemes)
Other colourways: HN52, 53,
53A, 335, 509.
Extremely rare.

HN51A
A Spook
Designer H. Tittensor.
Date 1916 - 36.
18cm (7ins) high.
Green robe with black cap.
Other colourways: HN50,
51, 51B, 58, 512, 625, 1218,
flambé glaze and miniature.
Est. £1700-2300.

HN48A
Lady with Rose
Designer E.W. Light.
Date 1916 - 36.
24cm (9.5ins) high.
Cream, black and orange.
Other colourways: HN52A, 68,
304, 336, 515, 517, 584, 624.
Est. £1400-2000.

HN51B
A Spook
Designer H. Tittensor.
Date 1916 - 36.
18cm (7ins) high.
Blue robe with red cap.
Other colourways: HN50,
51, 51A, 58, 512, 625, 1218,
flambé glaze and miniature.
Extremely rare.

HN49
**Under the
Gooseberry Bush**
Designer C.J. Noke.
Date 1916 - 38.
9cm (3.5ins) high.
Green, red and brown.
Est. £1300-1800.

HN52
Lady of the Fan
Designer E.W. Light.
Date 1916 - 36.
24cm (9.5ins) high.
Mustard and black.
Other colourways: HN48,
53, 53A, 335, 509.
Est. £1500-2000.

HN52A
Lady with Rose
Designer E.W. Light.
Date 1916 - 36.
24cm (9.5ins) high.
Yellow, black and orange.
Other colourways: HN48A, 68,
304, 336, 515, 517, 584, 624.
Extremely rare.

HN56
The Land of Nod
First Version
Designer H. Tittensor.
Date 1916 - 38.
24.5cm (9.75ins) high.
Ivory and green.
Other colourways: HN56A, 56B.
Est. £3500-4500.

HN53
Lady of the Fan
Designer E.W. Light.
Date 1916 - 36.
24cm (9.5ins) high.
Deep purple and grey.
Other colourways: HN48, 52,
53A, 335, 509.
Est. £1500-2000.

HN56A
The Land of Nod
First Version
Designer H. Tittensor.
Date 1916 - 38.
24.5cm (9.75ins) high.
Grey and green.
Other colourways: HN56, 56B.
Est. £3500-4500.

HN53A
Lady of the Fan
Designer E.W. Light.
Date 1916 - 36.
24cm (9.5ins) high.
Green and blue.
Other colourways: HN48, 52,
53, 335, 509.
Extremely rare

HN56B
The Land of Nod
First Version
Designer H. Tittensor.
Date 1916 - 38.
24.5cm (9.75ins) high.
Pale grey and red.
Other colourways: HN56, 56A.
Est. £3500-4500.

HN54
The Ermine Muff
(Also called 'Lady Ermine' and
'The Lady with Ermine Muff')
Designer C.J. Noke.
Date 1916 - 38.
21.5cm (8.5ins) high.
Blue, white and pale green.
Other colourways: HN332, 671.
Est. £1500-2000.

HN57
The Curtsey
First Version
Designer E.W. Light.
Date 1916 - 36.
28cm (11ins) high.
Orange lustre dress.
(Designed to be a pair with HN57A
with complimentary colourways)
Other colourways: HN57B, 66A,
327, 334, 363, 371, 518, 547, 629, 670.
Extremely rare.

HN55
A Jester
Second Version (Model 171)
Designer C.J. Noke.
Date 1916 - 38.
26cm (10.25ins) high.
Black, lilac, green and gold.
Other colourways: HN45A,
45B, 308, 630, 1333; also
recorded in black and white.
Est. £3000-4000.

HN57A
The Flounced Skirt
(Also called 'The Bow')
Designer E.W. Light.
Date 1916 - 38.
24.5cm (9.75ins) high.
Orange lustre dress.
Other colourways: HN66,
77, 78, 333.
Extremely rare.

HN57B
The Curtsey
First Version
Designer E.W. Light.
Date 1916 - 36.
28cm (11ins) high.
Lilac dress.
Other colourways: HN57,
66A, 327, 334, 363, 371, 518,
547, 629, 670.
Est. £1400-1900.

HN62
A Child's Grace
Designer L. Perugini.
Date 1916 - 38.
17cm (6.75ins) high.
Green, yellow, white and black.
Other colourways: HN62A, 510.
Extremely rare.

HN58
A Spook
Designer H. Tittensor.
Date 1916 - 36.
18cm (7ins) high.
Colour not recorded.
Other colourways: HN50, 51,
51A, 51B, 512, 625, 1218; also
known in flambé glaze and in
miniature.
Extremely rare.

HN62A
A Child's Grace
Designer L. Perugini.
Date 1916 - 38.
17cm (6.75ins) high.
Yellow, white and green.
Other colourways: HN62, 510.
Very rare.

HN59
Upon her Cheeks she Wept
Designer L. Perugini.
Date 1916 - 38.
23cm (9ins) high.
Light grey and yellow.
Other colourways: HN511, 522.
Est. £3000-4000.

HN63
The Little Land
Designer H. Tittensor.
Date 1916 - 36.
19cm (7.5ins) high.
Green and yellow.
Other colourways: HN67.
Est. £3000-4000.

HN60
Shy Anne
Designer L. Perugini.
Date 1916 - 36.
19.5cm (7.75ins) high.
Blue and yellow.
Other colourways: HN64,
65, 568.
Very rare.

HN64
Shy Anne
Designer L. Perugini.
Date 1916 - 36.
19.5cm (7.75ins) high.
Pale blue and yellow.
Other colourways: HN60,
65, 568.
Est. £3000-4000.

HN61
Katharine
Designer C.J. Noke.
Date 1916 - 38.
14.5cm (5.75ins) high.
Green and white.
Other colourways: HN74,
341, 471, 615, 793.
Est. £1200-1600.

HN65
Shy Anne
Designer L. Perugini.
Date 1916 - 36.
19.5cm (7.75ins) high.
Pale blue dress with trimmings
at hem.
Other colourways: HN60,
64, 568.
Est. £3000-4000.

HN66
The Flounced Skirt
(Also known as 'The Bow')
Designer E.W. Light.
Date 1916 - 38.
24.5cm (9.75ins) high.
Lilac dress.
Other colourways: HN57A,
77, 78, 333.
Est. £1200-1600.

HN70
Pretty Lady
Designer H. Tittensor.
Date 1916 - 38.
24cm (9.5ins) high.
Grey.
Other colourways: HN69, 302,
330, 361, 384, 565, 700, 763, 783.
Est. £1200-1600.

HN66A
The Curtsey
First Version
Designer E.W. Light.
Date 1916 - 36.
28cm (11ins) high.
Lilac dress.
Other colourways: HN57, 57B, 327,
334, 363, 371, 518, 547, 629, 670.
(This figure is possibly a
renumbered version of HN57B)
Est. £1200-1600.

HN71
A Jester
First Version (Model 170)
Designer C.J. Noke.
Date 1917 - 38.
25.5cm (10ins) high.
Pale green, black and orange.
Other colourways: HN45, 71A,
320, 367,412, 426, 446, 552,616,
627, 1295, 1702, 2016, 3922.
Est. £2200-3200.

HN67
The Little Land
Designer H. Tittensor.
Date 1916 - 36.
19cm (7.5ins) high.
Lilac dress with black trim.
Other colourways: HN63.
Est. £3000-4000.

HN71A
A Jester
First Version (Model 170)
Designer C.J. Noke.
Date 1917 - 38.
25.5cm (10ins) high.
Dark green, black and orange.
Other colourways: HN45, 71, 320,
367, 412, 426, 446, 552, 616, 627,
1295, 1702, 2016, 3922.
Est. £2200-3200.

HN68
Lady With Rose
Designer E.W. Light.
Date 1916 - 36.
24cm (9.5ins) high.
Yellow and green.
Other colourways: HN48A, 52A,
304, 336, 515, 517, 584, 624.
Est. £1400-2000.

HN72
An Orange Vendor
Designer C.J. Noke.
Date 1917 - 38.
16cm (6.25ins) high.
Green, white and orange.
Other colourways: HN508,
521, 1966.
(Ebay 24.7.04 sold £565)
Est. £700-1000.

HN69
Pretty Lady
Designer H. Tittensor.
Date 1916 - 38.
24cm (9.5ins) high.
Pale grey floral dress.
Other colourways: HN70, 302,
330, 361, 384, 565, 700, 763, 783.
Extremely rare.

HN73
A Lady of the Elizabethan Period
First Version (Model 165)
(Also known as 'Elizabethan Lady')
Designer E.W. Light.
Date 1917 - 38.
24cm (9.5ins) high.
Dark blue-green.
Other colourways: HN40,
40A, 411.
Very rare.

HN74
Katharine
Designer C.J. Noke.
Date 1917 - 38.
14.5cm (5.75ins) high.
Pale blue dress with green spots.
Other colourways: HN61, 341,
471, 615, 793.
Extremely rare.

HN79
Shylock
Designer C.J. Noke.
Date 1917 - 38.
Height not known.
Multicoloured robe with
yellow sleeves.
Other colourways: HN317.
Extremely rare.

HN75
Blue Beard
(With Plume on Turban)
First Version (Model 188)
Designer E.W. Light.
Date 1917 - 36.
28cm (11ins) high.
Pale blue, cream, brown and
yellow.
Other colourways: HN410.
Est. £4000-5000.

HN80
Fisherwomen
(Also known as 'Looking for the
Boats' and 'Waiting for the Boats')
Designer C.J. Noke.
Date 1917 - 38.
30cm (11.75ins) high.
Blue and yellow dress with
pink shawl.
Other colourways:
HN349, 359, 631.
Extremely rare.

HN76
The Carpet Vendor
First Version (Model 163)
Designer C.J. Noke.
Date 1917 - 36.
16cm (6.25ins) high.
Orange, blue and green.
Other colourways: HN38, 350;
also in flambé glaze.
Est. £1600-2200.

HN81
A Shepherd
First Version (Model 193)
Designer C.J. Noke.
Date 1918 - 38.
34.5cm (13.5ins) high.
Brown, black and cream.
Other colourways: HN617, 632.
Extremely rare.

HN77
The Flounced Skirt
(Also known as 'The Bow')
Designer E.W. Light.
Date 1917 - 38.
24.5cm (9.75ins) high.
Yellow dress with black trimmings.
Other colourways: HN57A,
66, 78, 333.
Est. £1300-1800.

HN82
The Afternoon Call
(Also known as 'Making a Call' and
'Lady with the Ermine Muff')
Designer E.W. Light.
Date 1918 - 38.
18cm (7ins) high.
Grey, white and cream.
Est. £2500-3500.

HN78
The Flounced Skirt
(Also known as 'The Bow')
Designer E.W. Light.
Date 1917 - 38.
24.5cm (9.75ins) high.
Yellow lustre floral dress.
Other colourways: HN57A,
66, 77, 333.
Est. £1300-1800.

HN83
The Lady Anne
Designer E.W. Light.
Date 1918 - 38.
24cm (9.5ins) high.
Yellow dress.
Other colourways: HN87, 93.
Est. £2500-3500.

HN84
A Mandarin
(Also known as 'Chinese
Mandarin' and 'The Mikado)'
First Version (Model 189)
Designer C.J. Noke.
Date 1918 - 36.
26cm (10.25ins) high.
Green and mauve.
Other colourways: HN316, 318,
382, 611, 746, 787, 791.
Extremely rare.

HN89
Spooks
(Also known as 'Double Spook')
Designer C.J. Noke.
Date 1918 - 36.
18.5cm (7.25ins) high.
Dark green robes, red caps.
Other colourways: HN88, 372.
Est. £2500-3200.

HN85
Jack Point
Designer C.J. Noke.
Date 1918 - 38.
41.5cm (16.25ins) high.
Red chequered costume,
green base.
Other colourways: HN91,
99, 2080, 3920, 3925.
Extremely rare.

HN90
Doris Keene as Cavallini
First Version (Model 205)
Designer C.J. Noke.
Date 1918 - 36.
28cm (11ins) high.
Dark green and white.
Other colourways: HN467.
Est. £1300-1800.

HN86
Out for a Walk
Designer E.W. Light.
Date 1918 - 36.
25.5cm (10ins) high.
Grey, white and black.
Other colourways: HN443, 748.
Est. £1800-2500.

HN91
Jack Point
Designer C.J. Noke.
Date 1918 - 38.
41.5cm (16.25ins) high.
Green and black chequered
costume.
Other colourways: HN85, 99,
2080, 3920, 3925.
Est. £2500-3300.

HN87
The Lady Anne
Designer E.W. Light.
Date 1918 - 38.
24cm (9.5ins) high.
Pale green and white.
Other colourways: HN83, 93.
Est. £2500-3500.

HN92
The Welsh Girl
(Also known as 'Myfanwy Jones')
Designer E.W. Light.
Date 1918 - 36.
30.5cm (12ins) high.
White and brown.
Other colourways: HN39, 456,
514, 516, 519, 520, 660, 668,
669, 701, 792.
Extremely rare.

HN88
Spooks
(Also known as 'Double Spook')
Designer C.J. Noke.
Date 1918 - 36.
18.5cm (7.25ins) high.
Pale green robes, black caps.
Other colourways: HN89, 372.
Est. £2500-3200.

HN93
The Lady Anne
Designer E.W. Light.
Date 1918 - 38.
24cm (9.5ins) high.
Blue and white.
Other colourways: HN83, 87.
Est. £2500-3500.

HN94
The Young Knight
Designer C.J. Noke.
Date 1918 - 36.
24cm (9.5ins) high.
Purple, yellow, green and black.
Extremely rare.

HN99
Jack Point
Designer C.J. Noke.
Date 1918 - 38.
41.5cm (16.25ins) high.
Green and purple.
Other colourways: HN85,
91, 2080, 3920, 3925.
Est. £2000-2800.

HN95
Europa and the Bull
First Version (Model 203)
Designer E.W. Light.
Date 1918 - 36.
24.5cm (9.75ins) high.
Lilac, brown and yellow.
Est. £3000-4500.

HN300
The Mermaid
Designer H. Tittensor.
Date 1918 - 36.
18cm (7ins) high.
Pale green and cream, red
berries in hair, darker base.
Other colourways: HN97.
Extremely rare.

HN96
Doris Keene as Cavallini
Second Version (Model 220)
(Also known as 'Romance')
Designer C.J. Noke.
Date 1918 - 36.
26.5cm (10.5ins) high.
Black and white.
Other colourways: HN345.
Est. £1600-2200.

HN301
Moorish Piper Minstrel
Designer C.J. Noke.
Date 1918 - 38.
34.5cm (13.5ins) high.
Purple, yellow and orange.
(Made as a pair with HN34, 'Moorish
Minstrel')
Other colourways: HN328, 416.
Est. £1500-2000.

HN97
The Mermaid
(Also recorded in flambé glaze
with both dark and fair hair)
Designer H. Tittensor.
Date 1918 - 36.
18cm (7ins) high.
Pale green and cream.
Other colourways: HN300.
Est. £500-650.

HN302
Pretty Lady
Designer H. Tittensor.
Date 1918 - 38.
24cm (9.5ins) high.
Green and purple.
Other colourways: HN69,
70, 330, 361, 384, 565, 700,
763, 783.
Est. £1100-1500.

HN98
Guy Fawkes
First Version (Model 226)
Designer C.J. Noke.
Date 1918 - 49.
26.5cm (10.5ins) high.
Red cloak with black hat and
robe.
Other colourways: HN347, 445.
(Also in Sung glaze)
Est. £950-1300.

HN303
Motherhood
First Version (Model 93)
Designer P. Stabler.
Date 1918 - 36.
20.5cm (8ins) high.
White dress with
black patterns.
Other colourways: HN28, 30.
Extremely rare.

HN304
Lady With Rose
Designer E.W. Light.
Date 1918 - 36.
24cm (9.5ins) high.
Lilac dress with brown pattern.
Other colourways: HN48A,
52A, 68, 336, 515, 517, 584, 624.
Extremely rare.

HN309
**A Lady of the Elizabethan
Period.**
Second Version (Model 232)
(Also known as 'An Elizabethan
Lady')
Designer E.W. Light.
Date 1918 - 38.
24cm (9.5ins) high.
Yellow, dark green and blue.
Est. £1750-2500.

HN305
A Scribe
Designer C.J. Noke.
Date 1918 - 36.
15cm (6ins) high.
Blue, orange and green.
Other colourways: HN324,
1235.
Est. £900-1200.

HN310
Dunce
Designer C.J. Noke.
Date 1918 - 36.
26.5cm (10.5ins) high.
Black and white patterned
costume with a green base.
Other colourways: HN6, 357.
Extremely rare.

HN306
Milking Time
Designer P. Stabler.
Date 1913 - 38.
16.5cm (6.5ins) high.
Light blue dress with black
markings.
Other colourways: HN3.
Very rare.

HN311
Dancing Figure
Designer not known.
Date 1918 - 38.
45cm (17.75ins) high.
Pink.
Extremely rare.

HN307
The Sentimental Pierrot
Designer C.J. Noke.
Date 1918 - 36.
14cm (5.5ins) high.
Black and white.
Other colourways: HN36.
Est. £3000-4000.

HN312
Spring
First Version (Model 215)
Designer possibly P. Stabler.
Date 1918 - 38.
19cm (7.5ins) high.
Yellow and grey.
Other colourways: HN472.
Series: The Seasons (Series One)
Est. £900-1200.

HN308
A Jester
Second Version (Model 171)
Designer C.J. Noke.
Date 1918 - 38.
26cm (10.25ins) high.
Black, lilac, green and gold.
Other colourways: HN45A, 45B, 55,
630; also known in black and white.
(This figure appears to be a
later version of HN55)
Extremely rare.

HN313
Summer
First Version (Model 219)
Designer possibly P. Stabler.
Date 1918 - 38.
19cm (7.5ins) high.
Pale green and lilac.
Other colourways: HN473.
Series: The Seasons (Series One)
Est. £900-1200.

HN314
Autumn
First Version (Model 222)
Designer possibly P. Stabler.
Date 1918 - 38.
19cm (7.5ins) high.
Pink and lilac.
Other colourways: HN474.
Series: The Seasons (Series One)
Est. £800-1100.

HN319
A Gnome
Designer H. Tittensor.
Date 1918 - 38.
16cm (6.25ins) high.
Brown and green.
Other colourways:
HN380, 381.
Very rare.

HN315
Winter
First Version
Designer not known.
Date 1918 - 38.
19cm (7.50ins) high.
Pale green and lilac.
Other colourways: HN475.
Series: The Seasons (Series One)
Est. £800-1100.

HN320
A Jester
First Version (Model 170)
Designer C.J. Noke.
Date 1918 - 38.
25.5cm (10ins) high.
Green and gold.
Other colourways: HN45, 71, 71A,
367, 412, 426, 446, 552, 616, 627,
1295, 1702, 2016, 3922.
Est. £3000-4000.

HN316
A Mandarin
First Version (Model 189)
(Also known as 'Chinese
Mandarin' and 'The Mikado')
Designer C.J. Noke.
Date 1918 - 36.
26cm (10.25ins) high.
Yellow, grey and black.
Other colourways: HN84, 318,
382, 611, 746, 787, 791.
Est. £3000-4000.

HN321
Digger (New Zealand)
Designer E.W. Light.
Date 1918 - 38.
28.5cm (11.25ins) high.
Mottled dark green.
Est. £1100-1500.

HN317
Shylock
Designer C.J. Noke.
Date 1918 - 38.
Height not known.
Blue, brown, grey and green.
Other colourways: HN79.
Very rare.

HN322
Digger (Australian)
Designer E.W. Light.
Date 1918 - 38.
28.5cm (11.25ins) high.
Brown.
Other colourways: HN353.
Est. £1100-1500.

HN318
A Mandarin
First Version (Model 189)
(Also known as 'Chinese
Mandarin' and 'The Mikado')
Designer C.J. Noke.
Date 1918 - 36.
26cm (10.25ins) high.
Gold and brown.
Other colourways: HN84, 316,
382, 611, 746, 787, 791.
Est. £3000-4000.

HN323
Blighty
Designer E.W. Light.
Date 1918 - 38.
29cm (11.5ins) high.
Green.
Other colourways: Khaki version
with same HN number.
Est. £1100-1500.

HN324
A Scribe
Designer C.J. Noke.
Date 1918 - 38.
15cm (6ins) high.
Brown, orange, green and grey.
Other colourways: HN305,
1235.
Est. £800-1100.

HN329
The Gainsborough Hat
Designer H. Tittensor.
Date 1918 - 36.
22cm (8.75ins) high.
Patterned blue dress:
Other colourways: HN46, 46A,
47, 352, 383, 453, 675. 705.
Extremely rare.

HN325
Pussy
(Also known as 'The Black Cat')
Designer F.C. Stone.
Date 1918 - 38.
19cm (7.5ins) high.
Patterned white dress with
black cat.
Other colourways: HN18, 507.
Extremely rare.

HN330
Pretty Lady
Designer H. Tittensor.
Date 1918 - 38.
24cm (9.5ins) high.
Blue patterned dress.
Other colourways: HN69,
70, 302, 361, 384, 565, 700,
763, 783.
Extremely rare.

HN326
Madonna of the Square
Designer P. Stabler.
Date 1918 - 36.
18cm (7ins) high.
Grey.
Other colourways: HN10, 10A,
11, 14, 27, 573, 576, 594,
613, 764, 1968, 1969, 2034.
Est. £700-950.

HN331
A Lady of the Georgian Period
Designer E.W. Light.
Date 1918 - 36.
26cm (10.25ins) high.
Dark green overskirt,
patterned yellow underskirt.
Other colourways: HN41, 444,
690, 702.
Est. £1600-2200.

HN327
The Curtsey
First Version
Designer E.W. Light.
Date 1918 - 36.
28cm (11ins) high.
Pale blue.
Other colourways: HN57, 57B,
66A, 334, 363, 371, 518, 547,
629, 670.
Est. £1300-1700.

HN332
Lady Ermine
(Also known as 'The Lady with
Ermine Muff' and 'The Ermine Muff)
Designer C.J. Noke.
Date 1918 - 38.
21.5cm (8.5ins) high.
Yellow and green skirt, red coat
and hat.
Other colourways: HN54, 671.
Extremely rare.

HN328
Moorish Piper Minstrel
Designer C.J. Noke.
Date 1918 - 38.
34.5cm (13.5ins) high.
Brown and green striped robe.
Other colourways: HN301, 416.
Extremely rare.

HN333
The Flounced Skirt
(Also known as 'The Bow')
Designer E.W. Light.
Date 1918 - 38.
24.5cm (9.75ins) high.
Dark green and blue dress.
Other colourways: HN57A,
66, 77, 78.
Est. £1300-1800.

HN334
The Curtsey
First Version
Designer E.W. Light.
Date 1918 - 36.
28cm (11ins) high.
Purple dress.
Other colourways: HN57,
57B, 66A, 327, 363, 371, 518,
547, 629, 670.
Est. £1300-1800.

HN339
In Grandma's Days
Designer C.J. Noke.
Date 1919 - 38.
22cm (8.75ins) high.
Green and lemon.
Other colourways: HN340, 388,
442; also called 'A Lilac Shawl'
HN44, 44A; 'The Poke Bonnet'
HN362, 612, 765.
Est. £1300-1800.

HN335
Lady of the Fan
Designer E.W. Light.
Date 1919 - 36.
24cm (9.5ins) high.
Dark blue.
Other colourways: HN48, 52,
53, 53A, 509.
Est. £1400-1900.

HN340
In Grandma's Days
Designer C.J. Noke.
Date 1919 - 38.
22cm (8.75ins) high.
Yellow, orange and lavender.
Other colourways: HN339, 388,
442; also called 'A Lilac Shawl'
HN44, 44A; 'The Poke Bonnet'
HN362, 612, 765.
Est. £1300-1800.

HN336
Lady with Rose
Designer E.W. Light.
Date 1919 - 36.
24cm (9.5ins) high
Multicoloured dress with brown
patterning.
Other colourways: HN48A, 52A,
68, 304, 515, 517, 584, 624.
Extremely rare.

HN341
Katharine
Designer C.J. Noke.
Date 1919 - 38.
14.5cm (5.75ins) high.
Red.
Other colourways: HN61, 74,
471, 615, 793.
Est. £1100-1500.

HN337
The Parson's Daughter
Designer H. Tittensor.
Date 1919 - 38.
25.5cm (10ins) high.
Lilac and brown.
Other colourways: HN338, 441,
564, 790, 1242, 1356, 2018.
Est. £900-1200.

HN342
The Lavender Woman
(Also known as 'The Lavender Girl'
and 'Any Old Lavender')
Designer P. Stabler.
Date 1919 - 36.
21.5cm (8.5ins) high.
Dark green dress, lavender shawl.
Other colourways: HN22, 23,
23A, 569, 744.
Est. £1700-2300.

HN338
The Parson's Daughter
Designer H. Tittensor.
Date 1919 - 38.
25.5cm (10ins) high.
Green dress with red shawl.
Other colourways: HN337, 441,
564, 790, 1242, 1356, 2018.
Est. £900-1200.

HN343
An Arab
Designer C.J. Noke.
Date 1919 - 38.
42cm (16.5ins) high.
Purple and yellow costume.
Other colourways: HN33, 378;
also called 'The Moor' HN1308,
1366, 1425, 1657, 2082, 3642, 3926.
Extremely rare.

HN344
Henry Irving as Cardinal Wolsey
Designer C.J. Noke.
Date 1919 - 49.
33.5cm (13.25ins) high.
Red.
Est.£1600-2200.

HN345
Doris Keene as Cavallini
Second Version (Model 220)
(Also known as 'Romance')
Designer C.J. Noke.
Date 1919 - 49.
26.5cm (10.5ins) high.
Black dress white shawl, dark collar
and striped muff.
Other colourways: HN96.
Est.£1600-2300.

HN346
Tony Weller
First Version. (Model 254)
Designer C.J. Noke.
Date 1919 - 38.
26.5cm (10.5ins) high.
Green coat with blue rug.
Other colourways: HN368, 684.
Extremely rare.

HN347
Guy Fawkes
First Version (Model 226)
Designer C.J. Noke.
Date 1919 - 38.
26.5cm (10.5ins) high.
Brown and orange cloak.
Other colourways: HN98, 445;
also in Sung glaze.
Very rare.

HN348
The Carpet Vendor Second
Version (Model 163A)
Designer C.J. Noke.
Date 1919 - 36.
16cm (6.25ins) high.
Turquoise, long chequered carpet.
Other colourways: HN38A.
Extremely rare.

*Picture
not available
at present*

HN349
Fisherwoman
(Also known as 'Looking for the
Boats' and 'Waiting for the Boats')
Designer C.J. Noke.
Date 1919 - 38.
30cm (11.75ins) high.
Yellow, lilac, black and red.
Other colourways: HN80,
359, 631.
Extremely rare.

HN350
The Carpet Vendor
First Version (Model 163)
Designer C.J. Noke.
Date 1919 - 36.
16cm (6.25ins) high
Blue and green.
Other colourways: HN38, 76; also
recorded in flambé glaze.
Est. £1700-2300.

HN351
Picardy Peasant (woman)
Designer P. Stabler.
Date 1919 - 38.
24cm (9.5ins) high.
Blue striped skirt, light blue top
and spotted hat.
Other colourways: HN4, 5,
17A, 513.
Est. £2500-3500.

HN352
The Gainsborough Hat
Designer H. Tittensor.
Date 1919 - 36.
22cm (8.75ins) high.
Yellow dress with purple hat.
Other colourways: HN46, 46A, 47,
329, 383, 453, 675, 705.
Extremely rare.

HN353
Digger (Australian)
Designer E.W. Light.
Date 1919 - 38.
28.5cm (11.25ins) high.
Brown.
Other colourways: HN322.
Very rare.

HN354
A Geisha
First Version (Model 238)
(Also known as 'The Japanese Lady')
Designer H. Tittensor.
Date 1919 - 38.
27.5cm (10.75ins) high.
Yellow, blue kimono with pink cuffs.
Other colourways: HN376, 376A,
387, 634, 741, 779, 1321, 1322.
Est. £2500-3500.

HN359
Fisherwoman
(Also known as 'Looking for the
Boats' and 'Waiting for the Boats')
Designer C.J. Noke.
Date 1919 - 38.
29.8cm (11.75 ins) high.
Lilac, green and red.
Other colourways: HN80,
349, 631.
Very rare.

HN355
Dolly
First Version (Model 245)
Designer C.J. Noke.
Date 1919 - 38.
19.5cm (7.75ins) high.
Pale blue.
Est. £3000-4000.

HN361
Pretty Lady
Designer H. Tittensor.
Date 1919 - 38.
24cm (9.5ins) high.
Blue-green dress.
Other colourways: HN69, 70,
302, 330, 384, 565, 700, 763, 783.
Est. £1100-1500.

HN356
Sir Thomas Lovell
Designer C.J. Noke.
Date 1919 - 36.
19.5cm (7.75ins) high.
Brown, red and orange.
Est. £1800-2500.

HN362
The Poke Bonnet
Designer C.J. Noke.
Date 1919 - 38.
22cm (8.75ins) high.
Green, yellow and red.
Other colourways: HN612, 765;
'A Lilac Shawl' HN44, 44A;
'In Grandma's Days' HN339,
340, 388, 442.
Est. £1300-1800.

HN357
Dunce
Designer C.J. Noke.
Date 1919 - 36.
26.5cm (10.5 ins) high.
Light spotted brown.
Other colourways: HN6, 310.
Very rare.

HN363
The Curtsey
First Version
Designer E.W. Light.
Date 1919 - 36.
28cm (11ins) high.
Peach and lilac.
Other colourways: HN57,
57B, 66A, 327, 334, 371, 518,
547, 629, 670.
Extremely rare.

HN358
An Old King
Designer C.J. Noke.
Date 1919 - 38.
24.5cm (9.75 ins) high.
Purple and green.
Other colourways: HN623,
1801, 2134.
Extremely rare.

HN364
A Moorish Minstrel
Designer C.J. Noke.
Date 1920 - 38.
34.5cm (13.5ins) high.
Green, orange and blue,
Other colourways: HN34,
415, 797.
Est. £1700-2300.

HN365
Double Jester
Designer C.J. Noke.
Date 1920 - 38.
Height not known.
Green, brown and purple.
Extremely rare.

HN370
Henry VIII
First Version (Model 271)
Designer C.J. Noke.
Date 1920 - 38.
Height not known.
Green, brown, gold and
purple.
Other colourways: HN673.
Extremely rare.

HN366
A Mandarin
Second Version (Model 260)
Designer C.J. Noke.
Date 1920 - 38.
21cm (8.25ins) high.
Yellow and blue costume.
Other colourways: HN455, 641.
Extremely rare.

HN371
The Curtsey
First Version
Designer E.W. Light.
Date 1920 - 36.
28cm (11ins) high.
Yellow dress.
Other colourways: HN57, 57B,
66A, 327, 334, 363, 518, 547,
629, 670.
Extremely rare.

HN367
A Jester
First Version (Model 170)
Designer C.J. Noke.
Date 1920 - 38.
25.5cm (10ins) high.
Green, black and red.
Other colourways: HN45, 71,
71A, 320, 412, 426, 446, 552, 616,
627, 1295, 1702, 2016, 3922.
Est. £2000-2500.

HN372
Spooks
(Also known as 'Double Spook')
Designer C.J. Noke.
Date 1920 - 36.
18.5cm (7.25ins) high.
Brown.
Other colourways:, HN88, 89.
Est. £2000-2500.

HN368
Tony Weller
First Version (Model 254)
Designer C.J. Noke.
Date 1920 - 38.
26.5cm (10.5ins) high.
Green, yellow and brown.
Other colourways: HN346, 684.
Est. £700-900.

HN373
Boy on Crocodile
Designer C.J. Noke.
Date 1920 - 36.
12.5cm (5ins) high,
length: 38cm (15ins)
Green-brown.
Other colourways:
Also recorded
in flambé glaze.
Extremely rare.

HN369
Cavalier
First Version (Model 268)
Designer not known.
Date 1920 - 36.
Height not known.
Blue-green, yellow
and black.
Extremely rare.

*Picture
not available
at present*

HN374
Lady and Blackamoor
First Version (Model 267)
Designer H. Tittensor.
Date 1920 - 36.
18.5cm (7.25ins) high.
Green and blue.
Extremely rare.

*Picture
not available
at present*

HN375
Lady and Blackamoor
Second Version (Model 273)
Designer H. Tittensor.
Date 1920 - 36.
18.5cm (7.25ins) high.
Purple, yellow and pink.
Other colourways: HN377, 470.
Extremely rare.

Picture not available at present

HN379
Ellen Terry as Queen Catharine
Designer C.J. Noke.
Date 1920 - 49.
32cm (12.5ins) high.
Purple, white and blue.
Est. £1100-1500.

HN376
A Geisha
First Version (Model 238)
(Also known as 'The Japanese Lady')
Designer H. Tittensor.
Date 1920 - 36.
27.5cm (10.75ins) high.
Lilac, peach, red and yellow.
Other colourways: HN354, 376A,
387, 634, 741, 779, 1321, 1322.
Est. £2000-3000.

HN380
A Gnome
Designer H. Tittensor.
Date 1920 - 38.
16cm (6.25ins) high.
Purple.
Other colourways:
HN319, 381.
Extremely rare.

HN376A
A Geisha
First Version (Model 238)
(Also known as 'The Japanese Lady')
Designer H. Tittensor.
Date 1920 - 36.
27.5cm (10.75ins) high.
Blue, lilac and peach.
Other colourways: HN354, 376, 387,
634, 741, 779, 1321, 1322.
Est. £2000-3000.

HN381
A Gnome
Designer H. Tittensor.
Date 1920 - 38.
16cm (6.25ins) high.
Green.
Other colourways:
HN319, 380.
Extremely rare.

HN377
Lady and Blackamoor
Second Version (Model 273)
Designer H. Tittensor.
Date 1920 - 36.
18.5cm (7.25ins) high.
Green and pink.
Other colourways: HN375, 470.
Extremely rare.

Picture not available at present

HN382
A Mandarin
First Version (Model 189)
(Also known as 'Chinese
Mandarin' and 'The Mikado')
Designer C.J. Noke.
Date 1920 - 36.
26cm (10.25ins) high.
Green.
Other colourways: HN84, 316,
318, 611, 746, 787, 791.
Est. £3000-4000.

HN378
An Arab
Designer C.J. Noke.
Date 1920 - 38.
42cm (16.5ins) high.
Brown, green and yellow.
Other colourways: HN33,
343; also called 'The Moor'
HN1308, 1366, 1425,
1657, 2082, 3642, 3926.
Est. £1600-2200.

HN383
The Gainsborough Hat
Designer H. Tittensor.
Date 1920 - 36.
22cm (8.75ins) high.
Green striped dress.
Other colourways: HN46, 46A,
47, 329, 352, 453, 675, 705.
Extremely rare.

HN384
Pretty Lady
Designer H. Tittensor.
Date 1920 - 38.
24cm (9.5ins) high.
Red dress with striped skirt.
Other colourways: HN69,
70, 302, 330, 361, 565, 700,
763, 783.
Est. £1100-1500.

HN389
Dolly
Second Version (Model 279)
(Also known as 'The Little Mother')
Designer H. Tittensor.
Date 1920 - 38.
28cm (11ins) high.
Pink dress and fair hair.
Other colourways: HN390, HN469.
Extremely rare.

HN385
St George
First Version (Model 191)
Designer S. Thorogood.
Date 1920 - 38.
41cm (16ins) high.
Purple, gold, grey, white and red.
Other colourways: HN386,
1800, 2067.
Est. £2000-2750.

HN390
Dolly
Second Version (Model 279)
(Also known as 'The Little Mother')
Designer H. Tittensor.
Date 1920 - 38.
28cm (11ins) high.
Pink dress and dark hair.
Other colourways: HN389, 469.
Extremely rare.

HN386
St George
First Version (Model 191)
Designer S. Thorogood.
Date 1920 - 38.
41cm (16ins) high.
Blue, brown, white and gold.
Other colourways: HN385,
1800, 2067.
Est. £2000-2750.

HN391
The Princess
Designer L. Harradine.
Date 1920 - 36.
23.5cm (9.25ins) high.
Purple and green.
Other colourways: HN392,
420, 430, 431, 633.
Extremely rare.

HN387
A Geisha
First Version (Model 238)
(Also known as 'The Japanese
Lady')
Designer H. Tittensor.
Date 1920 - 36.
27.5cm (10.75ins) high.
Blue kimono with yellow cuffs.
Other colourways: HN354, 376,
376A, 634, 741, 779, 1321, 1322.
Est. £2000-3000.

HN392
The Princess
Designer L. Harradine.
Date 1920 - 36.
23.5cm (9.25ins) high.
Yellow, cream, green
and pink.
Other colourways:
HN391, 420, 430, 431, 633.
Extremely rare.

HN388
In Grandma's Days
Designer C.J. Noke.
Date 1920 - 38.
22cm (8.75ins) high.
Pattened blue dress.
Other colourways: HN339, 340,
442; also called 'A Lilac Shawl'
HN44, 44A; 'The Poke Bonnet'
HN362, 612, 765.
Extremely rare.

HN393
The Necklace
(Also known as 'Lady without
Bouquet')
Designer G. Lambert.
Date 1920 - 36.
23cm (9ins) high.
Purple, green and yellow.
Other colourways: HN394.
Extremely rare.

HN394
The Necklace
Designer G. Lambert.
Date 1920 - 36.
23cm (9ins) high.
Green, orange, pink and yellow.
Other colourways: HN393.
Very rare.

HN399
Japanese Fan
Designer H. Tittensor.
Date 1920 - 36.
12.5cm (5ins) high.
Dark blue, green and yellow.
Other colourways: HN405,
439, 440; also as a lidded bowl
in flambé glaze.
Est. £1500-2500.

HN395
Contentment
Designer L. Harradine.
Date 1920 - 38.
18.5cm (7.25ins) high.
Green, lilac and yellow.
Other colourways: HN396,
421, 468, 572, 685, 686, 1323.
Est. £1000-1400.

HN400
Puff and Powder
Designer L. Harradine.
Date 1920 - 36.
16.5cm (6.5ins) high.
Green and blue bodice with
yellow skirt.
Other colourways: HN397,
398, 432, 433.
Extremely rare.

HN396
Contentment
Designer L. Harradine.
Date 1920 - 38.
18.5cm (7.25ins) high.
Blue, yellow and pink.
Other colourways: HN395,
421, 468, 572, 685, 686, 1323.
Est. £1000-1400.

HN401
Marie
First Version (Model 281)
Designer L. Harradine.
Date 1920 - 38.
18cm (7ins) high.
Cream, blue and yellow skirt
with pink bodice.
Other colourways: HN434,
502, 504, 505, 506.
Very rare.

HN397
Puff and Powder
Designer L. Harradine.
Date 1920 - 36.
16.5cm (6.5ins) high.
Brown, yellow and white.
Other colourways: HN398,
400, 432, 433.
Est. £1700-2200.

HN402
Betty
First Version (Model 282)
Designer L. Harradine.
Date 1920 - 38.
19cm (7.5ins) high.
Pink, brown, yellow and
black
Other colourways: HN403,
435, 438, 477, 478.
Very rare.

HN398
Puff and Powder
Designer L. Harradine.
Date 1920 - 36.
16.5cm (6.5ins) high.
Lilac and purple spot skirt.
Other colourways: HN397,
400, 432, 433.
Extremely rare.

HN403
Betty
First Version (Model 282)
Designer L. Harradine.
Date 1920 - 38.
19cm (7.5ins) high.
Green and cream skirt, blue
and yellow bodice.
Other colourways: HN402,
435, 438, 477, 478.
Very rare.

HN404
King Charles
Designers: C.J. Noke and
H. Tittensor.
Date 1920 - 51.
42.5cm (16.75ins) high.
Black and white with pink base.
Other colourways: HN2084, 3459.
Est. £1100-1500.

HN409
Omar Khayyam
First Version (Model 284)
Designer C.J. Noke.
Date 1920 - 38.
15cm (6ins) high.
Black and yellow.
Other colourways: HN408.
Extremely rare.

HN405
Japanese Fan
Designer H. Tittensor.
Date 1920 - 36.
12.5cm (5ins) high.
Pale yellow.
Other colourways: HN399, 439,
440; also recorded as a lidded
bowl in flambé glaze.
Extremely rare.

HN410
Blue Beard
(Without plume on turban)
First Version (Model 188)
Designer E.W. Light.
Date 1920 - 36.
28cm (11ins) high.
Dark green and blue.
Other colourways: HN75.
Est. £3000-4000.

HN406
The Bouquet
(Also known as 'The Nosegay')
Designer G. Lambert.
Date 1920 - 36.
23cm (9ins) high.
Pale blue and lemon.
Other colourways: HN414,
422, 428, 429, 567, 794.
Est. £1400-2000.

HN411
A Lady of the Elizabethan
Period
First Version (Model 165)
(Also known as 'Elizabethan Lady')
Designer E.W. Light.
Date 1920 - 38.
24cm (9.5ins) high.
Purple, black and white.
Other colourways: HN40,
40A, 73.
Est. £1250-1750.

HN407
Omar Khayyam and the
Beloved
Designer C.J. Noke.
Date 1920 - 36.
25.5cm (10ins) high.
Colour not known.
Other colourways: HN419,
459, 598.
Extremely rare.

HN412
A Jester
First Version (Model 170)
Designer C.J. Noke.
Date 1920 - 38.
25.5cm (10ins) high.
Green and red stripes.
Other colourways: HN45, 71,
71A, 320, 367, 426, 446, 552,
616, 627, 1295, 1702, 2016, 3922.
Very rare.

HN408
Omar Khayyam
First Version (Model 284)
Designer C.J. Noke.
Date 1920 - 38.
15cm (6ins) high.
Dark blue, brown and green.
Other colourways: HN409.
Extremely rare.

HN413
The Crinoline
Designer G. Lambert.
Date 1920 - 38.
16cm (6.25ins) high.
Pale blue and lemon.
Other colourways: HN8, 9,
9A, 21, 21A, 566, 628.
Est. £1100-1500.

HN414
The Bouquet
(Also known as 'The Nosegay')
Designer G. Lambert.
Date 1920 - 36.
23cm (9ins) high.
Blue, pink and yellow.
Other colourways: HN406, 422,
428, 429, 567, 794.
Extremely rare.

HN419
Omar Khayyam and the Beloved
Designer C.J. Noke.
Date 1920 - 36.
25.5cm (10ins) high.
Dark blue, yellow and green.
Other colourways: HN407,
459, 598.
Extremely rare.

HN415
Moorish Minstrel
Designer C.J. Noke.
Date 1920 - 38.
34.5cm (13.5ins) high.
Yellow and green.
Other colourways: HN34,
364, 797.
Est. £1500-2000.

HN420
The Princess
Designer L. Harradine.
Date 1920 - 36.
23.5cm (9.25ins) high.
Pink and yellow dress with
purple cape.
Other colourways: HN391, 392,
430, 431, 633.
Extremely rare.

HN416
Moorish Piper Minstrel
Designer C.J. Noke.
Date 1920 - 38.
34.5cm (13.5ins) high.
Yellow and green striped robe.
Other colourways: HN301, 328.
Extremely rare.

HN421
Contentment
Designer L. Harradine.
Date 1920 - 38.
18.5cm (7.25ins) high.
Pale green, pink and lemon.
Other colourways: HN395,
396, 468, 572, 685, 686, 1323.
Est. £1000-1500.

HN417
One of the Forty
First Version Models 288,289)
(Also known as 'Chu Chin Chow
with Beads')
Designer H. Tittensor.
Date 1920 - 36.
19.5-21cm (7.75-8.25ins) high.
Blue and green.
Other colourways: HN490, 495,
501, 528, 648, 677, 1351, 1352.
Extremely rare.

HN422
The Bouquet
(Also known as 'The Nosegay')
Designer G. Lambert.
Date 1920 - 36.
23cm (9ins) high.
Yellow and pink stripes.
Other colourways: HN406,
414, 428, 429, 567, 794.
Extremely rare.

HN418
One of the Forty
Second Version (Model 298)
(Also known as 'Chu Chin
Chow with Sack')
Designer H. Tittensor.
Date 1920 - 36.
18.5cm (7.25ins) high.
Striped green robes.
Other colourways: HN494, 498,
647, 666, 704, 1353.
Extremely rare.

HN423
One of the Forty
Third Version (Model 291)
(Also known as 'Chu Chin Chow'
in various descriptions)
Designer H. Tittensor.
Date 1921 - 36.
7-7.5cm (2.75-3ins) high.
Produced in a variety of colours.
Est. £500-900.

HN423A
One of the Forty
Fourth Version (Model 295)
(Also known as 'Chu Chin
Chow' in various descriptions)
Designer H. Tittensor.
Date 1921 - 36.
7-7.5cm (2.75-3ins) high.
Produced in a variety of
colour finishes.
Est. £500-900.

HN423B
One of the Forty
Fifth Version (Model 296)
(Also known as 'Chu Chin
Chow' in various descriptions)
Designer H. Tittensor.
Date 1921 - 36.
7-7.5cm (2.75-3ins) high.
Produced in a variety of
colour finishes.
Est. £500-900.

HN423C
One of the Forty
Sixth Version (Model 299)
(Also known as 'Chu Chin Chow'
in various descriptions)
Designer H. Tittensor.
Date 1921 - 36.
7-7.5cm (2.75-3ins) high.
Produced in a variety of colour
finishes.
Est. £500-900.

HN423D
One of the Forty
Seventh Version (Model 300)
(Also known as 'Chu Chin
Chow' in various descriptions)
Designer H. Tittensor.
Date 1921 - 36.
7-7.5cm (2.75-3ins) high.
Produced in a variety of colour
finishes.
Est. £500-900.

HN423E
One of the Forty
Eighth Version (Model 301)
(Also known as 'Chu Chin
Chow' in various descriptions)
Designer H. Tittensor.
Date 1921 - 36.
7-7.5cm (2.75-3ins) high.
Produced in a variety of colour
finishes.
Est. £500-900.

HN423F
One of the Forty
Ninth Version (Model 304)
(Also known as 'Chu Chin Chow'
in various descriptions)
Designer H. Tittensor.
Date 1921 - 38.
7-7.5cm (2.75-3ins) high.
Produced in a variety of colour finishes.
(Models 304, 317, and 318 have also
been recorded without HN numbers)
Est. £500-900.

HN424
Sleep
Second Version (Model 287)
Designer P. Stabler.
Date 1921 - 36.
15cm (6ins) high.
Blue.
Other colourways:
HN692, 710.
Est. £1000-1400.

HN425
The Goosegirl
First Version
Designer L. Harradine.
Date 1921 - 36.
20.5cm (8ins) high.
Blue stripes.
Designed to be a pair with
HN449 'Fruit Gathering'
Other colourways: HN436,
437, 448, 559, 560.
Extremely rare.

HN426
A Jester
First Version (Model 170)
Designer C.J. Noke.
Date 1921 - 38.
25.5cm (10ins) high.
Pink and black.
Other colourways: HN45, 71,
71A, 320, 367, 412, 446, 552, 616,
627, 1295, 1702, 2016, 3922.
Est. £2000-3000.

HN427
One of the Forty
Tenth Version (Model 303)
Designer H. Tittensor.
Date 1921 - 36.
Height not known.
Dark green.
Very rare.

HN428
The Bouquet
(Also known as 'The Nosegay')
Designer G. Lambert.
Date 1921 - 36.
23cm (9ins) high.
Green and blue.
Other colourways: HN406,
414, 422, 429, 567, 794.
Est. £1400-1800.

HN433
Puff and Powder
Designer L. Harradine.
Date 1921 - 36.
16.5cm (6.5ins) high.
Green spotted skirt, lilac
spotted overdress.
Other colourways: HN397, 398,
400, 432.
Est. £1700-2200.

HN429
The Bouquet
(Also known as 'The Nosegay')
Designer G. Lambert.
Date 1921 - 36.
23cm (9ins) high.
Green and dark red.
Other colourways: HN406, 414,
422, 428, 567, 794.
Est. £1400-1800.

HN434
Marie
First Version (Model 281)
Designer L. Harradine.
Date 1921 - 38.
18cm (7ins) high.
Yellow and orange striped skirt.
Other colourways: HN401,
502, 504, 505, 506.
Extremely rare.

HN430
The Princess
Designer L. Harradine.
Date 1921 - 36.
23.5cm (9.25ins) high.
Green floral dress and blue-green
striped cloak.
Other colourways: HN391, 392,
420, 431, 633.
Extremely rare.

HN435
Betty
First Version (Model 282)
Designer L. Harradine.
Date 1921 - 38.
19cm (7.5ins) high.
Blue skirt with yellow spots.
Other colourways: HN402,
403, 438, 477, 478.
Extremely rare.

HN431
The Princess
Designer L.Harradine.
Date 1921 - 36.
23.5cm (9.25ins) high.
White and yellow spotted
dress and yellow cloak.
Other colourways: HN391,
392, 420, 430, 633.
Extremely rare.

HN436
The Goosegirl
First Version
Designer L. Harradine.
Date 1921 - 36.
20.5cm (8ins) high.
Green and blue spotted skirt.
Other colourways: HN425,
437, 448, 559, 560.
Est. £1600-2000.

HN432
Puff and Powder
Designer L. Harradine.
Date 1921 - 36.
16.5cm (6.5ins) high.
Lilac skirt spotted with orange.
Other colourways: HN397,
398, 400, 433.
Extremely rare.

HN437
The Goosegirl
First Version
Designer L. Harradine.
Date 1921 - 36.
20.5cm (8ins) high.
Brown and lilac.
Other colourways: HN425, 436,
448, 559, 560.
Est. £1600-2000.

HN438
Betty
First Version (Model 282)
Designer L. Harradine.
Date 1921 - 38.
19cm (7.5ins) high.
Pale blue and cream.
Other colourways: HN402,
403, 435, 477, 478.
Extremely rare.

HN443
Out for a Walk
Designer E.W. Light.
Date 1921 - 36.
25.5cm (10ins) high.
Brown skirt.
Other colourways:
HN86, 748.
Extremely rare.

HN439
Japanese Fan
Designer H. Tittensor.
Date 1921 - 36.
12.5cm (5ins) high.
Blue costume with green spots.
Other colourways: HN399,
405, 440; also recorded in
flambé glaze.
Extremely rare.

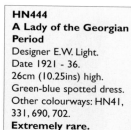

HN444
**A Lady of the Georgian
Period**
Designer E.W. Light.
Date 1921 - 36.
26cm (10.25ins) high.
Green-blue spotted dress.
Other colourways: HN41,
331, 690, 702.
Extremely rare.

HN440
Japanese Fan
Designer H. Tittensor.
Date 1921 - 36.
12.5cm (5ins) high.
Orange and cream.
Other colourways: HN399,
405, 439; also recorded in
flambé glaze.
Est. £1700-2200.

HN445
Guy Fawkes
First Version (Model 226)
Designer C.J. Noke.
Date 1921 - 38.
26.5cm (10.5ins) high.
Black costume and hat with
green cloak.
Other colourways: HN98, 347;
also recorded in Sung glaze.
Very rare.

HN441
The Parson's Daughter
Designer H. Tittensor.
Date 1921 - 38.
25.5cm (10ins) high.
Yellow dress with orange spots.
Other colourways: HN337, 338, 564,
790, 1242, 1356, 2018.
Est. £800-1100.

HN446
A Jester
First Version (Model 170)
Designer C.J. Noke.
Date 1921 - 38.
25.5cm (10ins) high.
Green, black and blue.
Other colourways: HN45, 71,
71A, 320, 367, 412, 426, 552,
616, 627, 1295, 1702, 2016, 3922.
Est. £2000-2500.

HN442
In Grandma's Days
Designer C.J. Noke.
Date 1921 - 38.
22cm (8.75ins) high.
Green shawl with white
spotted dress.
Other colourways: HN339, 340,
388; also called 'A Lilac Shawl'
HN44, 44A; 'The Poke Bonnet'
HN362, 612, 765.
Extremely rare.

HN447
Lady with Shawl
Designer L. Harradine.
Date 1921 - 1936.
33.5cm (13.25ins) high.
Green and cream striped dress
and spotted cloak.
Other colourways: HN458,
626, 678, 679
Est. £1600-2200.

HN448
The Goosegirl
First Version
Designer L. Harradine.
Date 1921 - 36.
20.5cm (8ins) high.
Blue stripes.
Other colourways: HN425,
436, 437, 559, 560.
Extremely rare.

HN449
Fruit Gathering
Designer L. Harradine.
Date 1921 - 36.
20.5cm (8ins) high.
Blue skirt with striped bouse.
(This figure was designed to
be a pair with HN425 'The
Goosegirl')
Other colourways: HN476,
503, 561, 562, 706, 707.
Extremely rare.

HN450
Chu Chin Chow
First Version (Model 308)
Designer C.J. Noke.
Date 1921 - 36.
17cm (6.75ins) high.
Red coat with green hat.
Other colourways: HN460, 461.
Very rare.

HN451
An Old Man
Designer not known.
Date 1921 - 38.
7.5cm (3ins) high.
Green, blue and red.
Extremely rare.

OUR PRICING POLICY has been to acquire individual pieces
from recent sales at either English auction houses or from the
internet. This information is shown on many of the figures within
this book, but we realise that you cannot take an individual sale
at auction or on the internet and expect that price to be the
general valuation of that particular piece; prices can be high or
low, it's all according to how many bidders want that particular
item, so taking that into consideration, we have made our
valuations within this book on many sales, not just one or two,
and from our findings we show an estimated spread valuation
which gives the average buying and selling price from which each
individual can use their own discretion.

HN453
The Gainsborough Hat
Designer H. Tittensor.
Date 1921 - 36.
22cm (8.75ins) high.
Red, green and blue.
Other colourways: HN46, 46A,
47, 329, 352, 383, 675, 705.
Extremely rare.

HN454
The Smiling Buddha
Designer C.J. Noke.
Date 1921 - 36.
16cm (6.25ins) high.
Blue and green.
Other colourways: Also
recorded in flambé and
Sung glazes.
Est. £1500-2000.

HN455
A Mandarin
Second Version (Model 260)
Designer C.J. Noke.
Date 1921 - 38.
21cm (8.25ins) high.
Green costume.
Other colourways: HN366, 641.
Extremely rare.

HN456
The Welsh Girl
(Also known as 'Myfanwy Jones')
Designer E.W. Light.
Date 1921 - 36.
30.5cm (12ins) high.
Green, white and brown.
Other colourways: HN39, 92,
514, 516, 519, 520, 660, 668,
669, 701, 792.
Est. £2200-3000.

HN457
Crouching Nude
Designer not known.
Date 1921 - 36.
14cm (5.5ins) high.
Cream with green base.
Est. £1100-1500.

HN458
Lady with Shawl
Designer L. Harradine.
Date 1921 - 36.
33.5cm (13.25ins) high.
Pink dress, multicoloured
shawl.
Other colourways: HN447,
626, 678, 679.
Extremely rare.

HN463
Polly Peachum
First Version (Model 320)
Designer L. Harradine.
Date 1921 - 49.
16.5cm (6.5ins) high.
Pink and blue.
Other colourways: HN465,
550, 589, 614, 680, 693.
Series: Beggar's Opera.
Est. £400-500.

HN459
**Omar Khayyam
and the Beloved**
Designer C.J. Noke.
Date 1921 - 36.
25.5cm (10ins) high.
Purple, lilac, green and orange.
Other colourways: HN407, 419,
598.
Very rare.

HN464
Captain MacHeath
Designer L. Harradine.
Date 1921 - 49.
18cm (7ins) high.
Red, black and yellow.
Other colourways: HN590, 1256.
Series: Beggar's Opera.
Est. £350-450.

HN460
Chu Chin Chow
First Version (Model 308)
Designer C.J. Noke.
Date 1921 - 36.
17cm (6.75ins) high.
Blue and pale green.
Other colourways: HN450, 461.
Extremely rare.

HN465
Polly Peachum
First Version (Model 320)
Designer L. Harradine.
Date 1921 - 49.
16.5cm (6.5ins) high.
Red and white.
Other colourways: HN463,
550, 589, 614, 680, 693.
Series: Beggar's Opera.
Est. £400-500.

HN461
Chu Chin Chow
First Version (Model 308)
Designer C.J. Noke.
Date 1921 - 36.
17cm (6.75ins) high.
Red and black.
Other colourways: HN450, 460.
Extremely rare.

HN466
Tulips
Designer not known.
Date 1921 - 36.
24cm (9.5ins) high.
Green dress.
Other colourways: HN488,
672, 747, 1334.
Extremely rare.

HN462
Motherhood
Second Version (Model 329)
Designer not known.
Date 1921 - 38.
23.5cm (9.25ins) high.
Green, light brown and white.
Other colourways: HN570,
703, 743.
Est. £2000-3000.

HN467
Doris Keane as Cavallini
First Version (Model 205)
Designer C. J. Noke.
Date 1921 - 36.
28cm (11ins) high.
Dark green with gold jewellery.
Other colourways: HN90.
Very rare.

HN468
Contentment
Designer L. Harradine.
Date 1921 - 38.
18.5cm (7.25ins) high.
Spotted green dress.
Other colourways: HN395,
396, 421, 572, 685, 686, 1323.
Est. £1300-1800.

HN473
Summer
First Version (Model 219)
Designer not known.
Date 1921 - 38.
19cm (7.5ins) high.
Patterned pale green robe.
Other colourways: HN313.
Series: The Seasons (Series One)
Extremely rare.

HN469
Dolly
Second Version (Model 279)
(Also known as 'The Little Mother')
Designer H. Tittensor.
Date 1921 - 38.
28cm (11ins) high.
White dress.
Other colourways: HN389, 390.
Extremely rare.

HN474
Autumn
First Version (Model 222)
Designer not known.
Date 1921 - 38.
19cm (7.5ins) high.
Patterned pink robe.
Other colourways: HN314.
Series: The Seasons (Series One)
Extremely rare.

HN470
Lady and Blackamoor
Second Version (Model 273)
Designer H. Tittensor.
Date 1921 - 36.
18.5cm (7.25ins) high.
Lilac and green dress.
Other colourways: HN375, 377.
Extremely rare.

*Picture
not available
at present*

HN475
Winter
First Version (Model 223)
Designer not known.
Date 1921 - 38.
19cm (7.5ins) high.
Patterned pale green robe.
Other colourways: HN315.
Series: The Seasons (Series One)
Extremely rare.

HN471
Katharine
Designer C. J. Noke.
Date 1921 - 38.
14.5cm (5.75ins) high.
Spotted green dress.
Other colourways: HN61,
74, 341, 615, 793.
Est. £1000-1400.

HN476
Fruit Gathering
Designer L. Harradine.
Date 1921 - 36.
20.5cm (8ins) high.
Lilac and lemon.
Other colourways: HN449,
503, 561, 562, 706, 707.
Est. £1500-2000.

HN472
Spring
First Version (Model 215)
Designer not known.
Date 1921 - 38.
19cm (7.5ins) high.
Patterned lilac robe.
Other colourways: HN312.
Series: The Seasons (Series One)
Est. £800-1100.

HN477
Betty
First Version (Model 282)
Designer L. Harradine.
Date 1921 - 38.
19cm (7.5ins) high.
Spotted green skirt.
Other colourways: HN402,
403, 435, 438, 478.
Extremely rare.

HN478
Betty
First Version (Model 282)
Designer L. Harradine.
Date 1921 - 38.
19cm (7.5ins) high.
White spotted skirt.
Other colourways: HN402,
403, 435, 438, 477.
Very rare.

HN483
One of the Forty
Twelfth Version (Model 319)
Designer H. Tittensor.
Date 1921 - 38.
Height not known.
Green striped robes and brown
hat.
Other colourways: HN481, 491,
646, 667, 712, 1336, 1350; also
recorded in flambé glaze.
Extremely rare.

HN479
The Balloon Seller
First Version (Model 321)
(Also known as 'The Balloon
Woman')
Designer L. Harradine.
Date 1921 - 38.
23cm (9ins) high.
Dark blue, pink, red and lilac.
Other colourways: HN486, 548,
583, 697.
Est. £1000-1400.

HN484
One of the Forty
Thirteenth Version (Model 327)
Designer H. Tittensor.
Date 1921 - 38.
15cm (6ins) high.
Green mottled robes.
Other colourways: HN482,
492, 645, 663, 713.
Extremely rare.

HN480
One of the Forty
Eleventh Version (Model 328)
Designer H. Tittensor.
Date 1921 - 38.
17cm (6.75ins) high.
Brown and yellow with blue hat.
Other colourways: HN493, 497,
499, 664, 714.
Est. £1200-1800.

HN485
Lucy Lockett
First Version (Model 360)
Designer L. Harradine.
Date 1921 - 49.
15cm (6ins) high.
Yellow and red.
Series: Beggar's Opera.
Est. £750-1100.

HN481
One of the Forty
Twelfth Version (Model 319)
Designer H. Tittensor.
Date 1921 - 36.
Height not known.
Dark spotted robe.
Other colourways: HN483,
491, 646, 667, 712, 1336, 1350;
also recorded in flambé glaze.
Extremely rare.

HN486
The Balloon Seller
First Version (Model 321)
(Also known as 'The Balloon
Woman')
Designer L. Harradine.
Date 1921 - 38.
23cm (9ins) high.
Blue dress without a hat.
Other colourways: HN479,
548, 583, 697.
Extremely rare.

HN482
One of the Forty
Thirteenth Version (Model 327)
Designer H. Tittensor.
Date 1921 - 38.
15cm (6ins) high.
White robe with spotted waistband.
Other colourways: HN484, 492,
645, 663, 713.
Extremely rare.

HN487
Pavlova
(Also known as
'Swan Song')
Designer C. J. Noke.
Date 1921 - 38.
11cm (4.25ins) high.
White with black base.
Other colourways:
HN676.
Extremely rare.

HN488
Tulips
Designer not known.
Date 1921 - 36
24cm (9.5ins) high.
Ivory.
Other colourways: HN466,
672, 747, 1334.
Extremely rare.

HN493
One of the Forty
Eleventh Version (Model 328)
Designer H. Tittensor.
Date 1921 - 38.
17cm (6.75ins) high.
Blue and black.
Other colourways: HN480,
497, 499, 664, 714.
Extremely rare.

HN489
Polly Peachum
Second Version
(Also known 'Polly Peachum-Curtsey'
or 'Curtsey') (Model 316)
Designer L. Harradine.
Date 1921 - 38.
11cm (4.25ins) high.
Turquoise and white.
Other colourways:
HN549, 620, 694, 734.
Series: Beggar's Opera.　**Est. £250-350.**

HN494
One of the Forty
Second Version (Model 298)
(Also known as 'Chu Chin
Chow with Sack')
Designer H. Tittensor.
Date 1921 - 36.
18.5cm (7.25ins) high.
White robes.
Other colourways: HN418, 498,
647, 666, 704, 1353.
Extremely rare.

HN490
One of the Forty
First Version (Model 289)
(Also known as 'Chu Chin Chow
with Beads')
Designer H. Tittensor.
Date 1921 - 38.
21cm (8.25ins) high.
Blue and brown chequered coat.
Other colourways: HN417, 495,
501, 528, 648, 677, 1351, 1352.
Extremely rare.

HN495
One of the Forty
First Version (Model 289)
(Also known as 'Chu Chin
Chow with Beads')
Designer H. Tittensor.
Date 1921 - 38.
21cm (8.25ins) high.
Brown, yellow and blue.
Other colourways: HN417, 490,
501, 528, 648, 677, 1351, 1352.
Extremely rare.

HN491
One of the Forty
Twelfth Version (Model 319)
Designer H. Tittensor.
Date 1921 - 36.
Height not known.
White robes, green hat.
Other colourways: HN481,
483, 646, 667, 712, 1336, 1350.
(Also recorded in flambé glaze)
Extremely rare.

HN496
One of the Forty
Fourteenth Version (Model 313)
Designer H. Tittensor.
Date 1921 - 38.
19.5cm (7.75ins) high.
Yellow and black checks with
yellow vase and hat.
Other colourways: HN500,
649, 665, 1354.
Extremely rare.

HN492
One of the Forty
Thirteenth Version (Model 327)
Designer H. Tittensor.
Date 1921 - 38.
15cm (6ins) high.
White and yellow.
Other colourways: HN482,
484, 645, 663, 713.
Extremely rare.

HN497
One of the Forty
Eleventh Version (Model 328)
Designer H. Tittensor.
Date 1921 - 38.
17cm (6.75ins) high.
Brown, black, red and green.
Other colourways: HN480, 493,
499, 664, 714.
Very rare.

HN498
One of the Forty
Second Version (Model 298)
(Also known as 'Chu Chin Chow
with Sack')
Designer H. Tittensor.
Date 1921 - 36.
18.5cm (7.25ins) high.
Dark striped coat, pale trousers.
Other colourways: HN418, 494,
647, 666, 704, 1353.
Extremely rare.

HN499
One of the Forty
Eleventh Version (Model 328)
Designer H. Tittensor.
Date 1921 - 38.
17cm (6.75ins) high.
Green and cream.
Other colourways: HN480,
493, 497, 664, 714.
Extremely rare.

HN500
One of the Forty
Fourteenth Version (Model 313)
Designer H. Tittensor.
Date 1921 - 38.
19.5cm (7.75ins) high.
Yellow checks with red hat.
Other colourways: HN496,
649, 665, 1354.
Extremely rare.

HN501
One of the Forty
First Version (Model 288)
(Also known as 'Chu Chin Chow
with Beads')
Designer H. Tittensor.
Date 1921 - 38.
21cm (8.25ins) high.
Green striped coat.
Other colourways: HN417, 490,
495, 528, 648, 677, 1351, 1352.
Extremely rare.

HN502
Marie
First Version (Model 281)
Designer L. Harradine.
Date 1921 - 38.
18cm (7ins) high.
White, blue and red.
Other colourways: HN401,
434, 504, 505, 506.
Extremely rare.

HN503
Fruit Gathering
Designer L. Harradine.
Date 1921 - 36.
20.5cm (8ins) high.
Brown and blue check dress.
Other colourways: HN449,
476, 561, 562, 706, 707.
Est. £1500-2000.

HN504
Marie
First Version (Model 281)
Designer L. Harradine.
Date 1921 - 38.
18cm (7ins) high.
Blue and green dress with
red spots.
Other colourways: HN401,
434, 502, 505, 506.
Extremely rare.

HN505
Marie
First Version (Model 281)
Designer L. Harradine.
Date 1921 - 38.
18cm (7ins) high.
Blue bodice, green and lilac
skirt.
Other colourways: HN401,
434, 502, 504, 506.
Extremely rare.

HN506
Marie
First Version (Model 281)
Designer L. Harradine.
Date 1921 - 38.
18cm (7ins) high.
Blue and green striped
bodice, lilac spotted skirt.
Other colourways: HN401,
434, 502, 504, 505.
Extremely rare.

HN507
Pussy
(Also known as 'The Black Cat')
Designer F.C. Stone.
Date 1921 - 38.
19cm (7.5ins) high.
Blue spotted dress.
Other colourways: HN18, 325.
Extremely rare.

HN508
An Orange Vendor
Designer C.J. Noke.
Date 1921 - 38.
16cm (6.25ins) high.
Red, tan, orange and cream.
Other colourways: HN72, 521,
1966.
Est. £800-1000.

HN513
Picardy Peasant (woman)
Designer P. Stabler.
Date 1921 - 38.
24cm (9.5ins) high.
Blue.
Other colourways: HN4, 5, 17A,
351.
Extremely rare.

HN509
Lady of the Fan
Designer E.W. Light.
Date 1921 - 36.
24cm (9.5ins) high.
Lilac, blue and green spotted
dress.
Other colourways: HN48, 52, 53,
53A, 335.
Extremely rare.

HN514
The Welsh Girl
(Also known as 'Myfanwy Jones')
Designer E.W. Light.
Date 1921 - 36.
30.5cm (12ins) high.
Green skirt with spotted apron.
Other colourways: HN39, 92, 456,
516, 519, 520, 660, 668, 669, 701,
792.
Extremely rare.

HN510
A Child's Grace
Designer L. Perugini.
Date 1921 - 38.
17cm (6.75ins) high.
Green chequered dress with
green base.
Other colourways: HN62, 62A.
Extremely rare.

HN515
Lady with Rose
Designer E.W. Light.
Date 1921 - 36.
24cm (9.5ins) high.
Lilac stripes on green dress.
Other colourways: HN48A,
52A, 68, 304, 336, 517, 584,
624.
Extremely rare.

HN511
Upon her Cheeks she Wept
Designer L. Perugini.
Date 1921 - 38.
23cm (9ins) high.
Lilac dress with large spots.
Other colourways: HN59, 522.
Extremely rare.

HN516
The Welsh Girl
(Also known as 'Myfanwy Jones')
Designer E.W. Light.
Date 1921 - 36.
30.5cm (12ins) high.
Lilac check dress with black cloak.
Other colourways: HN39, 92,
456, 514, 519, 520, 660, 668, 669,
701, 792.
Extremely rare.

HN512
A Spook
Designer H. Tittensor.
Date 1921 - 36.
18cm (7ins) high.
Purple and lilac.
Other colourways: HN50,
51, 51A, 51B, 58, 625, 1218;
also recorded in flambé
glaze and in miniature.
Very rare.

HN517
Lady with Rose
Designer E.W. Light.
Date 1921 - 36.
24cm (9.5ins) high.
Lilac dress with orange spots.
Other colourways: HN48A,
52A, 68, 304, 336, 515, 584, 624.
Extremely rare.

HN518
The Curtsey
First Version
Designer E.W. Light.
Date 1921 - 36.
28cm (11ins) high.
Lilac skirt with orange spots.
Other colourways: HN57, 57B,
66A, 327, 334, 363, 371, 547,
629, 670.
Extremely rare.

HN523
Sentinel
Designer not known.
Date 1921 - 38.
44.5cm (17.5ins) high.
Blue, red and black.
Extremely rare.

HN519
The Welsh Girl
(Also known as 'Myfanwy Jones')
Designer E.W. Light.
Date 1921 - 36.
30.5cm (12ins) high.
Blue and lilac.
Other colourways: HN39, 92,
456, 514, 516, 520, 660, 668,
669, 701, 792.
Extremely rare.

HN524
Lucy Lockett
Second Version (Model 360)
Designer L. Harradine.
Date 1921 - 49.
15cm (6ins) high.
Orange and brown.
Series: Beggar's Opera.
(Ebay 16.3.04 sold £300)
Est. £300-400.

HN520
The Welsh Girl
(Also known as 'Myfanwy Jones')
Designer E.W. Light
Date 1921 - 36.
30.5cm (12ins) high.
Spotted lilac dress.
Other colourways: HN39, 92,
456, 514, 516, 519, 660, 668,
669, 701, 792.
Extremely rare.

HN525
The Flower Seller's Children
Designer L. Harradine.
Date 1921 - 49.
21cm (8.25ins) high.
Green and blue.
Other colourways: HN551,
1206, 1342, 1406.
Extremely rare.

HN521
An Orange Vendor
Designer C.J. Noke.
Date 1921 - 38.
16cm (6.25ins) high.
Pale blue with black collar and
purple hood.
Other colourways: HN72,
508, 1966.
Extremely rare.

HN526
The Beggar
First Version (Model 348)
Designer L. Harradine.
Date 1921 - 49.
16.5cm (6.5ins) high.
Green, red and blue.
Other colourways: HN591.
Series: Beggar's Opera.
Est. £400-550.

HN522
**Upon her Cheeks
she Wept**
Designer L. Perugini.
Date 1921 - 38.
23cm (9ins) high.
Lilac dress with small spots.
Other colourways: HN59, 511.
Extremely rare.

HN527
The Highwayman
Designer L. Harradine.
Date 1921 - 49.
16.5cm (6.5ins) high.
Red, green and black.
Other colourways: HN592, 1257.
Series: Beggar's Opera.
Est. £300-350.

HN528
One of the Forty
First Version (Model 289)
(Also known as 'Chu Chin Chow
with Beads')
Designer H. Tittensor.
Date 1921 - 38.
21cm (8.25ins) high.
Brown robes.
Other colourways: HN417, 490,
495, 501, 648, 677, 1351, 1352.
Extremely rare.

HN529
Mr Pickwick
First Version (Model 352)
Designer L. Harradine.
Date 1922 - 32.
9.5cm (3.75ins) high.
Black, cream, white and tan.
Other colourways: M41.
Series: Dickens (Series One)
(Re-numbered as a Miniature
M41 in 1932)
Est. £35-45.

HN530
Fat Boy
First Version (Model 356)
Designer L. Harradine.
Date 1922 - 32.
9cm (3.5ins) high.
Pale blue, black, tan and white.
Other colourways: M44.
Series: Dickens (Series One)
(Re-numbered as a Miniature M44
in 1932)
Est. £35-45.

HN531
Sam Weller
Designer L. Harradine.
Date 1922 - 32.
10cm (4ins) high.
Yellow, white, red and brown.
Other colourways: M48.
Series: Dickens (Series One)
(Re-numbered as a Miniature
M48 in 1932)
Est. £35-45.

HN532
Mr Micawber
First Version (Model 357)
Designer L. Harradine.
Date 1922 - 32.
9cm (3.5ins) high.
Tan, black, white and yellow.
Other colourways: M42.
Series: Dickens (Series One)
(Re-numbered as a Miniature
M42 in 1932)
Est. £35-45.

HN533
Sairey Gamp
First Version (Model 358)
Designer L. Harradine.
Date 1922 - 32.
10cm (4ins) high.
Green, white and brown.
Other colourways: M46.
Series: Dickens (Series One)
(Re-numbered as a Miniature
M46 in 1932)
Est. £35-45.

HN534
Fagin
First Version
Designer L. Harradine.
Date 1922 - 32.
10cm (4ins) high.
Dark brown and orange.
Other colourways: M49.
Series: Dickens (Series One)
(Re-numbered as a Miniature
M49 in 1932)
Est. £35-45.

HN535
Pecksniff
First Version (Model 373)
Designer L. Harradine.
Date 1922 - 1932.
9.5cm (3.75ins) high.
Brown, white and tan.
Other colourways: M43.
Series: Dickens (Series One)
(Re-numbered as a Miniature
M43 in 1932)
Est. £35-45.

HN536
Stiggins
Designer L. Harradine.
Date 1922 - 32.
9.5cm (3.75 ins) high.
Black, tan and white.
Other colourways: M50.
Series: Dickens (Series One)
(Re-numbered as a Miniature
M50 in 1932)
Est. £35-45.

HN537
Bill Sykes
First Version.
Designer L. Harradine.
Date 1922 - 32.
9.5cm (3.75ins) high.
Black, white and brown.
Other colourways: M54.
Series: Dickens (Series One)
(Re-numbered as a Miniature
M54 in 1932)
Est. £35-45.

HN538
Buz Fuz
Designer L. Harradine.
Date 1922 - 32.
9.5cm (3.75ins) high.
Black, white and brown.
Other colourways: M53.
Series: Dickens (Series One)
(Re-numbered as a Miniature
M53 in 1932)
Est. £35-45.

HN539
Tiny Tim
Designer L. Harradine.
Date 1922 - 32.
9cm (3.5ins) high.
Black, white, brown and blue.
Other colourways: M56.
Series: Dickens (Series One)
(Re-numbered as a Miniature
M56 in 1932)
Est. £35-45.

HN540
Little Nell
Designer L. Harradine.
Date 1922 - 32.
10cm (4ins) high.
Pink and white.
Other colourways: M51.
Series: Dickens (Series One)
(Re-numbered as a Miniature
M51 in 1932)
Est. £35-45.

HN541
Alfred Jingle
Designer L. Harradine.
Date 1922 -32.
9.5cm (3.75ins) high.
Black and brown.
Other colourways: M52.
Series: Dickens (Series One)
(Re-numbered as a
Miniature M52 in 1932)
Est. £35-45.

HN542
The Cobbler
First Version (Model 362)
Designer C.J. Noke.
Date 1922 - 39.
19cm (7.5ins) high.
Green, yellow and brown.
Other colourways: HN543, 682.
Est. £450-600.

HN543
The Cobbler
First Version (Model 362)
Designer C.J. Noke.
Date 1922 - 38.
19cm (7.5ins) high.
Green, yellow and brown.
Other colourways: HN542,
682. (This figure is as HN542
but with a special firing)
Extremely rare.

HN544
Tony Weller
Second Version (Model 364)
Designer L. Harradine.
Date 1922 - 32.
9cm (3.5ins) high.
Green, yellow and red.
Other colourways: M47.
Series: Dickens (Series One)
(Re-numbered as a Miniature
M47 in 1932)
Est. £35-45.

HN545
Uriah Heep
First Version (Model 376)
Designer L. Harradine.
Date 1922 - 32.
10cm (4ins) high.
Black, grey and white.
Other colourways: M45.
Series: Dickens (Series One)
(Re-numbered as a Miniature
M45 in 1932)
Est. £35-45.

HN546
Artful Dodger
Designer L. Harradine.
Date 1922 - 32.
9.5cm (3.75ins) high.
Brown, white and black.
Other colourways: M55.
Series: Dickens (Series One)
(Re-numbered as a Miniature
M55 in 1932)
Est. £35-45.

HN547
The Curtsey
First Version
Designer E.W. Light.
Date 1922 - 36.
28cm (11ins) high.
Yellow and green skirt with
blue bodice.
Other colourways: HN57, 57B,
66A, 327, 334, 363, 371, 518,
629, 670.
Very rare.

HN548
The Balloon Seller
First Version (Model 321)
(Also known as 'The Balloon
Woman')
Designer L. Harradine.
Date 1922 - 38.
23cm (9ins) high.
Blue dress with black shawl.
Other colourways: HN479, 486,
583, 697.
Very rare.

HN553
Pecksniff
Second Version (Model 385)
Designer L. Harradine.
Date 1923 - 39.
18cm (7ins) high.
Black white and tan.
Other colourways: HN1891.
Series: Dickens (Series Two)
Est. £150-250.

HN549
Polly Peachum
Second Version (Model 316)
(Also 'Polly Peachum - Curtsey' or 'Curtsey')
Designer L. Harradine. Date 1922-49.
11cm (4.25ins) high.
Pink and white.
Other colourways:
HN489, 620, 694, 734.
Series: Beggar's Opera.
(Ebay 3.10.04 sold £210)
Est. £200-300.

HN554
Uriah Heep
Second Version (Model 384)
Designer L. Harradine.
Date 1923 - 39.
18.5cm (7.25ins) high.
Black and white.
Other colourways: HN1892.
Series: Dickens (Series Two)
Est. £150-250.

HN550
Polly Peachum
First Version (Model 320)
Designer L. Harradine.
Date 1922 - 49.
16.5cm (6.5ins) high.
Pink and white.
Other colourways: HN463,
465, 589, 614, 680, 693.
Series: Beggar's Opera.
Est. £250-350.

HN555
Fat Boy
Second Version (Model 381)
Designer L. Harradine.
Date 1923 - 39.
18cm (7ins) high.
Blue, white, brown and cream.
Other colourways: HN1893.
Series: Dickens (Series Two)
Est. £150-250.

HN551
The Flower Seller's Children
Designer L. Harradine.
Date 1922 - 49.
21cm (8.25ins) high.
Blue, yellow and orange.
Other colourways: HN525,
1206, 1342, 1406.
Extremely rare.

HN556
Mr. Pickwick
Second Version (Model 379)
Designer L. Harradine.
Date 1923 - 39.
18cm (7ins) high.
Blue, yellow, white and tan.
Other colourways: HN1894.
Series: Dickens (Series Two)
Est. £150-250.

HN552
A Jester
First Version (Model 170)
Designer C.J. Noke.
Date 1922 - 38.
25.5cm (10ins) high.
Black and red.
Other colourways: HN45,
71, 71A, 320, 367, 412, 426,
446, 616, 627, 1295, 1702,
2016, 3922.
Est. £2000-2500.

HN557
Mr. Micawber
Second Version (Model 380)
Designer L. Harradine.
Date 1923 - 39.
18cm (7ins) high.
Brown, tan, white and black.
Other colourways: HN1895.
Series: Dickens (Series Two)
*(Auction Bonhams Edinburgh
sold £100 plus comm.)*
Est. £150-250.

HN558
Sairey Gamp
Second Version (Model 382)
Designer L. Harradine.
Date 1923 - 39.
18cm (7ins) high.
Black, grey and white.
Other colourways: HN1896.
Series: Dickens (Series Two)
Est. £350-475.

HN563
Man in Tudor Costume
Designer not known.
Date 1923 - 38.
9cm (3.5ins) high.
Orange striped tunic, green tights,
black cloak.
Est. £1600-2200.

HN559
The Goosegirl
First Version.
Designer L. Harradine.
Date 1923 - 36.
20.5cm (8ins) high.
Pink dress and cream apron.
Other colourways: HN425,
436, 437, 448, 560.
Est. £1800-2500.

HN564
The Parson's Daughter
Designer H. Tittensor.
Date 1923 - 49.
25.5cm (10ins) high.
Red, yellow and coloured
patchwork skirt.
Other colourways: HN337, 338,
441, 790, 1242, 1356, 2018.
*(Auction PSA 23.6.04 sold
£175 plus comm.)*
Est. £200-250.

HN560
The Goosegirl
First Version
Designer L. Harradine.
Date 1923 - 36.
20.5cm (8ins) high.
Pink and white skirt with
pink blouse.
Other colourways: HN425,
436, 437, 448, 559.
Very rare.

HN565
Pretty Lady
Designer H. Tittensor.
Date 1923 - 38.
24cm (9.5ins) high.
Orange and lilac.
Other colourways: HN69, 70,
302, 330, 361, 384, 700, 763, 783.
Est. £900-1250.

HN561
Fruit Gathering
Designer L. Harradine.
Date 1923 - 36.
20.5cm (8ins) high.
White, green and pink.
Other colourways: HN449,
476, 503, 562, 706, 707.
Extremely rare.

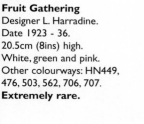

HN566
The Crinoline
Designer G. Lambert.
Date 1923 - 38.
16cm (6.25ins) high.
Cream, brown and green.
Other colourways: HN8, 9,
9A, 21, 21A, 413, 628.
Est. £1100-1500.

HN562
Fruit Gathering
Designer L. Harradine.
Date 1923 - 36.
20.5cm (8ins) high.
Pink, white and green.
Other colourways: HN449,
476, 503, 561, 706, 707.
Est. £1400-1900.

HN567
The Bouquet
(Also known as 'The Nosegay')
Designer G. Lambert.
Date 1923 - 36.
23cm (9ins) high.
Pink and cream.
Other colourways: HN406,
414, 422, 428, 429, 794.
Est. £1600-2200.

HN568
Shy Anne
Designer L. Perugini.
Date 1923 - 36.
19.5cm (7.75ins) high.
Green spotted dress, mauve,
pink ribbon.
Other colourways: HN60, 64, 65.
Est. £2200-3500.

HN569
The Lavender Woman
(Also known as 'The Lavender Girl'
and 'Any Old Lavender')
Designer P. Stabler.
Date 1924 - 36.
21.5cm (8.75ins) high.
Pink, brown and lilac.
Other colourways: HN22, 23,
23A, 342, 744.
Est. £1850-2250.

HN570
Motherhood
Second Version (Model 329)
Designer not known.
Date 1923 - 38.
23.5cm (9.25ins) high.
Pink, cream and green.
Other colourways: HN462,
703, 743.
Est. £3000-4000.

HN571
Falstaff
First Version (Model 401)
Designer C.J. Noke.
Date 1923 - 38.
18cm (7ins) high.
Brown and pale green.
Other colourways: HN575,
608, 609, 619, 638, 1216, 1606.
Est. £1100-1400.

HN572
Contentment
Designer L. Harradine.
Date 1923 - 38.
18.5cm (7.25ins) high.
Yellow and orange.
Other colourways:
HN395, 396, 421, 468,
685, 686, 1323.
Est. £950-1250.

HN573
Madonna of the Square
Designer P. Stabler.
Date 1923 - 36.
18cm (7ins) high.
Orange.
Other colourways: HN10, 10A,
11, 14, 27, 326, 576, 594, 613,
764, 1968, 1969, 2034.
Extremely rare.

As Doulton's chief modeller, Charles Noke
was very keen to revive the Staffordshire figure
tradition of the 18th century and in 1909 he
offered the opportunity to well known sculptors
of the day to design small ceramic figures. By
1912 he had collected enough to launch the 'HN'
series of models. Harry Nixon was in charge of
the figure-painting department and his initials
were taken for the series.

HN575
Falstaff
First Version (Model 401)
Designer C.J. Noke.
Date 1923 - 38.
18cm (7ins) high.
Yellow, cream and brown.
Other colourways: HN571,
608, 609, 619, 638, 1216, 1606.
Est. £1000-1300.

HN576
Madonna of the Square
Designer P. Stabler.
Date 1923 - 36.
18cm (7ins) high.
Green, orange and black.
Other colourways: HN10, 10A,
11, 14, 27, 326, 573, 594, 613,
764, 1968, 1969, 2034.
Est. £850-1150.

HN577
The Chelsea Pair (woman)
Designer L. Harradine.
Date 1923 - 38.
15cm (6ins) high.
White, blue and red.
Other colourways: HN578.
Est. £350-450.

HN578
The Chelsea Pair (woman)
Designer L. Harradine.
Date 1923 - 38.
15cm (6ins) high.
White skirt with red blouse,
Other colourways: HN577.
Est. £350-450.

HN583
The Balloon Seller
First Version (Model 321)
(Also known as 'The Balloon Woman')
Designer L. Harradine.
Date 1923 - 49.
23cm (9ins) high.
Green, pink and cream with
coloured balloons.
Other colourways: HN479, 486,
548, 697.
Est. £500-750.

HN579
The Chelsea Pair (man)
Designer L. Harradine.
Date 1923 - 38.
15cm (6ins) high.
Red, black, white and yellow.
Other colourways: HN580.
Est. £350-450.

HN584
Lady with Rose
Designer E.W. Light.
Date 1923 - 36.
24cm (9.5ins) high.
Pink and green.
Other colourways: HN48A,
52A, 68, 304, 336, 515, 517, 624.
Extremely rare.

HN580
The Chelsea Pair (man)
Designer L. Harradine.
Date 1923 - 38.
15cm (6ins) high.
Red, blue and black.
Other colourways: HN579.
Est. £350-450.

HN585
Harlequinade
First Version
Designer L. Harradine.
Date 1923 - 40.
18cm (7ins) high.
Green, yellow, black and purple.
Other colourways: HN635,
711, 780.
Est. £2000-3000.

HN581
The Perfect Pair
Designer L. Harradine.
Date 1923 - 38.
18cm (7ins) high.
Pink, red, grey and white.
Est. £500-750.

HN586
Boy with Turban
(Also known as 'Eastern Boy')
Designer L. Harradine.
Date 1923 - 36.
9.5cm (3.75ins) high.
Green, white and blue.
Other colourways: HN587,
661, 662, 1210, 1212, 1213,
1214, 1225.
Est. £600-800.

HN582
Grossmith's 'Tsang Ihang'
Perfume of Tibet
Designer not known.
Date 1923 - not known.
29cm (11.5ins) high.
Yellow, white, black and blue.
Est. £450-600.

HN587
Boy with Turban
(Also known as 'Eastern Boy')
Designer L. Harradine.
Date 1923 - 36.
9.5cm (3.75ins) high.
Green, red, white and blue.
Other colourways: HN586, 661,
662, 1210, 1212, 1213, 1214, 1225.
Est. £600-800.

HN588
Spring
Second Version (Model 426)
(Also known as 'Girl with
Yellow Frock')
Designer L. Harradine.
Date 1923 - 38.
16cm (6.25ins) high.
Yellow and pink dress.
Very rare.

HN593
Nude on Rock
Designer not known.
Date 1924 - 38.
17cm (6.75ins) high.
Blue.
Extremely rare.

HN589
Polly Peachum
First Version (Model 320)
Designer L. Harradine.
Date 1924 - 49.
16.5cm (6.5ins) high.
Pink and yellow.
Other colourways: HN463,
465, 550, 614, 680, 693.
Series: Beggar's Opera.
Very rare.

HN594
Madonna of the Square
Designer P. Stabler.
Date 1924 - 36.
18cm (7ins) high.
Green and brown.
Other colourways: HN10, 10A,
11, 14, 27, 326, 573, 576, 613,
764, 1968, 1969, 2034.
Extremely rare.

HN590
Captain MacHeath
Designer L. Harradine.
Date 1924 - 49.
18cm (7ins) high.
Red, yellow and black.
Other colourways: HN464, 1256.
Series: Beggar's Opera.
Est. £500-650.

HN595
Grief
Designer C.J. Noke.
Date 1924 - 38.
4.5cm (1.75ins) high.
Blue.
Est. £900-1200.

HN591
The Beggar
First Version (Model 348)
Designer L. Harradine.
Date 1924 - 49.
16.5cm (6.5ins) high.
Green, red and blue.
Other colourways: Same
colours as HN526 but with
different glaze.
Series: Beggar's Opera.
Est. £400-550.

HN596
Despair
Designer C.J. Noke.
Date 1924 - 38.
12cm (4.75ins) high.
Blue.
Extremely rare.

*Picture
not available
at present*

HN592
The Highwayman
Designer L. Harradine.
Date 1924 - 49.
16.5cm (6.5ins) high.
Green and red.
Other colourways: HN1257.
Same colours as HN527 but
with different glaze.
Series: Beggar's Opera.
Est. £400-550.

HN597
The Bather
First Version (Model 428)
Designer L. Harradine.
Date 1924 - 38.
19.5cm (7.75ins) high.
Grey and purple.
Other colourways: HN687,
781, 782, 1238, 1708.
Est. £1400-2000.

HN598
Omar Khayyam and the Beloved
Designer C.J. Noke.
Date 1924 - 36.
25.5cm (10ins) high.
Pink, green and blue.
Other colourways: HN407, 419, 459.
Extremely rare.

HN603A
Child Study
First Version
Designer L. Harradine.
Date 1924 - 38.
12cm (4.75ins) high.
White with primroses on base.
Other colourways: HN603B, 1441; also recorded in flambé glaze.
Est. £400-550.

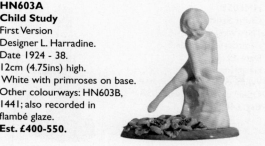

HN599
Masquerade (man)
First Version (Model 420)
Designer L. Harradine.
Date 1924 - 36.
17cm (6.75ins) high.
Red, white and brown.
Other colourways: HN636, 683.
Est. £500-700.

HN603B
Child Study
First Version
Designer L. Harradine.
Date 1924 - 38.
12cm (4.75ins) high.
White with kingcups on base.
Other colourways: HN603A, 1441; also recorded in flambé glaze.
Est. £400-550.

HN600
Masquerade (woman)
First Version (Model 417)
Designer L. Harradine.
Date 1924 - 49.
17cm (6.75ins) high.
Pink, white and red.
Other colourways: HN637, 674.
Est. £500-700.

HN604A
Child Study
Second Version
Designer L. Harradine.
Date 1924 - 38.
14cm (5.5ins) high.
White with primroses on base.
Other colourways: HN604B, 1442, 1443.
Est. £400-550.

HN601
A Mandarin
Third Version (Model 346)
Designer C.J. Noke.
Date 1924 - 38.
25.5cm (10ins) high.
Red and green.
Est. £2750-3750.

HN604B
Child Study
Second Version
Designer L. Harradine.
Date 1924 - 38.
14cm (5.5ins) high.
White with kingcups on base.
Other colourways: HN604A, 1442, 1443.
Est. £400-550.

Since the beginning of Royal Doulton Figurines there has always been the option to collect certain figures in a different variation of colours or glazes. Each figure with a different colour or glaze has a unique HN number, an example being Charles Noke's 'The Moor', which was originally called 'An Arab'. The Moor is available in seven different colourways and 'An Arab' in three different colourways. Noke also tried out various glaze effects on his figures including a glossy red flambé of which 'The Moor' HN3642 is a good example.

HN605A
Child Study
Third Version
Designer L. Harradine.
Date 1924 - 38.
Height not known.
White with primroses on base.
Other colourways: HN605B.
Est. £400-550.

HN605B
Child Study
Third Version
Designer L. Harradine.
Date 1924 - 38.
Height not known.
White with kingcups on base.
Other colourways: HN605A.
Est. £400-550.

HN609
Falstaff
First Version (Model 401)
Designer C.J. Noke.
Date 1924 - 38.
18cm (7ins) high.
Green.
Other colourways: HN571,
575, 608, 619, 638, 1216, 1606.
Extremely rare.

HN606A
Female Study
Designer L. Harradine.
Date 1924 - 36.
12.5cm (5ins) high.
White with primroses on base.
Other colourways: HN606B;
also recorded in flambé glaze.
Est. £400-550.

HN610
Henry Lytton as Jack Point
Designer C.J. Noke.
Date 1924 - 49.
16.5cm (6.5ins) high.
Black, brown, red and blue.
Est. £500-650.

HN606B
Female Study
Designer L. Harradine.
Date 1924 - 36.
12.5cm (5ins) high.
White with kingcups on base.
Other colourways: HN606A;
also recorded in flambé glaze.
Est. £400-550.

HN611
A Mandarin
First Version (Model 189)
(Also known as 'Chinese
Mandarin' and 'The Mikado')
Designer C.J. Noke.
Date 1924 - 36.
26cm (10.25ins) high.
Yellow.
Other colourways: HN84,
316, 318, 382, 746, 787, 791.
Est. £2750-4000.

This book can be purchased through
Bookshops, Antique Centres and Antique &
Collectors Fairs throughout the UK, but if you have a
problem in obtaining a copy please contact us on our
website www.bookbasket.co.uk or write to us at
Gemini Publications Ltd. 30a Monmouth Street,
Bath, BA1 2AN, England, UK.
Tel: 01225 484877
and from abroad +44 (0)1225 484877.
Email sales@bookbasket.co.uk

HN612
The Poke Bonnet
Designer C.J. Noke.
Date 1924 - 38.
24cm (9.5ins) high.
Green, red and yellow.
Other colourways: HN362, 765;
'A Lilac Shawl' HN44, 44A; 'In
Grandma's Days' HN339, 340,
388, 442.
Est. £1100-1500.

HN608
Falstaff
First Version (Model 401)
Designer C.J. Noke.
Date 1924 - 38.
18cm (7ins) high.
Red.
Other colourways: HN571,
575, 609, 619, 638, 1216, 1606.
Extremely rare.

HN613
Madonna of the Square
Designer P. Stabler.
Date 1924 - 36.
18cm (7ins) high.
Pink, green and yellow.
Other colourways: HN10, 10A,
11, 14, 27, 326, 573, 576, 594,
764, 1968, 1969, 2034.
Est. £850-1250.

HN614
Polly Peachum
First Version (Model 320)
Designer L. Harradine.
Date 1924 - 49.
16.5cm (6.5ins) high.
Blue and pink.
Other colourways: HN463,
465, 550, 589, 680, 693.
Series: Beggar's Opera.
Est. £500-700.

HN619
Falstaff
First Version (Model 401)
Designer C.J. Noke.
Date 1924 - 38.
18cm (7ins) high.
Brown, yellow and green.
Other colourways: HN571,
575, 608, 609, 638, 1216,
1606.
Very rare.

HN615
Katharine
Designer C.J. Noke.
Date 1924 - 38.
14.5cm (5.75ins) high.
Red, green, white and yellow.
Other colourways: HN61, 74,
341, 471, 793.
Est. £1100-1500.

HN620
Polly Peachum
Second Version (Model 316)
(Also known as 'Polly Peachum-
Curtsey' or 'Curtsey')
Designer L. Harradine.
Date 1924 - 38.
11cm (4.25ins) high.
Pink and lemon.
Other colourways:
HN489, 549, 694, 734.
Series: Beggar's Opera. **Est. £400-550.**

HN616
A Jester
First Version (Model 170)
Designer C.J. Noke.
Date 1924 - 38.
25.5cm (10ins) high.
Heraldic black and white tunic.
Other colourways: HN45, 71,
71A, 320, 367, 412, 426, 446,
552, 627, 1295, 1702, 2016, 3922.
Extremely rare.

HN621
Pan on Rock
Designer not known.
Date 1924 - 36.
13.5cm (5.25ins) high.
Cream on a green base.
Other colourways: HN622.
Very rare.

HN617
A Shepherd
First Version (Model 193)
Designer C.J. Noke.
Date 1924 - 38.
34.5cm (13.5ins) high.
Purple.
Other colourways: HN81, 632.
Very rare.

HN622
Pan on Rock
Designer not known.
Date 1924 - 38.
13.5cm (5.25ins) high.
Cream on a black base.
Other colourways: HN621.
Very rare.

HN618
Falstaff
Second Version (Model 353)
Designer C.J. Noke.
Date 1924 - 38.
18cm (7ins) high.
Green, brown, red and black.
Other colourways: HN2054.
Very rare.

HN623
An Old King
Designer C.J. Noke.
Date 1924 - 38.
24.5cm (9.75ins) high.
Green, red and grey.
Other colourways: HN358,
1801, 2134.
Extremely rare.

HN624
Lady with Rose
Designer E.W. Light.
Date 1924 - 36.
24cm (9.5ins) high.
Blue-green, pink and black.
Other colourways: HN48A, 52A,
68, 304, 336, 515, 517, 584.
Exremely rare.

HN629
The Curtsey
First Version
Designer E.W. Light.
Date 1924 - 36.
28cm (11ins) high
Green dress with black trim.
Other colourways: HN57,
57B, 66A, 327, 334, 363, 371,
518, 547, 670.
Extremely rare.

HN625
A Spook
Designer H. Tittensor.
Date 1924 - 36.
18cm (7ins) high.
Yellow.
Other colourways: HN50, 51,
51A, 51B, 58, 512, 1218; also
recorded in flambé glaze and
in miniature.
Est. £1650-2250.

HN630
A Jester
Second Version (Model 171)
Designer C.J. Noke.
Date 1924 - 38.
26cm (10.25ins) high.
Brown.
Other colourways: HN45A,
45B, 55, 308, 1333.
Est. £3000-4000.

HN626
Lady with Shawl
Designer L. Harradine.
Date 1924 - 36.
33.5cm (13.25ins) high.
White, green, yellow and pink.
Other colourways: HN447, 458,
678, 679.
Extremely rare.

HN631
Fisherwomen
(Also known as 'Looking for the
Boats' and 'Waiting For The Boats')
Designer C.J. Noke.
Date 1924 - 38.
30cm (11.75ins) high.
Mauve, brown and green.
Other colourways: HN80,
349, 359.
Very rare.

HN627
A Jester
First Version (Model 170)
Designer C.J. Noke.
Date 1924 - 38.
25.5cm (10ins) high.
Brown checks.
Other colourways: HN45, 71,
71A, 320, 367, 412, 426, 446, 552,
616, 1295, 1702, 2016, 3922.
Est. £3000-4000.

HN632
A Shepherd
First Version (Model 193)
Designer C.J. Noke.
Date 1924 - 38.
34.5cm (13.5ins) high.
Blue and white.
Other colourways:
HN81, 617.
Extremely rare.

HN628
The Crinoline
Designer G. Lambert.
Date 1924 - 38
16cm (6.25ins) high.
Yellow and blue checks.
Other colourways: HN8, 9,
9A, 21, 21A, 413, 566.
Extremely rare.

HN633
The Princess
Designer L. Harradine.
Date 1924 - 36.
23.5cm (9.25ins) high.
Black and white.
Other colourways: HN391,
392, 420, 430, 431.
Extremely rare.

HN634
A Geisha
First Version (Model 238)
(Also known as 'The Japanese Lady')
Designer H. Tittensor.
Date 1924 - 36.
27.5cm (10.75ins) high.
Black and white kimono.
Other colourways: HN354, 376, 376A,
387, 741, 779, 1321, 1322.
Est. £2300-3300.

HN639
Elsie Maynard
First Version (Model 421)
Designer C.J. Noke.
Date 1924 - 49.
18cm (7ins) high.
Mauve, blue, red and pink.
Est. £550-700.

HN635
Harlequinade
First Version
Designer L. Harradine.
Date 1924 - 40.
18cm (7ins) high.
Gold.
Other colourways: HN585,
711, 780.
Est. £2000-2800.

HN640
Charley's Aunt
First Version (Model 161)
Designer A. Toft.
Date 1924 - 36.
18cm (7ins) high.
Green and mauve spotted dress.
Other colourways: HN35.
Est. £800-1100.

HN636
Masquerade (man)
First Version (Model 420)
Designer L. Harradine.
Date 1924 - 36.
17cm (6.75ins) high.
Gold.
Other colourways: HN599, 683.
Est. £500-650.

HN641
A Mandarin
Second Version (Model 260)
Designer C.J. Noke.
Date 1924 - 38.
21cm (8.25ins) high.
Yellow, gold and blue.
Other colourways: HN366, 455.
Extremely rare.

HN637
Masquerade (woman)
First Version (Model 417)
Designer L. Harradine.
Date 1924 - 38.
17cm (6.75ins) high.
Gold.
Other colourways: HN600, 674.
Est. £500-650.

HN642
Pierrette
First Version (Model 445)
Designer L. Harradine.
Date 1924 - 38.
18.5cm (7.25ins) high.
Red.
Other colourways: HN643, 644,
691, 721, 731, 732, 784.
Est. £1200-1500.

HN638
Falstaff
First Version (Model 401)
Designer C.J. Noke.
Date 1924 - 38.
18cm (7ins) high.
Red and cream.
Other colourways: HN571,
575, 608, 609, 619, 1216, 1606.
Very rare.

HN643
Pierrette
First Version (Model 445)
Designer L. Harradine.
Date 1924 - 38.
18.5cm (7.25ins) high.
Red, white and black.
Other colourways: HN642, 644,
691, 721, 731, 732, 784.
Est. £1200-1500.

HN644
Pierrette
First Version (Model 445)
Designer L. Harradine.
Date 1924 - 38.
18.5cm (7.25ins) high.
White and black.
Other colourways: HN642,
643, 691, 721, 731, 732, 784.
(Ebay 13.3.04 sold £1299)
Est. £1200-1500.

HN645
One of the Forty
Thirteenth Version (Model 327)
Designer H. Tittensor.
Date 1924 - 38.
15cm (6ins) high.
Blue, white and black.
Other colourways: HN482, 484,
492, 663, 713.
Extremely rare.

HN646
One of the Forty
Twelfth Version (Model 319)
Designer H. Tittensor.
Date 1924 - 36.
Height not known.
Cream, black and blue.
Other colourways: HN481, 483,
491, 667, 712, 1336, 1350; Also
recorded in flambé glaze.
Very rare.

HN647
One of the Forty
Second Version (Model 298)
(Also known as 'Chu Chin
Chow with Sack')
Designer H. Tittensor.
Date 1924 - 36.
18.5cm (7.25ins) high.
Blue, white and black.
Other colourways: HN418, 494,
498, 666, 704, 1353.
Extremely rare.

HN648
One of the Forty
First Version (Model 289)
(Also known as 'Chu Chin
Chow with Beads')
Designer H. Tittensor.
Date 1924 - 38.
21cm (8.25ins) high.
Blue, white and black.
Other colourways: HN417, 490,
495, 501, 528, 677, 1351, 1352.
Extremely rare.

HN649
One of the Forty
Fourteenth Version (Model 313)
Designer H. Tittensor.
Date 1924 - 38.
19.5cm (7.75ins) high.
Blue, white and black.
Other colourways: HN496, 500,
665, 1354.
Extremely rare.

HN650
Crinoline Lady
Designer not known.
Date 1924 - 38.
7.5cm (3ins) high.
Grey, pale green and white.
Other colourways: HN651,
652, 653, 654, 655.
Est. £1150-1450.

HN651
Crinoline Lady
Designer not known.
Date 1924 - 38.
7.5cm (3ins) high.
Orange, green, black and white.
Other colourways: HN650,
652, 653, 654, 655.
Est. £1150-1450.

HN652
Crinoline Lady
Designer not known.
Date 1924 - 38.
7.5cm (3ins) high.
Purple.
Other colourways: HN650,
651, 653, 654, 655.
Est. £1150-1450.

HN653
Crinoline Lady
Designer not known.
Date 1924 - 38.
7.5cm (3ins) high.
Black and white.
Other colourways: HN650,
651, 652, 654, 655.
Est. £1150-1450.

HN654
Crinoline Lady
Designer not known.
Date 1924 - 38.
7.5cm (3ins) high.
Red and purple.
Other colourways: HN650,
651, 652, 653, 655.
Est. £1150-1450.

HN659
Mam'selle
Designer L. Harradine.
Date 1924 - 38.
17.8cm (7ins) high.
Dark blue and red.
Other colourways:
HN658, 724, 786.
Est. £1700-2300.

HN655
Crinoline Lady
Designer not known.
Date 1924 - 38.
7.5cm (3ins) high.
Blue, white and black.
Other colourways: HN650,
651, 652, 653, 654.
Est. £1150-1450.

HN660
The Welsh Girl
(Also known as 'Myfanwy Jones')
Designer E.W. Light.
Date 1924 - 36.
30.5cm (12ins) high.
Blue and white.
Other colourways: HN39, 92,
456, 514, 516, 519, 520, 668, 669,
701, 792.
Very rare.

HN656
The Mask
First Version
Designer L. Harradine.
Date 1924 - 38.
17cm (6.75ins) high.
Blue, orange and purple.
Other colourways: HN657,
729, 733, 785, 1271.
Est. £1400-2000.

HN661
Boy with Turban
(Also known as 'Eastern Boy')
Designer L. Harradine.
Date 1924 - 36.
9.5cm (3.75ins) high.
Blue.
Other colourways: HN586,
587, 662, 1210, 1212, 1213,
1214, 1225.
Est. £600-800.

HN657
The Mask
First Version
Designer L. Harradine.
Date 1924 - 38.
17cm (6.75ins) high.
Black and white.
Other colourways: HN656,
729, 733, 785, 1271.
Est. £1600-2200.

HN662
Boy with Turban
(Also known as 'Eastern Boy')
Designer L. Harradine.
Date 1924 - 36.
9.5cm (3.75ins) high.
Black and white.
Other colourways: HN586,
587, 661, 1210, 1212, 1213,
1214, 1225.
Est. £600-800.

HN658
Mam'selle
Designer L. Harradine.
Date 1924 - 38.
18cm (7ins) high.
Black and white.
Other colourways:
HN659, 724, 786.
Est. £1700-2300.

HN663
One of the Forty
Thirteenth Version (Model 327)
Designer H. Tittensor.
Date 1924 - 38.
15cm (6ins) high.
Yellow and black.
Other colourways: HN482,
484, 492, 645, 713.
Very rare.

HN664
One of the Forty
Eleventh Version (Model 328)
Designer H. Tittensor.
Date 1924 - 38.
17cm (6.75ins) high.
Yellow, black and green.
Other colourways: HN480, 493, 497, 499, 714.
Est. £1400-1900.

HN665
One of the Forty
Fourteenth Version (Model 313)
Designer H. Tittensor.
Date 1924 - 38.
19.5cm (7.75ins) high.
Yellow, green and black.
Other colourways: HN496, 500, 649, 1354.
(Ebay 11.3.04 sold £1900)
Est. £1850-2500.

HN666
One of the Forty
Second Version (Model 298)
Designer H. Tittensor.
Date 1924 - 36.
18.5cm (7.25ins) high.
Yellow, cream and black.
Other colourways: HN418, 494, 498, 647, 704, 1353.
Very rare.

HN667
One of the Forty
Twelfth Version (Model 319)
Designer H. Tittensor.
Date 1924 - 36.
Height not known.
Yellow and black.
Other colourways: HN481, 483, 491, 646, 712, 1336, 1350; Also recorded in flambé glaze.
Very rare.

HN668
The Welsh Girl
(Also known as 'Myfanwy Jones')
Designer E.W. Light.
Date 1924 - 36.
30.5cm (12ins) high.
Yellow, cream, pink and black.
Other colourways: HN39, 92, 456, 514, 516, 519, 520, 660, 669, 701, 792.
Est. £3000-4000.

HN669
The Welsh Girl
(Earthenware and smaller than original figure.)
(Also known as 'Myfanwy Jones')
Designer E.W. Light.
Date 1924 - 36.
21.5cm (8.5ins) high.
Yellow, black, white and green.
Other colourways: HN39, 92, 456, 514, 516, 519, 520, 660, 668, 701, 792.
Est. £3000-4000.

HN670
The Curtsey
First Version
Designer E.W. Light.
Date 1924 - 36.
28cm (11ins) high.
Pink, yellow, cream and black.
Other colourways: HN57, 57B, 66A, 327, 334, 363, 371, 518, 547, 629.
Est. £1300-1800.

HN671
Lady Ermine
(Also known as 'The Ermine Muff' and 'Lady with Ermine Muff')
Designer C.J. Noke.
Date 1924 - 38.
21.5cm (8.5ins) high.
Yellow and green.
Other colourways: HN54, 332.
Extremely rare.

HN672
Tulips
Designer not known.
Date 1924 - 36.
24cm (9.5ins) high.
Green, lilac, yellow and blue.
Other colourways: HN466, 488, 747, 1334.
Est. £1600-2100.

HN673
Henry VIII
First Version (Model 271)
Designer C.J. Noke.
Date 1924 - 38.
Height not known.
Brown and lilac.
Other colourways: HN370.
Extremely rare.

HN674
Masquerade (woman)
First Version (Model 417)
Designer L. Harradine.
Date 1924 - 38.
17cm (6.75ins) high.
Orange and yellow checks.
Other colourways: HN600, 637.
(Ebay19.8.04 sold £460)
Est. £500-650.

HN679
Lady with Shawl
Designer L. Harradine.
Date 1924 - 36.
33.5cm (13.25ins) high.
Black, blue, white and yellow.
Other colourways: HN447, 458,
626, 678.
Extremely rare.

HN675
The Gainsborough Hat
Designer H. Tittensor.
Date 1924 - 36.
22cm (8.75ins) high.
Cream, yellow and black.
Other colourways: HN46, 46A,
47, 329, 352, 383, 453, 705.
Est. £1600-2200.

HN680
Polly Peachum
First Version (Model 320)
Designer L. Harradine.
Date 1924 - 49.
16.5cm (6.5ins) high.
White spotted dress.
Other colourways: HN463,
465, 550, 589, 614, 693.
Series: Beggar's Opera.
Extremely rare.

HN676
Pavlova
(Also known as
Swan Song')
Designer C.J. Noke.
Date 1924 - 38.
11cm (4.25ins) high.
White and green.
Other colourways:
HN487.
Very rare.

HN681
The Cobbler
Second Version (Model 589)
Designer C.J. Noke.
Date 1924 - 38.
21.5cm (8.5ins) high.
Red and green.
Other colourways:
HN1251, 1283.
Extremely rare.

HN677
One of the Forty
First Version (Models 288, 289)
(Also known as 'Chu Chin Chow
with Beads')
Designer H. Tittensor.
Date 1924 - 38.
21cm (8.25ins) high.
Yellow, cream, black and red.
Other colourways: HN417, 490,
495, 501, 528, 648, 1351, 1352.
Very rare.

HN682
The Cobbler
First Version (Model 362)
Designer C.J. Noke.
Date 1924 - 38.
19cm (7.5ins) high.
Red and green.
Other colourways:
HN542, 543.
Extremely rare.

HN678
Lady with Shawl
Designer L. Harradine.
Date 1924 - 36.
33.5cm (13.25ins) high.
Black, white and yellow.
Other colourways: HN447,
458, 626, 679.
Est. £2500-3500.

HN683
Masquerade (man)
First Version (Model 420)
Designer L. Harradine.
Date 1924 - 36.
17cm (6.75ins) high.
Green, cream, black and orange.
Other colourways: HN599, 636.
Est. £500-650.

HN684
Tony Weller
First Version (Model 254)
Designer C.J. Noke.
Date 1924 - 38.
26.5cm (10.5ins) high.
Green, red, orange and brown.
Other colourways: HN346, 368.
Est. £700-950.

HN685
Contentment
Designer L. Harradine.
Date 1924 - 38.
18.5cm (7.25ins) high.
Black and white floral dress.
Other colourways:
HN395, 396, 421, 468,
572, 686, 1323.
Extremely rare.

HN686
Contentment
Designer L. Harradine.
Date 1924 - 38.
18.5cm (7.25ins) high.
Black and white stripes.
Other colourways: HN395,
396, 421, 468, 572, 685, 1323.
Extremely rare.

HN687
The Bather
First Version (Model 428)
Designer L. Harradine.
Date 1924 - 49.
19.5cm (7.75ins) high.
Dark blue.
Other colourways: HN597,
781, 782, 1238, 1708.
Est. £850-1100.

HN688
A Yeoman of the Guard
Designer L. Harradine.
Date 1924 - 38.
14.5cm (5.75ins) high.
Red, brown, white and gold.
Other colourways: HN2122.
(This figure was made
as a pair to HN689
'A Chelsea Pensioner')
Est. £400-550.

HN689
A Chelsea Pensioner
Designer L. Harradine.
Date 1924 - 38.
14.5cm (5.75ins) high.
Red, black and brown.
(This figure was made as a pair to
HN688 'A Yeoman of the Guard')
Est. £900-1200.

HN690
A Lady of the Georgian Period
Designer E.W. Light.
Date 1925 - 36.
26cm (10.25ins) high.
Pink and white striped dress
with yellow overdress.
Other colourways: HN41, 331,
444, 702.
Extremely rare.

HN691
Pierrette
First Version (Model 445)
Designer L. Harradine.
Date 1925 - 38.
18.5cm (7.25ins) high.
Gold.
Other colourways: HN642,
643, 644, 721, 731, 732, 784.
Est. £1600-2200.

HN692
Sleep
Second Version (Model 287)
Designer P. Stabler.
Date 1925 - 36.
15cm (6ins) high.
Gold.
Other colourways: HN424, 710.
Est. £950-1300.

HN693
Polly Peachum
First Version (Model 320)
Designer L. Harradine.
Date 1925 - 49.
16.5cm (6.5ins) high.
Dark pink and green.
Other colourways: HN463,
465, 550, 589, 614, 680.
Series: Beggar's Opera.
Est. £500-650.

HN694
Polly Peachum
Second Version (Model 316)
(Also known as 'Polly Peachum-Curtsey' or 'Curtsey')
Designer L. Harradine.
Date 1925 - 49.
11cm (4.25ins) high.
Dark green and pink.
Other colourways:
HN489, 549, 620, 734.
Series: Beggar's Opera. **Est. £500-650.**

HN695
Lucy Lockett
Third Version (Model 360)
Designer L. Harradine.
Date 1925 - 49.
15cm (6ins) high.
Yellow and brown.
Other colourways: HN696.
Series: Beggar's Opera.
Est. £500-650.

HN696
Lucy Lockett
Third Version
Designer L. Harradine.
Date 1925 - 49.
15cm (6ins) high.
Pale blue.
Other colourways: HN695.
Series: Beggar's Opera.
Extremely rare.

HN697
The Balloon Seller
First Version (Model 321)
(Also known as 'The Balloon Woman')
Designer L. Harradine.
Date 1925 - 38.
23cm (9ins) high.
Blue and red.
Other colourways: HN479, 486, 548, 583.
Extremely rare.

HN698
Polly Peachum
Third Version (Model 462)
Designer L. Harradine.
Date 1925 - 49.
5.5cm (2.25ins) high.
Rose pink and white.
Other colourways:
HN699, 757, 758, 759, 760, 761, 762, M21, M22, M23.
Series: Beggar's Opera.
Est. £500-650.

HN699
Polly Peachum
Third Version
Designer L. Harradine.
Date 1925 - 49.
5.5cm (2.25ins) high.
Pale blue and white.
Other colourways:
HN698, 757, 758, 759, 760, 761, 762, M21, M22, M23.
Series: Beggar's Opera.
Est. £500-650.

HN700
Pretty Lady
Designer H. Tittensor.
Date 1925 - 38.
24cm (9.5ins) high.
Yellow, green and black.
Other colourways: HN69, 70, 302, 330, 361, 384, 565, 763, 783.
Est. £1100-1450.

HN701
The Welsh Girl
(Also known as 'Myfanwy Jones')
Designer E.W. Light.
Date 1925 - 36.
30.5cm (12ins) high.
Multicoloured costume
with black cloak.
Other colourways: HN39, 92, 456, 514, 516, 519, 520, 660, 668, 669, 792.
Extremely rare.

HN702
A Lady of the Georgian Period
Designer E.W. Light.
Date 1925 - 36.
26cm (10.25ins) high.
Pink striped skirt with
green overdress.
Other colourways: HN41, 331, 444, 690.
Extremely rare.

HN703
Motherhood
Second Version (Model 329)
Designer not known.
Date 1925 - 38.
23.5cm (9.25ins) high.
Purple, red and black.
Other colourways: HN462, 570, 743.
Extremely rare.

HN704
One of the Forty
Second Version (Model 298)
(Also known as 'Chu Chin Chow
with Sack')
Designer H. Tittensor.
Date 1925 - 36.
18.5cm (7.25ins) high.
Red chequered robe.
Other colourways: HN418, 494,
498, 647, 666, 1353.
Extremely rare.

HN705
The Gainsborough Hat
Designer H. Tittensor.
Date 1925 - 36.
22cm (8.75ins) high.
Purple and blue.
Other colourways: HN46, 46A,
47, 329, 352, 383, 453, 675.
Est. £1500-2000.

HN706
Fruit Gathering
Designer L. Harradine.
Date 1925 - 36.
20.5cm (8ins) high.
Purple and yellow.
Other colourways: HN449,
476, 503, 561, 562, 707.
Very rare.

HN707
Fruit Gathering
Designer L. Harradine.
Date 1925 - 36.
20.5cm (8ins) high.
Red. lilac and cream.
Other colourways: HN449,
476, 503, 561, 562, 706.
Est. £1375-1800.

HN708
Shepherdess
First Version (Model 469)
Designer L. Harradine.
Date 1925 - 48.
9cm (3.5ins) high.
Blue and green.
Other colourways: M18, M20.
Series: Miniatures.
Est. £1100-1500.

HN709
Shepherd
Second Version (Model 470)
Designer L. Harradine.
Date 1925 - 38.
9cm (3.5ins) high.
Blue and green.
Other colourways: M17, M19.
Est. £1100-1500.

HN710
Sleep
Second Version (Model 287)
Designer P. Stabler.
Date 1925 - 36.
15cm (6ins) high.
Blue.
Other colourways: HN424, 692.
(This figure has a matt vellum finish)
Est. £950-1250.

HN711
Harlequinade
First Version
Designer L. Harradine.
Date 1925 - 40.
18cm (7ins) high.
Black and white.
Other colourways:
HN585, 635, 780.
Est. £2200-2750.

HN712
One of the Forty
Twelfth Version (Model 319)
Designer H. Tittensor.
Date 1925 - 36.
Height not known.
Red and black.
Other colourways: HN481, 483,
491, 646, 667, 1336, 1350; also
recorded in a flambé glaze.
Very rare.

HN713
One of the Forty
Thirteenth Version (Model 327)
Designer H. Tittensor.
Date 1925 - 38.
15cm (6ins) high.
Red.
Other colourways: HN482,
484, 492, 645, 663.
Extremely rare.

HN714
One of the Forty
Eleventh Version (Model 328)
Designer H. Tittensor.
Date, 1925 - 38.
17cm (6.75ins) high.
Red, black and blue.
Other colourways: HN480,
493, 497, 499, 664.
Est. £1375-1800.

HN719
Butterfly
(Also known as 'Butterfly
Woman')
Designer L. Harradine.
Date 1925 - 40.
16.5cm (6.5ins) high.
Pink, black, yellow and white.
Other colourways: HN720,
730, 1203, 1456.
Est. £1600-2100.

HN715
The Proposal (female)
Designer L. Harradine.
Date 1925 - 40.
14.5cm (5.75ins) high.
Dark red and black.
Other colourways:
HN716, 788.
(Made as a pair to HN725
'The Proposal' - man)
Est. £800-1100.

HN720
Butterfly
(Also known as 'Butterfly
Woman')
Designer L. Harradine.
Date 1925 - 40.
16.5cm (6.5ins) high.
Orange, white and black.
Other colourways: HN719,
730, 1203, 1456.
Est. £1600-2100.

HN716
Proposal (female)
Designer L. Harradine.
Date 1925 - 40.
14.5cm (5.75ins) high.
White and black.
Other colourways:
HN715, 788.
Est. £1200-1700.

HN721
Pierrette
First Version (Model 445)
Designer L. Harradine.
Date 1925 - 38.
18.5cm (7.25ins) high.
Black and white stripes.
Other colourways: HN642,
643, 644, 691, 731, 732, 784.
Est. £1600-2100.

HN717
Clownette
(Also known as 'Lady Clown')
Designer L. Harradine.
Date 1925 - 38.
19cm (7.5ins) high.
White and red stripes and
black squares.
Other colourways: HN718,
738, 770, 1263.
Est. £2600-3500.

HN722
Mephisto
Designer L. Harradine.
Date 1925 - 38.
16.5cm (6.5ins) high.
Black tunic with red cloak.
Other colourways: HN723.
Est. £2200-3200.

HN718
Clownette
(Also known as 'Lady Clown')
Designer L. Harradine.
Date 1925 - 38.
19cm (7.5ins) high.
White and red stripes and
black spots.
Other colourways: HN717, 738,
770, 1263.
Extremely rare.

HN723
Mephisto
Designer L. Harradine.
Date 1925 - 38.
16.5cm (6.5ins) high.
Red tunic and cloak.
Other colourways: HN722.
Est. £2200-3200.

HN724
Mam'selle
Designer L. Harradine.
Date 1925 - 38.
18cm (7ins) high.
White, yellow and red.
Other colourways: HN658,
659, 786.
Est. £2000-2500.

HN729
The Mask
First Version
Designer L. Harradine.
Date 1925 - 38.
17cm (6.75ins) high.
Red and black.
Other colourways: HN656,
657, 733, 785, 1271.
Est. £1650-2200.

HN725
The Proposal (male)
Designer not known.
Date 1925 - 38.
14cm (5.5ins) high.
Red, white and black.
Other colourways: HN1209.
(Made as a pair to HN717
'The Proposal' - female)
Est. £1200-1600.

HN730
Butterfly
(Also known as 'Butterfly
Woman')
Designer L. Harradine.
Date 1925 - 40.
16.5cm (6.5ins) high.
Blue, yellow and black.
Other colourways: HN719, 720,
1203, 1456.
Est. £1350-1800.

HN726
A Victorian Lady
Designer L. Harradine.
Date 1925 - 38.
19.5cm (7.75ins) high.
Purple, black, red and yellow.
Other colourways: HN727, 728,
736, 739, 740, 742, 745, 1208, 1258,
1276, 1277, 1345, 1452, 1529.
Est. £500-650.

HN731
Pierrette
First Version (Model 445)
Designer L. Harradine.
Date 1925 - 38.
18.5cm (7.25ins) high.
Black and white spotted dress.
Other colourways: HN642,
643, 644, 691, 721, 732, 784.
Est. £1600-2200.

HN727
A Victorian Lady
Designer L. Harradine.
Date 1925 - 38.
19.5cm (7.75ins) high.
Pink and pale green.
Other colourways: HN726,
728, 736, 739, 740, 742, 745,
1208, 1258, 1276, 1277, 1345,
1452, 1529.
Est. £250-350.

HN732
Pierrette
First Version (Model 445)
Designer L. Harradine.
Date 1925 - 38.
18.5cm (7.25ins) high.
Black and white.
Other colourways: HN642,
643, 644, 691, 721, 731, 784.
Est. £1600-2200.

HN728
A Victorian Lady
Designer L. Harradine.
Date 1925 - 52.
19.5cm (7.75ins) high.
Purple, pink and cream.
Other colourways:
HN726, 727, 736, 739, 740, 742,
745, 1208, 1258, 1276, 1277,
1345, 1452, 1529.
(Ebay 29.4.04 sold £205)
Est. £200-300.

HN733
The Mask
First Version
Designer L. Harradine.
Date 1925 - 38.
17cm (6.75ins) high.
White costume with
black squares.
Other colourways: HN656,
657, 729, 785, 1271.
Est. £1600-2200.

HN734
Polly Peachum
Second Version (Model 316)
(Also known as 'Polly Peachum-
Curtsey' or 'Curtsey')
Designer L. Harradine.
Date 1925 - 49.
11cm (4.25ins) high.
Black and white spots.
Other colourways:
HN489, 549, 620, 694.
Series: Beggar's Opera. **Est. £800-1100.**

HN735
Shepherdess
Second Version (Model 455)
(Also known as 'Milkmaid')
Designer L. Harradine.
Date 1925 - 38.
18cm (7ins) high.
Blue, red, white and black.
Other colourways: HN750.
(Made as a pair to HN751
'Shepherd')
Est. £1300-1700.

HN736
A Victorian Lady
Designer L. Harradine.
Date 1925 - 38.
19.5cm (7.75ins) high.
Red and purple.
Other colourways:
HN726, 727, 728, 739, 740, 742,
745, 1208, 1258, 1276, 1277,
1345, 1452, 1529.
Est. £300-400.

Foreign Currency Rates at 8th October 2004 was:
A simple calculation to find the difference on a daily rate
is as follows:

> £100 x 1.79 = $179 US Dollars
> £100 x 1.45 = €145 Euros
> £100 x 2.25 = $225 Canadian Dollar
> £100 x 2.46 = $246 Australian Dollar

Example: A Figurine; estimated cost £120 would be
calculated: £120 x 1.79 (US current rate) = $214.80 in US
dollars. To find the rate in reverse, divide the rate,
$100 divided by 1.79 = £55.87 GB Pounds.

HN738
Clownette
(Also known as 'Lady Clown')
Designer L. Harradine.
Date 1925 - 38.
19cm (7.5ins) high.
Black, white and red.
Other colourways: HN717,
718, 770, 1263.
Extremely rare.

HN739
A Victorian Lady
Designer L. Harradine.
Date 1925 - 38.
19.5cm (7.75ins) high.
Red, lilac and yellow.
Other colourways: HN726, 727,
728, 736, 740, 742, 745, 1208, 1258,
1276, 1277, 1345, 1452, 1529.
Est. £500-700.

HN740
A Victorian Lady
Designer L. Harradine.
Date 1925 - 38.
19.5cm (7.75ins) high.
Pink and white.
Other colourways:
HN726, 727, 728, 736, 739, 742,
745, 1208, 1258, 1276, 1277,
1345, 1452, 1529.
Est. £450-650.

HN741
A Geisha
First Version (Model 238)
(Also known as 'The Japanese Lady')
Designer H. Tittensor.
Date 1925 - 36.
27.5cm (10.75ins) high.
Multicoloured.
Other colourways: HN354, 376,
376A, 387, 634, 779, 1321, 1322.
Extremely rare.

HN742
A Victorian Lady
Designer L. Harradine.
Date 1925 - 38.
19.5cm (7.75ins) high.
White dress with blue spots, black
and white check shawl.
Other colourways:
HN726, 727, 728, 736, 739, 740,
745, 1208, 1258, 1276, 1277, 1345,
1452, 1529.
Est. £500-700.

HN743
Motherhood
Second Version (Model 329)
Designer not known.
Date 1925 - 38.
23.5cm (9.25ins) high.
Blue and yellow stripes.
Other colourways: HN462,
570, 703.
Extremely rare.

HN744
The Lavender Woman
(Also known as 'The Lavender Girl'
and 'Any Old Lavender')
Designer P. Stabler.
Date 1925 - 36.
21.5cm (8.5ins) high.
Blue.
Other colourways: HN22, 23,
23A, 342, 569.
Est. £1650-2200.

HN745
A Victorian Lady
Designer L. Harradine.
Date 1925 - 38.
19.5cm (7.75ins) high.
Pink and green.
Other colourways: HN726,
727, 728, 736, 739, 740, 742,
1208, 1258, 1276, 1277, 1345,
1452, 1529.
Est. £500-700.

HN746
A Mandarin
First Version (Model 189)
(Also known as 'A Chinese
Mandarin' and 'The Mikado')
Designer C.J. Noke.
Date 1925 - 36.
26cm (10.25ins) high.
Yellow, lilac and black.
Other colourways: HN84, 316,
318, 382, 611, 787, 791.
Est. £3000-4000.

HN747
Tulips
Designer not known.
Date 1925 - 36.
24cm (9.5ins) high.
Lilac and green.
Other colourways:
HN466, 488, 672, 1334.
Est. £1200-1600.

HN748
Out For a Walk
Designer E.W. Light.
Date 1925 - 36.
25.5cm (10ins) high.
Green, red and white.
Other colourways: HN86, 443.
Est. £2200-3000.

HN749
London Cry, Strawberries
Designer L. Harradine.
Date 1925 - 36.
17cm (6.75ins) high.
Cream, red and brown.
Other colourways: HN772.
Est. £1200-1600.

HN750
Shepherdess
Second Version (Model 455)
(Also known as 'Milkmaid')
Designer L. Harradine.
Date 1925 - 38.
18cm (7ins) high.
Pink and yellow.
Other colourways: HN735.
Est. £1300-1700.

HN751
Shepherd
Third Version (Model 453)
Designer L. Harradine.
Date 1925 - 38.
18cm (7ins) high.
Green, black, white and red.
(Made as a pair to HN735
'Shepherdess')
Est. £1300-1700.

HN752
**London Cry, Turnips and
Carrots**
Designer L. Harradine.
Date 1925 - 38.
17cm (6.75ins) high.
Purple, red, green and black.
Other colourways: HN771.
Est. £1100-1600.

HN753
The Dandy
Designer L. Harradine.
Date 1925 - 36.
17cm (6.75ins) high.
Red, white, green and black.
(Made as a pair to HN754
'The Belle')
Est. £900-1200.

HN754
The Belle
First Version (Model 477)
Designer L. Harradine.
Date 1925 - 38.
16.5cm (6.5ins) high.
Multicoloured.
Other colourways: HN776.
(This figure was made as a
pair to HN753 'The Dandy')
Est. £800-1100.

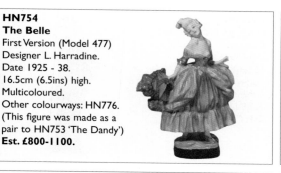

HN755
**Mephistopheles and
Marguerite**
Designer C.J. Noke.
Date 1925 - 49.
19.5cm (7.75ins) high.
Purple and orange.
Other colourways: HN775.
Est. £1200-1650.

HN756
The Modern Piper
Designer L. Harradine.
Date 1925 - 40.
21.5cm (8.5ins) high.
Lilac, cream and green.
(An earlier version of this
figure had a blue hat with
a feather)
Est. £2000-2500.

HN757
Polly Peachum
Third Version (Model 462)
Designer L. Harradine.
Date 1925 - 49.
5.5cm (2.25ins) high.
Red.
Other colourways: HN698,
699, 758, 759, 760, 761,
762; M21, M22, M23.
Series: Beggar's Opera.
Est. £550-700.

HN758
Polly Peachum
Third Version (Model 462)
Designer L. Harradine.
Date 1925 - 49
5.5cm (2.25ins) high.
Pink and orange.
Other colourways: HN698,
699, 757, 759, 760, 761,
762; M21, M22, M23.
Series: Beggar's Opera.
Est. £550-700.

HN759
Polly Peachum
Third Version (Model 462)
Designer L. Harradine.
Date 1925 - 49.
5.5cm (2.25ins) high.
Yellow and white with
black spots.
Other colourways:
HN698, 699, 757, 758, 760,
761, 762; M21, M22, M23.
Series: Beggar's Opera. **Est. £550-700.**

HN760
Polly Peachum
Third Version (Model 462)
Designer L. Harradine.
Date 1925 - 49.
5.5cm (2.25ins) high.
Multicoloured.
Other colourways: HN698,
699, 757, 758, 759, 761,
762; M21, M22, M23.
Series: Beggar's Opera.
Est. £550-700.

HN761
Polly Peachum
Third Version (Model 462)
Designer L. Harradine.
Date 1925 - 49.
5.5cm (2.25ins) high.
Purple and blue.
Other colourways: HN698,
699, 757, 758, 759, 760,
762; M21, M22, M23.
Series: Beggar's Opera.
Est. £550-700.

HN762
Polly Peachum
Third Version (Model 462)
Designer L. Harradine.
Date 1925 - 49.
5.5cm (2.25ins)
Red, white and pink.
Other colourways: HN698,
699, 757, 758, 759, 760,
761; M21, M22, M23.
Series: Beggar's Opera.
Est. £550-700.

HN763
Pretty Lady
Designer H. Tittensor.
Date 1925 - 38.
24cm (9.5ins) high.
Orange, green and white.
Other colourways: HN69, 70,
302, 330, 361, 384, 565, 700, 783.
Extremely rare.

HN764
Madonna of the Square
Designer P. Stabler.
Date 1925 - 36.
18cm (7ins) high.
Blue, purple and yellow.
Other colourways: HN10, 10A,
11, 14, 27, 326, 573, 576, 594,
613, 1968, 1969, 2034.
Very rare.

HN769
Harlequinade Masked
Designer L. Harradine.
Date 1925 - 38.
16.5cm (6.5ins) high.
Yellow, red and blue.
Other colourways: HN768,
1274, 1304.
Est. £2000-2700

HN765
The Poke Bonnet
Designer C.J. Noke.
Date 1925 - 38.
24cm (9.5ins) high.
Dark green, purple and blue.
Other colourways: HN362, 612;
'A Lilac Shawl' HN44, 44A; and
'In Grandma's Days' HN339,
340, 388, 442.
Extremely rare.

HN770
Clownette
(Also known as 'Lady Clown')
Designer L. Harradine.
Date 1925 - 38.
19cm (7.5ins) high.
Green and white.
Other colourways: HN717, 718,
738, 1263.
Est. £2700-3700.

HN766
Irish Colleen
Designer L. Harradine.
Date 1925 - 36.
16.5cm (6.5ins) high.
Red, black, grey and white.
Other colourways: HN767.
Est. £2000-2700.

HN771
London Cry, Turnips and Carrots
Designer L. Harradine.
Date 1925 - 38.
17cm (6.75ins) high.
Lavender, brown and cream.
Other colourways: HN752.
Est. £1200-1600.

HN767
Irish Colleen
Designer L. Harradine.
Date 1925 - 36.
16.5cm (6.5ins) high.
Black, green and red.
Other colourways: HN766.
Est. £2000-2700.

HN772
London Cry, Strawberries
Designer L. Harradine.
Date 1925 - 36
17cm (6.75ins) high.
Lilac, green and cream.
Other colourways: HN749.
Est. £1200-1600.

HN768
Harlequinade Masked
Designer L. Harradine.
Date 1925 - 38.
16.5cm (6.5ins)
Black, red and green checks.
Other colourways: HN769,
1274, 1304.
Very rare.

HN773
The Bather
Second Version (Model 486)
Designer L. Harradine.
Date 1925 - 38.
19cm (7.5ins) high.
Red, black and purple.
Other colourways: HN774, 1227.
Est. £1750-2450.

HN774
The Bather
Second Version (Model 486)
Designer L. Harradine.
Date 1925 - 38.
19cm (7.5ins) high.
Dark blue and red.
Other colourways: HN773, 1227.
Est. £1750-2450.

HN779
Geisha
First Version (Model 238)
(Also known as 'The Japanese Lady')
Designer H. Tittensor.
Date 1926 - 36.
27.5cm (10.75ins) high.
Red and purple.
Other colourways: HN354, 376,
376A, 387, 634, 741, 1321, 1322.
Est. £2600-3500.

HN775
Mephistopheles and
Marguerite
Designer C.J. Noke.
Date 1925 - 49.
19.5cm (7.75ins) high.
Cream and red.
Other colourways: HN755.
Est. £950-1250.

HN780
Harlequinade
First Version
Designer L. Harradine.
Date 1926 - 40.
18cm (7ins) high.
Blue, pink and brown.
Other colourways: HN585,
635, 711.
Est. £2000-2700.

HN776
The Belle
First Version (Model 477)
Designer L. Harradine.
Date 1925 - 38.
16.5cm (6.5ins)
Colour not known.
Other colourways: HN754.
Very rare.

HN781
The Bather
First Version (Model 428)
Designer L. Harradine.
Date 1926 - 38.
19.5cm (7.75ins) high.
Green and blue.
Other colourways: HN597,
687, 782, 1238, 1708.
Very rare.

HN777
Bo-Peep
First Version (Model 484)
Designer L. Harradine.
Date 1926 - 36.
17cm (6.75ins) high.
Dark blue.
Other colourways:
HN1202, 1327, 1328.
Est. £1650-2200.

HN782
The Bather
First Version (Model 428)
Designer L. Harradine.
Date 1926 - 38.
19.5cm (7.75ins) high.
Purple and black.
Other colourways: HN597,
687, 781, 1238, 1708.
Very rare.

HN778
Captain
First Version (Model 485)
Designer L. Harradine.
Date 1926 - 36.
18cm (7ins) high.
Red, white and black.
Est. £1300-1750.

HN783
Pretty Lady
Designer H. Tittensor.
Date 1926 - 38.
24cm (9.5ins) high.
Blue.
Other colourways: HN69, 70,
302, 330, 361, 384, 565, 700, 763.
Est. £1100-1450.

HN784
Pierrette
First Version (Model 445)
Designer L. Harradine.
Date 1926 - 38.
18.5cm (7.25ins) high.
Pink and black.
Other colourways: HN642,
643, 644, 691, 721, 731, 732.
Est. £1500-2000.

HN789
The Flower Seller
Designer L. Harradine.
Date 1926 - 38.
22cm (8.75ins) high.
Green, yellow, cream and white.
Est. £750-1000.

HN785
The Mask
First Version
Designer L. Harradine.
Date 1926 - 38.
17cm (6.75ins) high.
Blue, pink and black.
Other colourways: HN656,
657, 729, 733, 1271.
Est. £1700-2250.

HN790
The Parson's Daughter
Designer H. Tittensor.
Date 1926 - 38.
25.5cm (10ins) high.
Multicoloured.
Other colourways: HN337,
338, 441, 564, 1242, 1356, 2018.
Est. £950-1300.

HN786
Mam'selle
Designer L. Harradine.
Date 1926 - 38.
18cm (7ins) high.
Pink and black.
Other colourways: HN658,
659, 724.
Est. £2000-2600.

HN791
A Mandarin
First Version (Model 189)
(Also known as 'A Chinese
Mandarin' and 'The Mikado')
Designer C.J. Noke.
Date 1926 - 36.
26cm (10.25ins) high.
Purple and black.
Other colourways: HN84,
316, 318, 382, 611, 746, 787.
Est. £3000-4000.

HN787
A Mandarin
First Version (Model 189)
(Also known as 'A Chinese
Mandarin' and 'The Mikado')
Designer C.J. Noke.
Date 1926 - 36.
26cm (10.25ins) high.
Pink and orange with black flowers.
Other colourways: HN84, 316, 318,
382, 611, 746, 791.
Very rare.

HN792
The Welsh Girl
(Also known as 'Myfanwy Jones')
Designer E.W. Light.
Date 1926 - 36.
30.5cm (12ins) high.
Pink and blue.
Other colourways: HN39, 92,
456, 514, 516, 519, 520, 660, 668,
669 701.
Very rare.

HN788
The Proposal (female)
Designer L. Harradine.
Date 1926 - 40.
14.5cm (5.75ins) high.
Pink.
Other colourways:
HN715, 716.
Very rare.

HN793
Katharine
Designer C.J. Noke.
Date 1926 - 38.
14.5cm (5.75ins) high.
Lilac with green spots.
Other colourways: HN61,
74, 341, 471, 615.
Est. £1100-1500.

HN794
The Bouquet
(Also known as 'The Nosegay')
Designer G. Lambert.
Date 1926 - 36.
23cm (9ins) high.
Blue, green and red.
Other colourways: HN406,
414, 422, 428, 429, 567.
Very rare.

HN795
Pierrette
Second Version (Model 498)
Designer L. Harradine.
Date 1926 - 38.
9cm (3.5ins) high.
Pink.
Other colourways: HN796.
Very rare.

HN796
Pierrette
Second Version (Model 498)
Designer L. Harradine.
Date 1926 - 38.
9cm (3.5ins) high.
White and silver.
Other colourways: HN795.
Very rare.

HN797
Moorish Minstrel
Designer C.J. Noke.
Date 1926 - 49.
34.5cm (13.5ins) high.
Purple.
Other colourways: HN34, 364, 415.
Est. £1650-2200.

HN798
Tête-à-Tête
First Version (Model 487)
Designer L. Harradine.
Date 1926 - 38.
14.5cm (5.75ins) high.
Pink, tan, blue and red.
Other colourways: HN799.
Est. £1350-1750.

HN799
Tête-à-Tête
First Version (Model 487)
Designer L. Harradine.
Date 1926 - 40.
14.5cm (5.75ins) high.
Blue, purple, brown and red.
Other colourways: HN798.
Est. £1300-1750.

HN1201
Hunts Lady
Designer L. Harradine.
Date 1926 - 38.
21cm (8.25ins) high.
Grey brown and cream.
(This figure was made as a
pair to HN1226 'Huntsman')
Est. £1500-2000.

HN1202
Bo-Peep
First Version (Model 484)
Designer L. Harradine.
Date 1926 - 36.
17cm (6.75ins) high.
Purple, pink black and green.
Other colourways: HN777,
1327, 1328.
Very rare.

HN1203
Butterfly
(Also known as 'Butterfly
Woman')
Designer L. Harradine.
Date 1926 - 40.
16.5cm (6.5ins) high.
Black and gold.
Other colourways: HN719,
720, 730, 1456.
Very rare.

HN1204
Angela
(Also known as 'Fanny')
First Version (Model 513)
Designer L. Harradine.
Date 1926 - 40.
18.5cm (7.25ins) high.
Pink, purple and red.
Other colourways: HN1303.
Est. £1100-1500.

HN1205
Miss 1926
Designer L. Harradine.
Date 1926 - 38.
18.5cm (7.25ins) high.
Black coat with white fur
collar and cuffs.
Other colourways: HN1207.
Est. £2500-3500.

HN1206
**The Flower
Seller's Children**
Designer L. Harradine.
Date 1926 - 49.
21cm (8.25ins) high.
Purple, blue and yellow.
Other colourways:
HN525, 551, 1342, 1406.
Est. £1000-1300.

HN1207
Miss 1926
Designer L. Harradine.
Date not known.
18.5cm (7.25ins) high.
Black coat with black fur collar.
Other colourways: HN1205.
Very rare.

HN1208
A Victorian Lady
Designer L. Harradine.
Date 1926 - 38.
19.5cm (7.75ins) high.
Green dress with purple
and red shawl.
Other colourways: HN726,
727, 728, 736, 739, 740, 742,
745, 1258, 1276, 1277, 1345,
1452, 1529.
Est. £500-650.

HN1209
The Proposal (male)
Designer not known.
Date 1926 - 38.
14cm (5.5ins) high.
Blue, cream and pink.
Other colourways: HN725.
Est. £1350-1750.

HN1210
Boy with Turban
(Also known as 'Eastern Boy')
Designer L. Harradine.
Date 1926 - 36.
9.5cm (3.75ins) high.
Orange, white and black.
Other colourways: HN586,
587, 661, 662, 1212, 1213,
1214, 1225.
Est. £600-700.

HN1214
Boy with Turban
(Also known as 'Eastern Boy')
Designer L. Harradine.
Date 1926 - 36.
9.5cm (3.75ins) high.
Black, green and white.
Other colourways: HN586,
587, 661, 662, 1210, 1212,
1213, 1225.
Est. £600-700.

HN1211
Quality Street
Designer L. Harradine.
Date 1926 - 36.
19cm (7.5ins) high.
Red, grey and white.
Other colourways:
HN1211A.
Est. £700-1000.

HN1215
The Pied Piper
First Version
Designer L. Harradine.
Date 1926 - 38.
22cm (8.75ins) high.
Black, yellow and red.
Other colourways: HN2102.
Est. £1100-1500.

HN1211A
Quality Street
Designer L. Harradine.
Date 1926 - 36.
19cm (7.5ins) high.
Lilac.
Other colourways: HN1211.
Est. £700-1000.

HN1216
Falstaff
First Version (Model 401)
Designer C.J. Noke.
Date 1926 - 49.
18cm (7ins) high.
Multicoloured.
Other colourways: HN571,
575, 608, 609, 619, 638, 1606.
Est. £1000-1400.

HN1212
Boy with Turban
(Also known as 'Eastern Boy')
Designer L. Harradine.
Date 1926 - 36.
9.5cm (3.75ins) high.
Purple, red, lilac and green.
Other colourways: HN586,
587, 661, 662, 1210, 1213,
1214, 1225.
Est. £600-700.

HN1217
The Prince of Wales
Designer L. Harradine.
Date 1926 - 38.
18.5cm (7.25ins) high.
Red, white and brown.
Est. £800-1100.

HN1213
Boy with Turban
(Also known as 'Eastern Boy')
Designer L. Harradine.
Date 1926 - 36.
9.5cm (3.75ins) high.
White and black.
Other colourways: HN586,
587, 661, 662, 1210, 1212,
1214, 1225.
Est. £600-700.

HN1218
A Spook
Designer H. Tittensor.
Date 1926 - 36.
7.6cm (3ins) high.
Multicoloured.
Other colourways: HN50,
51A, 51B, 58, 512, 625;
(also recorded in flambé glaze
and in a miniature version.)
Est. £1200-1600.

HN1219
Negligée
Designer L. Harradine.
Date 1927 - 36.
12.5cm (5ins) high.
Yellow and blue with blue
hair band.
Other colourways: HN1228,
1272, 1273, 1454.
Est. £1100-1450.

HN1224
The Wandering Minstrel
Designer L. Harradine.
Date 1927 - 36.
18cm (7ins) high.
Purple, black, blue and red.
Est. £1500-2000.

HN1220
Lido Lady
First Version
Designer L. Harradine.
Date 1927 - 36.
17cm (6.75ins) high.
Pale blue and purple.
Other colourways: HN1229.
Est. £900-1100.

HN1225
Boy with Turban
(Also known as 'Eastern Boy')
Designer L. Harradine.
Date 1927 - 36.
9.5cm (3.75ins) high.
Yellow and blue.
Other colourways: HN586, 587,
661, 662, 1210, 1212, 1213, 1214.
Est. £550-750.

HN1221
Lady Jester
First Version (Model 531)
Designer L. Harradine.
Date 1927 - 38.
18.5cm (7.25ins) high.
Black, brown and blue.
Other colourways: HN1222, 1332.
Est. £1500-2100.

HN1226
The Huntsman
First Version (Model 503)
Designer L. Harradine.
Date 1927 - 38.
21.5cm (8.5ins) high.
Red and white.
(This figure was made as a pair
to HN1201 'Hunts Lady')
Est. £1400-2000.

HN1222
Lady Jester
First Version (Model 531)
Designer L. Harradine.
Date 1927 - 38.
18.5cm (7.25ins) high.
Black and white.
Other colourways: HN1221, 1332.
Est. £1500-2100.

HN1227
The Bather
Second Version (Model 486)
Designer L. Harradine.
Date 1927 - 38.
19cm (7.5ins) high.
Pink and black.
Other colourways: HN773, 774.
Est. £2000-2600.

HN1223
A Geisha
Second Version (Model 528)
Designer C.J. Noke.
Date 1927 - 38.
17cm (6.75ins) high.
Blue, black and orange.
Other colourways: HN1234,
1292, 1310.
Est. £900-1200.

HN1228
Negligée
Designer L. Harradine.
Date 1927 - 36.
12.5cm (5ins) high.
Yellow, blue with red hair
band.
Other colourways: HN1219,
1272, 1273, 1454.
Est. £1100-1450.

HN1229
Lido Lady
First Version
Designer L. Harradine.
Date 1927 - 36.
17cm (6.75ins) high.
Pink.
Other colourways: HN1220.
Est. £1650-2200.

HN1234
A Geisha
Second Version (Model 528)
Designer C.J. Noke.
Date 1927 - 38.
17cm (6.75ins) high.
Purple, yellow and red.
Other colourways: HN1223,
1292, 1310.
Est. £800-1100.

HN1230
Baba
Designer L. Harradine.
Date 1927 - 38.
9cm (3.5ins) high.
Blue, black, purple and yellow.
Other colourways: HN1243,
1244, 1245, 1246, 1247, 1248.
Est. £700-850.

HN1235
A Scribe
Designer C.J. Noke.
Date 1927 - 38.
15cm (6ins) high.
Brown, cream, orange and blue.
Other colourways: HN305, 324.
Est. £900-1200.

HN1231
Cassim
First Version (Model 555)
Designer L. Harradine.
Date 1927 - 38.
9.5cm (3.75ins) high.
Turquoise. yellow, black
and blue
Other colourways:
HN1232.
Est. £700-850.

HN1236
Tête-à-Tête
Second Version (Model 538)
Designer C.J. Noke.
Date 1927 - 38.
7.5cm (3ins) high.
Purple, white and red.
Other colourways: HN1237.
Est. £1500-2000.

HN1232
Cassim
First Version (Model 555)
Designer L. Harradine.
Date 1927 - 38.
9.5cm (3.75ins) high.
Orange, white and black.
Other colourways:
HN1231.
Est. £600-800.

HN1237
Tête-à-Tête
Second Version (Model 538)
Designer C.J. Noke.
Date 1927 - 38.
7.5cm (3ins) high.
Pink, orange and blue.
Other colourways:
HN1236.
Series: Miniatures.
Est. £1500-2000.

HN1233
Susanna
Designer L. Harradine.
Date 1927 - 36.
15cm (6ins) high.
Pink and white.
Other colourways:
HN1288, 1299.
Est. £1000-1350.

HN1238
The Bather
First Version (Model 428)
Designer L. Harradine.
Date 1927 - 38.
19.5cm (7.75ins) high.
Red and black.
Other colourways: HN597,
687, 781, 782, 1708.
Est. £1300-1750.

HN1242
The Parson's Daughter
Designer H. Tittensor.
Date 1927 - 38.
25.5cm (10ins) high.
Lilac and yellow.
Other colourways: HN337,
338, 441, 564, 790, 1356, 2018.
Est. £900-1200.

HN1247
Baba
Designer L. Harradine.
Date 1927 - 38.
9cm (3.5ins) high.
Black, orange and white.
Other colourways:
HN1230, 1243, 1244, 1245,
1246, 1248.
Est. £650-900.

HN1243
Baba
Designer L. Harradine.
Date 1927 - 38.
9cm (3.5ins) high.
Orange.
Other colourways: HN1230,
1244, 1245, 1246, 1247, 1248.
Est. £600-800.

HN1248
Baba
Designer L. Harradine.
Date 1927 - 38.
9cm (3.5ins) high.
Green and orange.
Other colourways: HN1230,
1243, 1244, 1245, 1246, 1247.
Est. £650-900.

HN1244
Baba
Designer L. Harradine.
Date 1927 - 38.
9cm (3.5ins) high.
Yellow and green.
Other colourways: HN1230,
1243, 1245, 1246, 1247, 1248.
Est. £650-900.

HN1249
Circe
Designer L. Harradine.
Date 1927 - 36.
19cm (7.5ins) high.
Green, pink and orange.
Other colourways:
HN1250, 1254, 1255.
Est. £1500-2000.

HN1245
Baba
Designer L. Harradine.
Date 1927 - 38.
9cm (3.5ins) high.
White, purple and black.
Other colourways: HN1230,
1243, 1244, 1246, 1247, 1248.
Est. £650-900.

HN1250
Circe
Designer L. Harradine.
Date 1927 - 36.
19cm (7.5ins) high.
Orange and black.
Other colourways:
HN1249, 1254, 1255.
Est. £1500-2000.

HN1246
Baba
Designer L. Harradine.
Date 1927 - 38.
9cm (3.5ins) high.
Green.
Other colourways: HN1230,
1243, 1244, 1245, 1247, 1248.
Est. £650-900.

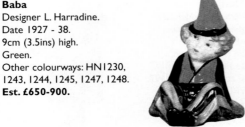

HN1251
The Cobbler
Second Version (Model 589)
Designer C.J. Noke.
Date 1927 - 38.
21.5cm (8.5ins) high.
Black and red.
Other colourways: HN681, 1283.
Est. £900-1200.

HN1252
Kathleen
First Version (Model 560)
Designer L. Harradine.
Date 1927 - 38.
19cm (7.5ins) high.
Lilac, purple and pink.
Other colourways: HN1253,
1275, 1279, 1291, 1357, 1512.
Est. £500-600.

HN1257
The Highwayman
Designer L. Harradine.
Date 1927 - 49.
16.5cm (6.5ins) high.
Green and red.
Other colourways:
HN527, 592.
Series: Beggar's Opera.
Est. £400-500.

HN1253
Kathleen
First Version (Model 560)
Designer L. Harradine.
Date 1927 - 38.
19cm (7.5ins) high.
Red, purple and black.
Other colourways: HN1252,
1275, 1279, 1291, 1357, 1512.
Est. £500-600.

HN1258
A Victorian Lady
Designer L. Harradine.
Date 1927 - 38.
19.5cm (7.75ins) high.
Purple and blue.
Other colourways: HN726, 727,
728, 736, 739, 740, 742, 745, 1208,
1276, 1277, 1345, 1452, 1529.
Est. £500-600.

HN1254
Circe
Designer L. Harradine.
Date 1927 - 36.
19cm (7.5ins) high.
Orange and red.
Other colourways:
HN1249, 1250, 1255.
Very rare.

HN1259
The Alchemist
Designer L. Harradine.
Date 1927 - 38.
29cm (11.5ins) high.
Green, black, blue and red.
Other colourways: HN1282.
Est. £950-1350.

HN1255
Circe
Designer L. Harradine.
Date 1927 - 38.
19cm (7.5ins) high.
Blue.
Other colourways:
HN1249, 1250, 1254.
Very rare.

HN1260
Carnival
Designer L. Harradine.
Date 1927 - 36.
21.5cm (8.5ins) high.
Red, purple and black.
Other colourways:
HN1278.
Est. £2500-3000.

HN1256
Captain MacHeath
Designer L. Harradine.
Date 1927 - 49.
18cm (7ins) high.
Red, black and yellow.
Other colourways: HN464, 590.
Series: Beggar's Opera.
Est. £500-600.

HN1261
Sea Sprite
First Version (Model 565)
Designer L. Harradine.
Date 1927 - 38.
13.5cm (5.25ins) high.
Red, purple and black.
Est. £500-600.

HN1262
Spanish Lady
Designer L. Harradine.
Date 1927 - 40.
21cm (8.25ins) high.
Black and red.
Other colourways: HN1290, 1293, 1294, 1309.
Est. £700-1000.

HN1267
Carmen
First Version (Model 537)
Designer L. Harradine.
Date 1928 - 38.
18cm (7ins) high.
Red and black.
Other colourways:
HN1300.
Est. £650-900.

HN1263
Clownette
(Also known as 'Lady Clown')
Designer L. Harradine.
Date 1927 - 38.
19cm (7.5ins) high.
Purple suit with coloured spots.
Other colourways: HN717, 718, 738, 770.
Est. £3000-4000.

HN1268
Yum-Yum
First Version (Model 519)
Designer L. Harradine.
Date 1928 - 36.
12.5cm (5ins) high.
Pink, red, green and cream.
Other colourways: HN1287.
(Made as a pair to
HN1266 'Ko-Ko')
Est. £700-900.

HN1264
Judge and Jury
Designer J.G. Hughes.
Date 1927 - 38.
15cm (6ins) high.
Red, brown and white.
Very rare.

HN1269
Scotch Girl
Designer L. Harradine.
Date 1928 - 38.
19cm (7.5ins) high.
Red, black and green.
Est. £1400-2000.

HN1265
Lady Fayre
Designer L. Harradine.
Date 1928 - 38.
14.5cm (5.75ins) high.
Lilac and red.
Other colourways: HN1557.
Est. £450-550.

HN1270
The Swimmer
First Version
Designer L. Harradine.
Date 1928 - 38.
19cm (7.5ins) high.
Black and red towel, spotted
swim-suit.
Other colourways: HN1326, 1329.
Est. £1650-2200.

HN1266
Ko-Ko
First Version (Model 518)
Designer L. Harradine.
Date 1928 - 36.
12.5cm (5ins) high.
Black, yellow and white.
Other colourways: HN1286.
(Made as a pair to
HN1268 'Yum-Yum')
Est. £700-900.

HN1271
The Mask
First Version
Designer L. Harradine.
Date 1928 - 38.
17cm (6.75ins) high.
Black, blue and red costume
with blue and white spots.
Other colourways: HN656,
657, 729, 733, 785.
Est. £1600-2100.

HN1272
Negligée
Designer L. Harradine.
Date 1928 - 36.
12.5cm (5ins) high.
Red and black.
Other colourways: HN1219,
1228, 1273, 1454.
Est. £1100-1400.

HN1277
A Victorian Lady
Designer L. Harradine.
Date 1928 - 38.
19.5cm (7.75ins) high.
Red, pink, yellow and blue.
Other colourways: HN726, 727,
728, 736, 739, 740, 742, 745, 1208,
1258, 1276, 1345, 1452, 1529.
Est. £500-650.

HN1273
Negligée
Designer L. Harradine.
Date 1928 - 36.
12.5cm (5ins) high.
Pink and white.
Other colourways:
HN1219, 1228, 1272, 1454.
Est. £1100-1400.

HN1278
Carnival
Designer L. Harradine.
Date 1928 - 36.
21.5cm (8.5ins) high.
Pale blue, yellow, orange and
purple.
Other colourways: HN1260.
Est. £2500-3500.

HN1274
Harlequinade Masked
Designer L. Harradine.
Date 1928 - 38.
16.5cm (6.5ins) high.
Orange and black.
Other colourways: HN768,
769, 1304.
Est. £1800-2500.

HN1279
Kathleen
First Version (Model 560)
Designer L. Harradine.
Date 1928 - 38.
19cm (7.5ins) high.
Red and black.
Other colourways: HN1252,
1253, 1275, 1291, 1357, 1512.
Est. £450-550.

HN1275
Kathleen
First Version (Model 560)
Designer L. Harradine.
Date 1928 - 38.
19cm (7.5ins) high.
Pink, white and black.
Other colourways: HN1252,
1253, 1279, 1291, 1357, 1512.
Very rare.

HN1280
Blue Bird
Designer L. Harradine.
Date 1928 - 38
12cm (4.75ins) high.
Cream with red and pink base.
Est. £500-650.

HN1276
A Victorian Lady
Designer L. Harradine.
Date 1928 - 38.
19.5cm (7.75ins) high.
Purple, red, yellow and green.
Other colourways: HN726,
727, 728, 736, 739, 740, 742,
745, 1208, 1258, 1277, 1345,
1452, 1529.
Est. £500-650.

HN1281
Scotties
Designer L. Harradine.
Date 1928 - 36.
13cm (5.25ins) high.
Red, yellow and black.
Other colourways: HN1349.
*(Auction BBC 'Flog-it' 31.8.04
sold £700 plus comm.)*
Est. £900-1450.

HN1282
The Alchemist
Designer L. Harradine.
Date 1928 - 38.
29cm (11.5ins) high.
Purple, black and red.
Other colourways: HN1259.
Est. £950-1250.

HN1283
The Cobbler
Second Version (Model 589)
Designer C.J. Noke.
Date 1928 - 49.
21.5cm (8.5ins) high.
Pale green, yellow and red.
Other colourways: HN681,
1251.
Est. £450-550.

HN1284
Lady Jester
Second Version (Model 578)
Designer L. Harradine.
Date 1928 - 38.
11cm (4.25ins) high.
Purple, white and red.
Other colourways: HN1285.
Est. £1300-1700.

HN1285
Lady Jester
Second Version (Model 578)
Designer L. Harradine.
Date 1928 - 38.
11cm (4.25ins) high.
Red, pink and pale blue.
Other colourways: HN1284.
Est. £1300-1700.

HN1286
Ko-Ko
First Version (Model 518)
Designer L. Harradine.
Date 1938 - 49.
12.5cm (5ins) high.
Purple, red and brown.
Other colourways: HN1266.
Est. £650-950.

HN1287
Yum-Yum
First Version (Model 519)
Designer L. Harradine.
Date 1928 - 36.
12.5cm (5ins) high.
Purple, pink and cream.
Other colourways: HN1268.
Est. £650-950.

HN1288
Susanna
Designer L. Harradine.
Date 1928 - 36.
15cm (6ins) high.
Red and black.
Other colourways:
HN1233, 1299.
Est. £950-1350.

HN1289
Midinette
First Version (Model 598)
Designer L. Harradine.
Date 1928 - 38.
23cm (9ins) high.
Purple, pink, yellow and blue.
Other colourways: HN1306.
Est. £1800-2400.

HN1290
Spanish Lady
Designer L. Harradine.
Date 1928 - 40.
21cm (8.25ins) high.
Lilac, yellow and black.
Other colourways:
HN1262, 1293, 1294, 1309.
Est. £650-850.

HN1291
Kathleen
First Version (Model 560)
Designer L. Harradine.
Date 1928 - 38.
19cm (7.5ins) high.
Red and yellow.
Other colourways: HN1252,
1253, 1275, 1279, 1357, 1512.
Est. £500-650.

HN1292
A Geisha
Second Version (Model 528)
Designer C.J. Noke.
Date 1928 - 38.
17cm (6.75ins) high.
Pink, black and lilac.
Other colourways: HN1223,
1234, 1310.
Est. £700-950.

HN1293
Spanish Lady
Designer L. Harradine.
Date 1928 - 40.
21cm (8.25ins) high.
Black with yellow flowers.
Other colourways: HN1262,
1290, 1294, 1309.
Est. £700-950.

HN1294
Spanish Lady
Designer L. Harradine.
Date 1928 - 40.
21cm (8.25ins) high.
Red and blue.
Other colourways: HN1262,
1290, 1293, 1309.
Est. £550-800.

HN1295
A Jester
First Version (Model 170)
Designer C.J. Noke.
Date 1928 - 49.
25.5cm (10ins) high.
Brown, black, orange and purple.
Other colourways: HN45, 71, 71A,
320, 367, 412, 426, 446, 552, 616,
627, 1702, 2016, 3922.
Est. £700-950.

HN1296
Columbine
First Version (Model 563)
Designer L. Harradine.
Date 1928 - 40.
15cm (6ins) high.
Orange and lilac.
Other colourways: HN1297,
1439.
Est. £650-850.

HN1297
Columbine
First Version (Model 563)
Designer L. Harradine.
Date 1928 - 40.
15cm (6ins) high.
Pink and purple.
Other colourways: HN1296, 1439.
Est. £650-900.

HN1298
Sweet and Twenty
First Version (Model 605)
Designer L. Harradine.
Date 1928 - 69.
15cm (6ins) high.
Red, grey and blue-green.
Other colourways:
HN1360, 1437, 1438,
1549, 1563, 1649.
(Ebay 10.7.04 sold £117)
Est. £125-170.

HN1299
Susanna
Designer L. Harradine.
Date 1928 - 36.
15cm (6ins) high.
Black, red and blue.
Other colourways: HN1233,
1288.
Est. £950-1350.

HN1300
Carmen
First Version (Model 537)
Designer L. Harradine.
Date 1928 - 38.
18cm (7ins) high.
Pale blue, pale green and lilac.
Other colourways: HN1267.
Est. £1600-2250.

HN1301
Young Mother with Child
(Also known as 'Gypsy Woman
with Child)
Designer not known.
Date 1928 - 38.
37cm (14.5ins) high.
Green, cream, black and red.
Extremely rare.

HN1302
The Gleaner
(Also known as 'Gypsy Girl with Flowers')
Designer not known.
Date 1928 - 36.
37cm (14.5ins) high.
Red, brown and cream.
Extremely rare.

HN1307
An Irishman
Designer H. Fenton.
Date 1928 - 38.
17cm (6.75ins) high.
Green, red, brown and blue.
Est. £1600-2200.

HN1303
Angela
First Version (Model 513)
(Also known as 'Fanny')
Designer L. Harradine.
Date 1928 - 40.
18.5cm (7.25ins) high.
Purple and orange.
Other colourways: HN1204.
Est. £1800-2400.

HN1308
The Moor
Designer C.J. Noke.
Date 1929 - 38.
42cm (16.5ins) high.
Blue and orange.
Other colourways: HN1366, 1425, 1657, 2082, 3642, 3926; 'An Arab" HN33, 343, 378.
Est. £1400-1700.

HN1304
Harlequinade Masked
Designer L. Harradine.
Date 1928 - 38.
16.5cm (6.5ins) high.
Dark blue background with coloured spots.
Other colourways: HN768, 769, 1274.
Est. £1800-2400.

HN1309
Spanish Lady
Designer L. Harradine.
Date 1929 - 40.
21cm (8.25ins) high.
Black, purple and orange.
Other colourways: HN1262, 1290, 1293, 1294.
Est. £850-1200.

HN1305
Siesta
Designer L. Harradine.
Date 1928 - 40.
12cm (4.75ins) high.
Red and lilac.
Est. £1800-2400.

HN1310
A Geisha
Second Version (Model 528)
Designer C.J. Noke.
Date 1929 - 38.
17cm (6.75ins) high.
Green and yellow.
Other colourways: HN1223, 1234, 1292.
Est. £700-950.

HN1306
Midinette
First Version (Model 598)
Designer L. Harradine.
Date 1928 - 38.
23cm (9ins) high.
Red and pale green.
Other colourways: HN1289.
Est. £1800-2400.

HN1311
Cassim
Second Version (Model 555)
Designer L. Harradine.
Date 1929 - 38.
9.5cm (3.75ins) high.
Colour not known but mounted on a pink lidded bowl.
Other colourways: HN1312.
Very rare.

*Picture
not available
at present*

HN1312
Cassim
Second Version (Model 555)
Designer L. Harradine.
Date 1929 - 38.
9.5cm (3.75ins) high.
Green, blue, orange and black
and mounted on green bowl.
Other colourways: HN1311.
Very rare.

*Picture
not available
at present*

HN1317
The Snake Charmer
Designer not known.
Date 1929 - 38.
11.5cm (4.5ins) high.
Green, red and black.
Est. £800-1100.

HN1313
Sonny
Designer L. Harradine.
Date 1929 - 38.
9cm (3.5ins) high.
Pink.
Other colourways: HN1314.
Est. £550-750.

HN1318
Sweet Anne
Designer L. Harradine.
Date 1929 - 49.
18cm (7ins) high.
Blue and pale green.
Other colourways: HN1330,
1331, 1453, 1496, 1631, 1701.
(Ebay 28.6.04 sold for £102)
Est. £100-150.

HN1314
Sonny
Designer L. Harradine.
Date 1929 - 38.
9cm (3.5ins) high.
Blue.
Other colourways: HN1313.
Est. £550-750.

HN1319
Darling
First Version (Model 89)
Designer C. Vyse.
Date 1929 - 59.
19cm (7.5ins) high.
White with black base.
Other colourways: HN1,
1371, 1372, 4140.
Est. £80-100.

HN1315
Old Balloon Seller
First Version (Model 607)
Designer L. Harradine.
Date 1929 - 98.
18cm (7ins) high.
Green, white and red.
Other colourways: HN3737.
*(Auction Bonhams sold £94 and
W&H 27.9.04 sold £90 plus comm.)*
(Ebay 26.5.04 sold £124)
Est. £125-150.

HN1320
Rosamund
First Version (Model 618)
Designer L. Harradine.
Date 1929 - 37.
18.5cm (7.25ins) high.
Lilac and blue.
Est. £1200-1650.

HN1316
Toys
Designer L. Harradine.
Date 1929 - 38.
Height not known.
Green, yellow, white and red.
Very rare.

*Picture
not available
at present*

HN1321
A Geisha
First Version (Model 238)
(Also known as 'The Japanese Lady')
Designer H. Tittensor.
Date 1929 - 36.
27.5cm (10.75ins) high.
Green.
Other colourways: HN354, 376,
376A, 387, 634, 741, 779, 1322.
Very rare.

HN1322
A Geisha
First Version (Model 238)
(Also known as 'The Japanese
Lady')
Designer H. Tittensor.
Date 1929 - 36.
27.5cm (10.75ins) high.
Pink and blue.
Other colourways: HN354, 376,
376A, 387, 634, 741, 779, 1321.
Very rare.

HN1327
Bo-Peep
First Version (Model 484)
Designer L. Harradine.
Date 1929 - 36.
17cm (6.75ins) high.
Multicoloured.
Other colourways: HN777,
1202, 1328.
Est. £1400-1800.

HN1323
Contentment
Designer L. Harradine.
Date 1929 - 38.
18.5cm (7.25ins) high.
Red, lilac and blue.
Other colourways: HN395,
396, 421, 468, 572, 685, 686.
Est. £900-1200.

HN1328
Bo-Peep
First Version (Model 484)
Designer L. Harradine.
Date 1929 - 36.
17cm (6.75ins) high.
Cream, blue and purple.
Other colourways: HN777,
1202, 1327.
Est. £1400-1800.

HN1324
Fairy
First Version (Model 629)
Designer L. Harradine.
Date 1929 - 38.
16.5cm (6.5ins) high.
Multicoloured.
Est. £850-1150.

HN1329
The Swimmer
First Version
Designer L. Harradine.
Date 1929 - 38.
19cm (7.5ins) high.
Pink.
Other colourways: HN1270, 1326.
Est. £1650-2100.

HN1325
The Orange Seller
(Made as a pair to HN1339
'Covent Garden')
Designer L. Harradine.
Date 1929 - 40.
18cm (7ins) high.
Lilac, green and orange.
Est. £650-850.

HN1330
Sweet Anne
Designer L. Harradine.
Date 1929 - 49.
18cm (7ins) high.
Pale blue, red, pink and
yellow.
Other colourways: HN1318,
1331, 1453, 1496, 1631, 1701.
Est. £160-210.

HN1326
The Swimmer
First Version
Designer L. Harradine.
Date 1929 - 38.
19cm (7.5ins) high.
Pink, orange and purple.
Other colourways: HN1270, 1329.
Est. £1650-2000.

HN1331
Sweet Anne
Designer L. Harradine.
Date 1929 - 49.
18cm (7ins) high.
Pale blue, red and yellow.
Other colourways: HN1318,
1330, 1453, 1496, 1631, 1701.
Est. £160-210.

HN1332
Lady Jester
First Version (Model 531)
Designer L. Harradine.
Date 1929 - 38.
18.5cm (7.25ins) high.
Red, black and blue.
Other colourways: HN1221, 1222.
Est. £1600-2200.

HN1337
Priscilla
Designer L. Harradine.
Date 1929 - 38.
20.5cm (8ins) high.
Lilac and yellow.
Other colourways:
HN1340, 1495, 1501, 1559.
Est. £400-550.

HN1333
A Jester
Second Version (Model 171)
Designer C.J. Noke.
Date 1929 - 49.
26cm (10.25ins) high.
Blue tunic, yellow and black.
Other colourways: HN45A,
45B, 55, 308, 630; also
recorded in black and white.
Est. £2600-3500.

HN1338
The Courtier
Designer L. Harradine.
Date 1929 - 38.
11.5cm (4.5ins) high.
Red and white.
Est. £1400-1900.

HN1334
Tulips
Designer not known.
Date 1929 - 36.
24cm (9.5ins) high.
Pink and lilac.
Other colourways: HN466,
488, 672, 747.
Est. £1100-1450.

HN1339
Covent Garden
First Version (Model 631)
(Made as a pair to HN1325 'The
Orange Seller')
Designer L. Harradine.
Date 1929 - 38.
23cm (9ins) high.
Green, lilac, red and yellow.
Est. £1100-1400.

HN1335
Folly
Designer L. Harradine.
Date 1929 - 38.
23cm (9ins) high.
Lilac, yellow, black and orange.
Other colourways: HN1750.
Est. £1100-1500.

HN1340
Priscilla
Designer L. Harradine.
Date 1929 - 49.
20.5cm (8ins) high.
Red and purple.
Other colourways: HN1337,
1495, 1501, 1559.
Est. £200-300.

HN1336
One of the Forty
Twelfth Version (Model 319)
Designer H. Tittensor.
Date 1929 - 36.
Height not known.
Mottled red, orange and blue.
Other colourways: HN481, 483,
491, 646, 667, 712, 1350; also
in flambé glaze.
Est. £1850-2500.

HN1341
Marietta
Designer L. Harradine.
Date 1929 - 40.
20.5cm (8ins) high.
Red and black.
Other colourways:
HN1446, 1699.
Est. £650-850.

HN1342
The Flower Seller's Children
Designer L. Harradine.
Date 1929 - 93.
21cm (8.25ins) high.
Purple, lilac, yellow and red.
Other colourways: HN525,
551, 1206, 1406.
*(Auction PSA 23.6.04
sold £134 plus comm.)*
Est. £165-225.

HN1347
Moira
Designer L. Harradine.
Date 1929 - 38.
16.5cm (6.5ins) high.
Lilac, brown, pink and green.
Est. £1950-2500.

HN1343
Dulcinea
Designer L. Harradine.
Date 1929 - 36.
13cm (5.25ins) high.
Red, green, blue and black.
Other colourways: HN1419.
Est. £1400-1800.

HN1348
Sunshine Girl
First Version
Designer L. Harradine.
Date 1929 - 37.
12.5cm (5ins) high.
Orange, green and black.
Other colourways: HN1344.
Est. £2750-4000.

HN1344
Sunshine Girl
First Version
Designer L. Harradine.
Date 1929 - 38.
12.5cm (5ins) high.
Green, red and black.
Other colourways: HN1348.
Est. £2700-4000.

HN1349
Scotties
Designer L. Harradine.
Date 1929 - 36.
13cm (5.25ins) high.
Blue, grey and cream.
Other colourways: HN1281.
Est. £1600-2250.

HN1345
A Victorian Lady
Designer L. Harradine.
Date 1929 - 49.
19.5cm (7.75ins) high.
Green, brown and lilac.
Other colourways: HN726, 727,
728, 736, 739, 740, 742, 745, 1208,
1258, 1276, 1277, 1452, 1529.
Est. £250-300.

HN1350
One of the Forty
Twelfth Version (Model 319)
Designer H. Tittensor.
Date 1929 - 49.
Size not known.
Multicoloured.
Other colourways: HN481, 483,
491, 646, 667, 712, 1336; also
recorded in flambé glaze.
Extremely rare.

HN1346
Iona
Designer L. Harradine.
Date 1929 - 38.
19cm (7.5ins) high.
Pale green, lilac brown and black.
Est. £2000-2500.

HN1351
One of the Forty
First Version (Model 288)
(Also known as 'Chu Chin Chou
with Beads')
Designer H. Tittensor.
Date 1920 - 49.
21cm (8.25ins) high.
Red and purple.
Other colourways: HN417, 490,
495, 501, 528, 648, 677, 1352.
Est. £1800-2400.

HN1352
One of the Forty
First Version (Model 288)
(Also known as 'Chu Chin Chou
with Beads')
Designer H. Tittensor.
Date 1929 - 49.
21cm (8.25ins) high.
Multicoloured.
Other colourways: HN417, 490,
495, 501, 528, 648, 677, 1351.
Est. £1800-2400.

HN1357
Kathleen
First Version (Model 560)
Designer L. Harradine.
Date 1929 - 38.
19cm (7.5ins) high.
Pink and lilac.
Other colourways:
HN1252, 1253, 1275,
1279, 1291, 1512.
Est. £450-550.

HN1353
One of the Forty
Second Version (Model 298)
(Also known as 'Chu Chin Chou
with Sack')
Designer H. Tittensor.
Date 1929 - 36.
18.5cm (7.25ins) high.
Orange and purple.
Other colourways: HN418, 494,
498, 647, 666, 704.
Est. £1800-2400.

HN1358
Rosina
Designer L. Harradine.
Date 1929 - 37.
13cm (5.25ins) high.
Red and white.
Other colourways:
HN1364, 1556.
Est. £550-750.

HN1354
One of the Forty
Fourteenth Version (Model 313)
Designer H. Tittensor.
Date 1929 - 49.
19.5cm (7.75ins) high.
Multicoloured.
Other colourways: HN496, 500,
649, 665.
Est. £1800-2400.

HN1359
Two-A-Penny
Designer L. Harradine.
Date 1929 - 38.
20.5cm (8ins) high.
Red, yellow, green and white.
Est. £2200-3000.

HN1355
The Mendicant
Designer L. Harradine.
Date 1929 - 38.
21cm (8.25ins) high.
Brown.
Other colourways: HN1365
(This figure is the same as
HN1365 but with a minor
glaze difference)
Est. £120-150.

HN1360
Sweet and Twenty
First Version (Model 605)
Designer L. Harradine.
Date 1929 - 38.
15cm (6ins) high.
Blue and green.
Other colourways:
HN1298, 1437, 1438,
1549, 1563, 1649.
Est. £350-500.

HN1356
The Parson's Daughter
Designer H. Tittensor.
Date 1929 - 38.
25.5cm (10ins) high.
Green, red, blue and white.
Other colourways: HN337, 338,
441, 564, 790, 1242, 2018.
Est. £450-550.

HN1361
Mask Seller
Designer L. Harradine.
Date 1929 - 38.
21.5cm (8.5ins) high.
Black, green, white and red.
Other colourways: HN2103.
Est. £950-1400.

HN1362
Pantalettes
Designer L. Harradine.
Date 1929 - 42.
20.5cm (8ins) high.
Green, lilac, white and blue.
Other colourways: HN1412,
1507, 1709.
Est. £225-300.

HN1367
Kitty
First Version
Designer not known.
Date 1930 - 38.
10cm (4ins) high.
White, yellow, green
and lilac.
Very rare.

HN1363
Doreen
Designer L. Harradine.
Date 1929 - 40.
13cm (5.25ins) high.
Red and green.
Other colourways:
HN1389, 1390.
Est. £650-850.

HN1368
Rose
First Version
Designer L. Harradine.
Date 1930 - 95.
11.5cm (4.5ins) high.
Pink and white.
Other colourways: HN1387,
1416, 1506, 1654, 2123.
*(Auction PSA 23.6.04 sold £25
plus comm.)*
Est. £30-45.

HN1364
Rosina
Designer L. Harradine.
Date 1929 - 37.
13cm (5.25ins) high.
Purple and red.
Other colourways: HN1358,
1556.
Est. £550-750.

HN1369
Boy on Pig
Designer C.J. Noke.
Date 1930 - 38.
10cm (4ins) high.
Green and brown.
Other colourways: Also
known in flambé glaze.
Very rare.

HN1365
The Mendicant
Designer L. Harradine.
Date 1929 - 69.
21cm (8.25ins) high.
Brown, pink, blue and yellow.
Other colourways: HN1355
(This figure is the same as HN1355
but with minor glaze differences)
*(Auction PSA 10.3.04 sold
£120 plus comm.)*
Est. £130-180.

HN1370
Marie
Second Version (Model 662)
Designer L. Harradine.
Date 1930 - 88.
11.5cm (4.5ins) high.
Blue and lilac.
Other colourways: HN1388,
1417, 1489, 1531, 1635, 1655.
*(Auction PSA 23.6.04 sold £25 plus
comm.) (Ebay 12.6.04 sold £40)*
Est. £30-55.

HN1366
The Moor
Designer C.J. Noke.
Date 1930 - 49.
42cm (16.5ins) high.
Multicoloured.
Other colourways: HN1308,
1425, 1657, 2082, 3642, 3926;
'An Arab' HN33, 343, 378.
Est. £1400-1950.

HN1371
Darling
First Version (Model 89)
Designer C. Vyse.
Date 1930 - 38.
19cm (7.5ins) high.
Green.
Other colourways: HN1,
1319, 1372, 4140.
Est. £500-700.

HN1372
Darling
First Version (Model 89)
Designer C. Vyse.
Date 1930 - 38.
19cm (7.5ins) high.
Pink nightshirt, black base.
Other colourways: HN1,
1319, 1371, 4140.
Est. £500-700.

HN1377
Fairy
Seventh Version
Designer L. Harradine.
Date 1932 - 38.
4cm (1.5ins) high.
Lilac and green.
Very rare.

HN1373
Sweet Lavender
(Also called 'Any Old Lavender')
Designer L. Harradine.
Date 1930 - 49.
23cm (9ins) high.
Pale green, grey, red and black.
Est. £400-525.

HN1378
Fairy
Fourth Version (Model 671)
Designer L. Harradine.
Date 1930 - 38.
6.5cm (2.5ins) high.
Orange and green.
Other colourways:
HN1396, 1535.
Est. £550-750.

HN1374
Fairy
Second Version (Model 667)
Designer L. Harradine.
Date 1930 - 38.
10cm (4ins) high.
Cream and yellow.
Other colourways: HN1376,
1380, 1532.
Est. £1100-1500.

HN1379
Fairy
Fifth Version (Model 670)
Designer L. Harradine.
Date 1930 - 38.
6.5cm (2.5ins) high.
Blue and green.
Other colourways:
HN1394, 1534.
Est. £550-750.

HN1375
Fairy
Third Version (Model 669)
Designer L. Harradine.
Date 1930 - 38.
8cm (3.25ins) high.
Yellow and blue.
Other colourways:
HN1395, 1533, 1536.
Est. £1000-1450.

HN1380
Fairy
Second Version (Model 667)
Designer L. Harradine.
Date 1930 - 38.
10cm (4ins) high.
Multicoloured.
Other colourways: HN1374,
1376, 1532.
Est. £1100-1500.

HN1376
Fairy
Second Version (Model 667)
Designer L. Harradine.
Date 1930 - 38.
6.5cm (2.5ins) high. (Smaller
version of HN1374)
Yellow and cream.
Other colourways: HN1374,
1380, 1532.
Est. £550-750.

*Picture
not available
at present*

HN1387
Rose
First Version
Designer L. Harradine.
Date 1930 - 38.
11.5cm (4.5ins) high.
Blue, pink and orange.
Other colourways:
HN1368, 1416, 1506,
1654, 2123.
Est. £100-150.

HN1388
Marie
Second Version (Model 662)
Designer L. Harradine.
Date 1930 - 38.
11.5cm (4.5ins) high.
Pink and cream.
Other colourways: HN1370,
1417, 1489, 1531, 1635, 1655.
Est. £110-150.

HN1393
Fairy
Sixth Version (Model 668)
Designer L. Harradine.
Date 1930 - 38.
5cm (2ins) high.
Yellow and green.
Est. £550-750.

HN1389
Doreen
Designer L. Harradine.
Date 1930 - 40.
13cm (5.25ins) high.
Green and white.
Other colourways:
HN1363, 1390.
Est. £650-850.

HN1394
Fairy
Fifth Version Model 670)
Designer L. Harradine.
Date 1930 - 38.
6.5cm (2.5ins) high.
Yellow and green.
Other colourways:
HN1379, 1534.
Est. £550-750.

HN1390
Doreen
Designer L. Harradine.
Date 1929 - 40.
13cm (5.25ins) high.
Lavender, yellow and white.
Other colourways:
HN1363, 1389.
Est. £600-850.

HN1395
Fairy
Third Version (Model 669)
Designer L. Harradine.
Date 1930 - 38.
8cm (3.25ins) high.
Blue, green and white.
Other colourways:
HN1375, 1533, 1536.
Est. £1100-1500.

HN1391
Pierette
Third Version (Model 659)
Designer L. Harradine.
Date 1930 - 38.
23cm (9ins) high.
Red and green.
Other colourways: HN1749.
Est. £1100-1500.

HN1396
Fairy
Fourth Version (Model 671)
Designer L. Harradine.
Date 1930 - 38.
6.5cm (2.5ins) high.
Blue and white flowers.
Other colourways:
HN1378, 1535.
Est. £550-750.

HN1392
Paisley Shawl
First Version (Model 660)
Designer L. Harradine.
Date 1930 - 49.
23cm (9ins) high.
Cream floral dress, red shawl.
Other colourways: HN1460, 1707,
1739, 1987.
Est. £150-200.

HN1397
Gretchen
Designer L. Harradine.
Date 1930 - 40.
19.5cm (7.75ins) high.
Blue, tan, green and white.
Other colourways: HN1562.
(This figure was made as a
pair to HN1398 'Derrick')
Est. £400-550.

HN1398
Derrick
Designer L. Harradine.
Date 1930 - 40.
20.5cm (8ins) high.
Blue, red, tan and white.
(This figure was made as a
pair to HN1397 'Gretchen')
Est. £400-550.

HN1404
Betty
Second Version (Model 678)
Designer L. Harradine.
Date 1930 - 36.
11.5cm (4.5ins) high.
Lilac, pink and yellow.
Other colourways: HN1405,
1435, 1436.
Est. £1300-1800.

HN1399
The Young Widow
Designer L. Harradine.
Date 1930.
20.5cm (8ins) high.
Purple, blue, red and yellow.
Other colourways: 'The Little
Mother' HN1418, 1641.
Est. £1600-2150.

HN1405
Betty
Second Version (Model 678)
Designer L. Harradine.
Date 1930 - 36.
11.5cm (4.5ins) high.
Green.
Other colourways: HN1404,
1435, 1436.
Est. £1300-1800.

HN1400
The Windmill Lady
Designer L. Harradine.
Date 1930 - 37.
21.5cm (8.5ins) high.
Pale green, yellow, tan and orange.
Est. £2300-3200.

HN1406
**The Flower Seller's
Children**
Designer L. Harradine.
Date 1930 - 38.
21cm (8.25ins) high.
Yellow, pink, brown and blue.
Other colourways: HN525,
551, 1206, 1342.
Est. £900-1200.

HN1401
Chorus Girl
(Also known as 'Harlequinade')
Designer L. Harradine.
Date 1930 - 36.
21.5cm (8.5ins) high.
Red and orange.
Est. £1300-1800.

HN1407
The Winner
Designer not known.
Date 1930 - 38.
17cm (6.75ins) high.
Blue, white,
grey, green and red.
Very rare.

HN1402
Miss Demure
Designer L. Harradine.
Date 1930 - 75.
19cm (7.5ins) high.
Lilac, green and pink.
Other colourways: HN1440,
1463, 1499, 1560.
Est. £110-150.

HN1408
John Peel
Designer not known.
Date 1930 - 37.
22cm (8.75ins) high.
Red, white, green
and brown.
Other colourways:
'The Huntsman' HN1815.
Est. £2000-2700.

HN1409
Hunting Squire
Designer not known.
Date 1930 - 38.
25.5cm (10ins) high.
Red and grey.
Other colourways: Renamed
'The Squire' HN 1814.
Est. £2000-2500.

HN1414
Patricia
First Version (Model 682)
Designer L. Harradine.
Date 1930 - 49.
21.5cm (8.5ins) high.
Yellow, black and green.
Other colourways:
HN1431, 1462, 1567.
(Ebay 25.5.04. sold £250)
Est. £250-400.

HN1410
Abdullah
Designer L. Harradine.
Date 1930 - 37.
15cm (6ins) high.
Blue, lilac, black and green.
Other colourways: HN2104.
Est. £850-1100.

HN1416
Rose
First Version
Designer L. Harradine.
Date 1930 - 49.
11.5cm (4.5ins) high.
Lilac.
Other colourways: HN1368,
1387, 1506, 1654, 2123.
Est. £110-150.

HN1411
Charley's Aunt
Second Version (Model 681)
Designer H. Fenton.
Date 1930 - 38.
19cm (7.5ins) high.
Black and grey.
Other colourways: HN1554.
Est. £650-900.

HN1417
Marie
Second Version (Model 662)
Designer L. Harradine.
Date 1930 - 49.
11.5cm (4.5ins) high.
Pink.
Other colourways: HN1370,
1388, 1489, 1531, 1635, 1655.
Est. £110-150.

HN1412
Pantalettes
Designer L. Harradine.
Date 1930 - 49.
20.5cm (8ins) high.
Blue, green, white and pink.
Other colourways: HN1362,
1507, 1709.
Est. £250-350.

HN1418
The Little Mother
Second Version (Model 648)
Designer L. Harradine.
Date 1930 - 38.
20.5cm (8ins) high.
Purple, blue, orange and yellow.
Other colourways: HN1641,
1399. (Previously called 'The
Young Widow')
Est. £1900-2500.

HN1413
Margery
Designer L. Harradine.
Date 1930 - 49.
27.5cm (10.75ins) high.
Red, lilac and purple.
Est. £250-350.

HN1419
Dulcinea
Designer L. Harradine.
Date 1930 - 38.
13cm (5.25ins) high.
Red, pink and lilac.
Other colourways: HN1343.
Est. £1575-2000.

HN1420
Phyllis
First Version (Model 683)
Designer L. Harradine.
Date 1930 - 49.
23cm (9ins) high.
Purple, orange and pale green.
Other colourways: HN1430,
1486, 1698.
(Auction PSA 1.9.04 sold £200
plus comm.)
Est. £250-350.

HN1421
Barbara
First Version (Model 691)
Designer L. Harradine.
Date 1930 - 37.
18.5cm (7.25ins) high.
Cream and lilac.
Other colourways:
HN1432, 1461.
Est. £600-800.

HN1422
Joan
First Version (Model 693)
Designer L. Harradine.
Date 1930 - 49.
14cm (5.5ins) high.
Blue and grey.
Other colourways: HN2023
(minor glaze difference)
(Made as a pair to HN1427 'Darby')
(Ebay 19.8.04 sold £155)
Est. £160-210.

HN1423
Babette
Designer L. Harradine.
Date 1930 - 38.
12.5cm (5ins) high.
Red, green, white and yellow.
Other colourways: HN1424.
(Ebay 01.10.04 sold £753)
Est. £775-975.

HN1424
Babette
Designer L. Harradine.
Date 1930 - 38.
12.5cm (5ins) high.
Blue and white.
Other colourways: HN1423.
Est. £650-850.

HN1425
The Moor
Designer C.J. Noke.
Date 1930 - 49.
42cm (16.5ins) high.
Multicoloured.
Other colourways: HN1308,
1366, 1657, 2082, 3642, 3926;
'An Arab' HN33, 343, 378.
(Auction PSA 23.6.04. sold £500
plus comm.)
Est. £600-800.

HN1426
The Gossips
Designer L. Harradine.
Date 1930 - 49.
14.5cm (5.75ins) high.
Turquoise, white
and pink.
Other colourways:
HN1429, 2025.
Est. £650-950.

HN1427
Darby
Designer L. Harradine.
Date 1930 - 49.
14cm (5.5ins) high.
Pink, grey, black and blue.
Other colourways: HN2024
(minor glaze difference)
(Made as a pair to
HN1422 'Joan')
Est. £160-210.

HN1428
Calumet
Designer C.J. Noke.
Date 1930 - 49.
15cm (6ins) high.
Light brown, yellow, blue and red.
Other colourways:
HN1689, 2068.
Est. £550-650.

HN1429
The Gossips
Designer L. Harradine.
Date 1930 - 49.
14.5cm (5.75ins) high.
Red and cream.
Other colourways:
HN1426, 2025.
Est. £500-650.

HN1430
Phyllis
First Version (Model 683)
Designer L. Harradine.
Date 1930 - 38.
23cm (9ins) high.
Dark blue and pink.
Other colourways: HN1420,
1486, 1698.
Est. £600-850.

HN1435
Betty
Second Version (Model 678)
Designer L. Harradine.
Date 1930 - 36.
11.5cm (4.5ins) high.
Multicoloured.
Other colourways: HN1404,
1405, 1436.
Est. £1300-1700.

HN1431
Patricia
First Version (Model 682)
Designer L. Harradine.
Date 1930 - 49.
21.5cm (8.5ins) high.
Lilac, blue and yellow.
Other colourways: HN1414,
1462, 1567.
Est. £500-650.

HN1436
Betty
Second Version (Model 678)
Designer L. Harradine.
Date 1930 - 36.
11.5cm (4.5ins) high.
Green.
Other colourways: HN1404,
1405, 1435.
Est. £1300-1700.

HN1432
Barbara
First Version (Model 691)
Designer L. Harradine.
Date 1930 - 37.
18.5cm (7.25ins) high.
Lilac, yellow and red.
Other colourways:
HN1421, 1461.
Est. £600-800.

HN1437
Sweet and Twenty
First Version (Model 605)
Designer L. Harradine.
Date 1930 - 38.
15cm (6ins) high.
Red.
Other colourways:
HN1298, 1360, 1438,
1549, 1563, 1649.
Est. £450-600.

HN1433
The Little Bridesmaid
First Version (Model 700)
Designer L. Harradine.
Date 1930 - 51.
12.5cm (5ins) high.
Lilac, blue and pink.
Other colourways: HN1434, 1530.
Est. £70-90.

HN1438
Sweet and Twenty
First Version (Model 605)
Designer L. Harradine.
Date 1930 - 38.
15cm (6ins) high.
Multicoloured.
Other colourways:
HN1298, 1360, 1437,
1549, 1563, 1649.
Est. £450-600.

HN1434
The Little Bridesmaid
First Version (Model 700)
Designer L. Harradine.
Date 1930 - 49.
12.5cm (5ins) high.
Yellow and blue.
Other colourways: HN1433, 1530.
*(Auction PSA 22.10.03. sold £95
plus comm.)*
Est. £110-150.

HN1439
Columbine
First Version (Model 563)
Designer L. Harradine.
Date 1930 - 40.
15cm (6ins) high.
Mottled red and cream.
Other colourways: HN1296, 1297.
Est. £650-800.

HN1440
Miss Demure
Designer L. Harradine.
Date 1930 - 49.
18cm (7ins) high.
Blue and cream.
Other colourways:
HN1402, 1463, 1499, 1560.
Est. £400-500.

HN1445
Biddy
Designer L. Harradine.
Date 1931 - 37.
14cm (5.5ins) high.
Yellow and blue.
Other colourways:
HN1500, 1513.
Est. £175-225.

HN1441
Child Study
First Version
Designer L. Harradine.
Date 1931 - 38.
12.5cm (5ins) high.
Cream with green flowered base.
Other colourways: HN603A,
603B; also recorded in a
flambé glaze.
Est. £500-650.

HN1446
Marietta
Designer L. Harradine.
Date 1931 - 40.
20.5cm (8ins) high.
Pale green and lilac.
Other colourways:
HN1341, 1699.
Est. £750-950.

HN1442
Child Study
Second Version
Designer L. Harradine.
Date 1931 - 38.
16.5cm (6.5ins) high.
Cream with green flowered base.
Other colourways: HN604A, 604B, 1443.
Est. £500-650.

HN1447
Marigold
Designer L. Harradine.
Date 1931 - 49.
15cm (6ins) high.
Lilac and white.
Other colourways:
HN1451, 1555.
*(Auction PSA 23.6.04. sold
£150 plus comm.)*
Est. £175-250.

HN1443
Child Study
Second Version
Designer L. Harradine.
Date 1931 - 38.
12.5cm (5ins) high.
Cream with, green flowered base.
Other colourways: HN604A, 604B, 1442.
Est. £500-650.

HN1448
Rita
Designer L. Harradine.
Date 1931 - 38.
18cm (7ins) high.
Red patterned dress with
pale green shawl.
Other colourways: HN1450.
Est. £525-700.

HN1444
Pauline
First Version (Model 703)
Designer L. Harradine.
Date 1931 - 40.
14.5cm (5.75ins) high.
Blue and green.
Est. £225-300.

HN1449
The Little Mistress
Designer L. Harradine.
Date 1931 - 49.
15cm (6ins) high.
Pale green and blue.
*(Auction PSA 23.6.04. sold £180
plus comm.)*
Est. £200-300.

HN1450
Rita
Designer L. Harradine.
Date 1931 - 38.
18cm (7ins) high.
Blue, green and red.
Other colourways: HN1448.
Est. £525-700.

HN1455
Molly Malone
Designer L. Harradine.
Date 1931 - 37.
18cm (7ins) high.
Red, brown and white.
Est. £1925-2500.

HN1451
Marigold
Designer L. Harradine.
Date 1931 - 38.
15cm (6ins) high.
Yellow.
Other colourways:
HN1447, 1555.
Est. £400-500.

HN1456
Butterfly
(Also known as 'Butterfly
Woman')
Designer L. Harradine.
Date 1931 - 40.
16.5cm (6.5ins) high.
Lilac and green.
Other colourways: HN719,
720, 730, 1203.
Est. £1475-1975.

HN1452
A Victorian Lady
Designer L. Harradine.
Date 1931 - 49.
19.5cm (7.75ins) high.
Green and blue.
Other colourways: HN726, 727,
728, 736, 739, 740, 742, 745, 1208,
1258, 1276, 1277, 1345, 1529.
Est. £225-300.

HN1457
All-A-Blooming
Designer L. Harradine.
Date 1931 - 38.
16.5cm (6.5ins) high.
Red, yellow and cream.
Other colourways: HN1466.
Est. £925-1400.

HN1453
Sweet Anne
Designer L. Harradine.
Date 1931 - 49.
18cm (7ins) high.
Green and blue.
Other colourways: HN1318,
1330, 1331, 1496, 1631, 1701.
Est. £225-300.

HN1458
Monica
Designer L. Harradine.
Date 1931 - 49.
10cm (4ins) high.
Flowered cream dress.
Other colourways:
HN1459, 1467, 3617.
Est. £200-250.

HN1454
Negligée
Designer L. Harradine.
Date 1931 - 36.
12.5cm (5ins) high.
Pale pink.
Other colourways: HN1219,
1228, 1272, 1273.
Est. £1100-1500.

HN1459
Monica
Designer L. Harradine.
Date 1931 - 49.
10cm (4ins) high.
Lilac.
Other colourways:
HN1458, 1467, 3617.
Est. £200-250.

HN1460
Paisley Shawl
First Version (Model 660)
Designer L. Harradine.
Date 1931 - 49.
23cm (9ins) high.
Green, lilac and red.
Other colourways: HN1392,
1707, 1739, 1987.
Est. £275-375.

HN1464A
The Carpet Seller
(Hand closed)
First Version
Designer L. Harradine.
Date ? - 1969.
23.5cm (9.25ins) high.
Green and orange.
Other colourways:
HN1464 (hand open)
Est. £150-190.

HN1461
Barbara
First Version (Model 691)
Designer L. Harradine.
Date 1931 - 37.
18.5cm (7.25ins) high.
Green and lilac.
Other colourways:
HN1421, 1432.
Est. £650-900.

HN1465
Lady Clare
Designer L. Harradine.
Date 1931 - 37.
19.5cm (7.75ins) high.
Red and pink.
Est. £425-550.

HN1462
Patricia
First Version (Model 682)
Designer L. Harradine.
Date 1931 - 38.
21.5cm (8.5ins) high.
Green and blue.
Other colourways: HN1414,
1431, 1567.
Est. £475-650.

HN1466
All-A-Blooming
Designer L. Harradine.
Date 1931 - 38.
16.5cm (6.5ins) high.
Purple, red, green and white.
Other colourways: HN1457.
Est. £950-1300.

HN1463
Miss Demure
Designer L. Harradine.
Date 1931 - 49.
18cm (7ins) high.
Green and lilac.
Other colourways: HN1402,
1440, 1499, 1560.
Est. £400-500.

HN1467
Monica
Designer L. Harradine.
Date 1931 - 95.
10cm (4ins) high.
Lilac and red.
Other colourways:
HN1458, 1459, 3617.
(Ebay 23.5.04. sold £36)
*(Auction Brightwells 2.9.04
sold £35 plus comm.)*
Est. £40-55.

HN1464
The Carpet Seller
(Hand Open)
First Version (Model 610)
Designer L. Harradine.
Date 1929 - 69.
23.5cm (9.25ins) high.
Green, yellow and orange.
Other colourways: HN1464A
(hand closed)
Est. £325-425.

HN1468
Pamela
First Version (Model 711)
Designer L. Harradine.
Date 1931 - 37.
20.5cm (8ins) high.
Blue and red.
Other colourways:
HN1469, 1564.
Est. £650-850.

HN1469
Pamela
First Version (Model 711)
Designer L. Harradine.
Date 1931 - 37.
20.5cm (8ins) high.
Yellow, blue and pink.
Other colourways:
HN1468, 1564.
Est. £650-850.

HN1474
In the Stocks
First Version (Model 719)
(Also known as 'Love in the
Stocks' and 'Love locked in')
Designer L. Harradine.
Date 1931 - 38.
13cm (5.25ins) high.
Red, blue and brown.
Other colourways:
HN1475.
Est. £1250-1500.

HN1470
Chloe
First Version
Designer L. Harradine.
Date 1931 - 49.
15cm (6ins) high.
Yellow, red and purple.
Other colourways: HN1476,
1479, 1498, 1765, 1956.
Est. £250-325.

HN1475
In the Stocks
First Version (Model 719)
(Also known as 'Love in the
Stocks' and 'Love locked in')
Designer L. Harradine.
Date 1931 - 37.
13cm (5.25ins) high.
Green and cream.
Other colourways:
HN1474.
Est. £1250-1500.

HN1471
Annette
First Version (Model 713)
Designer L. Harradine.
Date 1931 - 38.
15cm (6ins) high.
Blue and white.
Other colourways:
HN1472, 1550.
Est. £275-350.

HN1476
Chloe
First Version
Designer L. Harradine.
Date 1931 - 38.
15cm (6ins) high.
Blue and pink.
Other colourways: HN1470,
1479, 1498, 1765, 1956.
Est. £130-180.

HN1472
Annette
First Version (Model 713)
Designer L. Harradine.
Date 1931 - 49.
15cm (6ins) high.
Green, red and white.
Other colourways:
HN1471, 1550.
Est. £275-350.

HN1478
Sylvia
Designer L. Harradine.
Date 1931 - 38.
26.5cm (10.5ins) high.
Orange and blue.
Est. £300-425.

HN1473
Dreamland
Designer L. Harradine.
Date 1931 - 37.
12cm (4.75ins) high.
Lilac, pink and blue.
Other colourways:
HN1481.
Est. £2000-2500.

HN1479
Chloe
First Version
Designer L. Harradine.
Date 1931 - 49.
15cm (6ins) high.
Lilac and pink.
Other colourways: HN1470,
1476, 1498, 1765, 1956.
Est. £300-425.

HN1480
Newhaven Fishwife
Designer H. Fenton.
Date 1931 - 37.
19.5cm (7.75ins) high.
Red, white, brown and black.
Est. £2200-3000.

HN1485
Greta
Designer L. Harradine.
Date 1931 - 53.
14cm (5.5ins) high.
Lilac and red.
Est. £165-225.

HN1481
Dreamland
Designer L. Harradine.
Date 1931 - 37.
12cm (4.75ins) high.
Orange, yellow and
purple.
Other colourways:
HN1473.
Est. £2000-2600.

HN1486
Phyllis
First Version (Model 683)
Designer L. Harradine.
Date 1931 - 49.
23cm (9ins) high.
Blue and pink.
Other colourways: HN1420,
1430, 1698.
Est. £400-550.

HN1482
Pearly Boy
First Version (Model 724)
Designer L. Harradine.
Date 1931 - 49.
14cm (5.5ins) high.
Brown, red and white.
Other colourways: HN1547.
Est. £125-165.

HN1487
Suzette
Designer L. Harradine.
Date 1931 - 50.
19cm (7.5ins) high.
Pink and white.
Other colourways: HN1577,
1585, 1696, 2026.
Est. £200-275.

HN1483
Pearly Girl
First Version (Model 723)
Designer L. Harradine.
Date 1931 - 49.
14cm (5.5ins) high.
Orange, brown and white.
Other colourways: HN1548.
Est. £125-165.

HN1488
Gloria
First Version (Model 727)
Designer L. Harradine.
Date 1932 - 38.
18cm (7ins) high.
Green, blue and red.
Other colourways: HN1700.
Est. £1000-1350.

HN1484
Jennifer
First Version (Model 726)
Designer L. Harradine.
Date 1931 - 49.
16.5cm (6.5ins) high.
Yellow, cream and blue.
Est. £350-450.

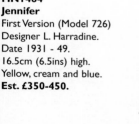

HN1489
Marie
Second Version (Model 662)
Designer L. Harradine.
Date 1932 - 49.
11.5cm (4.5ins) high.
Pale green and white.
Other colourways: HN1370,
1388, 1417, 1531, 1635, 1655.
Est. £110-150.

HN1490
Dorcas
Designer L. Harradine.
Date 1932 - 38.
18cm (7ins) high.
Pale blue and cream.
Other colourways:
HN1491, 1558.
Est. £300-400.

HN1495
Priscilla
Designer L. Harradine.
Date 1932 - 49.
20.5cm (8ins) high.
Blue, white and green.
Other colourways:
HN1337, 1340, 1501,
1559.
Est. £450-600.

HN1491
Dorcas
Designer L. Harradine.
Date 1932 - 38.
18cm (7ins) high.
Pale green and lilac.
Other colourways:
HN1490, 1558.
Est. £300-400.

HN1496
Sweet Anne
Designer L. Harradine.
Date 1932 - 67.
18cm (7ins) high.
Purple and lilac.
Other colourways:
HN1318, 1330, 1331,
1453, 1631, 1701.
Est. £110-150.

HN1492
Old Lavender Seller
Designer L. Harradine.
Date 1932 - 49.
16.5cm (6.5ins) high.
Green, orange and white.
Other colourways: HN1571.
Est. £500-650.

HN1497
Rosamund
Second Version (Model 729)
Designer L. Harradine.
Date 1932 - 38.
21.5cm (8.5ins) high.
Red and pink.
Other colourways: HN1551.
Est. £1100-1500.

HN1493
The Potter
Designer C.J. Noke.
Date 1932 - 92.
17cm (6.75ins) high.
Brown.
Other colourways:
HN1518, 1522.
(Ebay 25.9.04 sold £135)
Est. £140-190.

HN1498
Chloe
First Version
Designer L. Harradine.
Date 1932 - 38.
15cm (6ins) high.
Yellow and cream.
Other colourways: HN1470,
1476, 1479, 1765, 1956.
Est. £350-450.

HN1494
Gwendolen
Designer L. Harradine.
Date 1932 - 40.
15cm (6ins) high.
Green, cream and lilac.
Other colourways:
HN1503, 1570.
Est. £700-900.

HN1499
Miss Demure
Designer L. Harradine.
Date 1932 - 38.
18cm (7ins) high.
Yellow and pink.
Other colourways: HN1402,
1440, 1463, 1560.
Est. £300-420.

HN1500
Biddy
Designer L. Harradine.
Date 1932 - 37.
14cm (5.5ins) high.
Yellow.
Other colourways:
HN1445, 1513.
Est. £250-350.

HN1501
Priscilla
Designer L. Harradine.
Date 1932 - 38.
20.5cm (8ins) high.
Orange and green.
Other colourways: HN1337,
1340, 1495, 1559.
Est. £450-600.

HN1502
Lucy Ann
Designer L. Harradine.
Date 1932 - 51.
13cm (5.25ins) high.
Pink and lilac.
Other colourways: HN1565.
Est. £140-180.

HN1503
Gwendolen
Designer L. Harradine.
Date 1932 - 49.
15cm (6ins) high.
Orange.
Other colourways:
HN1494, 1570.
Est. £700-900.

HN1504
Sweet Maid
First Version (Model 739)
Designer L. Harradine.
Date 1932 - 36.
20.5cm (8ins) high.
Lilac and blue.
Other colourways: HN1505.
Est. £700-900.

HN1505
Sweet Maid
First Version (Model 739)
Designer L. Harradine.
Date 1932 - 36.
20.5cm (8ins) high.
Red, pink and green.
Other colourways: HN1504.
Est. £700-900.

HN1506
Rose
First Version
Designer L. Harradine.
Date 1932 - 38.
11.5cm (4.5ins) high.
Yellow.
Other colourways: HN1368,
1387, 1416, 1654, 2123.
Est. £110-150.

HN1507
Pantalettes
Designer L. Harradine.
Date 1932 - 49.
20.5cm (8ins) high.
Yellow and green.
Other colourways: HN1362,
1412, 1709.
Est. £450-600.

HN1508
Helen
First Version (Model 743)
Designer L. Harradine.
Date 1932 - 38.
20.5cm (8ins) high.
Green and red.
Other colourways:
HN1509, 1572.
Est. £700-950.

HN1509
Helen
First Version (Model 743)
Designer L. Harradine.
Date 1932 - 38.
20.5cm (8ins) high.
Blue, cream and red.
Other colourways:
HN1508, 1572.
Est. £700-950.

HN1510
Constance
First Version
Designer L. Harradine.
Date 1932 - 36.
17cm (6.75ins) high.
Yellow and lilac.
Other colourways: HN1511.
Est. £700-950.

HN1515
Dolly Vardon
Designer L. Harradine.
Date 1932 - 49.
21.5cm (8.5ins) high.
Red and lilac.
Other colourways: HN1514.
Est. £650-850.

HN1511
Constance
First Version
Designer L. Harradine.
Date 1932 - 36.
17cm (6.75ins) high.
Lilac.
Other colourways: HN1510.
Est. £700-950.

HN1516
Cicely
Designer L. Harradine.
Date 1932 - 49.
14cm (5.5ins) high.
Blue and cream.
Est. £600-750.

HN1512
Kathleen
First Version (Model 560)
Designer L. Harradine.
Date 1932 - 38.
19cm (7.5ins) high.
Lilac and blue.
Other colourways: HN1252,
1253, 1275, 1279, 1291, 1357.
Est. £450-550.

HN1517
Veronica
First Version (Model 751)
Designer L. Harradine.
Date 1932 - 51.
20.5cm (8ins) high.
Red, lilac and cream.
Other colourways: HN1519,
1650, 1943.
Est. £160-200.

HN1513
Biddy
Designer L. Harradine.
Date 1932 - 37.
14.5cm (5.75ins) high.
Pink, blue and white.
Other colourways:
HN1445, 1500.
Est. £110-150.

HN1518
The Potter
Designer C.J. Noke.
Date 1932 - 49.
17cm (6.75ins) high.
Green and purple.
Other colourways:
HN1493, 1522.
Est. £650-850.

HN1514
Dolly Vardon
Designer L. Harradine.
Date 1932 - 38.
21.5cm (8.5ins) high.
Multicoloured.
Other colourways: HN1515.
Est. £700-950.

HN1519
Veronica
First Version (Model 751)
Designer L. Harradine.
Date 1932 - 38.
20.5cm (8ins) high.
Pale blue and cream.
Other colourways: HN1517,
1650, 1943.
Est. £300-400.

HN1520
Eugene
Designer L. Harradine.
Date 1932 - 36.
14.5cm (5.75ins) high.
Green and pink.
Other colourways: HN1521.
Est. £750-950.

HN1525
Clarissa
First Version (Model 773)
Designer L. Harradine.
Date 1932 - 38.
25.5cm (10ins) high.
Green, yellow and red.
Other colourways: HN1687.
Est. £400-500.

HN1521
Eugene
Designer L. Harradine.
Date 1932 - 36.
14.5cm (5.75ins) high.
Orange, white and yellow.
Other colourways: HN1520.
Est. £750-950.

HN1526
Anthea
Designer L. Harradine.
Date 1932 - 40.
16.5cm (6.5ins) high.
Green, red and blue.
Other colourways:
HN1527, 1669.
Est. £650-850.

HN1522
The Potter
Designer C.J. Noke.
Date 1932 - 49.
17cm (6.75ins) high.
Green and purple.
Other colourways:
HN1493, 1518.
Est. £650-850.

HN1527
Anthea
Designer L. Harradine.
Date 1932 - 40.
16.5cm (6.5ins) high.
Lilac, cream and red.
Other colourways:
HN1526, 1669.
Est. £650-850.

HN1523
Lisette
Designer L. Harradine.
Date 1932 - 36.
13cm (5.25ins) high.
Red and lemon.
Other colourways:
HN1524, 1684.
Est. £800-1000.

HN1528
Bluebeard
Second Version (Model 745)
Designer L. Harradine.
Date 1932 - 49.
29cm (11.5ins) high.
Red, blue, green and purple.
Other colourways: HN2105.
Est. £500-650.

HN1524
Lisette
Designer L. Harradine.
Date 1932 - 36.
13cm (5.25ins) high.
Blue, yellow and pink.
Other colourways:
HN1523, 1684.
Est. £800-1000.

HN1529
A Victorian Lady
Designer L. Harradine.
Date 1932 - 38.
19.5cm (7.75ins) high.
Green, cream and orange.
Other colourways: HN726, 727,
728, 736, 739, 740, 742, 745, 1208,
1258, 1276, 1277, 1345, 1452.
Est. £300-400.

HN1530
The Little Bridesmaid
First Version (Model 700)
Designer L. Harradine.
Date 1932 - 38.
12.5cm (5ins) high.
Green and yellow.
Other colourways:
HN1433, 1434.
Est. £250-300.

HN1535
Fairy
Fourth Version (Model 671)
Designer L. Harradine.
Date 1932 - 38.
6.5cm (2.5ins) high.
Yellow.
Other colourways:
HN1378, 1396.
Est. £600-800.

HN1531
Marie
Second Version (Model 662)
Designer L. Harradine.
Date 1932 - 38.
11.5cm (4.5ins) high.
Green and yellow.
Other colourways: HN1370,
1388, 1417, 1489, 1635, 1655.
Est. £110-150.

HN1536
Fairy
Third Version (Model 669)
Designer L. Harradine.
Date 1932 - 38.
8cm (3.25ins) high.
Yellow, blue and green.
Other colourways: HN1375,
1395, 1533.
Est. £950-1350.

HN1532
Fairy
Second Version (Model 667)
Designer L. Harradine.
Date 1932 - 38.
10cm (4ins) high.
Multicoloured.
Other colourways: HN1374,
1376, 1380.
Est. £1100-1500.

HN1537
Janet
First Version (Model 785)
Designer L. Harradine.
Date 1932 - 95.
16.5cm (6.5ins) high.
Red, yellow and white.
Other colourways: HN1538,
1652, 1737.
*(Auction W&H 27.9.04
sold £50 plus comm.)*
(Ebay 8.9.04 sold £85) **Est. £75-100.**

HN1533
Fairy
Third Version (Model 669)
Designer L. Harradine.
Date 1932 - 38.
8cm (3.25ins) high.
Multicoloured.
Other colourways: HN1375,
1395, 1536.
Est. £1100-1500.

HN1538
Janet
First Version (Model 785)
Designer L. Harradine.
Date 1932 - 49.
16.5cm (6.5ins) high.
Purple, pink and white.
Other colourways: HN1537,
1652, 1737.
Est. £300-400.

HN1534
Fairy
Fifth Version (Model 670)
Designer L. Harradine.
Date 1932 - 38.
6.5cm (2.5ins) high.
Blue and yellow.
Other colourways:
HN1379, 1394.
Est. £600-800.

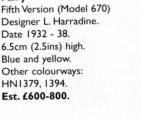

HN1539
A Saucy Nymph
Designer L. Harradine.
Date 1933 - 49.
11.5cm (4.5ins) high.
Green base.
Est. £250-350.

HN1540
'Little Child so Rare and Sweet'
First Version (Model 419)
Designer L. Harradine.
Date 1933 - 49.
12.5cm (5ins) high.
Cream with green base.
Est. £350-500.

HN1545
'Called Love, a little Boy, almost Naked, Wanton, Blind, Cruel now, and then as Kind'
Designer L. Harradine.
Date 1933 - 49.
9cm (3.5ins) high.
White with tan base.
Est. £500-700.

HN1541
'Happy Joy, Baby Boy'
Designer L. Harradine.
Date 1933 - 49.
16cm (6.25ins) high.
Cream with green base.
Est. £500-650.

HN1546
'Here a Little Child I Stand'
First Version
Designer L. Harradine.
Date 1933 - 49.
16cm (6.25ins) high.
Lilac with green base.
Est. £450-650.

HN1542
'Little Child so Rare and Sweet'
Second Version (Model 774)
Designer L. Harradine.
Date 1933 - 49.
12.5cm (5ins) high.
White with blue base.
Est. £350-500.

HN1547
Pearly Boy
First Version (Model 724)
Designer L. Harradine.
Date 1933 - 49.
14cm (5.5ins) high.
Green and lilac.
Other colourways: HN1482.
Est. £250-350.

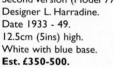

HN1543
'Dancing Eyes and Sunny Hair'
First Version
Designer L. Harradine.
Date 1938 - 49.
12.5cm (5ins) high.
White with blue base.
Est. £350-500.

HN1548
Pearly Girl
First Version (Model 723)
Designer L. Harradine.
Date 1933 - 49.
14cm (5.5ins) high.
Green and lilac.
Other colourways: HN1483.
Est. £250-350.

HN1544
'Do you Wonder where Fairies are that Folk Declare Have Vanished'
First Version
Designer L. Harradine.
Date 1933 - 49.
12.5cm (5ins) high.
Lilac with yellow base.
Est. £500-700.

HN1549
Sweet and Twenty
First Version (Model 605)
Designer L. Harradine.
Date 1933 - 49.
15cm (6ins) high.
Multicoloured.
Other colourways:
HN1298, 1360, 1437, 1438, 1563, 1649.
Est. £400-550.

HN1550
Annette
First Version (Model 713)
Designer L. Harradine.
Date 1933 - 49.
15cm (6ins) high.
Red and cream.
Other colourways:
HN1471, 1472.
Est. £220-300.

HN1555
Marigold
Designer L. Harradine.
Date 1933 - 49.
15cm (6ins) high.
Blue and pink.
Other colourways:
HN1447, 1451.
Est. £275-375.

HN1551
Rosamund
Second Version (Model 729)
Designer L. Harradine.
Date 1933 - 38.
21.5cm (8.5ins) high.
Blue and white.
Other colourways: HN1497.
Est. £1500-1950.

HN1556
Rosina
Designer L. Harradine.
Date 1933 - 37.
13cm (5.25ins) high.
Lilac and red.
Other colourways:
HN1358, 1364.
Est. £550-700.

HN1552
Pinkie
Designer L. Harradine.
Date 1933 - 38.
12.5cm (5ins) high.
Pink and yellow.
Other colourways: HN1553.
Est. £650-850.

HN1557
Lady Fayre
Designer L. Harradine.
Date 1933 - 38.
14.5cm (5.75ins) high.
Purple.
Other colourways: HN1265.
Est. £900-1200.

HN1553
Pinkie
Designer L. Harradine.
Date 1933 - 38.
12.5cm (5ins) high.
Yellow, red and blue.
Other colourways: HN1552.
Est. £650-850.

HN1558
Dorcas
Designer L. Harradine.
Date 1933 - 52.
18cm (7ins) high.
Purple and cream.
Other colourways:
HN1490, 1491.
Est. £150-200.

HN1554
Charley's Aunt
Second Version (Model 681)
Designer H. Fenton.
Date 1933 - 38.
19cm (7.5ins) high.
Purple, red and white.
Other colourways: HN1411.
Est. £650-900.

HN1559
Priscilla
Designer L. Harradine.
Date 1933 - 49.
20.5cm (8ins) high.
Purple and red.
Other colourways: HN1337,
1340, 1495, 1501.
Est. £500-700.

HN1560
Miss Demure
Designer L. Harradine.
Date 1933 - 49.
18cm (7ins) high.
Blue, red and cream.
Other colourways: HN1402,
1440, 1463, 1499.
Est. £400-500.

HN1565
Lucy Ann
Designer L. Harradine.
Date 1933 - 38.
13cm (5.25ins) high.
Pale green.
Other colourways: HN1502.
Est. £275-365.

HN1561
Willy-Won't He
Designer L. Harradine.
Date 1933 - 49.
15cm (6ins) high.
Blue, red and white.
Other colourways:
HN1584, 2150.
Est. £600-800.

HN1566
Estelle
Designer L. Harradine.
Date 1933 - 40.
20.5cm (8ins) high.
Lilac, pink and white.
Other colourways: HN1802.
(Ebay 5.10.04 sold £640.99)
Est. £700-950.

HN1562
Gretchen
Designer L. Harradine.
Date 1933 - 40.
19.5cm (7.75ins) high.
Purple, red and white.
Other colourways: HN1397.
Est. £525-700.

HN1567
Patricia
First Version (Model 682)
Designer L. Harradine.
Date 1933 - 49.
21.5cm (8.5ins) high.
Red and lilac.
Other colourways: HN1414,
1431, 1462.
Est. £750-950.

HN1563
Sweet and Twenty
First Version (Model 605)
Designer L. Harradine.
Date 1933 - 38.
15cm (6ins) high.
Black and pink.
Other colourways:
HN1298, 1360, 1437,
1438, 1549, 1649.
Est. £500-650.

HN1568
Charmian
Designer L. Harradine.
Date 1933 - 40.
16.5cm (6.5ins) high.
Red, pink and cream.
Other colourways:
HN1569, 1651.
Est. £550-750.

HN1564
Pamela
First Version (Model 711)
Designer L. Harradine.
Date 1933 - 37.
20.5cm (8ins) high.
Pink, blue and red.
Other colourways:
HN1468, 1469.
Est. £650-900.

HN1569
Charmian
Designer L. Harradine.
Date 1933 - 40.
16.5cm (6.5ins) high.
Cream, red and lilac.
Other colourways:
HN1568, 1651.
Est. £550-750.

HN1570
Gwendolen
Designer L. Harradine.
Date 1933 - 49.
15cm (6ins) high.
Pink and green.
Other colourways:
HN1494, 1503.
Est. £700-900.

HN1575
Daisy
First Version
Designer L. Harradine.
Date 1933 - 49.
9cm (3.5ins) high.
Blue floral dress with
pink sleeves.
Other colourways: HN1961.
Est. £250-300.

HN1571
Old Lavender Seller
Designer L. Harradine.
Date 1933 - 49.
16.5cm (6.5ins) high.
Orange, black, brown and cream.
Other colourways: HN1492.
Est. £550-750.

HN1576
Tildy
Designer L. Harradine.
Date 1933 - 39.
14cm (5.5ins) high.
Red, pink and cream.
Other colourways: HN1859.
Est. £700-900.

HN1572
Helen
First Version (Model 743)
Designer L. Harradine.
Date 1933 - 38.
20.5cm (8ins) high.
Red and lilac.
Other colourways:
HN1508, 1509.
Est. £700-900.

HN1577
Suzette
Designer L. Harradine.
Date 1933 - 49.
19cm (7.5ins) high.
Lilac and pink.
Other colourways: HN1487,
1585, 1696, 2026.
Est. £400-550.

HN1573
Rhoda
Designer L. Harradine.
Date 1933 - 40.
26cm (10.25ins) high.
Orange and green.
Other colourways:
HN1574, 1688.
Est. £350-450.

HN1578
The Hinged Parasol
Designer L. Harradine.
Date 1933 - 49.
16.5cm (6.5ins) high.
Yellow, red and blue.
Other colourways: HN1579.
Est. £600-750.

HN1574
Rhoda
Designer L. Harradine.
Date 1933 - 40.
26cm (10.25ins) high.
Brown and orange.
Other colourways:
HN1573, 1688.
Est. £350-450.

HN1579
The Hinged Parasol
Designer L. Harradine.
Date 1933 - 49.
16.5cm (6.5ins) high.
Lilac and red.
Other colourways: HN1578.
Est. £600-750.

HN1580
Rosebud
First Version (Model 807)
Designer L. Harradine.
Date 1933 - 38.
7.5cm (3ins) high.
Pink.
Other colourways:
HN1581.
Est. £450-600.

HN1581
Rosebud
First Version (Model 807)
Designer L. Harradine.
Date 1933 - 38.
7.5cm (3ins) high.
Blue.
Other colourways:
HN1580.
Est. £450-600.

HN1582
Marion
Designer L. Harradine.
Date 1933 - 40.
16.5cm (6.5ins) high.
Blue and purple.
Other colourways: HN1583.
(Ebay 5.6.04 sold £840)
Est. £850-1200.

HN1583
Marion
Designer L. Harradine.
Date 1933 - 40.
16.5cm (6.5ins) high.
Blue and orange.
Other colourways: HN1582.
(Ebay 5.6.04 sold £620)
Est. £650-1000.

HN1584
Willy-Won't He
Designer L. Harradine.
Date 1933 - 49.
15cm (6ins) high.
Red, blue and white.
Other colourways:
HN1561, 2150.
Est. £200-300.

HN1585
Suzette
Designer L. Harradine.
Date 1933 - 38.
19cm (7.5ins) high.
Green and yellow.
Other colourways: HN1487,
1577, 1696, 2026.
Est. £375-500.

HN1586
Camille
First Version (Model 815)
Designer L. Harradine.
Date 1933 - 49.
16.5cm (6.5ins) high.
Red, pink and cream.
Other colourways:
HN1648, 1736.
Est. £600-750.

HN1587
Fleurette
Designer L. Harradine.
Date 1933 - 49.
17cm (6.75ins) high.
Cream, red and pink.
(Ebay 26.9.04 sold £236)
Est. £250-400.

HN1588
The Bride
First Version (Model 810)
Designer L. Harradine.
Date 1933 - 38.
24cm (9.5ins) high.
White and yellow.
Other colourways: HN1600,
1762, 1841.
Est. £650-900.

HN1589
Sweet and Twenty
Second Version (Model 605a)
Designer L. Harradine.
Date 1933 - 49.
7.5cm (3ins) high.
Red, blue and pale green.
Other colourways:
HN1610.
(Auction PSA 22.10.03
sold £255 plus comm.)
Est. £300-400.

HN1598
Clothilde
Designer L. Harradine.
Date 1933 - 49.
18.5cm (7.25ins) high.
Lemon and pink.
Other colourways: HN1599.
Est. £475-650.

HN1606
Falstaff
First Version (Model 401)
Designer C.J. Noke.
Date 1933 - 49.
18cm (7ins) high.
Red, green and brown.
Other colourways: HN571,
575, 608, 609, 619, 638, 1216.
Est. £1000-1450.

HN1599
Clothilde
Designer L. Harradine.
Date 1933 - 49.
18.5cm (7.25ins) high.
Purple, blue and red.
Other colourways: HN1598.
Est. £475-650.

HN1607
Cerise
Designer L. Harradine.
Date 1933 - 49.
13cm (5.25ins) high.
Lilac and red.
Est. £250-300.

HN1600
The Bride
First Version (Model 810)
Designer L. Harradine.
Date 1933 - 49.
24cm (9.5ins) high.
Whitish pink.
Other colourways: HN1588,
1762, 1841.
Est. £650-850.

HN1610
Sweet and Twenty
Second Version (Model 605a)
Designer L. Harradine.
Date 1933 - 38.
7.5cm (3ins) high.
Red dress, green sofa.
Other colourways:
HN1589.
Est. £250-300.

HN1604
The Emir
Designer C.J. Noke.
Date 1933 - 49.
19cm (7.5ins) high.
Cream, red and yellow.
Other colourways: HN1605;
'Ibrahim' HN 2095.
Est. £500-650.

HN1617
Primroses
Designer L. Harradine.
Date 1934 - 49.
16.5cm (6.5ins) high.
Purple, red, white, brown
and yellow.
Est. £550-700.

HN1605
The Emir
Designer C.J. Noke.
Date 1933 - 49.
19cm (7.5ins) high.
Yellow, orange and purple.
Other colourways: HN1604;
'Ibrahim' HN 2095.
Est. £500-650.

HN1618
Maisie
Designer L. Harradine.
Date 1934 - 49.
16cm (6.25ins) high.
Yellow, red and blue.
Other colourways: HN1619.
Est. £300-450.

HN1619
Maisie
Designer L. Harradine.
Date 1934 - 49.
16cm (6.25ins) high.
Red, white and pink.
Other colourways: HN1618.
Est. £250-350.

HN1627
Curly Knob
Designer L. Harradine.
Date 1934 - 49.
16.5cm (6.5ins) high.
Blue, cream, green and red.
Est. £500-650.

HN1620
Rosabell
Designer L. Harradine.
Date 1934 - 40.
18cm (7ins) high.
Red, pink and green.
Est. £600-750.

HN1628
Margot
Designer L. Harradine.
Date 1934 - 40.
14.5cm (5.75ins) high.
Blue and yellow.
Other colourways:
HN1636, 1653.
Est. £550-750.

HN1621
Irene
Designer L. Harradine.
Date 1934 - 51.
17cm (6.75ins) high.
Lemon and red.
Other colourways:
HN1697, 1952.
Est. £250-320.

HN1629
Grizel
Designer L. Harradine.
Date 1934 - 38.
18cm (7ins) high.
Red, green and cream.
Est. £950-1300.

HN1622
Evelyn
Designer L. Harradine.
Date 1934 - 40.
15cm (6ins) high.
Cream, blue and red.
Other colourways: HN1637.
Est. £650-850.

HN1631
Sweet Anne
Designer L. Harradine.
Date 1934 - 38.
18cm (7ins) high.
Green, yellow, pink and red.
Other colourways: HN1318,
1330, 1331, 1453, 1496, 1701.
Est. £450-600.

HN1626
Bonnie Lassie
Designer L. Harradine.
Date 1934 - 53.
13cm (5.25ins) high.
Red, yellow and cream.
Est. £300-400.

HN1632
A Gentlewoman
Designer L. Harradine.
Date 1934 - 49.
18.5cm (7.25ins) high.
Lilac, green and white.
Est. £450-550.

HN1633
Clemency
Designer L. Harradine.
Date 1934 - 38.
18cm (7ins) high.
Cream, lilac, tan and pink.
flowered dress.
Other colourways:
HN1634, 1643.
Est. £650-850.

HN1638
Ladybird
Designer L. Harradine.
Date 1934 - 49.
19.5cm (7.75ins) high.
Pink.
Other colourways: HN1640.
Est. £1200-1500.

HN1634
Clemency
Designer L. Harradine.
Date 1934 - 49.
18cm (7ins) high.
Green, orange, pink and
cream.
Other colourways:
HN1633, 1643.
Est. £500-700.

HN1639
Dainty May
Designer L. Harradine.
Date 1934 - 49.
15cm (6ins) high.
Red, white and yellow.
Other colourways: HN1656.
Est. £200-275.

HN1635
Marie
Second Version (Model 662)
Designer L. Harradine.
Date 1934 - 49.
11.5cm (4.5 ins) high.
Blue, pink and white,
Other colourways: HN1370,
1388, 1417, 1489, 1531, 1655.
Est. £135-180.

HN1640
Ladybird
Designer L. Harradine.
Date 1934 - 38.
19.5cm (7.75ins) high.
Blue.
Other colourways: HN1638.
Est. £1500-2000.

HN1636
Margot
Designer L. Harradine.
Date 1934 - 40.
14.5cm (5.75ins) high.
Red, yellow and pink.
Other colourways:
HN1628, 1653.
Est. £650-850.

HN1641
The Little Mother
Second Version (Model 648)
Designer L. Harradine.
Date 1934 - 49.
20.5cm (8ins) high.
Red, dark green, cream with red
roses. Woman dark hair, boy fair.
Other colourways: HN1418;
Also known as 'The Young
Widow' HN1399.
Est. £1650-2200.

HN1637
Evelyn
Designer L. Harradine.
Date 1934 - 40.
15cm (6ins) high.
Cream, green, lilac and blue.
Other colourways: HN1622.
Est. £650-850.

HN1642
Granny's Shawl
Designer L. Harradine.
Date 1934 - 49.
15cm (6ins) high.
Red, cream and yellow.
Other colourways: HN1647.
Est. £250-350.

HN1643
Clemency
Designer L. Harradine.
Date 1934 - 38.
18cm (7ins) high.
Red, white and green.
Other colourways:
HN1633, 1634.
Est. £600-800.

HN1648
Camille
First Version (Model 815)
Designer L. Harradine.
Date 1934 - 49.
16.5cm (6.5ins) high.
Pale green and pink.
Other colourways:
HN1586, 1736.
Est. £700-850.

HN1644
Herminia
Designer L. Harradine.
Date 1934 - 38.
16.5cm (6.5ins) high.
Cream and pink.
Other colourways:
HN1646, 1704.
Est. £650-850.

HN1649
Sweet and Twenty
First Version (Model 605)
Designer L. Harradine.
Date 1934 - 36.
15cm (6ins) high.
Green, cream and
brown.
Other colourways:
1298, 1360, 1437,
1438, 1549, 1563.
Est. £500-650.

HN1645
Aileen
Designer L. Harradine.
Date 1934 - 38.
15cm (6ins) high.
Green, pink and blue.
Other colourways:
HN1664, 1803.
Est. £650-850.

HN1650
Veronica
First Version (Model 751)
Designer L. Harradine.
Date 1934 - 49.
20.5cm (8ins) high.
Pale green and pink.
Other colourways: HN1517,
1519, 1943.
Est. £500-700.

HN1646
Herminia
Designer L. Harradine.
Date 1934 - 38.
16.5cm (6.5ins) high.
Red, cream and blue.
Other colourways:
HN1644, 1704.
Est. £650-850.

HN1651
Charmian
Designer L. Harradine.
Date 1934 - 40.
16.5cm (6.5ins) high.
Red and green.
Other colourways:
HN1568, 1569.
Est. £650-900.

HN1647
Granny's Shawl
Designer L. Harradine.
Date 1934 - 49.
15cm (6ins) high.
Cream, blue, red and yellow.
Other colourways: HN1642.
Est. £300-450.

HN1652
Janet
First Version (Model 785)
Designer L. Harradine.
Date 1934 - 49.
16.5cm (6.5ins) high.
Red, pink and yellow.
Other colourways: 1537,
1538, 1737.
Est. £600-800.

HN1653
Margot
Designer L. Harradine.
Date 1934 - 40.
14.5cm (5.75ins) high.
Red and white.
Other colourways:
HN1628, 1636.
Est. £660-900.

HN1662
Delicia
Designer L. Harradine.
Date 1934 - 38.
14.5cm (5.75ins) high.
Lilac, pink and white.
Other colourways:
HN1663, 1681.
Est. £650-850.

HN1654
Rose
First Version
Designer L. Harradine.
Date 1934 - 38.
11.5cm (4.5ins) high.
Green and cream with pink
flowers on skirt.
Other colourways: HN1368,
1387, 1416, 1506, 2123.
Est. £135-200.

HN1663
Delicia
Designer L. Harradine.
Date 1934 - 38.
14.5cm (5.75ins) high.
Lilac, green and pink.
Other colourways:
HN1662, 1681.
Est. £650-850.

HN1655
Marie
Second Version (Model 662)
Designer L. Harradine.
Date 1934 - 38.
11.5cm (4.5ins) high.
Pink and white.
Other colourways: HN1370,
1388, 1417, 1489, 1531, 1635.
Est. £135-200.

HN1664
Aileen
Designer L. Harradine.
Date 1934 - 38.
15cm (6ins) high.
Pink and blue.
Other colourways:
HN1645, 1803.
Est. £750-1000.

HN1656
Dainty May
Designer L. Harradine.
Date 1934 - 49.
15cm (6ins) high.
Lilac and white.
Other colourways: HN1639.
Est. £300-400.

HN1665
Miss Winsome
Designer L. Harradine.
Date 1934 - 49.
17cm (6.75ins) high.
Lilac, green and white.
Other colourways: HN1666.
Est. £500-700.

HN1657
The Moor
Designer C.J. Noke.
Date 1934 - 49.
42cm (16.5ins) high.
Brownish red and black.
Other colourways: HN1308, 1366,
1425, 2082, 3642, 3926; also called
'An Arab' HN33, 343, 378.
Est. £1500-2000.

HN1666
Miss Winsome
Designer L. Harradine.
Date 1934 - 38.
17cm (6.75ins) high.
Green, brown and blue.
Other colourways: HN1665.
Est. £550-750.

HN1667
Blossom
Designer L. Harradine.
Date 1934 - 49.
17cm (6.75ins) high.
Orange patterned
shawl, blue child's dress.
Est. £1000-1300.

HN1668
Sibell
Designer L. Harradine.
Date 1934 - 49.
17cm (6.75ins) high.
Light green dress with
red overdress.
Other colourways:
HN1695, 1735.
(Auction PSA 10.3.04 sold
£300 plus comm.)
Est.. £350-500.

HN1669
Anthea
Designer L. Harradine.
Date 1934 - 40.
16.5cm (6.5ins) high.
Green, pink and cream.
Other colourways:
HN1526, 1527.
Est. £500-750.

HN1670
Gillian
First Version (Model 872)
Designer L. Harradine.
Date 1934 - 49.
19.5cm (7.75ins) high.
Pink dress with green bonnet.
Other colourways: HN1670A.
Est. £600-800.

HN1670A
Gillian
First Version (Model 872)
Designer L. Harradine.
Date not known.
19.5cm (7.75ins) high.
Green and white.
Other colourways: HN1670.
Est. £650-900.

HN1677
Tinkle Bell
Designer L. Harradine.
Date 1935 - 88.
12cm (4.75ins) high.
Pink.
(Ebay 23.5.04. sold for £33.50)
(Auction PSA 23.6.04. sold for
£40 plus comm.)
Est. £40-60.

HN1678
Dinky Doo
Designer L. Harradine.
Date 1934 - 96.
12cm (4.75ins) high.
Lilac, blue and white.
Other colourways:
HN2120, 3618.
(Ebay 28.5.04. sold for £32)
(Auction PSA 23.6.04. sold for
£32 plus comm.)
Est. £40-60.

HN1679
Babie
Designer L. Harradine.
Date 1935 - 92.
12cm (4.75ins) high.
Pale green, lilac and red.
Other colourways:
HN1842, 2121.
(Ebay 11.6.04. sold for £17)
Est. £25-50.

HN1680
Tootles
Designer L. Harradine.
Date 1935 - 75.
12cm (4.75ins) high.
Pink skirt, red bodice.
(Ebay 28.5.04. sold for £51)
Est. £50-70.

HN1681
Delicia
Designer L. Harradine.
Date 1935 - 38.
14.5cm (5.75ins) high.
Purple and green.
Other colourways:
HN1662, 1663.
Est. £600-800.

HN1682
Teresa
First Version (Model 883)
Designer L. Harradine.
Date 1935 - 49.
14.5cm (5.75ins) high.
Red dress with brown seat.
Other colourways: HN1683.
(Ebay 26.9.04 sold £720)
Est. £800-1000.

HN1686A
Cynthia
First Version (Model 889)
Designer L. Harradine.
Date 1935 - 49.
14.5cm (5.75ins) high.
Purple and red.
Other colourways:
HN1685, 1686.
Est. £600-800.

HN1683
Teresa
First Version (Model 883)
Designer L. Harradine.
Date 1935 - 38.
14.5cm (5.75ins) high.
Light blue dress with
brown seat.
Other colourways: HN1682.
Est. £1400-1750.

HN1687
Clarissa
First Version (Model 773)
Designer L. Harradine.
Date 1935 - 49.
25.5cm (10ins) high.
Blue, orange and green.
Other colourways: HN1525.
Est. £400-600.

HN1684
Lisette
Designer L. Harradine.
Date 1935 - 36.
13cm (5.25ins) high.
Pink, green and white.
Other colourways:
HN1523, 1524.
Est. £800-1100.

HN1688
Rhoda
Designer L. Harradine.
Date 1935 - 40.
26cm (10.25ins) high.
Orange skirt with red shawl.
Other colourways:
HN1573, 1574.
Est. £350-500.

HN1685
Cynthia
First Version (Model 889)
Designer L. Harradine.
Date 1935 - 49.
14.5cm (5.75ins) high.
Pink, yellow and turquoise.
Other colourways:
HN1686, 1686A.
Est. £600-800.

HN1689
Calumet
Designer C.J. Noke.
Date 1935 - 49.
15cm (6ins) high.
Green and brown with
blue bowl.
Other colourways:
HN1428, 2068.
Est. £500-700.

HN1686
Cynthia
First Version (Model 889)
Designer L. Harradine.
Date 1935 - 49.
14.5cm (5.75ins) high.
Blue, red and yellow.
Other colourways:
HN1685, 1686A.
Est. £600-800.

HN1690
June
First Version (Model 890)
Designer L. Harradine.
Date 1935 - 49.
19cm (7.5ins) high.
Green, white, red and pink.
Other colourways: HN1691,
1947, 2027.
Est. £500-700.

HN1691
June
First Version (Model 890)
Designer L. Harradine.
Date 1935 - 49.
19cm (7.5ins) high.
Yellow, green and pink.
Other colourways: HN1690,
1947, 2027.
Est. £300-450.

HN1692
Sonia
Designer L. Harradine.
Date 1935 - 49.
16.5cm (6.5ins) high.
White, pink, yellow and green.
Other colourways: HN1738.
Est. £600-800.

HN1693
Virginia
Designer L. Harradine.
Date 1935 - 49.
19cm (7.5ins) high.
Yellow and red.
Other colourways: HN1694.
Est. £660-900.

HN1694
Virginia
Designer L. Harradine.
Date 1935 - 49.
19cm (7.5ins) high.
Green over white spotted dress.
Other colourways: HN1693.
Est. £660-900.

HN1695
Sibell
Designer L. Harradine.
Date 1935 - 49.
17cm (6.75ins) high.
Green dress with orange
overdress.
Other colourways:
HN1668, 1735.
Est. £500-650.

HN1696
Suzette
Designer L. Harradine.
Date 1935 - 49.
19cm (7.5ins) high.
Green and white.
Other colourways: HN1487,
1577, 1585, 2026.
Est. £400-600.

HN1697
Irene
Designer L. Harradine.
Date 1935 - 49.
17cm (6.5ins) high.
Pink, green and white.
Other colourways:
HN1621, 1952.
Est. £500-700.

HN1698
Phyllis
First Version (Model 683)
Designer L. Harradine.
Date 1935 - 49.
23cm (9ins) high.
Green and white.
Other colourways: HN1420,
1430, 1486.
Est. £500-750.

HN1699
Marietta
Designer L. Harradine.
Date 1935 - 40.
20.5cm (8ins) high.
Green and red.
Other colourways:
HN1341, 1446.
Est. £1000-1500.

HN1700
Gloria
First Version (Model 727)
Designer L. Harradine.
Date 1935 - 38.
18cm (7ins) high.
Green and black.
Other colourways: HN1488.
Est. £1300-1750.

HN1701
Sweet Anne
Designer L. Harradine.
Date 1935 - 38.
18cm (7ins) high.
Pink floral dress with
blue trimmings.
Other colourways: 1318, 1330,
1331, 1453, 1496, 1631.
Est. £500-650.

HN1706
The Cobbler
Third Version (Model 891)
Designer C.J. Noke.
Date 1935 - 69.
20.5cm (8ins) high.
Green, brown, red and yellow.
Other colourways: HN1705.
Est. £150-200.

HN1702
A Jester
First Version (Model 170)
Designer C.J. Noke.
Date 1935 - 49.
25.5cm (10ins) high.
Brown and mauve with
orange trimmings.
Other colourways: HN45, 71,
71A, 320, 367, 412, 426, 446,
552, 616, 627, 1295, 2016, 3922.
Est. £300-400.

HN1707
Paisley Shawl
First Version (Model 660)
Designer L. Harradine.
Date 1935 - 49.
23cm (9ins) high.
Purple and lilac.
Other colourways: HN1392,
1460, 1739, 1987.
Est. £400-550.

HN1703
Charley's Aunt
Third Version
Designer A. Toft.
Date 1935 - 38.
15cm (6ins) high.
No base. Lilac dress, white shawl.
Est. £800-1000.

HN1708
The Bather
First Version (Model 428)
Designer L. Harradine.
Date 1935 - 38.
19cm (7.75ins) high.
Black, red and turquoise.
Other colourways: HN597, 687,
781, 782, 1238.
Same figure re-issued in 2000
in a limited edition. (HN4244)
Est. £1900-2500.

HN1704
Herminia
Designer L. Harradine.
Date 1935 - 38.
16.5cm (6.5ins) high.
Red dress with green hat
and shawl.
Other colourways:
HN1644, 1646.
Est. £750-1000.

HN1709
Pantalettes
Designer L. Harradine.
Date 1935 - 38.
20.5cm (8ins) high.
Red and pale blue.
Other colourways: HN1362,
1412, 1507.
Est. £550-750.

HN1705
The Cobbler
Third Version (Model 891)
Designer C.J. Noke.
Date 1935 - 49.
20.5cm (8ins) high.
Purple, blue, yellow and red.
Other colourways: HN1706.
Est. £450-650.

HN1710
Camilla
First Version
Designer L. Harradine.
Date 1935 - 49.
18cm (7ins) high.
Red and yellow dress.
Other colourways: HN1711.
Est. £750-1000.

HN1711
Camilla
First Version
Designer L. Harradine.
Date 1935 - 49.
18cm (7ins) high.
Green, white and yellow.
Other colourways: HN1710.
Est. £750-1000.

HN1712
Daffy Down Dilly
Designer L. Harradine.
Date 1935 - 75.
21cm (8.25ins) high.
Pale green, white and yellow.
Other colourways: HN1713.
Est. £150-250.

HN1713
Daffy Down Dilly
Designer L. Harradine.
Date 1935 - 49.
21cm (8.25ins) high.
Turquoise, white and yellow.
Other colourways: HN1712.
Est. £500-700.

HN1714
Millicent
Designer L. Harradine.
Date 1935 - 75.
20.5cm (8ins) high.
Red coat over white and
green dress.
Other colourways:
HN1715, 1860.
(Ebay 19.8.04 sold £721)
Est. £750-950.

HN1715
Millicent
Designer L. Harradine.
Date 1935 - 49.
20.5cm (8ins) high.
Lavender coat over
lavender floral dress.
Other colourways:
HN1714, 1860.
Est. £800-1000.

HN1716
Diana
First Version (Model 897)
Designer L. Harradine.
Date 1935 - 49.
14.5cm (5.75ins) high.
Pink, blue and red.
Other colourways:
HN1717, 1986.
Est. £300-400.

HN1717
Diana
First Version (Model 897)
Designer L. Harradine.
Date 1935 - 49.
14.5cm (5.75ins) high.
Turuoise and white.
Other colourways:
HN1716, 1986.
Est. £200-250.

HN1718
Kate Hardcastle
Designer L. Harradine.
Date 1935 - 49.
21cm (8.25ins) high.
Pink, white and pale green.
Other colourways: HN1719,
1734, 1861, 1919, 2028.
Est. £450-650.

HN1719
Kate Hardcastle
Designer L. Harradine.
Date 1935 - 49.
21cm (8.25ins) high.
Red, white and green.
Other colourways: HN1718,
1734, 1861, 1919, 2028.
Est. £450-650.

HN1720
Frangcon
Designer L. Harradine.
Date 1935 - 49.
19cm (7.5ins) high.
White, orange, lilac, red and yellow.
Other colourways: HN1721.
Est. £950-1250.

HN1721
Françcon
Designer L. Harradine.
Date 1935 - 49.
19cm (7.5ins) high.
Green and white.
Other colourways: HN1720.
Est. £700-950.

HN1726
Celia
Designer L. Harradine.
Date 1935 - 49.
29cm (11.5ins) high.
Pale lilac.
Other colourways: HN1727.
Est. £950-1280.

HN1722
The Coming of Spring
Designer L. Harradine.
Date 1935 - 49.
32cm (12.5ins) high.
Pinky yellow.
Other colourways: HN1723.
Est. £1350-1750.

HN1727
Celia
Designer L. Harradine.
Date 1935 - 49.
29cm (11.5ins) high.
Pale green.
Other colourways: HN1726.
Est. £650-850.

HN1723
The Coming of Spring
Designer L. Harradine.
Date 1935 - 49.
32cm (12.5ins) high.
Pale green.
Other colourways: HN1722.
Est. £1350-1750.

HN1728
The New Bonnet
Designer L. Harradine.
Date 1935 - 49.
18cm (7ins) high.
Pink, white and green.
Other colourways: HN1957.
Est. £450-650.

HN1724
Ruby
First Version
Designer L. Harradine.
Date 1935 - 49.
13cm (5.25ins) high.
Pink, white and red.
Other colourways: HN1725.
(Ebay 3.6.04. sold for £122)
Est. £150-250.

HN1729
Vera
Designer L. Harradine.
Date 1935 - 40.
11cm (4.25ins) high.
Pink dress, fair hair.
Other colourways: HN1730.
Same figure re-issued
in 2000 in limited edition
(HN4169)
Est. £450-650.

HN1725
Ruby
First Version
Designer L. Harradine.
Date 1935 - 49.
13cm (5.25ins) high.
Blue and white.
Other colourways: HN1724.
Est. £250-400.

HN1730
Vera
Designer L. Harradine.
Date 1935 - 38.
11cm (4.25ins) high.
Blue dress, fair hair.
Other colourways: HN1729.
Same figure re-issued
in 2000 in limited edition
(HN4169)
Est. £450-650.

HN1731
Daydreams
Designer L. Harradine.
Date 1934 - 96.
14cm (5.5ins) high.
Pale pink dress with blue trimmings.
Other colourways: HN1732,
1944.
(Ebay 24.5.04 sold for £62)
(Auction W&H 27.9.04
sold £75 plus comm.)
Est. £85-125.

HN1737
Janet
First Version (Model 785)
Designer L. Harradine.
Date 1935 - 49.
16.5cm (6.5ins) high.
Green, white and yellow.
Other colourways:
HN1537, 1538, 1652.
Est. £300-400.

HN1732
Daydreams
Designer L. Harradine.
Date 1935 - 49.
14cm (5.5ins) high.
Lilac and pink with
pink trimmings.
Other colourways:
HN1731, 1944.
Est. £350-480.

HN1738
Sonia
Designer L. Harradine.
Date 1935 - 49.
16.5cm (6.5ins) high.
Pale green, pink, lilac
and white.
Other colourways: HN1692.
Est. £600-800.

HN1734
Kate Hardcastle
Designer L. Harradine.
Date 1935 - 49.
21cm (8.25ins) high.
Green and white.
Other colourways: HN1718,
1719, 1861, 1919, 2028.
Est. £750-1000.

HN1739
Paisley Shawl
First Version (Model 660)
Designer L. Harradine.
Date 1935 - 49.
23cm (9ins) high.
Grey-green and red.
Other colourways: HN1392,
1460, 1707, 1987.
Est. £350-550.

HN1735
Sibell
Designer L. Harradine.
Date 1935 - 49.
17cm (6.75ins) high.
White and blue.
Other colourways:
HN1668, 1695.
Est. £500-750.

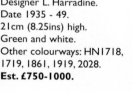

HN1740
Gladys
Designer L. Harradine.
Date 1935 - 49.
12.5cm (5ins) high.
Green dress, fair hair.
Other colourways:
HN1741. Same figure
re-issued in 2000 in
limited edition (HN4168)
Est. £450-650.

HN1736
Camille
First Version (Model 815)
Designer L. Harradine.
Date 1935 - 49.
16.5cm (6.5ins) high.
Pink and cream.
Other colourways:
HN1586, 1648.
Est. £825-1000.

HN1741
Gladys
Designer L. Harradine.
Date 1935 - 38.
12.5cm (5ins) high.
Lilac dress, fair hair.
Other colourways:
HN1740. Same figure
re-issued in 2000 in
limited edition
(HN4168),
Est. £450-650.

HN1742
Sir Walter Raleigh
Designer L. Harradine.
Date 1935 - 49.
26.5cm (10.5ins) high.
Green, blue and orange.
Other colourways:
HN1751, 2015.
Est. £1650-2000.

HN1747
Afternoon Tea
Designer P. Railston.
Date 1935 - 82.
13cm (5.25ins) high.
Pink, white and blue.
Other colourways:
HN1748.
*(Ebay 20.6.04.
sold £205)*
Est. £225-300.

HN1743
Mirabel
Designer L. Harradine.
Date 1935 - 49.
19.5cm (7.75ins) high.
Pale blue, red and green.
Other colourways: HN1744.
Est. £500-650.

HN1748
Afternoon Tea
Designer P. Railston.
Date 1935 - 49.
13cm (5.25ins) high.
Green dress.
Other colourways:
HN1747.
Est. £700-1000.

HN1744
Mirabel
Designer L. Harradine.
Date 1935 - 49.
19.5cm (7.75ins) high.
Pink & pale green.
Other colourways:
HN1743.
Est. £500-650.

HN1749
Pierrette
Third Version (Model 659)
Designer L. Harradine.
Date 1936 - 49.
23cm (9ins) high.
Purple, red, black and white.
Other colourways: HN1391.
Est. £1100-1500.

HN1745
The Rustic Swain
Designer L. Harradine.
Date 1935 - 49.
13cm (5.25ins) high.
Brown, red, green
and white
Other colourways:
HN1746.
Est. £1000-1250.

HN1750
Folly
Designer L. Harradine.
Date 1936 - 49.
23cm (9ins) high.
Purple, white and black,
multicoloured balloons.
Other colourways: HN1335.
Est. £1100-1500.

HN1746
The Rustic Swain
Designer L. Harradine.
Date 1935 - 49.
13cm (5.25ins) high.
Dark green, blue, white
and pink.
Other colourways:
HN1745.
Est. £1000-1250.

HN1751
Sir Walter Raleigh
Designer L. Harradine.
Date 1936 - 49.
29cm (11.5ins) high.
Orange and purple.
Other colourways:
HN1742, 2015.
(Same colours as HN2015 but with
minor glaze differences)
Est. £550-750.

HN1752
Regency
Designer L. Harradine.
Date 1936 - 49.
20.5cm (8ins) high.
Lilac, red and green.
Est. £550-700.

HN1757
Romany Sue
Designer L. Harradine.
Date 1936 - 49.
24cm (9.5ins) high.
Red, green, white and blue.
Other colourways: HN1758.
(Ebay 20.8.04 sold £536)
Est. £600-900.

HN1753
Eleanore
Designer L. Harradine.
Date 1936 - 49.
18cm (7ins) high.
Green, mauve, white and pink.
Other colourways: HN1754.
Est. £850-1100.

HN1758
Romany Sue
Designer L. Harradine.
Date 1936 - 49.
24cm (9.5ins) high.
Lilac, pink and yellow.
Other colourways: HN1757.
Est. £600-900.

HN1754
Eleanore
Designer L. Harradine.
Date 1936 - 49.
18cm (7ins) high.
Orange, blue, cream and white.
Other colourways: HN1753.
Est. £850-1100.

HN1759
The Orange Lady
Designer L. Harradine.
Date 1936 - 75.
22cm (8.75ins) high.
Pink, red, brown and orange.
Other colourways: HN1953.
*(Auction PSA 23.6.04 sold £100
and 1.9.04 sold £110 plus comm.)*
(Ebay 4.10.04 sold £145)
Est. £135-180.

HN1755
The Court Shoemaker
Designer L. Harradine.
Date 1936 - 49.
17cm (6.75ins) high.
Pink, purple, green and brown.
Est. £1100-1500.

HN1760
4 o'Clock
Designer L. Harradine.
Date 1936 - 49.
15cm (6ins) high.
Lilac and white.
Est. £660-900.

HN1756
Lizana
Designer L. Harradine.
Date 1936 - 49.
21.5cm (8.5ins) high.
Pink, green, red and purple.
Other colourways: HN1761.
Est. £500-700.

HN1761
Lizana
Designer L. Harradine.
Date 1936 - 38.
21.5cm (8.5ins) high.
Green dress leopard-skin cloak.
Other colourways HN1756.
Est. £500-700.

HN1762
The Bride
First Version (Model 810)
Designer L. Harradine.
Date 1936 - 49.
24cm (9.5ins) high.
Cream dress.
Other colourways: HN1588,
1600, 1841.
Est. £700-850.

HN1767
Nana
Designer L. Harradine.
Date 1936 - 49.
12cm (4.75ins) high.
Lilac and green.
Other colourways: HN1766.
Est. £100-150.

HN1763
Windflower
First Version (Model 926)
Designer L. Harradine.
Date 1936 - 49.
18.5cm (7.25ins) high.
Red top with cream floral skirt
and blue hat.
Other colourways: HN1764, 2029.
*(Auction PSA 10.3.04 sold for £150 plus
comm.) (Ebay 30.8.04 sold £280)*
Est. £200-320.

HN1768
Ivy
Designer L. Harradine.
Date 1936 - 79.
12cm (4.75ins) high.
Light blue dress, pink hat.
Other colourways: HN1769.
*(Auction W&H 27.9.04 sold £38
plus comm.)*
Est. £50-75.

HN1764
Windflower
First Version (Model 926)
Designer L. Harradine.
Date 1936 - 49.
18.5cm (7.25ins) high.
Blue top.
Other colourways:
HN1763, 2029.
Est. £350-450.

HN1769
Ivy
Designer L. Harradine.
Date 1936 - 38.
12cm (4.75ins) high.
Colour not recorded.
Other colourways: HN1768.
Rare.

HN1765
Chloe
First Version
Designer L. Harradine.
Date 1936 - 50.
15cm (6ins) high.
Light blue, grey and yellow.
Other colourways: HN1470,
1476, 1479, 1498, 1956.
Est. £150-200.

HN1770
Maureen
First Version (Model 924)
Designer L. Harradine.
19cm (7.5ins) high.
Pink, black and white.
Date 1936 - 59.
Other colourways: HN1771.
*(Auction PSA 26.5.04 sold for
£165 plus comm.)*
Est. £200-300.

HN1766
Nana
Designer L. Harradine.
Date 1936 - 49.
12cm (4.75ins) high.
Pink and blue.
Other colourways: HN1767.
*(Auction Brightwells 1.9.04 sold
£75 plus comm.)*
Est. £100-150.

HN1771
Maureen
First Version (Model 924)
Designer L. Harradine.
Date 1936 - 49.
19cm (7.5ins) high.
Lilac and white.
Other colourways: HN1770.
Est. £500-650.

HN1772
Delight
Designer L. Harradine.
Date 1936 - 67.
17cm (6.75ins) high.
Red, white and turquoise.
Other colourways: HN1773.
*(Auction PSA 6.8.03 sold for
£80 plus comm.)*
Est. £100-150.

HN1777
Spirit of the Wind
Designer R. Garbe.
Date 1933. Limited edition of 50
which sold out in 1939.
Height not known.
Matt ivory.
Other colourways: HN1825.
Extremely rare.

HN1773
Delight
Designer L. Harradine.
Date 1936 - 49.
17cm (6.75ins) high.
Turquoise, white and red.
Other colourways: HN1772.
Est. £300-425.

HN1778
Beethoven
Designer R. Garbe.
Date 1933. Limited edition of
25 which sold out in 1939.
56cm (22ins) high.
Matt ivory.
Extremely rare.

HN1774
Spring
Third Version (Model 796)
Designer R. Garbe.
Date 1933. Limited edition of 100
which sold out in 1939.
53.5cm (21ins) high.
Matt ivory.
Other colourways: HN1827.
Extremely rare.

HN1779
Macaw
Designer R. Garbe.
Date 1933 - 49.
37cm (14.5ins) high.
Ivory.
Other colourways: HN1829.
Extremely rare.

HN1775
Salome
First Version (Model 795)
Designer R. Garbe.
Date 1933. Limited edition of 100
which sold out in 1939.
20.5cm (8ins) high.
Ivory.
Other colourways: HN1828.
Extremely rare.

HN1780
Lady of the Snows
Designer R. Garbe.
Date 1933. Limited edition of 50
which sold out in 1939.
Height not known.
Other colourways: HN1830.
Extremely rare.

HN1776
West Wind
Designer R. Garbe.
Date 1933.
Limited edition of
25 which sold out
in 1939.
37cm (14.5ins) high.
Matt Ivory.
Other colourways: HN1826.
Extremely rare.

HN1791
**Old Balloon Seller and
Bulldog**
Designer L. Harradine.
Date 1932 - 38.
18cm (7ins) high.
Green, red and white, with
multicoloured balloons.
Other colourways: HN1912.
Extremely rare.

HN1792
Henry VIII
Second Version (Model 841)
Designer C.J. Noke.
Date 1933. Limited edition of
200 sold out in 1939.
29cm (11.5ins) high.
Multicoloured.
Est. £3000-4000.

HN1793
This Little Pig
Designer L. Harradine.
Date 1936 - 95
10cm (4ins) high.
Red.
Other colourways:
HN1794, 2125.
*(Auction PSA 23.6.04 sold £48
and W&H 27.9.04 sold £34 plus
comm.)(Ebay 9.7.04 sold £36)*
Est. £45-75.

HN1794
This Little Pig
Designer L. Harradine.
Date 1936 - 49.
10cm (4ins) high.
Blue.
Other colourways:
HN1793, 2125.
Est. £350-450.

HN1795
M'Lady's Maid
Designer L. Harradine.
Date 1936 - 49.
23cm (9ins) high.
Red and white.
Other colourways: HN1822.
Est. £1800-2500.

HN1796
Hazel
First Version (Model 936)
Designer L. Harradine.
Date 1936 - 49.
13cm (5.25ins) high.
Light green and red.
Other colourways: HN1797.
Est. £300-400.

HN1797
Hazel
First Version (Model 936)
Designer L. Harradine.
Date 1936 - 49.
13cm (5.25ins) high.
Pink, blue and cream.
Other colourways: HN1796.
Est. £300-400.

HN1798
Lily
First Version
Designer L. Harradine.
Date 1936 - 71.
12.5cm (5ins) high.
Pink and cream.
Other colourways: HN1799.
*(Auction PSA 23.6.04 sold for £48
plus comm.)*
Est. £50-85.

HN1799
Lily
First Version
Designer L. Harradine.
Date 1936 - 49.
12.5cm (5ins) high.
Light green and blue.
Other colourways: HN1798.
Est. £150-250.

HN1800
St. George
First Version (Model 191)
Designer S. Thorogood.
Date 1934 - 50.
40.5cm (16ins) high.
Purple, green, orange and grey
with white horse.
Other colourways: HN385,
386, 2067.
Est. £1500-2000.

HN1801
An Old King
Designer C.J. Noke.
Date 1937 - 54.
24.5cm (9.75ins) high.
Colour not known.
Other colourways: HN358,
623, 2134.
Extremely rare.

HN1802
Estelle
Designer L. Harradine.
Date 1937 - 40.
20.5cm (8ins) high.
Pink, lilac and green.
Other colourways: HN1566.
Est. £750-1000.

HN1807
Spring Flowers
Designer L. Harradine.
Date 1937 - 59.
18.5cm (7.25ins) high.
Yellow, pink, white and blue.
Other colourways: HN1945.
Est. £250-300.

HN1803
Aileen
Designer L. Harradine.
Date 1937 - 49.
15cm (6ins) high.
Cream and blue.
Other colourways:
HN1645, 1664.
Est. £1000-1300

HN1808
Cissie
Designer L. Harradine.
Date 1937 - 51.
12.5cm (5ins) high.
Green.
Other colourways: HN1809.
Est. £250-300.

HN1804
Granny
Designer L. Harradine.
Date 1937 - 49.
18cm (7ins) high.
Grey, cream, purple and brown.
Other colourways: HN1832.
Est. £1750-2500.

HN1809
Cissie
Designer L. Harradine.
Date 1937 - 93.
12.5cm (5ins) high.
Pink and yellow.
Other colourways: HN1808.
*(Auction PSA 22.10.03 sold for
£50 plus comm.)*
Est. £60-90.

HN1805
To Bed
Designer L. Harradine.
Date 1937 - 59.
15cm (6ins) high.
Pale green.
Other colourways: HN1806.
Est. £100-140.

HN1810
Bo-Peep
Second Version (Model 944)
Designer L. Harradine.
Date 1937 - 49.
12.5cm (5ins) high.
Blue.
Other colourways: HN1811.
Est. £250-300.

HN1806
To Bed
Designer L. Harradine.
Date 1937 - 49.
15cm (6ins) high.
Lilac.
Other colourways: HN1805.
Est. £225-325.

HN1811
Bo-Peep
Second Version (Model 944)
Designer L. Harradine.
Date 1937 - 95.
12.5cm (5ins) high.
Pink.
Other colourways: HN1810.
*(Auction PSA 6.8.03 sold for
£40 plus comm.)*
Est. £50-75.

HN1812
Forget-me-not
First Version (Model 932)
Designer L. Harradine.
Date 1937 - 49.
15cm (6ins) high.
Pink, cream and green.
Other colourways: HN1813.
Est. £550-750.

HN1819
Miranda
First Version (Model 942)
Designer L. Harradine.
Date 1937 - 49.
21.5cm (8.5ins) high.
Yellow, green, white and red.
Other colourways: HN1818.
Est. £1000-1400.

HN1813
Forget-me-not
First Version (Model 932)
Designer L. Harradine.
Date 1937 - 49.
15cm (6ins) high.
Red, white and blue.
Other colourways: HN1812.
Est. £400-600.

HN1820
Reflections
Designer L. Harradine.
Date 1937 - 38.
12.5cm (5ins) high.
Red, pink and green.
Other colourways:
HN1821, 1847, 1848.
Est. £1400-2000.

HN1814
The Squire
Designer not known.
Date 1937 - 49.
25.5cm (10ins) high.
Red and white and grey horse.
Other colourways:
'Hunting Squire' HN1409.
Est. £2000-3000.

HN1821
Reflections
Designer L. Harradine.
Date 1937 - 38.
12.5cm (5ins) high.
Green, orange
and red.
Other colourways:
HN1820, 1847, 1848.
Est. £1400-2000.

HN1815
The Huntsman
Second Version (Model 673)
Designer not known.
Date 1937 - 49.
22cm (8.75ins) high.
Red and white with brown horse.
Other colourways:
'John Peel' HN1408.
Est. £2000-3000.

HN1822
M'Lady's Maid
Designer L. Harradine.
Date 1937 - 49.
23cm (9ins) high.
Pink, white and yellow.
Other colourways: HN1795.
Est. £1800-2500.

HN1818
Miranda
First Version (Model 942)
Designer L. Harradine.
Date 1937 - 49.
21.5cm (8.5ins) high.
Blue, red, white and green.
Other colourways: HN1819.
Est. £1000-1400.

HN1825
Spirit of the Wind
Designer R. Garbe.
Date 1937 - 49.
Height not known.
Green and ivory.
Other colourways: HN1777.
Extremely rare.

HN1826
West Wind
Designer R. Garbe.
Date 1937 - 49.
37cm (14.5ins) high.
Tinted ivory.
Other colourways:
HN1776.
Extremely rare

HN1831
The Cloud
Designer R. Garbe.
Date 1937 - 49.
58.5cm (23ins) high.
Ivory and gold.
Extremely rare.

HN1827
Spring
Third Version (Model 796)
Designer R. Garbe.
Date 1937 - 49.
53.5cm (21ins) high.
Green, gold and ivory.
Other colourways: HN1774.
Extremely rare.

HN1832
Granny
Designer L. Harradine.
Date 1937 - 49.
18cm (7ins) high.
Red, yellow, white and green.
Other colourways: HN1804.
Est. £1500-2000.

HN1828
Salome
First Version (Model 795)
Designer R. Garbe.
Date 1937 - 49.
20.5cm (8ins) high.
Pale blue.
Other colourways: HN1775.
Extremely rare.

HN1833
Top o' the Hill
First Version (Model 965)
Designer L. Harradine.
Date 1937 - 71.
18cm (7ins) high.
Blue, green and white.
Other colourways: HN1834,
1849, 2127, 3735A.
*(Auction PSA 17.9.03 sold £60
plus comm.)*
Est. £75-125.

HN1829
Macaw
Designer R. Garbe.
Date 1937 - 49.
37cm (14.5ins) high.
Tinted ivory.
Other colourways: HN1779.
Extremely rare.

HN1834
Top o' the Hill
First Version (Model 965)
Designer L. Harradine.
Date 1937 to date.18cm (7ins) high.
Red, yellow and white.
Other colourways: HN1833,
1849, 2127, 3735A.
(Royal Doulton web price £170)
*(Auction PSA 23.6.04 sold £50 and
W&H 27.9.04 sold £62 plus comm.)*
(Ebay 28.6.04 sold £64) **Est. £75-115.**

HN1830
Lady of the Snows
Designer R. Garbe.
Date 1937 - 49.
Height not known.
Tinted ivory.
Other colourways: HN1780.
Extremely rare.

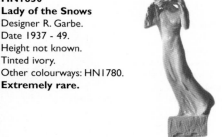

HN1835
Verena
Designer L. Harradine.
Date 1938 - 49.
21cm (8.25ins) high.
Light green, white and peach.
Other colourways: HN1854.
Est. £650-1000.

HN1836
Vanessa
First Version (Model 968)
Designer L. Harradine.
Date 1938 - 49.
19cm (7.5ins) high.
Blue, green and white.
Other colourways: HN1838.
Est. £600-800.

HN1841
The Bride
First Version (Model 810)
Designer L. Harradine.
Date 1938 - 49.
24cm (9.5ins) high.
Pale blue, white and yellow.
Other colourways: HN1588,
1600, 1762.
Est. £650-900.

HN1837
Mariquita
Designer L. Harradine.
Date 1938 - 49.
20.5cm (8ins) high.
Purple, red and white.
Est. £1300-1800.

HN1842
Babie
Designer L. Harradine.
Date 1938 - 49.
12cm (4.75ins) high.
Dark pink and green.
Other colourways:
HN1679, 2121.
Est. £120-170.

HN1838
Vanessa
First Version (Model 968)
Designer L. Harradine.
Date 1938 - 49.
19cm (7.5ins) high.
Pink and green.
Other colourways: HN1836.
Est. £600-800.

HN1843
Biddy Penny Farthing
Designer L. Harradine.
Date 1938 to date.
23cm (9ins) high.
Green and lilac with
multicoloured balloons.
(Made as a pair to HN1844
'Odds and Ends')
(Royal Doulton web price £175)
(Auction ASH 26.9.04 sold £90 plus comm.)
(Ebay 9.6.04 Sold £73) **Est. £95-150.**

HN1839
Christine
First Version (Model 939)
Designer L. Harradine.
Date 1938 - 49.
19.5cm (7.75ins) high.
Lilac and blue.
Other colourways: HN1840.
Est. £500-750.

HN1844
Odds and Ends
Designer L. Harradine.
Date 1938 - 49.
20.5cm (8ins) high.
Orange and green.
(Made as a pair to HN1843
'Biddy Penny Farthing')
Est. £1150-1650.

HN1840
Christine
First Version (Model 939)
Designer L. Harradine.
Date 1938 - 49.
19.5cm (7.75ins) high.
Pink, white and blue.
Other colourways: HN1839.
Est. £500-750.

HN1845
Modena
Designer L. Harradine.
Date 1938 - 49.
18.5cm (7.25ins) high.
Blue and pink with floral shawl.
Other colourways: HN1846.
Est. £1050-1450.

HN1846
Modena
Designer L. Harradine.
Date 1938 - 49.
18.5cm (7.25ins) high.
Red and green with floral shawl.
Other colourways: HN1845.
Est. £1050-1450.

HN1851
Antoinette
First Version (Model 980)
Designer L. Harradine.
Date 1938 - 49.
21cm (8.25ins) high.
Blue, white and lilac.
Other colourways: HN1850.
Est. £900-1200.

HN1847
Reflections
Designer L. Harradine.
Date 1938 - 49.
12.5cm (5ins) high.
Red, lilac and green.
Other colour ways:
HN1820, 1821, 1848.
(Auction PSA 23.6.04
sold £750
plus comm.)
Est. £900-1400.

HN1852
The Mirror
Designer L. Harradine.
Date 1938 - 49.
19cm (7.5ins) high.
Pink and pale green.
Other colourways: HN1853.
Est. £1400-2000.

HN1848
Reflections
Designer L. Harradine.
Date 1938 - 49.
12.5cm (5ins) high.
Pink, blue and green.
Other colourways:
HN1820, 1821, 1847.
Est. £1000-1400.

HN1853
The Mirror
Designer L. Harradine.
Date 1938 - 49.
19cm (7.5ins) high.
Blue and mauve.
Other colourways: HN1852.
Est. £1400-2000.

HN1849
Top o' the Hill
First Version (Model 965)
Designer L. Harradine.
Date 1938 - 75.
18cm (7ins) high.
Pink and green.
Other colourways: HN1833,
1834, 2127, 3735A.
Est. £95-135.

HN1854
Verena
Designer L. Harradine.
Date 1938 - 49.
21cm (8.25ins) high.
Blue and pink.
Other colourways: HN1835.
Est. £900-1200.

HN1850
Antoinette
First Version (Model 980)
Designer L. Harradine.
Date 1938 - 49.
21cm (8.25ins) high.
Red, white, green and pink.
Other colourways: HN1851.
Est. £900-1200.

HN1855
Memories
Designer L. Harradine.
Date 1938 - 49.
15cm (6ins) high.
Green, cream, lilac and red.
Other colourways:
HN1856, 1857, 2030.
Est. £350-450.

HN1856
Memories
Designer L. Harradine.
Date 1938 - 49.
15cm (6ins) high.
Pale blue, green and white.
Other colourways:
HN1855, 1857, 2030.
Est. £450-600.

HN1860
Millicent
Designer L. Harradine.
Date 1938 - 49.
20.5cm (8ins) high.
Blue, red and green.
Other colourways:
HN1714, 1715.
Est. £650-850.

HN1857
Memories
Designer L. Harradine.
Date 1938 - 49.
15cm (6ins) high.
Red, white and lilac.
Other colourways:
HN1855, 1856, 2030.
Est. £450-600.

HN1861
Kate Hardcastle
Designer L. Harradine.
Date 1938 - 49.
21cm (8.25ins) high.
Red, white, green and blue.
Other colourways: HN1718,
1719, 1734, 1919, 2028.
Est. £650-850.

HN1858
Dawn
(With head-dress)
First Version (Model 981)
Designer L. Harradine.
Date 1938 - 49.
26cm (10.25ins) high.
Pale green.
Other colourways: HN1858A.
Est. £1000-1400.

HN1862
Jasmine
First Version
Designer L. Harradine.
Date 1938 - 49.
19cm (7.5ins) high.
Blue, green, orange and white.
Other colourways:
HN1863, 1876.
*(Auction PSA 22.10.03 sold for
£550 plus comm.)*
Est. £700-950.

HN1858A
Dawn
(Without head-dress)
First Version (Model 981)
Designer L. Harradine.
Date 1938 - 1949.
24.5cm (9.75ins) high.
Pale green.
Other colourways: HN1858.
Est. £700-950.

HN1863
Jasmine
First Version
Designer L. Harradine.
Date 1938 - 49.
19cm (7.5ins) high.
Pale blue, green and white.
Other colourways:
HN1862, 1876.
Est. £700-900.

HN1859
Tildy
Designer L. Harradine.
Date 1934 - 39.
14cm (5.5ins) high.
Red, green and pink.
Other colourways:
HN1576.
Est. £600-900.

HN1864
Sweet and Fair
Designer L. Harradine.
Date 1938 - 49.
19cm (7.5ins) high.
Pink, blue, green and white.
Other colourways: HN1865.
Est. £1000-1400.

HN1865
Sweet and Fair
Designer L. Harradine.
Date 1938 - 49.
19cm (7.5ins) high.
Pale green, orange, white and blue.
Other colourways: HN1864.
Est. £1000-1400.

HN1870
Little Lady Make Believe
Designer L. Harradine.
Date 1938 - 49.
15cm (6ins) high.
Red, blue and green.
Est. £300-400.

HN1866
Wedding Morn
First Version
Designer L. Harradine.
Date 1938 - 49.
26.5cm (10.5ins) high.
Cream and yellow.
Other colourways: HN1867.
Est. £1300-1700.

HN1871
Annabella
Designer L. Harradine.
Date 1938 - 49.
12cm (4.75ins) high.
Pink, blue and green.
Other colourways:
HN1872, 1875.
Est. £450-600.

HN1867
Wedding Morn
First Version.
Designer L. Harradine.
Date 1938 - 49.
26.5cm (10.5ins) high.
Cream, red and yellow.
Other colourways: HN1866.
Est. £1300-1700.

HN1872
Annabella
Designer L. Harradine.
Date 1938 - 49.
12cm (4.75ins) high.
Blue, green and white.
Other colourways:
HN1871, 1875.
Est. £450-600.

HN1868
Serena
Designer L. Harradine.
Date 1938 - 49.
28cm (11ins) high.
Pink, blue and red.
Est. £500-650.

HN1873
Granny's Heritage
Designer L. Harradine.
Date 1938 - 49.
16cm (6.25ins) high.
Pink, green, grey and white.
Other colourways:
HN1874, 2031.
Est. £450-600.

HN1869
Dryad of the Pines
Designer R. Garbe.
Date 1938 - 49.
58.5cm (23ins) high.
Ivory and gold.
Extremely rare.

HN1874
Granny's Heritage
Designer L. Harradine.
Date 1938 - 49.
16cm (6.25ins) high.
Blue, brown and green.
Other colourways:
HN1873, 2031.
Est. £500-650.

HN1875
Annabella
Designer L. Harradine.
Date 1938 - 49.
12cm (4.75ins) high.
Red and white.
Other colourways:
HN1871, 1872.
Est. £500-650.

HN1880
The Lambeth Walk
Designer L. Harradine.
Date 1938 - 49.
25.5cm (10ins) high.
Blue, red and green.
Other colourways: HN1881.
Est. £1250-1750.

HN1876
Jasmine
First Version
Designer L. Harradine.
Date 1938 - 49.
19cm (7.5ins) high.
Blue, pink and green.
Other colourways:
HN1862, 1863.
Est. £700-1000.

HN1881
The Lambeth Walk
Designer L. Harradine.
Date 1938 - 49.
25.5cm (10ins) high.
Orange, pink and green.
Other colourways: HN1880.
Est. £1250-1750.

HN1877
Jean
First Version (Model 1000)
Designer L. Harradine.
Date 1938 - 49.
18.5cm (7.25ins) high.
Purple, pink and green.
Other colourways:
HN1878, 2032.
Est. £300-400.

HN1882
Nell Gwynn
Designer L. Harradine.
Date 1938 - 49.
16.5cm (6.5ins) high.
Orange, blue and white.
Other colourways: HN1887.
Est. £700-1000.

HN1878
Jean
First Version (Model 1000)
Designer L. Harradine.
Date 1938 - 49.
18.5cm (7.25ins) high.
Green with red shawl.
Other colourways:
HN1877, 2032.
Est. £250-330.

HN1883
Prudence
Designer L. Harradine.
Date 1938 - 49.
17cm (6.75ins) high.
Blue and white.
Other colourways: HN1884.
Est. £450-600.

HN1879
Bon Jour
Designer L. Harradine.
Date 1938 - 49.
17cm (6.75ins) high.
Green with red shawl.
Other colourways: HN1888.
Est. £700-900.

HN1884
Prudence
Designer L. Harradine.
Date 1938 - 49.
17cm (6.75ins) high.
Pink and white.
Other colourways: HN1883.
Est. £450-600.

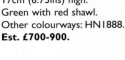

HN1885
Nadine
First Version
Designer L. Harradine.
Date 1938 - 49.
18.5cm (7.25ins) high.
Turquoise and green.
Other colourways: HN1886.
Est. £550-750.

HN1890
Lambing Time
First Version
Designer W.M. Chance.
Date 1938 - 81.
23.5cm (9.25ins) high.
Light and dark brown and white.
*(Auction PSA 23.6.04 sold for £110
plus comm)*
Est. £130-180.

HN1886
Nadine
First Version
Designer L. Harradine.
Date 1938 - 49.
18.5cm (7.25ins) high.
Pink and blue.
Other colourways: HN1885.
Est. £550-750.

HN1891
Pecksniff
Second Version (Model 385)
Designer L. Harradine.
Date 1938 - 52.
18cm (7ins) high.
Black, tan and white.
Other colourways: HN553.
Series: Dickens (Series Two)
Est. £200-300.

HN1887
Nell Gwynn
Designer L. Harradine.
Date 1938 - 49.
16.5cm (6.5ins) high.
Green, white and peach.
Other colourways: HN1882.
Est. £750-1000.

HN1892
Uriah Heep
Second Version (Model 384)
Designer L. Harradine.
Date 1938 - 52.
18.5cm (7.25ins) high.
Black and white.
Other colourways: HN554.
Series: Dickens (Series Two)
Est. £200-300.

HN1888
Bon Jour
Designer L. Harradine.
Date 1938 - 49.
17cm (6.75ins) high.
Red and green.
Other colourways: HN1879.
Est. £700-900.

HN1893
Fat Boy
Second Version (Model 381)
Designer L. Harradine.
Date 1938 - 52.
18cm (7ins) high.
Blue, white and cream.
Other colourways: HN555.
Series: Dickens (Series Two)
Est. £200-300.

HN1889
Goody Two Shoes
Designer L. Harradine.
Date 1938 - 49.
12cm (4.75ins) high.
Purple, white and green.
Other colourways:
HN1905, 2037.
Est. £250-300.

HN1894
Mr. Pickwick
Second Version (Model 379)
Designer L. Harradine.
Date 1938 - 52.
18cm (7ins) high.
Blue, cream and tan.
Other colourways: HN556.
Series: Dickens (Series Two)
Est. £200-300.

HN1895
Mr. Micawber
Second Version (Model 380)
Designer L. Harradine.
Date 1938 - 52.
18cm (7ins) high.
Black, white and tan.
Other colourways: HN557.
Series: Dickens (Series Two)
Est. £200-300.

HN1900
Midsummer Noon
Designer L. Harradine.
Date 1939 - 49.
11.5cm (4.5ins) high.
Blue, cream and white.
Other colourways:
HN1899, 2033.
Est. £900-1200.

HN1896
Sairey Gamp
Second Version (Model 382)
Designer L. Harradine.
Date 1938 - 52.
18cm (7ins) high.
Black, white and green.
Other colourways: HN558.
Series: Dickens (Series Two)
Est. £250-350.

HN1901
Penelope
Designer L. Harradine.
Date 1939 - 75.
17cm (6.75ins) high.
Red, green and white.
Other colourways: HN1902.
(Auction PSA 23.6.04 sold for
£150 plus comm.)
(Ebay 10.7.04 sold £155)
Est. £180-280.

HN1897
Miss Fortune
Designer L. Harradine.
Date 1938 - 49.
14.5cm (5.75ins) high.
Pink, blue, yellow and white.
Other colourways: HN1898.
Est. £350-500.

HN1902
Penelope
Designer L. Harradine.
Date 1939 - 49.
17cm (6.75ins) high.
Lilac, green, white and cream.
Other colourways: HN1901.
Est. £700-1000.

HN1898
Miss Fortune
Designer L. Harradine.
Date 1938 - 49.
14.5cm (5.75ins) high.
Blue, yellow and white.
Other colourways: HN1897.
Est. £400-600.

HN1903
Rhythm
Designer L. Harradine.
Date 1939 - 49.
17cm (6.75ins) high.
Pink.
Other colourways:
HN1904.
Est. £1350-1800.

HN1899
Midsummer Noon
Designer L. Harradine.
Date 1939 - 49.
11.5cm (4.5ins) high.
Pink, white and cream.
Other colourways:
HN1900. 2033.
Est. £350-500.

HN1904
Rhythm
Designer L. Harradine.
Date 1939 - 49.
17cm (6.75ins) high.
Blue.
Other colourways:
HN1903.
Est. £1650-2000.

HN1905
Goody Two Shoes
Designer L. Harradine.
Date 1939 - 49.
12cm (4.75ins) high.
Pink skirt, red overdress.
Other colourways:
HN1889, 2037.
Est. £95-150.

HN1910
Honey
Designer L. Harradine.
Date 1939 - 49.
17cm (6.75ins) high.
Blue and white.
Other colourways:
HN1909, 1963.
Est. £400-500.

HN1906
Lydia
First Version
Designer L. Harradine.
Date 1939 - 49.
11cm (4.25ins) high.
Pink and orange.
Other colourways:
HN1907, 1908.
Est. £250-350.

HN1911
Autumn Breezes
First Version (Model 1027)
Designer L. Harradine.
Date 1939 - 76.
18cm (7ins) high.
Green, lilac and pink.
Other colourways: HN1913,
1934, 2131, 2147, 3736.
(Ebay 11.6.04 sold for £85)
Est. £90-130.

HN1907
Lydia
First Version
Designer L. Harradine.
Date 1939 - 49.
11cm (4.25ins) high.
Green and white.
Other colourways:
HN1906, 1908.
Est. £250-350.

HN1912
Old Balloon Seller and Bulldog
Designer L. Harradine.
Date 1939 - 49.
18cm (7ins) high.
Colour not known.
Other colourways: HN1791.
Extremely rare.

HN1908
Lydia
First Version
Designer L. Harradine.
Date 1939 - 95.
11cm (4.25ins) high.
Red and white.
Other colourways:
HN1906, 1907.
(Auction W&H 27.9.04 sold £47 plus comm.)
Est. £60-90.

HN1913
Autumn Breezes
First Version (Model 1027)
Designer L. Harradine.
Date 1939 - 71.
18cm (7ins) high.
Light yellow-green and blue with green bonnet.
Other colourways: HN1911,
1934, 2131, 2147, 3736.
Est. £100-130.

HN1909
Honey
Designer L. Harradine.
Date 1939 - 49.
17cm (6.75ins) high.
Pink, red, blue and white.
Other colourways:
HN1910, 1963.
Est. £200-300.

HN1914
Paisley Shawl
Second Version (Model 1030)
Designer L. Harradine.
Date 1939 - 49.
16.5cm (6.5ins) high.
Light green dress with red shawl.
Other colourways: HN1988.
Est. £150-200.

HN1915
Veronica
Second Version (Model 1031)
Designer L. Harradine.
Date 1939 - 49.
14.5cm (5.75ins) high.
Red and cream with pale
green trimmings.
Est. £160-240.

HN1920
Windflower
Second Version (Model 977)
Designer L. Harradine.
Date 1939 - 49.
28cm (11ins) high.
Red, cream, pink and yellow.
Other colourways: HN1939.
Est. £1320-1750.

HN1916
Janet
Second Version (Model 1032)
Designer L. Harradine.
Date 1939 - 49.
12.5cm (5ins) high.
Pink and white dress with
blue bodice.
Other colourways: HN1964.
*(Auction PSA 11.8.04 sold £85
plus comm.)*
Est. £100-150.

HN1921
Roseanna
Designer L. Harradine.
Date 1940 - 49.
20.5cm (8ins) high.
Sage green, blue and yellow.
Other colourways: HN1926.
Est. £835-1100.

HN1917
Meryll
Designer L. Harradine.
Date 1939 - 40.
17cm (6.75ins) high.
Red jacket and green skirt.
Other colourways:
'Toinette' HN1940.
Est. £1300-1800.

HN1922
Spring Morning
First Version
Designer L. Harradine.
Date 1940 - 73.
18.5cm (7.25ins) high.
Pink overdress with
aqua-blue skirt.
Other colourways: HN1923.
Est. £105-160.

HN1918
Sweet Suzy
Designer L. Harradine.
Date 1939 - 49.
16.5cm (6.5ins) high.
Pink overdress with
green skirt.
Est. £550-750.

HN1923
Spring Morning
First Version
Designer L. Harradine.
Date 1940 - 49.
18.5cm (7.25ins) high.
Green and cream.
Other colourways: HN1922.
Est. £350-550.

HN1919
Kate Hardcastle
Designer L. Harradine.
Date 1939 - 49.
21cm (8.25ins) high.
Red, white and green.
Other colourways: HN1718,
1719, 1734, 1861, 2028.
Est. £750-1000.

HN1924
Fiona
First Version (Model 1040)
Designer L. Harradine.
Date 1940 - 49.
14.5cm (5.75ins) high.
Pink dress with lilac jacket.
Other colourways:
HN1925, 1933.
Est. £500-700.

HN1925
Fiona
First Version (Model 1040)
Designer L. Harradine.
Date 1940 - 49.
14.5cm (5.75ins) high.
Cream-white dress and
lilac jacket.
Other colourways:
HN1924, 1933.
Est. £500-700.

HN1930
Marguerite
Designer L. Harradine.
Date 1940 - 49.
20.5cm (8ins) high.
Lilac, purple and white.
Other colourways: HN1928,
1929, 1946.
Est. £650-850.

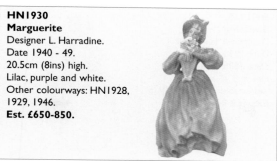

HN1926
Roseanna
Designer L. Harradine.
Date 1940 - 59.
20.5cm (8ins) high.
Red and pink.
Other colourways: HN1921.
Est. £200-300.

HN1931
Meriel
Designer L. Harradine.
Date 1940 - 49.
18.5cm (7.25ins) high.
Lemon and pink.
Other colourways: HN1932.
Est. £950-1250.

HN1927
The Awakening
First Version (Model 1043)
Designer L. Harradine.
Date 1940 - 49.
26cm (10.25ins) high.
Pale pink.
Est. £1500-1900.

HN1932
Meriel
Designer L. Harradine.
Date 1940 - 49.
18.5cm (7.25ins) high.
Green, blue and white.
Other colourways: HN1931.
Est. £950-1300

HN1928
Marguerite
Designer L. Harradine.
Date 1940 - 59.
20.5cm (8ins) high.
Pink.
Other colourways: HN1929,
1930, 1946.
Est. £200-300.

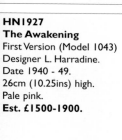

HN1933
Fiona
First Version (Model 1040)
Designer L. Harradine.
Date 1940 - 49.
14.5cm (5.75ins) high.
Multicoloured.
Other colourways:
HN1924, 1925.
(Ebay 25.4.04
sold £550)
Est. £550-750.

HN1929
Marguerite
Designer L. Harradine.
Date 1940 - 49.
20.5cm (8ins) high.
Pink and yellow.
Other colourways: HN1928,
1930, 1946.
Est. £800-1100.

HN1934
Autumn Breezes
First Version (Model 1027)
Designer L. Harradine.
Date 1940 to date.
18cm (7ins) high.
Red and white.
Other colourways: HN1911,
1913, 2131, 2147, 3736.
(Ebay 3.10.04 sold £72)
(Auction PSA 23.6.04. sold for £70)
Est. £80-120.

HN1935
Sweeting
Designer L. Harradine.
Date 1940 - 73.
15cm (6ins) high.
Pink and cream.
Other colourways: HN1938.
Est. £60-80.

HN1936
Miss Muffet
Designer L. Harradine.
Date 1940 - 67.
14cm (5.5ins) high.
Red and white.
Other colourways: HN1937.
(Auction PSA 23.6.04. sold for £70)
(Ebay 5.6.04. sold for £70)
Est. £80-120.

HN1937
Miss Muffet
Designer L. Harradine.
Date 1940 - 52.
14cm (5.5ins) high.
Green and white.
Other colourways: HN1936.
Est. £160-210.

HN1938
Sweeting
Designer L. Harradine.
Date 1940 - 49.
15cm (6ins) high.
Purple and red
patterned dress.
Other colourways: HN1935.
Est. £200-280.

HN1939
Windflower
Second Version (Model 977)
Designer L. Harradine.
Date 1940 - 49.
28cm (11ins) high.
Pink patterned skirt with red top.
Other colourways: HN1920.
Est. £1300-1750.

HN1940
Toinette
Designer L. Harradine.
Date 1940 - 49.
17cm (6.75ins) high.
Red, white and pink.
Other colourways:
'Meryll' HN1917.
Est. £900-1250.

HN1941
Peggy
Designer L. Harradine.
Date 1940 - 49.
12.5cm (5ins) high.
Red and white.
Other colourways: HN2038
(minor glaze difference)
Est. £80-120.

HN1942
Pyjams
Designer L. Harradine.
Date 1940 - 49.
13cm (5.25ins) high.
Pink and blue.
Est. £500-700.

HN1943
Veronica
First Version (Model 751)
Designer L. Harradine.
Date 1940 - 49.
20.5cm (8ins) high.
Red dress and blue hat
and trimmings.
Other colourways: HN1517,
1519, 1650.
Est. £600-800.

HN1944
Daydreams
Designer L. Harradine.
Date 1940 - 49.
14cm (5.5ins) high.
Red, white and blue.
Other colourways:
HN1731, 1732.
Est. £450-650.

HN1945
Spring Flowers
Designer L. Harradine.
Date 1940 - 49.
18.5cm (7.25ins) high.
Red, white and green.
Other colourways: HN1807.
Est. £650-850.

HN1950
Claribel
Designer L. Harradine.
Date 1940 - 49.
12cm (4.75ins) high.
Pink, white and purple.
Other colourways: HN1951.
Est. £240-320.

HN1946
Marguerite
Designer L. Harradine.
Date 1940 - 49.
20.5cm (8ins) high.
Pink dress with green bonnet.
Other colourways: HN1928,
1929, 1930.
Est. £825-1100.

HN1951
Claribel
Designer L. Harradine.
Date 1940 - 49.
12cm (4.75ins) high.
Red, white and pink.
Other colourways: HN1950.
Est. £240-320.

HN1947
June
First Version (Model 890)
Designer L. Harradine.
Date 1940 - 49.
19cm (7.5ins) high.
Red and white.
Other colourways: HN1690,
1691, 2027.
Est. £600-800.

HN1952
Irene
Designer L. Harradine.
Date 1940 - 50.
17cm (6.75ins) high.
Purple, white and blue.
Other colourways:
HN1621, 1697.
Est. £600-800.

HN1948
Lady Charmian
Designer L. Harradine.
Date 1940 - 73.
19.5cm (7.75ins) high.
Green and white dress
with red shawl.
Other colourways: HN1949.
Est. £120-160.

HN1953
The Orange Lady
Designer L. Harradine.
Date 1940 - 75.
22cm (8.75ins) high.
Green, brown and orange.
Other colourways: HN1759.
(Auction PSA 23.6.04. sold for £85
plus comm.)
Est. £100-140.

HN1949
Lady Charmian
Designer L. Harradine.
Date 1940 - 75.
19.5cm (7.75ins) high.
Red and white dress with
green shawl.
Other colourways: HN1948.
(Auction PSA 23.6.04. sold
for £75 and W&H 27.9.04 sold
£80 plus comm.)
Est. £100-150.

HN1954
The Balloon Man
Designer L. Harradine.
Date 1940 to date.
19cm (7.5ins) high.
Black, red and grey, with
multicoloured balloons.
(Royal Doulton web price £175)
(Ebay 29.9.04. sold for £77)
(Auction W&H 27.9.04 sold
£65 plus comm.)
Est. £80-160.

HN1955
Lavinia
Designer L. Harradine.
Date 1940 - 79.
12.5cm (5ins) high.
Red and white.
(Auction PSA 1.9.04 sold £40 plus comm.)
Est. £50-85.

HN1960
The Choice
Designer L. Harradine.
Date 1941 - 49.
18cm (7ins) high.
Purple and white.
Other colourways: HN1959.
Est. £900-1275.

HN1956
Chloe
First Version
Designer L. Harradine.
Date 1940 - 49.
15cm (6ins) high.
Red skirt with green ribbon.
Other colourways: HN1470,
1476, 1479, 1498, 1765.
Est. £390-520.

HN1961
Daisy
First Version
Designer L. Harradine.
Date 1941 - 49.
9cm (3.5ins) high.
Pink.
Other colourways: HN1575.
Est. £320-420.

HN1957
The New Bonnet
Designer L. Harradine.
Date 1940 - 49.
18cm (7ins) high.
Red, white and purple.
Other colourways: HN1728.
Est. £660-880.

HN1962
Genevieve
Designer L. Harradine.
Date 1941 - 75.
18cm (7ins) high.
Red and white.
Est. £165-220.

HN1958
Lady April
Designer L. Harradine.
Date 1940 - 59.
18cm (7ins) high.
Red, purple, white and blue.
Other colourways: HN1965.
(Ebay 19.8.04 sold £122)
Est. £150-200.

HN1963
Honey
Designer L. Harradine.
Date 1941 - 49.
17cm (6.75ins) high.
Red, yellow, blue and green.
Other colourways:
HN1909. 1910.
Est. £540-720.

HN1959
The Choice
Designer L. Harradine.
Date 1941 - 49.
18cm (7ins) high.
Red and pink.
Other colourways: HN1960.
Est. £900-1275.

HN1964
Janet
Second Version (Model 1032)
Designer L. Harradine.
Date 1941 - 49.
12.5cm (5ins) high.
Pink and white.
Other colourways: HN1916.
Est. £300-400.

HN1965
Lady April
Designer L. Harradine.
Date 1941 - 49.
18cm (7ins) high.
Green, blue, yellow and pink.
Other colourways: HN1958.
Est. £300-500.

HN1966
An Orange Vendor
Designer C.J. Noke.
Date 1941 - 49.
16cm (6.25ins) high.
Purple, black and orange.
Other colourways: HN72,
508, 521.
Est. £450-650.

HN1967
Lady Betty
Designer L. Harradine.
Date 1941 - 51.
16.5cm (6.5ins) high.
Red and blue.
Est. £200-300.

HN1968
Madonna of the Square
Designer P. Stabler.
Date 1941 - 49.
18cm (7ins) high.
Green.
Other colourways: HN10,
10A, 11, 14, 27, 326, 573, 576,
594, 613, 764, 1969, 2034.
Est. £700-900.

HN1969
Madonna of the Square
Designer P. Stabler.
Date 1941 - 49.
17.8cm (7ins) high.
Lilac.
Other colourways: HN10,
10A, 11, 14, 27, 326, 573, 576,
594, 613, 764, 1968, 2034.
Est. £700-900.

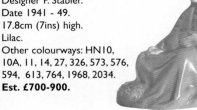

HN1970
Milady
Designer L. Harradine.
Date 1941 - 49.
16.5cm (6.5ins) high.
Pink and white.
Est. £650-850.

HN1971
Springtime
First Version (Model 459)
Designer L. Harradine.
Date 1941 - 49.
15cm (6ins) high.
Pink, green and blue.
Est. £600-850.

HN1972
Regency Beau
Designer H. Fenton.
Date 1941 - 49.
20.5cm (8ins) high.
Pink, white and green.
Est. £650-900.

HN1973
The Corinthian
Designer H. Fenton.
Date 1941 - 49.
19.5cm (7.75ins) high.
Green, red, cream and blue.
Est. £650-900.

HN1974
Forty Winks
Designer H. Fenton.
Date 1945 - 73.
17cm (6.75ins) high.
Green, white, red and tan.
(Made as a pair with
HN2094 'Uncle Ned')
*(Auction PSA 1.9.04 sold £80
plus comm.)*
Est. £100-150.

HN1975
The Shepherd
Forth Version (Model 1190)
Designer H. Fenton.
Date 1945 - 75.
21.5cm (8.5ins) high.
Tan, white and brown.
(Auction PSA 23.6.04 sold for £90
plus comm.)
Est. £100-150.

HN1980
Gwynneth
Designer L. Harradine.
Date 1945 - 52.
18cm (7ins) high.
Red and white.
Est. £175-225.

HN1976
Easter Day
Designer L. Harradine.
Date 1945 - 51.
19cm (7.5ins) high.
Green, blue and white.
Other colourways: HN2039.
Est. £275-350.

HN1981
The Ermine Coat
Designer L. Harradine.
Date 1945 - 67.
17cm (6.75ins) high.
Red, white and black.
(Auction PSA 22.10.03 sold
for £95 plus comm.)
Est. £110-150.

HN1977
Her Ladyship
Designer L. Harradine.
Date 1945 - 59.
18cm (7ins) high.
Green, red, white and cream.
Est. £200-250.

HN1982
Sabbath Morn
Designer L. Harradine.
Date 1945 - 59.
18.5cm (7.25ins) high.
Red, yellow and green.
Est. £125-175.

HN1978
Bedtime
First Version (Model 1214)
Designer L. Harradine.
Date 1945 - 97.
14cm (5.5ins) high.
White with black base.
Other colourways: HN2219.
(Auction PSA 23.6.04 sold for £28
plus comm.)
(Ebay 28.5.04 sold for £34)
Est. £35-50.

HN1983
Rosebud
Second Version (Model 1174)
Designer L. Harradine.
Date 1945 - 52.
19cm (7.5ins) high.
Pink, red and green.
(Auction PSA 1.9.04 sold £190
plus comm.)
Est. £240-350.

HN1979
Gollywog
Designer L. Harradine.
Date 1945 - 59.
14cm (5.5ins) high.
White, blue, red and green.
Other colourways: HN2040.
Est. £450-600.

HN1984
The Patchwork Quilt
Designer L. Harradine.
Date 1945 - 59.
15cm (6ins) high.
Multicoloured.
Est. £150-200.

HN1985
Darling
Second Version (Model 1264)
Designer C. Vyse.
Date 1946 - 97.
13cm (5.25ins) high.
White with black base.
Other colourways: HN3613.
(Auction PSA 11.8.04 sold for £25 plus comm.)
(Ebay 9.6.04 sold for £19)
Est. £30-50.

HN1990
Mary Jane
Designer L. Harradine.
Date 1947 - 52.
19cm (7.5ins) high.
Pink and white.
Est. £200-300.

HN1986
Diana
First Version (Model 897)
Designer L. Harradine.
Date 1946 - 75.
14.5cm (5.75ins) high.
Red, blue and white.
Other colourways:
HN1716, 1717.
Est. £80-100.

HN1991
Market Day
Designer L. Harradine.
Date 1947 - 55.
18.5cm (7.25ins) high.
Pink, white, blue and yellow.
Other colourways:
'A Country Lass' HN1991A
Est. £100-150.

HN1987
Paisley Shawl
First Version (Model 660)
Designer L. Harradine.
Date 1946 - 59.
23cm (9ins) high.
Red, blue and cream.
Other colourways: HN1392,
1460, 1707, 1739.
(Ebay 7.9.04 sold £149)
Est. £150-200.

HN1991A
A Country Lass
Designer L. Harradine.
Date 1975 - 81.
18.5cm (7.25ins) high.
Brown, white and blue.
Other colourways:
'Market Day' HN1991.
(Auction PSA 10.3.04 sold for £60 plus comm.)
Est. £75-120.

HN1988
Paisley Shawl
Second Version (Model 1030)
Designer L. Harradine.
Date 1946 - 75.
16.5cm (6.5ins) high.
Red, white and pink.
Other colourways: HN1914.
Est. £85-110.

HN1992
Christmas Morn
First Version (Model 1230)
Designer M. Davies.
Date 1947 - 96.
18cm (7ins) high.
Red and white.
(Auction Charterhouse 23.4.04 sold for £60 plus comm.)
(Ebay 30.9.04 sold £52)
Est. £70-115.

HN1989
Margaret
First Version (Model 1285)
Designer L. Harradine.
Date 1947 - 59.
18.5cm (7.25ins) high.
Red, white and green.
Est. £175-225.

HN1993
Griselda
Designer L. Harradine.
Date 1947 - 53.
14cm (5.5ins) high.
Lilac, white, green and cream.
Est. £200-300.

HN1994
Karen
First Version (Model 1237)
Designer L. Harradine.
Date 1947 - 55.
20.5cm (8ins) high.
Red, white and green.
Est. £250-350.

HN1999
Collinette
Designer L. Harradine.
Date 1947 - 49.
18.5cm (7.25ins) high.
Cream and red.
Other colourways: HN1998.
Est. £280-380.

HN1995
Olivia
First Version (Model 1267)
Designer L. Harradine.
Date 1947 - 51.
19cm (7.5ins) high.
Green, red, white and blue.
Est. £300-400.

HN2000
Jacqueline
First Version (Model 1234)
Designer L. Harradine.
Date 1947 - 51.
18.5cm (7.25ins) high.
Lilac and white.
Other colourways: HN2001.
Est. £250-340.

HN1996
Prue
Designer L. Harradine.
Date 1947 - 55.
17cm (6.75ins) high.
White, red and black.
Est. £200-250.

HN2001
Jacqueline
First Version (Model 1234)
Designer L. Harradine.
Date 1947 - 51.
18.5cm (7.25ins) high.
Pink and white.
Other colourways: HN2000.
Est. £250-300.

HN1997
Belle o' the Ball
Designer R. Asplin.
Date 1947 - 79.
15cm (6ins) high.
Red, brown
and white.
*(Auction PSA 1.9.04
sold £170
plus comm.)*
Est. £190-300.

HN2002
Bess
Designer L. Harradine.
Date 1947 - 69.
18.5cm (7.25ins) high.
Cream, red and white,
Other colourways: HN2003.
*(Ebay 10.6.04 sold £102)
(Auction PSA 11.8.04 sold £85
plus comm.)*
Est. £120-180.

HN1998
Collinette
Designer L. Harradine.
Date 1947 - 49.
18.5cm (7.25ins) high.
Cream and turquoise.
Other colourways: HN1999.
Est. £280-380.

HN2003
Bess
Designer L. Harradine.
Date 1947 - 50.
18.5cm (7.25ins) high.
Pink, red, purple and white.
Other colourways: HN2002.
Est. £300-400.

HN2004
A'Courting
Designer L. Harradine.
Date 1947 - 53.
18.5cm (7.25ins) high.
Black, white, red and grey.
Est. £250-300.

HN2009
Eleanor of Provence
Designer M. Davies.
Date 1948 - 53.
24cm (9.5ins) high.
Purple, green, white and red.
Series: Period Figures in
English History.
Est. £300-350.

HN2005
Henrietta Maria
First Version
Designer M. Davies.
Date 1948 - 53.
23.5cm (9.25ins) high.
Yellow overskirt and red skirt.
Series: Period Figures in
English History.
Est. £300-350.

HN2010
The Young Miss Nightingale
Designer M. Davies
Date 1948 - 53.
23cm (9ins) high.
Green, red, yellow and orange.
Series: Period Figures in
English History.
Est. £300-450.

HN2006
The Lady Anne Nevill
Designer M. Davies.
Date 1948 - 53.
23.5cm (9.5ins) high.
Purple, orange and white.
Series: Period Figures in
English History.
Est. £350-450.

HN2011
Matilda
Designer M. Davies.
Date 1948 - 53
23cm (9ins) high.
Purple, red and orange.
Series: Period Figures in
English History.
Est. £300-350.

HN2007
Mrs. Fitzherbert
Designer M. Davies.
Date 1948 - 53.
23cm (9ins) high.
Yellow, blue, red and cream.
Series: Period Figures in
English History.
Est. £250-350.

HN2012
Margaret of Anjou
First Version
Designer M. Davies.
Date 1948 - 53.
23.5cm (9.25ins) high.
Yellow, green and white.
Series: Period Figures in
English History.
Est. £350-450.

HN2008
Philippa of Hainault
First Version
Designer M. Davies.
Date 1948 - 53.
24cm (9.5ins) high.
Blue, green and red.
Series: Period Figures in
English History.
Est. £300-350.

HN2013
Angelina
Designer L. Harradine.
Date 1948 - 51.
18cm (7ins) high.
Red and white.
Est. £500-650.

HN2014
Jane
First Version (Model 1257)
Designer L. Harradine.
Date 1948 - 51.
16cm (6.25ins) high.
Red, pink and white.
Est. £600-850.

HN2019
Minuet
Designer M. Davies.
Date 1949 - 71.
18.5cm (7.25ins) high.
White and blue.
Other colourways: HN2066.
Est. £140-180.

HN2015
Sir Walter Raleigh
Designer L. Harradine.
Date 1948 - 55.
29cm (11.5ins) high.
Purple and orange.
Other colourways:
HN1742, 1751.
(Same colours as HN1751 but
with a minor glaze difference)
Est. £300-400.

HN2020
Deidre
Designer L. Harradine.
Date 1949 - 55.
18cm (7ins) high.
Pink, blue and white.
Est. £225-300.

HN2016
A Jester
First Version (Model 170)
Designer C.J. Noke.
Date 1949 - 97.
25.5cm (10ins) high.
Mauve, brown and orange.
Other colourways: HN45, 71,
71A, 320, 367, 412, 426, 446, 552,
616, 627, 1295, 1702, 3922.
(Auction Bonhams 27.07.04 sold £153 and
PSA 23.6.04 sold £135) **Est. £150-250.**

HN2021
Blithe Morning
Designer L. Harradine.
Date 1949 - 71.
18cm (7ins) high.
Mauve, cream, green and pink.
Other colourways: HN2065.
Est. £100-150.

HN2017
Silks and Ribbons
Designer L. Harradine.
Date 1949 - 2001.
16cm (6.25ins) high.
Green, white, orange and red.
(Auction PSA 23.6.04 sold for
£80 plus comm.)
Est. £100-150.

HN2022
Janice
First Version (Model 1314)
Designer M. Davies.
Date 1949 - 55.
18.5cm (7.25ins) high.
Cream, green and orange.
Other colourways: HN2165.
Est. £200-300.

HN2018
The Parson's Daughter
Designer H. Tittensor.
Date 1949 - 53.
25.5cm (10ins) high.
Multicoloured.
Other colourways: HN337, 338,
441, 564, 790, 1242, 1356.
Est. £300-400.

HN2023
Joan
First Version (Model 693)
Designer L. Harradine.
Date 1949 - 59.
14cm (5.5ins) high.
Blue and grey.
Other colourways: HN1422
(minor glaze difference)
(Ebay 11.6.04 sold £127)
Est. £130-180.

HN2024
Darby
Designer L. Harradine.
Date 1949 - 59.
14cm (5.5ins) high.
Pink, grey and blue.
Other colourways: HN1427
(minor glaze difference)
(Auction PSA 1.9.04 sold £180 plus comm.)
Est. £200-250.

HN2029
Windflower
First Version (Model 926)
Designer L. Harradine.
Date 1949 - 52.
18.5cm (7.25ins) high.
Pink, green and red.
Other colourways:
HN1763, 1764.
Est. £300-400.

HN2025
The Gossips
Designer L. Harradine.
Date 1949 - 67.
14.5cm (5.75ins) high.
Red, blue and cream.
Other colourways:
HN1426, 1429.
Est. £250-300.

HN2030
Memories
Designer L. Harradine.
Date 1949 - 59.
15cm (6ins) high.
White, pink and green.
Other colourways: HN1855,
1856, 1857.
(Ebay 25.5.04 sold £200)
Est. £200-300.

HN2026
Suzette
Designer L. Harradine.
Date 1949 - 59.
19cm (7.5ins) high.
Pink and white.
Other colourways: HN1487,
1577, 1585, 1696.
Est. £200-250.

HN2031
Granny's Heritage
Designer L. Harradine.
Date 1949 - 69.
16cm (6.25ins) high.
Lilac, yellow and green.
Other colourways:
HN1873, 1874.
Est. £300-400.

HN2027
June
First Version (Model 890)
Designer L. Harradine.
Date 1949 - 52.
19cm (7.5ins) high.
Yellow, pink and white.
Other colourways: HN1690,
1691, 1947.
Est. £250-350.

HN2032
Jean
First Version (Model 1000)
Designer L. Harradine.
Date 1949 - 59.
18.5cm (7.25ins) high.
Red, green and yellow.
Other colourways: HN1877, 1878.
(Auction PSA 22.10.03 sold for £110 plus comm.)
(Ebay 25.5.04 sold for £180)
Est. £200-250.

HN2028
Kate Hardcastle
Designer L. Harradine.
Date 1949 - 52.
21cm (8.25ins) high.
Green, white and red.
Other colourways: HN1718,
1719, 1734, 1861, 1919.
Est. £250-350.

HN2033
Midsummer Noon
Designer L. Harradine.
Date 1949 - 55.
11.5cm (4.5ins) high.
Pink, cream and red.
Other colourways:
HN1899, 1900.
Est. £300-450.

HN2034
Madonna of the Square
Designer P. Stabler.
Date 1949 - 51.
18cm (7ins) high.
Pale green.
Other colourways: HN10, 10A,
11, 14, 27, 326, 573, 576, 594,
613, 764, 1968, 1969.
Est. £350-450.

HN2039
Easter Day
Designer L. Harradine.
Date 1949 - 69.
19cm (7.5ins) high.
Multicoloured.
Other colourways: HN1976.
Est. £150-250.

HN2035
Pearly Boy
Second Version (Model 724)
Designer L. Harradine.
Date 1949 - 59.
14cm (5.5ins) high.
Brown, red and white.
(Auction PSA 6.8.03 sold for
£85 plus comm.)
Est. £100-150.

HN2040
Gollywog
Designer L. Harradine.
Date 1949 - 59.
14cm (5.5ins) high.
Blue, green and red.
Other colourways: HN1979.
Est. £150-250.

HN2036
Pearly Girl
Second Version (Model 723)
Designer L. Harradine.
Date 1949 - 59.
14cm (5.5ins) high.
Brown, orange and white.
(Auction PSA 6.8.03 sold for
£85 plus comm.)
Est. £100-150.

HN2041
The Broken Lance
Designer M. Davies.
Date 1949 - 75.
22cm (8.75ins) high.
White, blue, red and yellow.
Est. £250-350.

HN2037
Goody Two Shoes
Designer L. Harradine.
Date 1949 - 89.
12cm (4.75ins) high.
Red, white and pink.
Other colourways:
HN1889, 1905.
(Ebay 25.5.04 sold for £70)
Est. £70-120.

HN2042
Owd Willum
Designer L. Harradine.
Date 1949 - 73.
17cm (6.75ins) high.
Brown, green, tan and red.
(Auction PSA 1.9.04 sold
£110 plus comm.)
Est. £120-200.

HN2038
Peggy
Designer L. Harradine.
Date 1949 - 79.
12.5cm (5ins) high.
Red, orange and white.
Other colourways: HN1941
(minor glaze difference)
(Ebay 30.9.04 sold £48)
Est. £50-80.

HN2043
The Poacher
Designer L. Harradine.
Date 1949 - 59.
16cm (6.25ins) high.
Black, tan and brown.
Est. £150-200.

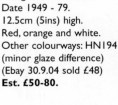

HN2044
Mary, Mary
Designer L. Harradine.
Date 1949 - 73.
12.5cm (5ins) high.
Pink, blue and green.
Series: Nursery Rhymes
(Series One)
(Ebay 3.10.04 sold £78)
Est. £80-120.

HN2049
Curly Locks
Designer M. Davies.
Date 1949 - 53.
11.5cm (4.5ins) high.
Pink blue and white.
Series: Nursery Rhymes
(Series One)
*(Auction PSA 1.9.04 sold
£190 plus comm.)*
Est. £220-300.

HN2045
She Loves Me Not
Designer L. Harradine.
Date 1949 - 62.
14cm (5ins) high.
Blue and green.
Series: Nursery Rhymes
(Series One)
Est. £100-140.

HN2050
Wee Willie Winkie
First Version (Model 1339)
Designer M. Davies.
Date 1949 - 53.
13cm (5.25ins) high.
Blue.
Series: Nursery Rhymes
(Series One)
Est. £150-200.

HN2046
He Loves Me
Designer L. Harradine.
Date 1949 - 62.
14cm (5.5ins) high.
Pink and green.
Series: Nursery Rhymes
(Series One)
Est. £100-140.

HN2051
St. George
Second Version (Model 1356)
Designer M. Davies
Date 1950 - 85.
18.5cm (7.25ins) high.
White, green, cream
and orange.
*(Auction PSA 3.12.03 sold
for £200 plus comm.)*
Est. £200-350.

HN2047
Once Upon a Time
Designer L. Harradine.
Date 1949 - 55.
11.5cm (4.5ins) high.
Pink, blue and green.
Series: Nursery Rhymes
(Series One)
Est. £250-300.

HN2052
Grandma
Designer L. Harradine.
Date 1950 - 59.
17cm (6.75ins) high.
Cream, red and blue.
Other colourways: HN2052A.
(Ebay 26.9.04 sold £170)
Est. £180-250.

HN2048
Mary Had a Little Lamb
Designer M. Davies.
Date 1949 - 88.
9cm (3.5ins) high.
Lilac and white.
Series: Nursery Rhymes
(Series One)
*(Auction PSA 10.3.04 sold for
£50 and W&H 27.9.04 sold
£57 plus comm.)*
Est. £65-110.

HN2052A
Grandma
Designer L. Harradine.
Date not known.
17cm (6.75ins) high.
Cream, red and brown.
Other colourways: HN2052.
Est. £200-250.

HN2053
The Gaffer
Designer L. Harradine.
Date 1950 - 59.
19cm (7.5ins) high.
Green, brown, red and orange.
Est. £175-250.

HN2057A
The Milkmaid
Second Version
Designer L. Harradine.
Date 1975 - 81.
17cm (6.75ins) high.
Brown, green and white.
Other colourways: 'The Jersey
Milkmaid' HN2057.
Est. £75-100.

HN2054
Falstaff
Second Version (Model 353)
Designer C.J. Noke.
Date 1950 - 92.
18cm (7ins) high.
Brown, cream and red.
Other colourways: HN618.
*(Auction PSA 23.6.04
sold £55 plus comm.)*
Est. £65-125.

HN2058
Hermione
Date 1950 - 52.
Designer M. Davies.
18.5cm (7.25ins) high.
Lilac, cream, white and red.
Est. £800-1100.

HN2055
The Leisure Hour
Designer M. Davies.
Date 1950 - 65.
17cm (6.75ins) high.
Brown, green and yellow.
(Ebay 25.7.04 sold £225)
Est. £200-300.

HN2059
The Bedtime Story
Designer L. Harradine.
Date 1950 - 96.
11.5cm (4.5ins) high.
Blue, pink and white.
*(Auction PSA 23.6.04 sold
£90 and W&H 27.9.04
sold £90 plus comm.)*
Est. £100-150.

HN2056
Susan
First Version (Model 1326)
Designer L. Harradine.
Date 1950 - 59.
18cm (7ins) high.
Lilac, pink and white.
(Ebay 26.5.04 sold £205)
Est. £200-300.

HN2060
Jack
Designer L. Harradine.
Date 1950 - 71.
14cm (5.5ins) high.
Green, black and white.
Series: Nursery Rhymes
(Series One)
Est. £90-140.

HN2057
The Jersey Milkmaid
Designer L. Harradine.
Date 1950 - 59.
17cm (6.75ins) high.
Red. blue and white.
Other colourways:
'The Milkmaid' HN2057A.
Est. £100-150.

HN2061
Jill
Designer L. Harradine.
Date 1950 - 71.
14cm (5.5ins) high.
Pink, green and white.
Series: Nursery Rhymes
(Series One)
Est. £90-140.

HN2062
Little Boy Blue
First Version (Model 1362)
Designer L. Harradine.
Date 1950 - 73.
14cm (5.5ins) high.
Blue and white.
Series: Nursery Rhymes
(Series One)
Est. £90-140.

HN2067
St. George
First Version (Model 191)
Designer S. Thorogood.
Date 1950 - 79.
40.5cm (16ins) high.
Red, purple, grey and white.
Other colourways: HN385,
386, 1800.
Est. £1000-1250.

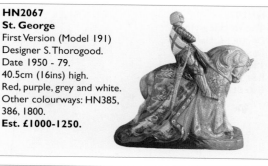

HN2063
Little Jack Horner
First Version (Model 1365)
Designer L. Harradine.
Date 1950 - 53.
11.5cm (4.5ins) high.
Red and white.
Series: Nursery Rhymes
(Series One)
Est. £300-400.

HN2068
Calumet
Designer C.J. Noke.
Date 1950 - 53.
15cm (6ins) high.
Green, blue, yellow and brown.
Other colourways: HN1428,
1689. (Minor glaze differences)
Est. £300-400.

HN2064
My Pretty Maid
Designer L. Harradine.
Date 1950 - 54.
14cm (5.5ins) high.
Turquoise, green and white.
Series: Nursery Rhymes
(Series One)
Est. £220-320.

HN2069
Farmer's Wife
First Version (Model 1221)
Designer L. Harradine.
Date 1951 - 55.
23.5cm (9.25ins) high.
Red, cream, green and brown.
Est. £300-400.

HN2065
Blithe Morning
Designer L. Harradine.
Date 1950 - 73.
18cm (7ins) high.
Red, blue and white.
Other colourways: HN2021.
*(Auction Charterhouse 24.4.04
sold £70 and PSA 1.9.04 sold
£60 plus comm.)*
(Ebay 10.6.04 sold £68)
Est. £80-140.

HN2070
Bridget
Designer L. Harradine.
Date 1951 - 73.
19.5cm (7.75ins) high.
Lilac, green, brown
and ogange.
*(Auction PSA 23.6.04
sold £160 plus comm.)*
(Ebay 10.7.04 sold £150)
Est. £180-250.

HN2066
Minuet
Designer M. Davies.
Date 1950 - 55.
18.5cm (7.25ins) high.
Red and white.
Other colourways: HN2019.
Est. £500-600.

HN2071
Bernice
Designer M. Davies.
Date 1951 - 53.
20.5cm (8ins) high.
Pink, blue and red.
Est. £500-700.

HN2072
The Rocking Horse
Designer L. Harradine.
Date 1951 - 53.
18cm (7ins) high.
Red, yellow, blue and white.
Est. £1400-2000.

HN2077
Rowena
Designer L. Harradine.
Date 1951 - 55.
19cm (7.5ins) high.
Red, lilac and pale green.
Est. £300-400.

HN2073
Vivienne
Designer L. Harradine.
Date 1951 - 67.
19.5cm (7.75ins) high.
Red, white and brown.
*(Auction PSA 23.6.04 sold
£95 plus comm.)*
Est. £120-170.

HN2078
Elfreda
Designer L. Harradine.
Date 1951 - 55.
18.5cm (7.25ins) high.
Purple, red and grey.
Est. £400-500.

HN2074
Marianne
First Version
Designer L. Harradine.
Date 1951 - 53.
18.5cm (7.25ins) high.
Red, blue and white.
Est. £500-700.

HN2079
Damaris
Designer M. Davies.
Date 1951 - 52.
19cm (7.5ins) high.
Green, purple, white and red.
Est. £800-1100.

HN2075
French Peasant
Designer L. Harradine.
Date 1951 - 55.
24cm (9.5ins) high.
Green, white and brown.
Est. £240-300.

HN2080
Jack Point
Designer C.J. Noke.
Date 1952 to date.
43cm (17ins) high.
Green, purple, blue and white.
Other colourways: HN85, 91, 99,
3920, 3925.
Series: Prestige.
(Royal Doulton web price £2750)
Retail £2750.

HN2076
Promenade
First Version (Model 1369)
Designer M. Davies.
Date 1951 - 53.
20.5cm (8ins) high.
Orange, white and blue.
*(Auction PSA 22.10.03
sold £810 plus comm.)*
Est. £1000-1500.

HN2081
Princess Badoura
First Version
Designer H. Tittensor, H.E. Stanton
and F. Van Allen Phillips.
Date 1952 to date.
51cm (20ins) high.
Pink, brown, gold and blue.
Other colourways: HN3921.
Series: Prestige.
(Royal Doulton web price £17,850)
Retail £17,850.

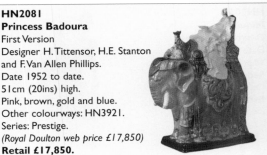

HN2082
The Moor
Designer C.J. Noke.
Date 1952 to date.
44.5cm (17.5ins) high.
Red, brown and black.
Other colourways: HN1308, 1366,
1425, 1657, 3642, 3926; Also known
as 'An Arab' HN33, 343, 378.
Series: Prestige.
(Auction PSA 22.10.03 sold £720 plus comm.)
(Royal Doulton web price £2250) **Est. £1000-1350.**

HN2088
Winter
Second Version (Model 1402)
Designer M. Davies.
Date 1952 - 59.
16cm (6.75ins) high.
Lilac, red and green.
Series: The Seasons
(Series Two)
Est. £180-250.

HN2084
King Charles
Designer C.J. Noke
and H. Tittensor.
Date 1952 - 92.
42.5cm (16.75ins) high.
Black, yellow and white.
Other colourways:
HN404, 3459.
*(Auction PSA 23.6.04
sold £710 plus comm.)*
Est. £800-1000.

HN2089
Judith
First Version (Model 1352)
Designer L. Harradine.
Date 1952 - 59.
17cm (6.75ins) high.
Red and pale blue.
Est. £180-250.

HN2085
Spring
Fourth Version (Model 1394)
Designer M. Davies.
Date 1952 - 59.
19.5cm (7.75ins) high.
Lilac, cream and green.
Series: The Seasons
(Series Two)
Est. £180-250.

HN2090
Midinette
Second Version (Model 1831)
Designer L. Harradine.
Date 1952 - 65.
18.5cm (7.25ins) high.
Pale blue, white and red.
Est. £150-200.

HN2086
Summer
Second Version (Model 1395)
Designer M. Davies.
Date 1952 - 59.
18.5cm (7.25ins) high.
Red, white, brown and green.
Series: The Seasons
(Series Two)
Est. £180-250.

HN2091
Rosemary
First Version (Model 1311)
Designer L. Harradine.
Date 1952 - 59.
18cm (7ins) high.
Red, white, blue and yellow.
Est. £255-350.

HN2087
Autumn
Second Version (Model 1400)
Designer M. Davies.
Date 1952 - 59.
18.5cm (7.25ins) high.
Red, lilac and green.
Series: The Seasons
(Series Two)
Est. £180-250.

HN2092
Sweet Maid
Second Version (Model 1325)
Designer L. Harradine.
Date 1952 - 55.
18.5cm (7.25ins) high.
Lilac and white.
Est. £250-300.

HN2093
Georgiana
Designer M. Davies.
Date 1952 - 55.
21.5cm (8.5ins) high.
Orange, white and blue.
Est. £800-1100.

HN2094
Uncle Ned
Designer H. Fenton.
Date 1952 - 65.
17cm (6.75ins) high.
Brown, green, cream and black.
(Made as a pair to HN1974
'Forty Winks')
Est. £150-200.

HN2095
Ibrahim
Designer C.J. Noke.
Date 1952 - 55.
19.5cm (7.75ins) high.
Pale brown, lemon and white.
Other colourways: 'The Emir'
HN1604, 1605.
Est. £250-300.

HN2096
Fat Boy
Third Version
(Adaption of Model 381)
Designer L. Harradine.
Date 1952 - 67.
18.5cm (7.25ins) high.
Blue, cream, green and yellow.
Series: Dickens (Series Three)
Est. £140-190.

HN2097
Mr. Micawber
Third Version
(Adaption of Model 380)
Designer L. Harradine.
Date 1952 - 67.
19cm (7.5ins) high.
Black, tan and orange.
Series: Dickens (Series Three)
Est. £140-190.

HN2098
Pecksniff
Third Version
(Adaption of Model 385)
Designer L. Harradine.
Date 1952 - 67.
18.5cm (7.25ins) high.
Black, orange and brown.
Series: Dickens (Series Three)
Est. £140-190.

HN2099
Mr. Pickwick
Third Version
(Adaption of Model 379)
Designer L. Harradine.
Date 1952 - 67.
19cm (7.5ins) high.
Black, tan and orange.
Series: Dickens (Series Three)
(Auction PSA 10.3.04 sold £130
plus comm.)
Est. £140-190.

HN2100
Sairey Gamp
Third Version
(Adaption of Model 382)
Designer L. Harradine.
Date 1952 - 67.
18.5cm (7.25ins) high.
Green, red and cream.
Series: Dickens (Series Three)
Est. £150-200.

HN2101
Uriah Heep
Third Version
(Adaption of Model 384)
Designer L. Harradine.
Date 1952 - 67.
18.5cm (7.25ins) high.
Black, green and yellow.
Series: Dickens (Series Three)
Est. £140-190.

HN2102
Pied Piper
First Version
Designer L. Harradine.
Date 1953 - 76.
22cm (8.75ins) high.
Red, black, cream and brown.
Other colourways: HN1215.
Est. £140-190.

HN2103
Mask Seller
Designer L. Harradine.
Date 1953 - 95.
21.5cm (8.5ins) high.
Green, black, yellow
and brown.
Other colourways: HN1361.
(Auction PSA 23.6.04 sold £150
plus comm.)
Est. £150-250.

HN2108
Baby Bunting
Designer M. Davies.
Date 1953 - 59.
13cm (5.25ins) high.
Brown, yellow and cream.
(Ebay 3.6.04 sold £80)
Est. £90-150.

HN2104
Abdullah
Designer L. Harradine.
Date 1953 - 62.
15cm (6ins) high.
Multicoloured.
Other colourways: HN1410.
(Auction PSA 23.6.04 sold
£150 plus comm.)
Est. £170-250.

HN2109
Wendy
Designer L. Harradine.
Date 1953 - 95.
12cm (4.75ins) high.
Pale blue and pink.
(Ebay 3.10.04 sold £70)
(Auction PSA 11.8.04 sold £35
plus comm.)
Est. £50-70.

HN2105
Bluebeard
Second Version (Model 745)
Designer L. Harradine.
Date 1953 - 92.
29cm (11.5ins) high.
Red, blue, purple and green.
Other colourways: HN1528.
(Auction PSA 22.10.03 sold £145
plus comm.)
Est. £160-220.

HN2110
Christmas Time
Designer M. Davies.
Date 1953 - 67.
18cm (7ins) high.
Red and white.
(Auction PSA 1.9.04 sold £160
plus comm.)
Est. £175-250.

HN2106
Linda
First Version (Model 1236)
Designer L. Harradine.
Date 1953 - 76.
12cm (4.75ins) high.
Red and white.
(Auction PSA 1.9.04 sold £80.
Brightwells 2.9.04 sold £115
plus comm.)
Est. £120-150.

HN2111
Betsy
Designer L. Harradine.
Date 1953 - 59.
18cm (7ins) high.
Lilac and white.
Est. £180-250.

HN2107
Valerie
First Version
Designer M. Davies.
Date 1953 - 95.
12.5cm (5ins) high.
Red, white and pink.
Other colourways: HN3620.
(Auction PSA 23.6.04 sold £30
plus comm.)
Est. £40-60.

HN2112
Carolyn
First Version (Model 1301)
Designer L. Harradine.
Date 1953 - 65.
18cm (7ins) high.
White, green, yellow and red.
(Ebay 27.7.04 sold £155)
Est. £150-225.

HN2113
Maytime
Designer L. Harradine.
Date 1953 - 67.
17cm (6.75ins) high.
Pink, blue and white.
Est. £120-175.

HN2118
Good King Wenceslas
First Version (Model 1444)
Designer M. Davies.
Date 1953 - 76.
23.5cm (9.25ins) high.
Orange, purple, brown and tan.
*(Auction PSA 1.9.04 sold £120
plus comm.)*
Est. £120-200.

HN2114
Sleepyhead
First Version
Designer M. Davies.
Date 1953 - 55.
12cm (4.75ins) high.
Orange, yellow, blue
and white.
Est. £1150-1500.

HN2119
Town Crier
First Version (Model 1424)
Designer M. Davies.
Date 1953 - 76.
21.5cm (8.5ins) high.
Red, green, yellow and mauve.
*(Auction PSA 23.6.04 sold £100
plus comm.)*
Est. £125-175.

HN2115
Coppelia
Designer M. Davies.
Date 1953 - 59.
18.5cm (7.25ins) high.
Red, blue and white.
Est. £300-400.

HN2120
Dinky Doo
Designer L. Harradine.
Date 1983 - 96.
12cm (4.75ins) high.
Pink, red and white.
Other colourways:
HN1678, 3618.
Est. £40-60.

HN2116
Ballerina
First Version
Designer M. Davies.
Date 1953 - 73.
19cm (7.5ins) high.
Lilac and purple.
Est. £130-180.

HN2121
Babie
Designer L. Harradine.
Date 1983 - 92.
12cm (4.75ins) high.
Pink and yellow.
Other colourways:
HN1679, 1842.
Est. £40-60.

HN2117
The Skater
First Version
Designer M. Davies.
Date 1953 - 71.
18cm (7ins) high.
White, blue, red and brown.
Est. £175-225.

HN2122
Yeoman of the Guard
Designer L. Harradine.
Date 1954 - 59.
14.5cm (5.75ins) high.
Red, brown, white and gold.
Other colourways: HN688.
Est. £300-450.

HN2123
Rose
First Version
Designer L. Harradine.
Date 1983 - 95.
11.5cm (4.5ins) high.
Lilac.
Other colourways: HN1368,
1387, 1416, 1506, 1654.
Est. £40-60.

HN2125
This Little Pig
Designer L. Harradine.
Date 1984 - 95.
10cm (4ins) high.
White.
Other colourways:
HN1793, 1794.
Est. £40-60.

HN2126
Top o' The Hill
Second Version (Model 3049)
Designer L. Harradine.
Remodeller P. Gee.
Date 1988.
10cm (4ins) high.
Green, lilac and white.
Other colourways: HN3499.
Series: 1. Miniatures.
Series: 2. R.D.I.C.C.
Est. £75-100.

HN2127
Top o' The Hill
First Version (Model 965)
Designer L. Harradine.
Date 1988.
18cm (7ins) high.
Yellow, green and white.
Other colourways: HN1833,
1834, 1849, 3735A.
Est. £180-230.

HN2128
River Boy
Designer M. Davies.
Date 1962 - 75.
10cm (4ins) high.
Blue and pale green.
*(Auction PSA 1.9.04 sold £75
plus comm.)*
Est. £75-120.

HN2129
Old Balloon Seller
Second Version (Model 3698)
Designer L. Harradine.
Remodeller W.K. Harper.
Date 1989 - 91.
9cm (3.5ins) high.
Green, red and white.
Series: Miniatures.
*(Auction PSA 1.9.04 sold £105
plus comm.)*
Est. £100-140.

HN2130
Balloon Seller
Second Version (Model 3748)
Designer L. Harradine.
Remodeller R. Tabbenor.
Date 1989 - 91.
10cm (4ins) high.
Green, grey and cream.
Series: Miniatures.
*(Auction PSA 1.9.04 sold £85
plus comm.)*
Est. £100-140.

HN2131
Autumn Breezes
First Version (Model 1027)
Designer L. Harradine.
Date 1990 - 94.
18cm (7ins) high.
Orange, white, black and yellow.
Other colourways: HN1911,
1913, 1934, 2147, 3736.
(Ebay 4.6.04 sold £131)
Est. £140-170.

HN2132
The Suitor
Designer M. Davies.
Date 1962 - 71.
18.5cm (7.25ins) high.
Blue, yellow, brown and white.
Est. £175-225.

HN2133
Faraway
Designer M. Davies.
Date 1958 - 62.
6.5cm (2.5ins) high.
Blue and white.
Series: Teenagers.
Est. £160-220.

HN2134
An Old King
Designer C.J. Noke.
Date 1954 - 92.
24.5cm (9.75ins) high.
Red, purple, green
and brown.
Other colourways: HN358,
623, 1801.
Est. £200-300.

HN2139
Giselle
Designer M. Davies.
Date 1954 - 69.
16cm (6.25ins) high.
Blue, green and white.
Est. £175-225.

HN2135
Gay Morning
Designer M. Davies.
Date 1954 - 67.
18cm (7ins) high.
Pink, blue and white.
Est. £120-170.

HN2140
Giselle,
The Forest Glade
Designer M. Davies.
Date 1954 - 65.
18.5cm (7.25ins) high.
Blue, green and white.
Est. £175-225.

HN2136
Delphine
Designer M. Davies.
Date 1954 - 67.
18.5cm (7.25ins) high.
Blue, lilac and tan.
(Auction PSA 3.12.03
sold £130 plus comm.)
Est. £150-200.

HN2141
Choir Boy
Designer M. Davies.
Date 1954 - 75.
12.5cm (5ins) high.
Red and white.
Est. £50-75.

HN2137
Lilac Time
Designer M. Davies.
Date 1954 - 69.
19cm (7.5ins) high.
Red and white.
Est. £150-200.

HN2142
Rag Doll
Designer M. Davies.
Date 1954 - 86.
12cm (4.75ins) high.
Red, white and blue.
Est. £50-85.

HN2138
La Sylphide
Designer M. Davies.
Date 1954 - 65.
18.5cm (7.25ins) high.
White, green and blue.
Est. £175-225.

HN2143
Friar Tuck
Designer M. Davies.
Date 1954 - 65.
20.5cm (8ins) high.
Brown, grey and tan.
(Auction Charterhouse 24.4.04
sold £130 and PSA 1.9.04 sold
£180 plus comm.)
Est. £170-300.

HN2144
The Jovial Monk
Designer M. Davies.
Date 1954 - 76.
19.5cm (7.75ins) high.
Brown and tan.
(Auction PSA 1.9.04 sold £100 plus comm.)
Est. £120-170.

HN2145
Wardrobe Mistress
Designer M. Davies.
Date 1954 - 67.
14.5cm (5.75ins) high.
White, green, red and blue.
Est. £200-250.

HN2146
The Tinsmith
Designer M. Nicoll.
Date 1962 - 67.
16.5cm (6.5ins) high.
Green, brown, white and black.
Est. £200-250.

HN2147
Autumn Breezes
First Version (Model 1027)
Designer L. Harradine.
Date 1955 - 71.
18cm (7ins) high.
Black and white.
Other colourways: HN1911,
1913, 1934, 2131, 3736.
Est. £140-180.

HN2148
The Bridesmaid
Second Version (Model 1481)
Designer M. Davies.
Date 1955 - 59.
14cm (5.5ins) high.
Lemon and pale blue.
Est. £100-140.

HN2149
Love Letter
First Version
(Model 1561)
Designer M. Davies.
Date 1958 - 76.
12.5cm (5ins) high.
Pale blue, pink
and white.
*(Auction PSA 11.8.04
sold £130 plus comm.)*
Est. £140-200.

HN2150
Willy-Won't He
Designer L. Harradine.
Date 1955 - 59.
15cm (6ins) high.
Blue, white, red and green.
Other colourways: HN1561,
1584 (minor glaze differences)
(Ebay 5.6.04 sold £170)
Est. £185-235.

HN2151
Mother's Help
Designer M. Davies.
Date 1962 - 69.
12.5cm (5ins) high.
Black and white.
Est. £100-150.

HN2152
Adrienne
Designer M. Davies.
Date 1964 - 76.
20.5cm (8ins) high.
Purple and yellow.
Other colourways: N2304,
'Fiona' HN3748, 'Joan' HN3217.
Est. £65-100.

HN2153
The One that Got Away
Designer M. Davies.
Date 1955 - 59.
16.5cm (6.5ins) high.
Brown, yellow, green and black.
Est. £150-200.

HN2154
A Child from Williamsburg
Designer M. Davies.
Date 1964 - 83.
14.5cm (5.75ins) high.
Blue and white.
Series: Figures of Williamsburg.
(Auction PSA 11.8.04 sold £45 and W&H 27.9.04 sold £45 plus comm.)
Est. £55-100.

HN2160
The Apple Maid
Designer L. Harradine.
Date 1957 - 62.
16.5cm (6.5ins) high.
Green, black, tan and white.
Est. £150-200.

HN2156
The Polka
Designer M. Davies.
Date 1955 - 69.
19cm (7.5ins) high.
Pale pink.
Est. £125-150.

HN2161
The Hornpipe
Designer M. Nicoll.
Date 1955 - 62.
23.5cm (9.25ins) high.
Blue and white.
Est. £375-475.

HN2157
A Gypsy Dance
First Version (Model 1492)
Designer M. Davies.
Date 1955 - 57.
18cm (7ins) high.
Lilac and white.
Est. £400-500.

HN2162
The Foaming Quart
Designer M. Davies.
Date 1955 - 92.
16cm (6.25ins) high.
Red and brown.
(Auction PSA 10.3.04 sold £85 plus comm.)
Est. £90-125.

HN2158
Alice
First Version (Model 1665)
Designer M. Davies.
Date 1960 - 81.
12.5cm (5ins) high.
Blue and white.
(Auction PSA 23.6.04 sold £55 plus comm.)
Est. £65-100.

HN2163
In The Stocks
Second Version (Model 1502)
Designer M. Nicoll.
Date 1955 - 59.
15cm (6ins) high.
Brown, red, green and black.
Est. £375-475.

HN2159
Fortune Teller
Designer L. Harradine.
Date 1955 - 67.
16.5cm (6.5ins) high.
Green, red, black and brown.
Est. £225-275.

HN2165
Janice
First Version (Model 1314)
Designer M. Davies.
Date 1955 - 65.
18.5cm (7.25ins) high.
Black, pale blue and white.
Other colourways: HN2022.
Est. £175-250.

HN2166
The Bride
Second Version (Model 1553)
Designer M. Davies.
Date 1956 - 76.
21cm (8.25ins) high.
Pink.
(Ebay 28.6.04 sold £100)
Est. £120-160.

HN2171
The Fiddler
Designer M. Nicoll.
Date 1956 - 62.
21.5cm (8.5ins) high.
Cream, red, brown and green.
Est. £450-650.

HN2167
Home Again
Designer M. Davies.
Date 1956 - 95.
9cm (3.5ins) high.
Red, green, tan and white.
Est. £60-90.

HN2172
Jolly Sailor
Designer M. Nicoll.
Date 1956 - 65.
16.5cm (6.5ins) high.
Blue, white, black, red and tan.
(Auction PSA 1.9.04 sold £360
plus comm.)
Est. £400-500.

HN2168
Esmeralda
Designer M. Davies.
Date 1956 - 59.
14.5cm (5.75ins) high.
Lemon, blue and red.
Est. £150-200.

HN2173
The Organ Grinder
Designer M. Nicoll.
Date 1956 - 65.
22cm (8.75ins) high.
Green, brown, cream and red.
Est. £450-600.

HN2169
Dimity
Designer L. Harradine.
Date 1956 - 59.
14.5cm (5.75ins) high.
Lilac, cream and green.
Est. £150-200.

HN2174
The Tailor
Designer M. Nicoll.
Date 1956 - 59.
10cm (4ins) high.
Cream, orange and blue.
Est. £350-450.

HN2170
Invitation
Designer M. Davies.
Date 1956 - 75.
14cm (5.5ins) high.
Pink, blue and white.
(Auction PSA 11.8.04 sold £48
plus comm.)
Est. £55-100.

HN2175
The Beggar
Second Version (Model 1574)
Designer L. Harradine.
Date 1956 - 62.
18cm (7ins) high.
Green and brown.
Series: Beggar's Opera.
Est. £250-350.

HN2176
Autumn Breezes
Second Version (Model 3949)
Designer L. Harradine.
Remodeller D. Frith.
Date 1991 - 95.
11cm (4.25ins) high.
Red and white.
Other colourways: HN2180.
Series: Miniatures.
*(Auction PSA 22.10.03 sold £45
plus comm.)* **Est. £50-90.**

HN2181
Summer's Day
First Version (Model 1582)
Designer M. Davies.
Date 1957 - 62.
15cm (6ins) high.
White.
Est. £135-180.

HN2177
My Teddy
Designer M. Davies.
Date 1962 - 67.
8cm (3.25ins) high.
Pale green, white and orange.
Est. £200-275.

HN2183
Boy from Williamsburg
Designer M. Davies.
Date 1969 - 83.
14cm (5.5ins) high.
Blue, brown and pink.
Series: Figures of Williamsburg.
*(Auction PSA 1.9.04 Sold £75
plus comm.)*
Est. £90-120.

HN2178
Enchantment
Designer M. Davies.
Date 1957 - 82.
20.5cm (8ins) high.
Pale blue and cream.
(Ebay 28.6.04 sold £51.50)
*(Auction W&H 27.9.04 sold
£45 plus comm.)*
Est. £55-85.

HN2184
Sunday Morning
Designer M. Davies.
Date 1963 - 69.
19cm (7.5ins) high.
Red, white and brown.
Est. £150-200.

HN2179
Noelle
Designer M. Davies.
Date 1957 - 67.
17cm (6.75ins) high.
Red, white and black.
Est. £200-250.

HN2185
Columbine
Second Version (Model 1589)
Designer M. Davies.
Date 1957 - 69.
18.5cm (7.25ins) high.
Pale pink.
Series: Teenagers.
(Ebay 23.5.04 sold £44)
Est. £50-125.

HN2180
Autumn Breezes
Second Version (Model 3949)
Designer L. Harradine.
Remodeller D. Frith.
Date 1991 - 95.
11cm (4.25ins) high.
Red, lilac and purple.
Other colourways: HN2176.
Series: 1. Miniatures. 2. Signature.
Est. £90-120.

HN2186
Harlequin
First Version (Model 1590)
Designer M. Davies.
Date 1957 - 69.
19cm (7.5ins) high.
Blue and white.
Series: Teenagers.
*(Auction PSA 10.3.04
sold £70 plus comm.)*
Est. £75-140.

HN2191
Sea Sprite
Second Version (Model 1595)
Designer M. Davies.
Date 1958 - 62.
18.5cm (7.25ins) high.
Pink, white and pale blue.
Series: Teenagers.
Est. £180-230.

HN2203
Teenager
Designer M. Davies.
Date 1957 - 62.
18.5cm (7.25ins) high.
Orange and white.
Series: Teenagers.
(Auction PSA 10.3.04 sold
£100 plus comm.)
Est. £130-200.

HN2192
Wood Nymph
Designer M. Davies.
Date 1958 - 62.
19cm (7.5ins) high.
Blue/green and white.
Series: Teenagers.
Est. £180-230.

HN2204
Long John Silver
First Version
Designer M. Nicoll.
Date 1957 - 65.
23cm (9ins) high.
Black, white, red and green.
Est. £240-300.

HN2193
Fair Lady
First Version (Model 1832)
Designer M. Davies.
Date 1963 - 96.
19cm (7.5ins) high.
Pale green and yellow.
Other colourways: HN2832,
2835, 'Kay' HN3340.
(Auction W&H 27.9.04 sold
£45 plus comm.)
Est. £55-90.

HN2205
Master Sweep
Designer M. Nicoll.
Date 1957 - 62.
21.5cm (8.5ins) high.
Green, red, brown and black.
Est. £300-400.

HN2196
The Bridesmaid
Third Version (Model 1681)
Designer M. Davies.
Date 1960 - 76.
12.5cm (5ins) high.
Pink and pale blue.
(Ebay 20.8.04 sold £52)
Est. £55-80.

HN2206
Sunday Best
First Version (Model 2609)
Designer M. Davies.
Date 1979 - 84.
19cm (7.5ins) high.
Yellow, pink and white.
Other colourways: HN2698.
Est. £90-120.

HN2202
Melody
First Version
Designer M. Davies.
Date 1957 - 62.
16cm (6.25ins) high.
Turquoise, white and pink.
Series: Teenagers.
Est. £160-210.

HN2207
Stayed at Home
Designer M. Davies.
Date 1958 - 69.
12.5cm (5ins) high.
Green and white.
(Ebay 11.6.04 sold £56)
Est. £60-100.

HN2208
Silversmith of Williamsburg
Designer M. Davies.
Date 1960 - 83.
16cm (6.25ins) high.
Blue, red, brown and white.
Series: Figures of Williamsburg.
(Auction PSA 23.6.04 sold £70 plus comm.)
Est. £85-125.

HN2213
Contemplation
Designer M. Davies.
Date 1982 - 86.
30.5cm (12ins) high.
White.
Other colourways: HN2241.
Series: Images.
Est. £75-100.

HN2209
Hostess of Williamsburg
Designer M. Davies.
Date 1960 - 83.
18.5cm (7.25ins) high.
Pink and white.
Series: Figures of Williamsburg.
(Auction PSA 4.2.04 sold £55 plus comm.)
Est. £65-100.

HN2214
Bunny
Designer M. Davies.
Date 1960 - 75.
12.5cm (5ins) high.
Turquoise, white and pink.
Est. £80-120.

HN2210
Debutante
First Version (Model 1810)
Designer M. Davies.
Date 1963 - 67.
12.5cm (5ins) high.
Blue and white.
Est. £120-170.

HN2215
Sweet April
Designer M. Davies.
Date 1965 - 67.
19cm (7.5ins) high.
Pink, white and green.
Est. £165-200.

HN2211
Fair Maiden
Designer M. Davies.
Date 1967 - 94.
13cm (5.25ins) high.
Green, white and lemon.
Other colourways: HN2434.
(Auction PSA 26.5.04 sold £30 plus comm.)
Est. £35-55.

HN2216
Pirouette
Designer M. Davies.
Date 1959 - 67.
14.5cm (5.75ins) high.
Pale blue.
(Auction PSA 3.12.03 sold £70 plus comm.)
(Ebay 10.6.04 sold £65)
Est. £80-120.

HN2212
Rendezvous
Designer M. Davies.
Date 1962 - 71.
18.5cm (7.25ins) high.
Red and white.
Est. £150-200.

HN2217
Old King Cole
Designer M. Davies.
Date 1963 - 67.
17cm (6.75ins) high.
Brown, white, tan and yellow.
Est. £250-350.

HN2218
Cookie
Designer M. Davies.
Date 1958 - 75.
12cm (4.75ins) high.
Pink and white.
Est. £75-100.

HN2223
Schoolmarm
Designer M. Davies.
Date 1958 - 81.
18cm (7ins) high.
Brown, purple, grey and white.
Est. £125-170.

HN2219
Bedtime
First Version (Model 1214)
Designer L. Harradine.
Date 1992.
14cm (5.5ins) high.
Pink.
Comm: Peter Jones China.
Other colourways: HN1978.
Est. £45-70.

HN2224
Make Believe
Designer M. Nicoll.
Date 1984 - 88.
14.5cm (5.75ins) high.
White.
Other colourways: HN2225.
(Auction PSA 11.6.04 sold £40
plus comm.)
Est. £50-80.

HN2220
Winsome
Designer M. Davies.
Date 1960 - 85.
20.5cm (8ins) high.
Red and white.
Est. £75-95.

HN2225
Make Believe
Designer M. Nicoll.
Date 1962 - 88.
14.5cm (5.75ins) high.
Blue, green and tan.
Other colourways: HN2224.
(Auction PSA 23.6.04 sold £45
plus comm.)
(Ebay 4.6.04 sold £64)
Est. £70-100.

HN2221
Nanny
Designer M. Nicoll.
Date 1958 - 91.
16cm (6.25ins) high.
Blue, brown and white.
(Auction PSA 1.9.04 sold £95
plus comm.)
(Ebay 10.7.04 sold £125)
Est. £125-165.

HN2226
The Cellist
Designer M. Nicoll.
Date 1960 - 67.
21cm (8.25ins) high.
Black, brown and white.
(Auction PSA 1.9.04 sold £190
plus comm.)
Est. £200-300.

HN2222
Camellia
Designer M. Davies.
Date 1960 - 71.
19.5cm (7.75ins) high.
Pink and white.
(Auction PSA 4.2.04 sold £45
plus comm.)
Est. £55-90.

HN2227
**Gentleman from
Williamsburg**
Designer M. Davies.
Date 1960 - 83.
16cm (6.25ins) high.
Green, brown and white.
Series: Figures of Williamsburg.
(Auction PSA 1.9.04 sold £75
plus comm.)
Est. £80-120.

HN2228
Lady from Williamsburg
Designer M. Davies.
Date 1960 - 83.
15cm (6ins) high.
Green and white.
Series: Figures of Williamsburg.
*(Auction PSA 28.6.04 sold £75
plus comm.)*
Est. £80-140.

HN2234
Michele
Designer M. Davies.
Date 1967 - 93.
17cm (6.75ins) high.
Green and pink.
Other colourways: 'Autumn
Attraction' HN3612.
(Ebay 5.7.04 sold £40.99)
Est. £50-95.

HN2229
Southern Belle
First Version (Model 1425)
Designer M. Davies.
Date 1958 - 97.
19cm (7.5ins) high.
Red, blue and cream.
Other colourways: HN2425.
*(Auction PSA 23.6.04
sold £50 plus comm.)*
(Ebay 27.5.04 sold £67)
Est. £70-120.

HN2235
Dancing Years
Designer M. Davies.
Date 1965 - 71.
18cm (7ins) high.
Lilac, pink and white.
Est. £125-175.

HN2230
A Gypsy Dance
Second Version (Model 1671)
Designer M. Davies.
Date 1959 - 71.
18cm (7ins) high.
Lilac and cream.
Est. £130-180.

HN2236
Affection
Designer M. Davies.
Date 1962 - 94.
11.5cm (4.5ins) high.
Purple and white.
(Ebay 23.5.04 sold £31)
*(Auction W&H 27.9.04 sold
£28 plus comm.)*
Est. £35-60.

HN2231
Sweet Sixteen
First Version (Model 1625)
Designer M. Davies.
Date 1958 - 65.
18.5cm (7.25ins) high.
Pale blue, black and white.
Series: Teenagers.
Est. £175-225.

HN2237
Celeste
First Version (Model 1649)
Designer M. Davies.
Date 1959 - 71.
18cm (7ins) high.
Pale blue, black and white.
(Ebay 20.5.04 sold £60)
*(Auction PSA 1.9.04 sold £55
plus comm.)*
Est. £60-100.

HN2233
Royal Governor's Cook
Designer M. Davies.
Date 1960 - 83.
15cm (6ins) high.
Dark blue, brown, tan and white.
Series: Figures of Williamsburg.
*(Auction PSA 23.6.04
sold £150 plus comm.)*
Est. £180-250.

HN2238
My Pet
Designer M. Davies.
Date 1962 - 75.
7.5cm (3ins) high.
Blue, white and tan.
Est. £105-140.

HN2239
Wigmaker of Williamsburg
Designer M. Davies.
Date 1960 - 83.
19cm (7.5ins) high.
White, black and brown.
Series: Figures of Williamsburg.
(Auction PSA 22.10.03 sold £55 plus comm.)
Est. £60-100.

HN2240
Blacksmith of Williamsburg
Designer M. Davies.
Date 1960 - 83.
18cm (7ins) high.
White, brown, black and grey.
Series: Figures of Williamsburg.
(Auction PSA 23.6.04 sold £85 plus comm.)
Est. £100-150.

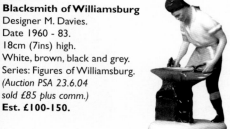

HN2241
Contemplation
Designer M. Davies.
Date 1982 - 86.
30.5cm (12ins) high.
Black.
Other colourways: HN2213.
Series: Images.
Est. £75-100.

HN2242
First Steps
First Version (Model 1656)
Designer M. Davies.
Date 1959 - 65.
17cm (6.75ins) high.
Blue, yellow and white.
Est. £200-250.

HN2243
Treasure Island
Designer M. Davies.
Date 1962 - 75.
12.5cm (5ins) high.
Blue, white and yellow.
Est. £90-120.

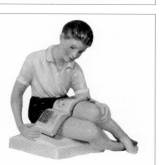

HN2244
Newsboy
Designer M. Nicoll.
Date 1959 - 65.
21.5cm (8.5ins) high.
Black, brown, green and cream.
(Also a Limited edition of 250 for Stoke's local newspaper 'Evening Sentinel', but not valued here)
(Auction PSA 23.6.04 sold £180 plus comm.)
Est. £225-350.

HN2245
The Basket Weaver
Designer M. Nicoll.
Date 1959 - 62.
16cm (6.25ins) high.
Pale blue, white and yellow.
Est. £200-250.

HN2246
Cradle Song
Designer M. Davies.
Date 1959 - 62.
14cm (5.5ins) high.
Green, brown and white.
Est. £200-250.

HN2247
Omar Khayyam
Second Version (Model 1870)
Designer M. Nicoll.
Date 1965 - 83.
16.5cm (6.5ins) high.
Brown, orange and red.
(Auction PSA 23.6.04 sold £80 plus comm.)
Est. £90-150.

HN2248
Tall Story
Designer M. Nicoll.
Date 1968 - 75.
16cm (6.25ins) high.
Blue, green, cream and brown.
Series: Sea Characters.
Est. £150-200.

HN2249
The Favourite
Designer M. Nicoll.
Date 1960 - 90.
19.5cm (7.75ins) high.
Blue, brown, grey and white.
(Auction PSA 11.8.04 sold £75 plus comm.)
Est. £85-130.

HN2254
Shore Leave
Designer M. Nicoll.
Date 1965 - 79.
21cm (8.25ins) high.
Black, brown, grey and white.
Series: Sea Characters.
Est. £120-160.

HN2250
The Toymaker
Designer M. Nicoll.
Date 1959 - 73.
15cm (6ins) high.
Brown, orange and red.
(Auction PSA 1.9.04 sold £180 plus comm.)
Est. £200-300.

HN2255
Teatime
Designer M. Nicoll.
Date 1972 - 95.
19cm (7.5ins) high.
Red, brown, grey
and white.
(Auction PSA 23.6.04 sold £75 plus comm.)
Est. £85-130.

HN2251
Masquerade
Second Version (Model 1690)
Designer M. Davies.
Date 1960 - 65.
21.5cm (8.5ins) high.
Pale blue and white.
Other colourways: HN2259.
Est. £135-180.

HN2256
Twilight
Designer M. Nicoll.
Date 1971 - 76.
12.5cm (5ins) high.
Green, blue, black,
grey and white.
(Auction PSA 22.19.03 sold £190 plus comm.)
Est. £210-300.

HN2252
The Joker
Second Version (Model 2024)
Designer M. Nicoll.
Date 1990 - 92.
21.5cm (8.5ins) high.
White, green and orange.
Series: Clowns.
Est. £120-160.

HN2257
Sea Harvest
Designer M. Nicoll.
Date 1969 - 76.
19.5cm (7.75ins) high.
Blue, black and brown.
Series: Sea Characters.
(Auction PSA 23.6.04 sold £80 plus comm.)
Est. £100-150.

HN2253
The Puppetmaker
Designer M. Nicoll.
Date 1962 - 73.
21cm (8.25ins) high.
Green, white, brown and red.
(Auction PSA 23.6.04 sold £195 plus comm.)
Est. £200-300.

HN2258
A Good Catch
Designer M. Nicoll.
Date 1966 - 86.
18.5cm (7.25ins) high.
Green, blue and grey.
Series: Sea Characters.
(Auction PSA 23.6.04 sold £80 and W&H 27.9.04 sold £80 plus comm.)
Est. £110-150.

HN2259
Masquerade
Second Version (Model 1690)
Designer M. Davies.
Date 1960 - 65.
21.5cm (8.5ins) high.
Red, white and cream.
Other colourways: HN2251.
Est. £135-200.

HN2264
Elegance
Designer M. Davies.
Date 1961 - 85.
19cm (7.5ins) high.
Green, orange and yellow.
(Auction PSA 23.6.04 sold
£55 plus comm.)
(Ebay 28.6.04 sold £62)
Est. £65-100.

HN2260
The Captain
Second Version (Model 1887)
Designer M. Nicoll.
Date 1965 - 82.
24cm (9.5ins) high.
Black, yellow and white.
Series: Sea Characters.
Est. £150-200.

HN2265
Sara
First Version (Model 2130)
Designer M. Davies.
Date 1981 - 2000.
19.5cm (7.75ins) high.
Red and white.
Other colourways: HN3308.
(Auction PSA 23.6.04
sold £55 plus comm.)
Est. £65-120.

HN2261
Marriage of Art and Industry
Designer M. Davies.
Date 1958. Limited edition of 12.
46cm (18ins) high.
Green.
Rare.

HN2266
Ballad Seller
Designer M. Davies.
Date 1968 - 73.
19.5cm (7.75ins) high.
Pink and white.
Est. £130-180.

HN2262
Lights Out
First Version
Designer M. Davies.
Date 1965 - 69.
12.5cm (5ins) high.
Blue, yellow, pink and white.
(Made as a pair to HN2270
'Pillow Fight')
Est. £100-150.

HN2267
Rhapsody
Designer M. Davies.
Date 1961 - 73.
18.5cm (7.25ins) high.
Blue/green and white.
Est. £65-100.

HN2263
Seashore
Designer M. Davies.
Date 1961 - 65.
9cm (3.5ins) high.
Yellow, pink and red.
Est. £150-200.

HN2268
Daphne
Designer M. Davies.
Date 1963 - 75.
21.5cm (8.5ins) high.
Pink, blue and white.
Est. £70-120.

HN2269
Leading Lady
Designer M. Davies.
Date 1965 - 76.
19.5cm (7.75ins) high.
Blue, yellow and red.
*(Auction PSA 1.9.04 sold £60
plus comm.)*
(Ebay 4.10.04 sold £132)
Est. £100-135.

HN2274
Golden Days
Designer M. Davies.
Date 1964 - 73.
10cm (4ins) high.
Yellow, blue, white and tan.
*(Auction PSA 23.6.04 sold £65
plus comm.)*
Est. £80-110.

HN2270
Pillow Fight
Designer M. Davies.
Date 1965 - 69.
13cm (5.25ins) high.
Pink and white.
(Made as a pair to HN2262
'Lights Out')
Est. £135-180.

HN2275
Sandra
Designer M. Davies.
Date 1969 - 97.
20.5cm (8ins) high.
Orange and white.
Other colourways: HN2401;
'Annette' HN3495.
*(Auction PSA 4.2.04 sold £50 plus
comm.)*
(Ebay 22.8.04 £45)
Est. £60-90.

HN2271
Melanie
Designer M. Davies.
Date 1965 - 81.
20.5cm (8ins) high.
Blue and yellow.
*(Auction PSA 17.9.03 sold
£40 plus comm.)*
Est. £60-100.

HN2276
Heart to Heart
Designer M. Davies.
Date 1961 - 71.
14cm (5.5ins) high.
Lilac, green, yellow
and white.
Est. £200-300.

HN2272
Repose
Designer M. Davies.
Date 1972 - 79.
13cm (5.25ins) high.
Pink, green and white.
*(Auction PSA 4.2.04
sold £90 plus comm.)*
Est. £120-160.

HN2277
Slapdash
Designer M. Nicoll.
Date 1990 - 94.
25.5cm (10ins) high.
Lilac, green, yellow and white.
Series: Clowns.
Est. £135-180.

HN2273
Denise
First Version (Model 1866)
Designer M. Davies.
Date 1964 - 71.
18.5cm (7.25ins) high.
Red and white.
Est. £150-200.

HN2278
Judith
Second Version (Model 2071)
Designer M. Nicoll.
Date 1986 N. America.
1987 - 89 Worldwide.
17cm (6.75ins) high.
Yellow and brown.
Other colourways: HN2313.
*(Auction PSA 1.9.04 sold £65
plus comm.)*
Est. £80-120.

HN2279
The Clockmaker
Designer M. Nicoll.
Date 1961 - 75.
18.5cm (7.5ins) high.
Green, orange and brown.
(Auction PSA 23.6.04
sold £140 plus comm.)
Est. £170-220.

HN2284
The Craftsman
Designer M. Nicoll.
Date 1961 - 65.
15cm (6ins) high.
Blue, tan and brown.
Est. £250-350.

HN2280
The Mayor
Designer M. Nicoll.
Date 1963 - 71.
21cm (8.25ins) high.
Red, gold, white and black.
Other colourways: Also known
in 19cm (7.5ins) high.
(Auction PSA 11.8.04 sold £155
plus comm.)
Est. £175-250.

HN2287
Symphony
Designer D.B. Lovegrove.
Date 1961 - 65.
14cm (5.25ins) high.
Yellow, grey and brown.
Est. £120-160.

HN2281
The Professor
Designer M. Nicoll.
Date 1965 - 81.
19.5cm (7.75ins) high.
Black, brown and white.
(Auction PSA 10.3.04 sold
£120 plus comm.)
Est. £160-200.

HN2304
Adrienne
Designer M. Davies.
Date 1964 - 91.
20.5cm (8ins) high.
Blue and yellow.
Other colourways: HN2152,
'Fiona' HN3748; 'Joan' HN3217.
Est. £80-105.

HN2282
The Coachman
Designer M. Nicoll.
Date 1963 - 71.
17cm (6.75ins) high.
Purple, green, blue and black.
(Auction PSA 10.3.04 sold £170
plus comm.)
Est. £200-260.

HN2305
Dulcie
Designer M. Davies.
Date 1981 - 84.
21cm (8.25ins) high.
Blue, white and purple.
Est. £120-150.

HN2283
Dreamweaver
(Matte)
Designer M. Nicoll.
Date 1972 - 76.
22cm (8.75ins) high.
Blue, green, brown and grey.
Est. £100-150.

HN2306
Reverie
Designer M. Davies.
Date 1964 - 81.
18cm (7ins) high.
Peach, crimson and white.
(Auction PSA 1.9.04 sold £75
and W&H 27.9.04 sold £60
plus comm.)
(Ebay 25.5.04 sold £85)
Est. £90-130.

HN2307
Coralie
Designer M. Davies.
Date 1964 - 88.
20.5cm (8ins) high.
Yellow and white.
Est. £65-90.

HN2312
Soirée
Designer M. Davies.
Date 1967 - 84.
19cm (7.5ins) high.
Green, white and cream.
Est. £70-100.

HN2308
Picnic
Designer M. Davies.
Date 1965 - 88.
9.5cm (3.75ins) high.
Yellow, green, tan and white.
(Auction PSA 23.6.04 sold
£45 plus comm.)
Est. 55-100.

HN2313
Judith
Second Version (Model 2071)
Designer M. Nicoll.
Date 1988. Limited edition of 1,000.
17cm (6.75ins) high.
Red, cream and yellow.
Other colourways: HN2278.
Comm: Guild of China and
Glass Retailers.
Est. £120-160.

HN2309
Buttercup
First Version (Model 1852)
Designer M. Davies.
Date 1964 - 97.
19cm (7.5ins) high.
Green, lemon and white.
Other colourways: HN2399.
(Auction PSA 10.3.04 sold £52
plus comm.)
Est. £70-100.

HN2314
Old Mother Hubbard
Designer M. Nicoll.
Date 1964 - 75.
21cm (8.25ins) high.
Green, white, black and brown.
(Auction PSA 23.6.04 sold £160
plus comm.)
Est. £200-250.

HN2310
Lisa
(Matte)
First Version
Designer M. Davies.
Date 1969 - 82.
19cm (7.5ins) high.
Purple and white.
Other colourways:
HN2394, 3265.
Est. £75-100.

HN2315
Last Waltz
Designer M. Nicoll.
Date 1967 - 93.
19.5cm (7.75ins) high.
Yellow and white.
Other colourways: HN2316.
(Auction PSA 1.9.04 sold £50
plus comm.)
Est. £70-100.

HN2311
Lorna
Designer M. Davies.
Date 1965 - 85.
21cm (8.25ins) high.
Green and yellow.
(Auction PSA 22.10.03 sold £45
and W&H 27.9.04 sold £55
plus comm.)
(Ebay 4.6.04 sold £95)
Est. £85-100.

HN2316
Last Waltz
Designer M. Nicoll.
Date 1987. Limited edition of 2,000.
19.5cm (7.75ins) high.
Pink, white and cream.
Other colourways: HN2315.
Series: M. Doulton Events.
Est. £150-1900.

HN2317
The Lobster Man
Designer M. Nicoll.
Date 1964 - 94.
19cm (7.5ins) high.
Blue, green, brown and grey.
Other colourways: HN2323.
Series: Sea Characters.
(Auction PSA 23.6.04 sold
£80 plus comm.)
(Ebay 4.6.04 sold £95)
Est. £100-150.

HN2322
The Cup of Tea
Designer M. Nicoll.
Date 1964 - 83.
19cm (7.5ins) high.
Dark blue, grey and white.
(Auction PSA 4.2.04 sold £70
plus comm.)
(Ebay 5.10.04 sold £100)
Est. £100-135.

HN2318
Grace
First Version
Designer M. Nicoll.
Date 1966 - 81.
19cm (7.5ins) high.
Green, white and tan.
(Auction PSA 23.6.04 sold
£55 plus comm.)
Est. £75-100.

HN2323
The Lobster Man
Designer M. Nicoll.
Date 1987 - 95.
19cm (7.5ins) high.
White, black and brown.
Other colourways: HN2317.
Series: Sea Characters.
Est. £170-250.

HN2319
The Bachelor
Designer M. Nicoll.
Date 1964 - 75.
17cm (6.75ins) high.
Green, brown, tan and blue.
Est. £150-200.

HN2324
Matador and Bull
First Version.
Designer M. Davies.
Date 1964 to date.
40.5cm (16ins) high.
Black, yellow and red.
(This model is being sold on
the Royal Doulton website
for £12,500; a smaller version,
HN4566 17.5cm is sold for £795)
Retail £12,500.

HN2320
Tuppence a Bag
Designer M. Nicoll.
Date 1968 - 95.
15cm (6ins) high.
Blue, green and orange.
(Ebay 6.7.04 sold £105.60)
Est. £110-150.

HN2325
The Master
Designer M. Davies.
Date 1967 - 92.
16.5cm (6.5ins) high.
Green, brown, white and grey.
(Auction PSA 23.6.04 sold
£80 plus comm.)
Est. £100-150.

HN2321
Family Album
Designer M. Nicoll.
Date 1966 - 73.
16cm (6.25ins) high.
Lilac, green, brown and white.
(Auction PSA 23.6.04 sold £110
plus comm.)
Est. £130-200.

HN2326
Antoinette
Second Version (Model 1904)
Designer M. Davies.
Date 1967 - 79.
16cm (6.25ins) high.
White and gold with white
rose in hand.
Other colourways:
'My Love' HN2339.
Est. £85-115.

HN2327
Katrina
First Version
Designer M. Davies.
Date 1965 - 69.
19.5cm (7.75ins) high.
Red and white.
Est. £150-200.

HN2332
Monte Carlo
Designer M. Davies.
Date 1982. Limited edition of 1,500.
21cm (8.25ins) high.
Green, red, blue and yellow.
Series: The Sweet and Twenties.
Est. £175-220.

HN2328
Queen of Sheba
Designer M. Davies.
Date 1982. Limited edition of 750.
23cm (9ins) high.
Orange, lilac, yellow and green.
Series: Les Femmes Fatales.
Est. £500-600.

HN2333
Jacqueline
Second Version (Model 2807)
Designer M. Davies.
Date 1982 Canada.
1983 Worldwide - 1991.
19cm (7.5ins) high.
Purple, yellow and blue.
Est. £80-120.

HN2329
Lynne
First Version
Designer M. Davies.
Date 1971 - 96.
18cm (7ins) high.
Green and white.
Other colourways: HN3740,
'Kathy' HN3305.
(Ebay 5.6.04 sold £39)
Est. £50-100.

HN2334
Fragrance
First Version (Model 1930)
Designer M. Davies.
Date 1966 - 95.
19cm (7.5ins) high.
Blue and white.
Other colourways: HN3311.
(Auction PSA 17.9.03 sold £48
plus comm.)
(Ebay 28.6.04 sold £58)
Est. £65-100.

HN2330
Meditation
Designer M. Davies.
Date 1971 - 83.
14.5cm (5.75ins) high.
Peach, white and cream.
Est. £125-175.

HN2335
Hilary
Designer M. Davies.
Date 1967 - 81.
18.5cm (7.25ins) high.
Blue, cream and white.
Est. £75-110.

HN2331
Cello
First Version
Designer M. Davies.
Date 1970. Limited edition of 750.
16cm (6.25ins) high.
Yellow, brown and white.
Series: Lady Musicians.
Est. £600-800.

HN2336
Alison
First Version
Designer M. Davies.
Date 1966 - 92.
19cm (7.5ins) high.
Blue, white and gold.
Other colourways: HN3264.
Est. £70-100.

HN2337
Loretta
Designer M. Davies.
Date 1966 - 81.
19.5cm (7.75ins) high.
Red and yellow.
(Auction PSA 23.6.04 sold
£55 and W&H 27.9.04 sold
£47 plus comm.)
Est. £70-100.

HN2342
Lucrezia Borgia
Designer M. Davies.
Date 1985. Limited edition of 750.
20.5cm (8ins) high.
Yellow, red, white and blue.
Series: Les Femmes Fatales.
Est. £500-625.

HN2338
Penny
Designer M. Davies.
Date 1968 - 95.
12cm (4.75ins) high.
Green and white.
Other colourways: HN2424.
(Auction PSA 11.8.04 sold £30
plus comm.)
Est. £40-60.

HN2343
Première
(Hand holds cloak)
Designer M. Davies.
Date 1969 - 79.
19.5cm (7.75ins) high.
Green, cream and yellow.
Other colourways: HN2343A.
(Auction PSA 22.10.03 sold £75
plus comm.)
Est. £100-150.

HN2339
My Love
First Version (Model 1904)
Designer M. Davies.
Date 1969 - 96.
16cm (6.25ins) high.
White & gold, red rose in hand.
Other colourways:
'Antoinette' HN2326.
(Ebay 24.5.04 sold £60)
(Auction Charterhouse 24.4.04
sold £60 plus comm.)   **Est. £70-110.**

HN2343A
Première
(Hand rests on cloak)
Designer M. Davies.
Date Not known - 1979.
19.5cm (7.75ins) high.
Green, cream and yellow.
Other colourways: HN2343.
Est. £90-120.

HN2340
Belle
Second Version (Model 2038)
Designer M. Davies.
Date 1968 - 88.
12cm (4.75ins) high.
Green and white.
Est. £35-50.

HN2344
Deauville
Designer M. Davies.
Date 1982. Limited edition
of 1,500.
21cm (8.25ins) high.
Yellow, orange and white.
Series: The Sweet and Twenties.
Est. £150-200.

HN2341
Chérie
Designer M. Davies.
Date 1966 - 92.
13cm (5.25ins) high.
Blue, yellow and white.
(Auction Brightwells 17.6.04
sold £35 plus comm.)
Est. £50-80.

HN2345
Clarissa
Second Version (Model 2001)
Designer M. Davies.
Date 1968 - 81.
20.5cm (8ins) high.
Green, yellow and white.
Est. £70-110.

HN2346
Kathy
First Version (Model 2813)
Designer M. Davies.
Date 1981 - 87.
12cm (4.75ins) high.
Cream, red and blue.
Series: Kate Greenaway.
Est. £90-120.

HN2356
Ascot
First Version (Model 1997)
Designer M. Nicoll.
Date 1968 - 95.
15cm (6ins) high.
Pale green, brown and yellow.
(Ebay 2.8.04 sold £53)
*(Auction PSA 11.8.04 sold £70
plus comm.)*
Est. £90-140.

HN2347
Nina
(Matte)
Designer M. Davies.
Date 1969 - 76.
19.5cm (7.75ins) high.
Blue and white.
Est. £70-90.

HN2359
The Detective
Designer M. Nicoll.
Date 1977 - 83.
23.5cm (9.25ins) high.
Brown, green and white.
Est. £150-200.

HN2348
Geraldine
(Matte)
Designer M. Davies.
Date 1972 - 76.
19cm (7.5ins) high.
Green and white.
Est. £70-90.

HN2361
The Laird (Small base)
Designer M. Nicoll.
Date 1969 - Not known.
21cm (8.25ins) high.
Green, white, tan and brown.
Other colourways: HN2361A
(Large base)
*(Auction PSA 22.10.03 sold
£80 plus comm.)*
(Ebay 30.9.04 sold £75)
Est. £100-140.

HN2349
Flora
Designer M. Nicoll.
Date 1966 - 73.
19.5cm (7.75ins) high.
Brown, blue, white and grey.
*(Auction PSA 1.9.04 sold £160
plus comm.)*
Est. £200-250.

HN2361A
The Laird (Large base)
Designer M. Nicoll.
Date Not known - 2001.
20.5cm (8ins) high.
Green, white, tan and brown.
Other colourways: HN2361
(Small base)
Est. £100-140.

HN2352
A Stitch in Time
Designer M. Nicoll.
Date 1966 - 81.
15cm (6ins) high.
Purple, orange, brown
and turquoise.
*(Auction PSA 23.6.04 sold
£95 plus comm.)*
Est. £120-165.

HN2362
The Wayfarer
Designer M. Nicoll.
Date 1970 - 76.
14cm (5.5ins) high.
Green, grey, white and brown.
*(Auction PSA 23.6.04 sold
£85 plus comm.)*
Est. £110-160.

HN2368
Fleur
First Version
Designer J. Bromley.
Date 1968 - 95.
19.5cm (7.75ins) high.
Green, gold and white.
Other colourways: HN2369;
'Flower of Love' HN2460, 3970.
Est. £80-100.

HN2373
Joanne
First Version (Model 2066)
Designer J. Bromley.
Date 1982 - 88.
13.cm (5.25ins) high.
White.
Series: Vanity Fair Ladies.
(Auction PSA 23.6.04
sold £55 plus comm.)
Est. £85-135.

HN2369
Fleur
First Version
Designer J. Bromley.
Date 1983 - 86.
19.5cm (7.75ins) high.
Orange and pale blue.
Other colourways: HN2368;
'Flower of Love' HN2460, 3970.
Est. £120-150.

HN2374
Mary
First Version (Model 2102)
Designer J. Bromley.
Date 1984 - 86.
19.5cm (7.75ins) high.
White and red.
Series: Vanity Fair Ladies.
Est. £100-130.

HN2370
Sir Edward
Designer J. Bromley.
Date 1979. Limited edition of 500.
27.5cm (10.75ins) high.
Red, grey and gold.
Series: The Age of Chivalry.
Est. £200-300.

HN2375
The Viking
(Matte)
Designer J. Bromley.
Date 1973 - 76.
22cm (8.75ins) high.
Blue, green, red and brown.
Est. £120-150.

HN2371
Sir Ralph
Designer J. Bromley.
Date 1979. Limited edition of 500.
26.5cm (10.5ins) high.
Turquoise, grey and black.
Series: The Age of Chivalry.
Est. £200-300.

HN2376
Indian Brave
Designer M. Davies.
Date 1967. Limited edition of 500.
39.5cm (15.5ins) high.
Black, white, tan and red.
Est. £2000-2500.

HN2372
Sir Thomas
Designer J. Bromley.
Date 1979. Limited edition of 500.
27.5cm (10.75ins) high.
Black and brown.
Series: The Age of Chivalry.
Est. £200-300.

HN2377
Georgina
First Version
Designer M. Davies.
Date 1981 - 86.
13cm (5.25ins) high.
Red, white and yellow.
Series: Kate Greenaway.
Est. £100-130.

HN2378
Simone
First Version
Designer M. Davies.
Date 1971 - 81.
19cm (7.5ins) high.
Green and white.
Est. £70-90.

HN2383
Breton Dancer
Designer M. Davies.
Date 1981. Limited edition of 750.
21.5cm (8.5ins) high.
Blue, cream and white.
Series: Dancers of the World.
Est. £300-400.

HN2379
Ninette
First Version (Model 2115)
Designer M. Davies.
Date 1971 - 97.
20.5cm (8ins) high.
Yellow and cream.
Other colourways: HN3417;
'Olivia HN3339.
*(Auction W&H 27.9.04
sold £52 plus comm.)*
(Ebay 9.6.04 sold £62) **Est. £65-100.**

HN2384
West Indian Dancer
Designer M. Davies.
Date 1981. Limited edition of 750.
22cm (8.75ins) high.
Yellow, white, lilac and green.
Series: Dancers of the World.
*(Auction PSA 22.10.03 sold £260
plus comm.)*
Est. £350-450.

HN2380
Sweet Dreams
First Version (Model 2044)
Designer M. Davies.
Date 1971 - 90.
12.5cm (5ins) high.
Multicoloured.
*(Auction PSA 23.6.04 sold
£120 plus comm.)*
Est. £150-180.

HN2385
Debbie
Designer M. Davies. Date 1969 - 82.
15cm (6ins) high.
Blue, gold and white.
Other colourways: HN2400; 'Lavender
Rose' HN3481; 'Memory Lane' HN3746;
'Moonlight Rose' HN3483; 'Old Country
Roses' HN3482; 'Tranquillity' HN3747.
*(Auction PSA 4.2.04 sold £32
plus comm.) (Ebay 20.6.04 sold £41)*
Est. £45-75.

HN2381
Kirsty
First Version (Model 2119)
Designer M. Davies.
Date 1971 - 96.
19.5cm (7.75ins) high.
Orange and white.
Other colourways: 'Janette'
HN3415.
(Ebay 10.6.04 sold £53)
Est. £60-100.

HN2386
**HRH Prince Philip Duke
of Edinburgh**
Designer M. Davies.
Date 1981. Limited edition of 1,500.
25.5cm (10ins) high.
Black and gold.
Est. £150-200.

HN2382
Secret Thoughts
First Version
Designer M. Davies.
Date 1971 - 88.
16.5cm (6.5ins) high.
Green, cream and white.
Est. £65-120.

HN2387
Helen of Troy
First Version
Designer M. Davies.
Date 1981. Limited edition of 750.
23.5cm (9.25ins) high.
Green, grey, gold and pink.
Series: Les Femmes Fatales.
Est. £500-600.

HN2388
Karen
Second Version (Model 2751)
Designer M. Davies.
Date 1982 - 99.
20.5cm (8ins) high.
Red, white and black.
Est. £135-170.

HN2393
Rosalind
Designer M. Davies.
Date 1970 - 75.
14cm (5.5ins) high.
Dark blue and white.
*(Auction PSA 1.9.04 sold £70
plus comm.)*
Est. £100-130.

HN2389
Angela
Second Version (Model 2063)
Designer M. Davies.
Date 1983 - 86.
19cm (7.5ins) high.
White.
Series: Vanity Fair Ladies.
Est. £80-100.

HN2394
Lisa
First Version
Designer M. Davies.
Date 1983 - 90.
19cm (7.5ins) high.
Purple, pink and yellow.
Other colourways:
HN2310, 3265.
Est. £60-90.

HN2390
Spinning
Designer M. Davies.
Date 1984. Limited edition of 750.
18.5cm (7.25ins) high.
Yellow, white, blue and pink.
Series: The Gentle Arts.
*(Auction PSA 22.10.03 sold
£330 plus comm.)*
Est. £450-650.

HN2395
Catherine
First Version (Model 2094)
Designer M. Davies.
Date 1983 - 84.
19cm (7.5ins) high.
Red, yellow and white.
Series: The Ladies of
Covent Garden.
Comm: Amex.
Est. £195-250.

HN2391
T'zu-hsi, Empress Dowager
Designer M. Davies.
Date 1983. Limited edition of 750.
20.5cm (8ins) high.
Red, white, blue and green.
Series: Les Femmes Fatales.
Est. £450-550.

HN2396
Wistful
First Version (Model 2567)
Designer M. Davies.
Date 1979 - 90.
16.5cm (6.5ins) high.
Peach, blue and cream.
Other colourways: HN2472.
*(Auction PSA 1.9.04 sold £55
plus comm.)*
(Ebay 3.10.04 sold £80)
Est. £70-110.

HN2392
Jennifer
Second Version (Model 2669)
Designer M. Davies.
Date 1982 - 92.
18cm (7ins) high.
Blue and white.
Est. £130-170.

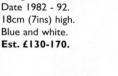

HN2397
Margaret
Second Version (Model 2729)
Designer M. Davies.
Date 1982 - 99.
19cm (7.5ins) high.
White and blue.
Other colourways: HN3496;
'Adele' HN2480; 'Camille' HN3171.
Series: Vanity Fair Ladies.
Est. £65-85.

HN2398
Alexandra
First Version (Model 2092)
Designer M. Davies.
Date 1970 - 76.
19.5cm (7.75ins) high.
Green, yellow and white.
(Ebay 23.5.04 sold £78)
Est. £85-120.

HN2410
Lesley
Designer M. Nicoll.
Date 1986 - 90.
20.5cm (8ins) high.
Orange, yellow, tan and blue.
Est. £100-135.

HN2399
Buttercup
First Version (Model 1852)
Designer M. Davies.
Date 1983 - 97.
19cm (7.5ins) high.
Red, yellow and white.
Other colourways: HN2309.
*(Auction PSA 17.9.03 sold
£52 plus comm.)*
Est. £75-120.

HN2417
The Boatman 'Skylark'
Designer M. Nicoll.
Date 1971 - 87.
16.5cm (6.5ins) high.
Yellow, green and cream.
Other colourway: HN2417A.
Series: Sea Characters.
*(Auction PSA 23.6.04 sold
£95 plus comm.)*
Est. £120-150.

HN2400
Debbie
Designer M. Davies.
Date 1983 - 95.
15cm (6ins) high.
Peach, white and lemon.
Other colourways: HN2385;
'Lavender Rose' HN3481; 'Memory
Lane' HN3746; 'Moonlight Rose'
HN3483; 'Old Country Roses'
HN3482; 'Tranquillity' HN3747.
(Ebay 22.8.04 sold £24)   **Est. £30-50.**

HN2417A
The Boatman 'Pilot'
Designer M. Nicoll.
Date 1971 - 87.
16.5cm (6.5ins) high.
Yellow, green and cream.
Other colourways: HN2417.
Series: Sea Characters.
Comm: Pilot Insurance Co.
Est. Price not available.

Picture
not available
at present, but the
same as HN2417
but with 'Pilot' on
the lifebelt.

HN2401
Sandra
Designer M. Davies.
Date 1983 - 92.
20.5cm (8ins) high.
Green and white.
Other colourways: HN2275;
'Annette' HN3495.
Est. £100-140.

HN2418
Country Love
Designer J. Bromley.
Date 1990. Limited edition
of 12,500.
20.5cm (8ins) high.
Pink, yellow and blue.
Comm: Lawleys By Post.
Est. £150-200.

HN2408
A Penny's Worth
Designer M. Nicoll.
Date 1986 - 90.
18cm (7ins) high.
Pale blue, white, yellow and tan.
*(Auction PSA 23.6.04 sold
£75 plus comm.)*
Est. £90-130.

HN2419
The Goose Girl
Second Version (Model 3900)
Designer J. Bromley.
Date 1990. Limited edition of 12,500.
20.5cm (8ins) high.
Blue, green and white.
Comm: Lawleys By Post.
Est. £150-180.

HN2420
The Shepherdess
Fourth Version (Model 3928)
Designer J. Bromley.
Date 1991. Limited edition of 12,500.
23cm (9ins) high.
Blue, white, peach and yellow.
Comm: Lawleys By Post.
Est. £150-200.

HN2424
Penny
Designer M. Davies.
Date 1983 - 92.
12cm (4.75ins) high.
Yellow and white.
Other colourways: HN2338.
(Ebay 28.6.04 sold £31)
Est. £40-60.

HN2421
Charlotte
First Version
Designer J. Bromley.
Date 1972 - 86.
17cm (6.75ins) high.
Purple, tan and white.
Other colourways: HN2423.
*(Auction PSA 17.9.03 sold
£52 plus comm.)*
Est. £70-120.

HN2425
Southern Belle
First Version (Model 1425)
Designer M. Davies.
Date 1983 - 94.
19cm (7.5ins) high.
Pale blue, pink and white.
Other colourways: HN2229.
Est. £90-120.

HN2422
Francine
Birds tail up)
Designer J. Bromley.
Date 1972 - 81.
13cm (5.25ins) high.
Green and white.
Other colourways: HN2422A
(Birds tail moulded to hand)
*(Auction PSA 1.9.04 sold £40 and
W&H 27.9.04 sold £45 plus comm.)*
Est. £55-80.

HN2426
Tranquility
Designer M. Davies.
Date 1981 - 86.
30.5cm (12ins) high.
Black.
Other colourways: HN2469.
Series: Images.
Est. £75-110.

HN2422A
Francine
(Birds tail moulded to hand)
Designer J. Bromley.
Date Not known - 1981.
12.7cm (5ins) high.
Green and white.
Other colourways: HN2422
(Birds tail up)
Est. £45-60.

HN2427
Virginals
Designer M. Davies.
Date 1971. Limited edition of 750.
16.5cm (6.5ins) high.
Green, yellow, white and brown.
Series: Lady Musicians.
(Ebay 11.6.04 sold £430)
Est. £550-800.

HN2423
Charlotte
First Version
Designer J. Bromley.
Date 1986 - 92.
17cm (6.75ins) high.
Pale blue, pink and pale brown.
Other colourways: HN2421.
(Ebay 20.8.04 sold £82)
Est. £110-150.

HN2428
The Palio
Designer M. Davies.
Date 1971. Limited edition
of 500.
45.5cm (18ins) high.
Brown, blue, red and yellow.
Est. £4000-5000.

HN2429
Elyse
Designer M. Davies.
Date 1972 - 95.
17cm (6.75ins) high.
Blue, white and red.
Other colourways:
HN2474, 4131.
*(Auction PSA 11.9.03 sold
£50 and W&H 27.9.04
sold £50 plus comm.)*
Est. £65-100.

HN2434
Fair Maiden
Designer M. Davies.
Date 1983 - 94.
13cm (5.25ins) high.
Red and white.
Other colourways: HN2211.
Est. £45-70.

HN2430
Romance
Second Version
Designer M. Davies.
Date 1972 - 81.
13cm (5.25ins) high.
Gold, green and white.
(Ebay 5.7.04 sold £78)
Est. £90-130.

HN2435
Queen of the Ice
Designer M. Davies.
Date 1983 - 86.
20.5cm (8ins) high.
Cream and gold.
Series: Enchantment.
Est. £90-120.

HN2431
Lute
Designer M. Davies.
Date 1972. Limited edition of 750.
16.5cm (6.5ins) high.
Pale blue, cream, white
and brown.
Series: Lady Musicians.
Est. £350-500.

HN2436
Scottish Highland Dancer
Designer M. Davies.
Date 1978. Limited edition of 750.
25.5cm (10ins) high.
Red, black, green
and white.
Series: Dancers of the World.
Est. £500-700.

HN2432
Violin
Designer M. Davies.
Date 1972. Limited edition of 750.
16.5cm (6.5ins) high.
Yellow, brown and white.
Series: Lady Musicians.
Est. £350-500.

HN2437
Queen of the Dawn
Designer M. Davies.
Date 1983 - 86.
21.5cm (8.5ins) high.
Cream and gold.
Series: Enchantment.
Est. £90-120.

HN2433
Peace
Designer M. Davies.
Date 1981 - 97.
20.5cm (8ins) high.
Black.
Other colourways: HN2470.
Series: Images.
Est. £55-70.

HN2438
Sonata
Designer M. Davies.
Date 1983 - 85.
16.5cm (6.5ins) high.
Cream.
Series: Enchantment.
Est. £90-120.

HN2439
Philippine Dancer
Designer M. Davies.
Date 1978. Limited edition of 750.
24.5cm (9.75ins) high.
Green, cream, yellow and red.
Series: Dancers of the World.
Est. £300-400.

HN2443A
The Judge
(Gloss)
First Version
Designer M. Nicoll.
Date 1976 - 92.
16.5cm (6.5ins) high.
Red, brown and white.
Other colourways:
HN2443 (matte)
(Auction PSA 23.6.04 sold
£75 plus comm.) **Est. £100-140.**

HN2440
Cynthia
Second Version (Model 2682)
Designer M. Davies.
Date 1984 - 92.
18.5cm (7.25ins) high.
Pale green and yellow.
Est. £120-160.

HN2444
Bon Appétit
(Matte)
Designer M. Nicoll.
Date 1972 - 76.
16cm (6.25ins) high.
Brown, tan and grey.
(Ebay 20.8.04 sold £76)
Est. £90-120.

HN2441
Pauline
Second Version (Model 2379)
Designer M. Davies.
Date 1983 Canada.
1984 Worldwide - 89.
18cm (7ins) high.
Peach and blue.
Est. £120-160.

HN2445
Parisian
(Matte)
Designer M. Nicoll.
Date 1972 - 75.
20.5cm (8ins) high.
Blue, brown and grey.
Est. £80-110.

HN2442
Sailor's Holiday
Designer M. Nicoll.
Date 1972 - 79.
15cm (6ins) high.
Orange, blue and white.
Series: Sea Characters.
Est. £150-200.

HN2446
Thanksgiving
(Matte)
Designer M. Nicoll.
Date 1972 - 76.
20.5cm (8ins) high.
Blue, red, grey and pink.
(Auction PSA 22.10.03
sold £75 plus comm.)
(Ebay 10.7.04 solld £92)
Est. £95-130.

HN2443
The Judge
(Matte)
First Version
Designer M. Nicoll.
Date 1972 - 76.
16.5cm (6.5ins) high.
Red, brown and white.
Other colourways: HN2443A
(Changed to gloss 1976)
Est. £100-145.

HN2455
The Seafarer
(Matte)
Designer M. Nicoll.
Date 1972 - 76.
21.5cm (8.5ins) high.
Yellow, blue, black and grey.
Series: Sea Characters.
Est. £120-150.

HN2460
Flower of Love
Designer J. Bromley.
Date 1991-1997
19.5cm (7.75ins) high.
White and lemon.
Other colourways: HN3970;
'Fleur' HN2368, 2369. Series:
Vanity Fair Ladies.
Est. £90-120.

HN2467
Melissa
First Version
Designer M. Davies.
Date 1981 - 94.
18cm (7ins) high.
Purple, white and cream.
*(Auction PSA 10.3.04 sold £55
plus comm.)*
Est. £70-120.

HN2461
Janine
Designer J. Bromley.
Date 1971 - 95.
20.5cm (8ins) high.
Green and white.
(Ebay 5.7.04 sold £67)
Est. £80-120.

HN2468
Diana
Second Version (Model 2209)
Designer M. Davies.
Date 1986 N. America.
1987 Worldwide - 99.
20.5cm (8ins) high.
White, pink and yellow.
Other colourways: HN3266.
*(Auction PSA 1.9.04 sold £45
plus comm.)*
(Ebay 27.7.04 sold £46) **Est. £60-100.**

HN2463
Olga
Designer J. Bromley.
Date 1972 - 75.
21cm (8.25ins) high.
Turquoise and yellow.
Est. £80-120.

HN2469
Tranquility
Designer M. Davies.
Date 1981 - 86.
30.5cm (12ins) high.
White.
Other colourways: HN2426.
Series: Images.
Est. £55-80.

HN2465
Elizabeth
Second Version (Model 2160)
Designer J. Bromley.
Date 1990 - 98.
21.5cm (8.5ins) high.
Blue, gold and white.
Est. £100-150.

HN2470
Peace
Designer M. Davies.
Date 1981 - 2000.
20.5cm (8ins) high.
White.
Other colourways: HN2433.
Series: Images.
(Ebay 29.9.04 sold £27)
Est. £35-60.

HN2466
Eve
Designer M. Davies.
Date 1984. Limited edition
of 750.
23.5cm (9.25ins) high.
Pale green, red and brown.
Series: Les Femmes Fatales.
Est. £500-650.

HN2471
Victoria
First Version
Designer M. Davies.
Date 1973 - 2000.
16.5cm (6.5ins) high.
Pink and white.
Other colourways: HN3416.
*(Auction PSA 1.9.04 sold
£50 plus comm.)*
(Ebay 21.5.04 sold £79)
Est. £90-125.

HN2472
Wistful
First Version (Model 2567)
Designer M. Davies.
Date 1985.
16.5cm (6.5ins) high.
Pale blue, red and white.
Other colourways: HN2396.
Series: M. Doulton Events.
Est. £110-150.

HN2477
Denise
Second Version (Model 2177)
Designer M. Davies.
Date 1987 - 96.
19cm (7.5ins) high.
White.
Other colourways:
'Summer Rose' HN3309.
Series: Vanity Fair Ladies.
(Ebay 23.5.04 sold £49)
Est. £55-85.

HN2473
At Ease
Designer M. Davies.
Date 1973 - 79.
15cm (6ins) high.
Lemon, white brown
and red.
Est. £110-150.

HN2478
Kelly
First Version
Designer M. Davies.
Date 1985 - 92.
19cm (7.5ins) high.
White and blue.
Other colourways: HN3222.
*(Auction PSA 26.5.04 sold £40
plus comm.)*
Est. £55-95.

HN2474
Elyse
Designer M. Davies.
Date 1986 N. America.
1987 Worldwide - 99.
17cm (6.75ins) high.
Green, white and pink.
Other colourways:
HN2429, 4131.
*(Auction PSA 1.9.04 sold £75
plus comm.)*
(Ebay 23.5.04 sold £94) **Est. £110-170.**

HN2479
Pamela
Second Version (Model 2179)
Designer M. Davies.
Date 1986 - 94.
18cm (7ins) high.
White and blue.
Other colourways: HN3223.
Series: Vanity Fair Ladies.
Est. £65-95.

HN2475
Vanity
Designer M. Davies.
Date 1973 - 92.
13cm (5.25ins) high.
Red and white.
*(Auction PSA 23.6.04 sold
£30 plus comm.)*
Est. £45-80.

HN2480
Adéle
Designer M. Davies.
Date 1987 - 92.
19cm (7.5ins) high.
White, green and blue.
Other colourways:
'Camille' HN3171; 'Margaret'
HN2397, 3496.
Est. £75-100.

HN2476
Mandy
Designer M. Davies.
Date 1982 - 92.
11.5cm (4.5ins) high.
White and yellow.
(Ebay 5.6.04 sold £21)
Est. £25-50.

HN2481
Maureen
Second Version (Model 2060)
Designer M. Davies.
Date 1987 - 92.
19cm (7.5ins) high.
White and purple.
Other colourways:
'Tina' HN3494.
Series: Vanity Fair Ladies.
Est. £75-100.

HN2482
Harp
Designer M. Davies.
Date 1973. Limited edition of 750.
23cm (9ins) high.
Gold, purple and pale green.
Series: Lady Musicians.
Est. £600-800.

HN2492
The Huntsman
Third Version (Model 2277)
Designer M. Nicoll.
Date 1974 - 79.
20.5cm (8ins) high.
Grey, cream, black and brown.
Est. £120-160.

HN2483
Flute
Designer M. Davies.
Date 1973. Limited edition of 750.
16cm (6.25ins) high.
Red, white and brown.
Series: Lady Musicians.
Est. £350-500.

HN2494
Old Meg
(Matte)
Designer M. Nicoll.
Date 1974 - 76.
20.5cm (8ins) high.
Blue, grey and brown.
Est. £90-120.

HN2484
Past Glory
Designer M. Nicoll.
Date 1973 - 79.
19cm (7.5ins) high.
Red, tan and black.
(Auction PSA 23.6.04 sold £190 plus comm.)
Est. £220-300.

HN2499
Helmsman
Designer M. Nicoll.
Date 1974 - 86.
21.5cm (8.5ins) high.
Brown, cream and yellow.
Series: Sea Characters.
(Auction PSA 11.8.04 £120 plus comm.)
Est. £150-200.

HN2485
Lunchtime
Designer M. Nicoll.
Date 1973 - 81.
20.5cm (8ins) high.
Brown, green and tan.
(Auction PSA 23.6.04 sold £75 plus comm.)
(Ebay 29.9.04 sold £84)
Est. £90-140.

HN2502
Queen Elizabeth II
First Version (Model 2244)
Designer M. Davies.
Date 1973. Limited edition of 750.
19.5cm (7.75ins) high.
Pale blue, dark blue and white.
Est. £550-650.

HN2487
Beachcomber
(Matte)
Designer M. Nicoll.
Date 1973 - 76.
16.5cm (6.5ins) high.
Purple, orange and grey.
Est. £90-120.

HN2520
The Farmer's Boy
Designer W.M. Chance.
Date 1938 - 60.
22cm (8.75ins) high.
White, tan and green.
Est. £650-750.

HN2521
Dapple Grey
Designer W.M. Chance.
Date 1938 - 60.
18cm (7ins) high.
White, grey, red and
brown.
Est. £1200-1700.

HN2545
Carmen
Second Version (Model 2198)
Designer E.J. Griffiths.
Date 1974 - 79.
29cm (11.5ins) high.
Blue, white and black.
Series: Haute Ensemble.
Est. £120-160.

HN2542
Boudoir
Designer E.J. Griffiths.
Date 1974 - 79.
31cm (12.25ins) high.
Pale blue and pink.
Series: Haute Ensemble.
Est. £150-200.

HN2546
Buddies
(Matte)
First Version (Model 2206)
Designer E.J. Griffiths.
Date 1973 - 76.
16cm (6.25ins) high.
Blue, brown and green.
*(Auction PSA 1.9.04 sold £80
plus comm.)*
Est. £100-140.

HN2543
Eliza (with moulded flowers)
First Version (Model 2202)
Designer E.J. Griffiths.
Date 1974 - 79.
30cm (11.75ins) high.
Red, white and yellow.
Other colourways: HN2543A.
Series: Haute Ensemble.
Est. £105-150.

HN2547
Mountie 1973
Designer D.V. Tootle.
Date 1973. Limited edition of
1,500 to mark centennial year of
Royal Canadian Mounted Police
and sold only in Canada.
20.5cm (8ins) high.
Red, gold and tan.
Est. £300-400.

HN2543A
Eliza (with painted flowers)
First Version (Model 2202)
Designer E.J. Griffiths.
Date 1974 - 79.
30cm (11.75ins) high.
Red, white and yellow.
Other colourways: HN2543.
Series: Haute Ensemble.
Est. £100-120.

HN2554
Masque
Designer D.V. Tootle.
Date 1973 - 75.
21.5cm (8.5ins) high.
Dark blue and white.
Other colourways: HN2554A.
Est. £150-200.

HN2544
A la Mode
Designer E.J. Griffiths.
Date 1974 - 79.
31cm (12.25ins) high.
Dark green.
Series: Haute Ensemble.
Est. £105-150.

HN2554A
Masque (Hand holds mask to face)
Designer D.V. Tootle.
Date 1975 - 82.
21.5cm (8.5ins) high.
Dark blue and white.
Other colourways: HN2554.
*(Auctions PSA 10.3.04 sold £90
plus comm.)*
(Ebay 21.7.04 sold £71)
Est. £110-150.

HN2555
Mountie 1873
Designer D.V. Tootle.
Date 1973. Limited edition of
1,500 to mark centennial year of
Royal Canadian Mounted Police,
sold only in Canada.
20.5cm (8ins) high.
Red and cream.
Est. £300-400.

HN2680
Taking Things Easy
Designer M. Nicoll.
Date 1987 - 96.
18cm (7ins) high.
Cream, blue and tan.
Other colourways: HN2677.
*(Auction PSA 23.6.04
sold £125 plus comm.)*
Est. £160-200.

HN2671
Good Morning
(Matte)
Designer M. Nicoll.
Date 1974 - 76.
20.5cm (8ins) high.
Pink, white, blue, grey and brown.
Est. £100-140.

HN2683
Stop Press
Designer M. Nicoll.
Date 1977 - 81.
19cm (7.5ins) high.
Blue, brown, white and grey.
Est. £100-140.

HN2677
Taking Things Easy
Designer M. Nicoll.
Date 1975 - 87.
18cm (7ins) high.
Blue, brown and white.
Other colourways: HN2680.
Est. £100-140.

HN2693
October
First Version (Model 2225)
Designer M. Davies.
Date 1987.
19.5cm (7.75ins) high.
White dress with flowers.
Other colourways: HN2695-2697,
2703, 2707, 2708, 2711, 2790, 2794,
3165, 3166; 'Gillian' HN3742.
Series: Figure of the Month.
Comm: Home Shopping Net. USA. **Est. £75-100.**

HN2678
The Carpenter
Designer M. Nicoll.
Date 1986 - 92.
20.5cm (8ins) high.
Blue, white, grey and brown.
*(Auction PSA 23.6.04 sold
£180 plus comm.)*
Est. £220-300.

HN2694
Fiona
Second Version (Model 2230)
Designer M. Davies.
Date 1974 - 81.
19cm (7.5ins) high.
Red and white.
Est. £75-100.

HN2679
Drummer Boy
Designer M. Nicoll.
Date 1976 - 81.
21.5cm (8.5ins) high.
Red, blue, grey and brown.
*(Auction PSA 01.9.04
sold £200 plus comm.)*
Est. £250-350.

HN2695
November
First Version (Model 2225)
Designer M. Davies.
Date 1987.
19.5cm (7.75ins) high.
White dress with flowers.
Other colourways: HN2693, 2696,
2697, 2703, 2707, 2708, 2711, 2790,
2794, 3165, 3166; 'Gillian' HN3742.
Series: Figure of the Month.
Comm: Home Shopping Net. USA. **Est. £75-100.**

HN2696
December
First Version (Model 2225)
Designer M. Davies.
Date 1987.
19.5cm (7.75ins) high.
White dress with Christmas rose.
Other colourways: HN2693, 2695,
2697, 2703, 2707, 2708, 2711, 2790,
2794, 3165, 3166; 'Gillian' HN3742.
Series: Figure of the Month.
Comm: Home Shopping Net. USA. **Est. £70-100.**

HN2701
Deborah
First Version
Designer M. Davies.
Date 1983 - 84.
19.5cm (7.75ins) high.
Green, white and pink.
Series: The Ladies of
Covent Garden.
Comm: Amex.
Est. £200-250.

HN2697
January
First Version (Model 2225)
Designer M. Davies.
Date 1987.
19.5cm (7.75ins) high.
White dress with snowdrop flowers.
Other colourways: HN2693, 2695,
2696, 2703, 2707, 2708, 2711, 2790,
2794, 3165, 3166; 'Gillian' HN3742.
Series: Figure of the Month.
Comm: Home Shopping Net. USA. **Est. £70-100.**

HN2702
Shirley
Designer M. Davies.
Date 1985 - 97.
18.5cm (7.25ins) high.
White and pink.
Est. £80-115.

HN2698
Sunday Best
First Version (Model 2609)
Designer M. Davies.
Date 1985 - 95.
19cm (7.5ins) high.
Pink and white.
Other colourways: HN2206.
Comm: Home Shopping
Network, USA.
Est. £70-115.

HN2703
February
First Version (Model 2225)
Designer M. Davies.
Date 1987.
19.5cm (7.75ins) high.
White dress with violet flowers.
Other colourways: HN2693, 2695-
2697, 2707, 2708, 2711, 2790, 2794,
3165, 3166; 'Gillian' HN3742.
Series: Figure of the Month.
Comm: Home Shopping Net. USA. **Est. £70-100.**

HN2699
Cymbals
Designer M. Davies.
Date 1974. Limited edition of 750.
19cm (7.5ins) high.
Green, white and gold.
Series: Lady Musicians.
Est. £350-450.

HN2704
Pensive Moments
Designer M. Davies.
Date 1975 - 81.
12.5cm (5ins) high.
Blue, lemon and white.
(Ebay 10.6.04 sold £50)
Est. £60-120.

HN2700
Chitarrone
Designer M. Davies.
Date 1974. Limited edition of 750.
20.5cm (8ins) high.
Blue, white and lemon.
Series: Lady Musicians.
Est. £350-500.

HN2705
Julia
First Version
Designer M. Davies.
Date 1975 - 90.
19cm (7.5ins) high.
Red, yellow and white.
Other colourways: HN2706.
*(Auction PSA 23.6.04 sold £55
plus comm.)*
(Ebay 20.8.04 sold £84)
Est. £90-135.

HN2706
Julia
First Version
Designer M. Davies.
Date 1985 - 93.
19cm (7.5ins) high.
Pale pink and green.
Other colourways: HN2705.
Est. £90-120.

HN2711
May
Second Version (Model 2225)
Designer M. Davies.
Date 1987.
19.5cm (7.75ins) high.
White & green with lily of valley.
Other colourways: HN2693,
2695-2697, 2703, 2707, 2708, 2790,
2794, 3165, 3166; 'Gillian' HN3742.
Series: Figure of the Month.
Comm: Home Shopping Net. USA. **Est. £75-100.**

HN2707
March
First Version (Model 2225)
Designer M. Davies.
Date 1987.
19.5cm (7.75ins) high.
White and green with anemones.
Other colourways: HN2693,
2695-2697, 2703, 2708, 2711, 2790,
2794, 3165, 3166; 'Gillian' HN3742.
Series: Figure of the Month.
Comm: Home Shopping Net. USA. **Est. £75-100.**

HN2712
Mantilla
Designer E.J. Griffiths.
Date 1974 - 79.
29cm (11.5ins) high.
Black, red and white.
Other colourways: HN3192.
Series: Haute Ensemble.
Est. £160-200.

HN2708
April
First Version (Model 2225)
Designer M. Davies.
Date 1987.
19.5cm (7.75ins) high.
White and tan with sweat peas.
Other colourways: HN2693,
2695-2697, 2703, 2707, 2711, 2790,
2794, 3165, 3166; 'Gillian' HN3742.
Series: Figure of the Month.
Comm: Home Shopping Net. USA. **Est. £75-100.**

HN2713
Tenderness
Designer E.J. Griffiths.
Date 1982 - 97.
30.5cm (12ins) high.
White.
Other colourways: HN2714.
Series: Images.
Est. £50-85.

HN2709
Regal Lady
Designer M. Davies.
Date 1975 - 83.
19cm (7.5ins) high.
Cream, gold and turquoise.
Est. £90-120.

HN2714
Tenderness
Designer E.J. Griffiths.
Date 1982 - 92.
30.5cm (12ins) high.
Black.
Other colourways: HN2713.
Series: Images.
Est. £65-90.

HN2710
Jean
Second Version (Model 2359)
Designer M. Davies.
Date 1983 - 86.
14.5cm (5.75ins) high.
White.
Series: Vanity Fair Ladies.
Est. £90-120.

HN2715
Patricia
Second Version (Model 2252)
Designer M. Davies.
Date 1982 - 85.
19cm (7.5ins) high.
White.
Series: Vanity Fair Ladies.
(Ebay 24.5.04. sold £145)
Est. £150-180.

HN2716
Cavalier
Second Version (Model 2199)
Designer E.J. Griffiths.
Date 1976 - 82.
25.5cm (10ins) high.
Brown, green, white and red.
Est. £90-130.

HN2717
**Private, 2nd South Carolina
Regiment, 1781**
Designer E.J. Griffiths.
Date 1975. Limited edition of 350.
29cm (11.5ins) high.
Blue, white, cream and red.
Series: Soldiers of the Revolution.
Est. £550-700.

HN2718
Lady Pamela
Designer D.V. Tootle.
Date 1974 - 81.
20.5cm (8ins) high.
Lilac, white and pink.
Est. £75-100.

HN2719
Laurianne
Designer D.V. Tootle.
Date 1974 - 79.
16.5cm (6.5ins) high.
Blue and white.
(Ebay 5.7.04. sold £66)
Est. £75-130.

HN2720
Family
First Version
Designer E.J. Griffiths.
Date 1981 - 2002.
30.5cm (12ins) high.
White.
Other colourways: HN2721.
Series: Images.
Est. £75-100.

HN2721
Family
First Version
Designer E.J. Griffiths.
Date 1981 - 92.
30.5cm (12ins) high.
Black
Other colourways: HN2720.
Series: Images.
Est. £60-100.

HN2722
Veneta
Designer W.K. Harper.
Date 1974 - 81.
19.5cm (7.75ins) high.
Orange, green and white.
Est. £75-100.

HN2723
Grand Manner
Designer W.K. Harper.
Date 1975 - 81.
19.5cm (7.75ins) high.
Lilac, yellow, green and blue.
Est. £85-110.

HN2724
Clarinda
Designer W.K. Harper.
Date 1975 - 81.
21.5cm (8.5ins) high.
Blue, white and brown.
Est. £85-110.

HN2725
Santa Claus
First Version
Designer W.K. Harper.
Date 1982 - 93.
24cm (9.5ins) high.
Red, white and brown.
Est. £160-200.

HN2726
Centurian
Designer W.K. Harper.
Date 1982 - 84.
23.5cm (9.25ins) high.
Purple, red, grey, and orange.
(Auction PSA 4.2.04. sold £100)
Est. £120-170.

HN2732
Thank You
First Version (Model 2830)
Designer W.K. Harper.
Date 1982 Canada.
1983 Worldwide - 86.
21cm (8.25ins) high.
White, grey, brown and blue.
Est. £100-150.

HN2727
Little Miss Muffet
Designer W.K. Harper.
Date 1984 - 87.
16cm (6.25ins) high.
White, pink and green.
Series: Nursery Rhymes
(Series Two)
Est. £75-100.

HN2733
Officer of the Line
Designer W.K. Harper.
Date 1982 Canada.
1983 Worldwide - 86.
23cm (9ins) high.
Red, white, brown and yellow.
Series: Sea Characters.
(Auction PSA 23.6.04. sold £135)
Est. £160-220.

HN2728
Rest Awhile
Designer W.K. Harper.
Date 1981 - 84.
20.5cm (8ins) high.
Blue, brown, purple and white.
Est. £100-140.

HN2734
Sweet Seventeen
Designer D.V. Tootle.
Date 1975 - 93.
19cm (7.5ins) high.
White with orange trimmings.
*(Auction PSA 10.3.04.
sold £45)*
Est. £55-100.

HN2729
Song of the Sea
Designer W.K. Harper.
Date 1982 Canada.
1983 Worldwide - 91.
18.5cm (7.25ins) high.
Green, blue, grey and white.
Series: Sea Characters.
*(Auction PSA 23.6.04 sold £100
plus comm.)*
Est. £150-200.

HN2735
Young Love
Designer D.V. Tootle.
Date 1975 - 90.
25.5cm (10ins) high.
Cream floral skirt, blue
and brown.
Est. £225-300.

HN2731
Thanks Doc
Designer W.K. Harper.
Date 1975 - 90.
22cm (8.75ins) high.
Brown and white.
Est. £100-150.

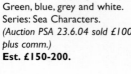

HN2736
Tracy
Designer D.V. Tootle.
Date 1983 - 94.
19cm (7.5ins) high.
White and pink.
Other colourways: HN3291.
Series: Vanity Fair Ladies.
(Ebay 25.9.04 sold £77)
Est. £75-120.

HN2737
Harlequin
Second Version (Model 2145)
Designer D.V. Tootle.
Date 1982 to date.
32cm (12.5ins) high.
Multicoloured.
Other colourways: HN3287, 4058.
Series: Prestige.
(Royal Doulton web price £1995)
(Auction PSA 22.10.03 sold £700
plus comm.) **Est. £900-1500.**

HN2738
Columbine
Third Version (Model 2440)
Designer D.V. Tootle.
Date 1982 to date.
32cm (12.5ins) high.
Blue, white, pink and orange.
Other colourways: HN3288, 4059.
Series: Prestige.
(Royal Doulton web price £1995)
(Auction PSA 22.10.03 sold £650
plus comm.) **Est. £850-1300.**

HN2739
Ann
First Version (Model 2292)
Designer D.V. Tootle.
Date 1983 - 85.
19.5cm (7.75ins) high.
White.
Series: Vanity Fair Ladies.
Est. £80-110.

HN2740
Becky
First Version
Designer D.V. Tootle.
Date 1987 - 92.
20.5cm (8ins) high.
Yellow, green, cream and red.
(Auction W&H 27.9.04 sold £60
plus comm.)
Est. £75-120.

HN2741
Sally
First Version
Designer D.V. Tootle.
Date 1987 - 91.
14cm (5.5ins) high.
Red, lilac and white.
(Ebay 26.5.04 sold £57)
Est. £60-100.

HN2742
Sheila
Designer D.V. Tootle.
Date 1983 Canada.
1984 Worldwide - 91.
21cm (8.25ins) high.
Pale blue and white.
Est. £70-100.

HN2743
Meg
Designer D.V. Tootle.
Date 1987 - 91.
21.5cm (8.5ins) high.
Yellow, white and lilac.
Est. £80-110.

HN2744
Modesty
Designer D.V. Tootle.
Date 1987 - 91.
21cm (8.25ins) high.
White.
Est. £80-100.

HN2745
Florence
Designer D.V. Tootle.
Date 1987 - 92.
20.5cm (8ins) high.
Purple and white.
Est. £110-150.

HN2746
May
First Version (Model 3456)
Designer D.V. Tootle.
Date 1987 - 92.
20.5cm (8ins) high.
Blue, red, green and tan.
Other colourways: HN3251.
(Auction W&H 27.9.04 sold
£70 plus comm.)
Est. £90-130.

HN2747
First Love
Designer D.V. Tootle.
Date 1987 - 97.
33cm (13ins) high.
White.
Series: Images.
Est. £60-90.

HN2752
**Major, 3rd New Jersey
Regiment, 1776**
Designer E.J. Griffiths.
Date 1975. Limited edition of 350.
25.5cm (10ins) high.
Blue, white and brown.
Series: Soldiers of the Revolution.
Est. £750-1000.

HN2748
Wedding Day
Designer D.V. Tootle.
Date 1987 to date.
32cm (12.5ins) high.
White.
Series: Images.
(Royal Doulton web price £185)
(Auction PSA 1.9.04 sold £65
plus comm.)
(Ebay 5.7.04 sold £58)
Est. £75-160.

HN2753
Serenade
Designer E.J. Griffiths.
Date 1983 - 85.
23cm (9ins) high.
Cream.
Series: Enchantment.
Est. £65-95.

HN2749
Lizzie
Designer D.V. Tootle.
Date 1988 - 91.
21.5cm (8.5ins) high.
Red, white, blue and green.
Est. £70-100.

HN2754
**Private, 3rd North Carolina
Regiment, 1778**
Designer E.J. Griffiths.
Date 1976. Limited edition of 350.
28cm (11ins) high.
Cream, green and brown.
Series: Soldiers of the Revolution.
Est. £500-750.

HN2750
Wedding Vows
First Version
Designer D.V. Tootle.
Date 1988 - 92.
20.5cm (8ins) high.
White.
Est. £80-120.

HN2755
**Captain, 2nd New York
Regiment, 1775**
Designer E.J. Griffiths.
Date 1976. Limited edition
of 350.
26cm (10.25ins) high.
Brown, blue and tan.
Series: Soldiers of the
Revolution.
Est. £500-750.

HN2751
Encore
First Version
Designer D.V. Tootle.
Date 1988 - 89.
25.5cm (10ins) high.
White and blue.
Series: Reflections.
Est. £80-120.

HN2756
Musicale
Designer E.J. Griffiths.
Date 1983 - 85.
23cm (9ins) high.
Cream.
Series: Enchantment.
Est. £65-95.

HN2757
Lyric
Designer E.J. Griffiths.
Date 1983 - 85.
16cm (6.25ins) high.
Cream.
Series: Enchantment.
Est. £60-90.

HN2762
Lovers
Designer D.V. Tootle.
Date 1981 - 97.
30.5cm (12ins) high.
White.
Other colourways: HN2763.
Series: Images.
Est. £70-100.

HN2758
Linda
Second Version (Model 2374)
Designer E.J. Griffiths.
Date 1984 - 88.
19.5cm (7.75ins) high.
White and pink.
(Ebay 5.6.04 sold £73)
Series: Vanity Fair Ladies.
Est. £80-110.

HN2763
Lovers
Designer D.V. Tootle.
Date 1981 - 92.
30.5cm (12ins) high.
Black.
Other colourways: HN2762.
Series: Images.
Est. £110-150.

HN2759
Private, Rhode Island Regiment, 1781
Designer E.J. Griffiths.
Date 1977. Limited edition
of 350.
30cm (11.75ins) high.
Grey, blue and brown.
Series: Soldiers of the
Revolution.
Est. £700-900.

HN2764
The Lifeboat Man
First Version
Designer W.K. Harper.
Date 1987 - 91.
24cm (9.5ins) high.
Yellow, white and brown.
Series: Sea Characters.
*(Auction PSA 22.10.03
sold £150 plus comm.)*
Est. £180-250.

HN2760
Private, Massachusetts Regiment, 1778
Designer E.J. Griffiths.
Date 1977. Limited edition of 350.
32cm (12.5ins) high.
Blue, red and tan.
Series: Soldiers of the Revolution.
Est. £600-800.

HN2765
Punch and Judy Man
Designer W.K. Harper.
Date 1981 - 90.
23.5cm (9.25ins) high.
Green, yellow and brown.
Est. £170-200.

HN2761
Private, Delaware Regiment, 1776
Designer E.J. Griffiths.
Date 1977. Limited edition of 350.
32cm (12.5ins) high.
Blue, red and tan.
Series: Soldiers of the Revolution.
Est. £600-800.

HN2766
Autumn Glory
Designer W.K. Harper.
Date 1988. Limited edition of 1,000.
30cm (11.75ins) high.
Grey and light brown.
Series: Reflections.
Comm: Home Shopping Network, USA
Est. £120-170.

HN2767
Pearly Boy
Third Version (Model 3674)
Designer W.K. Harper.
Date 1988.
19cm (7.5ins) high.
Black, white, blue and brown.
Other colourways: HN2767A.
Backstamped: Guild of Specialist
China and Glass Retailers.
Est. £85-120.

HN2767A
Pearly Boy
Third Version (Model 3674)
Designer W.K. Harper.
Date 1989 - 92.
19cm (7.5ins) high.
Black, white, blue and brown.
Other colourways: HN2767.
Est. £85-120.

HN2768
Pretty Polly
Designer W.K. Harper.
Date 1984 - 86.
15cm (6ins) high.
Pink, white, green, grey
and yellow.
Est. £85-120.

HN2769
Pearly Girl
Third Version (Model 3679)
Designer W.K. Harper.
Date 1988.
19cm (7.5ins) high.
Black, white, blue and brown.
Other colourways: HN2769A.
Backstamped: Guild of Specialist
China and Glass Retailers.
Est. £85-120.

HN2769A
Pearly Girl
Third Version (Model 3679)
Designer W.K. Harper.
Date 1989 - 92.
19cm (7.5ins) high.
Black, white, blue and brown.
Other colourways: HN2769.
Est. £85-120.

HN2770
New Companions
Designer W.K. Harper.
Date 1982 - 85.
19.5cm (7.75ins) high.
Black, white, purple and red.
Est. £95-130.

HN2771
Charlie Chaplin
Designer W.K. Harper.
Date 1989. Limited edition of 9500.
Commemorate 100 years of CC birth.
23cm (9ins) high.
Grey.
Series: Entertainers.
Comm: Lawleys By Post.
*(Auction PSA 22.10.03 sold £145 plus
comm.)*
Est. £185-230.

HN2772
Ritz Bell Boy
Designer W.K. Harper.
Date 1989 - 93.
20.5cm (8ins) high.
Black and white.
Est. £100-140.

HN2773
Robin Hood
First Version
Designer W.K. Harper.
Date 1985 - 90.
20.5cm (8ins) high.
Green, blue and brown.
*(Auction PSA 22.10.03 sold
£85 plus comm.)*
Est. £110-150.

HN2774
Stan Laurel
Designer W.K. Harper.
Date 1990. Limited edition of 9,500.
23.5cm (9.25ins) high.
Grey and black.
Series: Entertainers.
(Made as a pair with 'Oliver Hardy'
(HN2775) for centenary of
Laurel's birth)
Comm: Lawleys By Post.
Est. £175-250.

HN2775
Oliver Hardy
Designer W.K. Harper.
Date 1990. Limited edition of 9,500.
25.5cm (10ins) high.
Black, grey and white.
(Made as a pair with HN2774
'Stan Laurel')
Series: Entertainers.
Comm: Lawleys By Post.
Est. £175-250.

HN2780
**Corporal, 1st New Hampshire
Regiment, 1778**
Designer E.J. Griffiths.
Date 1975. Limited edition of 350.
33cm (13ins) high.
Green, white and red.
Series: Soldiers of the
Revolution.
Est. £500-700.

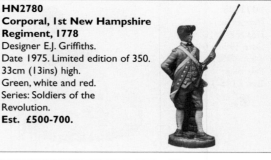

HN2776
Carpet Seller (Standing)
Second Version (Model 2769)
Designer W.K. Harper.
Date 1990 - 95.
23cm (9ins) high.
Flambé.
Series: Flambé.
Est. £200-250.

HN2781
The Lifeguard
Designer W.K. Harper.
Date 1992 - 95.
24cm (9.5ins) high.
Red, black and white.
(Auction PSA 22.10.03
sold £75 plus comm.)
Est. £90-120.

HN2777
Groucho Marx
Designer W.K. Harper.
Date 1991. Limited edition
of 9,500.
24cm (9.5ins) high.
Black, grey and white.
Series: Entertainers.
Comm: Lawleys By Post.
(Auction PSA 22.10.03
sold £130 plus comm.)
Est. £155-200.

HN2782
The Blacksmith
First Version
Designer W.K. Harper.
Date 1987 - 91.
23cm (9ins) high.
White, grey and brown.
Est. £100-130.

HN2778
Bobby
Designer W.K. Harper.
Date 1992 - 95.
23cm (9ins) high.
Black, white and grey.
Est. £90-120.

HN2783
Good Friends
Designer W.K. Harper.
Date 1985 - 90.
23cm (9ins) high.
Blue, white and brown.
Est. £100-130.

HN2779
**Private, 1st Georgia
Regiment, 1777**
Designer E.J. Griffiths.
Date 1975. Limited edition of 350.
28.5cm (11.25ins) high.
Light brown and white.
Series: Soldiers of the
Revolution.
Est. £500-700.

HN2784
The Guardsman
Designer W.K. Harper.
Date 1992 - 95.
24.5cm (9.75ins) high.
Red, black and white.
(Auction PSA 22.10.03 sold
£75 plus comm.)
Est. £90-120.

HN2788
Marjorie
Designer M. Davies.
Date 1980 - 84.
14cm (5.5ins) high.
Pale blue.
Est. £125-165.

HN2793
Clare
Designer M. Davies.
Date 1980 - 84.
19cm (7.5ins) high.
Floral lilac dress, yellow
hat and shawl.
Est. £100-130.

HN2789
Kate
First Version
Designer M. Davies.
Date 1978 - 87.
19cm (7.5ins) high.
White floral dress.
*(Auction PSA 4.2.04
sold £75 plus comm.)*
Est. £90-130.

HN2794
July
First Version (Model 2225)
Designer M. Davies.
Date 1987.
19.5cm (7.75ins) high.
White dress with flowers.
Other colourways: HN2693,
2695-2697, 2703, 2707, 2708, 2711,
2790, 3165, 3166; 'Gillian' HN3742.
Series: Figure of the Month.
Est. £70-100.

HN2790
June
Second Version (Model 2225)
Designer M. Davies.
Date 1987.
19.5cm (7.75ins) high.
White and pink with roses.
Other colourways: HN2693,
2695-2697, 2703, 2707, 2708, 2711,
2794, 3165, 3166; 'Gillian' HN3742.
Series: Figure of the Month.
Est. £70-100.

HN2795
French Horn
Designer M. Davies.
Date 1976. Limited edition of 750.
15cm (6ins) high.
Purple, turquoise and gold.
Series: Lady Musicians.
Est. £300-450.

HN2791
Elaine
First Version (Model 2652)
Designer M. Davies.
Date 1980 - 2000.
18.5cm (7.25ins) high.
Blue and white.
Other colourways:
HN3307, 3741, 4130.
*(Auction W&H 27.9.04 sold
£62 plus comm.)*
(Ebay 26.5.04 sold £75) **Est. £80-120.**

HN2796
Hurdy Gurdy
Designer M. Davies.
Date 1975. Limited edition of 750.
15cm (6ins) high.
Turquoise, white and gold.
Series: Lady Musicians.
Est. £350-450.

HN2792
Christine
Second Version (Model 2380)
Designer M. Davies.
Date 1978 - 94.
19.5cm (7.75ins) high.
Blue, yellow and white dress.
Other colourways: HN3172.
*(Auction PSA 1.9.04 sold £105
plus comm.)*
(Ebay 29.6.04 sold £77)
Est. £100-150.

HN2797
Viola d'Amore
Designer M. Davies.
Date 1976. Limited edition of 750.
15cm (6ins) high.
Yellow, blue and pink.
Series: Lady Musicians.
Est. £350-450.

HN2798
Dulcimer
Designer M. Davies.
Date 1975. Limited edition of 750.
16.5cm (6.5ins) high.
Lilac, gold, white and cream.
Series: Lady Musicians.
Est. £350-450.

HN2803
First Dance
Designer M. Davies.
Date 1977 - 92.
18.5cm (7.25ins) high.
Pale blue and white.
Other colourways: 'Samantha'
HN3304.
*(Auction W&H 27.9.04 sold
£47 plus comm.)*
(Ebay 23.5.04 sold £43)
Est. £55-100.

HN2799
Ruth
First Version
Designer M. Davies.
Date 1976 - 81.
16cm (6.25ins) high.
Green, white and pink.
Series: Kate Greenaway.
*(Auction PSA 22.10.03 sold
£85 plus comm.)*
Est. £100-150.

HN2804
Nicola
Designer M. Davies.
Date 1987.
18cm (7ins) high.
Red, lilac and white.
Other colourways: HN2839;
'Tender Moment' HN3303.
Series: M. Doulton Events.
Est. £110-150.

HN2800
Carrie
Designer M. Davies.
Date 1976 - 81.
16cm (6.25ins) high.
Turquoise, pink and white.
Series: Kate Greenaway.
*(Auction PSA 23.6.04
sold £105 plus comm.)*
Est. £125-160.

HN2805
Rebecca
First Version (Model 2663)
Designer M. Davies.
Date 1980 - 96.
19cm (7.5ins) high.
Pale blue, lilac and pink.
Est. £110-150.

HN2801
Lori
Designer M. Davies.
Date 1976 - 87.
15cm (6ins) high.
Yelow, pink and cream.
Series: Kate Greenaway.
*(Auction PSA 6.8.03
sold £65 plus comm.)*
Est. £80-120.

HN2806
Jane
Second Version (Model 2628)
Designer M. Davies.
Date 1982 - 86.
20.5cm (8ins) high.
Yellow, white and green.
Com: Barretts of Cambridge for
their bi-centenary and was sold
until the end of 1982.
Est. £100-125.

HN2802
Anna
First Version
Designer M. Davies.
Date 1976 - 82.
15cm (6ins) high.
White, pink and purple.
Series: Kate Greenaway.
*(Auction PSA 1.9.04 sold £90
plus comm.)*
Est. £80-110.

HN2807
Stephanie
First Version
Designer M. Davies.
Date 1977 - 82.
19cm (7.5ins) high.
Gold and white.
Other colourways: HN2811.
Est. £80-110.

HN2808
Balinese Dancer
Designer M. Davies.
Date 1982. Limited edition of 750.
22cm (8.75ins) high.
Green, gold, pink and yellow.
Series: Dancers of the World.
Est. £300-400.

HN2815
**Sergeant, 6th Maryland
Regiment, 1777**
Designer E.J. Griffiths.
Date 1976. Limited edition of 350.
35cm (13.75ins) high.
Light grey, white and blue.
Series: Soldiers of the Revolution.
Est. £500-650.

HN2809
North American Indian Dancer
Designer M. Davies.
Date 1982. Limited edition of 750.
21.5cm (8.5ins) high.
Yellow, pink and white.
Series: Dancers of the World.
Est. £300-400.

HN2816
Votes for Women
Designer W.K. Harper.
Date 1978 - 81.
24.5cm (9.75ins) high.
Grey, white and orange.
Est. £110-150.

HN2810
Solitude
Designer M. Davies.
Date 1977 - 83.
14cm (5.5ins) high.
Cream, orange, blue
and brown.
*(Auction W&H 27.9.04
sold £52 plus comm.)*
Est. £100-200.

HN2818
Balloon Girl
Designer W.K. Harper.
Date 1982 - 97.
16.5cm (6.5ins) high.
Yellow, green, white, grey
and red.
*(Auction PSA 23.6.04 sold
£150 plus comm.)*
(Ebay 9.6.04 sold £147)
Est. £175-225.

HN2811
Stephanie
First Version
Designer M. Davies.
Date 1983 - 94.
19cm (7.5ins) high.
Red and white.
Other colourways: HN2807.
*(Auction W&H 27.9.04 sold
£60 plus comm.)*
Est. £75-120.

HN2824
Harmony
First Version
Designer R. Jefferson.
Date 1978 - 84.
20.5cm (8ins) high.
Grey and white.
Est. £100-130.

HN2814
Eventide
Designer W.K. Harper.
Date 1977 - 91.
19cm (7.5ins) high.
Blue, white, yellow,
red and green.
Est. £95-140.

HN2825
Lady and the Unicorn
Designer R. Jefferson.
Date 1982. Limited edition
of 300.
22cm (8.75ins) high.
Blue, white, gold and red.
Series: Myths and
Maidens.
Est. £700-1000.

HN2826
Leda and the Swan
Designer R. Jefferson.
Date 1983. Limited edition
of 300.
24.5cm (9.75ins) high.
White swan, yellow dress,
green, red and blue.
Series: Myths and Maidens.
Est. £700-1000.

HN2827
Juno and the Peacock
Designer R. Jefferson.
Date 1984. Limited edition
of 300.
28cm (11ins) high.
Turquoise, lilac, green
and gold.
Series: Myths and Maidens.
Est. £700-1000.

HN2828
Europa and the Bull
Second Version (Model 2835)
Designer R. Jefferson.
Date 1985. Limited edition
of 300.
26.5cm (10.5ins) high.
Yellow, lilac, orange, and white.
Series: Myths and Maidens.
(Ebay 21.3.04 sold £542)
Est. £700-1000.

HN2829
Diana the Huntress
Designer R. Jefferson.
Date 1986. Limited edition of 300.
28.5cm (11.25ins) high.
Orange, yellow, green
and white.
Series: Myths and Maidens.
Est. £700-1000.

HN2830
Indian Temple Dancer
Designer M. Davies.
Date 1977. Limited edition of 750.
24cm (9.5ins) high.
Gold, brown, grey and green.
Series: Dancers of the World.
Est. £400-525.

HN2831
Spanish Flamenco Dancer
Designer M. Davies.
Date 1977. Limited edition of 750.
24cm (9.5ins) high.
Red, yellow and white.
Series: Dancers of the World.
Est. £600-800.

HN2832
Fair Lady
First Version (Model 1832)
Designer M. Davies.
Date 1977- 96.
19cm (7.5ins) high.
Red and white.
Other colourways: HN2193,
2835; 'Kay' HN3340.
Est. £75-110.

HN2833
Sophie
First Version (Model 2552)
Designer M. Davies.
Date 1977- 87.
16cm (6.25ins) high.
Red, pink and white.
Series: Kate Greenaway.
*(Auction PSA 23.6.04
sold £80 plus comm.)*
Est. £100-135.

HN2834
Emma
First Version (Model 2553)
Designer M. Davies.
Date 1977- 81.
15cm (6ins) high.
Pink, yellow, green and white.
Series: Kate Greenaway.
*(Auction PSA 1.9.04 sold £105
plus comm.)*
Est. £130-170.

HN2835
Fair Lady
First Version (Model 1832)
Designer M. Davies.
Date 1977- 96.
19cm (7.5ins) high.
Pink and white.
Other colourways: HN2193,
2832; 'Kay' HN3340.
Est. £75-100.

HN2836
Polish Dancer
Designer M. Davies.
Date 1980. Limited edition
of 750.
23.5cm (9.25ins) high.
Multicoloured.
Series: Dancers of the World.
Est. £300-450.

HN2841
Mother and Daughter
First Version
Designer E.J. Griffiths.
Date 1981 - 97.
21.5cm (8.5ins) high.
White.
Other colourways: HN2843.
Series: Images.
Est. £60-100.

HN2837
Awakening
Second Version (Model 2696)
Designer M. Davies.
Date 1981 - 97.
21.5cm (8.5ins) high.
Black.
Other colourways: HN2875.
Series: Images.
Est. £50-75.

HN2842
Innocence
First Version
Designer E.J. Griffiths.
Date 1979 - 83.
19cm (7.5ins) high.
Red.
Est. £80-120.

HN2838
Sympathy
Designer M. Davies.
Date 1981- 86.
30cm (11.75ins) high.
Black.
Other colourways: HN2876.
Series: Images.
Est. £70-90.

HN2843
Mother and Daughter
First Version
Designer E.J. Griffiths.
Date 1981 - 92.
21.5cm (8.5ins) high.
Black.
Other colourways: HN2841.
Series: Images.
Est. £60-100.

HN2839
Nicola
Designer M. Davies.
Date 1978 - 95.
18cm (7ins) high.
Lilac, yellow and white.
Other colourways: HN2804;
'Tender Moment' HN3303.
Est. £110-150.

HN2844
**Sergeant, Virginia 1st
Regiment Continental Light
Dragoons, 1777**
Designer E.J. Griffiths.
Date 1978. Limited edition
of 350.
37cm (14.5ins) high.
Brown, black, lemon and green.
Series: Soldiers of the Revolution.
Est. £1750-2500.

HN2840
Chinese Dancer
Designer M. Davies.
Date 1980. Limited edition of 750.
22cm (8.75ins) high.
Red floral tunic, green skirt,
purple and lilac.
Series: Dancers of the World.
Est. £300-400.

HN2845
**Private, Connecticut
Regiment, 1777**
Designer E.J. Griffiths.
Date 1978. Limited edition of 350.
30cm (11.75ins) high.
Brown, red, white and cream.
Series: Soldiers of the Revolution.
Est. £500-700.

HN2846
Private, Pennsylvania Rifle Battalion, 1776
Designer E.J. Griffiths.
Date 1978. Limited edition of 350.
21.5cm (8.5ins) high.
Grey and gold.
Series: Soldiers of the Revolution.
Est. £500-700.

HN2858
The Doctor
First Version
Designer W.K. Harper.
Date 1979 - 92.
19cm (7.5ins) high.
Black, grey, tan and pink.
(Auction PSA 23.6.04 sold £85 plus comm.)
Est. £110-150.

HN2851
Christmas Parcels
First Version (Model 2519)
Designer W.K. Harper.
Date 1978 - 82.
22cm (8.75ins) high.
Black, tan, blue and red.
(Auction PSA 23.6.04 sold £75 plus comm.)
Est. £90-130.

HN2859
The Statesman
Designer W.K. Harper.
Date 1988 - 90.
23.5cm (9.25ins) high.
Black, pink, brown and grey.
Other colourways: 'Sir John A. Macdonald' HN2860.
Est. £90-120.

HN2855
Embroidering
Designer W.K. Harper.
Date 1980 - 90.
19cm (7.5ins) high.
Grey, cream and brown.
(Auction PSA 23.6.04 sold £130 plus comm.)
Est. £150-200.

HN2860
Sir John A. MacDonald.
Designer W.K. Harper.
Date 1987.
23.5cm (9.25ins) high.
Black, pink and grey.
Other colourways: 'The Statesman' HN2859. Made to commemorate the centenary of Dominion of Canada General Insurance Co.
Est. £90-120.

HN2856
St. George
Third Version (Model 2565)
Designer W.K. Harper.
Date 1978 - 94.
42cm (16.5ins) high.
Cream, brown, pink and grey.
Est. £3500-4000.

HN2861
George Washington at Prayer
Designer L. Ispanky.
Date 1977. Limited edition of 750.
32cm (12.5ins) high.
Blue, red, grey and tan.
Est. £1000-1500.

HN2857
Covent Garden
Second Version (Model 3510)
Designer W.K. Harper.
Date 1988 - 90.
25.5cm (10ins) high.
Pale blue and white with coloured balloons and flowers.
Series: Reflections. (This figure was not introduced in the UK)
Est. £70-100.

HN2862
First Waltz
Designer M. Davies.
Date 1979 - 83.
19cm (7.5ins) high.
Red dress, white fan and sleeves.
Est. £120-160.

HN2863
Lucy
First Version (Model 2686)
Designer M. Davies.
Date 1980 - 84.
15cm (6ins) high.
Blue and white.
Series: Kate Greenaway.
Est. £90-120.

HN2868
Cleopatra
First Version
Designer M. Davies.
Date 1979. Limited
edition of 750.
19cm (7.5ins) high.
White, orange, blue
and black.
Series: Les Femmes
Fatales.
Est. £750-950.

HN2864
Tom
Designer M. Davies.
Date 1978 - 81.
14.5cm (5.75ins) high.
Blue, yellow and white.
Series: Kate Greenaway.
Est. £110-160.

HN2869
Louise
First Version (Model 2472)
Designer M. Davies.
Date 1979 - 86.
16cm (6.25ins) high.
Brown, yellow and white.
Series: Kate Greenaway.
Est. £100-135.

HN2865
Tess
Designer M. Davies.
Date 1978 - 83.
14.5cm (5.75ins) high.
Green, white and pink.
Series: Kate Greenaway.
Est. £95-125.

HN2870
Beth
First Version
Designer M. Davies.
Date 1979 - 83.
14.5cm (5.75ins) high.
Pink and white.
Series: Kate Greenaway.
Est. £150-190.

HN2866
Mexican Dancer
Designer M. Davies.
Date 1979. Limited edition of 750.
21.5cm (8.5ins) high.
Ornge, yellow and white.
Series: Dancers of the World.
Est. £300-400.

HN2871
Beat You To It
Designer M. Davies.
Date 1980 - 87.
18cm (7ins) high.
Pink, gold, white and blue.
Est. £125-170.

HN2867
Kurdish Dancer
Designer M. Davies.
Date 1979. Limited edition of 750.
21.5cm (8.5ins) high.
Blue and purple.
Series: Dancers of the World.
Est. £300-400.

HN2872
The Young Master
Designer M. Davies.
Date 1980 - 89.
18cm (7ins) high.
Brown, grey and purple.
*(Auction PSA 1.9.04 sold
£80 plus comm.)*
(Ebay 3.10.04 sold £112)
Est. £110-160.

HN2873
The Bride
Third Version (Model 2637)
Designer M. Davies.
Date 1980 - 89.
20.5cm (8ins) high.
White with gold trimming.
Est. £75-100.

HN2878
HM Queen Elizabeth II
Second Version (Model 3030)
Designer E.J. Griffiths.
Date 1983. Limited edition of 2,500.
26.5cm (10.5ins) high.
Blue, white and red.
Est. £150-200.

HN2874
The Bridesmaid
Fourth Version (Model 2639)
Designer M. Davies.
Date 1980 - 89.
13.5cm (5.25ins) high.
White with gold trimmings.
Est. £40-60.

HN2879
The Gamekeeper
Designer E.J. Griffiths.
Date 1984 - 92.
18cm (7ins) high.
Black, white, green and tan.
Est. £90-130.

HN2875
Awakening
Second Version (Model 2696)
Designer M. Davies.
Date 1981 - 97.
21.5cm (8.5ins) high.
White.
Other colourways: HN2837.
Series: Images.
Est. £40-60.

HN2880
Monique
Designer E.J. Griffiths.
Date 1984.
32cm (12.5ins) high.
Pale green.
Other colourways: 'Allure' HN3080.
Series: Elegance (Series One)
Est. £150-200.

HN2876
Sympathy
Designer M. Davies.
Date 1981 - 86.
30cm (11.75ins) high.
White.
Other colourways: HN2838.
Series: Images.
Est. £50-65.

HN2881
Lord Olivier as Richard III
Designer E.J. Griffiths.
Date 1985. Limited edition of 750.
29cm (11.5ins) high.
Black, brown, blue and red.
Est. £300-400.

HN2877
The Wizard
First Version
Designer A. Maslankowski.
Date 1979 to date.
25.5cm (10ins) high.
Blue, black and grey.
Other colourways:HN3121, 4069.
(Royal Doulton web price £170)
(Auction PSA 23.6.04 sold
£90 and W&H 27.9.04 sold £100
plus comm.) **Est. £125-170.**

HN2882
HM Queen Elizabeth The
Queen Mother
First Version
Designer E.J. Griffiths.
Date 1980. Limited edition of 1,500.
20.5cm (8ins) high.
Pink, white and blue.
Est. £350-500.

HN2883
HRH The Prince of Wales
First Version (Model 2877)
Designer E.J. Griffiths.
Date 1981. Limited edition of 1,500.
Made to commemorate the Royal
Wedding. (Made as a pair to HN2885)
20.5cm (8ins) high.
White, purple and black.
Est. £250-350.

HN2889
Captain Cook
Designer W.K. Harper.
Date 1980 - 84.
20.5cm (8ins) high.
Black, yellow and cream.
(Auction PSA 23.6.04 sold
£130 plus comm.)
(Ebay 5.6.04 sold £155)
Est. £160-220.

HN2884
HRH The Prince of Wales
Second Version (Model 2899)
Designer E.J. Griffiths.
Date 1981. Limited edition of 1,500.
(Made as a pair to HN2887)
20.5cm (8ins) high.
Black, red, brown and gold.
Est. £250-350.

HN2890
The Clown
Designer W.K. Harper.
Date 1979 - 88.
22cm (8.75ins) high.
Gold, white and grey.
Est. £135-185.

HN2885
Lady Diana Spencer
Designer E.J. Griffiths.
Date 1982. Limited edition of 1,500.
(Made as a pair to HN2883)
19.5cm (7.75ins) high.
Blue and white.
Est. £450-600.

HN2891
The Newsvendor
Designer W.K. Harper.
Date 1986. Limited edition of
2,500. Made to commemorate
the 150th Anniversary of the
Newspaper Society.
20.5cm (8ins) high.
Tan, white and grey.
Est. £150-200.

HN2887
HRH The Princess of Wales
Designer E.J. Griffiths.
Date 1982. Limited edition of 1,500.
(Made as a pair to HN2884)
19.5cm (7.75ins) high.
Cream and yellow.
Est. £800-1000.

HN2892
The Chief
Designer W.K. Harper.
Date 1979 - 88.
18cm (7ins) high.
Orange, tan, pink and grey.
(Auction PSA 1.9.04 sold £85
plus comm.)
Est. £100-150.

HN2888
**His Holiness Pope
John-Paul II**
Designer E.J. Griffiths.
Date 1982 - 92.
25.5cm (10ins) high.
White.
This figure commemorates the
visit to Britain by his Holiness.
(Auction PSA 11.8.04 sold
£80 plus comm.)
Est. £95-130.

HN2894
Balloon Clown
Designer W.K. Harper.
Date 1986 - 92.
23.5cm (9.25ins) high.
White and blue with
multicoloured balloons.
Est. £135-160.

HN2895
Morning Ma'am
Designer W.K. Harper.
Date 1986 - 89.
23cm (9ins) high.
Pale blue, brown and yellow.
(Auction PSA 23.6.04 sold
£85 plus comm.)
Est. £100-140.

HN2900
Ruth the Pirate Maid
Designer W.K. Harper.
Date 1981 - 85.
28.5cm (11.25ins) high.
Brown, cream, yellow and blue.
Series: Gilbert and Sullivan.
Est. £300-400.

HN2896
Good Day Sir
Designer W.K. Harper.
Date 1986 - 89.
21.5cm (8.5ins) high.
Purple, white and red.
(Auction PSA 11.8.04 sold
£65 plus comm.)
Est. £80-110.

HN2901
The Pirate King
Designer W.K. Harper.
Date 1981 - 85.
26cm (10.25ins) high.
Blue, tan, green and gold.
Series: Gilbert and Sullivan.
Est. £300-400.

HN2897
Francoise
Designer W.K. Harper.
Date 1984.
32cm (12.5ins) high.
White and cream.
Series: Elegance (Series One)
Est. £150-200.

HN2902
Elsie Maynard
Second Version (Model 2845)
Designer W.K. Harper.
Date 1982 - 85.
28.5cm (11.25ins) high.
Green, tan and white.
Series: Gilbert and Sullivan.
Est. £300-400.

HN2898
Ko-Ko
Second Version (Model 2653)
Designer W.K. Harper.
Date 1980 - 85.
27.5cm (10.75ins) high.
Blue, yellow, tan and red.
Series: Gilbert and Sullivan.
Est. £300-400.

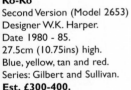

HN2903
Colonel Fairfax
Designer W.K. Harper.
Date 1982 - 85.
29cm (11.5ins) high.
Red, white and gold.
Series: Gilbert and Sullivan.
Est. £350-450.

HN2899
Yum-Yum
Second Version (Model 2704)
Designer W.K. Harper.
Date 1980 - 85.
27.5cm (10.75ins) high.
Green, white and yellow.
Series: Gilbert and Sullivan.
Est. £350-450.

HN2906
Paula
First Version (Model 2672)
Designer P. Parsons.
Date 1980 - 86.
19cm (7.5ins) high.
Yellow and white with
green trimmings.
Other colourways: HN3234.
(Auction PSA 1.9.04 sold £45
plus comm.)
Est. £60-115.

HN2907
The Piper
First Version (Model 2664)
Designer M. Abberley.
Date 1980 - 92.
20.5cm (8ins) high.
Green, brown, white and blue.
Est. £170-220.

HN2912
Frodo
Designer D. Lyttleton.
Date 1980 - 84.
11.5cm (4.5ins) high.
Black and white.
Series: Middle Earth (Tolkien)
*(Auction PSA 23.6.04 sold £75
plus comm.)*
Est. £90-130.

HN2908
HMS Ajax
Designer S. Keenan.
Date 1980. Limited edition of 950.
24.5cm (9.75ins) high.
Green, red, gold and blue.
Series: Ships' Figureheads.
Est. £250-300.

HN2913
Gollum
Designer D. Lyttleton.
Date 1980 - 84.
8cm (3.25ins) high.
Brown.
Series: Middle Earth (Tolkien)
*(Auction PSA 23.6.04 sold £80
plus comm.)*
Est. £95-135.

HN2909
Benmore
Designer S. Keenan.
Date 1980. Limited edition of 950.
23cm (9ins) high.
Red, blue, white and gold.
Series: Ships' Figureheads.
Est. £250-300.

HN2914
Bilbo
Designer D. Lyttleton.
Date 1980 - 84.
11cm (4.25ins) high.
Brown, yellow and tan.
Series: Middle Earth (Tolkien)
*(Auction PSA 23.6.04 sold £85
plus comm.)*
Est. £100-125.

HN2910
Lalla Rookh
Designer S. Keenan.
Date 1981. Limited edition of 950.
23cm (9ins) high.
Green, white, brown and gold.
Series: Ships' Figureheads.
Est. £250-350.

HN2915
Galadriel
Designer D. Lyttleton.
Date 1981 - 84.
14cm (5.5ins) high.
White.
Series: Middle Earth (Tolkien)
*(Auction PSA 23.6.04 sold £60
plus comm.)*
Est. £75-100.

HN2911
Gandalf
Designer D. Lyttleton.
Date 1980 - 84.
18cm (7ins) high.
Green and white.
Series: Middle Earth (Tolkien)
*(Auction PSA 23.6.04 Figure sold £110
plus comm. Lord of the Rings' display
stand sold £450 plus comm.)*
Est. £140-175. Figure.
Est. £550-650. Display stand.

HN2916
Aragorn
Designer D. Lyttleton.
Date 1981 - 84.
15cm (6ins) high.
Brown, black and green.
Series: Middle Earth (Tolkien)
*(Auction PSA 23.6.04 sold £60
plus comm.)*
Est. £75-100.

HN2917
Legolas
Designer D. Lyttleton.
Date 1981 - 84.
15cm (6ins) high.
Cream, yellow and tan.
Series: Middle Earth (Tolkien)
*(Auction PSA 23.6.04 sold £80
plus comm.)*
Est. £95-130.

HN2922
Gimli
Designer D. Lyttleton.
Date 1981 - 84.
14cm (5.5ins) high.
Brown, tan, white and blue.
Series: Middle Earth (Tolkien)
Est. £75-120.

HN2918
Boromir
Designer D. Lyttleton.
Date 1981 - 84.
16cm (6.25ins) high.
Brown, tan and green.
Series: Middle Earth (Tolkien)
*(Auction PSA 23.6.04 sold
£110 plus comm.)*
Est. £140-200.

HN2923
Barliman Butterbur
Designer D. Lyttleton.
Date 1982 - 84.
13cm (5.25ins) high.
Tan, white and brown.
Series: Middle Earth (Tolkien)
*(Auction PSA 1.9.04 sold £230
plus comm.)*
Est. £300-400.

HN2919
Rachel
First Version
Designer P. Gee.
Date 1981 - 84.
19.5cm (7.75ins) high.
Yellow, tan and green.
Other colourways: HN2936.
Est. £80-120.

HN2924
Tom Bombadil
Designer D. Lyttleton.
Date 1982 - 84.
14.5cm (5.75ins) high.
Black, brown and yellow.
Series: Middle Earth (Tolkien)
*(Auction PSA 23.6.04
sold £215 plus comm.)*
Est. £300-400.

HN2920
Yearning
Designer P. Gee.
Date 1982 - 86.
30cm (11.75ins) high.
White.
Other colourways: HN2921.
Series: Images.
Est. £55-75.

HN2925
Samwise
Designer D. Lyttleton.
Date 1982 - 84.
11.5cm (4.5ins) high.
Black, tan and brown.
Series: Middle Earth (Tolkien)
*(Auction PSA 23.6.04 sold £290
plus comm.)*
Est. £350-450.

HN2921
Yearning
Designer P. Gee.
Date 1982 - 86.
30cm (11.75ins) high.
Black.
Other colourways: HN2920.
Series: Images.
Est. £55-75.

HN2926
Tom Sawyer
Designer D. Lyttleton.
Date 1982 - 85.
13cm (5.25ins) high.
Blue, brown and tan.
Series: Characters from
Children's Literature.
Est. £70-100.

HN2927
Huckleberry Finn
Designer D. Lyttleton.
Date 1982 - 85.
18cm (7ins) high.
Brown and orange.
Series: Characters from
Children's Literature.
Est. £70-100.

HN2932
Hibernia
Designer S. Keenan.
Date 1983. Limited edition of 950.
24cm (9.5ins) high.
Grey, black, gold and white.
Series: Ships' Figureheads.
Est. £950-1350.

HN2928
Nelson
Designer S. Keenan.
Date 1981. Limited edition of 950.
22cm (8.75ins) high.
Blue, red, gold and green.
Series: Ships' Figureheads.
Est. £300-400.

HN2933
Kathleen
Second Version (Model 2965)
Designer S. Keenan.
Date 1983 Canada.
1984 Worldwide - 87.
16.5cm (6.5ins) high.
Yellow, green and orange.
Other colourways: HN3100.
(Ebay 29.6.04 sold £77)
Est. £90-130.

HN2929
Chieftan
Designer S. Keenan.
Date 1982. Limited edition of 950.
22cm (8.75ins) high.
Green, gold, black and brown.
Series: Ships' Figureheads.
Est. £450-600.

HN2934
Balloon Boy
Designer P. Gee.
Date 1984 - 98.
19cm (7.5ins) high.
Black, green, grey and white
with coloured balloons.
(Ebay 9.6.04 sold £150)
Est. £160-250.

HN2930
Pocahontas
Designer S. Keenan.
Date 1982. Limited edition of 950.
20.5cm (8ins) high.
White, gold, blue and red.
Series: Ships' Figureheads.
Est. £500-700.

HN2935
Balloon Lady
Designer P. Gee.
Date 1984 to date.
21cm (8.25ins) high.
Orange, purple and white with
coloured balloons.
(Royal Doulton web price £140)
(Ebay 9.7.04 sold £100)
*(Auction PSA 1.9.04 sold £90
plus comm.)*
Est. £100-150.

HN2931
Mary Queen of Scots
First Version (Model 2952)
Designer S. Keenan.
Date 1983. Limited edition of 950.
24cm (9.5ins) high.
Purple, gold, white and red.
Series: Ships' Figureheads.
Est. £700-1000.

HN2936
Rachel
First Version
Designer P. Gee.
Date 1985 - 97.
19.5cm (7.75ins) high.
Red, grey and cream.
Other colourways: HN2919.
*(Auction PSA 23.6.04 sold £70
plus comm.)*
(Ebay 4.6.04 sold £100)
Est. £100-150.

HN2937
Gail
First Version (Model 2732)
Designer P. Gee.
Date 1986 - 97.
19cm (7.5ins) high.
Red, yellow and cream.
(Auction W&H 27.9.04 sold
£62 plus comm.)
(Ebay 28.6.04 sold £70)
Est. £75-120.

HN2942
Prized Possessions
Designer R. Tabbenor.
Date 1982.
16.5cm (6.5ins) high.
Cream, grey, purple and green.
Series: RDICC.
Est. £250-350.

HN2938
Isadora
Designer P. Gee.
Date 1986 - 92.
20.5cm (8ins) high.
Lilac and purple.
Other colourways:
'Celeste' HN3322.
(Ebay 26.5.04 sold £98)
(Auction W&S 4.10.04 sold
£78 plus comm.)
Est. £100-150.

HN2943
The China Repairer
Designer R. Tabbenor.
Date 1982 Canada.
1983 Worldwide - 88.
17cm (6.75ins) high.
Pale blue, red and tan.
Est. £110-160.

HN2939
Donna
Designer P. Gee.
Date 1982 - 94.
19.5cm (7.75ins) high.
White.
Series: Vanity Fair Ladies.
Est. £70-100.

HN2944
The Rag Doll Seller
Designer R. Tabbenor.
Date 1984 - 95.
18cm (7ins) high.
White, green, lilac and yellow.
Est. £130-165.

HN2940
All Aboard
Designer R. Tabbenor.
Date 1982 - 86.
23.5cm (9.25ins) high.
Blue, black, tan and cream.
Series: Sea Characters.
Est. £125-165.

HN2945
Pride and Joy
First Version
Designer R. Tabbenor.
Date 1984.
18cm (7ins) high.
Gold, tan, white and green.
Series: RDICC.
Est. £110-150.

HN2941
Tom Brown
Designer R. Tabbenor.
Date 1983 - 85.
18cm (7ins) high.
Blue, white and cream.
Series: Characters from
Children's Literature.
Est. £55-100.

HN2946
Elizabeth
First Version (Model 2739)
Designer B. Franks.
Date 1982 - 86.
20.5cm (8ins) high.
Yellow, tan and green.
Est. £150-200.

HN2952
Susan
Second Version (Model 2749)
Designer P. Parsons.
Date 1982 - 93.
21.5cm (8.5ins) high.
Blue, pink, white and black.
Other colourways: HN3050.
(Auction PSA 10.3.04 sold £60 plus comm.)
Est. £80-120.

HN2953
Sleepy Darling
Designer P. Parsons.
Date 1981.
18.5cm (7.25ins) high.
Pale blue, cream and pink.
Series: RDICC.
Est. £100-135.

HN2954
Samantha
First Version (Model 2825)
Designer P. Parsons.
Date 1982 - 84.
18cm (7ins) high.
White.
Series: Vanity Fair Ladies.
(Auction PSA 22.10.03 sold £50 plus comm.)
(Ebay 28.7.04 sold £65)
Est. £80-130.

HN2955
Nancy
Designer P. Parsons.
Date 1982 - 94.
19cm (7.5ins) high.
White.
Series: Vanity Fair Ladies.
Est. £80-120.

HN2956
Heather
Designer P. Parsons.
Date 1982 - 2000.
15cm (6ins) high.
White.
Other colourways:
'Marie' HN3357.
Series: Vanity Fair Ladies.
Est. £60-100.

HN2957
Edith
Designer P. Parsons.
Date 1982 - 85.
14.5cm (5.75ins) high.
Green, pink and white.
Series: Kate Greenaway.
Est. £120-160.

HN2958
Amy
First Version (Model 2919)
Designer P. Parsons.
Date 1982 - 87.
15cm (6ins) high.
White, blue, red and yellow.
Series: Kate Greenaway.
Est. £95-135.

HN2959
Save Some for Me
Designer P. Parsons.
Date 1982 - 85.
18.5cm (7.25ins) high.
Blue, white and tan.
Series: Childhood Days.
Est. £85-120.

HN2960
Laura
First Version
Designer P. Parsons.
Date 1982 Canada.
1984 Worldwide - 94.
18.5cm (7.25ins) high.
Pale blue skirt with white,
floral overskirt.
Other colourways: HN3136.
Est. £100-135.

HN2961
Carol
Designer P. Parsons.
Date 1982 - 95.
19cm (7.5ins) high.
White with pink trimmings.
Series: Vanity Fair Ladies.
(Ebay 6.7.04 sold £75)
Est. £80-120.

HN2962
Barbara
Second Version (Model 2857)
Designer P. Parsons.
Date 1982 - 84.
20.5cm (8ins) high.
White.
Series: Vanity Fair Ladies.
Est. £100-135.

HN2967
Please Keep Still
Designer P. Parsons.
Date 1982 - 85.
11.5cm (4.5ins) high.
Yellow, white and blue.
Series: Childhood Days.
Est. £90-140.

HN2963
It Won't Hurt
Designer P. Parsons.
Date 1982 - 85.
19cm (7.5ins) high.
Brown, tan, blue and white.
Series: Childhood Days.
Est. £80-120.

HN2968
Juliet
First Version (Model 2720)
Designer P. Parsons.
Date 1983 - 84.
18cm (7ins) high.
White, blue and pink.
Series: Ladies of
Covent Garden.
Comm: Amex.
Est. £200-250.

*Picture
not available
at present*

HN2964
Dressing Up
First Version (Model 2954)
Designer P. Parsons.
Date 1982 - 85.
19cm (7.5ins) high.
White, yellow and blue.
Series: Childhood Days.
Est. £75-100.

HN2969
Kimberley
First Version (Model 2667)
Designer P. Parsons.
Date 1983 - 84.
20.5cm (8ins) high.
Yellow and white.
Other colourways:
'Yours Forever' HN3354.
Series: Ladies of Covent Garden.
Est. £180-235.

HN2965
Pollyanna
Designer P. Parsons.
Date 1982 - 85.
17cm (6.75ins) high.
White, tan and grey.
Series: Characters from
Children's Literature.
Est. £70-95.

HN2970
And One For You
Designer A. Hughes.
Date 1982 - 85.
16.5cm (6.5ins) high.
White and orange.
Series: Childhood Days.
Est. £70-100.

HN2966
And So To Bed
Designer P. Parsons.
Date 1982 - 85.
19cm (7.5ins) high.
Yellow and cream.
Series: Childhood Days.
Est. £100-135.

HN2971
As Good As New
Designer A. Hughes.
Date 1982 - 85.
16.5cm (6.5ins) high.
Blue, tan and green.
Series: Childhood Days.
Est. £85-110.

HN2972
Little Lord Fauntleroy
Designer A. Hughes.
Date 1982 - 85.
16cm (6.25ins) high.
Blue and white.
Series: Characters from
Children's Literature.
*(Auction PSA 23.6.04 sold £35
plus comm.)*
Est. £45-75.

HN2978
The Magpie Ring
Designer A. Hughes.
Date 1983 - 86.
20.5cm (8ins) high.
Cream.
Series: Enchantment.
Est. £85-130.

HN2974
Carolyn
Second Version (Model 2862)
Designer A. Hughes.
Date 1982 Canada.
1984 Worldwide - 86.
14cm (5.5ins) high.
Green, brown, yellow and white.
Est. £90-140.

HN2979
Fairyspell
Designer A. Hughes.
Date 1983 - 86.
13.5cm (5.25ins) high.
Cream.
Series: Enchantment.
Est. £85-130.

HN2975
Heidi
Designer A. Hughes.
Date 1983 - 85.
11.5cm (4.5ins) high.
Green, brown and white.
Series: Characters from
Children's Literature.
Est. £85-130.

HN2980
Just One More
Designer A. Hughes.
Date 1983 Canada.
1984 Worldwide - 85.
18cm (7ins) high.
Gold, green and blue.
Series: Childhood Days.
Est. £85-130.

HN2976
I'm Nearly Ready
Designer A. Hughes.
Date 1983 Canada.
1984 Worldwide - 85.
19cm (7.5ins) high.
Black, brown and white.
Series: Childhood Days.
Est. £85-130.

HN2981
Stick 'em Up
Designer A. Hughes.
Date 1983 Canada.
1984 Worldwide - 85.
18cm (7ins) high.
Blue, white and tan.
Series: Childhood Days.
Est. £85-130.

HN2977
Magic Dragon
Designer A. Hughes.
Date 1983 - 86.
12cm (4.75ins) high.
Cream and gold.
Series: Enchantment.
Est. £85-130.

HN2988
The Auctioneer
Designer R. Tabbenor.
Date 1986.
21.5cm (8.5ins) high.
Brown, black, yellow and grey.
Series: RDICC.
Est. £100-145.

HN2989
The Genie
Designer R. Tabbenor.
Date 1983 - 90.
24.5cm (9.75ins) high.
Blue and grey.
Other colourways: HN2999.
*(Auction PSA 1.9.04 sold £75
plus comm.)*
Est. £90-130.

HN2990
Shepherdess
Third Version (Model 3445)
Designer R. Tabbenor.
Date 1987 - 88.
20.5cm (8ins) high.
White, pale blue and tan.
Series: Reflections.
Est. £85-120.

HN2991
June
Third Version (Model 3359)
Designer R. Tabbenor.
Date 1988 - 94.
23cm (9ins) high.
Lilac, white and red.
Est. £100-135.

HN2992
Golfer
Designer R. Tabbenor.
Date 1988 - 91.
24cm (9.5ins) high.
Blue, grey, white and tan.
Series: Reflections.
Est. £85-120.

HN2993
Old Father Thames
Designer R. Tabbenor.
Date 1988. Limited edition of 500.
15cm (6ins) high.
Cream with gold
 trimmings.
Comm: Thames
 Water.
Est. £100-150.

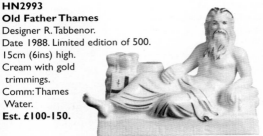

HN2994
Helen
Second Version (Model 3153)
Designer R. Tabbenor.
Date 1985 - 87.
12.5cm (5ins) high.
White.
Series: Vanity Fair Children.
Est. £45-65.

HN2995
Julie
First Version
Designer R. Tabbenor.
Date 1985 - 95.
12.5cm (5ins) high.
White.
Other colourways: HN3407.
Series: Vanity Fair Children.
(Ebay 3.10.04 sold £30)
Est. £30-50.

HN2996
Amanda
Designer R. Tabbenor.
Date 1986 - 2000.
13cm (5.25ins) high.
White and pink.
Other colourways: HN3406, 3632,
3634, 3635; 'Flower of the Month,
Child' series HN3323-3334.
Series: Vanity Fair Children.
Est. £40-65.

HN2997
Chic
Designer R. Tabbenor.
Date 1987 N. America.
1988 Worldwide - 90.
33cm (13ins) high.
Pale blue and light brown.
Series: Reflections.
Est. £110-150.

HN2998
Aperitif
Designer R. Tabbenor
Date 1988.
30.5cm (12ins) high.
Pale green.
Series: Reflections.
Comm: Home Shopping
Network, U.S.A.
Est. £110-150.

HN2999
The Genie
Designer R. Tabbenor.
Date 1990 - 95.
24.5cm (9.75ins) high.
Red.
Other colourways: HN2989.
Series: Flambé.
Est. £150-200.

HN3004
Emily In Autumn
First Version (Model 3156)
Designer P. Gee.
Date 1986.
20.5cm (8ins) high.
Yellow, brown and white.
Series: Seasons (Series Three)
Comm: Danbury Mint.
Est. £145-200.

HN3000
Sweet Bouquet
First Version
Designer P. Gee.
Date 1988.
33cm (13ins) high.
Pale blue and white.
Series: Reflections.
Comm: Home Shopping
Network, U.S.A.
Est. £110-150.

HN3005
Sarah In Winter
First Version (Model 3157)
Designer P. Gee.
Date 1986.
20.5cm (8ins) high.
White and pale green.
Series: Seasons (Series Three)
Comm: Danbury Mint.
Est. £145-200.

HN3001
Danielle
Second Version (Model 2766)
Designer P. Gee.
Date 1990 - 95.
18.5cm (7.25ins) high.
Pink and white.
Other colourways:
'Spring Song' HN3446.
Series: Vanity Fair Ladies.
Est. £70-95.

HN3006
Catherine In Spring
Second Version (Model 3155)
Designer P. Gee.
Date 1985.
21.5cm (8.5ins) high.
Peach and white.
Series: Seasons (Series Three)
Comm: Danbury Mint.
Est. £145-200.

HN3002
Marilyn
Designer P. Gee.
Date 1985 Canada.
1986 Worldwide - 95.
18.5cm (7.25ins) high.
White floral dress.
Est. £85-120.

HN3007
Mary, Countess Howe
Designer P. Gee.
Date 1990. Limited edition
of 5,000.
23.5cm (9.25ins) high.
Pink, blue and lemon.
Series: Gainsborough Ladies.
Est. £200-250.

HN3003
Lilian In Summer
Designer P. Gee.
Date 1985.
21.5cm (8.5ins) high.
White, pink and blue.
Series: Seasons (Series Three)
Comm: Danbury Mint.
Est. £145-200.

HN3008
**Sophia Charlotte, Lady
Sheffield**
Designer P. Gee.
Date 1990. Limited edition of 5,000.
26cm (10ins) high.
Yellow, white and turquoise.
Series: Gainsborough Ladies.
Est. £200-250.

HN3009
Honourable Frances Duncombe
Designer P. Gee.
Date 1991. Limited edition of 5,000.
24.5cm (9.75ins) high.
Blue, white and yellow.
Series: Gainsborough Ladies.
Est. £200-250.

HN3014
Nell
Designer P. Parsons.
Date 1982 - 87.
10cm (4ins) high.
White, pink and yellow.
Series: Kate Greenaway.
Est. £110-150.

HN3010
Isabella, Countess of Sefton
Designer P. Gee.
Date 1991. Limited edition of 5,000.
24.5cm (9.75ins) high.
Black, peach and white.
Series: Gainsborough Ladies.
Est. £200-250.

HN3015
Adornment
Designer P. Parsons.
Date 1989. Limited edition
of 750.
18.5cm (7.25ins) high.
Lilac and pink striped dress.
Series: Gentle Arts.
Est. £450-600.

HN3011
My Best Friend
Designer P. Gee.
Date 1990 - 2000.
20.5cm (8ins) high.
Pink, white and brown.
Est. £125-175.

HN3016
Graduate (female)
First Version
Designer P. Parsons.
Date 1984 - 92.
22cm (8.75ins) high.
Pink, black, yellow and white.
Est. £90-135.

HN3012
Painting
Designer P. Parsons.
Date 1987. Limited edition
of 750.
18.5cm (7.25ins) high.
Purple, red, brown and yellow.
Series: Gentle Arts.
Est. £450-600.

HN3017
Graduate (male)
First Version
Designer P. Parsons.
Date 1984 - 92.
23.5cm (9.25ins) high.
Grey, black and white.
Est. £90-135.

HN3013
James
Designer P. Parsons.
Date 1983 - 87.
15cm (6ins) high.
White, gold
and pale blue.
Series: Kate Greenaway.
Est. £250-350.

HN3018
Sisters
Designer P. Parsons.
Date 1983 to date.
21.5cm (8.5ins) high.
White.
Other colourways: HN3019.
Series: Images.
(Royal Doulton web price £39)
Retail £39.

HN3019
Sisters
Designer P. Parsons.
Date 1983 - 97.
21.5cm (8.5ins) high.
Black.
Other colourways: HN3018.
Series: Images.
Est. £45-65.

HN3026
Carefree
Designer R. Jefferson.
Date 1986 - 2001.
31cm (12.25ins) high.
White.
Other colourways: HN3029.
Series: Images.
Est. £40-60.

HN3020
Ellen
First Version
Designer P. Parsons.
Date 1984 - 87.
9cm (3.5ins) high.
Blue, white, orange and yellow.
Series: Kate Greenaway.
Est. £250-350.

HN3027
Windswept
Designer R. Jefferson.
Date 1985 N. America.
1987 Worldwide - 94.
31cm (12.25ins) high.
Pale blue.
Series: Reflections.
(Ebay 5.6.04 sold £31.50)
Est. £40-60.

HN3021
Polly Put the Kettle On
Designer P. Parsons.
Date 1984 - 87.
20.5cm (8ins) high.
Pink, white and black.
Series: Nursery Rhymes
(Series Two)
*(Auction PSA 11.8.04 sold £55
plus comm.)*
Est. £70-110.

HN3028
Panorama
Designer R. Jefferson.
Date 1985 N. America.
1987 Worldwide - 88.
32.5cm (12.75ins) high.
Pale blue.
Series: Reflections.
Est. £40-60.

HN3024
April Shower
Designer R. Jefferson.
Date 1983 - 86.
12cm (4.75ins) high.
Cream.
Series: Enchantment.
Est. £100-130.

HN3029
Carefree
Designer R. Jefferson.
Date 1986 - 97.
31cm (12.25ins) high.
Black.
Other colourways: HN3026.
Series: Images.
(Ebay 23.5.04 sold £76)
Est. £85-125.

HN3025
Rumpelstiltskin
Designer R. Jefferson.
Date 1983 - 86.
20.5cm (8ins) high.
Cream.
Series: Enchantment.
Est. £100-135.

HN3030
Little Bo Peep
Designer A. Hughes.
Date 1984 - 87.
20.5cm (8ins) high.
White with blue trimmings.
Series: Nursery Rhymes
(Series Two)
Est. £55-80.

HN3031
Wee Willie Winkie
Second Version (Model 3011)
Designer A. Hughes.
Date 1984 - 87.
19.5cm (7.75ins) high.
White and blue.
Series: Nursery Rhymes
(Series Two)
Est. £65-100.

HN3032
Tom, Tom, the Piper's Son
Designer A. Hughes.
Date 1984 - 87.
18cm (7ins) high.
Yellow, pink and white.
Series: Nursery Rhymes
(Series Two)
Est. £55-80.

HN3033
Springtime
Second Version (Model 3066)
Designer A. Hughes.
Date 1983.
20.5cm (8ins) high.
Yellow, cream and green.
Series: 1. Seasons (Series Four)
2. RDICC.
Est. £110-150.

HN3034
Little Jack Horner
Second Version (Model 3098)
Designer A. Hughes.
Date 1984 - 87.
18cm (7ins) high.
White, green and yellow.
Series: Nursery Rhymes
(Series Two)
Est. £55-80.

HN3035
Little Boy Blue
Second Version (Model 3099)
Designer A. Hughes.
Date 1984 - 87.
19.5cm (7.75ins) high.
Blue, white and yellow.
Series: Nursery Rhymes
(Series Two)
Est. £55-85.

HN3036
Kerry
Designer A. Hughes.
Date 1986 - 92.
13.5cm (5.25ins) high.
White.
Other colourways: HN3461.
Series: Vanity Fair Children.
*(Auction PSA 4.2.04
sold £30 plus comm.)*
Est. £40-65.

HN3037
Miranda
Second Version (Model 3298)
Designer A. Hughes.
Date 1987 - 90.
21.5cm (8.5ins) high.
Purple, lemon and cream.
Est. £100-135.

HN3038
Yvonne
Designer A. Hughes.
Date 1987 - 92.
22cm (8.75ins) high.
Turquoise and white.
Est. £85-120.

HN3039
Reflection
Designer A. Hughes.
Date 1987 - 91.
20.5cm (8ins) high.
Tan and white.
Series: Reflections.
Est. £75-110.

HN3040
Flower Arranging
Designer D. Brindley.
Date 1988. Limited edition of 750.
18.5cm (7.25ins) high.
Purple, lemon, green and pink.
Series: Gentle Arts.
Est. £400-550.

HN3041
The Lawyer
First Version
Designer P. Parsons.
Date 1985 - 95.
23cm (9ins) high.
Grey, white and black.
(Auction PSA 1.9.04 sold £85 plus comm.)
Est. £110-150.

HN3045
Demure
Designer P. Parsons.
Date 1985 N. America,
1987 Worldwide - 88.
32.5cm (12.75ins) high.
Blue, grey and white.
Series: Reflections.
Est. £100-145.

HN3042
Gilliam
(With shoulder straps)
Second Version (Model 2908)
Designer P. Parsons.
Date 1984 - 90.
21cm (8.25ins) high.
Green and white.
Other colourways: HN3042A
(without shoulder straps)
Series: M. Doulton Events.
Est. £100-135

HN3046
Debut
First Version
Designer P. Parsons.
Date 1985 N. America.
1986 Worldwide - 89.
32cm (12.5ins) high.
Pale blue, green and white.
Series: Reflections.
Est. £100-145

HN3042A
Gilliam
(Without shoulder straps)
Second Version (Model 2908)
Designer P. Parsons.
Date 1984 - 90.
21cm (8.25ins) high.
Green and white.
Other colourways: HN3042
(with shoulder straps)
Series: M. Doulton Events.
(Auction PSA 23.6.04 sold £45)

HN3047
Sharon
First Version (Model 3105)
Designer P. Parsons.
Date 1984 - 93.
14cm (5.5ins) high.
White, blue pink and yellow.
Other colourways: HN3455.
(Ebay 27.7.04 sold £46)
(Auction W&H 27.9.04 sold £30 plus comm.)
Est. £45-75.

HN3043
Lynsey
Designer P. Parsons.
Date 1985 - 95.
12cm (4.75ins) high.
White.
Series: Vanity Fair Children.
(Auction PSA 23.6.04 sold £30 plus comm.)
Est. £40-65.

HN3048
Tapestry Weaving
Designer P. Parsons.
Date 1985. Limited edition
of 750.
18.5cm (7.25ins) high.
Pink, white and brown.
Series: Gentle Arts.
Est. £500-700.

HN3044
Catherine
Second Version (Model 3044)
Designer P. Parsons.
Date 1985 - 96.
12.5cm (5ins) high.
White with blue flowers.
Other colourways: HN3451.
Series: Vanity Fair Children.
Est. £40-65.

HN3049
Writing
Designer P. Parsons.
Date 1986. Limited edition of 750.
18.5cm (7.25ins) high.
Yellow, white and brown.
Series: Gentle Arts.
Est. £500-600.

HN3050
Susan
Second Version (Model 2749)
Designer P. Parsons.
Date 1986 - 93.
21.5cm (8.5ins) high.
Pink, white and red.
Other colourways: HN2952.
(Ebay 7.7.04 sold £85)
Est. £100-150.

HN3055
Claudine
Designer A. Hughes.
Date 1984.
30.5cm (12ins) high.
Cream.
Series: Elegance (Series One)
Est. £150-200.

HN3051
Country Girl
First Version
Designer A. Hughes.
Date 1987 - 92.
19.5cm (7.75ins) high.
Blue and white.
Series: Reflections.
Est. £65-95.

HN3056
Danielle
First Version (Model 3136)
Designer A. Hughes.
Date 1984.
30.5cm (12ins) high.
Cream.
Series: Elegance (Series One)
Est. £150-200.

HN3052
A Winter's Walk
Designer A. Hughes.
Date 1987 N. America.
1988 Worldwide - 95.
31cm (12.25ins) high.
Pale blue, black and white.
Series: Reflections.
Est. £200-250.

HN3057
Sir Winston Churchill
First Version (Model 3162)
Designer A. Hughes.
Date 1985 to date.
26.5cm (10.5ins) high.
White.
(Royal Doulton web price £130)
(Auction PSA 22.10.03 sold £75 plus comm.)
Est. £90-130.

HN3053
Martine
Designer A. Hughes.
Date 1984.
34cm (13.5ins) high.
Other colourways: Reissued as
'Promenade' HN3072.
Cream and black.
Series: Elegance (Series One)
Est. £180-250.

HN3058
Andrea
First Version
Designer A. Hughes.
Date 1985 - 95.
13cm (5.25ins) high.
Blue and white.
Series: Vanity Fair Children.
Est. £45-65.

HN3054
Dominique
Designer A. Hughes.
Date 1984.
36cm (14ins) high.
Cream.
Other colourways:
'Paradise' HN3074.
Series: Elegance (Series One)
Est. £150-200.

HN3059
Sophistication
Designer A. Hughes.
Date 1987 - 90.
29cm (11.5ins) high.
Pale blue and white.
Series: Reflections.
Est. £95-130.

HN3060
Wintertime
First Version (Model 3221)
Designer A. Hughes.
Date 1985.
21.5cm (8.5ins) high.
Red and white.
Series: 1. Seasons (Series
Four) 2. RDICC.
Est. £100-135.

HN3069
Hiver (Winter)
Designer R. Jefferson.
Date 1988. Limited edition
of 300.
30cm (11.75ins) high.
White.
Series: Les Saisons.
Est. £500-700.

HN3061
Hope
First Version
Designer S. Mitchell.
Date 1984. Limited edition of 9,500.
21cm (8.25ins) high.
Pale blue and yellow.
Series: NSPCC Charity.
Comm: Lawleys By Post.
(Ebay 23.5.04 sold £95)
(Auction W&H 27.9.04 sold £60
plus comm.) **Est. £90-130.**

HN3070
Cocktails
Designer A. Hughes.
Date 1985 N. America.
1987 Worldwide - 95.
28cm (11ins) high.
Pale brown and cream.
Series: Reflections.
Est. £100-145.

HN3066
Printemps (Spring)
Designer R. Jefferson.
Date 1987. Limited edition of 300.
28.5cm (11.25ins) high.
White, green and brown.
Series: Les Saisons.
Est. £500-700.

HN3071
Flirtation
Designer A. Hughes.
Date 1985 N. America.
1987 Worldwide - 95.
25.5cm (10ins) high.
Pale blue, cream and tan.
Series: Reflections.
Est. £100-145.

HN3067
Eté (Summer)
Designer R. Jefferson.
Date 1989. Limited edition of 300.
30cm (11.75ins) high.
Yellow, white and green.
Series: Les Saisons.
Est. £500-700.

HN3072
Promenade
Second Version (Model 3112)
Designer A. Hughes.
Date 1985 N. America.
1987 Worldwide - 95.
33.5cm (13.25ins) high.
Pale brown and white.
Other colourways:
'Martine' HN3053.
Series: Reflections.
Est. £200-250.

HN3068
Automne (Autumn)
Designer R. Jefferson.
Date 1986. Limited edition of 300.
29cm (11.5ins) high.
Lilac, gold, red and cream.
Series: Les Saisons.
Est. £500-700.

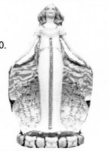

HN3073
Strolling
First Version
Designer A. Hughes.
Date 1985 N. America.
1987 Worldwide - 95.
37cm (14.5ins) high.
Pale green and white.
Series: Reflections.
Est. £200-250.

HN3074
Paradise
Designer A. Hughes.
Date 1985 N. America.
1987 Worldwide - 92.
35.5cm (14ins) high.
Pale brown and blue.
Other colourways:
'Dominique' HN3054.
Series: Reflections.
Est. £110-150.

HN3079
Sleeping Beauty
First Version
Designer A. Hughes.
Date 1987 - 89.
11.5cm
(4.5ins) high.
Green, brown
and white.
Est. £95-135.

HN3075
Tango
Designer A. Hughes.
Date 1985 N. America.
1987 Worldwide - 92.
33cm (13ins) high.
Pale blue, lemon and cream.
Series: Reflections.
Est. £110-150.

HN3080
Allure
Designer E.J. Griffiths.
Date 1985 N. America.
1987 Worldwide - 88.
32cm (12.5ins) high.
Pale green.
Other colourways:
'Monique' HN2880.
Series: Reflections.
Est. £80-130.

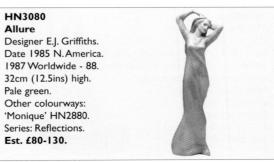

HN3076
Bolero
Designer A. Hughes.
Date 1985 N. America.
1987 Worldwide - 92.
34cm (13.5ins) high.
Pink and pale blue.
Series: Reflections.
Est. £110-150.

HN3082
Faith
First Version
Designer E.J. Grfiffiths.
Date 1986. Limited edition of 9,500.
21.5cm (8.5ins) high.
Pink, tan and white.
Series: NSPCC Charity.
Comm: Lawleys By Post.
(Ebay 23.5.04 sold £70)
*(Auction W&H 27.9.04 sold £64
plus comm.)* Est. £80-115.

HN3077
Windflower
Third Version (Model 3340)
Designer A. Hughes.
Date 1986 N. America.
1987 Worldwide - 92.
31cm (12.25ins) high.
Pale blue and white.
Series: Reflections.
*(Auction PSA 23.6.04 sold
£45 plus comm.)*
Est. £65-125.

HN3083
Sheikh
Designer E.J. Griffiths.
Date 1987 - 89.
24.5cm (9.75ins) high.
White, tan and blue.
Series: Reflections.
*(Auction PSA 4.2.04 sold
£40 plus comm.)*
Est. £55-100.

HN3078
Dancing Delight
Designer A. Hughes.
Date 1986 N. America.
1987 Worldwide - 88.
32.5cm (12.75ins) high.
Pale tan.
Series: Reflections.
Est. £100-145.

HN3084
Harvestime
Designer E.J. Griffiths.
Date 1988 - 90.
20.5cm (8ins) high.
Light blue, tan and grey.
Series: Reflections.
Est. £70-100.

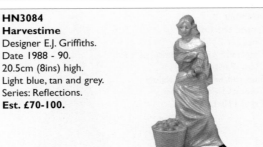

HN3085
Summer Rose
First Version (Model 3353)
Designer E.J. Griffiths.
Date 1987 N. America.
1988 Worldwide - 92.
21.5cm (8.5ins) high.
Pale blue, tan and yellow.
Series: Reflections.
Est. £85-120.

HN3090
Charisma
Designer P. Parsons.
Date 1986 N.America.
1987 Worldwide - 90.
32cm (12.5ins) high.
Pale blue, light brown and white.
Series: Reflections.
Est. £85-110.

HN3086
The Duchess of York
Designer E.J. Griffiths.
Date 1986. Limited edition of 1,500.
Commissioned to commemorate the
wedding of Sarah Ferguson to
HRH Prince Andrew.
21cm (8.25ins) high.
Cream and yellow.
Comm: Lawleys By Post.
Est. £300-400.

HN3091
Summer's Darling
First Version
Designer P. Parsons.
Date 1986 N. America.
1987 Worldwide - 95.
29cm (11.5ins) high.
Pale blue and light brown.
Series: Reflections.
Est. £85-110.

HN3087
Charity
First Version
Designer E.J. Griffiths.
Date 1987. Limited edition of 9,500.
21.5cm (8.5ins) high.
White, yellow and purple.
Series: NSPCC Charity.
Comm: Lawleys By Post.
(Ebay 23.5.04 sold £97)
(Auction W&H 27.9.04 sold £57
plus comm.) **Est. £90-125.**

HN3092
Cherry Blossom
Designer P. Parsons.
Date 1986 N. America.
1987 Worldwide - 89.
32.5cm (12.75ins) high.
Pale green, cream and brown.
Series: Reflections.
Est. £90-125.

HN3088
Kate Hannigan
Designer E.J. Griffiths.
Date 1989. Limited edition of 9,500.
23cm (9ins) high.
Light brown and peach.
Comm: Lawleys By Post.
(Auction PSA 23.6.04 sold £95
plus comm.)
Est. £120-170.

HN3093
Morning Glory
Designer P. Parsons.
Date 1986 N. America.
1987 Worldwide - 89.
33cm (13ins) high.
Light blue and green.
Series: Reflections.
Est. £85-110.

HN3089
Grace Darling
Designer E.J. Griffiths.
Date 1987. Limited edition of 9,500.
23cm (9ins) high.
Blue, red, brown and yellow.
Comm: Lawleys By Post.
Est. £110-150.

HN3094
Sweet Perfume
Designer P. Parsons.
Date 1986 N. America.
1987 Worldwide - 95.
33cm (13ins) high.
Pale blue, yellow and white.
Series: Reflections.
Est. £85-110.

HN3095
Happy Birthday
First Version
Designer P. Parsons.
Date 1987 - 94.
21.5cm (8.5ins) high.
Yellow, red and white.
Series: Special Occasions.
Est. £85-110.

HN3100
Kathleen
Second Version (Model 2965)
Designer S. Keenan.
Date 1986.
16.5cm (6.5ins) high.
Purple, cream and pink.
Other colourways: HN2933.
Series: M. Doulton Events.
Est. £100-135.

HN3096
Merry Christmas
Designer P. Parsons.
Date 1987 - 92.
20.5cm (8ins) high.
Green, red and white.
Series: Special Occasions.
Est. £85-110.

HN3105
The Love Letter
Second Version (Model 3195)
Designer R. Jefferson.
Date 1986 N.America.
1987 Worldwide - 88.
30.5cm (12ins) high.
Pale blue, white and light tan.
Series: Reflections.
Est. £95-135.

HN3097
Happy Anniversary
First Version (Model 3291)
Designer P. Parsons.
Date 1987 - 93.
16.5cm (6.5ins) high.
Lilac, pink and white.
(Ebay 26.5.04 sold £50)
Series: Special Occasions.
Est. £65-95.

HN3106
Secret Moment
Designer R. Jefferson.
Date 1986 N.America.
1987 Worldwide - 88.
31cm (12.25ins) high.
Pale blue and green.
Series: Reflections.
Est. £85-120.

HN3098
Dorothy
Designer P. Parsons.
Date 1987 - 90.
18cm (7ins) high.
Grey, black and white.
Est. £150-200.

HN3107
Daybreak
First Version
Designer R. Jefferson.
Date 1986 N.America.
1987 Worldwide - 88.
30cm (11.75ins) high.
White, green and yellow.
Series: Reflections.
Est. £85-120.

HN3099
Queen Elizabeth I
Designer P. Parsons.
Date 1986 U.K.
1987 Worldwide.
Limited edition of 5,000.
23cm (9ins) high.
Red, white and gold.
Series: Queens of the Realm.
(Auction PSA 23.6.04 sold £180
plus comm.)　**Est. £240-350.**

HN3108
Enchanting Evening
Designer R. Jefferson.
Date 1986 N.America.
1987 Worldwide - 92.
30cm (11.75ins) high.
Pale pink and blue.
Series: Reflections.
Est. £85-120.

HN3109
Pensive
Designer R. Jefferson.
Date 1986 N.America.
1987 Worldwide - 88.
33cm (13ins) high.
White, pale blue and yellow.
Series: Reflections.
Est. £85-120.

HN3114
Antony and Cleopatra
Designer R. Jefferson.
Date 1995. Limited edition of 150.
30.5cm (12ins) high.
Cream, gold and pale blue.
Series: Great Lovers.
Est. £650-1100.

HN3110
Enigma
Designer R. Jefferson.
Date 1986 N.America.
1987 Worldwide - 95.
32.5cm (12.75ins) high.
Cream and pink.
Series: Reflections.
Est. £85-120.

HN3115
Idle Hours
Designer A. Maslankowski.
Date 1986 N.America.
1987 Worldwide - 88.
31cm (12.25ins) high.
Pale blue and light brown.
Series: Reflections.
Est. £95-130.

HN3111
Robin Hood and Maid Marion
Designer R. Jefferson.
Date 1994. Limited edition of 150.
30.5cm (12ins) high.
Green, blue, cream and gold.
Series: Great Lovers.
Est. £650-1100.

HN3116
Park Parade
Designer A. Maslankowski.
Date 1987 N.America.
1988 Worldwide - 94.
30cm (11.75ins) high.
Pale brown, green and blue.
Series: Reflections.
Est. £150-200.

HN3112
Lancelot and Guinivere
Designer R. Jefferson.
Date 1996. Limited edition of 150.
30.5cm (12ins) high.
Green, lilac,
purple and cream.
Series: Great Lovers.
Est. £650-1100.

HN3117
Indian Maiden
Designer A. Maslankowski.
Date 1987 - 90.
30.5cm (12ins) high.
Light tan, blue and black.
Series: Reflections.
Est. £110-150.

HN3113
Romeo and Juliet
First Version
Designer R. Jefferson.
Date 1993. Limited edition of 150.
30.5cm (12ins) high.
Cream, green, purple and lilac.
Series: Great Lovers.
(Ebay 20.3.04 sold £560)
Est. £650-1100.

HN3118
Lorraine
First Version
Designer A. Maslankowski.
Date 1988 - 95.
20.5cm (8ins) high.
Blue and white.
*(Auction Bonhams, Oxford
sold £47 plus comm.)*
Est. £95-125.

HN3119
Partners
Designer A. Maslankowski.
Date 1990 - 92.
16.5cm (6.5ins) high.
Blue, black, yellow and grey.
Series: Clowns.
Est. £125-175.

HN3124
Thinking of You
First Version
Designer A. Maslankowski.
Date 1991 - 2001.
17cm (6.75ins) high.
White.
Other colourways: HN3490.
Series: Sentiments.
Est. £40-50.

HN3120
Spring Walk
Designer A. Maslankowski.
Date 1990 - 92.
33cm (13ins) high.
Pale blue and white.
Series: Reflections.
Est. £200-250.

HN3125
Queen Victoria
First Version
Designer P. Parsons.
Date 1987 U.K.
1988 Worldwide.
Limited edition of 5,000.
20.5cm (8ins) high.
Pink, gold, brown and white.
Series: Queens of the Realm.
Est. £400-600.

HN3121
Wizard
First Version
Designer A. Maslankowski.
Date 1990 - 95.
25.5cm (10ins) high.
Flambé.
Other colourways:
HN2877, 4069.
Series: Flambé.
Est. £200-250.

HN3126
Storytime
First Version
Designer P. Parsons.
Date 1987 - 92.
15cm (6ins) high.
Pale blue and cream.
Series: Reflections.
Est. £65-95.

HN3122
My First Pet
Designer A. Maslankowski.
Date 1991 - 97.
11.5cm (4.5ins) high.
Blue and white.
Series: Vanity Fair Children.
Est. £45-65.

HN3127
Playmates
Designer P. Parsons.
Date 1987 - 92.
21.5cm (8.5ins) high.
Pale blue, white and green.
Series: Reflections.
Est. £65-95.

HN3123
Sit
Designer A. Maslankowski.
Date 1991 - 2000.
11.5cm (4.5ins) high.
Yellow, tan and white.
Other colourways: HN3430.
Series: Vanity Fair Children.
(Auction PSA 23.6.04
sold £32 plus comm.)
Est. £40-55.

HN3128
Tomorrow's Dreams
First Version
Designer P. Parsons.
Date 1987 - 92.
16.5cm (6.5ins) high.
White and tan.
Series: Reflections.
Est. £70-100.

HN3129
Thankful
Designer P. Parsons.
Date 1987 - 99.
21.5cm (8.5ins) high.
White.
Other colourways: HN3135.
Series: Images.
Est. £40-55.

HN3135
Thankful
Designer P. Parsons.
Date 1987 - 94.
21.5cm (8.5ins) high.
Black.
Other colourways: HN3129.
Series: Images.
Est. £55-75.

HN3130
Sisterly Love
Designer P. Parsons.
Date 1987 - 95.
21.5cm (8.5ins) high.
Pale blue, tan and white.
Series: Reflections.
Est. £55-90.

HN3136
Laura
First Version
Designer P. Parsons.
Date 1988.
18.5cm (7.25ins) high.
Dark blue, lilac and white.
Other colourways: HN2960.
Produced exclusively for
M. Doulton Events that year.
Est. £110-150.

HN3132
Good Pals
Designer P. Parsons.
Date 1987 - 92.
16cm (6.25ins) high.
Pale blue, tan and white.
Series: Reflections.
Est. £55-90.

HN3137
Summertime
First Version (Model 2837)
Designer P. Parsons.
Date 1987.
20.5cm (8ins) high.
Pale blue, orange and white.
Series: 1. Seasons (Series
Four) 2. RDICC.
Est. £95-135.

HN3133
Dreaming
Designer P. Parsons.
Date 1987 - 95.
23cm (9ins) high.
Pale pink and cream.
Series: Reflections.
(Ebay 6.6.04 sold £29)
Est. £40-65.

HN3138
Eastern Grace
Designer P. Parsons.
Date 1988 - 89.
30.5cm (12ins) high.
Cream and blue.
Other colourways: HN3683.
Series: Reflections.
Est. £110-150.

HN3134
Ballet Class
First Version
Designer P. Parsons.
Date 1987 N.America,
1988 Worldwide - 92.
15cm (6ins) high.
White, tan and blue.
Series: Reflections.
Est. £55-90.

HN3139
Free As The Wind
Designer P. Parsons.
Date 1989 - 95.
1988 N.America,
1989 Worldwide - 95.
24cm (9.5ins) high.
Pale blue and white.
Series: Reflections.
Est. £95-135.

HN3140
Gaiety
Designer P. Parsons.
Date 1988 - 90.
26cm (10.25ins) high.
Pale green, blue
and white.
Series: Reflections.
Est. £95-135.

HN3145
Rose Arbour
Designer D. Brindley.
Date 1987 N.America.
1988 Worldwide - 90.
30.5cm (12ins) high.
Pale blue, tan and white.
Series: Reflections.
Est. £90-130.

HN3141
Queen Anne
Designer P. Parsons.
Date 1988. Limited edition of 5,000.
23cm (9ins) high.
Red, white, black and green.
Series: Queens of the Realm.
Comm: Lawleys By Post.
(Auction PSA 10.3.04
sold £150 plus comm.)
Est. £180-250.

HN3155
Water Maiden
Designer A. Hughes.
Date 1987 - 91.
30.5cm (12ins) high.
Blue and white.
Series: Reflections.
Est. £100-145.

HN3142
Mary, Queen of Scots
Second Version (Model 3602)
Designer P. Parsons.
Date 1989. Limited edition of 5,000.
23cm (9ins) high.
Blue, gold, black and purple.
Series: Queens of the Realm.
Comm: Lawleys By Post.
(Auction PSA 23.6.04
sold £195 plus comm.)
Est. £250-400.

HN3156
Bathing Beauty
First Version
Designer A. Hughes.
Date 1987 - 89.
24.5cm (9.75ins) high.
Grey and pink.
Series: Reflections.
Est. £200-250.

HN3143
Rosemary
Second Version (Model 2709)
Designer P. Parsons.
Date 1988 - 91.
19cm (7.5ins) high.
White and pink.
(Ebay 5.6.04 sold £69)
Est. £80-140.

HN3157
Free Spirit
First Version
Designer A. Hughes.
Date 1987 - 92.
26.5cm (10.5ins) high.
White.
Other colourways: HN3159.
Series: Images.
Est. £55-75.

HN3144
Florence Nightingale
Designer P. Parsons.
Date 1988. Limited edition of 5,000.
21cm (8.25ins) high.
Green, pink, red and cream.
Comm: Lawleys By Post.
(Auction PSA 23.6.04 sold £290
plus comm.)
(Ebay 22.8.04 sold £400)
Est. £350-500.

HN3159
Free Spirit
First Version
Designer A. Hughes.
Date 1987 - 92.
26.5cm (10.5ins) high.
Black.
Other colourways: HN3157.
Series: Images.
Est. £65-95.

HN3160
Shepherd
Fifth Version (Model 3448)
Designer A. Hughes.
Date 1988 - 89.
21.5cm (8.5ins) high.
Light grey, black, brown and yellow.
Series: Reflections.
Est. £110-145.

HN3161
Gardener
Designer A. Hughes.
Date 1988 - 91.
21cm (8.25ins) high.
Pale blue, white and pale brown.
Series: Reflections.
Est. £100-140.

HN3162
Breezy Days
Designer A. Hughes.
Date 1988 - 90.
21.5cm (8.5ins) high.
White, pale brown and blue.
Series: Reflections.
Est. £80-120.

HN3163
Country Maid
Designer A. Hughes.
Date 1988 - 91.
21cm (8.25ins) high.
Pink, blue, white and black.
Est. £110-150.

HN3164
Farmer's Wife
Second Version (Model 3595)
Designer A. Hughes.
Date 1988 - 91.
21.5cm (8.5ins) high.
Blue, brown and white.
Est. £90-130.

HN3165
August
First Version (Model 2225)
Designer M. Davies.
Date 1987.
19.5cm (7.75ins) high.
White dress with poppies.
Other colourways: HN2693, 2695-
2697, 2703, 2707, 2708, 2711, 2790,
2794, 3166; 'Gillian' HN3742.
Series: Figure of the Month.
Est. £70-95.

HN3166
September
First Version (Model 2225)
Designer M. Davies.
Date 1987.
19.5cm (7.75ins) high.
White and yellow dress with daisies.
Other colourways: HN2693,
2695-2697, 2703, 2707, 2708, 2711,
2790, 2794, 3165, 'Gillian' HN3742.
Series: Figure of the Month.
Est. £70-95.

HN3167
Hazel
Second Version (Model 1543)
Designer M. Davies.
Date 1988 - 91.
20.5cm (8ins) high.
White, blue and pink.
Est. £110-150.

HN3168
Jemma
Designer M. Davies.
Date 1988 - 91.
21cm (8.25ins) high.
Red, blue, white and yellow.
Est. £75-105.

HN3169
Jessica
First Version
Designer M. Davies.
Date 1988 - 95.
18cm (7ins) high.
White.
Other colourways: HN3497.
Series: Vanity Fair Ladies.
(Ebay 4.6.04 sold £62)
Est. £70-100.

HN3170
Caroline
First Version
Designer M. Davies.
Date 1989 - 92.
19cm (7.5ins) high.
White and blue.
Other colourways:
'Winter Welcome' HN3611.
Est. £80-100.

HN3175
Sweet Violets
Designer D. V. Tootle.
Date 1988 - 89.
26cm (10.25ins) high.
Pale blue, lemon and white.
Series: Reflections.
Est. £80-105.

HN3171
Camille
Second Version (Model 2729)
Designer M. Davies.
Date 1987.
19cm (7.5ins) high.
White, orange and green.
Other colourways: 'Adéle' HN2480;
'Margaret' HN2397, 3496.
Comm: Marks & Spencers for their
mail/order catalogue.
Est. £110-150.

HN3176
Young Dreams
Designer D. V. Tootle.
Date 1988 - 92.
16cm (6.25ins) high.
Pink, light blue and tan.
Est. £80-110.

HN3172
Christine
Second Version (Model 2380)
Designer M. Davies.
Date 1987. Limited edition of 1,000.
19.5cm (7.75ins) high.
Pink and white.
Other colourways: HN2792.
Comm: Guild of Specialist
China and Glass Retailers.
Est. £115-160.

HN3177
Harriet
First Version
Designer D. V. Tootle.
Date 1988 - 91.
18.5cm (7.25ins) high.
Pink, blue and white.
Est. £130-180.

HN3173
Natalie
First Version
Designer M. Davies.
Date 1988 - 96.
20.5cm (8ins) high.
Lemon and white.
Other colourways: HN3498.
Series: Vanity Fair Ladies.
Est. £85-110

HN3178
Polly
Designer D. V. Tootle.
Date 1988 - 91.
21cm (8.25ins) high.
Green, pink and lilac.
Est. £85-110

HN3174
Southern Belle
Second Version (Model 3646)
Designer M. Davies.
Remodeller R. Tabbenor.
Date 1988 - 97.
10cm (4ins) high.
Red and white.
Other colourways: HN3244.
Series: Miniatures.
Est. £65-95.

HN3179
Eliza
Second Version (Model 3630)
Designer D. V. Tootle.
Date 1988 - 92.
19cm (7.5ins) high.
Yellow, red and lilac.
Est. £85-110

HN3180
Phyllis
Second Version (Model 3623)
Designer D.V. Tootle.
Date 1988 - 91.
18.5cm (7.25ins) high.
Purple, red and white.
Est. £120-165.

HN3185
Traveller's Tale
Designer E.J. Griffiths.
Date 1988 - 89.
23.5cm (9.25ins) high.
Pale blue, white and grey.
Series: Reflections.
Est. £105-145.

HN3181
Moondancer
Designer D.V. Tootle.
Date 1988 - 90.
30cm (11.75ins) high.
Blue and white.
Series: Reflections.
This figure was not introduced
in the UK.
Est. £100-145.

HN3186
Entranced
Designer E.J. Griffiths.
Date 1988 - 89.
18.5cm (7.25ins) high.
Green, white and light brown.
Series: Reflections.
Est. £80-115.

HN3182
Stargazer
Designer D.V. Tootle.
Date 1988 - 90.
26.5cm (10.5ins) high.
Blue and white.
Series: Reflections.
This figure was not introduced
in the UK.
Est. £100-145.

HN3187
Balloons
Designer E.J. Griffiths.
Date 1988. Limited edition of 1,000.
21.5cm (8.5ins) high.
Pale blue and white with
multicoloured balloons.
Series: Reflections.
Comm: Home Shopping Network.
Est. £150-200.

HN3183
Tumbler
Designer D.V. Tootle.
Date 1989 - 91.
23cm (9ins) high.
Pink, yellow and white.
Other colourways:
'Tumbling' HN3283, 3289.
Series: 1. Clowns. 2.Reflections.
This figure was not introduced
in the UK.
Est. £125-175.

HN3188
Debutante
Second Version (Model 3330)
Designer E.J. Griffiths.
Date 1988. Limited edition of 1,000.
30.5cm (12ins) high.
Pale pink.
Series: Reflections.
Comm: Home Shopping Network.
Est. £120-160.

HN3184
Joy
First Version
Designer D.V. Tootle.
Date 1988 - 90.
17cm (6.75ins) high.
Pink and blue.
Series: Reflections.
This figure was not
introduced in the UK.
Est. £90-130.

HN3189
HM Queen Elizabeth the
Queen Mother
Third Version (Model 3925)
Designer E.J. Griffiths.
Date 1990. Limited edition of 2,500.
21cm (8.25ins) high.
Pale blue, pink, lilac and yellow.
Est. £300-400.

HN3190
Old Ben
Designer E.J. Griffiths.
Date 1990. Limited edition of 1,500.
15cm (6ins) high.
Blue, brown, black and white.
Comm: Newsvendors Benevolent
Society.
Est. £80-100.

HN3191
Brothers
Designer E.J. Griffiths.
Date 1991 to date.
21cm (8.25ins) high.
White.
Series: Images.
(Royal Doulton web price £39)
Retail £39.

HN3192
Mantilla
Designer E.J. Griffiths.
Date 1992. Limited edition of 1,992.
30cm (11.75ins) high.
Purple, red, black and white.
Other colourways: HN2712.
Introduced to commemorate
EXPO '92 in Seville.
Est. £150-200.

HN3195
The Farmer
First Version
Designer A. Hughes.
Date 1988 - 91.
23cm (9ins) high.
White, yellow and brown.
Est. £95-140.

HN3196
The Joker
First Version (Model 3531)
Designer A. Hughes.
Date 1988 - 90.
23.5cm (9.25ins) high.
Pale blue, red, tan and white.
Other colourways:
'Tip-Toe' HN3293.
Series: 1. Clowns. 2. Reflections.
Est. £110-160.

HN3197
Ballerina
Second Version (Model 3517)
Designer A. Hughes.
Date 1988. Limited edition of 1,000.
36cm (14ins) high.
White and light brown.
Series: Reflections.
Comm: Home Shopping Network.
Est. £135-185.

HN3198
Vanessa
Second Version (Model 3588)
Designer A. Hughes.
Date 1989 - 90.
21.5cm (8.5ins) high.
Black, green and white.
(Ebay 28.5.04 sold £62)
Est. £70-100.

HN3199
Maxine
Designer A. Hughes.
Date 1989 - 90.
21.5cm (8.5ins) high.
Purple, white and pink.
Est. £85-130.

HN3200
Gloria
Second Version (Model 3590)
Designer A. Hughes.
Date 1989 - 90.
22cm (8.75ins) high.
Pink and white.
Est. £100-135.

HN3201
Liberty
First Version
Designer A. Hughes.
Date 1989 - 90.
21cm (8.25ins) high.
Blue, red and white.
Est. £100-135.

HN3202
The Boy Evacuee
Designer A. Hughes.
Date 1989. Limited edition of 9,500.
21cm (8.25ins) high.
Green, blue and brown.
Series: Children of the Blitz.
Est. £250-350.

HN3207
Louise
Second Version (Model 3786)
Designer A. Hughes.
Date 1990 - 96.
19.cm (7.5ins) high.
Red and white.
Est. £100-135.

HN3203
The Girl Evacuee
Designer A. Hughes.
Date 1989. Limited edition of 9,500.
20.5cm (8ins) high.
Red, brown, blue and white.
Series: Children of the Blitz.
Est. £250-350.

HN3208
Emma
Second Version (Model 3787)
Designer A. Hughes.
Date 1990 - 98.
11.5cm (4.5ins) high.
Red and white.
Series: Miniatures.
*(Auction PSA 22.10.03 sold
£40 plus comm.)*
Est. £45-80.

HN3204
Emily
First Version (Model 3633)
Designer A. Hughes.
Date 1989 - 93.
21cm (8.25ins) high.
White and pale blue.
Series: Vanity Fair Ladies.
Est. £75-105.

HN3209
Claire
First Version (Model 3702)
Designer A. Hughes.
Date 1990 - 92.
21.5cm (8.5ins) high.
Pink and white
dress with roses.
Est. £70-95.

HN3205
Veronica
Third Version (Model 3631)
Designer A. Hughes.
Date 1989 - 92.
20.5cm (8ins) high.
White, pale blue and pink.
Series: Vanity Fair Ladies.
Est. £75-105.

HN3210
Christening Day
Designer P.A. Northcroft.
Date 1988 - 90.
21.5cm (8.5ins) high.
White, blue baby's shawl.
Other colourways: HN3211.
Series: Special Occasions.
Est. £65-95.

HN3206
Teresa
Second Version (Model 3713)
Designer A. Hughes.
Date 1989 - 92.
19.5cm (7.75ins) high.
White with holly and
Christmas Rose flowers.
Est. £85-110.

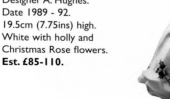

HN3211
Christening Day
Designer P.A. Northcroft.
Date 1988 - 90.
21.5cm (8.5ins) high.
White, pink baby's shawl.
Other colourways: HN3210.
Series: Special Occasions.
Est. £65-95.

HN3212
Christmas Morn
Second Version (Model 3640)
Designer M. Davies.
Remodeller R. Tabbenor.
Date 1988 - 98.
10cm (4ins) high.
Red and white.
Other colourways: HN3245.
Series: Miniatures.
(Ebay 29.5.04 sold £40)
Est. £45-80.

HN3217
Joan
Second Version (Model 1843)
Designer M. Davies.
Date 1988. Limited edition of 2,000.
20.5cm (8ins) high.
Yellow, white, green and black.
Other colourways:
'Adrienne' HN2152, 2304;
'Fiona' HN3748.
Est. £110-150.

HN3213
Kirsty
Second Version (Model 3640)
Designer M. Davies.
Remodeller P. Gee.
Date 1988 - 97.
9.5cm (3.75ins) high.
Purple and white.
Other colourways: HN3246,
3480, 3743.
Series: Miniatures.
Est. £40-60.

HN3218
Sunday Best
Second Version (Model 3671)
Designer M. Davies.
Remodeller P. Gee.
Date 1988 - 93.
9.5cm (3.75ins) high.
Green, yellow and white.
Other colourways: HN3312.
Series: Miniatures.
Est. £55-75.

HN3214
Elaine
Second Version (Model 3440)
Designer M. Davies.
Remodeller P. Gee.
Date 1988 - 98.
10cm (4ins) high.
Blue and white.
Other colourways:
HN3247, 3900.
Series: Miniatures.
(Ebay 29.5.04 sold £42) **Est. £45-75.**

HN3219
Sara
Second Version (Model 3672)
Designer M. Davies.
Remodeller P. Gee.
Date 1988 - 98.
9.5cm (3.75ins) high.
Pink and pale green.
Other colourways: HN3249.
Series: Miniatures.
(Auction PSA 23.6.04 sold £35 plus
comm.) (Ebay 8.7.04 sold £45) **Est. £55-85.**

HN3215
Ninette
Second Version (Model 3437)
Designer M. Davies.
Remodeller P. Gee.
Date 1988 - 97.
9cm (3.5ins) high.
Lilac, pink and cream.
Other colourways: HN3248,
3901. Series: Miniatures.
(Auction W&H 27.9.04 sold £24
plus comm.) **Est. £40-65.**

HN3220
Fragrance
Second Version (Model 3676)
Designer M. Davies.
Remodeller P. Gee.
Date 1988 - 92.
9.5cm (3.75ins) high.
Gold and white.
Other colourways: HN3250.
Series: Miniatures.
Est. £55-85.

HN3216
Fair Lady
Second Version (Model 3642)
Designer M. Davies.
Remodeller P. Gee.
Date 1988 - 95.
9.5cm (3.75ins) high.
Blue and pale yellow.
Other colourways: HN3336.
Series: Miniatures.
Est. £50-75.

HN3221
Country Rose
Designer M. Davies.
Date 1989 - 2000.
21.5cm (8.5ins) high.
White, pink, red and green.
Other colourways:
'Alyssa' HN4132.
Est. £100-135.

HN3222
Kelly
First Version
Designer M. Davies.
Date 1989.
19cm (7.5ins) high.
White and pale blue.
Other colourways: HN2478.
Comm: Kay's Mail Order Catalogue.
(Ebay 7.7.04 sold £44)
Est. £50-90.

HN3231
Autumntime
First Version (Model 3803)
Designer P. Parsons.
Date 1989.
20.5cm (8ins) high.
Red/brown, tan and white.
Series: 1. Seasons (Series Four) 2. RDICC.
Est. £100-135.

HN3223
Pamela
Second Version (Model 2179)
Designer M. Davies.
Date 1989.
18cm (7ins) high.
Pale blue, dark blue and white.
Other colourways: HN2479.
Series: M. Doulton Events.
Est. £100-135.

HN3232
Anne Bolelyn
Designer P. Parsons.
Date 1990. Limited edition of 9,500.
23cm (9ins) high.
Red, green and grey.
Series: Six Wives of Henry VIII.
Comm: Lawleys By Post.
(Auction Charterhouse 24.4.04 sold £160 plus comm.)
Est. £200-300.

HN3228
Devotion
Designer P. Parsons.
Date 1989 - 95.
24cm (9.5ins) high.
Pink, blue, pale green and white.
Series: Reflections.
Est. £130-180.

HN3233
Catherine of Aragon
Designer P. Parsons.
Date 1990. Limited edition of 9,500.
16.5cm (6.5ins) high.
Blue, green, white and brown.
Series: Six Wives of Henry VIII.
Comm: Lawleys By Post.
Est. £200-300.

HN3229
The Geisha
Third Version (Model 3132)
Designer P. Parsons.
Date 1989.
24cm (9.5ins) high.
Flambé.
Series: 1. Flambé.
2. RDICC.
Est. £180-250.

HN3234
Paula
Designer P. Parsons.
Date 1990 - 96.
19cm (7.5ins) high.
Pale blue and white.
Other colourways: HN2906.
Series: Vanity Fair Ladies.
(Auction PSA 3.12.03 sold £55 plus comm.)
Est. £70-100.

HN3230
HM Queen Elizabeth the Queen Mother as the Duchess of York
Second Version (Model 3779)
Designer P. Parsons.
Date 1989. Limited edition of 9,500.
23cm (9ins) high.
Pink, blue, brown and tan.
Comm: Lawleys By Post.
To celebrate Her Majesty's 90th birthday.
Est. £250-350.

HN3235
Mother and Child
First Version
Designer P. Parsons.
Date 1991 - 93.
19cm (7.5ins) high.
Pale blue and white.
Other colourways:
HN3348, 3353.
Est. £70-100.

HN3236
Falstaff
Third Version (Model 3697)
Designer C.J. Noke.
Remodeller R. Tabbenor.
Date 1989 - 90.
10cm (4ins) high.
Brown, orange, lilac and yellow.
Series: Miniatures.
*(Auction PSA 1.9.04 sold £30
plus comm.)*
Est. £40-60.

HN3244
Southern Belle
Second Version (Model 3646)
Designer M. Davies.
Remodeller R. Tabbenor.
Date 1989 - 96.
10cm (4ins) high.
Yellow, gold and turquoise.
Other colourways: HN3174.
Series: 1. Miniatures. 2. Signature.
Comm: Lawleys By Post.
Est. £85-110.

HN3245
Christmas Morn
Second Version (Model 3640)
Designer M. Davies.
Remodeller R. Tabbenor.
Date 1991 - 96.
10cm (4ins) high.
Green, gold and white.
Other colourways: HN3212.
Series: 1. Miniatures. 2. Signature.
Comm: Lawleys By Post.
Est. £70-95.

HN3246
Kirsty
Second Version (Model 3652)
Designer M. Davies.
Remodeller P. Gee.
Date 1989 - 96.
9.5cm (3.75ins) high.
Purple, gold and white.
Other colourways: HN3213,
3480, 3743.
Series: 1. Miniatures. 2. Signature.
Comm: Lawleys By Post. **Est. £70-95.**

HN3247
Elaine
Second Version (Model 3440)
Designer M. Davies.
Remodeller P. Gee. Date 1989 - 96.
10cm (4ins) high.
Blue, gold and white.
Other colourways:
HN3214, 3900.
Series: 1. Miniatures.
2. Signature.
Comm: Lawleys By Post. **Est. £70-95.**

HN3248
Ninette
Second Version (Model 3437)
Designer M. Davies.
Remodeller P. Gee.
Date 1989 - 96.
9cm (3.5ins) high.
Red, gold, green and white
Other colourways:
HN3215, 3901.
Series: 1.Miniatures. 2. Signature.
Comm. by Lawleys by Post. **Est. £70-100.**

HN3249
Sara
Second Version (Model 3672)
Designer M. Davies.
Remodeller P. Gee.
Date 1989 - 96.
9.5cm (3.75ins) high.
Blue, pink, white and gold.
Other colourways: HN3219.
Series: 1. Miniatures. 2. Signature.
Comm. by Lawleys by Post.
Est. £70-95.

HN3250
Fragrance
Second Version (Model 3676)
Designer M. Davies.
Remodeller P. Gee.
Date 1989 - 92.
9.5cm (3.75ins) high.
Red, white and gold.
Other colourways: HN3220.
Series: 1. Miniatures. 2. Signature.
Comm: Lawleys By Post.
(Ebay 7.7.04 sold £51) **Est. £65-100.**

HN3251
May
First Version (Model 3456)
Designer D.V. Tootle.
Date 1989. Limited edition of 2,000.
20.5cm (8ins) high.
Red, blue, grey and pink.
Other colourways: HN2746.
Comm: U.S.A. Direct Mail Service.
Est. £100-135.

HN3252
Fiona
Third Version Model 3634
Designer D.V. Tootle.
Date 1989 - 92.
18cm (7ins) high.
Red, green and blue.
Est. £95-130.

HN3253
Cheryl
Designer D.V. Tootle.
Date 1989 - 94.
19cm (7.5ins) high.
Red, white and grey.
Est. £125-165.

HN3258
Dawn
Second Version (Model 3729)
Designer D.V. Tootle.
Date 1990 - 92.
20.5cm (8ins) high.
Red, purple and white.
Est. £100-135.

HN3254
Happy Anniversary
Second Version (Model 3714)
Designer D.V. Tootle.
Date 1989 to date.
30.5cm (12ins) high.
White.
Series: Images.
Est. £60-90.

HN3259
Ann
Second Version (Model 3753)
Designer D.V. Tootle.
Date 1990 - 96.
20.5cm (8ins) high.
Pink, blue, green and white.
Other colourways:
'Lauren' HN3290.
(Ebay 19.8.04 sold £105)
Est. £120-165.

HN3255
Madaleine
Designer D.V. Tootle.
Date 1989 - 92.
19cm (7.5ins) high.
Pink, lilac, green and cream.
Exclusively for the USA.
Est. £85-110.

HN3260
Jane
Third Version (Model 3777)
Designer D.V. Tootle.
Date 1990 - 93.
19.5cm (7.75ins) high.
Blue, yellow, green and white.
Est. £120-145.

HN3256
**Queen Victoria and
Prince Albert**
Designer D.V. Tootle.
Date 1990. Limited edition of 2,500.
23.5cm (9.25ins) high.
Red, yellow, cream and pink.
Comm: Lawleys By Post.
Est. £350-450.

HN3261
The Town Crier
Second Version (Model 3724)
Designer M. Davies.
Remodeller R. Tabbenor.
Date 1989 - 91.
11.5cm (4.5ins) high.
Purple, yellow, green and black.
Series: Miniatures.
(Auction PSA 1.9.04 sold £35
plus comm.)
Est. £40-65.

HN3257
Sophie
Second Version (Model 3719)
Designer D.V. Tootle.
Date 1990 - 92.
20.5cm (8ins) high.
Blue, red, grey and yellow.
Est. £120-155.

HN3262
Good King Wenceslas
Second Version (Model 3735)
Designer M. Davies.
Remodeller R. Tabbenor.
Date 1989 - 92.
11cm (4.25ins) high.
Orange, black, blue and brown.
Series: Miniatures.
(Auction PSA 1.9.04 sold £35
plus comm.)
Est. £40-65.

HN3263
Beatrice
Designer M. Davies.
Date 1989 - 98.
18cm (7ins) high.
Blue, white and green.
Other colourways: HN3631;
'Kathryn' HN3413; 'Lucy' HN3653;
'Summer Serenade' HN3610;
'Wildflower of the Month' series
HN3341-3347, 3408-3412.
Est. £65-95.

HN3268
Buttercup
Second Version (Model 3868)
Designer M. Davies.
Remodeller R. Tabbenor.
Date 1990 - 98.
9.5cm (3.75ins) high.
Green, blue and white.
Other colourways: HN3908.
Series: Miniatures.
*(Auction PSA 22.10.03 sold £40
plus comm.)* **Est. £50-75.**

HN3264
Alison
First Version
Designer M. Davies.
Date 1989 - 93.
19cm (7.5ins) high.
Pale pink, white and yellow.
Other colourways: HN2336.
Est. £65-95.

HN3269
Christine
Third Version (Model 3774)
Designer M. Davies.
Remodeller P. Gee.
Date 1990 - 94.
10cm (4ins) high.
Orange, white and pink.
Other colourways: HN3337.
Series: Miniatures.
Est. £55-75.

HN3265
Lisa
First Version
Designer M. Davies.
Date 1989 - 95.
19cm (7.5ins) high.
Pink, blue and white.
Other colourways:
HN2310, 2394.
Est. £65-95.

HN3270
Karen
Third Version (Model 3885)
Designer M. Davies.
Remodeller R. Tabbenor.
Date 1990 - 95.
9.5cm (3.75ins) high.
Red, black and white.
Other colourways:
HN3338, 3749.
Series: Miniatures.
Est. £70-95.

HN3266
Diana
Second Version (Model 2209)
Designer M. Davies.
Date 1990.
20.5cm (8ins) high.
Pale blue, pink and white.
Other colourways: HN2468.
Series: M. Doulton Events.
*(Auction PSA 1.9.04 sold £80
plus comm.)*
Est. £100-150.

HN3271
Guy Fawkes
Second Version (Model 3746)
Designer C.J. Noke.
Remodeller P. Gee.
Date 1989 - 91.
11cm (4.25ins) high.
Red and black.
Series: Miniatures.
*(Auction PSA 22,10.03 sold £50
plus comm.)* *(Ebay 4.6.04 sold £28)*
Est. £55-75.

HN3267
Salome
Second Version (Model 2745)
Designer M. Davies.
Date 1990. Limited edition of 1,000.
24cm (9.5ins) high.
Blue, green, red and lilac.
*(Auction PSA 10.3.04 sold
£200 plus comm.)*
Est. £275-400.

HN3272
Dick Turpin
First Version
Designer G. Tongue.
Date 1989. Limited edition of 5,000.
30.5cm (12ins) high.
Black, red, green and white.
Comm: Lawleys By Post.
Est. £250-350.

HN3273
Annabel
Designer R. Tabbenor.
Date 1989 - 92.
13.5cm (5.25ins) high.
Yellow, blue, pink and white.
Est. £100-135.

HN3278
Lamp Seller
Designer R. Tabbenor.
Date 1990 - 95.
23cm (9ins) high.
Red.
Series: Flambé.
Est. £250-350.

HN3274
Over The Threshold
Designer R. Tabbenor.
Date 1989 - 98.
30.5cm (12ins) high.
White.
Series: Images.
Est. £70-95.

HN3279
Winning Putt
Designer R. Tabbenor.
Date 1991 - 95.
21.5cm (8.5ins) high.
Blue, yellow and grey.
Est. £85-130.

HN3275
Will He, Won't He
Designer R. Tabbenor.
Date 1990 - 94.
23cm (9ins) high.
Green, white and grey.
Series: Clowns.
Est. £110-145.

HN3280
Bridesmaid
Fifth Version (Model 3942)
Designer R. Tabbenor.
Date 1991 - 99.
21.5cm (8.5ins) high.
White.
Series: Images.
Est. £35-50.

HN3276
Teeing Off
Designer R. Tabbenor.
Date 1990 - 97.
21cm (8.25ins) high.
Yellow, cream and green.
Est. £110-150.

HN3281
Bride and Groom
Designer R. Tabbenor.
Date 1991 - 2000.
16cm (6.25ins) high.
White.
Series: Images.
Est. £35-50.

HN3277
The Carpet Seller (Sitting)
Third Version (Model 2584)
Designer R. Tabbenor.
Date 1990 - 95.
18cm (7ins) high.
Red.
Series: Flambé.
Est. £180-250.

HN3282
First Steps
Second Version (Model 2964)
Designer R. Tabbenor.
Date 1991 - 2001.
25.5cm (10ins) high.
White.
Series: Images.
Est. £70-95.

HN3283
Tumbling
Designer D.V. Tootle.
Date 1990 - 94.
23cm (9ins) high.
White, yellow, green and blue.
Other colourways: 3289;
'Tumbler' HN3183.
Series: Clowns.
Est. £135-190.

HN3288
Columbine
Third Version (Model 2440)
Designer D.V. Tootle.
Date 1993.
32cm (12.5ins) high.
Yellow, blue, red and white.
Other colourways:
HN2738, 4059.
Series: Prestige.
Comm: Harrods.
Est. £650-875.

HN3284
The Bride
Fourth Version (Model 3843)
Designer D.V. Tootle.
Date 1990 - 97.
21cm (8.25ins) high.
White.
Other colourways: HN3285.
Est. £90-130.

HN3289
Tumbling
Designer D.V. Tootle.
Date 1991. Limited edition
of 2,500.
23cm (9ins) high.
Pink, blue, white and yellow.
Other colourways: HN3283;
'Tumbler' HN3183.
Series: Clowns.
Comm: National Playing Fields Asso.
Est. £135-195.

HN3285
The Bride
Fourth Version (Model 3843)
Designer D.V. Tootle.
Date 1990 - 96.
21cm (8.25ins) high.
Ivory with yellow flowers.
Other colourways: HN3284.
Est. £90-130

HN3290
Lauren
First Version
Designer D.V. Tootle.
Date 1992.
20.5cm (8ins) high.
Yellow, purple, pink and white.
Other colourways:
'Ann' HN3259.
Comm: Great Universal Stores.
Est. £130-195.

HN3286
Alexandra
Second Version (Model 3821)
Designer D.V. Tootle.
Date 1990 - 2000.
19.5cm (7.75ins) high.
Yellow, white, green and peach.
Other colourways: HN3292.
*(Auction W&H 27.9.04 sold £50
plus comm.)*
Est. £80-115.

HN3291
Tracy
Designer D.V. Tootle.
Date 1993 - 99.
19cm (7.5ins) high.
White and pink.
Other colourways: HN2736.
Marketed in USA.
Est. £80-120.

HN3287
Harlequin
Second Version (Model 2145)
Designer D.V. Tootle.
Date 1993.
32cm (12.5ins) high.
Yellow, gold and black.
Other colourways:
HN2737, 4058.
Series: Prestige.
Comm: Harrods.
Est. £650-875.

HN3292
Alexandra
Second Version (Model 3821)
Designer D.V. Tootle.
Date 1994 - 2002.
19.5cm (7.75ins) high.
Pink, grey, yellow and white.
Other colourways: HN3286.
Est. £110-150.

HN3293
Tip-toe
Designer A. Hughes.
Date 1990 - 94.
23cm (9ins) high.
White, black, yellow and blue.
Other colourways:
'Joker' HN3196.
Series: Clowns.
Est. £130-180.

HN3298
Hold Tight
Designer A. Hughes.
Date 1990 - 93.
21.5cm (8.5ins) high.
White, green, pink and blue.
Est. £170-240.

HN3294
Daddy's Joy
Designer A. Hughes.
Date 1990. Limited edition of
12,500.
20.5cm (8ins) high.
White, green, pink and yellow.
Comm: Lawleys By Post.
Est. £130-180.

HN3299
Welcome Home
Designer A. Hughes.
Date 1991. Limited edition of 9,500.
21.5cm (8.5ins) high.
Grey, blue, orange and turquoise.
Series: Children of the Blitz.
Comm: Lawleys By Post.
Est. £155-225.

HN3295
The Homecoming
Designer A. Hughes.
Date 1990. Limited edition of 9,500.
18cm (7ins) high.
Pink, blue, white and green.
Series: Children of the Blitz.
Comm: Lawleys By Post.
(Auction PSA 23,6.04 sold
£150 plus comm.)
Est. £180-235.

HN3300
Dressing Up
Second Version (Model 4048)
Designer A. Hughes.
Date 1991. Limited edition
of 9,500.
17cm (6.75ins) high.
Blue, yellow and cream.
Comm: Lawleys By Post.
Est. £130-175.

HN3296
Fantasy
Designer A. Hughes.
Date 1990 - 92.
32cm (12.5ins) high.
White.
Series: Reflections.
Est. £170-250.

HN3301
Santa's Helper
Designer A. Hughes.
Date 1991 - 95.
16.5cm (6.5ins) high.
White, red, green and brown.
Comm: Lawleys By Post.
Est. £125-170.

HN3297
Milestone
Designer A. Hughes.
Date 1990 - 94.
18.5cm (7.25ins) high.
Blue, red, green and white.
Est. £130-175.

HN3302
Please Sir
Designer A. Hughes.
Date 1992. Limited edition of 7,500.
20.5cm (8ins) high.
Blue, grey, yellow and cream.
Comm: Lawleys By Post
with donation to 'National
Children's Home'.
Est. £135-165.

HN3303
Tender Moment
First Version
Designer M. Davies.
Date 1990 - 97.
18cm (7ins) high.
Pink, green and white.
Other colourways:
'Nicola' HN2804, 2839.
Series: Vanity Fair Ladies.
Est. £75-120.

HN3308
Sara
First Version (Model 2130)
Designer M. Davies.
Date 1990 - 96.
19.5cm (7.75ins) high.
Dark blue, pink and white.
Other colourways: HN2265.
Est. £100-145.

HN3304
Samantha
Second Version (Model 2439)
Designer M. Davies.
Date 1990 - 96.
18.5cm (7.25ins) high.
White, pink and green.
Other colourways:
'First Dance' HN2803.
Est. £75-110.

HN3309
Summer Rose
Second Version
Designer M. Davies.
Date 1991 - 97.
19cm (7.5ins) high.
White, pink and green.
Other colourways:
'Denise' HN2477.
(Ebay 3.10.04 sold £100)
Est. £95-125.

HN3305
Kathy
Second Version (Model 1910)
Designer M. Davies.
Date 1990 - 96.
18cm (7ins) high.
Pale blue and white.
Other colourways:
'Lynne' HN2329, 3740.
Est. £85-125.

HN3310
Diana
Third Version (Model 3948)
Designer M. Davies.
Remodeller D. Frith.
Date 1991 - 95.
11.5cm (4.5ins) high.
Pale blue and pink.
Series: Miniatures.
Est. £55-75.

HN3306
Megan
First Version
Designer M. Davies.
Date 1991 - 94.
19cm (7.5ins) high.
White and lemon.
Series: Vanity Fair Ladies.
Est. £60-90.

HN3311
Fragrance
First Version (Model 1930)
Designer M. Davies.
Date 1991.
19cm (7.5ins) high.
Red and white.
Other colourways: HN2334.
Series: M. Doulton Events.
Est. £95-130.

HN3307
Elaine
First Version (Model 2652)
Designer M. Davies.
Date 1990 - 2000.
18.5cm (7.25ins) high.
Pink and white.
Other colourways: HN2791,
3741, 4130.
Est. £100-130.

HN3312
Sunday Best
Second Version (Model 3671)
Designer M. Davies.
Remodeller P. Gee.
Date 1991 - 93.
9.5cm (3.75ins) high.
Blue, green, white and gold.
Other colourways: HN3218.
Series: 1. Miniatures. 2. Signature.
Comm: Lawleys By Post.
Est. £65-90.

HN3313
Morning Breeze
Designer P. Gee.
Date 1990 - 94.
20.5cm (8ins) high.
Dark and light blue dress
with orange shawl.
Est. £90-130.

HN3318
Lady Worsley
Designer P. Gee.
Date 1992. Limited edition of 5,000.
24cm (9.5ins) high.
Red dress, black hat and gold bodice.
Series: Reynolds Ladies.
Est. £155-200.

HN3314
Confucius
Designer P. Gee.
Date 1990 - 95.
23cm (9ins) high.
Flambé.
Series: Flambé.
Est. £175-245.

HN3319
Mrs. Hugh Bonfoy
Designer P. Gee.
Date 1992. Limited edition of 5,000.
24cm (9.5ins) high.
Pale blue and pink.
Series: Reynolds Ladies.
Est. £165-225.

HN3315
Waiting for a Train
Designer P. Gee.
Date 1991. Limited edition of 9,500.
22cm (8.75ins) high.
Yellow, black and brown
Comm: Lawleys By Post.
Est. £125-175.

HN3320
Countess Spencer
Designer P. Gee.
Date 1993. Limited edition of 5,000.
24cm (9.5ins) high.
Blue, red, black and white.
Series: Reynolds Ladies.
Est. £165-225.

HN3316
Amy
Second Version (Model 3932)
Designer P. Gee.
Date 1991.
21cm (8.25ins) high.
Blue, white and pink.
Series: Figure of the Year.
*(Auction PSA 1.9.04 sold £240
and W&H 27.9.04 sold £175 plus
comm.) (Ebay 23.5.04 sold £350)*
Est. £300-400.

HN3321
Gail
Second Version (Model 4022)
Designer P. Gee.
Date 1992 - 97.
9.5cm (3.75ins) high.
Red and white.
Series: Miniatures.
Est. £50-70.

HN3317
Countess of Harrington
Designer P. Gee.
Date 1992. Limited edition of 5,000.
24cm (9.5ins) high.
Pink, blue and green.
Series: Reynolds Ladies.
*(Auction PSA 22,10.03 sold
£120 plus comm.)*
Est. £150-300.

HN3322
Celeste
Second Version (Model 3217)
Designer P. Gee.
Date 1992.
20.5cm (8ins) high.
Yellow and black.
Other colourways:
'Isadora' HN2938.
Comm: Great Universal Stores.
Est. £110-150.

HN3323

June

Fourth Version (Model 3202)
Designer R. Tabbenor.
Date 1990 to date.
13.5cm (5.25ins) high.
White, pink and green.
Other colourways: HN3323-3334;
'Amanda' HN2996, 3406, 3632,
3634, 3635.
Series: Flower of the Month, Child.
Est. £12-25

HN3328

November

Second Version (Model 3202)
Designer R. Tabbenor.
Date 1990 to date.
13.5cm (5.25ins) high.
White, lilac and green.
Other colourways: HN3323-3334;
'Amanda' HN2996, 3406, 3632,
3634, 3635.
Series: Flower of the Month, Child.
Est. £12-25

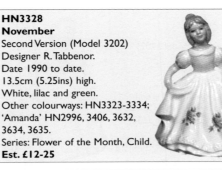

HN3324

July

Second Version (Model 3202)
Designer R. Tabbenor.
Date 1990 to date.
13.5cm (5.25ins) high.
White, blue and green.
Other colourways: HN3323-3334;
'Amanda' HN2996, 3406, 3632,
3634, 3635.
Series: Flower of the Month, Child.
Est. £12-25

HN3329

December

Second Version (Model 3202)
Designer R. Tabbenor.
Date 1990 to date.
13.5cm (5.25ins) high.
White, red and green.
Other colourways: HN3323-3334;
'Amanda' HN2996, 3406, 3632,
3634, 3635.
Series: Flower of the Month, Child.
Est. £12-25

HN3325

August

Second Version (Model 3202)
Designer R. Tabbenor.
Date 1990 to date.
13.5cm (5.25ins) high.
White, purple, blue and green.
Other colourways: HN3323-3334;
'Amanda' HN2996, 3406, 3632,
3634, 3635.
Series: Flower of the Month, Child.
Est. £12-25

HN3330

January

Second Version (Model 3202)
Designer R. Tabbenor.
Date 1990 to date.
13.5cm (5.25ins) high.
White, yellow and green.
Other colourways: HN3323-3334;
'Amanda' HN2996, 3406, 3632,
3634, 3635.
Series: Flower of the Month, Child.
Est. £12-25

HN3326

September

Second Version (Model 3202)
Designer R. Tabbenor.
Date 1990 to date.
13.5cm (5.25ins) high.
White, lilac and green.
Other colourways: HN3323-3334;
'Amanda' HN2996, 3406, 3632,
3634, 3635.
Series: Flower of the Month, Child.
Est. £12-25

HN3331

February

Second Version (Model 3202)
Designer R. Tabbenor.
Date 1990 to date.
13.5cm (5.25ins) high.
White, blue and green.
Other colourways: HN3323-3334;
'Amanda' HN2996, 3406, 3632,
3634, 3635.
Series: Flower of the Month, Child.
Est. £12-25

HN3327

October

Second Version (Model 3202)
Designer R. Tabbenor.
Date 1990 to date.
13.5cm (5.25ins) high.
White, lilac and green.
Other colourways: HN3323-3334;
'Amanda' HN2996, 3406, 3632,
3634, 3635.
Series: Flower of the Month, Child.
Est. £12-25

HN3332

March

Second Version (Model 3202)
Designer R. Tabbenor.
Date 1990 to date.
13.5cm (5.25ins) high.
White, purple and green.
Other colourways: HN3323-3334;
'Amanda' HN2996, 3406, 3632,
3634, 3635.
Series: Flower of the Month, Child.
Est. £12-25

HN3333
April
Second Version (Model 3202)
Designer R. Tabbenor.
Date 1990 to date.
13.5cm (5.25ins) high.
White, purple, pink and green.
Other colourways: HN3323-3334;
'Amanda' HN2996, 3406, 3632,
3634, 3635.
Series: Flower of the Month, Child.
Est. £12-25

HN3338
Karen
Third Version (Model 3885)
Designer M. Davies.
Remodeller R. Tabbenor.
Date 1991 - 94.
9.5cm (3.75ins) high.
Purple, white and gold.
Other colourways:
HN3270, 3749.
Series: 1. Miniatures. 2. Signature.
Comm: Lawleys By Post. **Est. £75-100.**

HN3334
May
Third Version (Model 3202)
Designer R. Tabbenor.
Date 1990 to date.
13.5cm (5.25ins) high.
White, blue and green.
Other colourways: HN3323-3334;
'Amanda' HN2996, 3406, 3632,
3634, 3635.
Series: Flower of the Month, Child.
Est. £12-25

HN3339
Olivia
Second Version (Model 2115)
Designer M. Davies.
Date 1992.
20.5cm (8ins) high.
Red, pink and white.
Other colourways:
'Ninette' HN2379, 3417.
Comm: Great Universal Stores.
Est. £125-165.

HN3335
A Jester
Third Version (Model 3906)
Designer C.J. Noke.
Remodeller R. Tabbenor.
Date 1990.
10cm (4ins) high.
Purple, yellow, beige and brown.
Series: 1. Miniatures. 2. RDICC.
(Auction PSA 1.9.04 sold £75 plus comm.)
Est. £85-130.

HN3340
Kay
Designer M. Davies.
Date 1991.
19cm (7.5ins) high.
Blue and white.
Other colourways:
'Fair Lady' HN2193, 2832, 2835.
Comm: Great Universal Stores.
Est. £85-120.

HN3336
Fair Lady
Second Version (Model 3642)
Designer M. Davies.
Remodeller P. Gee.
Date 1991 - 94.
9.5cm (3.75ins) high.
Red, white, gold and purple.
Other colourways: HN3216.
Series: 1. Miniatures. 2. Signature.
Comm: Lawleys By Post.
Est. £60-90.

HN3341
January
Third Version (Model 2447)
Designer M. Davies. Date 1991.
18cm (7ins) high.
White dress with snowdrops.
Other colourways: HN3341-3347,
3408-3412; 'Beatrice' HN3263, 3631;
'Kathryn' HN3413; 'Lucy' HN3653;
'Summer Serenade' HN3610.
Series: Wildflower of the Month.
Comm: Sears, Canada. **Est. £70-95.**

HN3337
Christine
Third Version (Model 3774)
Designer M. Davies.
Remodeller P. Gee.
Date 1991 - 94.
10cm (4ins) high.
Black, gold, yellow and white.
Other colourways: HN3269.
Series: 1. Miniatures. 2. Signature.
Comm: Lawleys By Post.
Est. £75-100.

HN3342
February
Third Version (Model 2447)
Designer M. Davies. Date 1991.
18cm (7ins) high.
White dress with anemones.
Other colourways: HN3341-3347,
3408-3412; 'Beatrice' HN3263, 3631;
'Kathryn' HN3413; 'Lucy' HN3653;
'Summer Serenade' HN3610.
Series: Wildflower of the Month.
Comm: Sears, Canada. **Est. £70-95.**

HN3343
March
Third Version (Model 2447)
Designer M. Davies. Date 1991.
18cm (7ins) high.
White dress with violets.
Other colourways: HN3341-3347,
3408-3412; 'Beatrice' HN3263, 3631;
'Kathryn' HN3413; 'Lucy' HN3653;
'Summer Serenade' HN3610.
Series: Wildflower of the Month.
Comm: Sears, Canada. **Est. £70-95.**

HN3344
April
Third Version (Model 2447)
Designer M. Davies. Date 1991.
18cm (7ins) high.
White dress with primroses.
Other colourways: HN3341-3347,
3408-3412; 'Beatrice' HN3263, 3631;
'Kathryn' HN3413; 'Lucy' HN3653;
'Summer Serenade' HN3610.
Series: Wildflower of the Month.
Comm: Sears, Canada. **Est. £70-95.**

HN3345
May
Fourth Version (Model 2447)
Designer M. Davies. Date 1991.
18cm (7ins) high.
White dress with Lady's Smock.
Other colourways: HN3341-3347,
3408-3412; 'Beatrice' HN3263, 3631;
'Kathryn' HN3413; 'Lucy' HN3653;
'Summer Serenade' HN3610.
Series: Wildflower of the Month.
Comm: Sears, Canada. **Est. £70-95.**

HN3346
June
Fifth Version (Model 2447)
Designer M. Davies. Date 1991.
18cm (7ins) high.
White dress with roses.
Other colourways: HN3341-3347,
3408-3412; 'Beatrice' HN3263, 3631;
'Kathryn' HN3413; 'Lucy' HN3653;
'Summer Serenade' HN3610.
Series: Wildflower of the Month.
Comm: Sears, Canada. **Est. £70-95.**

HN3347
July
Third Version (Model 2447)
Designer M. Davies. Date 1991.
18cm (7ins) high.
White dress with harebells.
Other colourways: HN3341-3347,
3408-3412; 'Beatrice' HN3263, 3631;
'Kathryn' HN3413; 'Lucy' HN3653;
'Summer Serenade' HN3610.
Series: Wildflower of the Month.
Comm: Sears, Canada. **Est. £70-95.**

HN3348
Mother and Child
First Version
Designer P. Parsons.
Date 1991 - 93.
19cm (7.5ins) high.
White, pink and blue.
Other colourways:
HN3235, 3353.
Est. £80-115.

HN3349
Jane Seymour
Designer P. Parsons.
Date 1991. Limited edition of 9,500.
23cm (9ins) high.
Orange, brown, yellow and blue.
Series: Six Wives of Henry VIII.
Comm: Lawley's by post.
(Ebay 4.6.04 sold £262)
Est. £270-400.

HN3350
Henry VIII
Third Version (Model 4251)
Designer P. Parsons.
Date 1991. Limited edition of 1991.
24cm (9.5ins) high.
Brown, red, gold and white.
Comm: Lawleys By Post.
Est. £750-1000.

HN3351
Congratulations
Designer P. Parsons.
Date 1991 to date.
28cm (11ins) high.
White.
Series: Images.
(Royal Doulton web price £69)
Retail £69.

HN3353
Mother and Child
First Version
Designer P. Parsons.
Date 1992 - 99.
19cm (7.5ins) high.
White.
Other colourways:
HN3235, 3348.
Series: Vanity Fair Series.
Marketed in Canada.
Est. £75-125.

HN3354
Yours Forever
Designer P. Parsons.
Date 1992 - 97.
20.5cm (8ins) high.
Pink and lemon.
Other colourways:
'Kimberley' HN2969.
Series: Vanity Fair Ladies.
Est. £70-100.

HN3359
L'Ambitieuse
Designer V. Annand.
Date 1991. Limited edition
of 5,000.
21cm (8.25ins) high.
Pink, white and pale blue.
Series: RDICC.
Est. £140-200.

HN3355
Just For You
First Version
Designer P. Parsons.
Date 1992 - 98.
21cm (8.25ins) high.
White.
Series: Vanity Fair Ladies.
Est. £70-100.

HN3360
Katie
First Version
Designer V. Annand.
Date 1992 - 97.
21cm (8.25ins) high.
Yellow, white, blue and pink.
Est. £100-145.

HN3356
Anne of Cleves
Designer P. Parsons.
Date 1991. Limited edition of 9,500.
16cm (6.25ins) high.
Yellow, green, white and brown.
Series: Six Wives of Henry VIII.
Comm: Lawley's by post.
Est. £600-900.

HN3361
First Steps
Third Version (Model 3964)
Designer V. Annand.
Date 1992.
12.5cm (5ins) high.
Pink and white.
Series: Little Cherubs.
Comm: Lawleys By Post.
Est. £55-80.

HN3357
Marie
Third Version (Model 2770)
Designer P. Parsons.
Date 1992.
15cm (6ins) high.
White, pink and yellow.
Other colourways:
'Heather' HN2956.
Comm: Great Universal Stores.
Est. £85-125.

HN3362
Well Done
Designer V. Annand.
Date 1992.
10cm (4ins) high.
Pink, blue and white.
Series: Little Cherubs.
Comm: Lawleys By Post.
(Auction W&H 27.9.04 sold £44 plus comm.)
Est. £55-80.

HN3358
Loyal Friend
Designer V. Annand.
Date 1991 - 95.
21cm (8.25ins) high.
Green, white pink and brown.
Est. £140-200.

HN3363
Peek A Boo
Designer V. Annand.
Date 1992.
6.5cm (2.5ins) high.
Pink.
Series: Little Cherubs.
Comm: Lawleys By Post.
Est. £55-80.

HN3364
What Fun
Designer V. Annand.
Date 1992.
9.5cm (3.75ins) high.
Pink and white.
Series: Little Cherubs.
Comm: Lawleys By Post.
Est. £55-80.

HN3369
Hannah
First Version (Model 3369)
Designer N. Pedley.
Date 1991 - 96.
21cm (8.25ins) high.
Pale pink, blue and lemon.
Other colourways: HN3655.
(Ebay 2.8.04 sold £62)
Est. £80-120.

HN3365
Patricia
Third Version (Model 4197)
Designer V. Annand.
Date 1993.
21.5cm (8.5ins) high.
Red, white and black.
Series: Figure of the Year.
*(Auction W&H 27.9.04 sold £60
plus comm.)*
(Ebay 12.6.04 sold £129)
Est. £100-155.

HN3370
Bunny's Bedtime
Designer N. Pedley.
Date 1991. Limited edition of 9,500.
15cm (6ins) high.
Pale blue, pink, and light brown.
Series: RDICC.
Est. £100-130.

HN3366
Wimbledon
Designer V. Annand.
Date 1995. Limited edition of 5,000.
20.5cm (8ins) high.
Pink, blue, white and brown.
Series: British Sporting Heritage.
Est. £220-300.

HN3371
Puppy Love
Designer N. Pedley.
Date 1991. Limited edition of 9,500.
19cm (7.5ins) high.
Orange, brown and blue.
Series: Age of Innocence.
(Ebay 5.6.04 sold £68)
*(Auction PSA 1.9.04 sold £80
comm.)*
Est. £90-150.

HN3367
Henley
Designer V. Annand.
Date 1993. Limited edition
of 5,000.
20.5cm (8ins) high.
Pink, green, yellow and brown.
Series: British Sporting Heritage.
Est. £170-260.

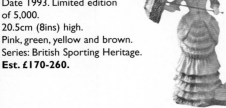

HN3372
Making Friends
Designer N. Pedley.
Date 1991. Limited edition of 9,500.
14cm (5.5ins) high.
White, yellow, orange and pink.
Series: Age of Innocence.
Est. £100-150.

HN3368
Alice
Second Version (Model 3947)
Designer N. Pedley.
Date 1991 - 96.
21cm (8.25ins) high.
Pale blue, white and pink.
Est. £120-150.

HN3373
Feeding Time
Designer N. Pedley.
Date 1991. Limited edition of 9,500.
19cm (7.5ins) high.
Yellow, tan and white.
Series: Age of Innocence.
Est. £100-150.

HN3374
Linda
Third Version (Model 3971)
Designer N. Pedley.
Date 1991 - 95.
21cm (8.25ins) high.
Blue, turquoise and white.
Est. £120-160.

HN3375
Mary
Second Version (Model 3970)
Designer N. Pedley.
Date 1992.
21.5cm (8.5ins) high.
Blue, pink and white.
Series: Figure of the Year.
*(Auction PSA 1.9.04 sold £152
and W&H 27.9.04 sold £135
plus comm.)*
Est. £175-250.

HN3376
Single Red Rose
Designer N. Pedley.
Date 1992 - 95.
20.5cm (8ins) high.
Red, white and yellow.
Est. £100-140.

HN3377
First Outing
Designer N. Pedley.
Date 1992. Limited edition of 9,500.
19cm (7.5ins) high.
Peach, white, green and brown.
Series: Age of Innocence.
Est. £130-180.

HN3378
Summer's Day
Second Version (Model 3955)
Designer T. Potts.
Date 1991 - 96.
21.5cm (8.5ins) high.
Pink, blue and white.
Est. £90-140.

HN3379
Kimberley
Second Version (Model 4050)
Designer T. Potts.
Date 1992 - 97.
21.5cm (8.5ins) high.
Blue and white.
Other colourways:
HN3382, 3864.
Series: Vanity Fair Ladies.
Est. £90-120.

HN3380
Sarah
First Version (Model 4196)
Designer T. Potts.
Date 1993.
20.5cm (8ins) high.
Yellow, pink, white and blue.
Series: M. Doulton Events.
Est. £110-150.

HN3381
Maria
Designer T. Potts.
Date 1993 - 99.
21.5cm (8.5ins) high.
White and yellow.
Series: 1. Roadshow Events.
2. Vanity Fair Ladies.
*(Auction PSA 7.4.04 sold £48
plus comm.)*
Est. £60-100.

HN3382
Kimberley
Second Version (Model 4050)
Designer T. Potts.
Date 1993 - 96.
21.5cm (8.5ins) high.
Pink, yellow and white.
Other colourways:
HN3379, 3864.
Marketed for the USA.
Est. £90-130.

HN3383
Sally
Second Version
Designer T. Potts.
Date 1995 - 97.
21cm (8.25ins) high.
Red.
Other colourways:
HN3851, 4160.
Comm: Freemans.
Est. £60-100.

HN3384
Sarah
Second Version
Designer T. Potts.
Date 1995 - 2000.
20.5cm (8ins) high.
Pink and red.
Other colourways:
HN3852, 3857.
(Ebay 10.7.04 sold £74)
Est. £80-120.

HN3392
Christopher Columbus
Designer A. Maslankowski.
Date 1992. Limited edition of 1,492.
To commemorate the 500 years since
he set sail.
30.5cm (12ins) high.
Brown, red, green and white,
*(Auction PSA 22.10.03 sold £310
plus comm.)*
Est. £370-550.

HN3388
Forget Me Not
Second Version (Model 3975)
Designer A. Maslankowski.
Date 1991 - 2002.
15cm (6ins) high.
White.
Series: Sentiments.
Est. £40-50.

HN3393
With Love
Designer A. Maslankowski.
Date 1992 to date.
15cm (6ins) high.
White and pink.
Other colourways: HN3492.
Series: Sentiments.
(Royal Doulton web price £31.50)
Retail £31.50.

HN3389
Loving You
Designer A. Maslankowski.
Date 1991 to date.
16cm (6.25ins) high.
White.
Series: Sentiments.
(Royal Doulton web price £31.50)
(Ebay 27.5.04 sold £41)
Est. £40-55.

HN3394
Sweet Dreams
Second Version (Model 4075)
Designer A. Maslankowski.
Date 1992 - 98.
15cm (6ins) high.
White.
Series: Sentiments.
Est. £35-50.

HN3390
Thank You
Second Version (Model 3992)
Designer A. Maslankowski.
Date 1991 to date.
16cm (6.25ins) high.
White.
Other colourways:
'Thank You Mother' HN4251.
Series: Sentiments.
(Royal Doulton web price £31.50)
(Ebay 24.5.04 sold £25) **Est. £25-35.**

HN3395
Little Ballerina
Designer A. Maslankowski.
Date 1992 to date.
15cm (6ins) high.
White dress, pink shoes.
Other colourways: HN3431.
(Ebay 29.9.04 sold £25)
Est. £25-45.

HN3391
Reward
Designer A. Maslankowski.
Date 1992 - 96.
11.5cm (4.5ins) high.
Pink, grey and white.
Series: Vanity Fair Children.
Est. £45-75.

HN3396
Buddies
Second Version (Model 4121)
Designer A. Maslankowski.
Date 1992 - 96.
11cm (4.25ins) high.
Pink, white and beige.
Series: Vanity Fair Children.
Est. £45-65.

HN3397
Let's Play
Designer A. Maslankowski.
Date 1992 - 96.
10cm (4ins) high.
Pale green, tan and white.
Series: Vanity Fair Children.
Est. £45-60.

HN3398
The Ace
Designer R. Tabbenor.
Date 1991 - 95.
25.5cm (10ins) high.
White.
Est. £80-120.

HN3399
Father Christmas
Designer R. Tabbenor.
Date 1992 - 99.
23cm (9ins) high.
Red, black and white.
Est. £110-160.

HN3400
God Bless You
Designer R. Tabbenor.
Date 1992 to date.
20.5cm (8ins) high.
White.
Series: Images.
(Royal Doulton web price £29)
Retail £29.

HN3401
Gardening Time
Designer R. Tabbenor.
Date 1992 - 94.
12.5cm (5ins) high.
Blue, green, yellow and grey.
Est. £85-130.

HN3402
Samurai Warrior
Designer R. Tabbenor.
Date 1992. Limited edition of 950.
23cm (9ins) high.
Red.
Series: Flambé.
Est. £180-250.

HN3403
Lt. General
Ulysses S. Grant
Designer R. Tabbenor.
Date 1993. Limited edition of
5,000 for USA market.
30cm (11.75ins) high.
Blue, red, white and brown.
Est. £400-600.

HN3404
General Robert E. Lee
Designer R. Tabbenor.
Date 1993. Limited edition of
5,000 for USA market.
29cm (11.5ins) high.
Grey, red, white and brown.
Est. £400-600.

HN3405
Field Marshall Montgomery
Designer R. Tabbenor.
Date 1994. Limited edition of 1944.
To commemorate the D.Day landings.
30cm (11.75ins) high.
Khaki and brown.
Est. £400-600.

HN3406
Amanda
Designer R. Tabbenor.
Date 1993 - 99.
13.5cm (5.25ins) high.
White and pink.
Other colourways: HN2996, 3632,
3634, 3635; 'Flower of the Month,
Child' series HN3323-3334.
Series: Vanity Fair Children.
Marketed in USA.
Est. £40-60.

HN3407
Julie
First Version
Designer R. Tabbenor.
Date 1993 - 99.
12.5cm (5ins) high.
White and blue.
Other colourways: HN2995.
Marketed in USA.
Est. £40-60.

HN3408
August
Third Version (Model 2447)
Designer M. Davies. Date 1991.
18cm (7ins) high.
White dress with poppies.
Other colourways: HN3341-3347,
3408-3412; 'Beatrice' HN3263, 3631;
'Kathryn' HN3413; 'Lucy' HN3653;
'Summer Serenade' HN3610.
Series: Wildflower of the Month.
Comm: Sears, Canada. **Est. £65-85.**

HN3409
September
Third Version (Model 2447)
Designer M. Davies. Date 1991.
18cm (7ins) high.
White dress with blue flowers.
Other colourways: HN3341-3347,
3408-3412; 'Beatrice' HN3263, 3631;
'Kathryn' HN3413; 'Lucy' HN3653;
'Summer Serenade' HN3610.
Series: Wildflower of the Month.
Comm: Sears, Canada. **Est. £65-85.**

HN3410
October
Third Version (Model 2447)
Designer M. Davies. Date 1991.
18cm (7ins) high.
White dress with buttercups.
Other colourways: HN3341-3347,
3408-3412; 'Beatrice' HN3263, 3631;
'Kathryn' HN3413; 'Lucy' HN3653;
'Summer Serenade' HN3610.
Series: Wildflower of the Month.
Comm: Sears, Canada. **Est. £65-85.**

HN3411
November
Third Version (Model 2447)
Designer M. Davies. Date 1991.
18cm (7ins) high.
White dress with pink flowers.
Other colourways: HN3341-3347,
3408-3412; 'Beatrice' HN3263, 3631;
'Kathryn' HN3413; 'Lucy' HN3653;
'Summer Serenade' HN3610.
Series: Wildflower of the Month.
Comm: Sears, Canada. **Est. £65-85.**

HN3412
December
Third Version (Model 2447)
Designer M. Davies. Date 1991.
18cm (7ins) high.
White dress with Christmas roses.
Other colourways: HN3341-3347,
3408-3412; 'Beatrice' HN3263, 3631;
'Kathryn' HN3413; 'Lucy' HN3653;
'Summer Serenade' HN3610.
Series: Wildflower of the Month.
Comm: Sears, Canada. **Est. £65-85.**

HN3413
Kathryn
First Version
Designer M. Davies. Date 1992.
18cm (7ins) high. Blue and white.
Other colourways: 'Beatrice'
HN3263, 3631; 'Lucy' HN3653;
'Summer Serenade' HN3610;
'Wildflower of the Month' series
HN3341-3347, 3408-3412.
Comm: Great Universal Stores
Est. £65-85.

HN3414
Rebecca
Second Version (Model 4012)
Designer M. Davies.
Remodeller D. Frith.
Date 1992 - 97.
9cm (3.5ins) high.
Pale blue and pink.
Series: Miniatures.
Est. £45-75.

HN3415
Janette
Designer M. Davies.
Date 1992.
19.5cm (7.75ins) high.
Blue, white and green.
Other colourways:
'Kirsty' HN2381.
Comm: Great Universal Stores.
Est. £110-150.

HN3416
Victoria
First Version
Designer M. Davies.
Date 1992.
16.5cm (6.5ins) high.
Blue, white, yellow
and pink.
Other colourways: HN2471.
Series: Roadshow Events.
Est. £140-200.

HN3417
Ninette
First Version (Model 2115)
Designer M. Davies.
Date 1992.
20.5cm (8ins) high.
Orange, white and gold.
Other colourways: HN2379,
'Olivia' HN3339.
Series: Roadshow Events.
Est. £140-200.

HN3422
Joanne
Second Version (Model 4091)
Designer N. Pedley.
Date 1993 - 98.
19cm (7.5ins) high.
White and pink.
Other colourways:
'Annabelle' HN4090.
Est. £100-135.

HN3418
Bedtime
Second Version (Model 4012)
Designer N. Pedley.
Date 1991. Limited edition of 9,000.
18.5cm (7.25ins) high.
Pink, white, tan and yellow.
Comm: Lawleys By Post.
Est. £90-130.

HN3423
Birthday Girl
Designer N. Pedley.
Date 1993 - 2000.
15cm (6ins) high.
White and pink.
Series: Vanity Fair Children.
Est. £55-75.

HN3419
Angela
Third Version (Model 4040)
Designer N. Pedley.
Date 1992.
21.5cm (8.5ins) high.
Blue, pink, lemon and white.
Series: M. Doulton Events.
(Ebay 23.5.04 sold £82)
Est. £90-150.

HN3424
My First Figurine
Designer N. Pedley.
Date 1993 - 98.
11cm (4.25ins) high.
Red, white and pink.
*(Auction W&H 27.9.04 sold £30
plus comm.)*
Est. £40-65.

HN3420
Ashley
Designer N. Pedley.
Date 1992 - 99.
20.5cm (8ins) high.
Lilac and white.
Series: Vanity Fair Ladies.
(Ebay 10.6.04 sold £46)
*(Auction PSA 1.9.04 sold £45
plus comm.)*
Est. £55-85.

HN3425
Almost Grown
Designer N. Pedley.
Date 1993 - 97.
11.5cm (4.5ins) high.
Pale green, white and beige.
Est. £40-55.

HN3421
Nicole
First Version
Designer N. Pedley.
Date 1993 - 97.
19cm (7.5ins) high.
Cream and pink.
Other colourways: HN3686.
Est. £65-95.

HN3426
Best Wishes
First Version
Designer N. Pedley.
Date 1993 - 95.
15cm (6ins) high.
Red, blue and white.
Est. £65-100.

HN3427
Gift of Love
Designer N. Pedley.
Date 1993 - 2000.
19cm (7.5ins) high.
White, pink and lemon.
Series: Vanity Fair Ladies.
Est. £60-90.

HN3428
Discovery
Designer A. Munslow.
Date 1992.
30.5cm (12ins) high.
Matte white.
Series: RDICC.
Est. £60-80.

HN3429
Napoleon at Waterloo
Designer A. Maslankowski.
Date 1992. Limited edition of 1,500.
29cm (11.5ins) high.
Cream, brown, black and green.
(Auction PSA 23.6.04 sold £450
plus comm.)
Est. £550-750.

HN3430
Sit
Designer A. Maslankowski.
Date 1992 - 96.
11.5cm (4.5ins) high.
Pink, brown and white.
Other colourways: HN3123.
Series: Vanity Fair Children.
Marketed in USA.
Est. £45-75.

HN3431
Little Ballerina
Designer A. Maslankowski.
Date 1993. Limited edition of 2,000.
15cm (6ins) high.
Pink.
Other colourways: HN3395.
Marketed in USA.
Est. £45-75.

HN3432
Duke of Wellington
Designer A. Maslankowski.
Date 1993. Limited edition of 1,500.
30.5cm (12ins) high.
Black, blue, cream and yellow.
Est. £550-750.

HN3433
Winston S. Churchill
Second Version (Model 4205)
Designer A. Maslankowski.
Date 1993. Limited edition of 5,000.
30.5cm (12ins) high.
Black, brown and grey.
(Auction PSA 22.10.03 sold £230
plus comm.)
Est. £275-400.

HN3434
Ballet Shoes
Designer A. Maslankowski.
Date 1993 - 2001.
8cm (3.25ins) high.
White.
Est. £45-65.

HN3435
Daddy's Girl
Designer A. Maslankowski.
Date 1993 - 98.
10cm (4ins) high.
Pink, white and tan.
Series: Vanity Fair Children.
Est. £45-65.

HN3436
HM Queen Elizabeth II
Third Version (Model 4665)
Designer A. Maslankowski.
Date 1992. Limited edition of 5,000.
To commemorate Coronation
anniversary.
21cm (8.25ins) high.
Lilac, brown and yellow.
Comm: Lawleys By Post.
(Auction PSA 10.3.04 sold £200
plus comm.) **Est. £300-450.**

HN3437
Mary
Third Version (Model 4044)
Designer A. Maslankowski.
Date 1993 - 96.
8cm (3.25ins) high.
White.
Other colourways: HN3485.
Series: Holy Family.
Marketed in USA.
Est. £30-40.

HN3442
Eliza Farren,
Countess of Derby
Designer P. Gee.
Date 1993. Limited edition of 5,000.
22cm (8.75ins) high.
White, pale brown and blue.
Series: RDICC.
Est. £120-160.

HN3438
Joseph
First Version
Designer A. Maslankowski.
Date 1993 - 96.
14.5cm (5.75ins) high.
White.
Other colourways: HN3486.
Series: Holy Family.
Marketed in USA.
Est. £30-40.

HN3443
Gift of Freedom
Designer P. Gee.
Date 1993 to date.
24.5cm (9.75ins) high.
White.
Series: Images.
(Royal Doulton web price £59)
Retail £59.

HN3439
The Skater
Second Version (Model 4084)
Designer P. Gee.
Date 1992 - 97.
20.5cm (8ins) high.
Red, blue and white.
Est. £125-175.

HN3444
Piper
Second Version (Model 4243)
Designer P. Gee.
Date 1993. Limited edition of 750.
25.5cm (10ins) high.
Black, white, red and green.
Comm: Site of the Green.
Est. £140-200.

HN3440
HM Queen Elizabeth II
Fourth Version (Model 4062)
Designer P. Gee.
Date 1992. Limited edition of 3,500.
To commemorate anniversary
of Coronation.
19cm (7.5ins) high.
Pink, lemon and white.
*(Auction PSA 23.6.04 sold £110
plus comm.)*
Est. £145-195.

HN3445
Amy's Sister
Designer P. Gee.
Date 1993 - 96.
20.5cm (8ins) high.
Red, blue, white and yellow.
Est. £80-120.

HN3441
Barbara
Third Version (Model 4106)
Designer P. Gee.
Date 1993. Limited edition of 9,500.
20.5cm (8ins) high.
Pink lilac and lemon.
Series: RDICC.
Est. £170-250.

HN3446
Spring Song
Designer P. Gee.
Date 1993 - 96.
18.5cm (7.25ins) high.
Yellow and white.
Other colourways:
'Danielle' HN3001.
Series: The Seasons (Series Five)
Comm: Guild of Specialist
Retailers, UK.
Est. £55-70.

HN3447
Jennifer
Third Version (Model 4293)
Designer P. Gee.
Date 1994.
19.5cm (7.75ins) high.
Pink and white.
Series: Figure of the Year.
*(Auction PSA 1.9.04 sold £85
and W&H 27.9.04 sold £70
plus comm.)*
Est. £110-150.

HN3452
Our First Christmas
Designer P. Parsons.
Date 1993 - 98.
29cm (11.5ins) high.
White.
Series: Images.
Est. £50-75.

HN3448
Charles Dickens
Designer P. Gee.
Date 1994. Limited edition of 5,000.
10cm (4ins) high.
Black, grey and white.
Comm: Pascoe & Company.
*(Auction PSA 22.10.03 sold £45
plus comm.)*
Est. £55-80.

HN3453
Juliet
Second Version (Model 4202)
Designer P. Parsons.
Date 1994. Limited edition of 5,000.
15cm (6ins) high.
Red, green, grey and pink.
Series: Shakespearean Ladies.
Comm: Lawleys By Post.
Est. £165-200.

HN3449
Catherine Howard
Designer P. Parsons.
Date 1992. Limited edition of 9,500.
21cm (8.25ins) high.
Purple, yellow and white.
Series: Six Wives of Henry VIII.
Comm: Lawleys By Post.
(Ebay 4.6.04 sold £211)
Est. £275-375.

HN3454
Flowers For Mother
Designer P. Parsons.
Date 1994 - 97.
14.5cm (5.75ins) high.
Pink, white and yellow.
Est. £45-65.

HN3450
Catherine Parr
Designer P. Parsons.
Date 1992. Limited edition of 9,500.
16cm (6.25ins) high.
Red and white.
Series: Six Wives of Henry VIII.
Comm: Lawleys By Post.
Est. £275-375.

HN3455
Sharon
First Version (Model 3105)
Designer P. Parsons.
Date 1994 - 99.
14cm (5.5ins) high.
White and pink.
Other colourways: HN3047.
Est. £55-70.

HN3451
Catherine
Second Version (Model 3044)
Designer P. Parsons.
Date 1993 - 99.
12.5cm (5ins) high.
White.
Other colourways: HN3044.
Est. £40-60.

HN3456
Grandpa's Story
Designer P. Parsons.
Date 1994 - 2000.
15cm (6ins) high.
Green, blue, pink and white.
(Ebay 5.10.04 sold £97)
Est. £120-170.

HN3457
When I Was Young
Designer P. Parsons.
Date 1994 - 2000.
14cm (5.5ins) high.
Pink, blue and green.
Est. £150-200.

HN3462
Boy Scout
Designer A. Hughes.
Date 1994. Limited edition of 9,500.
19.5cm (7.75ins) high.
Green, black and brown.
Comm: Lawleys By Post.
Est. £140-200.

HN3458
Henry VIII
Fourth Vervion (Model 4251)
Designer P. Parsons.
Date 1994. Limited edition of 9,500.
23.5cm (9.25ins) high.
Brown, black, red and white.
Comm: Lawleys By Post.
Est. £300-400.

HN3470
Croquet
Designer V. Annand.
Date 1996. Limited edition of 5,000.
21.5cm (8.5ins) high.
Red, blue and white.
Series: British Sporting Heritage.
Est. £180-250.

HN3459
King Charles
Designer C.J. Noke
and H. Tittensor.
Date 1992. Limited edition of 350
to mark 350th anniversary of the
beginning of the Civil War.
42.5cm (16.75ins) high.
Gold, purple, white and cream.
Other colourways: HN404, 2084.
Est. £1000-1500.

HN3471
Ascot
Second Version (Model 4123)
Designer V. Annand.
Date 1994. Limited edition of 5,000.
21.5cm (8.5ins) high.
Purple and pink.
Series: British Sporting Heritage.
Est. £185-250.

HN3460
Brother and Sister
Designer A. Hughes.
Date 1993 to date.
19.5cm (7.75ins) high.
White.
Series: Images.
(Royal Doulton web price £39)
Retail £39.

HN3472
La Loge
Designer V. Annand.
Date 1992. Limited edition of 7,500.
21.5cm (8.5ins) high.
White, yellow, pink and black.
Comm: Lawleys By Post.
Est. £250-350.

HN3461
Kerry
Designer A. Hughes.
Date 1993 - 99.
13.5cm (5.25ins) high.
White.
Other colourways: HN3036.
Marketed in USA.
Est. £35-50.

HN3473
Les Parapluies
Designer V. Annand.
Date 1993. Limited edition of 7,500.
21cm (8.25ins) high.
Blue and white.
Comm: Lawleys By Post.
Est. £275-400.

HN3474
Lise
Designer V. Annand.
Date 1994. Limited edition of 7,500.
21.5cm (8.5ins) high.
Lilac, yellow and purple.
Comm: Lawleys By Post.
Est. £180-250.

HN3475
Marie Sisley (Mrs)
Designer V. Annand.
Date 1994. Limited edition of 7,500.
21.5cm (8.5ins) high.
Yellow, grey and red.
Comm: Lawleys By Post.
Est. £250-350.

HN3476
Bridesmaid
Sixth Version (Model 4217)
Designer V. Annand.
Date 1994 - 97.
13.5cm (5.25ins) high.
Pink and white.
Other colourways:
'Flowergirl' HN3479.
Est. £55-70.

HN3477
Springtime
Third Version (Model 4189)
Designer V. Annand.
Date 1993 - 96.
20.5cm (8ins) high.
Pink, yellow and cream.
Series: The Seasons (Series Six)
Est. £145-195.

HN3478
Summertime
Second Version (Model 4217)
Designer V. Annand.
Date 1994 - 96.
21.5cm (8.5ins) high.
Green, yellow and lilac.
Series: The Seasons (Series Six)
Est. £135-175.

HN3479
Flowergirl
First Version (Model 4217)
Designer V. Annand.
Date 1994 - 97.
12.5cm (5ins) high.
Pink and white.
Other colourways:
'Bridesmaid' HN3476.
Marketed in North America.
Est. £55-70.

HN3480
Kirsty
Second Version (Model 3652)
Designer M. Davies.
Remodeller P. Gee.
Date 1993 - 97.
9.5cm (3.75ins) high.
Blue and white.
Other colourways: HN3213,
3246, 3743.
Series: Miniatures.
Marketed in Canada.   **Est. £45-65.**

HN3481
Lavender Rose
Designer M. Davies.
Date 1993 - 95.
15cm (6ins) high.
White, pink and green.
Other colourways: 'Debbie' HN2385,
2400; 'Moonlight Rose' HN3483;
'Old Country Roses' HN3482;
'Memory Lane' HN3746;
'Tranquillity' HN3747.
Est. £45-70.

HN3482
Old Country Roses
First Version
Designer M. Davies.
Date 1993 - 95.
15cm (6ins) high.
White, red, yellow and green.
Other colourways: 'Debbie' HN2385,
2400; 'Lavender Rose' HN3481;
'Moonlight Rose' HN3483; 'Memory
Lane' HN3746; 'Tranquillity'
HN3747.   **Est. £45-70.**

HN3483
Moonlight Rose
Designer M. Davies.
Date 1993 - 95.
15cm (6ins) high.
White, blue and lilac.
Other colourways: 'Debbie' HN2385,
2400; 'Lavender Rose' HN3481;
'Old Country Roses' HN3482;
'Memory Lane' HN3746;
'Tranquillity' HN3747.
Est. £45-70.

HN3484
Jesus
Designer A. Maslankowski.
Date 1993 - 96.
6.5cm (2.5ins) high.
White and pale brown.
Other colourways: HN3487.
Series: Holy Family.
Marketed in USA.
Est. £25-30.

HN3489
Vice Admiral Lord Nelson
Designer A. Maslankowski.
Date 1993. Limited edition of 950.
32cm (12.5ins) high.
Dark blue, cream and yellow.
Est. £550-750.

HN3485
Mary
Third Version (Model 4044)
Designer A. Maslankowski.
Date 1993 - 96.
8cm (3.25ins) high.
Blue and white.
Other colourways: HN3437.
Series: Holy Family.
Marketed in USA.
Est. £40-65.

HN3490
Thinking of You
First Version
Designer A. Maslankowski.
Date 1993.
17cm (6.75ins) high.
White dress with pink sash.
Other colourways: HN3124.
Series: 1. Roadshow and Events.
2. Sentiments.
Commissioned for Collectors
Events in UK.   **Est. £50-65.**

HN3486
Joseph
First Version
Designer A. Maslankowski.
Date 1993 - 96.
14.5cm (5.75ins) high.
Brown and white.
Other colourways: HN3438.
Series: Holy Family.
Marketed in USA.
Est. £40-55.

HN3491
Friendship
Designer A. Maslankowski.
Date 1994 to date.
15cm (6ins) high.
White.
Series: Sentiments.
(Royal Doulton web price £31.50)
Retail £31.50.

HN3487
Jesus
Designer A. Maslankowski.
Date 1993 - 96.
6.5cm (2.5ins) high.
White.
Other colourways: HN3484.
Series: Holy Family.
Marketed in USA.
Est. £20-30.

HN3492
With Love
Designer A. Maslankowski.
Date 1994 - 97.
14.5cm (5.75ins) high.
White dress and pink sash.
Other colourways: HN3393.
Series: Sentiments.
Marketed in Canada.
Est. £35-45.

HN3488
Christmas Day
Designer A. Maslankowski.
Date 1993 - 99.
15cm (6ins) high.
White.
Other colourways: HN4062.
Series: Sentiments.
Est. £35-55.

HN3493
Christmas Parcels
Second Version (Model 4363)
Designer A. Maslankowski.
Date 1994 - 98.
15cm (6ins) high.
White.
Other colourways: HN4063.
Series: Sentiments.
Est. £35-50.

HN3494
Tina
Designer M. Davies.
Date 1993.
19cm (7.5ins) high.
Blue, white and lilac.
Other colourways:
'Maureen' HN2481.
Comm: Great Universal Stores.
Est. £50-75.

HN3499
Top o' the Hill
Second Version (Model 3049)
Designer L. Harradine.
Remodeller P. Gee.
Date 1993 - 98.
10cm (4ins) high.
Red, yellow and white.
Other colourways: HN2126.
Series: Miniatures.
*(Auction PSA 22.10.03 sold £40
plus comm.)* **Est. £55-100.**

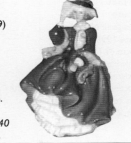

HN3495
Annette
Second Version (Model 2005)
Designer M. Davies.
Date 1993.
20.5cm (8ins) high.
Pale green and cream.
Other colourways:
'Sandra' HN2275, 2401.
Est. £120-150.

HN3600
Dawn
Third Version (Model 4219)
Designer N. Pedley.
Date 1993 - 98.
19cm (7.5ins) high.
Pink and white.
Series: Vanity Fair Ladies.
Est. £80-120.

HN3496
Margaret
Second Version (Model 2729)
Designer M. Davies.
Date 1993 - 99.
19cm (7.5ins) high.
White and pale green.
Other colourways: HN2397;
'Adele' HN2480; 'Camille' HN3171.
Marketed in USA.
Est. £90-130.

HN3601
Helen
Third Version (Model 4208)
Designer N. Pedley.
Date 1993 to date.
20.5cm (8ins) high.
Blue, white and yellow.
Other colourways: HN3687,
3763, 3886; 'Miss Kay' HN3659.
(Ebay 27.7.04 sold £87)
Est. £90-130.

HN3497
Jessica
First Version
Designer M. Davies.
Date 1993.
18cm (7ins) high.
White and pale blue.
Other colourways: HN3169.
Marketed in North America.
Est. £65-95.

HN3602
Flowergirl
Second Version (Model 4070)
Designer N. Pedley.
Date 1993 - 96.
13.5cm (5.25ins) high.
Cream and pink.
Est. £40-60.

HN3498
Natalie
First Version
Designer M. Davies.
Date 1993 - 99.
20.5cm (8ins) high.
White and yellow.
Other colourways: HN3173.
Marketed in USA.
Est. £70-90.

HN3603
Sharon
Second Version (Model 4297)
Designer N. Pedley.
Date 1994.
20.5cm (8ins) high.
Blue, peach and tan.
Series: M. Doulton Events.
*(Auction PSA 4.2.04 sold £60
plus comm.)*
(Ebay 28.5.04 sold £75)
Est. £80-120.

HN3604
Diane
Designer N. Pedley.
Date 1994.
22cm (8.75ins) high.
Pink, lilac, white and blue.
Series: RDICC.
*(Auction PSA 22.10.03 sold £80
plus comm.)*
Est. £100-140.

HN3605
First Performance
Designer N. Pedley.
Date 1994 - 98.
16cm (6.25ins) high.
White, pink and brown.
Est. £55-85.

HN3606
A Posy for You
Designer N. Pedley.
Date 1994 - 97.
12cm (4.75ins) high.
Blue, yellow and white.
Est. £45-70.

HN3607
Special Friend
Designer N. Pedley.
Date 1994 - 98.
11cm (4.25ins) high.
Blue, white, brown and cream.
*(Auction W&H 27.9.04 sold £30
plus comm.)*
Est. £40-65.

HN3608
Good Companion
Designer N. Pedley.
Date 1994 - 99.
21cm (8.25ins) high.
White, pink and brown.
Series: Vanity Fair Ladies.
Est. £70-100.

HN3609
Kathleen
Third Version (Model 4299)
Designer N. Pedley.
Date 1994 - 2000.
21cm (8.25ins) high.
Yellow and white.
Other colourways: HN3880;
'Brianna' HN4126.
Series: Vanity Fair Ladies.
Est. 70-100.

HN3610
Summer Serenade
Designer M. Davies.
Date 1993 - 96.
18cm (7ins) high.
Blue and white.
Other colourways: 'Beatrice' HN3263,
3631; 'Kathryn' HN3413; 'Lucy'
HN3653; 'Wildflower of the Month'
series HN3341-3347, 3408-3412.
Series: Seasons (Series Five)
Comm: Great Universal Stores.   **Est. 65-85.**

HN3611
Winter Welcome
Designer M. Davies.
Date 1993 - 96.
19cm (7.5ins) high.
Russet and white.
Other colourways:
 'Caroline' HN3170.
Series: Seasons (Series Five)
Comm: Guild of Spec. China and
Glass Retailers, UK.
Est. £65-85.

HN3612
Autumn Attraction
Designer M. Davies.
Date 1993 - 96.
17cm (6.75ins) high.
Gold, yellow and white.
Other colourways:
 'Michele' HN2234.
Series: Seasons (Series Five)
Est. £65-85.

HN3613
Darling
Second Version (Model 1264)
Designer C. Vyse.
Date 1993.
13cm (5.25ins) high.
White and pale blue.
Other colourways: HN1985.
Est. £45-70.

HN3617
Monica
Designer L. Harradine.
Date 1993 - 99.
10cm (4ins) high.
Yellow, pink, green and white.
Other colourways: HN1458,
1459, 1467.
Est. £45-70.

HN3623
Lady Eaton
Designer V. Annand.
Date 1994. Limited edition
of 2,500. To celebrate 125th
Anni. Thomas Eaton Co.
19cm (7.5ins) high.
Blue, pink, yellow and white.
Other colourways:
'Janice' HN3624.
Est. £200-250.

HN3618
Dinky Doo
Designer L. Harradine.
Date 1994 - 2002.
11.5cm (4.75ins) high.
Pale blue and white.
Other colourways:
HN1678, 2120.
Est. £30-50.

HN3624
Janice
Second Version (Model 4134)
Designer V. Annand.
Date 1994 - 97.
19cm (7.5ins) high.
Pale blue, pink, lemon and white.
Other colourways:
'Lady Eaton' HN3623.
Comm: Great Universal Stores.
Est. £110-150.

HN3620
Valerie
First Version
Designer M. Davies.
Date 1994 - 99.
12.5cm (5ins) high.
Pink, white, blue
and yellow.
Other colourways: HN2107.
Est. £35-55.

HN3625
Anniversary
Designer V. Annand.
Date 1994 - 98.
22cm (8.75ins) high.
White, black, blue and pink.
Est. £250-300.

HN3621
Autumntime
Second Version (Model 4216)
Designer V. Annand.
Date 1995 - 96.
22cm (8.75ins) high.
Turquoise, white and brown.
Series: The Seasons (Series Six)
Est. £165-225.

HN3626
Lily
Second Version
Designer V. Annand.
Date 1995.
24cm (9.5ins) high.
Yellow and purple.
Series: 1. Lady Doulton 1995.
2. M. Doulton Events.
*(Auction PSA 4.2.04 sold £70
plus comm.) (Ebay 8.7.04 sold £77)*
Est. £100-135.

HN3622
Wintertime
Second Version (Model 4198)
Designer V. Annand.
Date 1996.
21.5cm (8.5ins) high.
Red, pink, green and white.
Series: The Seasons (Series Six)
*(Auction W&H 27.9.04 sold £90
plus comm.)*
Est. £125-175.

HN3627
England
Designer V. Annand.
Date 1996 - 98.
20.5cm (8ins) high.
Pink and blue.
Series: Ladies of the British Isles.
*(Auction PSA 23.6.04 sold £105
plus comm.)*
Est. £145-195.

HN3628
Ireland
Designer V. Annand.
Date 1996 - 98.
19.5cm (7.75ins) high.
White and green.
Series: Ladies of the
British Isles.
*(Auction PSA 23.6.04 sold £100
plus comm.)*
Est. £145-195.

HN3633
Shakespeare
Designer R. Tabbenor.
Date 1994. Limited edition of 1,564.
30cm (11.75ins) high.
Brown, white and cream.
Comm: Lawleys By Post.
Est. £450-600.

HN3629
Scotland
Designer V. Annand.
Date 1995 - 98.
19.5cm (7.75ins) high.
White, pink and green.
Series: Ladies of the
British Isles.
*(Auction PSA 23.6.04 sold £130
plus comm.)*
Est. £150-225.

HN3634
Amanda
Designer R. Tabbenor.
Date 1995.
13.5cm (5.25ins) high.
Blue and white.
Other colourways: HN2996,
3406, 3632, 3635; 'Flower of
the Month, Child' series
HN3323-3334.
Comm: Youngs, Canada.
Est. £40-50.

HN3630
Wales
Designer V. Annand.
Date 1995 - 98.
21.5cm (8.5ins) high.
Green, white and red.
Other colourways:
'Welsh Lady' HN4712
Series: Ladies of the British Isles.
Est. £200-300.

HN3635
Amanda
Designer R. Tabbenor.
Date 1995 - 95.
13.5cm (5.25ins) high.
Pink and white.
Other colourways: HN2996,
3406, 3632, 3634; 'Flower of
the Month, Child' series
HN3323-3334.
Est. £40-50.

HN3631
Beatrice
Designer M. Davies.
Date 1994 - 98.
18cm (7ins) high.
White.
Other colourways: HN3263;
'Kathryn' HN3413; 'Lucy' HN3653;
'Summer Serenade' HN3610;
'Wildflower of the Month' series
HN3341-3347, 3408-3412.
Est. £65-85.

HN3636
Captain Hook
Designer R. Tabbenor.
Date 1993 - 96.
23.5cm (9.25ins) high.
Blue, brown and red.
Series: Character Sculptures.
Est. £100-130.

HN3632
Amanda
Designer R. Tabbenor.
Date 1994 - 96.
13.5cm (5.25ins) high.
White, pink and green.
Other colourways: HN2996,
3406, 3634, 3635; 'Flower of
the Month, Child' series
HN3323-3334.
Series: Vanity Fair Children.
Est. £40-50.

HN3637
Dick Turpin
Second Version
Designer R. Tabbenor.
Date 1993 - 96.
23cm (9ins) high.
Black, white, red and brown.
Series: Character Sculptures.
Est. £100-130.

HN3638
D'Artagnan
First Version
Designer R. Tabbenor.
Date 1993 - 96.
23cm (9ins) high.
Blue, dark red, brown and black.
Series: Character Sculptures.
Est. £100-130.

HN3643
Pauline
Third Version (Model 4134)
Designer N. Pedley.
Date 1994.
18.5cm (7.25ins) high.
Dark red, white and blue.
Other colourways: HN3656.
Series: Roadshow Events.
Est. £70-95.

HN3639
Sherlock Holmes
Designer R. Tabbenor.
Date 1995 - 96.
19cm (7.5ins) high.
Brown and green.
Series: Character Sculptures.
Est. £100-130.

HN3644
Deborah
Second Version
Designer N. Pedley.
Date 1995.
19cm (7.5ins) high.
Yellow, pink and white.
Series: Figure of the Year.
(Auction W&H 27.9.04 sold
£60 plus comm.)
Est. £80-130.

HN3640
W. G. Grace
Designer R. Tabbenor.
Date 1995. Limited edition
of 9,500.
20.5cm (8ins) high.
Cream, white and red.
Comm: Lawleys By Post.
Est. £140-190.

*Picture
not available
at present*

HN3645
Lindsay
Designer N. Pedley.
Date 1994 - 98.
20.5cm (8ins) high.
Cream, white and blue.
Other colourways:
'Katie' HN4123.
Est. £90-120.

HN3641
Robert Burns
Second Version
Designer R. Tabbenor.
Date 1996 - 98.
19cm (7.5ins) high.
Brown and green.
Est. £170-250.

HN3646
Claire
Second Version (Model 4317)
Designer N. Pedley.
Date 1994 - 2000.
20.5cm (8ins) high.
White and pale blue.
Other colourways: 'Kaitlyn'
HN4128; 'Molly' HN4091;
'Rosemary' HN3691, 3698.
Est. £75-100.

HN3642
The Moor
Designer C.J. Noke.
Date 1994 - 95.
42cm (16.5ins) high.
Flambé.
Other colourways: HN1308, 1366,
1425, 1657, 2082, 3926; 'An Arab'
HN33, 343, 378.
Series: Flambé.
Est. £900-1300.

HN3647
Holly
Designer N. Pedley.
Date 1994 - 2000.
20.5cm (8ins) high.
Red, green and pink.
(Auction W&H 27.9.04 sold £75
plus comm.)
Est. £100-135.

HN3648
Sweet Sixteen
Second Version
Designer N. Pedley.
Date 1994 - 98.
20.5cm (8ins) high.
Pink and white.
Other colourways: 'Angela'
HN3690; 'Kelly' HN3912.
(Ebay 5.8.04 sold £75)
Est. £85-125.

HN3653
Lucy
Second Version
Designer M. Davies.
Date 1994 - 97.
18cm (7ins) high. White.
Other colourways: 'Beatrice'
HN3263, 3631; 'Kathryn' HN3413;
'Summer Serenade' HN3610;
'Wildflower of the Month' series
HN3341-3347, 3408-3412.
Comm: Great Universal Stores. **Est. £65-85.**

HN3649
Hannah
Second Version
Designer N. Pedley.
Date 1994 - 98.
10cm (4ins) high.
Blue, pink and white.
Other colourways: HN3870.
Series: Miniatures.
Est. £60-75.

HN3654
Young Melody
Designer N. Pedley.
Date 1994 - 96.
11cm (4.25ins) high.
White and yellow.
Est. £40-65.

HN3650
Mother's Helper
Designer N. Pedley.
Date 1994 - 2000.
11.5cm (4.5ins) high.
Pink, cream and white.
(Ebay 3.10.04 sold £35)
Est. £35-55.

HN3655
Hannah
First Version
Designer N. Pedley.
Date 1995.
21cm (8.25ins) high.
Blue and white.
Other colourways: HN3369.
Est. £95-140.

HN3651
Hello Daddy
Designer N. Pedley.
Date 1994 - 2000.
14.5cm (5.75ins) high.
Pale green, black and white.
Est. £55-70.

HN3656
Pauline
Third Version
Designer N. Pedley.
Date 1994.
18.5cm (7.25ins) high.
Red and white.
Other colourways: HN3643.
Comm: Littlewoods.
Est. £90-130.

HN3652
First Recital
Designer N. Pedley.
Date 1994 - 96.
11.5cm (4.5ins) high.
Blue and white.
*(Auction PSA 1.9.04 sold £30
plus comm.)*
Est. £40-65.

HN3657
Quiet, They're Sleeping
Designer N. Pedley.
Date 1994 - 97.
14cm (5.5ins) high.
White, blue and pink.
Comm: Lawleys By Post.
Est. £65-95.

HN3658
Charlotte
Second Version
Designer N. Pedley.
Date 1995 - 96.
20.5cm (8ins) high.
Blue.
Comm: Littlewoods.
(Ebay 19.7.04 sold £60)
Est. £75-110.

HN3663
Special Treat
Designer N. Pedley.
Date 1995 - 97.
15cm (6ins) high.
Pink, yellow and white.
Est. £55-75.

HN3659
Miss Kay
Designer N. Pedley.
Date 1994.
21cm (8.25ins) high.
Pink and white.
Other colourways: 'Helen'
HN3601, 3687, 3763, 3886.
Comm: Kay's Catalogue
(Auction W&H 27.9.04 sold £65
plus comm.)
Est. £80-110.

HN3664
Wistful
Second Version
Designer P. Gee.
Date 1994 - 2002.
31cm (12.25ins) high.
White.
Series: Images.
Est. £30-45.

HN3660
Happy Birthday
Second Version
Designer N. Pedley.
Date 1995 - 99.
20.5cm (8ins) high.
Pink, green and white.
(Auction W&H 27.9.04 sold £65
plus comm.)
Est. £80-110.

HN3665
Tomorrow's Dreams
Second Version
Designer P. Gee.
Date 1995 to date.
21.5cm (8.5ins) high.
White.
Series: Images.
(Royal Doulton web price £39)
Retail £39.

HN3661
Gemma
Designer N. Pedley.
Date 1995 - 98.
20.5cm (8ins) high.
Green, pink and white.
Est. £80-100.

HN3674
Ophelia
Designer P. Parsons.
Date 1995. Limited edition of 5,000.
18cm (7ins) high.
Pink, green, lilac and white.
Series: Shakespearean Ladies.
Comm: Lawleys By Post.
Est. £175-225.

HN3662
Take Me Home
Designer N. Pedley.
Date 1995 - 99.
20.5cm (8ins) high.
White and pink.
(Auction PSA 3.12.03 sold £60
plus comm.)
(Ebay 9.6.04 sold £60)
Est. £70-110.

HN3675
Richard the Lionheart
Designer P. Parsons.
Date 1995 - 2002.
25.5cm (10ins) high.
Blue, tan, red and white.
Est. £185-250.

HN3676
Desdemona
Designer P. Parsons.
Date 1995. Limited edition of 5,000.
23cm (9ins) high.
Blue and white.
Series: Shakespearean Ladies.
Comm: Lawleys By Post.
Est. £175-225.

HN3681
Joan of Arc
Designer P. Parsons.
Date 1996 - 98.
25.5cm (10ins) high.
Cream and blue.
*(Auction PSA 23.6.04 sold £120
plus comm.)*
Est. £150-200.

HN3677
Cinderella
First Version
Designer P. Parsons.
Date 1995. Limited edition of 2,000.
20.5cm (8ins) high.
Blue and white.
Series: The Disney Princess
Collection.
Est. £150-200.

HN3682
Princess Elizabeth
Designer P. Parsons.
Date 1996. Limited edition of 5,000.
21.5cm (8.5ins) high.
Red, brown and pink.
Series: Tudor Roses.
Comm: Lawleys By Post.
Est. £225-325.

HN3678
Snow White
Designer P. Parsons.
Date 1995. Limited edition of 2,000.
21cm (8.25ins) high.
Blue, red and yellow.
Series: The Disney Princess
Collection.
Est. £180-220.

HN3683
Eastern Grace
Designer P. Parsons.
Date 1995. Limited edition of 2,500.
32cm (12.5ins) high. Flambé.
Other colourways: HN3138.
Series: Flambé.
*(Auction PSA 22.10.03 sold £140
plus comm.)*
Est. £180-250.

HN3679
Titania
Designer P. Parsons.
Date 1995. Limited edition of 5,000.
22cm (8.75ins) high.
Yellow, pink and blue.
Series: Shakespearean Ladies.
Comm: Lawleys By Post.
Est. £200-250.

HN3684
What's The Matter?
Designer N. Pedley.
Date 1995 - 98.
14cm (5.5ins) high.
White and yellow.
Est. £55-80.

HN3680
Lady Jane Grey
Designer P. Parsons.
Date 1995. Limited edition of 5,000.
21cm (8.25ins) high.
Green, red, white and gold.
Series: Tudor Roses.
Comm: Lawleys By Post.
*(Auction PSA 10.3.04 sold £190
plus comm.)*
Est. £250-350.

HN3685
Hometime
Designer N. Pedley.
Date 1995 - 97.
15cm (6ins) high.
Blue, brown and white.
Est. £65-85.

HN3686
Nicole
First Version
Designer N. Pedley.
Date 1995.
19cm (7.5ins) high.
Pink and cream.
Other colourways: HN3421.
Comm: Birks, Canada.
Est. £80-100.

HN3691
Rosemary
Third Version
Designer N. Pedley.
Date 1995 U.K. 1996
Canada - 97.
20.5cm (8ins) high.
Purple, white and yellow.
Other colourways: HN3698;
'Claire' HN3646; 'Kaitlyn'
HN4128; 'Molly' HN4091.
Est. £110-135.

HN3687
Helen
Third Version
Designer N. Pedley.
Date 1995 - 96.
19cm (7.5ins) high.
Green.
Other colourways: HN3601;
3763, 3886; 'Miss Kay' HN3659.
Comm: Express Gifts.
Est. £85-120.

HN3692
Old Country Roses
Second Version
Designer N. Pedley.
Date 1995 - 99.
20.5cm (8ins) high.
Yellow, red and white.
(Ebay 9.6.04 sold £183)
Est. £190-225.

HN3688
Emily
Second Version
Designer N. Pedley.
Date 1995.
21cm (8.25ins) high.
Yellow, blue and white.
Series: RDICC.
Est. £120-150.

HN3693
April
Fourth Version
Designer N. Pedley.
Date 1995 - 97.
20.5cm (8ins) high.
Yellow, white and green.
Est. £105-140.

HN3689
Jacqueline
Third Version
Designer N. Pedley.
Date 1995.
20.5cm (8ins) high.
Green and white.
Series: Roadshow Events.
Est. £85-120.

HN3694
Caroline
Second Version
Designer N. Pedley.
Date 1995 - 98.
20.5cm (8ins) high.
Pink, yellow, blue and white.
*(Auction PSA 1.9.04 sold £50
plus comm.)*
Est. £70-100.

HN3690
Angela
Fourth Version
Designer N. Pedley.
Date 1995 - 97.
20.5cm (8ins) high.
Other colourways: 'Kelly' HN3912;
'Sweet Sixteen' HN3648.
Comm: Great Universal Stores.
Est. £80-110.

HN3695
Storytime
Second Version
Designer N. Pedley.
Date 1995 - 98.
10cm (4ins) high.
White, red and brown.
*(Auction PSA 10.3.04 sold £30
plus comm.)*
Est. £40-60.

HN3696
Faithful Friend
Designer N. Pedley.
Date 1995 - 97.
15cm (6ins) high.
Peach, yellow, black and white.
Est. £50-65.

HN3701
Camellias
Designer V. Annand.
Date 1995 - 98.
21.5cm (8.5ins) high.
Pink and white.
Series: Flowers of Love.
Est. £135-185.

HN3697
Home at Last
Designer N. Pedley.
Date 1995 - 99.
14.5cm (5.75ins) high.
Green, brown and cream.
*(Auction PSA 10.3.04 sold £40
plus comm.)*
Est. £50-65.

HN3702
Le Bal
Designer V. Annand.
Date 1995. Limited
edition of 5,000.
21.5cm (8.5ins) high.
Yellow, orange and white.
Series: RDICC.
(Ebay 10.6.04 sold £77)
Est. £90-150.

HN3698
Rosemary
Third Version
Designer N. Pedley.
Date 1995 - 97.
20.5cm (8ins) high.
Yellow and purple.
Other colourways: HN3691;
'Claire' HN3646; 'Kaitlyn'
HN4128; 'Molly' HN4091.
Est. £100-135.

HN3703
Belle
Third Version
Designer V. Annand.
Date 1996.
20.5cm (8ins) high.
Yellow and red.
Series: Figure of the Year.
*(Auction W&H 27.9.04 sold £70
plus comm.)*
Est. £100-145.

HN3699
Grace
Second Version
Designer N. Pedley.
Date 1996 - 2001.
20.5cm (8ins) high.
Green and white.
Series: Vanity Fair Ladies.
Est. £100-130.

HN3704
First Violin
Designer V. Annand.
Date 1995. Limited edition
of 1,500.
23cm (9ins) high.
Grey and yellow.
Series: Edwardian String Quartet.
Comm: Lawleys By Post.
Est. £180-260.

*Picture
not available
at present*

HN3700
Forget-Me-Nots
Designer V. Annand.
Date 1995 - 98.
23cm (9ins) high.
Lilac and blue.
Series: Flowers of Love.
Est. £135-180.

HN3705
Second Violin
Designer V. Annand.
Date 1995. Limited edition of 1,500.
23cm (9ins) high.
Grey and pink.
Series: Edwardian String Quartet.
Comm: Lawleys By Post.
Est. £180-260.

HN3706
Viola
Designer V. Annand.
Date 1995. Limited edition
of 1,500.
22cm (8.75ins) high.
Grey and green.
Series: Edwardian String Quartet.
Comm: Lawleys By Post.
Est. £180-260.

*Picture
not available
at present*

HN3711
Jane
Fourth Version
Designer V. Annand.
Date 1997. Limited edition of 1997.
23cm (9ins) high.
Green, white and red.
Series: Lady Doulton, 1997.
(Ebay 25.5.04 sold £60)
Est. £65-100.

HN3707
Cello
Second Version
Designer V. Annand.
Date 1995. Limited edition
of 1,500.
18cm (7ins) high.
Grey and blue.
Series: Edwardian String Quartet.
Comm: Lawleys By Post.
Est. £180-260.

*Picture
not available
at present*

HN3712
New Baby
Designer V. Annand.
Date 1997 - 2002.
5cm (2ins) high.
White and pink.
Other colourways:
HN3713.
Series: Name
Your Own.
Est. £40-50.

HN3708
Katherine
Designer V. Annand.
Date 1996.
23cm (9ins) high.
Peach.
Series: Lady Doulton, 1996.
Est. £110-150.

HN3713
New Baby
Designer V. Annand.
Date 1997 - 2002.
5cm (2ins) high.
White and blue.
Other colourways:
HN3712.
Series: Name
Your Own.
Est. £40-50.

HN3709
Rose
Second Version
Designer V. Annand.
Date 1996 - 2000.
21.5cm (8.5ins) high.
Peach, green and white.
Series: Flowers of Love.
*(Ebay 7.9.04 sold £122 and
3.10.04 sold £92)*
Est. £100-150.

HN3714
Emma
Third Version
Designer V. Annand.
Date 1997 to date.
21.5cm (8.5ins) high.
Red and white.
Other colourways:
'Madison' HN4204.
Series: In Vogue.
Est. £55-75.

HN3710
Primrose
Designer V. Annand.
Date 1996 - 98.
23cm (9ins) high.
Yellow and cream.
Series: Flowers of Love.
(Ebay 28.5.04 sold £86)
Est. £100-150.

HN3715
Sophie
Fourth Version
Designer V. Annand.
Date 1997 - 2001.
22cm (8.75ins) high.
Pale green and white.
Series: In Vogue.
Est. £75-100.

HN3716
Isabel
First Version
Designer V. Annand.
Date 1997 - 2001.
21.5cm (8.5ins) high.
Pale blue, pink and white.
Series: Chelsea.
Est. £80-110.

*Picture
not available
at present*

HN3721
Pied Piper
Second Version (Resin)
Designer A. Maslankowski.
Date 1993 - 96.
22cm (8.75ins) high.
Yellow, red, black and green.
Series: Character Sculptures.
Est. £95-145.

HN3717
Olivia
Third Version
Designer V. Annand.
Date 1997 - 2002.
22cm (8.75ins) high.
Lilac, pink and white.
Other colourways:
 'Brittany' HN4206.
Series: Chelsea.
Est. £55-75.

HN3722
The Wizard
Second Version (Resin)
Designer A. Maslankowski.
Date 1994 - 96.
25.5cm (10ins) high.
Light blue, grey, orange and brown.
Other colourways: HN3732.
Series: Character Sculptures.
Est. £110-150.

HN3718
**The Charge of
the Light Brigade**
First Version
Designer A. Maslankowski.
Date 1995 to date.
43cm (17ins) high.
Brown, black, blue and white.
Series: Prestige.
*(Royal Doulton website price is £11,500;
the smaller version HN4486 is priced
at £945)* **Retail £11,500.**

HN3723
Au Revoir
First Version
Designer A. Maslankowski.
Date 1995 - 98.
19.5cm (7.75ins) high.
White and gold.
Other colourways:
 'Fond Farewell' HN3815.
Series: Elegance (Series Two)
Est. £75-95.

HN3719
Long John Silver
Second Version (Resin)
Designer A. Maslankowski.
Date 1993 - 96.
22cm (8.75ins) high.
Brown, purple and yellow.
Series: Character Sculptures.
Est. £100-130.

HN3724
Summer Breeze
Designer A. Maslankowski.
Date 1995 - 98.
19.5cm (7.75ins) high.
White, cream and gold.
Other colourways:
 'Moonlight Stroll' HN3954.
Series: Elegance (Series Two)
Est. £75-95.

HN3720
Robin Hood
Second Version (Resin)
Designer A. Maslankowski.
Date 1993 - 96.
26.5cm (10.5ins) high.
Brown, yellow and green.
Series: Character Sculptures.
Est. £125-175.

HN3725
Spring Morning
Second Version
Designer A. Maslankowski.
Date 1995 - 98.
19.5cm (7.75ins) high.
Cream and gold.
Other colourways:
 'Summer Scent' HN3955.
Series: Elegance (Series Two)
Est. £75-95.

HN3726
Dinnertime
Designer A. Maslankowski.
Date 1995 - 98.
11.5cm (4.5ins) high.
White, grey, tan and green.
Series: Vanity Fair Children.
Est. £40-55.

HN3731
Ballet Class
Second Version
Designer A. Maslankowski.
Date 1996 - 2003.
15cm (6ins) high.
White and lemon.
Series: Images.
Est. £30-40.

HN3727
Christmas Carols
Designer A. Maslankowski.
Date 1995 - 99.
15cm (6ins) high.
White.
Other colourways: HN4061.
Series: Sentiments.
Est. £45-55.

HN3732
The Wizard
Second Version (Resin)
Designer A. Maslankowski.
Date 1995 - 96.
25.5cm (10ins) high.
Orange and blue.
Other colourways: HN3722.
Series: Character Sculptures.
Comm: Lawleys By Post.
Est. £110-150.

HN3728
Free Spirit
Second Version
Designer A. Maslankowski.
Date 1995 - 98.
19cm (7.5ins) high.
Cream and gold.
Other colourways:
'Spring Serenade' HN3956.
Series: Elegance (Series Two)
Est. £70-90.

HN3733
Christmas Angel
Designer A. Maslankowski.
Date 1996 - 98.
14.5cm (5.75ins) high.
White.
Other colourways: HN4060.
Series: Sentiments.
Est. £40-55.

HN3729
Au Revoir
Second Version
Designer A. Maslankowski.
Date 1996 - 99.
16.5cm (6.5ins) high.
White.
Series: Sentiments.
Est. £45-55.

HN3734
Top o' the Hill
Second Version
Designer L. Harradine.
Remodeller P. Gee.
Date 1995 - 96.
9.5cm (3.75ins) high.
Red, gold and white.
Other colourways: HN2126, 3499.
Series: 1. Signature. 2. Miniatures.
Comm: Lawleys By Post.
Est. £85-110.

HN3730
Innocence
Second Version
Designer A. Maslankowski.
Date 1996 - 2000.
9cm (3.5ins) high.
Pink, brown and white.
*(Auction PSA 1.9.04 sold £30
plus comm.)*
Est. £35-55.

HN3735
Victoria
Second Version
Designer M. Davies.
Remodeller P. Gee.
Date 1995 - 96.
9cm (3.5ins) high.
Purple.
Other colourways: HN3744, 3909.
Series: 1. Signature. 2. Miniatures.
Comm: Lawleys By Post.
Est. £85-110.

HN3735A
Top o' the Hill
First Version
Designer L. Harradine.
Date 1997. Limited edition of 3,500.
18cm (7ins) high.
Dark blue and white.
Other colourways: HN1833,
1834, 1849, 2127.
Est. £115-155.

HN3736
Autumn Breezes
First Version
Designer L. Harradine.
Date 1997 - 98.
19cm (7.5ins) high.
Yellow and blue.
Other colourways: HN1911,
1913, 1934, 2131, 2147.
Series: M. Doulton Events.
(Auction PSA 23.6.04 sold £95
plus comm.) **Est. £115-155.**

HN3737
Old Balloon Seller
First Version
Designer L. Harradine.
Date 1999.
19cm (7.5ins) high.
Yellow, blue, purple, green and white.
Other colourways: HN1315.
Series: M. Doulton Events.
Est. £135-175.

HN3740
Lynne
First Version
Designer M. Davies.
Date 1995.
18cm (7ins) high.
White, blue and red.
Other colourways:
HN2329, 'Kathy' HN3305.
Series: Roadshow Events.
Est. £140-185.

HN3741
Elaine
First Version
Designer M. Davies.
Date 1995.
19cm (7.5ins) high.
Red and white.
Other colourways: HN2791,
3307, 4130.
Series: Roadshow Events.
Est. £140-185.

HN3742
Gillian
Third Version
Designer M. Davies.
Date 1995 - 97.
19.5cm (7.75ins) high.
Pink and white.
Other colourways:
'Figure of the Month' series
HN2693, 2695-2697, 2703, 2707,
2708, 2711, 2790, 2794, 3165, 3166.
Comm: Great Universal Studios.   **Est. £70-100.**

HN3743
Kirsty
Second Version
Designer M. Davies.
Remodeller P. Gee.
Date 1995.
9.5cm (3.75ins) high.
Yellow.
Other colourways: HN3213,
3246, 3480.
Series: Miniatures.
Comm: Great Universal Studios.   **Est. £40-55.**

HN3744
Victoria
Second Version
Designer M. Davies.
Remodeller P. Gee.
Date 1995 - 98.
8cm (3.25ins) high.
Pink and white.
Other colourways:
HN3735, 3909.
Series: Miniatures.
Est. £55-75.

HN3746
Memory Lane
Designer M. Davies.
Date 1996.
14cm (5.5ins) high.
Blue and white.
Other colourways: 'Debbie'
HN2385, 2400; 'Lavender Rose'
HN3481; 'Moonlight' Rose'
HN3483; 'Old Country Roses'
HN3482; 'Tranquillity' 3747.
(Ebay 5.7.04 sold £25) **Est. £35-60.**

HN3747
Tranquillity
Designer M. Davies.
Date 1996.
14cm (5.5ins) high.
Pink and white.
Other colourways: 'Debbie'
HN2385, 2400; 'Lavender Rose'
HN3481; 'Moonlight Rose';
'Old Country Roses' HN3482;
'Memory Lane' HN3746.
Est. £35-60.

HN3748
Fiona
Fourth Version
Designer M. Davies.
Date 1996 - 2002.
19cm (7.5ins) high.
Pale yellow and tartan.
Other colourways:
'Adrienne' HN2152, 2305;
'Joan' HN3217.
Est. £70-90.

HN3754
For You
Designer T. Potts.
Date 1996 to date.
21.5cm (8.5ins) high.
Blue, pink and white.
Other colourways: HN3863.
Series: Name Your Own.
Est. £45-65.

HN3749
Karen
Third Version
Designer M. Davies.
Remodeller R. Tabbenor.
Date 1997.
10cm (4ins) high.
White and gold.
Other colourways:
HN3270, 3338.
Series: Miniatures.
Est. £70-90.

HN3755
Strolling
Second Version
Designer T. Potts.
Date 1996 - 99.
20.5cm (8ins) high.
Red, white and yellow.
Est. £90-120.

HN3750
Gulliver
Designer D. Biggs.
Date 1995 - 96.
21.5cm (8.5ins) high.
Blue, red, white, green and yellow.
Series: Character Sculptures.
Est. £120-145.

HN3756
Pamela
Third Version
Designer T. Potts.
Date 1996.
20.5cm (8ins) high.
Pink, lilac, white and blue.
Series: RDICC.
Est. £100-130.

HN3751
Cyrano de Bergerac
Designer D. Biggs.
Date 1995 - 96.
21.5cm (8.5ins) high.
Blue, white, red, black and brown.
Series: Character Sculptures.
Est. £120-145.

HN3757
Jean
Third Version
Designer T. Potts.
Date 1996 - 97.
17cm (6.75ins) high.
Blue and white.
Other colourways: HN3862.
Comm: Kay's Mail Order
Catalogue.
Est. £70-90.

*Picture
not available
at present*

HN3752
Fagin
Second Version (Resin)
Designer A. Dobson.
Date 1995 - 96.
21.5cm (8.5ins) high.
Black, brown, green and red.
Series: Character Sculptures.
Est. £100-135.

HN3758
Bride of the Year
Designer T. Potts.
Date 1996.
20.5cm (8ins) high.
Peach and white.
Other colourways:
'Wedding Morn' HN3853.
Comm: Kay's Mail Order Catalogue.
Est. £100-130.

HN3759
Stephanie
Second Version
Designer T. Potts.
Date 1996.
21cm (8.25ins) high.
Lilac and pink.
Series: Roadshow Events.
(Auction PSA 10.3.04 sold £60 plus comm.)
Est. £75-100.

HN3764
Welcome
Designer N. Pedley.
Date 1996.
14.5cm (5.75ins) high.
White.
Series: Club Membership Figure.
(Auction PSA 23.6.04 sold £20 plus comm.)
Est. £25-45.

HN3760
Laura
Second Version
Designer N. Pedley.
Date 1996 - 99.
20.5cm (8ins) high.
Blue and white.
(Ebay 20.8.04 sold £108)
Est. £95-130.

HN3765
Kate
Second Version
Designer N. Pedley.
Date 1996.
20.5cm (8ins) high.
Red, pink and white.
Other colourways: HN3882.
Comm: Kay's Mail Order Catalogue.
Est. £85-110.

HN3761
Sleepyhead
Second Version
Designer N. Pedley.
Date 1996 - 98.
10cm (4ins) high.
White, tan and green.
Est. £50-70.

HN3766
Anita
Designer N. Pedley.
Date 1996.
20.5cm (8ins) high.
Yellow green and white.
Comm: Kay's Mail Order Catalogue.
Est. £70-90.

Picture not available at present

HN3762
Time For Bed
Designer N. Pedley.
Date 1996 - 98.
13.5cm (5.25ins) high.
Pink, white and brown.
Est. £50-70.

HN3767
Christine
Fourth Version
Designer N. Pedley.
Date 1996 - 98.
20.5cm (8ins) high.
Blue.
Est. £100-135.

HN3763
Helen
Third Version
Designer N. Pedley.
Date 1996.
21cm (8.25ins) high.
Pink.
Other colourways: HN3601, 3687, 3886; 'Miss Kay' HN3659.
Comm: Sears, Canada.
Est. £80-110.

HN3768
Off to School
Designer N. Pedley.
Date 1996 - 98.
13.5cm (5.25ins) high.
Grey and dark blue.
(Auction PSA 22.10.03 sold £95 and W&H 27.9.04 sold £40 plus comm.)
Est. £100-150.

HN3769
Winter's Day
Designer N. Pedley.
Date 1996 - 97.
19.5cm (7.75ins) high.
Red and white.
Series: RDICC.
Est. £110-150.

HN3790
Sophie
Third Version
Designer A. Maslankowski.
Date 1996 - 97.
24cm (9.5ins) high.
Green and cream.
Other colourways: HN3791,
3792, 3793.
Series: Charleston.
Est. £50-70.

HN3770
Sir Francis Drake
(Resin)
Designer D. Biggs.
Date 1996.
21.5cm (8.5ins) high.
Yellow, orange, green and red.
Series: Character Sculptures.
Est. £100-130.

HN3791
Sophie
Third Version
Designer A. Maslankowski.
Date 1996 - 97.
24cm (9.5ins) high.
Blue and cream.
Other colourways: HN3790,
3792, 3793.
Series: Charleston.
Est. £50-70.

HN3780
The Bowls Player
(Resin)
Designer J. Jones.
Date 1996.
15cm (6ins) high.
White, yellow, red and green.
Series: Character Sculptures.
Est. £100-130.

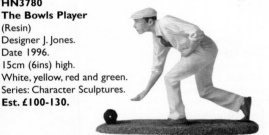

HN3792
Sophie
Third Version
Designer A. Maslankowski.
Date 1996 - 97.
24cm (9.5ins) high.
Pink and cream.
Other colourways: HN3790,
3791, 3793.
Series: Charleston.
*(Auction PSA 4.2.04 sold £42 plus
comm.)* **Est. £50-70.**

HN3785
Bill Sykes
Second Version (Resin)
Designer A. Dobson.
Date 1996.
23cm (9ins) high.
Brown, purple and grey.
Series: Character Sculptures.
Est. £100-130.

HN3793
Sophie
Third Version
Designer A. Maslankowski.
Date 1996 - 97.
24cm (9.5ins) high.
Gold and cream.
Other colourways: HN3790,
3791, 3792.
Series: Charleston.
Est. £50-70.

HN3786
**Oliver Twist and
The Artful Dodger**
(Resin)
Designer A. Dobson.
Date 1996.
20.5cm (8ins) high.
Blue, brown, black and green.
Series: Character Sculptures.
Est. £110-150.

HN3794
Harriet
Second Version
Designer A. Maslankowski.
Date 1996 - 97.
23.5cm (9.25ins) high.
Green and cream.
Other colourways: HN3795,
3796, 3797.
Series: Charleston.
*(Auction PSA 7.4.04 sold £45
plus comm.)* **Est. £55-85.**

HN3795
Harriet
Second Version
Designer A. Maslankowski.
Date 1996 - 97.
23.5cm (9.25ins) high.
Blue and cream.
Other colourways: HN3794,
3796, 3797.
Series: Charleston.
Est. £55-85.

HN3800
Eliza
Third Version
Designer A. Maslankowski.
Date 1996 - 97.
24cm (9.5ins) high.
Pink and cream.
Other colourways: HN3798,
3799, 3801.
Series: Charleston.
Est. £50-85.

HN3796
Harriet
Second Version
Designer A. Maslankowski.
Date 1996 - 97.
23.5cm (9.25ins) high.
Pink and cream.
Other colourways: HN3794,
3795, 3797.
Series: Charleston.
Est. £55-85.

HN3801
Eliza
Third Version
Designer A.Maslankowski.
Date 1996 - 97.
24cm (9.5ins) high.
Gold and cream.
Other colourways: HN3798,
3799, 3800.
Series: Charleston.
Est. £50-85.

HN3797
Harriet
Second Version
Designer A. Maslankowski.
Date 1996 - 97.
23.5cm (9.25ins) high.
Ivory, gold and cream.
Other colourways: HN3794,
3795, 3796.
Series: Charleston.
Est. £55-85.

HN3802
Daisy
Second Version
Designer A. Maslankowski.
Date 1996 - 97.
23.5cm (9.25ins) high.
Blue and cream.
Other colourways: HN3803,
3804, 3805.
Series: Charleston.
Est. £60-90.

HN3798
Eliza
Third Version
Designer A. Maslankowski.
Date 1996 - 97.
24cm (9.5ins) high.
Green and cream.
Other colourways: HN3799,
3800, 3801.
Series: Charleston.
Est. £50-85.

HN3803
Daisy
Second Version
Designer A. Maslankowski.
Date 1996 - 97.
23.5cm (9.25ins) high.
Blue and cream.
Other colourways: HN3802,
3804, 3805.
Series: Charleston.
Est. £60-90.

HN3799
Eliza
Third Version
Designer A. Maslankowski.
Date 1996 - 97.
24cm (9.5ins) high.
Blue and cream.
Other colourways: HN3798,
3800, 3801.
Series: Charleston.
Est. £50-85.

HN3804
Daisy
Second Version
Designer A. Maslankowski.
Date 1996 - 97.
23.5cm (9.25ins) high.
Pink and cream.
Other colourways: HN3802,
3803, 3805.
Series: Charleston.
Est. £60-90.

HN3805
Daisy
Second Version
Designer A. Maslankowski.
Date 1996 - 97.
23.5cm (9.25ins) high.
Gold and cream.
Other colourways: HN3802,
3803, 3804.
Series: Charleston.
Est. £60-90.

HN3806
Emily
Third Version
Designer A. Maslankowski.
Date 1996 - 97.
23cm (9ins) high.
Green and cream.
Other colourways: HN3807,
3808, 3809.
Series: Charleston.
Est. £50-60.

HN3807
Emily
Third Version
Designer A. Maslankowski.
Date 1996 - 97.
23cm (9ins) high.
Blue and cream.
Other colourways: HN3806,
3808, 3809.
Series: Charleston.
*(Auction PSA 7.4.04 sold £30
plus comm.)* **Est. £40-60.**

HN3808
Emily
Third Version
Designer A. Maslankowski.
Date 1996 - 97.
23cm (9ins) high.
Pink and cream.
Other colourways: HN3806,
3807, 3809.
Series: Charleston.
Est. £40-60.

HN3809
Emily
Third Version
Designer A. Maslankowski.
Date 1996 - 97.
23cm (9ins) high.
Gold and cream.
Other colourways: HN3806,
3807, 3808.
Series: Charleston.
Est. £40-60.

HN3810
Charlotte
Third Version
Designer A. Maslankowski.
Date 1996 - 97.
23.5cm (9.25ins) high.
Green and cream.
Other colourways: HN3811,
3812, 3813.
Series: Charleston.
Est. £100-145.

HN3811
Charlotte
Third Version
Designer A. Maslankowski.
Date 1996 - 97.
23.5cm (9.25ins) high.
Blue and cream.
Other colourways: HN3810,
3812, 3813.
Series: Charleston.
Est. £100-145.

HN3812
Charlotte
Third Version
Designer A. Maslankowski.
Date 1996 - 97.
23.5cm (9.25ins) high.
Pink and cream.
Other colourways: HN3810,
3811, 3813.
Series: Charleston.
Est. £100-145.

HN3813
Charlotte
Third Version
Designer A. Maslankowski.
Date 1996 - 97.
23.5cm (9.25ins) high.
Gold and cream.
Other colourways: HN3810,
3811, 3812.
Series: Charleston.
Est. £100-145.

HN3814
The Cricketer
First Version
Designer A. Maslankowski.
Date 1996 - 96.
21cm (8.25ins) high.
White.
Est. £85-120.

HN3815
Fond Farewell
Designer A. Maslankowski.
Date 1997 - 99.
20.5cm (8ins) high.
Red and blue.
Other colourways:
'Au Revoir' HN3723.
*(Auction PSA 10.3.04 sold £45
plus comm.)*
Est. £60-100.

HN3822
James I
(1603 - 1625)
Designer D.V. Tootle.
Date 1996. Limited edition of 1,500.
23cm (9ins) high.
Grey, gold and red.
Series: Stuart Kings.
Comm: Lawleys By Post.
Est. £250-350.

HN3816
Ellen
Second Version
Designer A. Maslankowski.
Date 1997.
22cm (8.75ins) high.
Blue.
Other colourways: HN3819.
Series: Charleston.
Est. £60-80.

HN3824
Charles I
(1625 - 1649)
Designer D.V. Tootle.
Date 1997. Limited edition of 1,500.
25.5cm (10ins) high.
White and green.
Series: Stuart Kings.
Comm: Lawleys By Post.
Est. £250-350.

HN3819
Ellen
Second Version
Designer A. Maslankowski.
Date 1997.
22cm (8.75ins) high.
Ivory and gold.
Other colourways: HN3816.
Series: Charleston.
Est. £60-80.

HN3825
Charles II
(1660 - 1685)
Designer D.V. Tootle.
Date 1996. Limited edition
of 1,500.
23cm (9ins) high.
Cream and purple.
Series: Stuart Kings.
Comm: Lawleys By Post.
Est. £250-350.

HN3820
Lillie Langtry
Designer D.V. Tootle.
Date 1996. Limited edition of 5,000.
22cm (8.75ins) high.
Pink.
Series: Victorian and Edwardian
actresses. Comm: Lawleys By Post.
Est. £135-185.

HN3826
Ellen Terry
Designer D.V. Tootle.
Date 1996. Limited edition
of 5,000.
23cm (9ins) high.
Yellow, red and blue.
Series: Victorian and
Edwardian actresses.
Comm: Lawleys By Post.
Est. £160-240.

HN3821
Alfred The Great
Designer D.V. Tootle.
Date 1996 - 97.
23.5cm (9.25ins) high.
Red, gold and green.
Est. £160-220.

HN3827
The Performance
Designer D.V. Tootle.
Date 1997 - 2001.
26cm (10.25ins) high.
White.
Series: Images.
Est. £95-130.

HN3828
The Ballerina
Third Version
Designer D.V. Tootle.
Date 1997 - 2001.
14cm (5.5ins) high.
White.
Series: Images.
Est. £45-60.

HN3833
Aurora
Designer P. Parsons.
Date 1996. Limited edition of 2,000.
19cm (7.5ins) high.
Blue.
Series: The Disney Princess Collection.
Est. £85-110.

HN3829
Happy Birthday
Third Version
Designer D.V. Tootle.
Date 1997 - 2002.
19cm (7.5ins) high.
White.
Series: Images.
Est. £35-45.

HN3834
Mary Tudor
Designer P. Parsons.
Date 1997. Limited edition of 5,000.
16cm (6.25ins) high.
Yellow, purple and peach.
Series: Tudor Roses.
Comm: Lawleys By Post.
Est. £200-250.

HN3830
Belle
Fourth Version
Designer P. Parsons.
Date 1996. Limited edition
of 2,000.
20.5cm (8ins) high.
Yellow.
Series: The Disney
Princess Collection.
Est. £140-185.

*Picture
not available
at present*

HN3835
Scheherazade
Designer P. Parsons.
Date 1996. Limited edition of 1,500.
26.5cm (10.5ins) high.
Green and red.
Series: Fabled Beauties.
Comm: Lawleys By Post.
Est. £200-275.

HN3831
Ariel
Designer P. Parsons.
Date 1996. Limited edition of 2,000.
21cm (8.25ins) high.
White.
Series: The Disney Princess
Collection.
Est. £140-200.

HN3836
**Queen Elizabeth II and The
Duke of Edinburgh**
Designer P. Parsons.
Date 1997. Limited edition of 750,
to celebrate their Golden
Wedding.
23.5cm (9.25ins) high.
White and dark blue.
Est. £270-350.

HN3832
Jasmine
Second Version
Designer P. Parsons.
Date 1996. Limited edition of 2,000.
19cm (7.5ins) high.
Lilac.
Series: The Disney Princess
Collection.
Est. £140-200.

HN3838
Margaret Tudor
Designer P. Parsons.
Date 1997. Limited edition of 5,000.
16.5cm (6.5ins) high.
Green and gold.
Series: Tudor Roses.
Comm: Lawleys By Post.
Est. £200-275.

HN3839
Cruella De Vil
Designer P. Parsons.
Date 1997. Limited edition of 2,000.
20.5cm (8ins) high.
Black and white.
Series: Disney Villains.
Est. £140-190.

HN3844
Nefertiti
Designer P. Parsons.
Date 1998. Limited edition of 950.
26.5cm (10.5ins) high.
Cream, blue and tan.
Series: Egyptian Queens.
Comm: Lawleys By Post.
Est. £220-300.

HN3840
Maleficent
Designer P. Parsons.
Date 1997. Limited edition of 2,000.
20.5cm (8ins) high.
Purple and black.
Series: Disney Villains.
Est. £140-190.

HN3845
Elizabeth Bennet
Designer P. Parsons.
Date 1998. Limited edition of 3,500.
22cm (8.75ins) high.
White and pink.
Series: Literary Heroines.
Comm: Lawleys By Post.
Est. £140-190.

HN3841
Rapunzel
Designer P. Parsons.
Date 1998. Limited edition
of 1,500.
25.5cm (10ins) high.
Purple and yellow.
Series: Fabled Beauties.
Comm: Lawleys By Post.
Est. £200-250.

*Picture
not available
at present*

HN3846
Tess of the D'Urbervilles
Designer P. Parsons.
Date 1998. Limited edition of 3,500.
21cm (8.25ins) high.
White, red and brown.
Series: Literary Heroines.
Comm: Lawleys By Post.
Est. £140-190.

HN3842
Jane Eyre
Designer P. Parsons.
Date 1997. Limited edition of 3,500.
21cm (8.25ins) high.
Blue, white and black.
Series: Literary Heroines.
Comm: Lawleys By Post.
Est. £160-230.

HN3847
The Queen
Designer P. Parsons.
Date 1998. Limited edition of 2,000.
22cm (8.75ins) high.
Red, purple, black and white
Series: Disney Villains.
Est. £110-150.

HN3843
Emma
Fourth Version.
Designer P. Parsons.
Date 1997. Limited edition of 3,500.
21cm (8.25ins) high.
Lemon, pink, white and brown.
Series: Literary Heroines.
Comm: Lawleys By Post.
Est. £140-190.

HN3848
The Witch
First Version
Designer P. Parsons.
Date 1998. Limited edition of 2,000.
18cm (7ins) high.
Black and white.
Series: Disney Villains.
Est. £110-150.

HN3849
Moll Flanders
Designer P. Parsons.
Date 1999. Limited edition of 3,500.
21.5cm (8.5ins) high.
Pink, cream and white.
Series: Literary Heroines.
Est. £140-190.

HN3854
Amy
Third Version
Designer T. Potts.
Date 1996 - 99.
20.5cm (8ins) high.
Pink.
Est. £75-100.

HN3850
Jessica
Second Version
Designer N. Pedley.
Date 1997.
20.5cm (8ins) high.
Pale purple and green.
Series: Figure of the Year.
*(Auction PSA 1.9.04 sold £55 and
W&H 27.9.04 sold £50 plus comm.)*
Est. £75-100.

HN3855
Lambing Time
Second Version
Designer T. Potts.
Date 1996 - 98.
20.5cm (8ins) high.
Ivory and gold.
Series: Elegance (Series Two)
Est. £55-70.

HN3851
Sally
Second Version
Designer T. Potts.
Date 1996 - 98.
21cm (8.25ins) high.
Blue and white.
Other colourways:
HN3383, 4160.
Est. £75-100.

HN3856
Country Girl
Second Version
Designer T. Potts.
Date 1996 - 98.
20.5cm (8ins) high.
Ivory and gold.
Series: Elegance (Series Two)
Est. £55-70.

HN3852
Sarah
Second Version
Designer T. Potts.
Date 1996 - 99.
20.5cm (8ins) high.
Green.
Other colourways:
HN3384, 3857.
Est. £85-120.

HN3857
Sarah
Second Version
Designer T. Potts.
Date 1996. Limited edition of 1996.
20.5cm (8ins) high.
Pink.
Other colourways:
HN3384, 3852.
Series: Visitor Centre.
*(Auction PSA 23.6.04 sold £75
plus comm.)* **Est. £100-145.**

HN3853
Wedding Morn
Second Version
Designer T. Potts.
Date 1996 - 99.
20.5cm (8ins) high.
Ivory and gold.
Other colourways:
'Bride of the Year' HN3758.
Est. £100-150.

HN3858
Lucy
Third Version
Designer T. Potts.
Date 1997 - 99.
21.5cm (8.5ins) high.
Pink, black and white.
(Ebay 27.7.04 sold £46)
Est. £50-90.

HN3859
Sweet Bouquet
Second Version
Designer T. Potts.
Date 1997. Special edition
of 250.
20.5cm (8ins) high.
Ivory and gold.
Series: Elegance (Series Two)
Est. £55-85.

*Picture
not available
at present*

HN3864
Kimberley
Second Version
Designer T. Potts.
Date 1997. Special edition of 2,000.
21.5cm (8.5ins) high.
Pink, white, yellow and brown.
Other colourways:
HN3379, 3382.
Series: Visitor Centre.
*(Auction PSA 3.12.03 sold £65
plus comm.)* **Est. £80-120.**

HN3860
Morning Walk
Designer T. Potts.
Date 1997 - 98.
20.5cm (8ins) high.
Ivory and gold.
Series: Elegance (Series Two)
Est. £55-85.

HN3865
Anna of the Five Towns
Designer T. Potts.
Date 1997 - 98.
20.5cm (8ins) high.
Pink, brown and white.
Series: 1. Arnold Bennett.
2. Visitor Centre.
Est. £75-110.

HN3861
Centre Stage
Designer T. Potts.
Date 1996.
20.5cm (8ins) high.
Blue.
Other colourways:
'Courtney' HN3869.
Comm: Great Universal Stores.
Est. £50-80.

HN3866
Bon Voyage
Designer T. Potts.
Date 1998 - 2001.
23cm (9ins) high.
Pink and white.
Est. £75-110.

HN3862
Jean
Third Version
Designer T. Potts.
Date 1997. Special edition of 350.
17cm (6.75ins) high.
Blue and white.
Other colourways: HN3757.
Comm: Seaway China.
Est. £100-125.

HN3867
The Countess of Chell
Designer T. Potts.
Date 1998.
21.5cm (8.5ins) high.
Pale pink and gold.
Series: 1. Arnold Bennett.
2. Visitor Centre.
Est. £50-80.

HN3863
For You
Designer T. Potts.
Date 1997- 99.
20.5cm (8ins) high.
Pink.
Other colourways: HN3754.
Series: Name Your Own.
Est. £50-80.

HN3868
Danielle
Third Version
Designer T. Potts.
Date 1998.
22cm (8.75ins) high.
Orange.
Comm: Great Universal Stores.
Est. £50-80.

*Picture
not available
at present*

HN3869
Courtney
Designer N. Pedley.
Date 1999. Special edition of 250.
20.5cm (8ins) high.
Blue.
Other colourways:
'Centre Stage' HN3861.
Comm: Seaway China.
Est. £60-80.

HN3876
Kitty
Second Version
Designer N. Pedley.
Date 1997 - 2000.
11.5cm (4.5ins) high.
White and blue.
Est. £40-65.

HN3870
Hannah
Second Version
Designer N. Pedley.
Date 1995 - 96.
10cm (4ins) high.
Red, pink and gold.
Other colourways: HN3649.
Series: 1. Signature.
2. Miniatures.
Est. £70-90.

HN3877
On The Beach
Designer N. Pedley.
Date 1997 - 99.
9cm (3.5ins) high.
Pink and yellow.
Est. £45-70.

HN3871
Susan
Third Version
Designer N. Pedley.
Date 1997.
20.5cm (8ins) high.
Pink and white.
Series: RDICC.
Est. £90-120.

HN3878
Julie
Second Version
Designer N. Pedley.
Date 1997 - 2001.
20.5cm (8ins) high.
Pink and white.
Est. £60-80.

HN3872
Lauren
Second Version
Designer N. Pedley.
Date 1997.
23cm (9ins) high.
Cream, pink and yellow.
Series: Roadshow Events.
Est. £70-90.

HN3879
Linda
Fourth Version.
Designer N. Pedley.
Date 1997.
20.5cm (8ins) high.
Yellow.
Comm: Great Universal Stores.
Est. £60-80.

*Picture
not available
at present*

HN3875
Joy
Second Version
Designer N. Pedley.
Date 1997.
13cm (5.25ins) high.
White.
Series: Club Membership Figure.
*(Ebay 8.7.04 sold £20 and
16.6.04 sold £15)*
Est. £25-45.

HN3880
Kathleen
Third Version
Designer N. Pedley.
Date 1997.
21.5cm (8.5ins) high.
Pink.
Other colourways: HN3609;
'Brianna' HN4126.
Comm: Great Universal Stores.
Est. £60-80.

HN3882
Kate
Second Version
Designer N. Pedley.
Date 1997.
20.5cm (8ins) high.
Pink and white.
Other colourways: HN3765.
Comm: Pascoe & Company.
Est. £75-100.

HN3888
Louise
Third Version
Designer N. Pedley.
Date 1997 - 2000.
20.5cm (8ins) high.
White, pink and blue.
Est. £65-90.

HN3883
Chloe
Second Version
Designer N. Pedley.
Date 1997 - 98.
20.5cm (8ins) high.
Yellow.
Other colourways: HN3914;
'Amber' HN4125.
Comm: Index Catalogue Co.
(Ebay 29.9.04 sold £50)
Est. £55-80.

HN3889
Flowers For You
Designer N. Pedley.
Date 1997 - 99.
14.5cm (5.75ins) high.
Yellow.
Est. £40-55.

HN3885
Melissa
Second Version
Designer N. Pedley.
Date 1997 - 99.
21cm (8.25ins) high.
Purple and cream.
Est. £65-90.

HN3890
Geoffrey Boycott
Designer R. Tabbenor.
Date 1996. Limited edition of 8,114.
24cm (9.5ins) high.
White.
Comm: Lawleys By Post.
Est. £65-90.

HN3886
Helen
Third Version
Designer N. Pedley.
Date 1997 - 99.
20.5cm (8ins) high.
Cream and red.
Other colourways: HN3601,
3687, 3763, 'Miss Kay' HN3659.
Est. £95-135.

HN3891
Sir Henry Doulton
Designer R. Tabbenor.
Date 1997. Limited edition of 1997.
22cm (8.75ins) high.
Grey and black.
Est. £150-200.

HN3887
Megan
Second Version
Designer N. Pedley.
Date 1997 - 2000.
20.5cm (8ins) high.
White and pale blue.
Other colourways:
'Jasmine' HN4127.
Series: Vanity Fair Ladies.
Est. £65-90.

HN3900
Elaine
Second Version
Designer M. Davies.
Remodeller P. Gee.
Date 1997.
10cm (4ins) high.
White and gold.
Other colourways:
HN3214, 3247.
Series: Miniatures.
Comm: Great Universal Stores.   **Est. £40-55.**

HN3901
Ninette
Second Version
Designer M. Davies.
Remodeller P. Gee. Date 1997.
9cm (3.5ins) high.
White and yellow.
Other colourways:
HN3215, 3248.
Series: Miniatures.
Comm: Index Catalogue Co.
Est. £40-55.

HN3906
Eleanor
First Version
Designer M. Davies.
Date 1998.
20.5cm (8ins) high.
Pink and yellow.
Series: Peggy Davies
Collection.
Est. £75-110.

HN3902
Lily
Third Version
Designer M. Davies.
Date 1998.
19.5cm (7.75ins) high.
Green and white.
Series: Peggy Davies Collection.
Est. £65-90.

HN3907
Patricia
Fourth Version
Designer M. Davies.
Date 1998.
19.5cm (7.75ins) high.
Yellow, peach and white.
Series: Peggy Davies Collection.
Est. £75-110.

HN3903
Mary
Fourth Version
Designer M. Davies.
Date 1998.
18cm (7ins) high.
Red and pink.
Series: Peggy Davies Collection.
Est. £65-90.

HN3908
Buttercup
Second Version
Designer M. Davies.
Remodeller P. Gee.
Date 1998.
9cm (3.5ins) high. Colour: Pink.
Other colourways: HN3268.
Series: Miniatures.
Comm: Great Uni. Stores.
(Auction PSA 22.10.03 sold £30
plus comm.) (Ebay 3.6.04 sold £26) Est. £30-60.

HN3904
Valerie
Second Version
Designer M. Davies.
Date 1998.
19.5cm (7.75ins) high.
Blue and pink.
Series: Peggy Davies Collection.
Est. £80-110.

HN3909
Victoria
Second Version
Designer M. Davies.
Remodeller P. Gee.
Date 1998.
9cm (3.5ins) high.
Pale blue.
Other colourways:
HN3735, 3744.
Series: Miniatures.
Comm: Index Catalogue Co. Est. £40-55.

HN3905
Christine
Fifth Version
Designer M. Davies.
Date 1998.
19cm (7.5ins) high.
White and pink.
Series: Peggy Davies Collection.
Est. £85-110.

HN3911
First Prize
Designer N. Pedley.
Date 1997 - 99.
13.5cm (5.25ins) high.
Brown, black, white and blue.
(Auction PSA 4.2.04 sold £42
plus comm.)
Est. £60-90.

HN3912
Kelly
Second Version
Designer N. Pedley.
Date 1997 - 98.
20.5cm (8ins) high.
Pink.
Other colourways: 'Angela'
HN3690; 'Sweet Sixteen' HN3648.
Comm: Home Shopping.
Est. £60-80.

HN3917
Summer Blooms
First Version
Designer N. Pedley.
Date 1997.
22cm (8.75ins) high.
Pale blue.
Series: The Seasons
(Series Seven)
Comm: Guild of Specialist
China and Glass Retailers.
Est. £70-95.

HN3913
First Bloom
Designer N. Pedley.
Date 1997.
20.5cm (8ins) high.
Blue and white.
Other colourways:
"Mackenzie" HN4109.
Series: Roadshow Events.
Est. £60-80

HN3918
Autumn Flowers
Designer N. Pedley.
Date 1997.
21.5cm (8.5ins) high.
Red and yellow.
Series: The Seasons
(Series Seven)
Comm: Guild of Specialist China
and Glass Retailers.
Est. £70-95.

*Picture
not available
at present*

HN3914
Chloe
Second Version
Designer N. Pedley.
Date 1997 - 2002.
20.5cm (8ins) high.
Pink.
Other colourways: HN3883;
'Amber' HN4125.
Marketed in Canada.
Est. £75-110.

HN3919
Winter Bouquet
Designer N. Pedley.
Date 1997.
22cm (8.75ins) high.
Red.
Series: The Seasons
(Series Seven)
Comm: Guild of Specialist China
and Glass Retailers.
Est. £70-95.

*Picture
not available
at present*

HN3915
Colleen
Designer N. Pedley.
Date 1997 - 2002.
20.5cm (8ins) high.
White and lemon.
Marketed in Canada.
Est. £75-110.

HN3920
Jack Point
Designer C.J. Noke.
Date 1996. Limited edition of 250.
43cm (17ins) high.
Blue, red and gold.
Other colourways: HN85, 91,
99, 2080, 3925.
*(A version of this is sold on
Royal Doulton web £2750)*
Retail £2750.

HN3916
Spring Posy
Designer N. Pedley.
Date 1997.
22cm (8.75ins) high.
Green.
Series: The Seasons
(Series Seven)
Comm: Guild of Specialist
China and Glass Retailers.
Est. £70-100.

*Picture
not available
at present*

HN3921
Princess Badoura
First Version
Designer H. Tittensor,
Harry E. Stanton and
F. Van Allen Phillips.
Date 1996 - 99.
50.5cm (20ins) high.
Blue, red and gold.
Other colourways: HN2081.
Series: Prestige.
(This figure is out of production) **Est. £12000-15000.**

HN3922
A Jester (Parian)
First Version (Model 170)
Designer C.J. Noke.
Date 1997. Limited edition of 950.
26.5cm (10.5ins) high.
Green, pink and gold.
Other colourways: HN45, 71, 71A,
320, 367, 412, 426, 446, 552, 616,
627, 1295, 1702, 2016.
Comm: Lawleys By Post.
Est. £175-225.

HN3924
Lady Jester (Parian)
Third Version
Designer W.K. Harper.
Date 1998. Limited edition of 950.
24cm (9.5ins) high.
Pink and green.
Comm: Lawleys By Post.
Est. £175-225.

HN3925
Jack Point
Designer C.J. Noke.
Date 1998. Limited edition of 85.
41.5cm (16.25ins) high.
Lilac, blue, green, black and
orange.
Other colourways: HN85, 91,
99, 2080, 3920.
Est. £2500-3000.

HN3926
The Moor
Designer C.J. Noke.
Date 1999. Limited edition of 99.
44.5cm (17.5ins) high.
Purple and black.
Other colourways: HN1308,
1366, 1425, 1657, 2082, 3642;
'An Arab' HN33, 343, 378.
Series: RDICC.
(Royal Doulton web price £2250)
Retail £2250.

HN3930
Constance
Second Version
Designer A. Maslankowski.
Date 1997.
22cm (8.75ins) high.
Blue.
Other colourways: HN3933.
Series: Charleston.
Est. £65-95.

HN3933
Constance
Second Version
Designer A. Maslankowski.
Date 1997.
22cm (8.75ins) high.
Ivory and gold.
Other colourways: HN3930.
Series: Charleston.
Est. £65-95.

HN3934
Across the Miles
Designer A. Maslankowski.
Date 1997 - 99.
10cm (4ins) high.
White.
Series: Sentiments.
Est. £40-50.

HN3935
Best Friends
First Version
Designer A. Maslankowski.
Date 1997 - 99.
7.5cm (3ins) high.
White, blue and black.
Est. £40-50.

HN3936
Goose Girl
Third Version
Designer A. Maslankowski.
Date 1997 - 98.
28cm (11ins) high.
White.
Series: Images.
Est. £40-50.

HN3938
Mother and Child
Second Version
Designer A. Maslankowski.
Date 1997 to date.
29cm (11.5ins) high.
White.
Series: Images.
Est. £40-50.

HN3940
Angel
Designer A. Maslankowski.
Date 1997 - 99.
29cm (11.5ins) high.
White.
Series: Images.
Est. £45-60.

HN3947
Henry V at Agincourt
Designer A. Maslankowski.
Date 1997 to date.
51cm (20ins) high.
Grey, red, blue and gold.
Series: Prestige.
*(Royal Doulton web price
£12,500)*
Retail £12,500.

HN3942
Graduation (girl)
Designer A. Maslankowski.
Date 1997 - 2002.
29cm (11.5ins) high.
White.
Series: Images.
Est. £55-75.

HN3948
Loving Thoughts
First Version
Designer A. Maslankowski.
Date 1997 - 99.
16cm (6.25ins) high.
White.
Series: Sentiments.
Est. £40-50.

HN3944
**HM Queen Elizabeth The
Queen Mother**
Third Version
Designer A. Maslankowski.
Date 1997 Limited edition of 5,000.
26.5cm (10.5ins) high.
Lilac.
Comm: Lawleys By Post.
*(Auction PSA 10.3.04 sold £90
plus comm.)*
Est. £125-175.

HN3949
Forever Yours
First Version
Designer A. Maslankowski.
Date 1998 - 2001.
9.5cm (3.75ins) high.
White.
Series: Sentiments.
Est. £40-50.

HN3945
Millie
First Version
Designer A. Maslankowski.
Date 1997.
22cm (8.75ins) high.
Green.
Other colourways: HN3946.
Series: Charleston.
Est. £75-100.

*Picture
not available
at present*

HN3950
Star Performer
Designer A. Maslankowski.
Date 1997 to date.
10cm (4ins) high.
White and pink.
Series: Images.
Est. £30-40.

HN3946
Millie
First Version
Designer A. Maslankowski.
Date 1997.
22cm (8.75ins) high.
Ivory and gold.
Other colourways: HN3945.
Series: Charleston.
Est. £75-100.

*Picture
not available
at present*

HN3951
Stage Struck
Designer A. Maslankowski.
Date 1997 to date.
9cm (3.5ins) high.
White and blue.
Series: Images.
Est. £30-40.

HN3952
The Messiah
Designer A. Maslankowski.
Date 1997 - 99.
28cm (11ins) high.
White.
Series: Images.
Est. £60-85.

HN3957
Eleanor of Aquitaine (1122 - 1204)
Designer A. Maslankowski.
Date 1997. Limited edition of 5,000.
23cm (9ins) high.
Blue, brown and gold.
Series: Plantagenet Queens.
Comm: Lawleys By Post.
(Auction PSA 23.6.04 sold £190
plus comm.)
Est. £225-300.

HN3953
Christmas Lantern
Designer A. Maslankowski.
Date 1997 - 98.
15cm (6ins) high.
White.
Series: Sentiments.
Est. £35-50.

HN3958
Country Girl
Third Version
Designer A. Maslankowski.
Date 1998 - 99.
27.5cm (10.75ins) high.
White.
Series: Images.
Est. £45-65.

HN3954
Moonlight Stroll
Designer A. Maslankowski.
Date 1997 - 99.
19.5cm (7.75ins) high.
Blue and cream.
Other colourways:
'Summer Breeze' HN3724.
Est. £95-135.

HN3959
The Graduate (male)
Second Version
Designer A. Maslankowski.
Date 1998 - 2001.
29cm (11.5ins) high.
White.
Series: Images.
(Auction PSA 10.3.04 sold £25
plus comm.)
Est. £35-55.

HN3955
Summer Scent
Designer A. Maslankowski.
Date 1997 - 99.
19.5cm (7.75ins) high.
Pink, cream and blue.
Other colourways:
'Spring Morning' HN3725.
Est. £90-130.

HN3970
Flower of Love
Designer J. Bromley.
Date 1996 - 97.
18.5cm (7.25ins) high.
Red.
Other colourways: HN2460;
'Fleur' HN2368, 2369.
(Auction ASH 5.9.04 sold £60
plus comm.)
Est. £75-120.

HN3956
Spring Serenade
Designer A. Maslankowski.
Date 1997 - 99.
19cm (7.5ins) high.
Green and cream.
Other colourways:
'Free Spirit' HN3728.
Est. £90-130.

HN3971
Best Wishes
Second Version
Designer J. Bromley.
Date 1998 to date.
22.5cm (8.75ins) high.
Green, pink and white.
Other colourways: 'Kate' HN4233;
'Forever Yours' HN4501.
Series: Name Your Own.
(Includes Metal plaque for
engraved name) **Est. £75-100.**

HN3972
Sweet Lilac
Designer J. Bromley.
Date 2000.
22.5cm (8.75ins) high.
Mauve, lilac and cream
Series: RDICC.
Est. £100-135.

HN3991
Cinderella
Second Version
Designer J. Bromley.
Date 1997. Limited edition of 2,950.
Date 2000. Limited edition of 2,000.
25.5cm (10ins) high.
1st. Iss. Pink. 2nd. Iss. Blue.
Series: 1st. Fairytale Princesses.
Comm: Compton/Woodhouse.
Est. £150-200.

HN3975
Lauren
Third Version
Designer D. Hughes.
Date 1999.
23cm (9ins) high.
Pink.
Series: Figure of the Year.
*(Auction PSA 3.12.03 sold £80
and W&H 27.9.04 sold £85
plus comm.)*
Est. £100-135.

HN3992
Ellen
Third Version
Designer J. Bromley.
Date 1997.
21cm (8.25ins) high.
Pink and beige.
Series: Lady of the Year.
Comm: Compton/Woodhouse.
*(Auction Charterhouse 24.4.04 sold
£70 plus comm.)*
Est. £90-130.

HN3976
Rachel
Second Version
Designer D. Hughes.
Date 2000.
21cm (8.25ins) high.
Pink, white and lilac.
Series: Figure of the Year.
Est. £75-110.

HN3993
Carmen
Third Version
Designer M. Halson.
Date 1997 Limited edition of 12,500.
24cm (9.5ins) high.
Red, gold and black.
Comm: Compton/Woodhouse.
*(Auction Charterhouse 24.4.04 sold
£90 plus comm.)*
Est. £120-160.

HN3977
Melissa
Third Version
Designer D. Hughes.
Date 2001.
21.5cm (8.5ins) high.
Blue, white and pink.
Series: Figure of the Year.
Est. £70-100.

HN3994
Red Red Rose
Designer R. Hughes.
Modeller: J. Bromley.
Date 1997. Limited edition
of 12,500.
23cm (9ins) high.
Pink and gold.
Series: Language of Love.
Comm:Compton/Woodhouse.
Est. £100-135.

HN3978
Sarah
Third Version
Designer D. Hughes.
Date 2002.
21cm (8.25ins) high.
Green.
Series: Figure of the Year.
Est. £70-100.

HN3995
Sophie
Fifth Version
Designer J. Bromley.
Date 1998.
21cm (8.25ins) high.
Pink and gold.
Series: Lady of the Year.
Comm: Compton/Woodhouse.
Est. £90-125.

HN3996
Miss Violet
Designer M. Evans.
Date 1998. Limited edition
of 12,500.
14cm (5.5ins) high.
Purple and lilac.
Series: Pretty Maids.
Comm: Compton/Woodhouse.
Est. £55-75.

*Picture
not available
at present*

HN4001
My True Love
Designer J. Bromley.
Date 1999. Limited edition of 12,500.
23cm (9ins) high.
White and red.
Comm: Compton/Woodhouse.
Est. £90-140.

HN3997
Miss Maisie
Designer M. Evans
Date 1998. Limited edition
of 12,500.
14cm (5.5ins) high.
Blue, pink and green.
Series: Pretty Maids.
Comm: Compton/Woodhouse.
Est. £55-75.

*Picture
not available
at present*

HN4003
Alice
Fourth Version
Designer J. Bromley.
Date 1999.
22.5cm (8.75ins) high.
Yellow and red.
Series: Lady of the Year.
Comm: Compton/Woodhouse.
(Ebay 28.5.04 sold £77)
Est. £80-120.

HN3998
Miss Tilly
Designer M. Evans
Date 1998. Limited edition
of 12,500.
14cm (5.5ins) high.
Green and pink.
Series: Pretty Maids.
Comm: Compton/Woodhouse.
Est. £55-75.

*Picture
not available
at present*

HN4015
Eleanor
Second Version
Designer J. Bromley
Date 2001.
23cm (9ins) high.
Green and cream.
Series: Lady of the Year.
Comm: Compton/Woodhouse.
Est. £100-135.

HN3999
**Shall I Compare Thee To A
Summer's Day**
Designer J. Bromley.
Date 1998. Limited edition of 12,500.
23cm (9ins) high.
White, gold and blue.
Series: Language of Love.
Comm: Compton/Woodhouse.
Est. £100-135.

HN4016
A Love So Tender
Designer M. Halson.
Date 2001. Limited edition of 7,500.
Height not known.
White.
Series: Lady of the Year.
Comm: Compton/Woodhouse.
Est. £55-75.

HN4000
Sleeping Beauty
Second Version
Designer S. Curzon.
Modeller: J. Bromley.
Date 1998. Limited edition
of 4,950.
19cm (7.5ins) high.
White and gold.
Series: Fairytale Princesses.
Comm: Compton/Woodhouse.
Est. £145-200.

HN4017
Ellie
Second Version
Designer J. Bromley
Date 2003.
22.5cm (8.75ins) high.
Purple and lilac.
Series: Lady of the Year.
Comm: Compton/Woodhouse.
Est. £110-145.

HN4021
Amen
Designer D.V. Tootle.
Date 1997 to date.
11cm (4.25ins) high.
White.
Series: Images.
(Royal Doulton web price £29)
Retail £29.

HN4026
Best Friends
Second Version
Designer D.V. Tootle.
Date 1998.
18cm (7ins) high.
White.
Series: Images Figure of
the Year.
Est. £45-60.

HN4022
William III (1650 - 1702)
Designer D.V. Tootle.
Date 1998. Limited edition of 1,500.
26cm (10.25ins) high.
Red, white and cream.
Series: Stuart Kings.
Comm: Lawleys By Post.
Est. £350-500.

HN4027
The Ballet Dancer
Designer D.V. Tootle.
Date 1998 - 2000.
23.5cm (9.25ins) high.
White.
Series: Images.
Est. £45-60.

HN4023
Sarah Bernhardt
Designer D.V. Tootle.
Date 1998. Limited edition of 5,000.
23cm (9ins) high.
Green and cream.
Series: Victorian and
Edwardian Actresses.
Comm: Lawleys By Post.
Est. £140-185.

HN4028
Ballet Lesson
Designer D.V. Tootle.
Date 1998 - 2001.
12.5cm (5ins) high.
White.
Series: Images.
Est. £30-40.

HN4024
Prima Ballerina
Designer D.V. Tootle.
Date 1998 - 2000.
21cm (8.25ins) high.
White.
Series: Images.
Est. £45-60.

HN4030
Leap-Frog
Designer D.V. Tootle.
Date 1999 - 2001.
21.5cm (8.5ins) high.
White.
Series: Images.
Est. £45-60.

HN4025
The Dance
First Version.
Designer D.V. Tootle.
Date 1998 - 2002.
18cm (7ins) high.
White.
Series: Images.
Est. £45-60.

HN4031
Carol Singer (Boy)
Designer D.V. Tootle.
Date 1999. Limited edition of 6,000.
15cm (6ins) high.
White.
Series: Images Christmas Choir.
Est. £20-30.

HN4032
Carol Singer (Girl)
Designer D.V. Tootle.
Date 1999. Limited edition of 6,000.
12.5cm (5ins) high.
White.
Series: Images Christmas Choir.
Est. £25-35.

HN4037
Melchior
Designer D.V. Tootle.
Date 1999. Limited edition of 2,000.
Height not known.
White.
Series: 1. Images: The Christmas Story.
2. Millennium.
Est. £12-20 each.

HN4033
The Promise
Designer D.V. Tootle.
Date 1999.
16cm (6.25ins) high.
White.
Series: Images Figure of
the Year.
Est. £55-75.

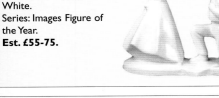

HN4038
Caspar
Designer D.V. Tootle.
Date 1999. Limited edition of 2,000.
Height not known.
White.
Series: 1. Images: The Christmas Story.
2. Millennium.
*(Auction PSA 10.3.04 (2 pieces) with
HN4038 sold £22 plus comm.)*
Est. £12-20 each.

HN4034
Mary and Jesus
Designer D.V. Tootle.
Date 1999. Limited edition of 2,000.
Height not known.
White.
Series: 1. Images: The Christmas Story.
2. Millennium.
Est. £12-20 each.

HN4039
Boy Shepherd
Designer D.V. Tootle.
Date 1999. Limited edition of 2,000.
Height not known.
White.
Series: 1. Images: The Christmas Story.
2. Millennium.
Est. £12-20 each.

HN4035
Joseph
Second Version
Designer D.V. Tootle.
Date 1999. Limited edition of 2,000.
Height not known.
White.
Series: 1. Images: The Christmas Story.
2. Millennium.
Est. £12-20 each.

HN4040
Kathryn
Second Version
Designer V. Annand.
Date 1997 to date.
21.5cm (8.5ins) high.
Lemon and white.
Other colourways:
'Alexis' HN4205.
Series: Chelsea.
Est. £50-75.

HN4036
Balthazar
Designer D.V. Tootle.
Date 1999. Limited edition
of 2,000.
Height not known.
White.
Series: 1. Images: The Christmas Story.
2. Millennium.
*(Auction PSA 10.3.04 (2 pieces) with
HN4038 sold £22 plus comm.)*
Est. £12-20 each.

HN4041
Rebecca
Third Version
Designer V. Annand.
Date 1998.
23cm (9ins) high.
Blue and yellow.
Series: Figure of the Year.
*(Auction W&H 27.9.04 sold £62
plus comm.)*
Est. £75-120.

HN4042
Janet
Third Version
Designer V. Annand.
Date 1998.
23cm (9ins) high.
Pink and white.
Series: RDICC.
Est. £100-145.

HN4047
Georgina
Second Version
Designer V. Annand.
Date 1998 - 2001.
21cm (8.25ins) high.
Peach and white.
Series: Chelsea.
Est. £65-85.

HN4043
Samantha
Third Version
Designer V. Annand.
Date 1998.
21cm (8.25ins) high.
Blue and white.
Series: Roadshow Events.
Est. £80-110.

*Picture
not available
at present*

HN4048
Natalie
Second Version
Designer V. Annand.
Date 1999 - 2001.
21cm (8.25ins) high.
Pink, cream and lilac.
Series: In Vogue.
Est. £80-110.

HN4044
Abigail
First Version
Designer V. Annand.
Date 1998 - 2001.
21cm (8.25ins) high.
Lilac and cream.
Series: In Vogue.
Est. £65-85.

HN4049
Jessica
Third Version
Designer V. Annand.
Date 1999 - 2001.
21.5cm (8.5ins) high.
Yellow, white and peach.
Series: In Vogue.
Est. £80-110.

HN4045
Blossomtime
Designer V. Annand.
Date 1998.
20.5cm (8ins) high.
Pink.
Series: Annabelle Doulton
Collection.
Comm: Lawleys By Post.
Est. £300-400.

HN4050
Hannah
Third Version
Designer V. Annand.
Date. 1998. Special edition of 250.
22cm (8.75ins) high.
Blue, pink and white.
Other colourways: HN4051, 4052.
(Note: The only difference in all
these figurines is the backstamp)
Comm: Hadleigh.
Est. £80-110.

HN4046
Ellie
First Version
Designer V. Annand.
Date 1998 - 2001.
21cm (8.25ins) high.
Pink and lemon.
Other colourways:
'Alison' HN4207.
Series: Chelsea.
Est. £65-85.

HN4051
Hannah
Third Version
Designer V. Annand.
Date 1998. Special edition of 250.
22cm (8.75ins) high.
Blue, pink and white.
Other colourways: HN4050, 4052.
(Note: The only difference in all
these figurines is the backstamp)
Comm: Collectibles.
Est. £80-110.

HN4052
Hannah
Third Version
Designer V. Annand.
Date 1999 - 2000.
21.5cm (8.5ins) high.
Blue, pink and white.
Other colourways: HN4050, 4051.
(Note: The only difference in all
these figurines is the backstamp)
Est. £80-110.

HN4057
Romeo and Juliet
Second Version
Designer D. V. Tootle.
Date 1999. Limited edition of 300.
30.5cm (12ins) high.
White, gold and pink.
Series: Prestige.
(Royal Doulton web price £1595)
Retail. £1595.

HN4053
Joy
Third Version
Designer V. Annand.
Date 1999 - 2000.
20.5cm (8ins) high.
Pink and white.
Other colourways: HN4054.
Est. £80-110.

HN4058
Harlequin
Second Version
Designer D. V. Tootle.
Date 1999. Limited edition of 200.
30.5cm (12ins) high.
Pink, blue, gold and white.
Other colourways: HN2737, 3287.
Series: 1. Millennium.
2. Prestige.
Comm: Lawleys By Post.
Est. £1200-1500.

HN4054
Joy
Third Version
Designer V. Annand.
Date 1999 - 2000.
20.5cm (8ins) high.
Red, pink and white.
Other colourways: HN4053.
Est. £80-110.

HN4059
Columbine
Third Version
Designer D. V. Tootle.
Date 1999. Limited edition of 200.
30.5cm (12ins) high.
Pink, blue and white.
Other colourways: HN2738, 3288.
Series: 1. Millennium.
2. Prestige.
Comm: Lawleys By Post.
Est. £1200-1500.

HN4055
Kneeling Shepherd
Designer D. V. Tootle.
Date 1999. Limited edition of 2,000.
Height not known.
White.
Series: 1. Images: The Christmas Story.
2. Millennium.
Est. £12-20 each.

HN4060
Christmas Angel
Designer A. Maslankowski.
Date 1997 - 98.
14.5cm (5.75ins) high.
White.
Other colourways: HN3733.
Series: Sentiments.
(Gold backstamp for Canadian
market)
Est. £40-50.

HN4056
Standing Shepherd
Designer D. V. Tootle.
Date 1999. Limited edition of 2,000.
Height not known.
White.
Series: 1. Images: The Christmas Story.
2. Millennium.
Est. £12-20 each.

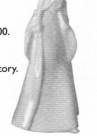

HN4061
Christmas Carols
Designer A. Maslankowski.
Date 1997 - 98.
15cm (6ins) high.
White.
Variations: HN3727.
Series: Sentiments.
Gold backstamp for Canadian market.
Est. £40-50.

HN4062
Christmas Day
Designer A. Maslankowski.
Date 1997 - 98.
15cm (6ins) high.
White.
Other colourways: HN3488.
Series: Sentiments.
Gold backstamp for Canadian market.
Est. £40-50.

HN4067
Christmas Garland
Designer A. Maslankowski.
Date 1998 - 2000.
15cm (6ins) high.
White.
Series: Sentiments.
Est. £40-50.

HN4063
Christmas Parcels
Second Version
Designer A. Maslankowski.
Date 1997 - 98.
15cm (6ins) high.
White.
Other colourways: HN3493.
Series: Sentiments.
Gold backstamp for Canadian market.
Est. £40-50.

HN4068
Happy Anniversary
Third Version
Designer A. Maslankowski.
Date 1998 to date.
14.5cm (5.75ins) high.
White.
Series: Sentiments.
(Royal Doulton web price £31.50)
(Ebay 14.7.04 sold £28)
Est. £30-40.

HN4064
The Kiss (boy)
Designer A. Maslankowski.
Date 1998 to date.
16cm (6.25ins) high.
White.
Series: Images.
Est. £20-30.

HN4069
Wizard (Parian)
First Version
Designer A. Maslankowski.
Date 1998. Limited edition of 1,500.
25.5cm (10ins) high.
Pink and green.
Other colourways: HN2877, 3121.
Comm: Lawleys By Post.
Est. £150-185.

HN4065
The Kiss (girl)
Designer A. Maslankowski.
Date 1998 to date.
15cm (6ins) high.
White.
Series: Images.
Est. £20-30.

HN4070
Good Luck
Designer A. Maslankowski.
Date 1999 to date.
15cm (6ins) high.
White.
Series: Sentiments.
(Royal Doulton web price £31.50)
Retail £31.50.

HN4066
Philippa of Hainault (1314 - 1369)
Second Version
Designer A. Maslankowski.
Date 1998. Limited edition of 5,000.
18cm (7ins) high.
Green and red.
Series: Plantagenet Queens.
Comm: Lawleys By Post.
Est. £150-200.

HN4071
Heathcliff and Cathy
Designer A. Maslankowski.
Date 1999. Limited edition of 750.
32cm (12.5ins) high.
Pale blue, green, brown and white.
Series: Literary Lovers.
Est. £450-600.

HN4073
Margaret of Anjou (1430 - 1482)
Second Version
Designer A. Maslankowski.
Date 1998. Limited edition of 5,000.
19cm (7.5ins) high.
Purple, pink and white.
Series: Plantagenet Queens.
Comm: Lawleys By Post.
Royal Doulton web price £249.99)
(Auction PSA 23.6.04 sold £130)
Est. £160-250.

HN4079
Hebe, Handmaiden to the Gods
Designer A. Maslankowski.
Date 1999. Limited edition of 250.
36cm (14ins) high.
White parian body, purple and
gold base.
Series: The Immortals and Aurora.
Est. £500-600.

HN4074
Sophia Dorothea (1666 - 1726)
Designer A. Maslankowski.
Date 1998. Limited edition of 2,500.
24cm (9.5ins) high.
Pink, red and white.
Series: Georgian Queens.
Comm: Lawleys By Post.
Est. £150-185.

HN4080
Ceres, Goddess of Plenty
Designer A. Maslankowski.
Date 1999. Limited edition of 250.
36cm (14ins) high.
White parian body, red and gold base.
Series: The Immortals and Aurora.
Est. £500-600.

HN4076
Missing You
Designer A. Maslankowski.
Date 1999 - 2001.
14.5cm (5.75ins) high.
White.
Series: Sentiments.
Est. £35-45.

HN4081
Artemis, Goddess of the Hunt
Designer A. Maslankowski.
Date 1999. Limited edition of 250.
36cm (14ins) high.
White parian body, green and
gold base.
Series: The Immortals and Aurora.
Est. £500-600.

HN4077
Kindred Spirits
Designer A. Maslankowski.
Date 2000.
15cm (6ins) high.
White.
Series: Images Figure of
the Year.
Est. £45-65.

HN4082
Erato, the Parnassian Muse
Designer A. Maslankowski.
Date 1999. Limited edition of 250.
36cm (14ins) high.
White parian body, blue and gold base.
Series: The Immortals and Aurora.
Est. £500-650.

HN4078
**Aurora, Goddess
of the Dawn**
Designer A. Maslankowski.
Date 1999. Limited edition of 250.
46cm (18ins) high.
White parian body, white and gold base.
Series: The Immortals and Aurora.
Est. £1000-1200.

HN4083
Wisdom
First Version
Designer A. Maslankowski.
Date 1999 - 2001.
Height not known.
White.
Series: Sentiments.
Comm: Great Uni. Stores.
*(Auction PSA 22.10.03 sold £30
plus comm.)*
Est. £35-50.

HN4084
Noel
Designer A. Maslankowski.
Date 1999.
15cm (6ins) high.
White.
Series: Sentiments.
Est. £35-50.

HN4085
Remembering You
Designer A. Maslankowski.
Date 2002.
15cm (6ins) high.
White.
Series: Sentiments.
(Ebay 4.6.04 sold £17)
Est. £20-30.

HN4086
HM Queen Elizabeth The Queen Mother
Fourth Version
Designer A. Maslankowski.
Date 2000. Limited edition of 2,000.
23cm (9ins) high.
Pale blue, tan and white.
Est. £155-200.

HN4088
Storytime (Boy)
Designer A. Maslankowski.
Date 2000 - 2003.
10cm (4ins) wide.
White.
Series: Images.
Est. £20-30.

HN4089
Storytime (Girl)
Designer A. Maslankowski.
Date 2000 to date.
11.5cm (4.5ins) high.
White.
Series: Images.
(Royal Doulton web price £29)
Retail £29.

HN4090
Annabelle
Designer N. Pedley.
Date 1998. Special edition of 2,500.
19cm (7.5ins) high.
Pink.
Other colourways:
'Joanne' HN3422.
Marketed in USA.
Est. £100-140.

HN4091
Molly
Designer N. Pedley.
Date 1997.
20.5cm (8ins) high.
Yellow and red.
Other colourways: 'Claire'
HN3646; 'Kaitlyn' HN4128;
'Rosemary' HN3691, 3698.
Comm: Debenhams.
Est. £70-95.

HN4092
Charlotte
Fourth Version
Designer N. Pedley.
Date 1998 - 2002.
21.5cm (8.5ins) high.
Blue and white.
Other colourways: HN4303.
Est. £70-95.

HN4093
Emily
Fourth Version
Designer N. Pedley.
Date 1998 to date.
21cm (8.25ins) high.
Dark and pale green and white.
(Royal Doulton web price £110)
Retail £110.

HN4094
Rosie
Designer N. Pedley.
Date 1998 to date.
20.5cm (8ins) high.
Pink, tan and white.
(Royal Doulton web price £115)
Retail £115.

HN4095
Anna
Second Version
Designer N. Pedley.
Date 1998 - 2000.
17cm (6.75ins) high.
Pink and white.
Series: Vanity Fair Ladies.
Est. £60-85.

HN4100
Special Occasion
Designer N. Pedley.
Date 1998 - 2002.
21cm (8.25ins) high.
Red, pink and white.
Est. £90-130.

HN4096
Harmony
Second Version
Designer N. Pedley.
Date 1998.
14.5cm (5.75ins) high.
White.
Series: Club Membership Figure.
(Auction PSA 23.6.04 sold £15
plus comm.)
(Ebay 8.7.04 sold £20)
Est. £20-35.

HN4101
Kirsten
Designer N. Pedley.
Date 1998 - 2000.
20.5cm (8ins) high.
Pale blue, white and pink.
Series: Vanity Fair Ladies.
Est. £60-85.

HN4097
Hope
Second Version
Designer N. Pedley.
Date 1998 - 99.
21.5cm (8.5ins) high.
Pink.
Series: Charity (Breast Cancer)
(Ebay 20.8.04 sold £100)
Est. £120-175.

HN4102
Pride and Joy
Second Version
Designer N. Pedley.
Date 1998 to date.
11.5cm (4.5ins) high.
Pale blue, tan, green and white
Series: Name Your Own.
(Name can be engaved on base)
(Royal Doulton web price £49)
Retail £49.

HN4098
Suzanne
First Version
Designer N. Pedley.
Date 1998 - 2001.
21.5cm (8.5ins) high.
Lilac, pink and white.
Series: Vanity Fair Ladies.
Est. £70-95.

HN4103
Sugar and Spice
Designer N. Pedley.
Date 1998 to date.
11cm (4.25ins) high.
Pink and light brown.
Series: Name Your Own.
(Name can be engaved on base)
(Ebay 4.6.04 sold £44)
Est. £45-60.

HN4099
Ruth
Second Version
Designer N. Pedley.
Date 1998 - 2001.
20.5cm (8ins) high.
Pink and white.
Series: Vanity Fair Ladies.
Est. £60-85.

HN4109
Mackenzie
Designer N. Pedley.
Date 1998. Special edition of 350.
20.5cm (8ins) high.
Blue.
Other colourways:
'First Bloom' HN3913.
Comm: Seaway China.
Est. £60-85.

HN4110
Jane
Fifth Version
Designer N. Pedley.
Date 1998.
21cm (8.25ins) high.
Pink.
Comm: Great Universal Stores.
Est. £55-75.

*Picture
not available
at present*

HN4115
Brenda
Designer N. Pedley.
Date 1999 to date.
21.5cm (8.5ins) high.
White and pink.
Series: Vanity Fair Ladies.
Marketed in Canada.
Est. £85-115

HN4111
Alice
Third Version
Designer N. Pedley.
Date 1998 - 2001.
21cm (8.25ins) high.
Pink and white.
Comm: Index Mail Order Catalogue.
Est. £55-75.

HN4116
Barbara
Fourth Version
Designer N. Pedley.
Date 1999 to date.
21cm (8.25ins) high.
White and pale green.
Series: Vanity Fair Ladies.
Marketed in Canada.
Est. £85-115

HN4112
Nicole
Second Version
Designer N. Pedley.
Date 1999.
20.5cm (8ins) high.
Red, green and cream.
Series: RDICC.
*(Auction PSA 3.12.03 sold
£100 plus comm.)*
Est. £120-170.

*Picture
not available
at present*

HN4117
Melody
Second Version
Designer N. Pedley.
Date 1999.
14cm (5.5ins) high.
Blue and white.
Series: Club Membership Figure.
Est. £40-55.

HN4113
Sweet Poetry
Designer N. Pedley.
Date 1999 - 2002.
20.5cm (8ins) high.
Lilac, pink and white.
Est. £100-140.

HN4118
Special Gift
Designer N. Pedley.
Date 1999.
14cm (5.5ins) high.
White and pink.
Other colourways: HN4129.
Marketed in Canada.
Est. £40-55.

HN4114
Mary
Fifth Version
Designer N. Pedley.
Date 1999 - 2002.
21.5cm (8.5ins) high.
Red, pink and white.
Est. £90-120.

HN4123
Katie
Second Version
Designer N. Pedley.
Date 1998 - 2002.
20.5cm (8ins) high.
Blue and white.
Other colourways:
'Lindsay' HN3645.
Comm: Debenhams.
Est. £55-75.

HN4124
Julia
Second Version
Designer N. Pedley.
Date 1999.
20.5cm (8ins) high.
Pink.
Series: M. Doulton Events.
Est. £60-85.

HN4129
Special Gift
Designer N. Pedley.
Date 1999 - 2000.
14cm (5.5ins) high.
Peach.
Other colourways: HN4118.
Series: Visitor Centre.
Est. £35-50.

HN4125
Amber
Designer N. Pedley.
Date 1999 to date.
20.5cm (8ins) high.
White and yellow.
Other colourways:
Chloe' HN3883, 3914.
Marketed in USA.
Est. £60-85.

HN4130
Elaine
First Version
Designer M. Davies.
Date 1998. Limited edition of 2,500.
18.5cm (7.25ins) high.
Red and white.
Other colourways: HN2791,
3307, 3741.
Comm: Great Uni. Stores.
Est. £90-130.

HN4126
Brianna
Designer N. Pedley.
Date 1999 to date.
21.5cm (8.5ins) high.
White and green.
Other colourways: 'Kathleen'
HN3609, 3880.
Marketed in USA.
Est. £60-85.

HN4131
Elyse
Designer M. Davies.
Date 1998. Limited edition of 2,500.
14.5cm (5.75ins) high.
Pink.
Other colourways:
HN2429, 2474.
Comm: Great Uni. Stores.
Est. £90-130.

HN4127
Jasmine
Third Version
Designer N. Pedley.
Date 1999 to date.
20.5cm (8ins) high.
Pink and white.
Other colourways:
'Megan' HN3887.
Marketed in USA.
Est. £60-85.

HN4132
Alyssa
Designer M. Davies.
Date 1999 to date.
21.5cm (8.5ins) high.
Blue and white.
Other colourways:
'Country Rose' HN3221.
Marketed in USA.
Est. £60-85.

HN4128
Kaitlyn
Designer N. Pedley.
Date 1999 to date.
20.5cm (8ins) high.
Pink and white.
Other colourways: 'Claire'
HN3646; 'Molly' HN4091;
'Rosemary' HN3691, 3698.
Marketed in USA.
Est. £60-85.

HN4140
Darling
First Version (Model 89)
Designer C. Vyse.
Remodeller W.K. Harper.
Date 1998. Limited edition of 1,913.
19.5cm (7.75ins) high.
Pale blue.
Other colourways: HN1, 1319,
1371, 1372.
Comm: Lawleys By Post.
Est. £65-95.

HN4141
The Mask
Second Version
Designer L. Harradine.
Remodeller W.K. Harper.
Date 1999. Limited edition of 1,500.
24cm (9.5ins) high.
Black, blue and pink.
Comm: Lawleys By Post.
*(Auction PSA 22.10.03 sold £130
plus comm.)*
Est. £160-200.

HN4151
Faith
Second Version
Designer N. Pedley.
Date 1999 - 2000.
20.5cm (8ins) high.
Pale blue, pink and white.
Series: Charity (Breast Cancer)
Est. £85-120.

HN4152
Madeline
Designer N. Pedley.
Date 1999 to date.
21cm (8.25ins) high.
Lemon and white.
Est. £65-85.

HN4153
Marianne
Second Version
Designer N. Pedley.
Date 1999 - 2002.
21cm (8.25ins) high.
Red and white.
Other colourways:
'Jane' HN4210.
Est. £65-90.

HN4154
Natasha
Designer N. Pedley.
Date 1999 - 2001.
21cm (8.25ins) high.
Yellow, red and white.
Est. £130-180.

HN4155
Lynne
Second Version
Designer N. Pedley.
Date 1999 - 2002.
21cm (8.25ins) high.
Pink and white.
Est. £65-85.

HN4156
Beth
Second Version
Designer N. Pedley.
Date 1999 - 2002.
21cm (8.25ins) high.
Lilac, white and yellow.
Other colourways:
'Lydia' HN4211.
Est. £60-80.

HN4157
Kelly
Third Version
Designer N. Pedley.
Date 1999 to date.
20.5cm (8ins) high.
Pale green and white.
(Royal Doulton web price £80,50)
Retail £80.50.

HN4158
Michelle
Designer N. Pedley.
Date 1999 - 2002.
21cm (8.25ins) high.
Blue and white.
Est. £60-80.

HN4160
Sally
Second Version
Designer T. Potts.
Date 1998. Limited edition of 1,500.
21cm (8.25ins) high.
Pink and turquoise.
Other colourways:
HN3383, 3851.
Series: Visitor Centre.
Est. £85-110.

HN4161
The Open Road
Designer T. Potts.
Date 1999 - 2001.
23cm (9ins) high.
Pink and white.
Est. £100-135.

HN4166
Wisdom
Second Version
Designer T. Potts.
Date 1999 Limited edition of 500.
48.5cm (19ins) high.
Brown, black and gold.
Series: Art Deco.
Est. £500-700.

HN4162
Clara Hamps
Designer T. Potts.
Date 1999 - 2001.
21.5cm (8.5ins) high.
Blue and white.
Series: 1. Arnold Bennett.
2. Visitor Centre.
Est. £100-135.

HN4167
Sophia Baines
Designer T. Potts.
Date 2000 - 2001.
20.5cm (8ins) high.
Blue and white.
Series: 1. Arnold Bennett
2. Visitor Centre.
Est. £100-135.

HN4163
Ecstasy
Designer T. Potts.
Date 1999. Limited edition of 500.
43cm (17ins) high.
Brown, black and gold.
Series: Art Deco.
Est. £500-700.

HN4168
Gladys
Designer L. Harradine.
Remodeller T. Potts.
Date 2000. Limited edition
of 2,000.
11cm (4.25ins) high.
Green.
(Re-issued from original
figure HN1740, 1741)
Comm: Lawleys By Post.
Est. £70-90.

HN4164
Destiny
Designer T. Potts.
Date 1999. Limited edition of 500.
48.5cm (19ins) high.
Brown, black and gold.
Series: Art Deco.
Est. £500-700.

HN4169
Vera
Designer L. Harradine.
Remodeller T. Potts.
Date 2000. Limited edition
of 2,000.
11cm (4.25ins) high.
Pink and white.
(Re-issued from originaal
figure HN1729, 1730)
Comm: Lawleys By Post.
Est. £70-90.

HN4165
Optimism
Designer T. Potts.
Date 1999. Limited edition of 500.
40.5cm (16ins) high.
Brown, black and gold.
Series: Art Deco.
Est. £500-700.

HN4174
The Land of Nod
Second Version
Designer H. Tittensor.
Remodeller R. Tabbenor.
Date 2000. Limited edition of 2,500.
19.5cm (7.75ins) high.
Pale blue and pale brown.
Comm: Lawleys By Post.
Est. £70-90.

HN4175
Santa Claus
Second Version
Designer R. Tabbenor.
Date 2000 to date.
25cm (9.75ins) high.
Red, brown, black and white.
Est. £100-140.

HN4193
Sweet Dreams
Third Version
Designer P. Parsons.
Date 1999 - 2002.
30.5cm (12ins) high.
Lemon, blue and cream.
Series: Impressions.
Est. £70-100.

HN4179
Princess Badoura
Second Version
Designer R. Tabbenor.
Date 2001. Limited edition
of 500.
19cm (7.5ins) high.
Pink, red, brown, blue, gold
and grey.
(Royal Doulton web price £630)
Retail £630.

HN4194
Summer Blooms
Second Version
Designer P. Parsons.
Date 1999 to date.
33cm (13ins) high.
Pink, cream and blue.
Series: Impressions.
Est. £70-100.

HN4190
Ankhesenamun
Designer P. Parsons.
Date 1998. Limited edition of 950.
26.5cm (10.5ins) high.
Green and brown
Series: Egyptian Queens.
Comm: Lawleys By Post.
(Royal Doulton web price £395)
Retail £395.

HN4195
Summer Fragrance
Designer P. Parsons.
Date 1999 - 2000.
30.5cm (12ins) high.
Cream, pink and green.
Series: Impressions.
Est. £100-140.

HN4191
Hatshepsut
Designer P. Parsons.
Date 1999. Limited edition
of 950.
26.5cm (10.5ins) high.
Cream, blue, brown, russet and gold.
Series: Egyptian Queens.
Comm: Lawleys By Post.
Est. £250-350.

HN4196
Daybreak
Second Version
Designer P. Parsons.
Date 1999 to date.
33cm (13ins) high.
Blue, cream and pink.
Series: Impressions.
(Ebay 2.8.04 sold £66)
Est. £70-100.

HN4192
Tender Moment
Second Version
Designer P. Parsons.
Date 1999 to date.
30.5cm (12ins) high.
Lilac, pink and cream.
Series: Impressions.
Est. £70-100.

HN4197
Secret Thoughts
Second Version
Designer P. Parsons.
Date 1999 to date.
33cm (13ins) high.
Cream and pink.
Series: Impressions.
Est. £70-100.

HN4198
Sunset
Designer P. Parsons.
Date 2000 to date.
18cm (7ins) high.
Blue, white and cream.
Series: Impressions.
Est. £70-100.

HN4202
Joanne
Third Version
Designer V. Annand.
Date 2000 - 2002.
22.5cm (9ins) high.
Green, blue and lemon.
Series: In Vogue.
Est. £70-90.

HN4199
Sunrise
Designer P. Parsons.
Date 2000 to date.
18cm (7ins) high.
Lemon, blue and white.
Series: Impressions.
Est. £70-100.

HN4203
Rebecca
Fourth Version
Designer V. Annand.
Date 2000 - 2002.
23cm (9ins) high.
Pink, green and cream.
Series: In Vogue.
Est. £70-90.

HN4200
Scarlett OHara
Designer V. Annand.
Date 1999 - 2000.
23cm (9ins) high.
Dark and pale green and yellow.
Series: Classic Movies.
Est. £150-200.

*Picture
not available
at present*

HN4204
Madison
Designer V. Annand.
Date 2000 to date.
21.5cm (8.5ins) high.
Green.
Other colourways:
'Emma' HN3714.
Marketed in USA.
Est. £60-85.

HN4201A
Chloe
Third Version
Designer J. Bromley.
Date 2000. Limited edition of 2,000.
21.5cm (8.5ins) high.
Cream and pink.
Series: Lady of the Year.
Comm: by Compton/Woodhouse.
Est. £85-110.

HN4205
Alexis
Designer V. Annand.
Date 2000. to date.
21.5cm (8.5ins) high.
Lemon and rose.
Other colourways:
'Kathryn' HN4040.
Marketed in USA.
Est. £60-85.

HN4201B
Millennium Celebration
Designer V. Annand.
Date 1999 - 2001.
21cm (8.25ins) high.
Lemon and turquoise.
Other colourways:
HN4321, 4325.
Comm: Great Universal Stores.
Est. £70-90.

HN4206
Brittany
Designer V. Annand.
Date 2000 to date.
22cm (8.75ins) high.
Pink.
Other colourways:
'Olivia' HN3717.
Marketed in USA.
Est. £60-85.

HN4207
Allison
Designer V. Annand.
Date 2000 to date.
21cm (8.25ins) high.
Pale blue.
Other colourways:
'Ellie' HN3717.
Marketed in USA.
Est. £60-85.

HN4212
Millie
Designer N. Pedley.
Date 1999.
20.5cm (8ins) high.
Pink and white.
Other editions, 'Jasmine'
HN4127; 'Megan' HN3887.
Comm: by Debenham
Est. £60-85.

HN4208
Zoe
Designer V. Annand.
Date 2000 to date.
21cm (8.25ins) high.
Lilac.
Series: Chelsea.
Est. £55-75.

HN4213
With All My Love
Designer N. Pedley.
Date 2000. Limited edition of 2,500.
12.5cm (5ins) high.
White and blue.
Other colourways: HN4241.
Series: Sentiments.
Marketed in Canada.
Est. £60-85.

HN4209
Melinda
Designer V. Annand.
Date 2000 - 2002.
21cm (8.25ins) high.
Peach and white.
Series: Chelsea.
Est. £55-75.

HN4214
Christmas Day 1999
Designer N. Pedley.
Date 1999.
20.5cm (8ins) high.
Red.
Series: Christmas Figures.
*(Auction PSA 1.9.04 sold £75
plus comm.)*
Est. £90-150.

*Picture
not available
at present*

HN4210
Jayne
First Version
Designer N. Pedley.
Date 1999 - 2001.
21cm (8.25ins) high.
Yellow and blue.
Other colourways:
'Marianne' HN4153.
Comm: Great Universal Stores.
Est. £75-100.

HN4215
Happy Birthday 2000
Designer N. Pedley.
Date 2000.
23cm (9ins) high.
Pink and white.
Series: Happy Birthday.
Est. £55-75.

HN4211
Lydia
Second Version
Designer N. Pedley.
Date 1999 - 2001.
21cm (8.25ins) high.
Red.
Other colourways:
'Beth' HN4156.
Comm: Great Universal Stores.
Est. £75-100.

HN4216
Wedding Celebration
Designer N. Pedley.
Date 2000 - 02
22.5cm (8.75ins) high.
Ivory and pink.
Other colourways: HN4229.
Series: Name Your Own.
(Name can be engaved on base)
Est. £60-90.

HN4220
Camilla
Second Version
Designer N. Pedley.
Date 2000 - 02.
21.5cm (8.5ins) high.
Pink and white.
Est. £70-100.

HN4221
Susannah
Designer N. Pedley.
Date 2000 to date.
20.5cm (8ins) high.
Cream, white and yellow.
Series: Country Maids.
Est. £65-85.

HN4222
Fair Maid
Designer N. Pedley.
Date 2000 - 02.
20.5cm (8ins) high.
Pale blue, white and brown.
Series: Country Maids.
Est. £65-85.

HN4223
Josephine
Designer N. Pedley.
Date 2000 to date.
21.5cm (8.5ins) high.
Blue and white.
Other colourways:
'Caroline' HN4395.
Series: Vanity Fair Ladies.
(Royal Doulton web price £105)
Retail £105.

HN4225
Summer Duet
Designer N. Pedley.
Date 1999. Limited edition of 1,500.
15cm (6ins) high.
Ivory and gold.
Series: Ivory and Gold.
Comm: Lawleys By Post.
Est. £40-55.

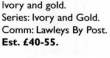

HN4226
After the Rain
Designer N. Pedley.
Date 1999. Limited edition of 1,500.
15cm (6ins) high.
Ivory and gold.
Series: Ivory and Gold.
Comm: Lawleys By Post.
Est. £40-55.

HN4231
Ellen
Fourth Version
Designer J. Bromley.
Date 2000 - 02.
21.5cm (8.5ins) high.
Red, pink and white.
Est. £100-145.

HN4227
Off to the Pond
Designer N. Pedley.
Date 1999. Limited edition of 1,500.
15cm (6ins) high.
Ivory and gold.
Series: Ivory and Gold.
Comm: Lawleys By Post.
Est. £40-55.

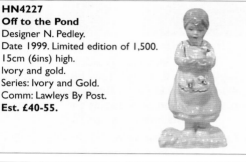

HN4232
Specially for You
Designer J. Bromley.
Date: 2000 to date.
21.5cm (8.5ins) high.
Lilac, green and white.
(Royal Doulton web price £185)
Retail £185.

HN4228
Helping Mother
Designer N. Pedley.
Date 1999. Limited edition of 1,500.
15cm (6ins) high.
Ivory and gold.
Series: Ivory and Gold.
Comm: Lawleys By Post.
Est. £40-55.

HN4233
Kate
Third Version
Designer J. Bromley.
Date 2000.
21.5cm (8.5ins) high.
Pink.
Other colourways: 'Best Wishes'
HN3971; 'Forever Yours' HN4501.
Series: Charity Figure 2000.
Comm: Compton/Woodhouse.
Est. £85-110.

HN4229
Wedding Celebration
Designer N. Pedley.
Date 2000 - 02.
22cm (8.75ins) high.
White and pink.
Other colourways: HN4216.
Series: Name Your Own.
Est. £75-100.

HN4234
Special Celebration
Designer J. Bromley.
Date 2001 to date.
23cm (9ins) high.
Cream and purple.
(Royal Doulton web price £205)
Retail £205.

HN4230
Susan
Fourth Version
Designer J. Bromley.
Date 2000.
21.5cm (8.5ins) high.
Pink and yellow.
Series: M. Doulton Events.
Est. £100-155.

*Picture
not available
at present*

HN4235
Belle
Fifth Version
Designer J. Bromley.
Date 2001 to date.
21.5cm (8.5ins) high.
Purple and white.
(Royal Doulton web price £205)
Retail £205.

HN4236
Just For You
Second Version
Designer J. Bromley.
Date 2002 to date.
21.5cm (8.5ins) high.
Pink and white.
(Royal Doulton web price £185)
Retail £185.

HN4242
Christmas Day 2000
Designer N. Pedley.
Date 2000.
21cm (8.25ins) high.
Green, white and red.
Series: Christmas Day.
Est. £85-110.

HN4237
Georgina
Third Version
Designer J. Bromley.
Date 2002.
23.5cm (9.25ins) high.
Pink and white.
Series: Lady of the Year.
Comm: Compton/Woodhouse.
Est. £85-110.

HN4243
Charity
Second Version
Designer N. Pedley.
Date 2000 - 01.
21cm (8.25ins) high.
Pink and white.
Series: Charity Breast Cancer.
Est. £85-110.

HN4238
Francesca
Designer D. Hughes.
Date 2001. Limited edition of 2,500.
21.5cm (8.5ins) high.
Red and white.
Comm: Home Shopping Ltd.
Est. £85-110.

HN4244
The Bather
First Version
Designer L. Harradine.
Remodeller N. Pedley.
Date 2000. Limited edition of 2,000.
18.5cm (7.25ins) high.
Dark blue.
(re-issued from original model
HN1708)
Series: Bathers.
Est. £150-200.

HN4240
Flower of Scotland
Designer N. Pedley.
Date 2000 - 03.
21.5cm (8.5ins) high.
Blue, green and white.
(Royal Doulton web price £135)
Retail £135.

HN4245
The Sunshine Girl
Second Version
Designer L. Harradine.
Remodeller N. Pedley.
Date 2000. Limited edition
of 2,000.
11.5cm (4.5ins) high.
Red, green and white.
Series: Bathers.
Est. £150-200.

HN4241
With All My Love
Designer N. Pedley.
Date 2000 - 01.
12.5cm (5ins) high.
Pink and white.
Other colourways: HN4213.
Series: Visitor Centre.
Est. £35-50.

HN4246
The Swimmer
Second Version
Designer L. Harradine.
Remodeller N. Pedley.
Date 2000. Limited edition of 2,000.
18.5cm (7.25ins) high.
Blue, black and red.
Series: Bathers.
Est. £150-200.

HN4247
Lido Lady
Second Version
Designer L. Harradine.
Remodeller N. Pedley.
Date 2000 - 01.
17cm (6.75ins) high.
Pink.
Series: 1. Bathers. 2. RDICC.
Est. £110-150.

HN4252
The Sorcerer
Designer A. Maslankowski.
Date 2000 - 02.
23.5cm (9.25ins) high.
Purple, blue, white, red and yellow.
Series: Mystical Figures.
Est. £165-225.

HN4248
Jennifer
Fourth Version
Designer N. Pedley.
Date 2000 to date.
21cm (8.25ins) high.
Lemon and white.
(Royal Doulton web price £125)
Retail £125.

HN4253
The Sorceress
Designer A. Maslankowski.
Date 2000 - 02.
24cm (9.5ins) high.
Purple, blue, yellow, red and white.
Series: Mystical Figures.
Est. £125-175.

HN4249
Dairy Maid
Designer N. Pedley.
Date 2000 - 02.
21cm (8.25ins) high.
White, pink and yellow.
Series: Country Maids.
Est. £65-100.

HN4254
Many Happy Returns
Designer A. Maslankowski.
Date 2000 to date.
15cm (6ins) high.
White.
Series: Sentiments.
(Royal Doulton web price £31.50)
Retail £31.50.

HN4250
Greetings
Designer A. Maslankowski.
Date 2000.
14.5cm (5.75ins) high.
Yellow and white.
Series: 1. Club Membership
Figure. 2. Sentiments.
Est. £30-45.

HN4255
Happy Christmas
Designer A. Maslankowski.
Date 2000 to date.
16cm (6.25ins) high.
White.
Series: Sentiments.
(Royal Doulton web price £31.50)
Retail £31.50.

HN4251
Thank You Mother
Designer A. Maslankowski.
Date 2000 - 03.
16cm (6.25ins) high.
White and lilac.
Other colourways: Also
called 'Thank You' HN3390.
Series: Sentiments.
Marketed in Canada.
Est. £45-55

HN4256
Carol Singer with Lantern
Designer D.V. Tootle.
Date 2000. Limited edition of 6,000.
16cm (6.25ins) high.
White.
Series: Images Christmas Choir.
Est. £25-35.

HN4257
Special Friends
Designer A. Maslankowski.
Date 2001.
17cm (6.75ins) high.
White.
Series: Images Figure of
the Year.
Est. £55-75.

HN4263
Edward VI
Designer P. Parsons.
Date 2000. Limited edition of 5,000.
21cm (8.25ins) high.
Gold, red, brown and cream.
Comm: Lawleys By Post.
Est. £200-275.

HN4258
Embrace
Designer A. Maslankowski.
Date 2001.
15cm (6ins) high.
White.
Series: Club Membership Figure.
Est. £30-40.

HN4264
Cleopatra
Second Version
Designer P. Parsons.
Date 2001. Limited edition of 950.
25.5cm (10ins) high.
Pale blue, tan and red.
Series: Egyptian Queens.
Comm: Doulton-Direct.
(Royal Doulton web price £395)
Retail £395.

HN4260
Henrietta-Maria
(Wife of Charles I)
Second Version
Designer P. Parsons.
Date 2000. Limited edition of 2,500.
23cm (9ins) high.
Red, white, yellow and blue.
Series: Stuart Queens.
Comm: Doulton Direct.
(Royal Doulton web price £249.99)
Retail £249.99.

HN4265
Cherished Memories
Designer P. Parsons.
Date 2001 - 02.
32.5cm (12.75ins) high.
Lemon.
Series: 1. RDICC. 2. Impressions.
Est. £85-115.

*Picture
not available
at present*

HN4261
Tender Greeting
Designer P. Parsons.
Date 2000 - 02.
28cm (11ins) high.
Light green, white and grey.
Series: Impressions.
Est. £90-120.

HN4266
Anne of Denmark
(Wife of James I)
Designer P. Parsons.
Date 2001. Limited edition of 2,500.
23cm (9ins) high.
Green, red and white.
Series: Stuart Queens.
Comm: Doulton-Direct.
(Royal Doulton web price £250)
Retail £250.

HN4262
In Loving Arms
Designer P. Parsons.
Date 2000 - 02.
30.5cm (12ins) high.
Pink and cream.
Series: Impressions.
Est. £90-120.

HN4267
Catherine of Braganza
(Wife of Charles II)
Designer P. Parsons.
Date 2001. Limited edition of 2,500.
23cm (9ins) high.
Orange, white, green and brown.
Series: Stuart Queens.
Comm: Doulton-Direct.
(Royal Doulton web price £265)
Retail £265.

HN4270
Spring
Fifth Version
Designer M. King.
Date 2000. Limited edition
of 2,000.
21.5cm (8.5ins) high.
Yellow and white.
Series: The Seasons (Series Eight)
Comm: Compton/Woodhouse.
Est. £100-130.

Picture not available at present

HN4281
Debut
Second Version
Designer A. Hughes.
Date 2000. Limited edition of 2,000.
23cm (9ins) high.
White.
Series: Images.
Comm: Lawleys By Post.
Est. £35-50.

HN4271
Summer
Third Version
Designer M. King.
Date 2000. Limited edition
of 2,000.
21.5cm (8.5ins) high.
Yellow, white and blue.
Series: The Seasons (Series Eight)
Comm: Compton/Woodhouse.
Est. £100-130.

Picture not available at present

HN4282
Encore
Second Version
Designer A. Hughes.
Date 2000. Limited edition of 2,000.
23cm (9ins) high.
White.
Series: Images.
Comm: Lawleys By Post.
Est. £35-50.

HN4272
Autumn
Third Version
Designer M. King.
Date 2000. Limited edition
of 2,000.
21.5cm (8.5ins) high.
Purple.
Series: The Seasons (Series Eight)
Comm: Compton/Woodhouse.
Est. £100-130.

Picture not available at present

HN4283
Trumpet Player
Designer A. Hughes.
Date 2000. Limited edition of 1,500.
24cm (9.5ins) high.
White.
Series: The Age of Jazz.
Comm: Lawleys By Post.
Est. £35-50.

HN4273
Winter
Third Version
Designer M. King.
Date 2000. Limited edition of 2,000.
21.5cm (8.5ins) high.
Red.
Series: The Seasons (Series Eight)
Comm: Compton/Woodhouse.
Est. £100-130.

HN4284
Saxophone Player
Designer A. Hughes.
Date 2000. Limited edition of 1,500.
24cm (9.5ins) high.
White.
Series: The Age of Jazz.
Comm: Lawleys By Post.
Est. £35-50.

HN4280
Love Everlasting
Designer A. Hughes.
Date 2000 to date.
16.5cm (6.5ins) high.
White.
Series: Images.
(Royal Doulton web price £39)
Retail £39.

HN4285
The Age of Swing
Designer A. Hughes.
Date 2000. Limited edition of 1,500.
20.5cm (8ins) high.
White.
Comm: Lawleys By Post.
Est. £40-55.

HN4286
Doctor
Second Version
Designer A. Hughes.
Date 2001 - 02.
23.5cm (9.25ins) high.
Brown, grey and black.
Est. £135-175.

HN4300
Bells Across the Valley
Designer N. Pedley.
Date 2000 to date.
21cm (8.5ins) high.
Lilac and white.
(Royal Doulton web price £160)
Retail £160.

HN4287
Nurse
Designer A. Hughes.
Date 2001 to date.
21.5cm (8.5ins) high.
White, blue, red and tan.
(Royal Doulton web price £230)
(Ebay 7.7.04 sold £127)
*(Auction ASH 26.9.04 sold £75
plus comm.)*
Est. £125-175.

HN4301
Lorraine
Second Version
Designer N. Pedley.
Date 2000 to date.
21cm (8.25ins) high.
Blue. green and cream.
(Royal Doulton web price £99)
(Ebay 19.7.04 sold £74)
Est. £75-110.

HN4289
Lawyer
Second Version
Designer A. Hughes.
Date 2001 - 03.
22cm (8.75ins) high.
Black, white, red and brown.
(Royal Doulton web price £175)
*(Auction PSA 4.2.04 sold £60 plus
comm.)*
Est. £85-135.

HN4302
Sweet Music
Designer N. Pedley.
Date 2001 to date.
21.5cm (8.5ins) high.
Pink and white.
(Royal Doulton web price £115)
Retail £115.

HN4290
Carol Singer (Brother)
Designer D.V. Tootle.
Date 2000. Limited edition
of 6,000.
16cm (6.25ins) high.
White.
Series: Images Christmas Choir.
Est. £25-30.

HN4303
Charlotte
Fourth Version
Designer N. Pedley.
Date 2000 - 01.
21.5cm (8.5ins) high.
Green and white.
Other colourways: HN4092.
Comm: Great Universal Stores.
Est. £70-95.

HN4291
Carol Singer (Sister)
Designer D.V. Tootle.
Date 2000. Limited edition of 6,000.
16cm (6.25ins) high.
White.
Series: Images Christmas Choir.
Est. £25-30.

HN4304
Catherine
Third Version
Designer N. Pedley.
Date 2001 to date.
21.5cm (8.5ins) high.
Pale blue and white.
(Royal Doulton web price £120)
Retail £120.

HN4305
Milk Maid
Third Version
Designer N. Pedley.
Date 2001 - 02.
20.5cm (8ins) high.
Pale blue, cream,
white and pink.
Series: Country Maids.
Est. £65-95.

HN4310
Janet
Fourth Version
Designer N. Pedley.
Date 2001 - 02.
21cm (8.25ins) high.
Pale blue.
Est. £65-95.

HN4306
Congratulations to You
Designer N. Pedley.
Date 2000 to date.
20.5cm (8ins) high.
Lilac and white.
Series: Name Your Own.
Est. £75-100.

HN4311
Margaret
Third Version
Designer N. Pedley.
Date 2001 to date.
21.5cm (8.5ins) high.
Pink and white.
Series: Vanity Fair Ladies.
*(Royal Doulton web price
£52.50)*
Retail £52.50.

HN4307
Christine
Sixth Version
Designer N. Pedley.
Date 2001.
20.5cm (8ins) high.
Red, white and tan.
Series: M. Doulton Events.
Est. £85-110.

HN4312
Pretty as a Picture
Designer N. Pedley.
Date 2001 to date.
14.5cm (5.75ins) high.
White and pink.
Series: Name Your Own.
(Royal Doulton web price £42)
(Ebay 10.6.04 sold £17)
Est. £20-40.

HN4308
Happy Birthday 2001
Designer N. Pedley.
Date 2001.
20.5cm (8ins) high.
Pale green and tan.
Series: Happy Birthday.
Est. £55-75.

HN4313
For Your Special Day
Designer N. Pedley.
Date 2001 - 03.
15cm (6ins) high.
Pale yellow and white.
Other colourways:
'Sweet Delight' HN4398.
Marketed in Canada.
Est. £35-45.

HN4309
Jacqueline
Fourth Version
Designer N. Pedley.
Date 2001.
21.5cm (8.5ins) high.
Pink, lemon and white.
Series: RDICC.
Est. £100-130.

HN4314
New Dawn
Designer N. Pedley.
Date 2001 - 02.
21.5cm (8.5ins) high.
Pink and lilac.
Series: Charity (Breast Cancer)
('New Dawn' was also produced
in 7 different colours and
auctioned off, where the proceeds
went to Breast Cancer Research)
Est. £75-100.

HN4315
Christmas Day 2001
Designer N. Pedley.
Date 2001 - 01.
22cm (8.75ins) high.
Dark green, white and red.
Series: Christmas Figures.
Est. £65-90.

HN4320
Claudia
Designer V. Annand.
Date 2000 - 02.
21cm (8.25ins) high.
Pale blue.
Other colourways:
'Amelia' HN4327.
Series: In Vogue.
*(Auction W&H 27.9.04 sold
£50 plus comm.)*
Est. £70-95.

HN4316
Maid of the Meadow
Designer N. Pedley.
Date 2001 - 02.
21.5cm (8.5ins) high.
Tan, yellow and white.
Series: Country Maids.
Est. £65-90.

HN4321
Millennium Celebration
Designer V. Annand.
Date 2000.
21cm (8.25ins) high.
Yellow and turquoise.
Other colourways: HN4201B, 4325.
(Australian backstamp on this figure)
Est. £65-90.

HN4317
Gentle Breeze
Designer N. Pedley.
Date 2001 - 02.
21.5cm (8.5ins) high.
Red, white and pink.
Est. £85-110.

HN4322
Becky
Second Version
Designer V. Annand.
Date 2001 to date.
22cm (8.75ins) high.
Lilac.
Series: Chelsea.
(Royal Doulton web price £105)
Retail £105.

HN4318
Loving Thoughts
Second Version
Designer N. Pedley.
Date 2001 to date.
20.5cm (8ins) high.
Green, lilac and tan.
Est. £70-95.

HN4323
Katie
Third Version
Designer V. Annand.
Date 2001 to date.
20.5cm (8ins) high.
Pale blue and white.
Series: Chelsea.
(Royal Doulton web price £135)
(Ebay 28.5.04. sold £62)
Est. £65-125.

HN4319
Sweetheart
Designer N. Pedley.
Date 2001 to date.
20.5cm (8ins) high.
Pink.
(Royal Doulton web price £130)
Retail £130.

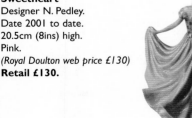

HN4324
The Bride
Fifth Version
Designer V. Annand.
Date 2000 - 03.
21.5cm (8.5ins) high.
Pink and white.
Series: In Vogue.
Est. £65-85.

HN4325
Millennium Celebration
Designer V. Annand.
Date 2000.
20.5cm (8.25ins) high.
Turquoise and yellow.
Other colourways: HN4201B, 4321.
(Canadian backstamp on this figure)
Est. £65-90.

HN4350
Christmas Eve
Designer A. Maslankowski.
Date 2000 - 02.
14.5cm (5.75ins) high.
White.
Series: Sentiments.
Marketed in Canada.
Est. £45-55.

HN4326
Bethany
Designer V. Annand.
Date 2001 - 03.
21.5cm (8.5ins) high.
Yellow and white.
Series: Chelsea.
(Auction PSA 22.10.03. sold £35
plus comm.)
Est. £45-60.

HN4351
Sweetheart (Boy)
Designer A. Maslankowski.
Date 2000 - 03.
15cm (6ins) high.
White.
Series: Images.
(Royal Doulton web price £29)
Retail £29.

HN4327
Amelia
Designer V. Annand.
Date 2002 - 03.
21.5cm (8.5ins) high.
Black, gold and silver.
Other colourways:
'Claudia' HN4320.
Series: In Vogue.
(Royal Doulton web price £15)
Retail £125.

HN4352
Sweetheart (Girl)
Designer A. Maslankowski.
Date 2000 - 03.
16.5cm (6.5ins) high.
White.
Series: Images.
(Royal Doulton web price £29)
Retail £29.

HN4328
Applause
Designer V. Annand.
Date 2002.
21.5cm (8.5ins) high.
Yellow, orange and white.
Series: RDICC.
Est. £85-110.

HN4353
Liberty
Second Version
Designer A. Maslankowski.
Date 2000. Limited edition of 1,500.
26cm (10.25ins) high.
Brown and pink.
Comm: Lawleys By Post.
Est. £65-90.

HN4329
Finishing Touch
Designer V. Annand.
Date 2002 to date.
23cm (9ins) high.
White and blue.
Series: In Vogue.
(Royal Doulton web price £125)
Retail £125.

HN4354
Felicity
Designer A. Maslankowski.
Date 2000. Limited edition of 1,500.
26cm (10.25ins) high.
Brown and pink.
Comm: Lawleys By Post.
Est. £65-90.

HN4356
Sister and Brother
Designer A. Maslankowski.
Date 2001 to date.
18.5cm (7.25ins) high.
White.
Series: Images.
(Royal Doulton web price £39)
Retail £39.

HN4362
Moonlight Gaze
Designer T. Potts.
Date 2002.
20.5cm (8ins) high.
Blue.
Series: Lady of the Year.
Comm: Doulton-Direct.
Est. £100-135.

HN4357
Perfect Pose
Designer A. Maslankowski.
Date 2001 - 03.
16cm (6.25ins) high.
White.
Series: Images.
Est. £20-25.

HN4363
Farewell Daddy
Designer T. Potts.
Date 2002 Limited edition of 2,500.
26.5cm (10.5ins) high.
Khaki.
Series: Nostalgia.
Comm. Doulton-Direct.
(Royal Doulton web price £250)
*(Auction ASH 12.9.04 sold £125
plus comm.)*
Est. £150-190.

HN4358
First Lesson
Designer A. Maslankowski.
Date 2001 - 03.
16cm (6.25ins) high.
White.
Series: Images.
(Royal Doulton web price £29)
Retail £29.

HN4364
Women's Land Army
Designer T. Potts.
Date 2002. Limited edition of 2,500.
22cm (8.75ins) high.
Brown and green.
Series: Nostalgia.
Comm: Doulton-Direct.
Est. £150-190.

HN4360
Arnold Bennett
Designer T. Potts.
Date 2001.
21.5cm (8.5ins) high.
Brown, grey, black and white.
Series: 1. Arnold Bennett.
2. Visitor Centre.
*(Auction ASH 19.9.04 sold £55
plus comm.)*
Est. £100-135.

HN4366
The Batsman
Designer T. Potts.
Date 2003. Limited edition of 2,500.
22cm (8.75ins) high.
Blue, green, white and yellow.
Comm: Doulton-Direct.
(Royal Doulton web price £175)
Retail £175.

HN4361
Land Girl
Designer T. Potts.
Date 2001 Limited edition of 2,500.
22cm (8.75ins) high.
Brown, tan, yellow and black.
Series: Nostalgia.
Comm: Doulton-Direct.
(Royal Doulton web price £159.60)
Retail £159.60.

HN4370
Skating
Designer A. Maslankowski.
Date 2001.
16cm (6.25ins) high.
White.
Series: Sentiments.
Marketed in Canada.
Est. 50-65.

HN4371
St. George
Fourth Version
Designer A. Maslankowski.
Date 2001. Limited edition of 50.
43cm (17ins) high.
Grey, white, yellow and red.
Series: Prestige.
Retail: £10,000.

HN4376
Surprise
Designer A. Maslankowski.
Date 2001 - 02.
18.5cm (7.25ins) high.
White.
Series: Images.
Est. £25-35.

HN4372
HM Queen Elizabeth II
Fifth Version
Designer A. Maslankowski.
Date 2001 Limited edition of 1,500.
21.5cm (8.5ins) high.
White and gold.
Est. £150-200.

HN4377
Keep In Touch
Designer A. Maslankowski.
Date 2002.
18cm (7ins) high.
White.
Series: Images Figure of the Year.
Est. £45-60.

HN4373
Bridesmaid
Seventh Version
Designer A. Maslankowski.
Date 2001 to date.
16.5cm (6.5ins) high.
White.
Series: Images.
(Royal Doulton web price £29)
Retail £29.

HN4378
Prayers
Designer A. Maslankowski.
Date 2002 to date.
15cm (6ins) high.
White.
Series: Images.
(Royal Doulton web price £29)
Retail £29.

HN4374
Pageboy
Designer A. Maslankowski.
Date 2001 - 02.
16cm (6.25ins) high.
White.
Series: Images.
(Royal Doulton web price £29)
Retail £29.

HN4379
Wedding Vows
Second Version
Designer A. Maslankowski.
Date 2002 to date.
26.5cm (10.5ins) high.
White.
Series: Images.
(Royal Doulton web price £59)
Retail £59.

HN4375
Independence
Designer A. Maslankowski.
Date 2002.
23cm (9ins) high.
White.
Series: 1. Images.
2. Save the Children Charity.
Est. £45-60.

HN4380
From This Day Forward
Designer N. Lee.
Date 2000.
25.5cm (10ins) high.
White.
Series: Images.
Comm: Compton/ Woodhouse.
Est. £55-75.

HN4390
Julia
Third Version
Designer N. Pedley.
Date 2001 - 02.
21.5cm (8.5ins) high.
Peach and lilac.
Est. £80-100.

HN4396
Serenity
Designer N. Pedley.
Date 2001 - 03.
21cm (8.25ins) high.
Blue and lilac.
(Royal Doulton web price £120)
Retail £120.

HN4391
Anna
Third Version
Designer N. Pedley.
Date 2001 to date.
21cm (8.25ins) high.
White and pale blue.
Series: Vanity Fair Ladies.
(Royal Doulton web price £49.50)
Retail £49.50.

HN4397
Thoughts for You
Designer N. Pedley.
Date 2001.
21cm (8.25ins) high.
Blue, yellow and white.
Series: Name Your Own.
Comm: Great Universal Store.
Est. £55-80.

HN4392
My Love
Second Version
Designer N. Pedley.
Date 2001 to date.
21cm (8.25ins) high.
Red.
Series: Name Your Own.
(Royal Doulton web price £135)
Retail £135.

HN4398
Sweet Delight
Designer N. Pedley.
Date 2001 to date.
15cm (6ins) high.
Pink.
Other colourways:
'For Your Special Day' HN4313.
Series: Visitor Centre.
Est. £30-40.

HN4393
Happy Birthday 2002
Designer N. Pedley.
Date 2002.
21cm (8.25ins) high.
Blue.
Series: Happy Birthday.
Est. £55-80.

HN4399
Bathing Beauty
Second Version
Designer N. Pedley.
Date 2001. Limited edition of 1,000.
18.5cm (7.25ins) high.
Blue, pink and yellow.
Other colourways: HN4599.
Series: Leslie Harradine Tribute.
Est. £85-110.

HN4395
Caroline
Third Version
Designer N. Pedley.
Date 2001.
21cm (8.25ins) high.
Yellow.
Other colourways:
'Josephine' HN4223.
Comm: Great Universal Store.
Est. £55-80.

HN4400
Brighton Belle
Designer N. Pedley.
Date 2001. Limited edition of 1,000.
18cm (7ins) high.
Pink.
Other colourways: HN4600
Series: Leslie Harradine Tribute.
Est. £85-110.

HN4401
Summer's Darling
Second Version
Designer N. Pedley.
Date 2001. Limited edition of 1,000.
10.5cm (4.25ins) high.
Green and mauve.
Other colourways: HN4601
Series: Leslie Harradine Tribute.
Est. £85-110.

HN4406
Summer Stroll
Designer N. Pedley.
Date 2002 to date.
21cm (8.25ins) high.
White, pink and yellow.
(Royal Doulton web price £120)
(Ebay 20.3.04. sold £130)
Est. £120-150.

HN4402
Taking The Waters
Designer N. Pedley.
Date 2001. Limited edition of 1,000.
16cm (6.25ins) high.
Purple and yellow.
Other colourways: HN4602
Series: Leslie Harradine Tribute.
Est. £85-110.

HN4407
Hannah
Fourth Version
Designer N. Pedley.
Date 2002 to date.
21cm (8.25ins) high.
Blue, lemon and white.
(Royal Doulton web price £125)
Retail £125.

HN4403
Samantha
Fourth Version
Designer N. Pedley.
Date 2002 to date.
21cm (8.25ins) high.
Pale pink.
(Royal Doulton web price £125)
(Ebay 6.7.04 sold £50)
Est. £70-100.

HN4408
Scarlett
Designer N. Pedley.
Date 2002 to date.
20.5cm (8ins) high.
Red.
(Royal Doulton web price £175)
Retail £175.

HN4404
Gillian
Fourth Version
Designer N. Pedley.
Date 2002 - 03.
21cm (8.25ins) high.
Green, yellow and white.
(Royal Doulton web price £120)
Retail £120.

HN4409
Perfect Gift
Designer N. Pedley.
Date 2002 to date.
20.5cm (8ins) high.
Pale pink and white.
Series: Name Your Own.
(Royal Doulton web price £87.50)
Retail £87.50.

HN4405
Angela
Fifth Version
Designer N. Pedley.
Date 2002 - 03.
20.5cm (8ins) high.
White and pale green.
(Royal Doulton web price £120)
Retail £120.

HN4410
Policeman
Designer A. Hughes.
Date 2001 - 03.
22cm (8.75ins) high.
Dark blue, white and tan.
Est. £90-125.

HN4411
Fireman
Designer A. Hughes.
Date 2002 - 03.
20.5cm (8ins) high.
Dark blue, yellow and tan.
Est. £110-150.

HN4416
Porthos
Designer A. Hughes.
Date 2001. Limited edition of 950.
24cm (9.5ins) high.
Brown, tan and white.
Comm: Doulton-Direct.
Est. £150-200.

HN4412
Judge
Second Version
Designer A. Hughes.
Date 2002 to date.
17cm (6.75ins) high.
Red, blue, white and brown.
(Royal Doulton web price £143.50)
Retail £143.50.

HN4417
D'Artagnan
Second Version
Designer A. Hughes.
Date 2001. Limited edition
of 950.
22cm (8.75ins) high.
Brown, tan and white.
Comm: Doulton-Direct.
Est. £150-200.

HN4413
Sleepyhead
Third Version
Designer A. Hughes.
Date 2002 to date.
15cm (6ins) high.
White.
Series: Images.
(Royal Doulton web price £29)
Retail £29.

HN4418
Railway Sleeper
Designer T. Potts.
Date 2001. Limited edition of 2,500.
18cm (7ins) high.
Brown, black and green.
Series: Nostalgia.
Comm: Doulton-Direct.
(Royal Doulton web price £195)
Retail £195.

HN4414
Athos
Designer A. Hughes.
Date 2001. Limited edition of 950.
22cm (8.75ins) high.
Black, cream and white.
Comm: Doulton-Direct.
Est. £150-200.

HN4420
**Prince Albert, Duke of York
(Wedding Day)**
Designer V. Annand.
Date 2002. Limited edition of 1,000.
23cm (9ins) high.
Blue, purple, white and gold.
(Sold as a pair with HN4421)
(Royal Doulton web price £420)
Retail £420 pair.

HN4415
Aramis
Designer A. Hughes.
Date 2001. Limited edition of 950.
23.5cm (9.25ins) high.
Dark blue, black and white.
Comm: Doulton-Direct.
Est. £150-200.

HN4421
**Elizabeth Bowes-Lyon
(Wedding Day)**
Designer V. Annand.
Date 2002. Limited edition of 1,000.
21cm (8.25ins) high.
White, gold and purple.
(Sold as a pair with HN4420)
(Royal Doulton web price £420)
Retail £420 pair.

HN4422
Christmas Day 2002
Designer V. Annand.
Date 2002.
20.5cm (8.25ins) high.
Red, white, green and cream.
Series: Christmas Figures.
Est. £85-110.

HN4428
Here A Little Child I Stand
Second Version
Designer V. Annand.
Date 2002. Limited edition of 1,000.
12cm (4.75ins) high.
Blue, green and pink.
Series: Leslie Harradine Tribute.
Comm: Doulton-Direct.
Est. £65-85.

HN4423
Jenny
Designer V. Annand.
Date 2002 to date.
20.5cm (8ins) high.
Lilac.
Series: Chelsea.
(Royal Doulton web price £95)
(Ebay 28.5.04. sold £48.50)
Est. £50-85.

HN4429
**Do You Wonder Where
The Fairies Are**
Second Version
Designer V. Annand.
Date 2002. Limited edition of 1,000.
12cm (4.75ins) high.
Green and yellow.
Series: Leslie Harradine Tribute.
Comm: Doulton-Direct.
Est. £65-85.

HN4424
Antique Dealer
Designer V. Annand.
Date 2002 to date.
17cm (6.75ins) high.
Grey, red and brown.
(Royal Doulton web price £143.50)
*(Auction ASH 26.9.04 sold £105
plus comm.)*
Est. £115-140.

HN4430
Special Moments
Designer C. Froud.
Date 2002 to date.
21.5cm (8.5ins) high.
Pink and white.
(Royal Doulton web price £135)
Retail £135.

HN4426
Elizabeth
Third Version
Designer J. Bromley.
Date 2003.
21cm (8.25ins) high.
Peach, yellow and white.
Series: Figure of the Year.
*(Auction W&H 27.9.04 sold £50
plus comm.)*
Est. £65-100.

HN4431
Jasmine
Fourth Version
Designer C. Froud.
Date 2002 to date.
20.5cm (8ins) high.
Red and white.
(Royal Doulton web price £165)
Retail £165.

HN4427
Baby's First Christmas
Designer V. Annand.
Date 2002 - 03.
10cm (4ins) high.
White, red and green.
Series: Name Your Own.
Est. £25-35.

HN4442
Cherish
Designer A. Maslankowski.
Date 2002.
15cm (6ins) high.
White.
Series: 1. Club Membership Figure.
2. Sentiments.
(Ebay 22.8.04. sold £29)
Est. £30-50.

HN4443
Happy Holidays
Designer A. Maslankowski.
Date 2002 - 03.
16cm (6.25ins) high.
White.
Series: Sentiments.
Marketed in Canada.
Est £40-50.

HN4448
Father and Son
Designer A. Maslankowski.
Date 2002 - 03.
22cm (8.75ins) high.
White.
Series: Images.
(Royal Doulton web price £69)
(Ebay 23.5.04. sold £40)
Est. £40-70.

HN4444
Witch
Second Version
Designer A. Maslankowski.
Date 2002 - 03.
25cm (9.75ins) high.
Dark blue, black and dark red.
Est. £120-160.

HN4449
A Gift For You
Designer A. Maslankowski.
Date 2002 to date.
15cm (6ins) high.
White.
Series: Images.
(Royal Doulton web price £29)
Retail £29.

HN4445
Charmed
Designer A. Maslankowski.
Date 2003.
14cm (5.5ins) high.
White.
Series: 1. Club Membership Gift.
2. Sentiments.
(Auction W&H 27.9.04 sold £28
plus comm.)
Est. £35-50.

HN4450
Linda
Fifth Version
Designer N. Pedley.
Date 2002.
21cm (8.25ins) high.
Blue.
Series: M. Doulton Events.
Est. £85-110.

HN4446
Gift of Friendship
Designer A. Maslankowski.
Date 2003.
14cm (5.5ins) high.
White.
Series: Images Figure of
the Year.
Est. £35-50.

HN4451
Spring Morning
Third Version
Designer N. Pedley.
Date 2002 - 03.
20.5cm (8ins) high.
Green and white.
Series: Charity (Breast Cancer)
Est. £70-95.

HN4447
Christmas Dreams
Designer A. Maslankowski.
Date 2002 - 03.
15cm (6ins) high.
White.
Series: Images.
Est. £20-30.

HN4452
Suzanne
Second Version
Designer N. Pedley.
Date 2002.
21cm (8.25ins) high.
Yellow.
(Ebay 25.5.04. sold £65)
Est £70-95.

*Picture
not available
at present*

HN4453
Pride of Scotland
Designer N. Pedley.
Date 2002 to date.
20.5cm (8ins) high.
White, purple and lilac.
(Royal Doulton web price £125)
(Ebay 3.10.04 sold £87.50)
Est. £90-125.

HN4459
Lucy
Fourth Version
Designer N. Pedley.
Date 2002 to date.
20.5cm (8ins) high.
Lilac and white.
(Royal Doulton web price £120)
Retail £120.

HN4454
From The Heart
Designer N. Pedley.
Date 2002.
14.5cm (5.75ins) high.
Light blue.
Est. £40-50.

HN4461
Stephanie
Third Version
Designer N. Pedley.
Date 2002 to date.
20.5cm (8ins) high.
Pale green, yellow and white
(Royal Doulton web price £120)
Retail £120.

HN4456
Chloe
Fourth Version
Designer N. Pedley.
Date 2002 to date.
20.5cm (8ins) high.
Pale green and white.
(Royal Doulton web price £105)
Retail £105.

HN4463
Eleanor
Third Version
Designer N. Pedley.
Date 2003.
20.5cm (8ins) high.
Green and white.
Series: M. Doulton Events.
Est. £70-90.

HN4457
Georgia
Designer N. Pedley.
Date 2002 to date.
20.5cm (8ins) high.
Yellow and white.
(Ebay 6.7.04 sold £50)
(Royal Doulton web price £115)
Est. £55-85.

HN4464
Happy Birthday 2003
Designer N. Pedley.
Date 2003.
20.5cm (8ins) high.
Lilac and lemon.
Series: Happy Birthday.
(Auction ASH 19.9.04 sold £45
plus comm.)
Est. £50-80.

HN4458
Isabel
Second Version
Designer N. Pedley.
Date 2002 to date.
21cm (8.25ins) high.
Blue and white.
(Royal Doulton web price £125)
(Ebay 3.6.04. sold £46)
Est. £55-95.

HN4465
Lights Out
Second Version
Designer N. Pedley.
Date 2003.
16cm (6.25ins) high.
Pale blue, green, tan and white.
Series: RDICC.
Est. £50-70.

HN4466
The Recital
Designer N. Pedley.
Date 2003.
21cm (8.25ins) high.
Purple and cream.
Series: RDICC.
Est. £80-115.

HN4474
Queen Mary II
(Wife of William of Orange)
Designer P. Parsons.
Date 2002. Limited edition of 2,500.
22cm (8.75ins) high.
Purple, red, blue and gold.
Series: Stuart Queens.
Comm: Doulton-Direct.
(Royal Doulton web price £265)
Retail £265.

HN4467
Katrina
Second Version
Designer N. Pedley.
Date 2002 to date.
20.5cm (8ins) high.
Yellow and white.
Series: Vanity Fair Ladies.
(Royal Doulton web price £99)
Retail £99.

HN4475
Queen Victoria
Second Version
Designer P. Parsons.
Date 2003. Limited edition of 950.
14cm (5.5ins) high.
Pink, white and purple.
Comm: Doulton-Direct.
(Royal Doulton web price £275)
Retail £275.

HN4468
Deborah
Third Version
Designer N. Pedley.
Date 2002 to date.
21cm (8.25ins) high.
Blue and lilac.
(Royal Doulton web price £115)
Retail £115.

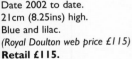

HN4476
HM Queen Elizabeth II
Sixth Version
Designer P. Parsons.
Date 2003. Limited edition of 2,000.
19.5cm (7.75ins) high.
Purple, gold and white.
Comm: Doulton-Direct.
(Royal Doulton web price £295)
Retail £295.

HN4469
Spirit of Scotland
Designer N. Pedley.
Date 2003 to date.
21cm (8.25ins) high.
Lilac and white.
Marketed in Scotland.
(Royal Doulton web price £120)
Retail £120.

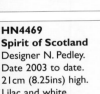

HN4481
Alexander the Great
Designer A. Maslankowski.
Date 2002. Limited edition of 50.
46cm (18ins) high.
Purple, lilac, black, brown and green.
Series: Prestige.
(Royal Doulton web price £12,500)
Retail £12,500.

HN4470
For Someone Special
Designer N. Pedley.
Date 2003.
14cm (5.5ins) high.
Blue and white.
Marketed in Canada.
Est. £40-55.

HN4482
Clever Boy
Designer A. Maslankowski.
Date 2003 to date.
16cm (6.25ins) high.
White.
Series: Images.
(Royal Doulton web price £29)
Retail £29.

HN4483
Clever Girl
Designer A. Maslankowski.
Date 2003 to date.
16cm (6.25ins) high.
White.
Series: Images.
(Royal Doulton web price £29)
Retail £29.

HN4488
Blacksmith
Second Version
Designer P. Parsons.
Date 2003 to date.
21.5cm (8.5ins) high.
White, brown and grey.
(Royal Doulton web price £143.50)
Retail £143.50.

HN4484
Father and Daughter
Designer A. Maslankowski.
Date 2003 to date.
21.5cm (8.5ins) high.
White.
Series: Images.
(Royal Doulton web price £75)
Retail £75.

HN4491
**Little Child So Rare
And Sweet**
Third Version
Designer V. Annand.
Date 2002. Limited edition of 1,000.
12cm (4.75ins) high.
Purple, pink and blue.
Series: Leslie Harradine Tribute.
Comm: Doulton-Direct.
Est. £65-85.

HN4485
Unity
Designer A. Maslankowski.
Date 2003.
17cm (6.75ins) high.
White.
Series: 1. Images.
2. Save the Children Charity.
Est. £65-90.

HN4492
Dancing Eyes and Sunny Hair
Second Version
Designer V. Annand.
Date 2002. Limited edition of 1,000.
12cm (4.75ins) high.
Pale green and blue.
Series: Leslie Harradine Tribute.
Comm: Doulton-Direct.
Est. £65-85.

HN4486
Charge of the Light Brigade
Second Version
Designer A. Maslankowski.
Date 2002. Limited edition of 500.
19.5cm (7.75ins) high.
Brown, blue, grey and green.
(Royal Doulton website price £945)
Retail £945.

HN4493
Annabel Vision in Red
Designer V. Annand.
Date 2003 to date.
21cm (8.25ins) high.
Red.
Series: Chelsea.
Marketed in Canada.
Est. £50-70.

HN4487
Farmer
Second Version
Designer A. Hughes.
Date 2003 to date.
20.5cm (8ins) high.
Brown, black, green, tan and white.
(Royal Doulton web price £143.50)
Retail £143.50.

HN4494
Home Guard
Designer V. Annand.
Date 2002. Limited edition of 2,500.
22cm (8.75ins) high.
Khaki and tan.
Series: Nostalgia.
Comm: Doulton-Direct.
(Royal Doulton web price £195)
Retail £195.

HN4495
Auxilliary Territorial Service
Designer V. Annand.
Date 2002. Limited edition of 2,500.
22cm (8.75ins) high.
Khaki and tan.
Series: Nostalgia.
Comm: Doulton-Direct.
(Royal Doulton web price £195)
(Auction ASH 22.8.04 sold £70
plus comm.)
Est. £95-155.

HN4500
Nadine
Second Version
Designer V. Annand.
Date 2003 to date.
21.5cm (8.5ins) high.
Black.
Series: In Vogue.
(Royal Doulton web price £99)
Retail £99.

HN4496
Taylor
Designer V. Annand.
Date 2003 to date.
21cm (8.25ins) high.
Pale yellow and blue.
Series: In Vogue.
(Royal Doulton web price £125)
(Ebay 19.8.04 sold £55)
Est. £60-100.

HN4501
Forever Yours
Second Version
Designer J. Bromley.
Date 2002 - 03.
22cm (8.75ins) high.
Pink.
Other colourways:
'Best Wishes' HN3971;
'Kate' HN4233.
Est. £65-90.

HN4497
Helen of Troy
Second Version
Designer V. Annand.
Date 2002. Limited edition of 950.
25cm (9.75ins) high.
White, yellow, tan and pink.
Series: Greek Mythology.
Comm: Doulton-Direct.
(Royal Doulton web price £199)
Retail £199.

HN4510
The Pilot Skipper
Designer Not known.
Date 2002.
17cm (6.75ins) high.
Yellow, white, grey and brown.
Comm: Pilot Insurance.
Est. £110-145.

HN4498
Women's Royal Navy Service
Designer V. Annand.
Date 2003. Limited edition of 2,500.
23cm (9ins) high.
Brown and dark blue.
Series: Nostalgia.
Comm: Doulton-Direct.
(Royal Doulton web price £195)
(Auction ASH 26.9.04 sold £80 plus
comm.) (Ebay 23.5.04. sold £98)
Est. £100-155.

HN4511
Fisherman
Designer M. Alcock.
Date 2003 to date.
18cm (7ins) high.
Brown, green and grey.
(Royal Doulton web price
£136.50)
(Auction ASH 22.8.04 sold £66
plus comm.)
Est. £90-125.

HN4499
Alana
Designer V. Annand.
Date 2003 to date.
21.5cm (8.5ins) high.
Black.
Series: In Vogue.
(Royal Doulton web price £99)
Retail £99.

HN4517
Footballer
Designer M. Alcock.
Date 2004 to date.
21cm (8.25ins) high.
White.
Series: Images.
(Royal Doulton web price £54)
Retail £54.

HN4518
Cricketer
Second Version
Designer M. Alcock.
Date 2004 to date.
21cm (8.25ins) high.
White.
Series: Images.
(Royal Doulton web price £49)
Retail £49.

HN4523
Faye
Designer N. Pedley.
Date 2003 to date.
21.5cm (8.5ins) high.
Green, grey and white.
(Royal Doulton web price £105)
Retail £105.

HN4519
Hockey Player
Designer M. Alcock.
Date 2004 to date.
21cm (8.25ins) high.
White.
Series: Images.
Est. £30-40.

HN4524
Jayne
Second Version
Designer N. Pedley.
Date 2003 to date.
20.5cm (8ins) high.
Pink and white.
Series: Vanity Fair Ladies.
(Royal Doulton web price £49.50)
(Ebay 10.6.04. sold £51)
Est. £50-75.

HN4520
April
Fifth Version
Designer N. Pedley.
Date 2003 to date.
21.5cm (8.5ins) high.
Pink and white.
(Royal Doulton web price £140)
Retail £140.

HN4525
Lisa
Second Version
Designer N. Pedley.
Date 2003 to date.
21cm (8.25ins) high.
White and yellow.
(Royal Doulton web price £99)
(Ebay 5.7.04. sold £59)
Est. £60-95.

HN4521
Ruby
Second Version
Designer N. Pedley.
Date 2003 to date.
21cm (8.25ins) high.
Red.
(Royal Doulton web price £135)
(Ebay 30.9.04 sold £63)
Est. £65-110.

HN4526
Christine
Seventh Version
Designer N. Pedley.
Date 2003.
21cm (8.25ins) high.
Blue and white.
Other colourways:
'Gillian' HN4404.
Comm: G.U.S.
Est. £65-85.

HN4522
Anne Marie
Designer N. Pedley.
Date 2003 to date.
21cm (8.25ins) high.
Green and white.
(Royal Doulton web price £115)
Retail £115.

HN4527
Nicole
Third Version
Designer N. Pedley.
Date 2003 to date.
21cm (8.25ins) high.
Pink and purple.
(Royal Doulton web price £160)
Retail £160.

HN4528
Hapy Birthday 2004
Designer N. Pedley.
Date 2004.
21cm (8.25ins) high.
Yellow.
Series: Happy Birthday.
(Royal Doulton web price £100)
Retail £100

HN4533
Beautiful Blossom
Designer J. Bromley.
Date 2003 to date.
22cm (8.75ins) high.
Lilac.
(Royal Doulton web price £160)
Retail £160.

HN4529
Love of Life
Designer N. Pedley.
Date 2003 - 04.
22cm (8.75ins) high.
Pink and white.
Series: Charity (Breast Cancer)
(Royal Doulton web price £130)
Retail £130.

HN4538
A Winter's Morn
Designer J. Bromley.
Date 2004.
22cm (8.75ins) high.
Red and white.
Other colourways: HN4622
Comm: Compton/Woodhouse.
Est. £90-125.

HN4530
Moonlight Serenade
Designer J. Bromley.
Date 2003 to date.
22.5cm (8.75ins) high.
Blue and white.
(Royal Doulton web price £160)
Retail £160.

HN4539
Megan
Third Version
Designer J. Bromley.
Date 2004.
22cm (8.75ins) high.
Mauve, white and lilac.
Series: Lady of the Year.
Comm: Compton/Woodhouse.
Est. £85-115.

HN4531
Message of Love
Designer J. Bromley.
Date 2003 to date.
23.5cm (9.25ins) high.
Purple, pink and white.
(Royal Doulton web price £185)
Retail £185.

HN4540
Merlin
Designer S. Ridge.
Date 2003. Limited edition of 950.
25cm (9.75ins) high.
Yellow, grey, brown and green.
Comm: Doulton-Direct.
(Royal Doulton web price £250)
Retail £250.

HN4532
Susan
Fifth Version
Designer J. Bromley.
Date 2004.
23cm (9ins) high.
Blue and white.
Series: Figure of the Year 2004.
(Royal Doulton web price £120)
(Ebay 10.7.04. sold £78)
Est. £80-115.

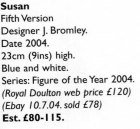

HN4541
King Arthur
Designer S. Ridge.
Date 2003. Limited edition of 950.
23cm (9ins) high.
Brown, tan, white, grey and red.
Comm: Doulton-Direct.
(Royal Doulton web price £295)
Retail £295.

HN4542
Graduate (female)
Second Version
Designer S. Ridge.
Date 2004 to date.
20.5cm (8ins) high.
White.
Series: Images.
(Royal Doulton web price £39)
Retail £39.

HN4553
The Dance
Second Version
Designer V. Annand.
Date 2004.
22cm (8.75ins) high.
Pale blue, white and pink.
Series: RDICC.
Est. £85-115.

HN4543
Graduate (male)
Third Version
Designer S. Ridge.
Date 2004 to date.
20.5cm (8ins) high.
White.
Series: Images.
(Royal Doulton web price £39)
Retail £39.

HN4554
Women's Auxiliary
Air Force
Designer V. Annand.
Date 2003 Limited edition of 2,500.
21cm (8.25ins) high.
Navy, grey and brown.
Series: Nostalgia
Comm: Doulton-Direct.
Est. £125-155.

HN4550
Mikaela
Designer V. Annand.
Date 2003 to date.
21.5cm (8.5ins) high.
Black.
Series: In Vogue.
(Royal Doulton web price £99)
Retail £99.

HN4555
Air Raid Precaution Warden
Designer V. Annand.
Date 2003. Limited edition of 2,500.
14cm (5.5ins) high.
Green grey and brown.
Series: Nostalgia
Comm: Doulton-Direct.
(Royal Doulton web price £195)
Retail £195.

HN4551
Daniella
Designer V. Annand.
Date 2003 to date.
21.5cm (8.5ins) high.
Black.
Series: In Vogue.
(Royal Doulton web price £99)
Retail £99.

HN4556
Hayley
Designer V. Annand.
Date: 2003 to date.
21.5cm (8.5ins) high.
Pink and light green.
Series: Chelsea Collection.
(Royal Doulton web price £130)
Retail £130.

HN4552
Christmas Day 2003
Designer V. Annand.
Date 2003.
22cm (8.75ins) high.
Red and white.
Series: Christmas Figures.
Est. £95-115.

HN4557
Alexandra
Third Version
Designer V. Annand.
Date 2003.
20.5cm (8ins) high.
Blue.
Other colourways:
'Jenny' HN4423.
Comm: G.U.S.
Est. £65-90.

HN4558
Christmas Day 2004
Designer V. Annand.
Date 2004.
21cm (8.25ins) high.
Dark red and white.
Series: Christmas Day.
(Royal Doulton web price £150)
Retail £150.

HN4560
The Secret
Designer A Maslankowski.
Date 2004.
16cm (6.25ins) high.
White.
Series: Image Figure of
the Year.
(Ebay 17.3.04. sold £32)
Est. £35-50.

HN4561
Hercules
Designer A. Maslankowski.
Date 2003. Limited edition of 50.
41cm (16.25ins) high.
Brown, grey and white.
Series: Prestige.
(Royal Doulton web price £10,500)
Retail £10,500.

HN4562
Mother and Daughter
Second Version
Designer A. Maslankowski.
Date 2003 to date.
19cm (7.5ins) high.
White.
Series: Images.
(Royal Doulton web price £65)
Retail £65.

HN4563
Studious Boy
Designer A. Maslankowski.
Date 2003 to date.
8cm (3.25ins) high.
White.
Series: Images.
*(Royal Doulton
web price £39)*
Retail £39.

HN4564
Studious Girl
Designer A. Maslankowski.
Date 2003 to date.
8cm (3.25ins) high.
White.
Series: Images.
*(Royal Doulton
web price £39)*
Retail £39.

HN4565
Hope
Third Version
Designer A. Maslankowski.
Date 2003.
15cm (6ins) high.
White.
Series: Holiday Collection.
Marketed in Canada.
Est. £35-45.

HN4566
Matador and Bull
Second Version
Designer A. Maslankowski.
Date 2004. Limited edition
of 250.
17.5cm (7ins) high.
Black, gold, mauve and yellow.
(Royal Doulton web price £795
A larger version, HN2324
40.6cm is sells for £12500)
Retail £795.

HN4567
Harmony
Third Version
Designer A. Maslankowski.
Date 2004.
18.5cm (7.25ins) high.
White.
Series: 1. Images.
2. Save The Children Charity.
Est. £50-70.

HN4570
Lifeboat Man
Second Version
Designer A. Hughes.
Date 2003 to date.
23cm (9ins) high.
Yellow and brown.
(Royal Doulton web price £136.50)
(Ebay 28.6.04. sold £100)
Est. £110-135.

HN4580
Irish Charm
Designer N. Pedley.
Date 2004 to date.
21.5cm (8.5ins) high.
Green and white.
Series: Classics.
Marketed in Ireland.
Est. £75-100.

HN4585
Thinking of You
Second Version
Designer N. Pedley.
Date 2003 to date.
21.5cm (8.5ins) high.
Lemon.
Series: Name Your Own.
Est. £70-90.

HN4581
Rose
Third Version
Designer N. Pedley.
Date 2004.
21cm (8.25ins) high.
Lemon and orange.
Series: M. Doulton Events.
Est. £75-100.

HN4586
Springtime
Fourth Version
Designer N. Pedley.
Date 2004.
15cm (6ins) high.
Yellow.
Series: Club Membership Figure.
Est. £50-75.

HN4582
Sweet Memories
Designer N. Pedley.
Date 2003 to date.
21cm (8.25ins) high.
Pink and white.
(Royal Doulton web price £125)
Retail £125.

HN4599
Bathing Beauty
Designer N. Pedley.
Date 2003. Limited edition of 200.
18.5cm (7.25ins) high.
Red and pink.
Other colourways: HN4399.
Series: Leslie Harradine Tribute.
Comm: Sinclairs.
Est. £145-195.

HN4583
Jessica
Fourth Version
Designer N. Pedley.
Date 2003 to date.
21.5cm (8.5ins) high.
Red and white.
(Royal Doulton web price £160)
Retail £160.

HN4600
Brighton Belle
Designer N. Pedley.
Date 2003. Limited edition of 200.
18cm (7ins) high.
Yellow and pink.
Other colourways: HN4400.
Series: Leslie Harradine Tribute.
Comm: Sinclairs.
Est. £145-195.

HN4584
Andrea
Second Version
Designer N. Pedley.
Date 2003 to date.
21cm (8.25ins) high.
Pale green.
(Royal Doulton web price £125)
Retail £125.

HN4601
Summer's Darling
Designer N. Pedley.
Date 2003. Limited edition of 200.
11cm (4.25ins) high.
Purple and pink.
Other colourways: HN4401.
Series: Leslie Harradine Tribute.
Comm: Sinclairs.
Est. £145-195.

HN4602
Taking the Waters
Designer N. Pedley.
Date 2003. Limited edition of 200.
16cm (6.25ins) high.
Black.
Other colourways: HN4402.
Series: Leslie Harradine Tribute.
Comm: Sinclairs.
Est. £145-195.

HN4603
Dawn
Fourth Version
Designer N. Pedley.
Date 2004 to date.
21cm (8.25ins) high.
Pink and white.
(Royal Doulton web price £110)
Retail £110.

HN4604
Happy Anniversary
Fourth Version
Designer N. Pedley.
Date 2004 to date.
21cm (8.25ins) high.
Blue, white and silver.
Other colourways:
HN4605, 4606.
Est. £90-130.

HN4605
Happy Anniversary
Fourth Version
Designer N. Pedley.
Date 2004 to date.
21cm (8.25ins) high.
Green and white.
Other colourways:
HN4604, 4606.
Est. £90-130.

HN4606
Happy Anniversary
Fourth Version
Designer N. Pedley.
Date 2004 to date.
21cm (8.25ins) high.
Red, pink and white.
Other colourways:
HN4604, 4605.
Est. £90-130.

HN4607
Magical Moments
Designer N. Pedley.
Date 2004 to date.
14.5cm (5.75ins) high.
Pink.
Marketed in Canada.
Retail: Late for press.

HN4608
Heart of Scotland
Designer N. Pedley.
Date 2004 to date.
20.5cm (8ins) high.
Green and red.
Est. £70-100.

HN4609
Free Spirit
Third Version
Designer N. Pedley.
Date 2004 - 05.
12cm (4.75ins) high.
Purple and white.
Series: Charity (Breast Cancer)
Retail: Late for press.

HN4610
Daybreak
Third Version
Designer N. Welch.
Date 2004 to date.
21cm (8.25ins) high.
White.
Est. £70-100.

*Picture
not available
at present*

HN4611
Moonlight
Designer N. Welch.
Date 2004 to date.
21cm (8.25ins) high.
Blue.
Est. £70-100.

*Picture
not available
at present*

HN4620
Sophie
Sixth Version
Designer J. Bromley.
Date 2004 to date.
21cm (8.25ins) high.
Blue and white.
(Royal Doulton web price £165)
Retail £165.

HN4635
Bowler
Designer T. Potts.
Date 2003. Limited edition of 2,500.
22cm (8.75ins) high.
White and green.
Comm: Doulton-Direct.
Est. £90-130.

HN4621
True Love
Designer J. Bromley.
Date 2004 to date.
21cm (8.25ins) high.
Purple, grey and gold.
(Royal Doulton web price £165)
(Auction ASH 19.9.04 sold £50 plus comm.)
Est. £70-135.

HN4641
Lady Godiva
Designer A. Maslankowski.
Date 2004 (Limited edition of 50)
35cm (13.75ins) high.
43cm (17ins) long.
White, grey, red, gold and brown.
Series: Classics.
Retail: Late for press.

HN4622
A Winter's Morn
Designer J. Bromley.
Date 2004.
22cm (8.75ins) high.
White.
Other colourways: HN4538.
Comm: Compton/Woodhouse.
Est. £70-125.

HN4643
Best Friends
Third Version
Designer A. Maslankowski.
Date 2004 to date.
21cm (8.25ins) high.
White.
Series: Images.
Retail: Late for press.

HN4624
Eleanor
Fourth Version
Designer J. Bromley.
Date 2004 to date.
22cm (8.75ins) high.
Dark red and pink.
Series: Classics.
Retail: Late for press.

HN4644
Two Become One
Designer A. Maslankowski.
Date 2004 to date.
26cm (10.25ins) high.
White.
Series: Images.
Retail: Late for press.

HN4625
Sweet Devotion
Designer J. Bromley.
Date 2004 to date.
Height not known.
Pink, black and white.
Comm: Home Shopping Exclusives.
Retail: Late for press.

HN4645
Family
Second Version
Designer A. Maslankowski.
Date 2004 to date.
26cm (10.25ins) high.
White.
Series: Images.
Retail: Late for press.

HN4650
Country Veterinary
Designer M. Alcock.
Date 2004 to date.
23cm (9ins) high.
Brown, black and white.
Series: Classics.
Retail: Late for press.

HN4663
Fleur
Designer N. Pedley.
Date 2004 to date.
20cm (7.75ins) high.
Pink and white.
Series: Classics.
Retail: Late for press.

HN4651
Town Veterinary
Designer M. Alcock.
Date 2004 to date.
14cm (5.5ins) high.
White, lilac and black.
Series: Classics.
Retail: Late for press.

HN4664
Abigail
Second Version
Designer N. Pedley.
Date 2004 to date.
21cm (8.25ins) high.
Red.
Series: Classics.
Retail: Late for press.

HN4660
Summer's Dream
Designer N. Pedley.
Date 2004 - 05.
21cm (8.25ins) high.
Orange and white.
Series: Charity (Breast Cancer)
Retail: Late for press.

HN4665
Laura
Designer N. Pedley.
Date 2004 to date.
21cm (8.25ins) high.
Pale turquoise and white.
Retail: Late for press.

HN4661
Naomi
Designer N. Pedley.
Date 2004 to date.
21cm (8.25ins) high.
Pale pink and white.
Series: Classics.
Retail: Late for press.

HN4666
Caitlyn
Designer N. Pedley.
Date 2004 to date.
21cm (8.25ins) high.
Dark red/black.
Series: Classics.
Retail: Late for press.

HN4662
Rosemary
Designer N. Pedley.
Date 2004 to date.
21cm (8.25ins) high.
Lilac and pink.
Retail: Late for press.

HN4667
Alison
Third Version
Designer N. Pedley.
Date 2004 to date.
Height not known.
Gold.
Comm: Home Shopping Exclusives.
Retail: Late for press.

ᘓᘏᘓ ADDENDA ᘓᘏᘓ

These four figurines were issued recently by Royal Doulton and we were not able to put them in their numerical order.

HN4018
Alison
Second Version
Designer N. Pedley.
Date 2004 to date.
Height not known.
Turquoise, pale green
and white.
Comm: Compton Woodhouse.
Retail: Late for press.

HN4559
Rose Garden
Designer V. Annand.
Date 2004 (Limited
edition of 250)
24cm (9.5ins) high.
35.5cm (13.75ins)
long.
Multicoloured.
Series: Classics.
Retail: Late for press.

HN4535
Simone
Second Version
Designer J. Bromley.
Date 2004 to date.
Height not known.
White.
Series: Sensual Collection.
Comm: Home Shopping Exclusives.
Retail: Late for press.

HN4712
Welsh Lady
Designer V. Annand.
Date 2004 to date.
21.5cm (8.5ins) high.
Red, white, grey and black.
Other colourways:
'Wales' HN3630.
Retail: Late for press.

AIL
SERIES

AIL1
Kiss
Designer A Maslankowski.
Date 2000. Limited edition of 950.
37.5cm (14.75ins) high.
White Parian.
Series: Art Is Life.
Est. £140-170.

AIL9
Ballerina
Designer A Maslankowski.
Date 2000. Limited edition of 1,250.
30.5cm (12ins) high.
White Parian.
Series: Art Is Life.
Est. £140-170.

AIL2
Love
Designer A Maslankowski.
Date 2000. Limited edition of 950.
29cm (11.5ins) high.
White Parian.
Series: Art Is Life.
Est. £140-170.

AIL10
Ballet Dancer
Designer A Maslankowski.
Date 2000. Limited edition of 1,250.
35.5cm (14ins) high.
White Parian.
Series: Art Is Life.
Est. £140-170.

AIL6
Girl Stretching
Designer A Maslankowski.
Date 2000. Limited edition of 2,000.
28cm (11.25ins) high.
White Parian.
Series: Art Is Life.
Est. £125-155.

This book can be purchased through
Bookshops, Antique Centres and Antique &
Collectors Fairs throughout the UK, but if you have a
problem in obtaining a copy please contact us on our
website www.bookbasket.co.uk or write to us at
Gemini Publications Ltd. 30a Monmouth Street,
Bath, BA1 2AN, England, UK.
Tel: 01225 484877
and from abroad +44 (0)1225 484877.
Email sales@bookbasket.co.uk

AIL7
Girl With Pony Tail
Designer A Maslankowski.
Date 2000. Limited edition of 2,000.
27cm (10.75ins) high.
White Parian.
Series: Art Is Life.
Est. £125-155.

Foreign Currency Rates at 8th October 2004:
A simple calculation to find the difference on a daily rate
is as follows:
£100 x 1.79 = $179 US Dollars
£100 x 1.45 = €145 Euros
£100 x 2.25 = $225 Canadian Dollar
£100 x 2.46 = $246 Australian Dollar
Example: A Figurine; estimated cost £120 would be
calculated: £120 x 1.79 (US current rate) = $214.80 in US
dollars. To find the rate in reverse, divide the rate,
$100 divided by 1.79 = £55.87 GB Pounds.

AIL8
Girl On Rock
Designer A Maslankowski.
Date 2000 Limited edition of 2,000.
23cm (9ins) high.
White Parian.
Series: Art Is Life.
Est. £100-130.

Pictures and Images
We are asking our readers to aid us in the next
edition by sending in any photographs available for
any of the HN figures that are missing in this book.
A prize draw will be organised at the end of the year
where those people who send in pictures will be put
into the draw and the first one out of the hat
will receive £100 and the next 20 will receive
a free copy of the next edition.

CL
SERIES

CL3980
Isobel
Designer T. Potts.
Date 1997 - 99.
26.5cm (10.5ins) high.
Yellow and blue.
Other colourways:
'Annabel' CL3981.
Est. £90-120.

CL3985
Stephanie
Designer T. Potts.
Date 1998 - 2001.
26.5cm (10.5ins) high.
Pink, lilac, grey and gold.
Other colourways:
'Faye' CL3984.
Est. £90-120.

CL3981
Annabel
Designer T. Potts.
Date 1998 - 2001.
26.5cm (10.5ins) high.
Yellow, grey and black.
Other colourways:
'Isobel' CL3980.
Est. £90-120.

CL3986
Felicity
Designer T. Potts.
Date 1997 - 99.
26.5cm (10.5ins) high.
Tan, yellow and pink.
Other colourways: 'CL4103';
'Bethany' CL3987.
Est. £90-120.

CL3982
Susanne
Designer T. Potts.
Date 1997 - 98.
26.5cm (10.5ins) high.
Yellow and peach.
Other colourways:
'Lucinda' CL3983.
Est. £90-120.

CL3987
Bethany
Designer T. Potts.
Date 1997 - 98.
26.5cm (10.5ins) high.
Yellow.
Other colourways:
'Felicity' CL3986, 4103.
Est. £90-120.

CL3983
Lucinda
Designer T. Potts.
Date 1998 - 2001.
26.5cm (10.5ins) high.
Green, tan, grey and cream.
Other colourways:
'Susanne' CL3982.
Est. £90-120.

CL3988
Penelope
Designer T. Potts.
Date 1997 - 99.
26.5cm (10.5ins) high.
Pink and gold.
Other colourways:
'Vanessa' CL3989.
Est. £90-120.

CL3984
Faye
Designer T. Potts.
Date 1998 - 2002.
26.5cm (10.5ins) high.
Green and white.
Other colourways:
'Stephanie' CL3985.
Est. £90-120.

CL3989
Vanessa
Designer T. Potts.
Date 1998 - 2001.
26.5cm (10.5ins) high.
White, lilac, grey and brown.
Other colourways:
'Penelope' CL3988.
Est. £90-120.

CL3990
From This Day Forth
Designer T. Potts.
Date 1997 - 99.
26.5cm (10.5ins) high.
White.
Est. £90-120.

CL3995
Kate
Designer T. Potts.
Date 1998 - 2000.
28cm (11ins) high.
Pink, white, grey and green.
Other colourways:
'Naomi' CL3996.
Est. £90-120.

CL3991
Christina
Designer T. Potts.
Date 1998 - 2001.
28.5cm (11.25ins) high.
Pink, grey and cream.
Other colourways:
'Theresa' CL3992.
Est. £90-120.

CL3996
Naomi
Designer T. Potts.
Date 1998 - 2001.
28cm (11ins) high.
Pink and cream.
Other colourways:
'Kate' CL3995.
Est. £90-120.

CL3992
Theresa
Designer T. Potts.
Date 1998 - 2000.
28.5cm (11.25ins) high.
Lemon, lilac and grey.
Other colourways:
'Christina' CL3991.
Est. £90-120.

CL3997
Lorna
Designer T. Potts.
Date 1998 - 99.
25.5cm (10ins) high.
Brown, grey and pink.
Other colourways:
'Harriet' CL3998.
Est. £90-120.

CL3993
Julia
Designer T. Potts.
Date 1998 - 2001.
28cm (11ins) high.
Pink and grey.
Other colourways:
'Chloe' CL4017;
'Helena' CL3994.
Est. £90-120.

CL3998
Harriet
Designer T. Potts.
Date 1998 - 2001.
25.5cm (10ins) high.
Green, tan and brown.
Other colourways:
'Lorne' CL3997.
Est. £90-120.

CL3994
Helena
Designer T. Potts.
Date 1998 - 2001.
27.5cm (11ins) high.
Peach, lilac and grey.
Other colourways:
'Chloe' CL4017;
'Julia' CL3993.
Est. £90-120.

CL3999
Virginia
Designer T. Potts.
Date 1998 - 99.
26.5cm (10.5ins) high.
Pale blue and grey.
Other colourways:
'Nicola' CL4000.
Est. £90-120.

CL4000
Nicola
Designer T. Potts.
Date 1998 - 2000.
26.5cm (10.5ins) high.
Lilac, grey and gold.
Other colourways:
'Virginia' CL3999.
Est. £90-120.

CL4005
Bernadette
Designer T. Potts.
Date 1999 - 2001.
28cm (11ins) high.
White, grey and orange.
Est. £90-120.

CL4001
Frances
Designer T. Potts.
Date 1998 - 99.
21.5cm (8.5ins) high.
Lemon and pink.
Other colourways:
'Eve' CL4002.
(Ebay 7.9.04 sold £103)
Est. £90-130.

CL4006
Tanya
Designer T. Potts.
Date 1999 - 2001.
28cm (11ins) high.
Red, grey and white.
Est. £90-120.

CL4002
Eve
Designer T. Potts.
Date 1998 - 2001.
21.5cm (8.5ins) high.
Green and grey.
Other colourways:
'Frances' CL4001.
Est. £90-120.

CL4007
Anyone For Tennis?
Designer T. Potts.
Date 1999 - 2001.
25.5cm (10ins) high.
Lilac, grey and white.
Est. £90-120.

CL4003
To Love and To Cherish
Designer T. Potts.
Date 1999 - 2001.
29cm (11.5ins) high.
Cream, pink and grey.
Est. £90-120.

CL4008
To The Fairway
Designer T. Potts.
Date 1999 - 2001.
25.5cm (10ins) high.
Blue, yellow, green, grey and red.
Est. £90-120.

CL4004
Simone
Designer T. Potts.
Date 1999 - 2001.
29cm (11.5ins) high.
Pink, grey, brown and yellow.
Est. £90-120.

CL4009
Elizabeth
Designer T. Potts.
Date 2000 - 02.
25.5cm (10ins) high.
Blue and lilac.
Est. £90-120.

CL4010
Philippa
Designer T. Potts.
Date 2000 - 02.
25.5cm (10ins) high.
Grey, white and silver.
(Ebay 3.10.04 sold £82)
Est. £90-120.

CL4016
Victoria
Designer T. Potts.
Date 2001 - 02.
28.5cm (11.25ins) high.
Blue, brown and gold.
Est. £90-120.

CL4011
Celebration
Designer T. Potts.
Date 2000 - 02.
25.5cm (10ins) high.
Silver, gold, grey and white.
Est. £90-120.

CL4017
Chloe
Designer T. Potts.
Date 2001 - 02.
27.5cm (10.75ins) high.
Black, grey and white.
Other colourways:
'Helena' CL3994;
'Julia' CL3993.
Comm: Compton/Woodhouse.
Est. £90-120.

CL4012
Gabrielle
Designer T. Potts.
Date 2000 - 01.
25.5cm (10ins) high.
Peach, lilac, grey and mauve.
Est. £90-120.

CL4103
Felicity
Designer T. Potts.
Date 2000.
26.5cm (10.5ins) high.
Bronze.
Other colourways: CL3986;
'Bethany' CL3987.
Est. £90-120.

CL4013
Taking the Reins
Designer T. Potts.
Date 2001 - 02.
29cm (11.5ins) high.
Lilac, black, beige, brown
and purple.
Est. £90-120.

CL4014
At the Races
Designer T. Potts.
Date 2001 - 02.
30.5cm (12ins) high.
Pink and grey.
Est. £90-120.

Foreign Currency Rates at 8th October 2004 was:
A simple calculation to find the difference on a daily rate
is as follows:
£100 x 1.79 = $179 US Dollars
£100 x 1.45 = €145 Euros
£100 x 2.25 = $225 Canadian Dollar
£100 x 2.46 = $246 Australian Dollar
Example: A Figurine; estimated cost £120 would be
calculated: £120 x 1.79 (US current rate) = $214.80 in US
dollars. To find the rate in reverse, divide the rate,
$100 divided by 1.79 = £55.87 GB Pounds.

The No.1 antiques and collectables magazine

Discover the hottest topics and latest happenings in the trade, all in one magazine – Antiques and Collectables is packed full of fascinating features written by experts, informative series and vital fairs and auctions listings. It's the must read monthly magazine for anyone interested in the antiques world whether you're a serious dealer or enthusiastic collector.

Subscriptions 01225 786814

Advertising 01225 786810

Antiques and Collectables, Units 3-4 Riverside Court, Lower Bristol Road, Bath, BA2 3DZ

www.antiques-collectables.co.uk

Antiques & Collectables is published by Merrick's Media on the second Wednesday of every month.

M SERIES

M1
Victorian Lady
Designer L. Harradine.
Date 1932 - 45.
9.5cm (3.75ins) high.
Green and pink.
Other colourways: M2, 25.
Est. £150-200.

M6
Sweet Anne
Designer L. Harradine.
Date 1932 - 45.
10cm (4ins) high.
Blue.
Other colourways: M5, 27.
Est. £150-200.

M2
Victorian Lady
Designer L. Harradine.
Date 1932 - 45.
9.5cm (3.75ins) high.
Green and lilac.
Other colourways: M1, 25.
(Auction PSA 23.6.04. sold £105 plus comm.)
Est. £150-200.

M7
Patricia
Designer L. Harradine.
Date 1932 - 45.
10cm (4ins) high.
Green and pink.
Other colourways: M8, 28.
(Auction PSA 22.10.03. sold £165 plus comm.)
Est. £200-265.

M3
Paisley Shawl
Designer L. Harradine.
Date 1932 - 38.
10cm (4ins) high.
Lilac.
Other colourways: M4, 26.
(Auction PSA 22.10.03. sold £120 plus comm.)
Est. £150-200.

M8
Patricia
Designer L. Harradine.
Date 1932 - 38.
10cm (4ins) high.
Yellow and orange.
Other colourways: M7, 28.
Est. £200-265.

M4
Paisley Shawl
Designer L. Harradine.
Date 1932 - 45.
10cm (4ins) high.
Green and lilac.
Other colourways:
M3, M26.
(Auction PSA 23.6.04. sold £95 plus comm.)
Est. £150-200.

M9
Chloe
Designer L. Harradine.
Date 1932 - 45.
7cm (2.75ins) high.
Pink.
Other colourways: M10, 29.
Est. £200-265.

M5
Sweet Anne
Designer L. Harradine.
Date 1932 - 45.
10cm (4ins) high.
Lilac and green.
Other colourways: M6, 27.
Est. £150-200.

M10
Chloe
Designer L. Harradine.
Date 1932 - 45.
7cm (2.75ins) high.
Lilac.
Other colourways: M9, 29.
Est. £200-265.

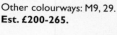

M11
Bridesmaid
Designer L. Harradine.
Date 1932 - 38.
9.5cm (3.75ins) high.
Pink and lilac.
Other colourways: M12, 30.
Est. £160-210.

M16
Pantalettes
Designer L. Harradine.
Date 1932 - 45.
9.5cm (3.75ins) high.
Pink.
Other colourways: M15, 31.
Est. £160-210.

M12
Bridesmaid
Designer L. Harradine.
Date 1932 - 45.
9.5cm (3.75ins) high.
Yellow and lilac.
Other colourways: M11, 30.
*(Auction PSA 23.6.04. sold £120
and 1.9.04 sold £95 plus comm.)*
Est. £140-170.

M17
Shepherd
Second Version (Model 470)
Designer L. Harradine.
Date 1932 - 38.
9.5cm (3.75ins) high.
Pink, green and purple.
Other colourways:
HN709, M19.
Est. £1100-1500.

M13
Priscilla
Designer L. Harradine.
Date 1932 - 38.
10cm (4ins) high.
Yellow and green.
Other colourways: M14, 24.
*(Auction PSA 22.10.03. sold £190
plus comm.)*
Est. £240-300.

M18
Shepherdess
First Version (Model 469)
Designer L. Harradine.
Date 1932 - 38.
9cm (3.5ins) high.
Green and lilac.
Other colourways:
HN708, M20.
Est. £1100-1500.

M14
Priscilla
Designer L. Harradine.
Date 1932 - 45.
10cm (4ins) high.
Lilac and pink.
Other colourways: M13, 24.
(Ebay 7.9.04 sold £235)
Est. £240-300.

M19
Shepherd
Second Version (Model 470)
Designer L. Harradine.
Date 1932 - 38.
9.5cm (3.75ins) high.
Brown, purple and green.
Other colourways:
HN709, M17.
Est. £1100-1500.

M15
Pantalettes
Designer L. Harradine.
Date 1932 - 45.
9.5cm (3.75ins) high.
Lilac.
Other colourways: M16, 31.
Est. £160-210.

M20
Shepherdess
First Version (Model 469)
Designer L. Harradine.
Date 1932 - 38.
9.5cm (3.75ins) high.
Yellow.
Other colourways:
HN708, M18.
Est. £1100-1500.

M21
Polly Peachum
Third Version (Model 462)
Designer L. Harradine.
Date 1932 - 45.
5.5cm (2.25ins) high.
Pink.
Other colourways:
HN698, 699, 757,
758, 759, 760, 761,
762, M22, 23.
Est. £220-300

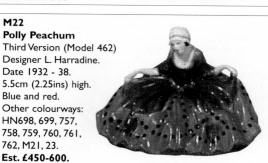

M22
Polly Peachum
Third Version (Model 462)
Designer L. Harradine.
Date 1932 - 38.
5.5cm (2.25ins) high.
Blue and red.
Other colourways:
HN698, 699, 757,
758, 759, 760, 761,
762, M21, 23.
Est. £450-600.

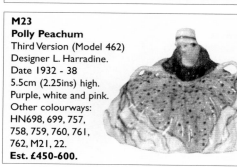

M23
Polly Peachum
Third Version (Model 462)
Designer L. Harradine.
Date 1932 - 38.
5.5cm (2.25ins) high.
Purple, white and pink.
Other colourways:
HN698, 699, 757,
758, 759, 760, 761,
762, M21, 22.
Est. £450-600.

M24
Priscilla
Designer L. Harradine.
Date 1932 - 45.
9.5cm (3.75ins) high.
Red.
Other colourways: M13, 14.
*(Auction PSA 23.6.04. sold
£140)*
Est. £165-225.

M25
Victorian Lady
Designer L. Harradine.
Date 1932 - 45.
9.5cm (3.75ins) high.
Lilac and pink.
Other colourways: M1, 2.
Est. £160-210.

M26
Paisley Shawl
Designer L. Harradine.
Date 1932 - 45.
9.5cm (3.75ins) high.
Green.
Other colourways: M3, 4.
Est. £160-210.

M27
Sweet Anne
Designer L. Harradine.
Date 1932 - 45.
10cm (4ins) high.
Red, yellow and blue.
Other colourways: M5, 6.
Est. £160-210.

M28
Patricia
Designer L. Harradine.
Date 1932 - 45.
10cm (4ins) high.
Lilac.
Other colourways: M7, 8.
Est. £165-225.

M29
Chloe
Designer L. Harradine.
Date 1932 - 45.
7cm (2.75ins) high.
Pink and yellow.
Other colourways: M9, 10.
Est. £200-275.

M30
Bridesmaid
Designer L. Harradine.
Date 1932 - 45.
9.5cm (3.75ins) high.
Pink and lilac.
Other colourways: M11, 12.
Est. £160-210.

M31
Pantalettes
Designer L. Harradine.
Date 1932 - 45.
10cm (4ins) high.
Blue and green.
Other colourways: M15, 16.
*(Auction PSA 23.6.04.
sold £210 plus comm.)*
Est. £250-350.

M36
Norma
Designer L. Harradine.
Date 1933 - 45.
11.5cm (4.5ins) high.
Red and green.
Other colourways: M37.
Est. £400-550.

M32
Rosamund
Designer L. Harradine.
Date 1932 - 45.
11cm (4.25ins) high.
Yellow.
Other colourways: M33.
Est. £350-500.

M37
Norma
Designer L. Harradine.
Date 1933 - 45.
11.5cm (4.5ins) high.
Red, white and blue.
Other colourways: M36.
Est. £500-650.

M33
Rosamund
Designer L. Harradine.
Date 1932 - 45.
11cm (4.25ins) high.
Red.
Other colourways: M32.
(Ebay 4.10.04 sold £212)
Est. £250-350.

M38
Robin
Designer L. Harradine.
Date 1933 - 45.
6.5cm (2.5ins) high.
Pink and lilac.
Other colourways: M39.
Est. £275-375.

M34
Denise
Designer L. Harradine.
Date 1933 - 45.
11.5cm (4.5ins) high.
Green, blue and red.
Other colourways: M35.
Est. £400-550.

M39
Robin
Designer L. Harradine.
Date 1933 - 45.
6.5cm (2.5ins) high.
Green and blue.
Other colourways: M38.
Est. £275-375.

M35
Denise
Designer L. Harradine.
Date 1933 - 45.
11.5cm (4.5ins) high.
Pink and blue.
Other colourways: M34.
Est. £450-625.

M40
Erminie
Designer L. Harradine.
Date 1933 - 45.
10cm (4ins) high.
Pink and white.
Est. £350-500.

M41
Mr. Pickwick
Designer L. Harradine.
Date 1932 - 83.
10cm (4ins) high.
Yellow and black.
Other colourways: HN529.
Series: Dickens
(Series One)
Est. £40-50.

M42
Mr. Micawber
Designer L. Harradine.
Date 1932 - 83.
10cm (4ins) high.
Black, yellow, orange and white.
Other colourways: HN532.
Series: Dickens (Series One)
Est. £40-50.

M43
Pecksniff
Designer L. Harradine.
Date 1932 - 82.
10.5cm (4.25ins) high.
Brown, black and red.
Other colourways: HN535.
Series: Dickens (Series One)
Est. £40-50.

M44
Fat Boy
Designer L. Harradine.
Date 1932 - 83.
11cm (4.25ins) high.
Blue, black and white.
Other colourways: HN530.
Series: Dickens (Series One)
Est. £40-50.

M45
Uriah Heep
Designer L. Harradine.
Date 1932 - 83.
10cm (4ins) high.
Black, grey and white.
Other colourways: HN545.
Series: Dickens (Series One)
Est. £40-50.

M46
Sairey Gamp
Designer L. Harradine.
Date 1932 - 83.
10cm (4ins) high.
Green, black, white and red.
Other colourways: HN533.
Series: Dickens (Series One)
Est. £40-50.

M47
Tony Weller
Designer L. Harradine.
Date 1932 - 81.
10cm (4ins) high.
Green, yellow, black and red.
Other colourways: HN544.
Series: Dickens (Series One)
Est. £40-50.

M48
Sam Weller
Designer L. Harradine.
Date 1932 - 81.
10cm (4ins) high.
Brown, white and yellow.
Other colourways: HN531.
Series: Dickens (Series One)
Est. £40-50.

M49
Fagin
Designer L. Harradine.
Date 1932 - 83.
10cm (4ins) high.
Brown and orange.
Other colourways: HN534.
Series: Dickens (Series One)
Est. £40-50.

M50
Stiggins
Designer L. Harradine.
Date 1932 - 81.
10cm (4ins) high.
Black, white and brown.
Other colourways: HN536.
Series: Dickens (Series One)
Est. £40-50.

M51
Little Nell
Designer L. Harradine.
Date 1932 - 83.
11cm (4.25ins) high.
Pink, white and black.
Other colourways: HN540.
Series: Dickens (Series One)
(Auction PSA 6.8.03. sold £30
plus comm.)
Est. £40-50.

M56
Tiny Tim
Designer L. Harradine.
Date 1932 - 83.
9.5cm (3.75ins) high.
Black, white and brown.
Other colourways: HN539.
Series: Dickens (Series One)
Est. £40-50.

M52
Alfred Jingle
Designer L. Harradine.
Date 1932 - 81.
9.5cm (3.75ins) high.
Black, brown and white.
Other colourways: HN541.
Series: Dickens (Series One)
(Auction PSA 6.8.03. sold £30
plus comm.)
Est. £40-50.

M64
Veronica
Designer L. Harradine.
Date 1934 - 49.
11.5cm (4.5ins) high.
Pink and blue.
Other colourways: M70.
Est. £350-450.

M53
Buz Fuz
Designer L. Harradine.
Date 1932 - 83.
10cm (4ins) high.
Black, white and red.
Other colourways: HN538.
Series: Dickens (Series One)
Est. £40-50.

M65
June
Designer L. Harradine.
Date 1935 - 49.
11.5cm (4.5ins) high.
Pink, yellow and lilac.
Other colourways: M71.
Est. £350-450.

M54
Bill Sykes
Designer L. Harradine.
Date 1932 - 81.
11cm (4.25ins) high.
Black, white and brown.
Other colourways: HN537.
Series: Dickens (Series One)
Est. £40-50.

M66
Monica
Designer L. Harradine.
Date 1935 - 49.
7.5cm (3ins) high.
Pink and blue.
Other colourways: M72.
(Auction PSA 23.6.04. sold £260
plus comm.)
Est. £300-450.

M55
Artful Dodger
Designer L. Harradine.
Date 1932 - 83.
11cm (4.25ins) high.
Black, white and brown.
Other colourways: HN546.
Series: Dickens (Series One)
Est. £40-50.

M67
Dainty May
Designer L. Harradine.
Date 1935 - 49.
10cm (4ins) high.
Pink and turquoise.
Other colourways: M73.
Est. £300-450.

M68
Mirabel
Designer L. Harradine.
Date 1936 - 49.
10cm (4ins) high.
Green and pink.
Other colourways: M74.
Est. £350-450.

M73
Dainty May
Designer L. Harradine.
Date 1936 - 49.
10cm (4ins) high.
Pink and lemon.
Other colourways: M67.
Est. £425-575.

M69
Janet
Designer L. Harradine.
Date 1936 - 49.
10cm (4ins) high.
Blue, green and white.
Other colourways: M75.
Est. £220-300.

M74
Mirabel
Designer L. Harradine.
Date 1936 - 49.
10cm (4ins) high.
Green, blue and red.
Other colourways: M68.
Est. £350-450.

M70
Veronica
Designer L. Harradine.
Date 1936 - 49.
11.5cm (4.5ins) high.
Green and pink.
Other colourways: M64.
Est. £450-575.

M75
Janet
Designer L. Harradine.
Date 1936 - 49.
10cm (4ins) high.
Purple and white.
Other colourways: M69.
Est. £350-450.

M71
June
Designer L. Harradine.
Date 1936 - 49.
11.5cm (4.5ins) high.
Lilac and green.
Other colourways: M65.
Est. £400-500.

M76
Bumble
Designer L. Harradine.
Date 1939 - 82.
10cm (4ins) high.
Red, brown white and green.
Series: Dickens (Series One)
Est. £40-50.

M72
Monica
Designer L. Harradine.
Date 1936 - 49.
7.5cm (3ins) high.
Blue, pink and white.
Other colourways: M66.
Est. £300-450.

M77
Captain Cuttle
Designer L. Harradine.
Date 1939 - 82.
10cm (4ins) high.
Black, white and yellow.
Series: Dickens (Series One)
Est. £40-50.

M78
Windflower
Designer L. Harradine.
Date 1939 - 49.
10cm (4ins) high.
Pink white and red.
Other colourways: M79.
Est. £400-550.

M83
Bo-Peep
Designer L. Harradine.
Date 1939 - 49.
10cm (4ins) high.
Purple, white and pink.
Other colourways: M82.
Est. £400-550.

M79
Windflower
Designer L. Harradine.
Date 1939 - 49.
10cm (4ins) high.
Green, white and blue.
Other colourways: M78.
Est. £400-550.

M84
Maureen
Designer L. Harradine.
Date 1939 - 49.
10cm (4ins) high.
Pink and black.
Other colourways: M85.
Est. £400-550.

M80
Goody Two Shoes
Designer L. Harradine.
Date 1939 - 49.
10cm (4ins) high.
Blue, white and pink.
Other colourways: M81.
(Auction PSA 10.3.04. sold £370
plus comm.)
Est. £450-650.

M85
Maureen
Designer L. Harradine.
Date 1939 - 49.
10cm (4ins) high.
Purple, black and white.
Other colourways: M84.
Est. £400-550.

M81
Goody Two Shoes
Designer L. Harradine.
Date 1939 - 49.
10cm (4ins) high.
Lilac, white and pink.
Other colourways: M80.
Est. £450-600.

M86
Mrs. Bardell
Designer L. Harradine.
Date 1949 - 82.
11cm (4.25ins) high.
Green, black and white.
Series: Dickens (Series One)
Est. £40-50.

M82
Bo-Peep
Designer L. Harradine.
Date 1939 - 49.
10cm (4ins) high.
Pink, white and blue.
Other colourways: M83.
Est. £400-550.

M87
Scrooge
Designer L. Harradine.
Date 1949 - 82.
10cm (4ins) high.
Brown and white.
Series: Dickens (Series One)
Est. £40-50.

M88
David Copperfield
Designer L. Harradine.
Date 1949 - 83.
11cm (4.25ins) high.
Black, white and light brown.
Series: Dickens (Series One)
Est. £40-50.

M201
Elaine
Designer M. Davies.
Remodeller not known.
Date 2004 to date.
5cm (2ins) high.
Blue and white.
Series: Miniatures.
(Royal Doulton web price £15)
(Ebay 11.6.04. sold £11)
Est. £10-15.

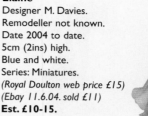

M89
Oliver Twist
Designer L. Harradine.
Date 1949 - 83.
11cm (4.25ins) high.
Black, white and light brown.
Series: Dickens (Series One)
Est. £40-50.

M202
Elizabeth
Designer B. Franks.
Remodeller not known.
Date 2004 to date.
5cm (2ins) high.
Yellow, green and white.
Series: Miniatures.
(Royal Doulton web price £15)
Retail £15.

M90
Dick Swiveller
Designer L. Harradine.
Date 1949 - 81.
11cm (4.25ins) high.
Black, yellow and light brown.
Series: Dickens (Series One)
Est. £40-50.

M203
Jane
Designer D.V. Tootles.
Remodeller not known.
Date 2004 to date.
5cm (2ins) high.
Blue, yellow, acqua and white.
Series: Miniatures.
(Royal Doulton web price £15)
(Ebay 11.6.04. sold £11)
Est. £10-15.

M91
Trotty Veck
Designer L. Harradine.
Date 1949 - 82.
11cm (4.25ins) high.
Black, white and brown.
Series: Dickens (Series One)
Est. £40-50.

M204
Karen
Designer M. Davies.
Remodeller not known.
Date 2004 to date.
5cm (2ins) high.
Red, black and white.
Series: Miniatures.
(Royal Doulton web price £15)
Retail £15.

M200
Christine
Designer M. Davies.
Remodeller not known.
Date 2004 to date.
5cm (2ins) high.
White, pink, yellow and blue.
Series: Miniatures.
(Royal Doulton web price £15)
Retail £15.

M205
Margaret
Designer M. Davies.
Remodeller not known.
Date 2004 to date.
5cm (2ins) high.
White and blue.
Series: Miniatures.
(Royal Doulton web price £15)
Retail £15.

M206
Ninette
Designer M. Davies.
Remodeller not known.
Date 2004 to date.
5cm (2ins) high.
Yellow, pink and white.
Series: Miniatures.
(Royal Doulton web price £15)
Retail £15.

M207
Rachel
Designer P. Gee.
Remodeller not known.
Date 2004 to date.
5cm (2ins) high.
Red, yellow and white.
Series: Miniatures.
(Royal Doulton web price £15)
Retail £15.

M208
Susan
Designer P. Parsons.
Remodeller not known.
Date 2004 to date.
5cm (2ins) high.
White, black and pink.
Series: Miniatures.
(Royal Doulton web price £15)
Retail £15.

M209
Victoria
Designer M. Davies.
Remodeller not known.
Date 2004 to date.
5cm (2ins) high.
Red, white and pink.
Series: Miniatures.
(Royal Doulton web price £15)
Retail £15.

Royal Doulton Miniatures were originally produced with
'HN' references, HN708 Shepherdess and HN709 Shepherd
designed by Leslie Harradine in 1925 are two good
examples. HN708 Shepherdess, became M18 and M20 same
Model 469, but different colourways, and HN709 Shepherd,
became M17 and M19 same Model 470, but again with
different colourways. HN698 and 699 Polly Peachum are
both Model 462, and were given a variety of other HN
numbers, but eventually Royal Doulton brought them into
the Miniature Series and gave them numbers M21, 22 and 23
as various colourways.

INDEX OF
Figure Names

A

A'Courting HN2004
A La Mode HN2544
Abdullah HN1410, 2104
Abigail (First Version) HN4044;
　(Second Version) HN4664
Ace HN3398
Across The Miles HN3934
Adéle HN2480
Adornment HN3015
Adrienne HN2152, 2304
Affection HN2236
After The Rain HN4226
Afternoon Call HN82
Afternoon Tea HN1747, 1748
Age of Swing HN4285
Aileen HN1645, 1664, 1803
Air Raid Precaution Warden HN4555
Ajax, HMS HN2908
Alana HN4499
Alchemist HN1259, 1282
Alexander the Great HN4481
Alexandra (First Version) HN2398;
　(Second Version) HN3286, 3292;
　(Third Version) HN4557
Alexis HN4205
Alfred Jingle HN54 (M52)
Alfred the Great HN3821
Alice (First Version) HN2158;
　(Second Version) HN3368;
　(Third Version) HN4111;
　(Fourth Version) HN4003
Alison (First Version) HN2336, 3264;
　(Second Version) 4018;
　(Third Version) 4667
All Aboard HN2940
All-a-Blooming HN1457, 1466
Allison HN4207
Allure HN3080
Almost Grown HN3425
Alyssa HN4132
Amanda HN2996, 3406, 3632, 3634, 3635
Amber HN4125
Amelia HN4327
Amen HN4021
Amy (First Version) HN2958;
　(Second Version) HN3316;
　(Third Version) HN3854
Amy's Sister HN3445
And One for You HN2970
And So To Bed HN2966
Andrea (First Version) HN3058;
　(Second Version) HN4584

Angel HN3940
Angela (First Version) HN1204, 1303;
　(Second Version) HN2389;
　(Third Version) HN3419;
　(Fourth Version) HN3690;
　(Fifth Version) HN4405
Angelina HN2013
Anita HN3766
Ankhesenamun HN4190
Ann (First Version) HN2739;
　(Second Version) HN3259
Anna (First Version) HN2802;
　(Second Version) HN4095;
　(Third Version) HN4391
Anna of the Five Towns HN3865
Annabel HN3273
Annabel CL3981
Annabel Vision in Red HN4493
Annabella HN1871, 1872, 1875
Annabelle HN4090
Anne Bolelyn HN3232
Anne Marie HN4522
Anne of Cleves HN3356
Anne of Denmark HN4266
Annette (First Version) HN1471, 1472, 1550;
　(Second Version) HN3495
Anniversary HN3625
Anthea HN1526, 1527, 1669
Antique Dealer HN4424
Antoinette (First Version) HN1850, 1851;
　(Second Version) HN2326
Antony and Cleopatra HN3114
Any Old Lavender HN22, 23, 23A, 342,
　569, 744, 1373
Anyone for Tennis CL4007
Aperitif HN2998
Applause HN4328
Apple Maid HN2160
April (First Version) HN2708;
　(Second Version) HN3333;
　(Third Version) HN3344;
　(Fourth Version) HN3693;
　(Fifth Version) HN4520
April Shower HN3024
Arab HN33, 343, 378
Aragorn HN2916
Aramis HN4415
Ariel HN3831
Arnold Bennett HN4360
Artemis, Goddess of the Hunt HN4081
Artful Dodger HN546 (M55)
A Stitch in Time HN2352
As Good As New HN2971
Ascot (First Version) HN2356;
　(Second Version) HN3471

Ashley HN3420
At Ease HN2473
Attentive Scholar HN26
At The Races CL4014
Athos HN4414
Auctioneer HN2988
August (First Version) HN3165;
　(Second Version) HN3325;
　(Third Version) HN3408
Au Revoir (First Version) HN3723;
　(Second Version) HN3729
Aurora HN3833
Aurora, Goddess of the Dawn HN4078
Automne (Autumn) HN3068
Autumn (First Version) HN314, 474;
　(Second Version) HN2087;
　(Third Version) HN4272
Autumn Attraction HN3612
Autumn Breezes (First Version) HN1911,
　1913, 1934, 2131, 2147, 3736;
　(Second Version) HN2176, 2180
Autumn Flowers HN3918
Autumn Glory HN2766
Autumntime (First Version) HN3231;
　(Second Version) HN3621
Auxiliary Territorial Service HN4495
Awakening (First Version) HN1927;
　(Second Version) HN2837, 2875

B

Baba HN1230, 1243, 1244, 1245, 1246,
　1247, 1248
Babette HN1423, 1424
Babie HN1679, 1842, 2121
Baby HN12
Baby Bunting HN2108
Baby's First Christmas HN4427
Bachelor HN2319
Balinese Dancer HN2808
Ballad Seller HN2266
Ballerina AIL9
Ballerina (First Version) HN2116;
　(Second Version) HN3197;
　(Third Version) HN3828
Ballet Class (First Version) HN3134;
　(Second Version) HN3731
Ballet Dancer AIL10
Ballet Dancer HN4027
Ballet Lesson HN4028
Ballet Shoes HN3434
Balloon Boy HN2934
Balloon Clown HN2894
Balloon Girl HN2818

Gypsy Dance (First Version) HN2157;
  (Second Version) HN2230
Gypsy Girl with Flowers HN1302
Gypsy Woman with Child HN1301

H

Hannah (First Version) HN3369, 3655;
  (Second Version) HN3649, 3870;
  (Third Version) HN4050, 4051, 4052;
  (Fourth Version) HN4407
Happy Anniversary (First Version) HN3097;
  (Second Version) HN3254;
  (Third Version) HN4068;
  (Fourth Version) HN4604, 4605, 4606
Happy Birthday (First Version) HN3095;
  (Second Version) HN3660;
  (Third Version) HN3829
Happy Birthday 2000 HN4215
Happy Birthday 2001 HN4308
Happy Birthday 2002 HN4393
Happy Birthday 2003 HN4464
Happy Birthday 2004 HN4528
Happy Christmas HN4255
Happy Joy, Baby Boy HN1541
Happy Holidays HN4443
Harlequin (First Version) HN2186;
  (Second Version) HN2737, 3287, 4058
Harlequinade (First Version) HN585, 635,
  711, 780;
  (Second Version) HN1401
Harlequinade Masked HN768, 769,
  1274, 1304
Harmony (First Version) HN2824;
  (Second Version) HN4096;
  (Third Version) HN4567
Harp HN2482
Harriet CL3998
Harriet (First Version) HN3177;
  (Second Version) HN3794, 3795,
  3796, 3797
Harvestime HN3084
Hatshepsut HN4191
Hayley HN4556
Hazel (First Version) HN1796, 1797;
  (Second Version) HN3167
He Loves Me HN2046
Heart of Scotland HN4608
Heart to Heart HN2276
Heathcliff and Cathy HN4071
Heather HN2956
Hebe, Handmaiden to the Gods HN4079
Heidi HN2975
Helen (First Version) HN1508, 1509, 1572;
  (Second Version) HN2994;
  (Third Version) HN3601, 3687,
  3763, 3886
Helen of Troy (First Version) HN2387;
  (Second Version) HN4497
Helena CL3994
Hello Daddy HN3651
Helmsman HN2499
Helping Mother HN4228
Henley HN3367
Henrietta Maria (First Version) HN2005;
  (Second Version) HN4260
Henry Irving As Cardinal Wolsey HN344
Henry Lytton As Jack Point HN610
Henry V at Agincourt HN3947
Henry VIII (First Version) HN370, 673;
  (Second Version) HN1792;
  (Third Version) HN3350;
  (Fourth Version) HN3458

Her Ladyship HN1977
Hercules HN4561
Here A Little Child I Stand
  (First Version) HN1546;
  (Second Version) HN4428
Herminia HN1644, 1646, 1704
Hermione HN2058
Hibemia HN2932
Highwayman HN527, 592, 1257
Hilary HN2335
Hinged Parasol HN1578, 1579
His Holiness Pope John-Paull II HN2888
Hiver (Winter) HN3069
HM Queen Elizabeth, The Queen Mother
  (First Version) HN2882;
  (Second Version) HN3189;
  (Third Version) HN3944;
  (Fourth Version) HN4086
HM Queen Elizabeth, The Queen Mother
  As The Duchess of York HN3230
HM Queen Elizabeth II
  (First Version) HN2502;
  (Second Version) HN2878;
  (Third Version) HN3436;
  (Fourth Version) HN3440;
  (Fifth Version) HN4372;
  (Sixth Version) HN4476
Hockey Player HN4519
Hold Tight HN3298
Holly HN3647
Home Again HN2167
Home at Last HN3697
Home Guard HN4494
Homecoming HN3295
Hometime HN3685
Honey HN1909, 1910, 1963
Honourable Frances Duncombe HN3009
Hope (First Version) HN3061;
  (Second Version) HN4097;
  (Third Version) HN4565
Hornpipe HN2161
Hostess of Williamsburg HN2209
HRH Prince Philip, Duke of Edinburgh
  HN2386
HRH The Prince of Wales
  (First Version) HN2883;
  (Second Version) HN2884
HRH The Princess of Wales HN2887
Huckleberry Finn HN2927
Hunting Squire HN1409
Hunts Lady HN1201
Huntsman (First Version) HN1226;
  (Second Version) HN1815;
  (Third Version) HN2492
Hurdy Gurdy HN2796

I

I'm Nearly Ready HN2976
Ibrahim HN2095
Idle Hours HN3115
Idle Scholar HN15, 16, 29
In Grandma's Days HN339, 340, 388, 442
In Loving Arms HN4262
In The Stocks (First Version) HN1474, 1475;
  (Second Version) HN2163
Independence HN4375
Indian Brave HN2376
Indian Maiden HN3117
Indian Temple Dancer HN2830
Innocence (First Version) HN2842;
  (Second Version) HN3730

Invitation HN2170
Iona HN1346
Ireland HN3628
Irene HN1621, 1697, 1952
Irish Colleen HN766, 767
Irish Charm HN4580
Irishman HN1307
Isabel (First Version) HN3716;
  (Second Version) HN4458
Isabella, Countess of Sefton HN3010
Isadora HN2938
Isobel CL3980
It Won't Hurt HN2963
Ivy HN1768, 1769

J

Jack HN2060
Jack Point HN85, 91, 99, 2080, 3920, 3925
Jacqueline (First Version) HN2000, 2001;
  (Second Version) HN2333;
  (Third Version) HN3689;
  (Fourth Version) HN4309
James HN3013
James I HN3822
Jane (First Version) HN2014;
  (Second Version) HN2806;
  (Third Version) HN3260;
  (Fourth Version) HN3711;
  (Fifth Version) HN4110;
  (Miniature) M203
Jane Eyre HN3842
Jane Seymour HN3349
Janet (First Version) HN1537, 1538,
  1652, 1737;
  (Second Version) HN1916, 1964;
  (Third Version) HN4042;
  (Fourth Version) HN4310;
  (Miniatures) M69, M75
Janette HN3415
Janice (First Version) HN2022, 2165;
  (Second Version) HN3624
Janine HN2461
January (First Version) HN2697;
  (Second Version) HN3330;
  (Third Version) HN3341
Japanese Fan HN399, 405, 439, 440
Japanese Lady HN354, 376, 376A, 387,
  634, 741, 779, 1321, 1322
Jasmine (First Version) HN1862, 1863, 1876
  (Second Version) HN3832;
  (Third Version) HN4127;
  (Fourth Version) HN4431
Jayne (First Version) HN4210;
  (Second Version) HN4524
Jean (First Version) HN1877, 1878, 2032;
  (Second Version) HN2710;
  (Third Version) HN3757, 3862
Jemma HN3168
Jennifer (First Version) HN1484;
  (Second Version) HN2392;
  (Third Version) HN3447;
  (Fourth Version) HN4248
Jenny HN4423
Jersey Milkmaid HN2057
Jessica (First Version) HN3169, 3497;
  (Second Version) HN3850;
  (Third Version) HN4049;
  (Fourth Version) HN4583
Jester (First Version) HN45, 71, 71A, 320,
  367, 412, 426, 446, 552, 616, 627,
  1295, 1702, 2016, 3922;

Miss Kay HN3659
Miss Maisie HN3997
Miss Muffet HN1936, 1937
Miss Tilly HN3998
Miss Violet HN3996
Miss Winsome HN1665, 1666
Missing You HN4076
M'ladys Maid HN1795, 1822
Modena HN1845, 1846
Modern Piper HN756
Modesty HN2744
Moira HN1347
Moll Flanders HN3849
Molly HN4091
Molly Malone HN1455
Monica HN1458, 1459, 1467, 3617;
    (Miniatures) M66, M72
Monique HN2880
Monte Carlo HN2332
Moondancer, HN3181
Moonlight HN4611
Moonlight Gaze HN4362
Moonlight Rose HN3483
Moonlight Serenade HN4530
Moonlight Stroll HN3954
Moor HN1308, 1366, 1425, 1657, 2082,
    3642, 3926
Moorish Minstrel HN34, 364, 415, 797
Moorish Piper Minstrel HN301, 328, 416
Morning Breeze HN3313
Morning Glory HN3093
Morning Ma'am HN2895
Morning Walk HN3860
Mother and Child
    (First Version) HN3235, 3348, 3353;
    (Second Version) HN3938
Mother and Daughter
    (First Version) HN2841, 2843;
    (Second Version) HN4562
Motherhood (First Version) HN28, 30, 303;
    (Second Version) HN462, 570, 703, 743
Mother's Help HN2151
Mother's Helper HN3650
Mountie 1973 HN2547
Mountie 1873 HN2555
Mr Micawber (First Version) HN532 (M42);
    (Second Version) HN557, 1895;
    (Third Version) 2097
Mr Pickwick (First Version) HN529 (M41);
    (Second Version) HN556, 1894;
    (Third Version) HN2099
Mrs Bardell (Miniature) M86
Mrs Fitzherbert HN2007
Mrs Hugh Bonfoy HN3319
Musicale HN2756
My Best Friend HN3011
My First Figurine HN3424
My First Pet, HN3122
My Love (First Version) HN2339;
    (Second Version) HN4392
My Pet HN2238
My Pretty Maid HN2064
My Teddy HN2177
My True Love HN4001
Myfanwy Jones HN39, 92, 456, 514, 516,
    519, 520, 660, 668, 669, 701, 792

N

Nadine (First Version) HN1885, 1886;
    (Second Version) HN4500
Nana HN1766, 1767

Nancy HN2955
Nanny HN2221
Naomi HN4661
Naomi CL3996
Napoleon at Waterloo HN3429
Natalie (First Version) HN3173, 3498;
    (Second Version) HN4048
Natasha HN4154
Necklace HN393, 394
Nefertiti HN3844
Negligee HN1219, 1228, 1272, 1273, 1454
Nell HN3014
Nell Gwynn HN1882, 1887
Nelson HN2928
New Baby HN3712, 3713
New Bonnet HN1728, 1957
New Companion HN2770
New Dawn HN4314
Newhaven Fishwife HN1480
Newsboy HN2244
Newsvendor HN2891
Nicola CL4000
Nicola HN2804, 2839
Nicole (First Version) HN3421, 3686;
    (Second Version) HN4112;
    (Third Version) HN4527
Nina HN2347
Ninette (First Version) HN2379, 3417;
    (Second Version) HN3215, 3248, 3901;
    (Miniature) M206
Noel HN4084
Noelle HN2179
Norma (Miniatures) M36, M37
North American Indian Dancer HN2809
Nosegay HN406, 414, 422, 428, 429,
    567, 794
November (First Version) HN2695;
    (Second Version) HN3328; (Third
    Version) HN3411
Nude on Rock HN593
Nurse HN4287

O

October (First Version) HN2693;
    (Second Version) HN3327;
    (Third Version) HN3410
Odds and Ends HN1844
Off To School HN3768
Off To The Pond HN4227
Officer of the Line HN2733
Old Balloon Seller
    (First Version) HN1315, 3737;
    (Second Version) HN2129
Old Balloon Seller and Bulldog
    HN1791, 1912
Old Ben HN3190
Old Country Roses
    (First Version) HN3482;
    (Second Version) HN3692
Old Father Thames HN2993
Old King HN358, 623, 1801, 2134
Old King Cole HN2217
Old Lavender Seller HN1492, 1571
Old Man HN451
Old Meg HN2494
Old Mother Hubbard HN2314
Olga HN2463
Oliver Hardy HN2775
Oliver Twist (Miniature) M89
Oliver Twist and The Artful Dodger
    HN3786

Olivia (First Version) HN1995;
    (Second Version) HN3339;
    (Third Version) HN3717
Omar Khayyam (First Version) HN408,
    409; (Second Version) HN2247
Omar Khayyam and the Beloved HN407,
    419, 459, 598
On the Beach HN3877
Once Upon a Time HN2047
One of the Forty (First Version) HN417,
    490, 495, 501, 528, 648, 677, 1351, 1352;
    (Second Version) HN418, 494, 498,
    647, 666, 704, 1353;
    (Third Version) HN423;
    (Fourth Version) HN423A;
    (Fifth Version) HN423B;
    (Sixth Version) HN423C;
    (Seventh Version) HN423D;
    (Eighth Version) HN423E;
    (Ninth Version) HN423F;
    (Tenth Version) HN427;
    (Eleventh Version) HN480, 493, 497,
    499, 664, 714;
    (Twelfth Version) HN481, 483, 491,
    646, 667, 712, 1336, 1350;
    (Thirteenth Version) HN482, 484, 492,
    645, 663, 713;
    (Fourteenth Version) HN496, 500, 649,
    665, 1354
One That Got Away HN2153
Ophelia HN3674
Open Road HN4161
Optimism HN4165
Orange Lady HN1759, 1953
Orange Seller HN1325
Orange Vendor HN72, 508, 521, 1966
Organ Grinder HN2173
Our First Christmas HN3452
Out for a Walk HN86, 443, 748
Over the Threshold HN3274
Owd Willum HN2042

P

Pageboy HN4374
Painting HN3012
Paisley Shawl (First Version) HN1392,
    1460, 1707, 1739, 1987;
    (Second Version) HN1914, 1988;
    (Miniatures) M3, M4, M26
Palio HN2428
Pamela (First Version) HN1468, 1469, 1564;
    (Second Version) HN2479, 3223;
    (Third Version) HN3756
Pan on Rock HN621, 622
Panorama HN3028
Pantalettes HN1362, 1412, 1507, 1709;
    (Miniatures) M15, M16, M31
Paradise HN3074
Parisian HN2445
Park Parade HN3116
Parson's Daughter HN337, 338, 441, 564,
    790, 1242, 1356, 2018
Partners HN3119
Past Glory HN2484
Patchwork Quilt HN1984
Patricia (First Version) HN1414, 1431,
    1462, 1567;
    (Second Version) HN2715;
    (Third Version) HN3365;
    (Fourth Version) HN3907;
    (Miniatures) M7, M8, M28

Paula HN2906, 3234
Pauline (First Version) HN1444;
  (Second Version) HN2441;
  (Third Version) HN3643, 3656
Pavlova HN487, 676
Peace HN2433, 2470
Pearly Boy (First Version) HN1482, 1547;
  (Second Version) HN2035;
  (Third Version) HN2767, 2767A
Pearly Girl (First Version) HN1483, 1548;
  (Second Version) HN2036;
  (Third Version) HN2769, 2769A
Pecksniff (First Version) HN535 (M43);
  (Second Version) HN553, 1891;
  (Third Version) HN2098
Pedlar Wolf HN7
Peek a Boo HN3363
Peggy HN1941, 2038
Penelope CL3988
Penelope HN1901, 1902
Penny HN2338, 2424
Penny's Worth, A HN2408
Pensive HN3109
Pensive Moments HN2704
Perfect Gift HN4409
Perfect Pair HN581
Perfect Pose HN4357
Performance HN3827
Philippa CL4010
Philippa of Hainault
  (First Version) HN2008;
  (Second Version) HN4066
Philippine Dancer HN2439
Phyllis (First Version) HN1420, 1430,
  1486, 1698;
  (Second Version) HN3180
Picardy Peasant (man) HN13, 17, 19
Picardy Peasant (woman) HN4, 5, 17A,
  351, 513
Picnic HN2308
Pied Piper (First Version) HN1215, 2102;
  (Second Version) HN3721
Pierrette (First Version) HN642, 643, 644,
  691, 721, 731, 732, 784;
  (Second Version) HN795, 796;
  (Third Version) HN1391, 1749
Pillow Fight HN2270
Pilot Skipper HN4510
Pinkie HN1552, 1553
Piper (First Version) HN2907;
  (Second Version) HN3444
Pirate King HN2901
Pirouette HN2216
Playmates HN3127
Please Keep Still HN2967
Please Sir HN3302
Poacher HN2043
Pocahontas HN2930
Poke Bonnet HN362, 612, 765
Policeman HN4410
Polish Dancer HN2836
Polka HN2156
Polly HN3178
Polly Peachum (First Version) HN463, 465,
  550, 589, 614, 680, 693;
  (Second Version) HN489, 549, 620,
  694, 734;
  (Third Version) HN698, 699, 757, 758,
  759, 760, 761, 762 (M21, M22, M23)
Polly Peachum Curtsey HN489, 549, 620,
  694, 734
Polly Put The Kettle On HN3021
Pollyanna HN2965

Porthos HN4416
Posy For You, A HN3606
Potter HN1493, 1518, 1522
Prayers HN4378
Premiere HN2343, 2343A
Pretty As A Picture HN4312
Pretty Lady HN69, 70, 302, 330, 361, 384,
  565, 700, 763, 783
Pretty Polly HN2768
Pride and Joy (First Version) HN2945;
  (Second Version) HN4102
Pride of Scotland HN4453
Prima Ballerina HN4024
Primrose HN3710
Primroses HN1617
Prince Albert, Duke of York HN4420
Prince of Wales HN1217
Princess HN391, 392, 420, 430, 431, 633
Princess Badoura (First Version)
  HN2081, 3921;
  (Second Version) HN4179
Princess Elizabeth HN3682
Printemps (Spring) HN3066
Priscilla HN1337, 1340, 1495, 1501, 1559;
  (Miniatures) M13, M14, 24
Private, 1st Georgia Regiment, 1777
  HN2779
Private, 2nd South Carolina Regiment,
  1781 HN2717
Private, 3rd North Carolina Regiment,
  1778 HN2754
Private, Connecticut Regiment, 1777
  HN2845
Private, Delaware Regiment, 1776
  HN2761
Private, Massachusetts Regiment, 1778
  HN2760
Private, Pennsylvania Rifle Battalion, 1776
  HN2846
Private, Rhode Island Regiment, 1781
  HN2759
Prized Possessions HN2942
Professor HN2281
Promenade (First Version) HN2076;
  (Second Version) HN3072
Promise HN4033
Proposal (man) HN725, 1209
Proposal (woman) HN715, 716, 788
Prudence HN1883, 1884
Prue HN1996
Puff and Powder HN397, 398, 400, 432, 433
Punch and Judy Man HN2765
Puppetmaker HN2253
Puppy Love HN3371
Pussy HN18, 325, 507
Pyjams HN1942

Q

Quality Street HN1211, 1211A
Queen HN3847
Queen Anne HN3141
Queen Elizabeth I HN3099
Queen Elizabeth II and the Duke of
  Edinburgh HN3836
Queen Mary II HN4474
Queen of Sheba HN2328
Queen of the Dawn HN2437
Queen of the Ice HN2435
Queen Sophia HN4074
Queen Victoria (First Version) HN3125;
  (Second Version) HN4475

Queen Victoria and Prince Albert
  HN3256
Quiet, They're Sleeping HN3657

R

Rachel (First Version) HN2919, 2936;
  (Second Version) HN3976;
  (Miniatures) M207
Rag Doll HN2142
Rag Doll Seller HN2944
Railway Sleeper HN4418
Rapunzel HN3841
Rebecca (First Version) HN2805;
  (Second Version) HN3414;
  (Third Version) HN4041;
  (Fourth Version) HN4203
Recital HN4466
Red Red Rose HN3994
Reflection HN3039
Reflections HN1820, 1821, 1847, 1848
Regal Lady HN2709
Regency HN1752
Regency Beau HN1972
Remembering You HN4085
Rendezvous HN2212
Repose HN2272
Rest Awhile HN2728
Return of Persephone HN31
Reverie HN2306
Reward HN3391
Rhapsody HN2267
Rhoda HN1573, 1574, 1688
Rhythm HN1903, 1904
Richard the Lionheart HN3675
Rita HN1448, 1450
Ritz Bell Boy HN2772
River Boy HN2128
Robert Burns (First Version) HN42;
  (Second Version) HN3641
Robin (Miniatures) M38, M39
Robin Hood (First Version) HN2773;
  (Second Version) HN3720
Robin Hood and Maid Marion HN3111
Rocking Horse HN2072
Romance (First Version) HN96, 345;
  (Second Version) HN2430
Romany Sue HN1757, 1758
Romeo and Juliet (First Version) HN3113;
  (Second Version) HN4057
Rosabell HN1620
Rosalind HN2393
Rosamund (First Version) HN1320;
  (Second Version) HN1497, 1551,
  (Miniatures) M32, 33
Rose (First Version) HN1368, 1387, 1416,
  1506, 1654, 2123;
  (Second Version) HN3709;
  (Third Version) HN4581
Rose Arbour HN3145
Roseanna HN1921, 1926
Rosebud (First Version) HN1580, 1581;
  (Second Version) HN1983
Rose Garden HN4559
Rosemary (First Version) HN2091;
  (Second Version) HN3143;
  (Third Version) HN3691, 3698;
  (Fourth Version) HN4662
Rosie HN4094
Rosina HN1358, 1364, 1556
Rowena HN2077
Royal Governor's Cook HN2233

Ruby (First Version) HN1724, 1725;
    (Second Version) HN4521
Rumpelstiltskin HN3025
Rustic Swain HN1745, 1746
Ruth (First Version) HN2799;
    (Second Version) HN4099
Ruth, The Pirate Maid HN2900

S

Sabbath Morn HN1982
Sailor's Holiday HN2442
Sairey Gamp (First Version) HN533 (M46);
    (Second Version) HN558, 1896;
    (Third Version) HN2100
Sally (First Version) HN2741;
    (Second Version) HN3383, 3851, 4160
Salome (First Version) HN1775, 1828;
    (Second Version) HN3267
Sam Weller HN531 (M48)
Samantha (First Version) HN2954;
    (Second Version) HN3304;
    (Third Version) HN4043;
    (Fourth Version) HN4403
Samurai Warrior HN3402
Samwise HN2925
Sandra HN2275, 2401
Santa Claus (First Version) HN2725;
    (Second Version) HN4175
Santa's Helper HN3301
Sara (First Version) HN2265, 3308;
    (Second Version) HN3219, 3249
Sarah (First Version) HN3380;
    (Second Version) HN3384, 3852, 3857;
    (Third Version) HN3978
Sarah Bernhardt HN4023
Sarah In Winter HN3005
Saucy Nymph HN1539
Save Some For Me HN2959
Saxophone Player HN4284
Scarlett HN4408
Scarlett O'Hara HN4200
Scheherazade HN3835
Schoolmarm HN2223
Scotch Girl HN1269
Scotland HN3629
Scotties HN1281, 1349
Scottish Highland Dancer HN2436
Scribe HN305, 324, 1235
Scrooge (Miniature) M87
Sea Harvest HN2257
Sea Sprite (First Version) HN1261;
    (Second Version) HN2191
Seafarer HN2455
Seashore HN2263
Second Violin HN3705
Secret HN4560
Secret Moment HN3106
Secret Thoughts (First Version) HN2382;
    (Second Version) HN4197
Sentimental Pierrot HN36, 307
Sentinel HN523
September (First Version) HN3166;
    (Second Version) HN3326;
    (Third Version) HN3409
Serena HN1868
Serenade HN2753
Serenity HN4396
Sergeant, 6th Maryland Regiment, 1777
    HN2815
Sergeant, Virginia 1st Regiment Continental
    Light Dragoons, 1777 HN2844

Shakespeare HN3633
Shall I Compare Thee To A Summer's Day
    HN3999
Sharon (First Version) HN3047, 3455;
    (Second Version) HN3603
She Loves Me Not HN2045
Sheikh HN3083
Sheila HN2742
Shepherd (First Version) HN81, 617, 632;
    (Second Version) HN709 (M17, M19);
    (Third Version) HN751;
    (Fourth Version) HN1975;
    (Fifth Version) HN3160
Shepherdess (First Version) HN708
    (M18, M20);
    (Second Version) HN735, 750;
    (Third Version) HN2990;
    (Fourth Version) HN2420
Sherlock Holmes HN3639
Shirley HN2702
Shore Leave, HN2254
Shy Anne HN60, 64, 65, 568
Shylock HN79, 317
Sibell HN1668, 1695, 1735
Siesta HN1305
Silks and Ribbons HN2017
Silversmith of Williamsburg HN2208
Simone CL4004
Simone (First Version) HN2378;
    (Second Version) HN4535
Single Red Rose HN3376
Sir Edward HN2370
Sir Francis Drake HN3770
Sir Henry Doulton HN3891
Sir John A MacDonald HN2860
Sir Ralph HN2371
Sir Thomas HN2372
Sir Thomas Lovell HN356
Sir Walter Raleigh HN1742, 1751, 2015
Sir Winston Churchill
    (First Version) HN3057;
    (Second Version) HN3433
Sister and Brother HN4356
Sisterly Love HN3130
Sisters HN3018, 3019
Sit HN3123, 3430
Skater (First Version) HN2117;
    (Second Version) HN3439
Skating HN4370
Slapdash HN2277
Sleep HN24, 24A, 25, 25A, 424, 692, 710
Sleeping Beauty (First Version) HN3079;
    (Second Version) HN4000
Sleepy Darling HN2953
Sleepy Scholar HN15, 16, 29
Sleepyhead (First Version) HN2114;
    (Second Version) HN3761;
    (Third Version) HN4413
Smiling Buddha HN454
Snake Charmer HN1317
Snow White HN3678
Soiree HN2312
Solitude HN2810
Sonata HN2438
Song of the Sea HN2729
Sonia HN1692, 1738
Sonny HN1313, 1314
Sophia Baines HN4167
Sophia Charlotte, Lady Sheffield HN3008
Sophia Dorothea HN4074
Sophie (First Version) HN2833;
    (Second Version) HN3257;
    (Third Version) HN3790, 3791,
    3792, 3793;

    (Fourth Version) HN3715;
    (Fifth Version) HN3995;
    (Sixth Version) HN4620
Sophistication HN3059
Sorcerer HN4252
Sorceress HN4253
Southern Belle
    (First Version) HN2229, 2425;
    (Second Version) HN3174, 3244
Spanish Flamenco Dancer HN2831
Spanish Lady HN1262, 1290, 1293,
    1294, 1309
Special Celebration HN4234
Special Friend HN3607
Special Friends HN4257
Special Gift HN4118, 4129
Special Moments HN4430
Special Occasion HN4100
Special Treat HN3663
Specially For You HN4232
Spinning HN2390
Spirit of Scotland HN4469
Spirit of the Wind HN1777, 1825
Spook HN50, 51, 51A, 51B, 58, 512,
    625, 1218
Spooks HN88, 89, 372
Spring (First Version) HN312, 472;
    (Second Version) HN588;
    (Third Version) HN1774, 1827;
    (Fourth Version) HN2085;
    (Fifth Version) HN4270
Spring Flowers HN1807, 1945
Spring Morning
    (First Version) HN1922, 1923;
    (Second Version) HN3725;
    (Third Version) HN4451
Spring Posy HN3916
Spring Serenade HN3956
Spring Song HN3446
Spring Walk HN3120
Springtime (First Version) HN1971;
    (Second Version) HN3033;
    (Third Version) HN3477;
    (Fourth Version) HN4586
Squire HN1814
St George (First Version) HN385, 386,
    1800, 2067;
    (Second Version) HN2051;
    (Third Version) HN2856;
    (Fourth Version) HN4371
Stage Struck HN3951
Standing Shepherd HN4056
Stan Laurel HN2774
Stargazer HN3182
Star Performer HN3950
Statesman HN2859
Stayed At Home HN2207
Stephanie CL3985
Stephanie (First Version) HN2807, 2811;
    (Second Version) HN3759;
    (Third Version) HN4461
Stick 'em Up HN2981
Stiggins HN536 (M50)
Stitch in Time HN2352
Stop Press HN2683
Storytime (First Version) HN3126;
    (Second Version) HN3695
Storytime (boy) HN4088
Storytime (girl) HN4089
Strolling (First Version) HN3073;
    (Second Version) HN3755
Studious Boy HN4563
Studios Girl HN4564

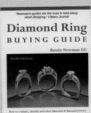

Figures by SERIES

Age of Chivalry
Sir Edward HN2370
Sir Ralph HN2371
Sir Thomas HN2372

Age of Innocence
Feeding Time HN3373
First Outing HN3377
Making Friends HN3372
Puppy Love HN3371

Age of Jazz
Saxaphone Player HN4284
Trumpet Player HN4283

Annabelle Doulton Collection
Blossomtime HN4045

Arnold Bennett
Anna of the Five Towns HN3865
Arnold Bennett HN4360
Clara Hamps HN4162
Countess of Chell HN3867
Sophia Baines HN4167

Art Deco
Destiny HN4164
Ecstasy HN4163
Optimism HN4165
Wisdom (Second Version) HN466

Art is Life
Ballerina AIL9
Ballet Dancer AIL10
Girl on Rock AIL8
Girl Stretching AIL6
Girl with Pony Tail AIL7
Kiss AIL1
Love AIL2

Bathers Collection
Bather (Second Version) HN4244
Lido Lady (Second Version) HN4247
Sunshine Girl (Second Version) HN4245
Swimmer (Second Version) HN4246

Beggar's Opera
Beggar (First Version) HN526, 591
   (Second Version) HN2175
Captain MacHeath HN464, 590, 1256
Highwayman HN527, 592, 1257
Lucy Lockett (First Version) HN485
   (Second Version) HN524
   (Third Version) HN695, 696
Polly Peachum (First Version)
   .... HN463, 465, 550, 589, 614, 680, 693

(Second Version)
.... HN489, 549, 620, 694, 734
(Third Version)
.... HN698, 699, 757, 758, 759, 760,
761, 762, M21, M22, M23

British Sporting Heritage
Ascot (First Version) HN3471
Croquet HN3470
Henley HN3367
Wimbledon HN3366

Character Sculptures (Resin)
Bill Sykes (Second Version) HN3785
Bowls Player HN3780
Captain Hook HN3636
Cyrano de Bergerac HN3751
D'Artagnan (First Version) HN3638
Dick Turpin (Second Version) ... HN3637
Fagin (Second Version) HN3752
Gulliver HN3750
Long John Silver (Second Version)
.... HN3719
Oliver Twist and The Artful Dodger
.... HN3786
Pied Piper (Second Version) HN3721
Robin Hood (Second Version) .. HN3720
Sherlock Holmes HN3639
Sir Francis Drake HN3770
Wizard (Second Version) ... HN3722, 3732

Character from Children's Literature
Heidi HN2975
Huckleberry Finn HN2927
Little Lord Fauntleroy HN2972
Pollyanna HN2965
Tom Brown HN2941
Tom Sawyer HN2926

Charities: Breast Cancer
1998 Hope (Second Version) HN4097
1999 Faith (Second Version) HN4151
2000 Charity (Second Version).... HN4243
2001 New Dawn HN4314
2002 Spring Morning (Third Version)
.... HN4451
2003 Love of Life HN4529
2004 Free Spirit (Third Version)
.... HN4609
2004 Summer's Dream HN4660

Charities: Compton & Woodhouse
2000 Kate (Third Version) HN4233

Charites: Save The Children
Harmony (Third Version) HN4567
Independence HN4375
Unity HN4485

Charleston
Charlotte (Third Version)
.... HN3810, 3811, 3812, 3813
Constance (Second Version)
.... HN3930, 3933
Daisy (Second Version)
.... HN3802, 3803, 3804, 3805
Eliza (Third Version)
.... HN3798, 3799, 3800, 3801
Ellen (Second Version) HN3816, 3819
Emily (Third Version)
.... HN3806, 3807, 3808, 3809
Harriet (Second Version)
.... HN3794, 3795, 3796, 3997
Millie (Second Version) HN3945, 3946
Sophie (Third Version)
.... HN3790, 3791, 3792, 3793

Chelsea
Annabel Vision in Red HN4493
Becky (Second Version) HN4322
Bethany HN4326
Ellie (First Version) HN4046
Georgina (Second Version) HN4047
Hayley HN4556
Isabel (First Version) HN3716
Jenny HN4423
Katie (Third Version) HN4323
Kathryn (Second Version) HN4040
Melinda HN4209
Olivia (Third Version) HN3717
Zoe HN4208

Childhood Days
And One for You HN2970
And So To Bed HN2966
As Good As New HN2971
Dressing Up (First Version) HN2964
I'm Nearly Ready HN2976
It Won't Hurt HN2963
Just One More HN2980
Please Keep Still HN2967
Save Some for Me HN2959
Stick 'em Up HN2981

Children of the Blitz
Boy Evacuee HN3202
Girl Evacuee HN3203
Homecoming HN3295
Welcome Home HN3299

Free Spirit (First Version) .... HN3157, 3159 (black)
From This Day Forward HN4380
Gift of Freedom HN3443
God Bless You HN3400
Goose Girl (Third Version) HN3936
Graduate (female) (Second Version) HN4542
Graduate (male) (Second Version) HN3959
(Third Version) HN4543
Graduation (girl) HN3942
Happy Anniversary (Second Version) HN3254
Happy Birthday (Third Version) HN3829
Harmony (Third Version) HN4567
Hockey Player HN4519
Independence HN4375
Kiss (boy) HN4064
Kiss (girl) HN4065
Lady Godiva HN4641
Leap-Frog HN4030
Love Everlasting HN4280
Lovers .... HN2762, 2763 (black)
Messiah HN3952
Mother and Child (Second Version) HN3938
Mother and Daughter (First Version) .... HN2841, HN2843 (black)
(Second Version) HN4562
Our First Christmas HN3452
Over the Threshold HN3274
Pageboy HN4374
Peace HN2433, 2470
Perfect Pose HN4357
Performance HN3827
Prayers HN4378
Prima Ballerina HN4024
Sister and Brother HN4356
Sisters .... HN3018, 3019 (black)
Sleepyhead (Third Version) HN4413
Stage Struck HN3951
Star Performer HN3950
Storytime (boy) HN4088
Storytime (girl) HN4089
Studious Boy HN4563
Studious Girl HN4564
Surprise HN4376
Sweetheart (boy) HN4351
Sweetheart (girl) HN4352
Sympathy .... HN2838 (black), 2876
Tenderness .... HN2713, 2714 (black)
Thankful .... HN3129, 3135 (black)
Tomorrow's Dreams (Second Version) HN3665
Tranquility .... HN2426 (black), 2469
Two Become One HN4644
Unity HN4485
Wedding Day HN2748
Wedding Vows (Second Version) .. HN4379
Wistful (Second Version) HN3664
Yearning .... HN2920, 2921 (black)

Images: Christmas Choir
Carol Singer (Boy) HN4031
Carol Singer (Brother) HN4290
Carol Singer (Girl) HN4032
Carol Singer (Sister) HN4291
Carol Singer with Lantern HN4256

Images: The Christmas Story
Balthazar HN4036
Boy Shepherd HN4039

Casper HN4038
Joseph (Second Version) HN4035
Kneeling Shepherd HN4055
Mary and Jesus HN4034
Melchior HN4037
Standing Shepherd HN4056

Images: Figure of the Year
1998 Best Friends (Second Version) HN4026
1999 Promise HN4033
2000 Kindred Spirits HN4077
2001 Special Friends HN4257
2002 Keep in Touch HN4377
2003 Gift of Friendship HN4446
2004 Secret HN4560

Imortals and Aurora
Artemis, Goddess of the Hunt . HN4081
Aruora, Goddess of the Dawn . HN4078
Ceres, Goddess of Plenty HN4080
Erato, The Parnassian Muse HN4082
Hebe, Handmaiden to the Gods HN4079

Impressions
Cherished Memories HN4265
Daybreak (Second Version) HN4196
In Loving Arms HN4262
Secret Thoughts (Second Version) HN4197
Summer Blooms (Second Version) HN4194
Summer Fragrance HN4195
Sunrise HN4199
Sunset HN4198
Sweet Dreams (Third Version) . HN4193
Tender Greeting HN4261
Tender Moment (Second Version) HN4192

In Vogue
Abigail (First Version) HN4044
Alana HN4499
Amelia HN4327
Bride (Fifth Version) HN4324
Claudia HN4320
Daniella HN4551
Emma(Third Version) HN3714
Finishing Touch HN4329
Jessica (Third Version) HN4049
Joanne (Third Version) HN4202
Mikaela HN4550
Nadine (Second Version) HN4500
Natalie (Second Version) HN4048
Rebecca (Fourth Version) HN4203
Sophie (Fourth Version) HN3715
Taylor HN4496

Ivory and Gold
After the Rain HN4226
Helping Mother HN4228
Off to the Pond HN4227
Summer Duet HN4225

Kate Greenaway
Amy (First Version) HN2958
Anna (First Version) HN2802
Beth (First Version) HN2870
Carrie HN2800
Edith HN2957
Ellen (First Version) HN3020
Emma (First Version) HN2834

Georgina (First Version) HN2377
James HN3013
Kathy (First Version) HN2346
Lori HN2801
Louise (First Version) HN2869
Lucy (First Version) HN2863
Nell HN3014
Ruth (First Version) HN2799
Sophie (First Version) HN2833
Tess HN2865
Tom HN2864

Ladies of Covent Gardens
Catherine (First Version) HN2395
Deborah (First Version) HN2701
Juliet (First Version) HN2968
Kimberley (First Version) HN2969

Ladies of the British Isles
England HN3627
Ireland HN3628
Scotland HN3629
Wales HN3630

Lady Doulton
1995 Lily (Second Version) HN3626
1996 Katherine HN3708
1997 Jane (Fourth Version) HN3711

Lady Musicians
Cello (First Version) HN2331
Chitarrone HN2700
Cymbals HN2699
Dulcimer HN2798
Flute HN2483
French Horn HN2795
Harp HN2482
Hurdy Gurdy HN2796
Lute HN2431
Viola d'Amore HN2797
Violin HN2432
Virginals HN2427

Lady of the Year
(Compton and Woodhouse)
1997 Ellen (Third Version) HN3992
1998 Sophie (Fifth Version) HN3995
1999 Alice (Fourth Version) HN4003
2000 Chloe (Third Version) ... HN4201A
2001 A Love So Tender HN4016
2001 Eleanor (Second Version) HN4015
2002 Georgina (Third Version) HN4237
2002 Moonlight Gaze HN4362
2003 Ellie (Second Version) HN4017
2004 Megan (Third Version) HN4539

Language of Love
Red Red Rose HN3994
Shall I Compare Thee To A Summer's Day HN3999

Les Femmes Fatales
Cleopatra (First Version) HN2868
Eve HN2466
Helen of Troy (First Version) HN2387
Lucrezia Borgia HN2342
Queen of Sheba HN2328
T'zu-hsi, Empress Dowager HN2391

Leslie Harradine Tribute
Bathing Beauty (Second Version) HN4399, 4599

Brighton Belle HN4400, 4600
Dancing Eyes and Sunny Hair
    (Second Version) HN4492
Do You Wonder Where the Fairies Are
    (Second Version) HN4429
Here A Little Child I Stand
    (Second Version) HN4428
Little Child So Rare and Sweet
    (Third Version) HN4491
Summer's Darling (Second Version)
    .... HN4401, 4601
Taking the Waters HN4402, 4602

Les Saisons
Automne (Autumn) HN3068
Eté (Summer) HN3067
Hiver (Winter) HN3069
Printemps (Spring) HN3066

Literary Heroines
Elizabeth Bennet HN3845
Emma (Fourth Version) HN3843
Jane Eyre HN3842
Moll Flanders HN3849
Tess of the D'Urbervilles HN3846

Literary Loves
Heathcliff and Cathy HN4071

Little Cherubs
First Steps (Third Version) HN3361
Peek A Boo HN3363
Well Done HN3362
What Fun HN3364

Michael Doulton Events
1984 Gillian (Second Version) ... HN3042
1985 Wistful (First Version) HN2472
1986 Kathleen (Second Version)
    .... HN3100
1987 Last Waltz HN2316
1987 Nicola HN2804
1988 Laura (First Version) HN3136
1989 Pamela (Second Version) ... HN3223
1990 Diana (Second Version) HN3266
1991 Fragrance (First Version) ... HN3311
1992 Angela (Third Version) HN3419
1993 Sarah (First Version) HN3380
1994 Sharon (Second Version) ... HN3603
1995 Lily (Second Version) HN3626
1997 Autumn Breezes (First Version)
    .... HN3736
1999 Julia (Second Version) HN4124
1999 Old Balloon Seller (First Version)
    .... HN3737
2000 Susan (Fourth Version) ... HN4230
2001 Christine (Sixth Version) ... HN4307
2002 Linda (Fifth Version) HN4450
2003 Eleanor (Third Version) ... HN4463
2004 Rose (Third Version) HN4581

Michael Doulton Signature Collection
Autumn Breezes (Second Version)
    .... HN2180
Christine (Third Version) HN3337
Christmas Morn (Second Version)
    .... HN3245
Elaine (Second Version) HN3247
Fair Lady (Second Version) HN3336
Fragrance (Second Version) HN3250
Hannah (Second Version) HN3870
Karen (Third Version) HN3338

Kirsty (Second Version) HN3246
Ninette (Second Version) HN3248
Sara (Second Version) HN3249
Southern Belle (Second Version)
    .... HN3244
Sunday Best (Second Version) ... HN3312
Top o' the Hill (Second Version)
    .... HN3734
Victoria (Second Version) HN3735

Middle Earth
Aragorn HN2916
Barliman Butterbur HN2923
Bilbo HN2914
Boromir HN2918
Frodo HN2912
Galadriel HN2915
Gandalf HN2911
Gimli HN2922
Gollum HN2913
Legolas HN2917
Samwise HN2925
Tom Bombadil HN2924

Millennium
Balthazar HN4036
Boy Hshepherd HN4039
Casper HN4038
Columbine (Third Version) HN4059
Harlequin (Second Version) HN4058
Joseph (Second Version) HN4035
Kneeling Shepherd HN4055
Mary and Jesus HN4034
Mechoir HN4037
Standing Shepherd HN4056

Miniatures: Character Studies
Balloon Seller (Second Version) ... HN2130
Falstaff (Third Version) HN3236
Good King Wencelas (Second Version)
    .... HN3262
Guy Fawkes (Second Version) ... HN3271
Jester (Third Version) HN3335
Old Balloon Seller (Second Version)
    .... HN2129
Town Crier, The (Second Version)
    .... HN3261

Miniatures: Ladies
Autumn Breezes (Second Version)
    .... HN2176, 2180
Buttercup (Second Version)
    .... HN3268, 3908
Christine (Third Version)... HN3269, 3337
Christmas Morn (Second Version)
    .... HN3212, 3245
Diana (Third Version) HN3310
Elaine (Second Version) ... HN3214, 3247
    (Third Version) 3900
Emma (Second Version) HN3208
Fair Lady (Second Version)
    .... HN3216, 3336
Fragrance (Second Version)
    .... HN3220, 3250
Gail (Second Version) HN3321
Hannah (Second Version) ... HN3649, 3870
Karen (Second Version) HN3270
    (Third Version) 3338, 3749
Kirsty (Second Version)
    .... HN3213, 3246, 3480, 3743
Ninette (Second Version)
    .... HN3215, 3248, 3901
Rebecca (Second Version) HN3414

Sara (Second Version) HN3219, 3249
Southern Belle (Second Version)
    .... HN3174, 3244
Sunday Best (Second Version)
    .... HN3218, 3312
Top o' the Hill (Second Version)
    .... HN2126, 3499, 3734
Victoria (Second Version)
    .... HN3735, 3744, 3909

Miniature Pretty Ladies
Christine M200
Elaine M201
Elizabeth M202
Jane M203
Karen M204
Margaret M205
Ninette M206
Rachel M207
Susan M208
Victoria M209

Mystical Figures
Sorcerer HN4252
Sorceress HN4253

Myths and Maidens
Diana the Huntress HN2829
Europa and the Bull (Second Version)
    .... HN2828
Juno and the Peacock HN2827
Lady and the Unicorn HN2825
Leda and the Swan HN2826

Name Your Own
Baby's First Christmas HN4427
Best Wishes (Second Version) .. HN3971
Congratulations to You HN4306
For You HN3754, 3863
My Love (Second Version) HN4392
New Baby HN3712, 3713
Perfect Gift HN4409
Pretty as a Picture HN4312
Pride and Joy (Second Version) HN4102
Sugar and Spice HN4103
Thinking of You (Second Version)
    .... HN4585
Thoughts for You HN4397
Wedding Celebration HN4216, 4229

National Society of the Prevention of Cruelty to Children Charity (NSPCC)
Charity (First Version) HN3087
Faith (First Version) HN3082
Hope (First Version) HN3061

Nostalgia
Air Raid Precaution Warden HN4555
Auxilary Territorial Service HN4495
Farewell Daddy HN4463
Home Guard HN4494
Land Girl HN4361
Railway Sleeper HN4418
Women's Auxiliary Air Force HN4554
Women's Land Army HN4364
Women's Royal Naval Service ... HN4498

Nursery Rhymes: Series One
Curly Locks HN2049
He Loves Me HN2046
Jack HN2060
Jill HN2061

Little Boy Blue (First Version) ... HN2062
Little Jack Horner (First Version)
.... HN2063
Mary Had a Little Lamb HN2048
Mary, Mary HN2044
My Pretty Maid HN2064
Once Upon a Time HN2047
She Loves Me Not HN2045
Wee Willie Winkie (First Version)
.... HN2050

Nursery Rhymes: Series Two
Little Bo Peep HN3030
Little Boy Blue (Second Version)
.... HN3035
Little Jack Horner (Second Version)
.... HN3034
Little Miss Muffet HN2727
Polly Put The Kettle On HN3021
Tom, Tom, The Piper's Son HN3032
Wee Willie Winkie (Second Version)
.... HN3031

Peggy Davis Collection
Christine (Fifth Version) HN3905
Eleanor (First Version) HN3906
Lily (Third Version) HN3902
Mary (Fourth Version) HN3903
Patricia (Fourth Version) HN3907
Valerie (Second Version) HN3904

Period Figures in English History
Eleanor of Provence HN2009
Henrietta Maria (First Version) HN2005
Lady Anne Nevill HN2006
Margaret of Anjou (First Version)
.... HN2012
Matilda HN2011
Mrs. Fitzherbert HN2007
Philippa of Hainault (First Version)
.... HN2008
Young Miss Nightingale HN2010

Plantagenet Queens
Eleanor of Aquitaine (1122-1204)
.... HN3957
Margaret of Anjou (Second Version)
.... HN4073
Philippa of Hainault (Second Version)
.... HN4066

Prestige
Alexander the Great HN4481
Charge of the Light Brigade
  (First Version) HN3718
  (Second Version) HN4486
Columbine (Third Version)
.............................HN2738, 3288, 4059
Harlequin (Second Version)
.... HN2737, 3287, 4058
Henvy V at Agincourt HN3947
Hercules HN4561
Jack Point HN2080
Moor, The HN2082
Princess Badoura (First Version)
.... HN2081, 3921
Romeo and Juliet (Second Version)
.... HN4057
St. George (Fourth Version) HN4371

Pretty Maids
Miss Maisie HN3997
Miss Tilly HN3998
Miss Violet HN3996

Queens of the Realm
Mary, Queen of Scots (Second Version)
.... HN3142
Queen Anne HN3141
Queen Elizabeth I HN3099
Queen Victoria (First Version) .. HN3125

Reflections
Allure HN3080
Apertif HN2998
Autumn Glory HN2766
Ballerina (Second Version) HN3197
Ballet Class (First Version) HN3134
Balloons HN3187
Bathing Beauty (First Version) .. HN3156
Bolero HN3076
Breezy Day HN3162
Charisma HN3090
Cherry Blossom HN3092
Chic HN2997
Cocktails HN3070
Country Girl (First Version) HN3051
Covent Garden (Second Version)
.... HN2857
Dancing Delight HN3078
Daybreak (First Version) HN3107
Debut (First Version) HN3046
Debutante (Second Version) HN3188
Demure HN3045
Devotion HN3228
Dreaming HN3133
Eastern Grace HN3138
Enchanting Evening HN3108
Encore (First Version) HN2751
Enigma HN3110
Entranced HN3186
Fantasy HN3296
Flirtation HN3071
Free as the Wind HN3139
Gaiety HN3140
Gardener HN3161
Golfer HN2992
Good Pals HN3132
Harvestime HN3084
Idle Hours HN3115
Indian Maiden HN3117
Joker, The (First Version) HN3196
Joy (First Version) HN3184
Love Letter, The (Second Version)
.... HN3105
Moondancer HN3181
Morning Glory HN3093
Panorama HN3028
Paradise HN3074
Park Parade HN3116
Pensive HN3109
Playmates HN3127
Promenade (Second Version) HN3072
Reflection HN3039
Rose Arbour HN3145
Secret Moment HN3106
Sheikh HN3083
Shepherd (Fifth Version) HN3160
Shepherdess (Third Version) HN2990
Sisterly Love HN3130
Sophistication HN3059
Spring Walk HN3120
Stargazer HN3182
Storytime (Second Version) HN3126
Strolling (First Version) HN3073
Summer Rose (First Version) .. HN3085
Summer's Darling (First Version)
.... HN3091

Sweet Bouquet (First Version) HN3000
Sweet Perfume HN3094
Sweet Violets HN3175
Tango HN3075
Tomorrow's Dreams (First Version)
.... HN3128
Traveller's Tale HN3185
Tumbler HN3183
Water Maiden HN3155
Windflower (Third Version) HN3077
Windswept HN3027
Winter's Walk, A HN3052

Reynolds Ladies
Countess of Harrington HN3317
Countess Spencer HN3320
Lady Worsley HN3318
Mrs. High Bonfoy HN3319

Royal Doulton International
Collectors Club (RDICC)
Applause HN4328
Auctioneer HN2988
Autumntime (First Version) HN3231
Barbara (Third Version) HN3441
Bunny's Bedtime HN3370
Cherished Memories HN4265
Dance (Second Version) HN4553
Diane HN3604
Discovery HN3428
Eliza Farren, Countess of Derby
.... HN3442
Emily (Second Version) HN3688
Geisha, The (Third Version) HN3229
Jacqueline (Fourth Version) HN4309
Janet (Third Version) HN4042
Jester (Third Version) HN3335
L'Ambiteuse HN3359
Le Bal HN3702
Lido Lady (Second Version) HN4247
Lights Out (Second Version) HN4465
Moor HN3926
Nicole (Second Version) HN4112
Pamela (Third Version) HN3756
Pride and Joy (First Version) HN2945
Prized Possessions HN2942
Recital, The HN4466
Sleepy Darling HN2953
Springtime (Second Version) HN3033
Summertime (First Version) HN3137
Susan (Third Version) HN3871
Sweet Lilac HN3972
Top o' the Hill (Second Version)
.... HN2126
Winter's Day HN3769
Wintertime (First Version) HN3060

Sea Characters
All Aboard HN2940
Boatman 'Pilot' HN2417A
Boatman 'Skylark' HN2417
Captain (Second Version) HN2260
Captain Cook HN2889
Good Catch, A HN2258
Helmsman HN2499
Lifeboat Man (First Version) HN2764
Lobster Man HN2317, 2323
Officer of the Line HN2733
Pilot Skipper, The HN4510
Sailor's Holiday HN2442
Seafarer HN2455
Sea Harvest HN2257
Shore Leaver HN2254

Lost treasure hunt

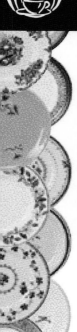

Pieces to be cherished

A dinner or tea service is not merely another piece of functional kitchenware. For many people, it has been an essential part of family life and wonderful occasions for years. It comprises one of their most treasured posessions.

A service may carry with it the beautiful memories associated with a wedding gift. Or it may have been lovingly built up over many years, only becoming a complete service when money finally allowed. Perhaps it was inherited and has immense sentimental value attached.

An incomplete set

Whatever the history, breaking such pieces can be very traumatic. The act of smashing a coffee cup or soup bowl is upsetting in itself, but the realisation that a collection is no longer complete carries a despair of its own. Where there was once a perfect eight piece setting there are now just seven pieces – and an empty space.

To continually revive their portfolio, tableware manufacturers are forced to cease production of patterns to make room for new, modern designs. It's an unfortunate fact of life, but they do not have the capacity to produce patterns indefinitely.

What can be done?

So what happens when the very piece you have broken is from a pattern that hasn't been produced for years? Tablewhere is here for you, ready to help you restore a treasured collection.

The elusive teacup or dinnerplate that you've been looking for may already be available from our warehouse containing over a million pieces. Thousands of patterns are represented, from hundreds of manufacturers, such as;

Wedgwood, Royal Doulton, Spode, Denby, Minton, Royal Albert, Johnson Brothers, Poole, Royal Worcester, Noritake, Midwinter, Hornsea, Royal Crown Derby, Masons, Adams, Villeroy & Boch, Paragon, M&S, Aynsley and many, many others.

The Tablewhere team

Heading the team are the buyers, who travel all over the country in order to gather those hard-to-find pieces. Although some stock is available from trade sources, the team are always eager to hear from members of the public with tableware to sell.

From there, the friendly and efficient customer service team keep detailed records of all the patterns and shapes in stock – from egg cups to soup tureens. They have an excellent success rate in finding replacements – around 85% — and will not give up until the customer is completely satisfied.

Kim Cotton, Managing director

The requests for replacements cover a vast array of different manufacturers, designs and decades, stretching back as far as the early 1900's. Famous designers amongst them include Susie Cooper, Clarice Cliff and Eric Ravillious.

The most frequently requested patterns were originally available from the 1960's to the 1980's, including:

- Royal Doulton's Yorktown, Rose Elegans and Old Colony;
- Wedgwood's Hathaway Rose and Florentine;
- Denby's Greenwheat, Gypsy and Memories;
- Hornsea's Contrast and Fleur, and;
- Midwinter's Spanish Garden and Stonehenge.

How can Tablewhere help you?

Whatever pattern you have, Tablewhere should be able to find replacement pieces for you. And since registering your requirements is free, with no obligation to buy, there's absolutely nothing to lose.

If you're thinking of starting a brand new collection and aren't sure what to do with the old one, don't hesitate to contact our buyers.

Getting in touch

Call us on 0845 130 6111 within the UK and you'll only pay the price of a local call. If you'd prefer to write, ensure your letter contains every detail of the relevant manufacturer, pattern and pieces, including a photograph or colour photocopy where identification is difficult. This information, together with full contact details will enable us to help you without delay.

For further information, or to submit your requirements online, visit the Tablewhere web site.

Tablewhere

Mail-order address:	**4 Queens Parade Close London N11 3FY**	Telephone:	**+44 (0) 20 8361 6111**
		Fax:	**+44 (0) 20 8361 4143**
Web site:	**www.tablewhere.co.uk**	Lines open:	**Monday to Saturday,**
Tel (UK local rate):	**0845 130 6111**		**9.00am until 5.00pm**

bookbasket

Gemini Publications
Publishers

30a Monmouth Street, Bath, BA1 2AN, England, UK
Telephone: 01225 484877 Fax: 01225 334619
Email sales@bookbasket.co.uk
Web: www.bookbasket.co.uk

TITLES FROM GEMINI PUBLICATIONS

Masonic Memorabilia for Collectors
By Bill Jackman. Edited by George Perrott.

This is the first book on Freemasonry artifacts to be published with a price guide. Packed with useful information with over 150 coloured illustrations. It covers china, glass, jewels of the craft, books, prints, etc., and gives tips on how to spot fakes; how to care for your collection and where to buy the best pieces.

Published 2002. ISBN 0-9530637-2-0.
Softback 240x170mm, 120 pages. Price £17.95.

Troika Ceramics of Cornwall (with Updated Price Supplement)
By George Perrott

Packed with useful information, plus over 200 coloured photographs. This book meets the demands of collectors and dealers for information on this innovative and unusual pottery. It covers shapes, designs and glazes with an informative section on marks. A price Guide covering those realized at auction and on the internet. A book well worth a space on your bookshelf.

Published March 2003. ISBN 0-9530637-3-9.
Softback. 240x170mm. 128 pages. Price £17.95

Pottery & Porcelain Marks, European, Oriental & USA
By E.G.Perrott.

Commencing with the Ming Dynasty of 1368, through to the 15th century 'Maiolica' period of the Italian Renaissance, the German and French 'Faience' of the 16th century, the early 17th century Dutch 'Delft' wares, then onto the great factories of Europe, Meissen, Sevres, and the English factories of Wedgwood, Minton, etc., to the USA factories of the 18th & 19th centuries.

Published 1997. ISBN 0-9530637-0-4
Hardback 250x175mm, 667 pages. Price £45.00.

The policy of Gemini Publications is to publish at least two books per year specialising in antique and collectable subjects. Our eventual aim is to find those subjects that are interesting and collectable but of which there isn't much information, or alternately up-date those books on collectables that have overrun their shelf life.
If you are a potential writer with an idea on any collectable subject give us a call, we might be able to help you.

Distributed by Gemini Publications Ltd., 30A Monmouth Street, Bath, BA1 2AN, England.
Telephone: 01225 484877 Fax: 01225 334619.